D0638827

MARQUAND

Also by Millicent Bell

Edith Wharton and Henry James: The Story of Their Friendship
Hawthorne's View of the Artist

MARQUAND

An American Life

MILLICENT BELL

An Atlantic Monthly Press Book

Little, Brown and Company — Boston–Toronto

FIRST EDITION

LIBRARY OF CONGRESS CATALOGING IN PUBLICATION DATA
Bell, Millicent.
Marquand: an American life.
"An Atlantic Monthly Press book."
Includes bibliographical references and index.
1. Marquand, John Phillips, 1893–1960—Biography.
2. Authors, American—20th century—Biography.
PS3525.A6695Z57 818'.5'209 [B] 79-12818
ISBN 0-316-08828-5

ATLANTIC–LITTLE, BROWN BOOKS
ARE PUBLISHED BY
LITTLE, BROWN AND COMPANY
IN ASSOCIATION WITH
THE ATLANTIC MONTHLY PRESS

VB
Designed by Susan Windheim

Published simultaneously in Canada
by Little, Brown & Company (Canada) Limited

PRINTED IN THE UNITED STATES OF AMERICA

To Gene and Meg

Contents

Illustrations follow page 226.

Prologue

The "ordeal by success," as Malcolm Cowley called it—is it possible writers still experience it today, when writing a successful book has become a recognized way of joining the upper middle class? Our great novelists of the early half of the century—Hemingway, Fitzgerald and Lewis, most notably—became rich and lived like rich men, but worried that their art suffered. Their lives contained an anguish that money only exacerbated. John P. Marquand, who first transferred the phrase "point of no return" from aviation to personal history, also made it to the top in that time, and *Life* called him "the most successful novelist in the United States." He had less exalted ideas about his gifts than those three contemporaries had of theirs—writing was something he found easy to do and he did it at first because he felt that he needed a lot of money and saw a way to make it. But there were unconscious compulsions that more decisively attached him to the effort of literature and something incalculable in his endowment, so that in time he became a "serious" writer. Again, he was successful—at least he made the money he wanted and was widely read—beyond almost anyone else in the field. But the highest tribute eluded him.

When, a year before his death, he was asked to speculate about his "eventual position in the history of the novel," he said: "When you are dead you are very dead, intellectually and artistically. The only hope is that there will be some raker in the dust heaps of the future—and there will be plenty of them—who may, in his opinion, discover something that will be of value to future generations." It would have pleased him, possibly, to imagine that he was due to receive, at the hand of a biographer or revisionist critic, nomination to the most exclusive of clubs, the company of the immortals—as will be seen in the pages that follow, the sense of unjustified exclusion was the compelling motive of his life. But he felt that he had sacrificed that chance, even if he had ever had it—and it is certainly not my intention now to surprise his uneasy ghost by thrusting upon him the honor we give to only one or two in a generation.

It *has* seemed to me that Marquand's best books have a claim upon our attention. His work belongs to a native mode not always regarded as highly as it should be—that of the novel of manners as composed in the past by Howells and Wharton, later by Lewis, and by Updike, Cheever, and O'Hara in our own time. Like the work of these writers at their best, his notation of social experience was shaped by hidden psychic energy into mythic structures. As he came to maturity, a past to which his own youth had belonged was coming to an end, the inheritance of older American habits and standards to which, as a nation, we still make a compromised reference. He had happened for quite private reasons to need to find a way of claiming relationship to that past in terms of attachment to an ancestral home and to family tradition. But his life was to be governed not only by the desire to regain a place in this past but by an urge to ride the crest of the future, to be a new man of the twentieth century, giving free expression to the cravings of the ego, unrestrained by the older disciplines or inhibitions. He stood at the threshold between two epochs. He could write about the changes overtaking the stable, older world of a small New England city and, hardly knowing that he did so, invest his depiction with the urgency of his private need for self-understanding.

Chiefly, I have wanted to tell the storywriter's own story, visible not only in the autobiography of his fiction but in the full factuality of an exceptionally available record. Marquand's personal history has seemed to me to be of such prototypical character as to justify my subtitle, "An American Life." It was, I think, so representative in its essentials as to constitute a kind of metonymy for all our lives, a work of the personal will and imagination collaborating with fate to produce an artistic fable of the general experience. It was Marquand's particular lot to be a novelist, of course, and the history of his professional career was also to prove itself, in this narrower sense, representative. His development as a literary producer, the drama of his relationship to the reading public and to magazine editors and agents and publishers, and the story of the "strings," as he called them, by which he was pulled in the progress of his career—all this is surely a case of the modern writer and as such would be worth setting forth for its typicality as well as for its vivid individual interest.

But, more generally than this, his was a profoundly American life. His dream of success, conceived in simple material terms yet involving longings for a vanished spiritual innocence, had the characteristic American confusion. Like many Americans he desired to come home again as the Big Success—but also to regain some grace that his youth had known. He would return to the scene of early humiliations, the town where he had been a shabby young nobody, the Harvard where he had been a greaseball, the Boston where he had been a hack writer outside the genteel pale, and "show them" who he really was: a true gentleman with a finer and more rightful claim than others upon everything that was best. Still more in the common grain were his domestic adventures, his love affairs, his marriages, his relation with his children, his encounters with sickness and age, his preoccupation with status and property, his sense of diminishing time and strength. These had no grandeur—and why should they? He was, except for his destiny, an ordinary man whose mundane experience was, as Tolstoy said of the life of Ivan Ilyich, "most simple and most ordinary and therefore most terrible." In the end, having had two wives, five children, and several extramarital love affairs, he died lonely. He had, by his own insistence, divorced both his wives, he had lost close touch with his children, he had not been able to make much of his relations with other women. He had, moreover, hardly any close and constant male friends and he had alienated himself from his relatives by an unseemly squabble over property. Still, he was a "successful" man, one who had managed to do a great deal of what he had wanted to do, seen much of the world, gained praise and esteem from his neighbors as well as from readers everywhere. If it is true, as historians are saying, that the "obscure" life tells us more about history than the life of a king or a statesman, then Marquand's private life has historic truth, even though it was the private life of a famous man. I have wanted to set it forth for our recognizing eyes in its "most ordinary and therefore most terrible" dailiness.

Like all private lives, of course, it was governed and enveloped by public History—of which Marquand was, indeed, acutely aware as an astute and informed witness, but one whose response to public events was, again, generally representative. He was of the generation of World War I, which affected him deeply, but unlike some of his literary contemporaries, he never claimed to have been "lost" or to have suffered invisible wounds. He played, in the aftermath, the rôle of the average ex-soldier who was trying to get up and on during the years of prosperity, more like his old college friends who went into advertising and journalism than the rebels of Greenwich Village or the Left Bank. He took a dim view of expatriation and after World War II would lecture his son on the obligation to be an American. He had the instincts of a critic of society, as his art would show, exposing sham and social arrogance in novel after novel, but his political conservatism was not disturbed by the Depression—which he managed to weather successfully. He read the newspapers alertly and saw the inevitability of World War II, and when it came, he participated, as a civilian, in the war services, managing to see the battlegrounds of Europe and the Pacific war sites as well as the corridors of the Pentagon, and to make the acquaintance of the generals in all three places. Like many civilians, he was bemused by the spectacle of military authority. After the war he continued to read the newspapers, to feel he had a part to play, and was ready to switch parties, just as the nation was, when he died in 1960.

Undeniably, he was also a uniquely gifted man. He was peculiar as gifted persons are, more inordinately driven and more woefully disappointed than most, suffering monstrously, and flashing a bizarre humor through the slits of his armor of conformity. But above all he was extraordinary in having realized the common dream instead of merely dreaming it to no or partial avail. He transmuted his wishes into fulfillments and came home exactly as in the heart's fairy tale—like the once-scorned swineherd who has proved his legitimacy as the king's son. But his power to enact his dreams explains much of his conduct of life, not only in the achievement of success but also in the achievement of failure. He dreamed early that he had suffered an unjust displacement. Perhaps he had. But though his parents had lost their money and though he was sent to the Newburyport public high school instead of to Groton or St. Mark's and though he went to Harvard on a scholarship and failed to make one of the snobbish undergraduate clubs, it is clear that his disinheritance was one only if he chose to think it so. His self-erected myth of disadvantage became, psychically speaking, his reality. And he did more than reread his early experience as myth: he continued to invite and assist experience so that it would conform to a foretold design. The early trials of the hero were followed by expected later ones, continuing ordeals while he suffered more snubs as his triumph was in the making. He labored during his first marriage under the conviction that his wife and her family looked down on him, and so they did—but as he might have anticipated, perhaps did unconsciously anticipate, in choosing her. His second wife would exasperate him by an executive urge weirdly lodged in a brilliantly inefficient personality; he would complain that he was being "run" and that nothing ran. And it is not likely that he was altogether unwilling to suffer the conditions of this marriage either, for they were part of a fatality he had chosen for himself and, with a power beyond the ordinary, brought into being.

Even the final defeat of his ambition to be a great writer was, perhaps, conceived—and enacted—by him in mythic terms that we may regard with a degree of suspicion. He thought of himself as one denied the grail because he had compromised his purity, had listened to the wrong advisers, served the market too well for too long. Again and again he made private statements in which he blamed those who had helped him to make a popular success in the market for having misdirected his talent—and blamed the burdens of marriage for having forced him to make compromises. Yet one cannot be absolutely sure that he did not willingly assent to the direction he received because, in fact, he had no intense conviction to oppose to it. He continued always to resent the holier-than-thou attitudes of writers who had not done what he had—and suspected that they simply lacked the ability to write an entertaining tale; he was sure that they underestimated the skill required to write magazine stories. Of course, he did experience a kind of illumination and conversion when he wrote *The Late George Apley* and turned decisively towards the book market. He felt that he would henceforth serve higher gods in his fiction. Yet there were some critics who still refused to credit him with a devotion to serious themes and reproached him because his lucid, easy prose remained formally conventional. He felt that he had not been able, in the end, to shake loose from his earlier reputation—however much he tried to elevate his art—that of the get-rich-quick literary trickster whose aesthetic soul had been sold to the devil of commerce. He had been cheated of his guerdon.

Marquand's impulse towards self-mythification was, undoubtedly, the hidden spring of his desire to write in the first place. He expressed his myth in his fiction, repeating again and again a story that was his version of his own past. His novels thus contain renditions of his experience converted to legend and may be used in composing a biography only if we remember to distinguish verifiable fact from the subject's self-image. But these fictional versions are deeply expressive of that dream Conrad's Stein speaks of when he says that a man is born to fall into it as into a sea, a destructive element he must submit to if he is to survive. Like Lord Jim, such a man is endowed with imagination. He is, indeed, an artist, who would have worked in the medium of life to compose himself according to the dream even if he had not worked in the medium of literature.

It is to be expected that he would also work at his own myth in the creating of an oral legend, a form of autobiography. He became a gifted storyteller and parodist who would recount some scene of his own life and take all parts and outrageously and tellingly exaggerate; these, naturally, were facilities that helped his writing. Today, a large number of stories are remembered that seem to have originated in his own telling of them—to illustrate, for example, one wife's impracticality or snobbery or the other's scattered energy and bossiness. These were, actually, truly based, but they gained something in the telling by a master satirist. Satire, of course, simplifies, if it does not distort, and unites with myth.

It is not easy for the biographer to distinguish "truth" in such a case. Only the most ample opportunity to collect the actualities of Marquand's life gives me any confidence that I have been able to separate the romance of his self-conceptions from his life as it was and to identify where the two became one as he compelled life to conform to his romance. Perhaps the difference between life and myth is not absolute, really. In conceiving ourselves we make ourselves, and dreams unfulfilled have a status in the definition of self equal to that of dreams fulfilled. In a way, such a dreamer as Marquand tries to write his own biography, insisting upon an outline he has conceived for it and imposing it upon the biographer's realistic intention. Thus, Marquand dictated that his story should begin with his family past.

He imagined the lives of previous Marquands and Curzons and made them a continuing obsession and an influence. From earliest youth he put together a continuity of ancestral lives connected with his own, and these gave a peculiar importance to one place where he had spent part—not the whole—of his youth: Curzon's Mill in Newburyport. His biography, as I was forced to recognize, truly began with these imagined lives, not as a conventional gesture towards genealogy but because his own sense of beginning was located in this past. Curzon's Mill, in the same way, was the veritable homeplace his willed attachment made it.

But, putting dreams aside, even active life, the biographer finds, is not so obviously separated into episodes of doing and nondoing. One might tend to think, for example, that Marquand's intervals of escape from his own struggles and problems—his long journeys to the Orient, particularly—were simply gaps in the story, time when "nothing happened," which one could virtually skip over. During these periods he became completely a spectator, and a spectator of cultures remote from his own. The human beings he encountered on these journeys were foreigners whose way of thinking and living and even speaking he could not understand. And yet these experiences of travel have a special importance in Marquand's life because in his imagination they did. They provided him with another kind of dream to be held in the back of the mind as a dimly figured backdrop to his own continued existence. In China, particularly, he glimpsed the lingering of a tradition still older than the one he had admired in his New England ancestors. But above all, his travel taught him how to bear himself as an observing stranger. It was still as such an observing stranger that he would then look again at his own familiar civilization, having learned an attitude of detachment from the traveler's uninvolvement.

And yet, despite what has been said, it is the biographer's duty to contend, as best he can, with his subject's propensity to manipulate him. He must oppose to the myths the irrefutable facts. I have tried in the following pages, therefore, to be faithful to the principle of objective verification at all points and to distinguish the Marquandian self-image from what could be independently descried in his character and actions. As a record of the audible and visible Marquand, the account I present has been based upon factual record and no particle of description or chronicle is unsupported. Such an account could be written only because its subject was (though I have called his private life "ordinary") important to himself and to others. He preserved the documents of his own history with scrupulous care in conscious anticipation of the biographer. From the moment he became successful he kept nearly every letter he received and copies of thousands sent to others. His fame, moreover, stimulated others to keep his letters. As a consequence, he himself assisted more than anyone in the construction of a record by which his own myth could be tested. Of course, his own voice, always quoted exactly from letters or other sources, is heard continuously, but the effect is demythifying rather than otherwise—for in these utterances, sprung from the occasions of life, a less romantic and a more tragic hero emerges.

I have, obviously, been indebted to many sources and persons for the evidence upon which my narrative is based. Most of my obligations are recognized in the notes that follow the text. I wish, however, to repeat here a particular declaration of grateful acknowledgment to the five children of John P. Marquand—John Phillips Marquand, Jr., Christina Marquand Welch, Blanche Ferry Marquand, Timothy Fuller Marquand and Elon Huntington Marquand—all of whom shared their recollections with me with great generosity and courage and gave me unlimited access to their father's and also to their mothers' unpublished papers. Marquand's publishers, Little, Brown and Company, opened their files to me so that I could more informedly trace the history of Marquand's professional life, and his lawyer, Brooks Potter, allowed me to study his files for the period of his stewardship of Marquand's affairs. Although both of Marquand's wives were dead when my research began, the three other women who played a part in his life all proved generously willing to tell me about their relations with him, and I acknowledge a particular debt in this book to the late Helen Howe, to Carol Brandt and to Marjorie Davis. To the libraries of Boston University, Harvard University and Yale University, holders of the bulk of Marquand's manuscripts, correspondence and other papers, I owe a debt of gratitude for their help and courtesy in assisting me to use the materials in their possession. Dr. Howard Gotlieb, curator of Special Collections at Mugar Library, Boston University, was a constantly helpful friend and adviser to me in the use of the collection in his care, and I owe him the first suggestion that this biography be written. Peter Davison, friend and editor, helped the book achieve final form.

MARQUAND

1

Curzon's Mill

Before passing Newburyport to drop its waters between Plum Island and Salisbury Beach, the Merrimack is met by a last tributary. It is the Artichoke, which rises and falls with the tide and once turned the wheel of a small gristmill close to the junction of the two rivers. Though a bridge crosses the smaller stream alongside the Mill, there is only an occasional rattle of its plank bed as a car passes over it to West Newbury. Above the point stands a knoll shaded by white pines. In a world grown noisier nearly everywhere the spot has, now, the peculiar quiet of places from which the modern age has managed to withdraw. The part of the Mill that juts over the water has been used as a sort of summerhouse by its owners in recent years. It is pleasant to be there on a hot day. One feels oneself suspended over a stream which, though invisibly advancing, seems motionless between its green banks.

Seventy years ago, when the Mill was in regular service, its great grooved stone—long since removed and lying like a giant sand dollar in the grass nearby—thundered sometimes at night and sometimes during the day, according to the tide. When a concrete dam was built on the river in 1906 to provide a water supply for Newburyport, the turning of the mill wheel ended after 228 years. John Marquand, who was thirteen that autumn, even then felt that some portentous change had overtaken his life. Many years later he would perceive the moment as the end point not only of his own childhood but of a stage of the general experience, of a historical epoch. He would say, then, that he was glad to have known the earlier time: "Sometimes when I regret that I was not born ten years later, so that my mind might now be more agile in coping with the startling changes witnessed by my generation, the mill is a consoling thought. I was on the earth enough at least to see it running, fulfilling the tail end of a contract that stretched back over two hundred–odd years." The contract the town had made in 1678, granting twelve acres of riverside land to a certain John Emery (provided that he would maintain a mill to grind the community's corn), had, in fact, become void long before 1906. But the ending Marquand meant was a metaphysical one. It seemed to him that his childhood had been spent, because of Curzon's Mill, in a past more remote than the final years of the nineteenth century and the first half dozen of the twentieth. This family homestead, which he visited on and off throughout his early years, seemed to be situated, along with the older people who lived there, on a sort of landing, where one could step off into that remoter past.

It was the scene of his earliest recollections. He was two years old when his parents brought him there to live for a whole year, and after that he looked forward to a vacation at the Mill every summer. He could remember coming late in the spring of 1898 when he was five. All the way up on the train from New York people talked excitedly about the Spanish-American War. He and his parents were met at Newburyport by Vitarl, his grandfather's stableman, who had driven to the station in a polished phaeton behind a dappled-gray pair whose sides shone like metal. In a moment they were off down High Street, its big, white houses floating by like sailing ships on their green lawns, and then out of town and down the familiar sand road, the horses trotting softly now, until the stone walls and stately drive of the Moseley place came into view. Beyond lay Curzon's Mill. With a dip down the hill they were there, seeing first the little brick building, where his parents and he always stayed. It looked like a city row house picked up from just such a street as they had been living on in New York City and planted down in a country field. It even had a side wall that was blank save for a single high window, as though the builder had expected someday to continue the row. Beyond was a flower garden set in a pattern of beds that resembled his mother's parlor carpet, and beyond that, the yellow-shingled main house with its central brick chimney and bay window. There was a horse chestnut in front of the house and a stone wall, and across the road a red-handled pump and a water trough hewn from a log. But his first glance, even then, he remembered, was towards the brown Mill at the foot of the bridge. He listened to hear if the wheel was turning.

A variety of pleasures was promised by the sight of the Mill. Sometimes the miller, James Knight, would let him ride up and down the grain lift. Sometimes he was allowed to fish from the second-story window. The river was full of fish; he had seen sturgeon leap straight out of the water, and once his aunt Greta had caught a four-pound perch as she leaned out of the window fishing with him, and he had had to run for someone to help them pull it up. Looking out the windows of the Mill he had a view on one side of the mud flats of the Merrimack covered with wild rice that grew thickly. On the other side he could look down on the red wooden bridge and the millpond and see how the Artichoke stretched away, half glittering in the sun, half murky green. There was a bend in the river where you lost sight of it, but just before that a great patch of white water lilies, which his grandmother was supposed to have planted. If someone took him down there in a rowboat, there would be small green turtles sitting on the leaves among the waxy flowers.

But nothing could compare with being beside the Mill on a "grinding day." He could remember a morning when he watched the horse-drawn drays come over the bridge, their barrels of corn rumbling against one another over the deeper rumble of the planks under wheels and hooves. One by one they stopped alongside the building so that the barrels would be hoisted by ropes into the second-story window. From within came another sound, a powerful humming. Standing well away on the grass bank, the child felt himself embraced by a vast, strange vibration, a purring, he thought, like that of a gigantic cat. Inside the Mill this sound was fuller, as though the cat were purring more contentedly while the corn was prepared for grinding into feed. The walls and rafters were covered with cobwebs and coated with white powder, and the light coming through the dusty windows had a pearly quality. He remembered watching Mr. Knight, whitened from head to foot, moving among the empty barrels of broken corncobs that were slowly being fed into the depths where the unseen millstones revolved. As the meal poured into a trough, Mr. Knight scooped it out with a flat wooden spoon. John came forward and thrust his hands into the meal, which was warm from the friction of the stones and had a sharp, sweet smell.

Throughout his childhood, the Mill remained obscurely wonderful to him. Once, when he was ten, he had been so eager to hear it that when the tide was about to rise he had run to turn the wheel which opened the sluice gates. He heard the swirling underneath the wooden floor and then, as he had seen Mr. Knight do, he pulled the lever which meshed the gears to send the trapped water through the raceway, turning the turbine and bringing the massive upper stone into motion with a roar over the sound of the rushing water. He remembered being scolded—his joy hardly diminishing, nonetheless—for having presumed to set the Mill going on a day when Mr. Knight was not planning to grind.

Jim Knight, to whom the Mill was rented, was one of those whose fascination to a young person makes for a greater influence than most familial intimacies. He was a small, quiet man with a genius for practical inventions of all sorts. But it was not of them that he would talk to the small boy who followed him about his tasks at the Mill and into the flower garden, which was also under his care. In his own boyhood, Knight had known the aging Whittier; he loved the nature poetry of the past century, and he tried to write poetry himself. He knew a great deal about flowers, about birds and fish and the small animals that could be found along the river, and he talked to the child with gentle enthusiasm about these things, which he saw with a child's or a poet's fresh surprise each day. "I think they were a good deal more important to him than people, and at that time our minds were completely sympathetic," Marquand remembered. And, long after Knight retired, he still liked to visit Curzon's Mill and to talk with Marquand again as they had when they were children and poets together. "He was still back in the world of horned pout and ducks and wild flowers which I had left a long time ago. I often wished that I could return there with him. He kept that attitude, I think, because he was essentially a poet, although he could not write. In the twenties, at the time of his death, when the material world was moving fast, he was an incongruous and beautiful figure and my memory of him is still a great deal stronger than my memories of bankers and editors."

The Mill, along with the Brick House, the Yellow House, the farm buildings and the land, comprised an estate that was owned by his grandfather Marquand—John Phillips Marquand, for whom he had been named—and his grandmother's sister, Mary Russell Curzon. Margaret Curzon Marquand, his father's mother, had died when he was three, an invalid whom he could remember seeing only once as she was being wheeled out of the Yellow House in a chaise to take the air. But these two other representatives of her generation, her husband and her sister, lived just long enough to leave a permanent and extraordinary impression on him. Of his great-aunt Mary he said towards the end of his life, "I have been impressed by her more than by almost anyone whom I ever met." With his grandfather, it appears, he felt an identity that was much more than one of name. His great-aunt died in 1911, when he was eighteen, and his grandfather when he was still younger, only a child of seven. Yet both, like Jim Knight, had given him the sense of having lived in that earlier world upon which the door had shut by the time he himself was an adult.

Mary Russell Curzon, who was born in 1825, was already in her seventies when he first met her. Like many old people she changed very little in the last ten or fifteen years of her life, and when she finally died he felt that she had always been just as she was when he began to know her as a child. Her routine of life was unvarying, and seemed to him later to be that of someone who maintained a constant sense of the function of human time and of her relation to nature. Nothing she did, though new generations might deem it eccentric, was without a sort of rationality, which he then perfectly understood. He remembered that when he would get up at Curzon's Mill he would find that she had already been awake for some time and was dressed in one of her long gingham dresses, which he afterwards realized were in the fashion of the 1870's. She had watered her house plants and dusted and ordered her parlor, taking care particularly to straighten the pictures on the walls because, as she once explained to him, the earth had shifted slightly in turning on its axis during the night. Now it was time for her walk. She had put a cotton bonnet over her gray, tightly braided hair, pinned a paisley shawl around her shoulders with a cameo, and taken the ivory-headed cane that had belonged to her father. (She loved to walk outdoors in all seasons, but he seemed to remember her best on late summer days with the first coolness of autumn, those days that had a certain melancholy in them, for they meant that he would soon be leaving Curzon's Mill.) When she came back, she fed scraps from a basket to the pigs and her dog, whom she called her "hairy dove," and worked awhile in her garden. Then, before the postman arrived, she was back in the house at her drop-leaf desk, ready to read her mail and to reply immediately to her correspondents, who were numerous. After lunch she worked on her hooked rug or sewed, but just as the sun began to go down she walked out again, now gathering chips and pine cones for kindling the long-room fire. When she came back into the house it was time to light the three or four kerosene lamps kept downstairs, her reluctant concession to modernity; at bedtime one took up a candle ready in its holder on a shelf near the foot of the stairs. The lamps were lit from paper spills, which she would make in the evening—neat, tight rolls of paper that would carry the fire from the hearth to the lamp. She taught young John how to twist them up, a skill he never forgot (many years later, he impressed his Park Avenue hostess by making some to light her guest's cigarettes). Then she drew closed the sliding wooden shutters of the parlor. "You never know who might want to be looking in," she once explained, throwing a suspicious glance into the country night. In the last hours of the evening she wrote in her diary and read, sometimes aloud if younger relatives like her great-nephew were present. She read him Dickens and the Waverley novels (Scott, she said, was considered such a daring writer in her girlhood that she had had to read him secretly at school, hiding the books under the lid of her desk).

Her old-fashionedness seemed to him, reflecting upon it later, to have abounded in symbolic tenacities. There was no plumbing indoors at the Yellow House except for a pump in the kitchen, and drinking water from a well across the road "had a delicious taste of moss and vegetation which might have made a public health officer suspicious," but before every meal a maid in a starched apron filled an elegant silver pitcher there for the dining table. His aunt distrusted sulfur matches, but she could use a flint and tinderbox, and Marquand never saw anyone use flint and steel again until, in the Gobi Desert, he "gave a Camel cigarette to a camel driver," who was, he noticed, "no more adroit than my great-aunt had been." She knew, too, how to use an ax, like the farm women of an earlier age; even in her eighties she split white pine for kindling sticks on a chopping block. When, one time, the ax slipped and cut her knee, she got out her sewing basket and sewed up the wound. And when notice was given that the dam would be built, which would stop the operation of the Mill, she made her gesture against the new age. She added to her daily round a walk to the bridge with a basket filled with old bones from the kitchen and threw them into the millpond. When the contractors finally drained the river in order to put in a coffer dam, the workmen were amazed and slightly awed at finding several bushels of assorted bits of animal skeletons on the riverbed.

As a child John Marquand had perfectly understood that his great-aunt was not eccentric and that these quaint ways of hers were simply due to her being a member of a generation most of whose other representatives were gone. Yet these vanished companions seemed to him to have just stepped across the threshold, and not until he was older did he realize how distant a time was represented by the stories he had heard from her, even about her own life and the lives of her parents, who were, after all, born in the eighteenth century. The history of the Curzon family, moreover, was full of enough romantic mystery to seem perfectly plausible only to a young boy. Yet when he was grown up he searched old family letters and journals for the facts and found that life had, in actuality, been no less romantic than legend.

The American immigrant, Richard Curzon, was a Derbyshire man from an old Norman-French family who had come for a tour of the Colonies and fallen in love with a niece of Peter Zenger, the New York printer whose trial for sedition was the first American law case concerned with freedom of the press. He returned to New York, married the girl, one Elizabeth Becker, and proceeded to make money in banking and shipping. Moving to Baltimore at the start of the Revolution, he enlarged his fortune in privateering, running his ships through the British blockade and sending them to prey on enemy vessels. His eldest son, Samuel, grew up in this derring-do period and founded a shipping firm of his own in New York. His boats carried guns for the American forces in 1779. This Curzon was apparently a clever and adventure-loving man, and he traveled a great deal on his own business missions and as a secret government agent, living for different periods in the West Indies. In 1786 he applied to Congress for the position of American consul, a post he would probably have received had he not just then been fatally wounded in a duel.

Of all the ghosts that jammed the dark corners of Curzon's Mill, this great-great-grandfather must have been the most entrancing to a youthful imagination. A miniature of him that belonged to Great-aunt Mary showed a young man with hair powdered in the fashion of the time, elegant frogged coat and waistcoat opening to a froth of lace at the neck. His face was fair and smooth, with a small, pursed mouth and eyebrows delicately arched over wide-set eyes. Altogether he looked just as he should have as the tragic hero of an "affair of honor." Which, in fact, he was. The man whose pistol inflicted his mortal wound was the brother of Elizabeth Burling, John Marquand's great-grandmother. It appears that the young Burling girl had been secretly married to Samuel Curzon—perhaps because he had feared his family's objections to her Quaker faith or perhaps because he was an undercover American agent in the Indies, where the Burlings were open partisans. But when the time came for her to declare herself legally married her husband was a British captive, and she was not believed. His child was five years old when Curzon returned and was met by the brother's challenge. Named Samuel, after him, his son continued to bear the Burling surname under the assumption that he was illegitimate.

Of the poignancy of the younger Samuel's orphaned and shame-haunted youth John Marquand probably did not know until, years later, he read his ancestor's journals. One day Samuel was told that his father (whom he had never seen) was dead. He remembered being then told that his uncle had killed him and that "it was on my account that he had done the deed." Shortly afterwards, the boy was sent to Boston to live with business partners of the Burlings, members of the prominent Perkins family, which virtually adopted him. So, his childhood was spent among good-natured strangers who wished him well but owed him nothing. It is said that when he was hardly grown he had gone to see his grandfather, Richard Curzon, in Baltimore, to demand some recognition of relationship, and had been coldly denied. Later, when he wished to marry Margaret Searle of Newburyport he had, at her family's insistence, succeeded in gaining from his relatives some acknowledgment that he had a right to the Curzon name. He then waited eight years, probably because of the hesitations of the Searles, before he could be married to her. He was now thirty-five. Some sense of identification with this grandparent may have been felt by Marquand when he discovered himself to be a kind of orphan with no firm attachment to persons and places, despite his respectable possession of two living parents. Later, he may have felt a sympathy with this man when he remembered hearing how he had purchased the Mill property on the Artichoke and settled his wife and children there so that they would have an anchorage in a home scene, though he was more often in New York or Boston when he was not away on a long voyage. Curzon's Mill would also become an anchorage for Marquand, one that he must strive to bring into his own hands and leave to his children.

And Marquand, who was nearly thirty when he married the socially prominent Christina Sedgwick, may have felt that he had continued to duplicate some of his great-grandfather's history. The Searles had undoubtedly looked askance at the man without a name. Margaret was the daughter of George Searle, an established merchant, and his wife Mary, who came from one of the town's proudest families. Mrs. Searle's grandmother had been a Kent. Her father and grandfather were Dudley and Joseph Atkins, of the Newburyport colonial aristocracy. Young Samuel Curzon (as we can now finally call him) was, also like Marquand himself, without any personal fortune. He had been taken into the Perkins office and sent out as a supercargo on their ships. His career had been rich in adventure—he had sailed around the Horn in pursuit of the furs of the Northwest and to Hawaii, where he had had an interview with King Kamehameha; he had fallen into the hands of the Inquisition in Peru and had been attacked by pirates and shipwrecked. But when he was in his fifties he had been forced, after all, to the humiliation of accepting a clerical job in the Boston office of his wife's brothers. A surviving miniature portrait shows him ruddy-faced, reddish hair brushed into an aggressive crest, his mouth somewhat pugnacious and his strong chin emphasized by a stiff cravat. He looks somewhat warily back at the viewer, like a man who has learned not to expect too much of fate. His great-grandson, of course, would succeed where Curzon had failed, in mounting above those who had once condescended to him.

To young John Marquand, listening to his great-aunt's stories, there were still many visible evidences and souvenirs of his great-grandfather at Curzon's Mill. It was he who had rebuilt the open fireplaces in the front rooms and inserted iron grates such as he had seen in English houses to accommodate coal—this in a land where firewood was plentifully available in one's own woodlot for the chopping, while coal had to be purchased. And he filled the house with curious objects brought back as presents for his family after each voyage—a mahogany bowl, nearly four feet in diameter, hewn out of a single tree, from the West Indies; an Inca mortar in the shape of a llama from Peru; a fire screen made of embroidered boot tops which he had worn when received by the Mexican viceroy; a marvelous cabinet or chest-on-chest from Spain, inlaid with tortoiseshell, ivory, mother-of-pearl and silver; a mineral specimen from a peak in the Andes; and pearls given him by the Hawaiian king. There were also several pictures painted on copper that were supposed to have been found nailed as patching to the bottom of one of his vessels, and a Spanish painting of John the Baptist, which he assured his family was an art object of great value. Neither the painted copper pictures nor the Spanish canvas proved, when John Marquand had them appraised later, to have any value at all. But to the boy who first knew the objects deposited at Curzon's Mill by Samuel Curzon, all had a fascination. He would say: "seen all together in the old house where he had left them and where they were tended ritually by his surviving daughter, they had a ghostly message, plus a glittering reality. They told their wordless tale of the sea and demonstrated better than words that the distant places from which they came were once physically and emotionally closer to Newburyport than they ever will be again." Perhaps in emulation, Samuel Curzon's great-grandson became himself a tireless traveler to the near and remote portions of the world, loving particularly China, Hawaii and the islands of the Caribbean, to which his great-grandfather had voyaged for the Perkinses. But he would observe: "I have been to all the places he visited, not once but several times, and to more besides, but he had an advantage. He traveled so slowly that background was never a blur, whereas I have always gone by fast ship or by air."

What Marquand must have envied still more, in later years, was the fashion in which, out of a life of many disappointments, Samuel Curzon had somehow wrested a sense of satisfaction. For a man who was only intermittently at home his homelife was remarkable. He retained a capacity for sentiment that contrasted sharply with the marital disillusionments of his great-grandson, as evidenced in the letter he wrote to his wife on her forty-eighth birthday: "Still, still we belong to each other, dear Peggy, with feelings as fresh and strong as those of 1808, as ready to be happy—still the same in hopes and wishes as regards each other and only differed in respect [of] the hopes we form of the world." Margaret Searle Curzon seems to have been a remarkable woman and the character of his great-grandmother even more than that of his great-grandfather might well have seemed to John Marquand to be of a vanished human type—sensitive and serene, strong and gentle, sustained by intelligence as well as by piety through the vicissitudes of her marriage. Her separations from her husband were long and trying to her—yet she could master her feelings as in this letter to her sister written in 1821, when after five years of marriage he was still a rolling stone, seldom at home and with little to show for his wanderings: "In all forms I must learn to bear disappointment and I had begun to think there was no new form in which it would reach me—but they are various as our hopes, our affections, our pride, our imagination can make them. I must learn more entirely than I have done to look beyond the present scene to permanent felicity." But she also learned to look for felicity in the family life at Curzon's Mill: days with her daughters, tasks that were never burdensome, and leisure filled with a sense of usefulness. Where, in modern life, John Marquand might have asked, are the rhythms of living that his great-aunts were taught, as their mother describes them in the summer when they were sixteen and thirteen years old? Elizabeth was observed practicing Spanish with her father as she helped him at the Mill, reading Milton and Shakespeare to her aunt, for whom she also filled the lamps and washed dishes, sewing her own gowns, doing household needlework, and also taking long walks in search of rare flowers in the woods. Mary, who cared for the hens and the chickens, rode her horse to town on all the errands of the house, read every book she could get hold of, and had, her mother said, "such energy in all her actions, such an intense perception of the ludicrous, of the beautiful and the sublime in all that passes before her, that with her by me I have no chance of losing my faculties." Mary, of course, was to grow old as Marquand's great-aunt already described, preserving still the qualities of her girlhood.

Above all, Margaret Curzon found Nature, a capitalized presence, always available as a companion. She loved the pretty river, which she watched as though it were indeed animated by friendly spirits: "I have been wandering around the point again and again looking to see the river break up but the ice seems loath to move tho' the strip of water increases by the flats. The ice has gone so quietly from the river that I have never seen it moving. I went out on the bank many times to look at it, but all our wide bend is free from ice. The hills and houses on the opposite bank have been mirrored in the grey water today and a gleam of rosy light spread all across it just before sunset. There seems to be no freshet but yesterday the high tide lifted the ice and it melted or sank away in a most mysterious manner. My days have been as quiet as the river. Yesterday I cut out some shirts and today have made good progress in making one." It is not difficult to see John Marquand's great-grandmother as a mental relative of her contemporaries Thoreau and Emerson; she is as much a representative of transcendental conviction of the essential spirit in all things.

Curzon's Mill had, in the days of Great-aunt Mary's girlhood, its direct connection with the intellectual currents of the time. The gentle ladies had apparently no hesitation in making their rural retreat a haven for escaping slaves bound for Canada, and had speeded many to the border, though one, young John heard with a shudder, had arrived dead in a trunk shipped from a southern Underground station and was buried somewhere on the place. The Curzon women had friends among the intellectuals of the day. Thomas Wentworth Higginson, the poets William Ellery Channing and Whittier, Elizabeth Peabody, Celia Thaxter and George Curtis were among those who came up to the Mill to visit. Elizabeth, in fact, had met some of the literary radicals when she went down to reside for a period at Brook Farm in West Roxbury, along, perhaps, with Margaret Fuller and Hawthorne, and it was there that she met her future husband, a young carpenter from upstate New York named John Hoxie.

Whittier, who lived not far from Curzon's Mill, seems to have been in love with them all, mother and daughters, and he also loved the Mill's "bowery stream," as he called it. He was accustomed to row down the Merrimack from Amesbury to visit; he once recorded coming in this fashion with a friend, picking up Mary, and having turned into the Artichoke, "floating lazily, along its dreamy shores, where the dropping ferns, azaleas and witch hazels mirror themselves in the still water, or as Marvell says, 'Where all things gaze themselves and doubt whether they be in it or without.'" The Curzon women were, to the transcendentally minded Whittier, priestesses of a divine Nature. So, indeed, he termed them in a poem inspired by an impromptu visit made one day when he had forgotten to take money for the bridge toll and had stopped to borrow. He found the "sprites of the river" hanging out the wash. The celibate Whittier may have come close to a romantic admiration for the vivacious and pretty Mary, and when she presented him with a bunch of catkins one day, he went home to write a little poem that declares, with the poet's melancholy vanity:

. . . maidens in the far off twilights
Singing my words to breeze and stream
Shall wonder if the old-time Mary
Were real or the rhymer's dream.

She was definitely wooed by other distinguished visitors, in any case. One of these was the artist William Morris Hunt. Another was William Ellery Channing. "She was delighted to tell of her last interview with Mr. Channing, and once she even told it to me, perhaps under the impression that I was older than I was," Marquand recalled. Channing's first wife having died because, according to rumor, of his neglect, he presented himself to Mary Curzon, only to be tartly told, "Ellery, you have killed off one wife, but you certainly won't kill me."

She remained unmarried despite this and similar opportunities, preserving in her own personality some quality of that mid-nineteenth-century "feminine" moment that was peculiarly epitomized by the life of the women of Curzon's Mill in their indifference to practical achievement and their cultivation of ethical refinement and love of the beautiful. Yet the "masculine" element of our culture, more matter-minded than idealistic, was what, in the end, sustained the life of Curzon's Mill after the death of Samuel Curzon in 1847. John Hoxie and Elizabeth came back after a while from Brook Farm, and the young carpenter applied himself to the task of running the Mill, making it a source of income for the first time in years. It was he who built the little red Brick House for his own family and developed the flower gardens and orchards, which Samuel Curzon had only had time to lay out. And Margaret, after rejecting the famous abolitionist Thomas Wentworth Higginson, married John Marquand's grandfather, a hardheaded young businessman who, like his own colonial ancestors in Newburyport, could make a fortune while keeping unshakable faith in the general rightness of the universe.

The Curzon story mingled in the legend-drenched air of the Mill with the history of the Marquands. Young John listened to the talk of the Marquand sisters, his father's sisters, Greta, Bessie and Molly—the last two unmarried and present there constantly from his childhood until they died in the 1930's. They told him the tale of a masculine ancestry that had once been mighty in Newburyport. The Marquands had been practical-minded, assertive men, beginning with Daniel Marquand, a Guernsey merchant and shipowner. He decided in 1732 to settle in the young port, which had in a generation become a focus of colonial shipping. Daniel had sensed an opportunity, having visited the place in his own ships which now joined the fleet, sending barrel staves cut from Merrimack Valley lumber to be exchanged for West Indies rum, picking up tobacco or flaxseed or rice from southern American ports and calling in England for hardware, spices and fine clothes or at Málaga for wine or Quebec for wheat. Soon he was able to build a spacious, two-story, gambrel-roofed house, which fronted the riverside so he could see his ships come in at his own dock. As his twentieth-century descendant stared hard at the picture of Daniel Marquand, which hung in the dining room at the Mill, he thought of what his aunts had told him about the expansive red waistcoat worn by the gentleman in the painting. He was said to have instructed his tailor to make it without false backing, "red cloth all the way around." Like his waistcoat, Marquand imagined, the eighteenth-century Newburyporter's character had possessed no hidden mysteries but was entirely and proudly what appeared on the surface. It conveyed a practical spirit quite the opposite of that elusive poetic strain that had come to him in the traditions of the Curzon ladies.

Daniel's son, Joseph, who was born in 1748, married Rebecca Coffin, daughter of a prosperous fellow merchant and member of the family that had furnished the island of Nantucket with its first governor. He seems to have been a man of attractively compounded daring and business sense, patriotism and pecuniary drive, hardheadedness and piety. During the Revolution he took the lead among Newburyport shipowners who, like the Curzons in Baltimore, turned their merchant vessels into practical men-of-war. Armed with letters of marque from Washington and swivel guns mounted on deck, the Marquand ships robbed and destroyed enemy shipping to the advantage of the American cause and their owners' pockets. The schooner *Washington*, of which he was part owner, was among the first Newburyport vessels to sail out upon this hazardous and profitable career in December 1775, and she was out on the dangerous wartime seas repeatedly during the next two years.

As the war progressed, Joseph Marquand and his partners sent out other vessels: the brig *Virgin*, 130 tons; the ship *Monmouth*, 200 tons; the ship *Unity*, 150 tons; the ship *Lyon*, 250 tons; and others. Though he suffered considerable losses at this risky business, he ranked fifth among the town's wealthiest citizens as late as 1786. Newburyport prospered during these years of national crisis and war, and homes were soon filled with rare merchandise snatched from British holds. The Marquand house on Water Street became a place of gay receptions where the finest European wines were served amid elegant furnishings. The house was long gone, and so was Joseph Marquand's money, John's aunts sadly told him, yet the whole precarious refinement of that early time was made visible by objects here and there that had come to rest at Curzon's Mill. There were, for example, four Chippendale chairs of the darkest mahogany, which had become as brittle as porcelain with age and on which he was forbidden to sit. Their preciousness and delicacy conveyed something even to a child. These, and a tall clock made in London along with a pair of silver candle snuffers he was shown, had a history that made the peril and glamor of privateering visible. At the opening of the Revolution, he was told, Joseph Marquand was rich enough to contribute two vessels to Benedict Arnold's Kennebec expedition. It was a Marquand privateer that took these items from a ship which was carrying them across the ocean to the governor-general of Canada.

All went so well for a while that there occurred an incident which John Marquand heard about again and again from members of the family, an anecdote which he in turn would recount many times when he was grown up. "There are two versions of this legend," he would say. "The first is that [Joseph Marquand] was called from his countinghouse to the head of Marquand Wharf to see two new fine prizes being escorted by one of his vessels into the harbor. When he saw them, he is supposed to have spoken as follows: 'Lord stay Thy hand; Thy servant hath enough.' The other version is more theatrical. In this, he is rowed out to view the prizes, and on this occasion his privateer captain presented him with a handsome and massive silver bowl taken from one of the ships. After gazing at it, he tossed it into the river, repeating the same words. Needless to say, to round out the anecdote, retribution soon followed. The Lord stayed His hand, and things went very badly afterwards. The Marquand privateer, *America*, disappeared with all hands, and finally the Newburyport Fire destroyed all of Joseph Marquand's property."

There was something in the historic climate of this story that John Marquand found fascinating, if somewhat obscure to the mind of a twentieth-century person like himself. "The speech of my great-great-grandfather's is a reflection of a certain facet of the latter eighteenth-century New England mind. To a modern it has a schizophrenic quality, an unreconciled split between God and privateering, but it is doubtful whether this contradiction disturbed many of Joseph Marquand's contemporaries." No pictures survived of Joseph Marquand, and he left behind no letters or journals like those Samuel Curzon had written; only a few receipted bills and a Waterford glass decanter with his initials on it turned up when John Marquand searched for clues to this ancestor's character. Yet he was, in some ways, the most thought-provoking of the ghosts at Curzon's Mill. That "unreconciled split" between God and privateering was the sort of untroubled self-contradiction that might have been the most enviable of all his ancestor's advantages.

It was self-contradiction, no doubt, that led Joseph Marquand to be a partisan of the party of Jefferson when the rest of his fellow merchants became fanatic supporters of the Federalists. The logic of self-interest certainly ranged him with them on the Federalist side. By the turn of the century, Newburyport had become a consolidated small capital of shipping wealth, with mounting fortunes made in neutral trade during the wars between the English and the French. It is said that until the Embargo of 1807, Newburyport holds were bringing into the port from the French West Indies goods worth $1,500,000 a year—molasses, coffee and sugar, which had been exchanged for fish and lumber and other New England products, and were then reshipped to northern European ports at double or triple profit. Republican foreign policy aroused the wrath of Newburyporters because it placed increasing restrictions on such a lucrative trade. Joseph Marquand and the few Republicans in the town who supported the national government must have been treated with lively animosity.

The town had, indeed, after the slump that followed the Revolution, been enjoying an extraordinary prosperity, one that went beyond the war boom which had made Joseph Marquand wealthy. There was more money and new money in the town; the shops displayed fineries of dress and home furnishings of a quality and variety rivaling what was offered in London and New York. And Newburyport had a cultural sparkle, too, that made her seem a Florence of early America, with crafts of every kind at a peak of activity, and men of intellect residing there, like the great lawyer Theophilus Parsons and practical inventors like Jacob Perkins, who designed machines for making nails, writing checks, gold-plating beads, et cetera, and Orlando Merrill, who invented the "waterline" ship-model method of construction, which is supposed to have revolutionized shipbuilding. It was in this period that many of those masterpieces of private architecture, which still stand on Newburyport's High Street, were built. To young John Marquand, as to every child in Newburyport, they would always speak of a time when the town had been an important place, a place of wealth and might and also of fleeting grace. To the older John Marquand they expressed a moment of American idyll when materialism and aesthetics were joined as they were not to be again.

The spectacle of Newburyport history in Joseph Marquand's time absorbed the twentieth-century novelist, who wrote and spoke of it throughout his life. In an early series of connected stories, which were published together as *Haven's End,* he mingled romantic invention with true history, showing the procession of changing times in the fortunes of the Swales and the Scarlets, who were recognizably the true-life Tracy and Bartlet families. The Tracys were colonial aristocrats who had lived with style in their fine brick town house until, after the Revolution, they suffered disastrous losses of their shipping to the British. Their case was similar, of course, to that of Joseph Marquand, who also lost shipping and assets towards the end of the war, and when the fire of 1811, which razed much of Newburyport's waterfront, destroyed all his warehouses and his Water Street home as well, his economic position was leveled irrecoverably. Economic authority in Newburyport passed to a new group represented by William Bartlet, a cordwainer's son who eventually opened the first American cotton mill and became the richest man of the community.

One of Joseph Marquand's contemporaries captivated the imagination of the grown John Marquand more than any other. This was Newburyport's most famous eccentric, the subject of a biography Marquand published in 1925, and of *Timothy Dexter Revisited,* the extensive revision he wrote just before his death thirty-five years later. Like Bartlet, "Lord" Timothy Dexter got rich in those days of "upward mobility," to use the phrase made famous by William Lloyd Warner (who became an acquaintance of Marquand's while conducting his social studies of Newburyport). A penniless leather dresser when he arrived in the city, he soon accumulated enough capital to invest in Continental currency and make other speculations that proved, to the astonishment of the prudent, to be extremely well calculated. Legendary are his sales, in the West Indies, of warming pans (convertible to sugar ladles!), and of mittens (reshipped to Russia!), and to Newcastle, England, of the proverbial coal (during a coal strike!). He became a rich man—and the town buffoon. He enjoyed his role of half-illiterate jester whose grotesque airs of grandeur were a telling parody, whether unconscious or deliberate, of the pretensions of the worthies—Tracys or Bartlets—of the town. With a nice instinct for social irony he purchased the Tracy house two years after Washington had been entertained there, and some years later moved to one of the grandest dwellings on High Street. This house, once owned by the Tracys' business partner, Jonathan Jackson, became a sort of sideshow and museum of oddity, its fence and lawn decorated by brightly painted wooden statues of famous personages, its garden containing an ornate tomb where Dexter rehearsed his own burial. Dexter's apologia, though there is nothing apologetic about it, was a bizarre and surprisingly shrewd little book called *A Pickle for the Knowing Ones,* which invited the reader's condescension by its egregious errors of spelling and total lack of punctuation only to somehow win his respect for the saucy wit of the writer.

There was something oddly ancestral, for John Marquand, about this comic figure from the past who consorted so incongruously with the dignified Curzons and Marquands. One cannot but wonder why he was so fond of the fellow, why his imagination harked back to him repeatedly, dwelling on his pranks as though they satisfied some deep identification. But was Marquand not, beneath his own liking for dignity and style, his respect for traditional values, another nose-thumber at settled authority? For old Joseph Marquand, who lived out his years in increasing alienation from the Tracys and the Bartlets of his day, a Timothy Dexter might have also provided some sour amusement. He did not purchase a fine mansion on High Street to replace his lost waterfront house, and he left his descendants a much-dwindled estate. An insider become outsider, he resigned from the congregation of the First Religious Society after hearing the minister proclaim antigovernment views from the pulpit. But his loyalty to the national government was rewarded. He was appointed Collector of Customs for Newburyport, holding the post until his death in 1817. Two months earlier he had served, with justified pride, one imagines, on the committee that welcomed President Monroe on his visit to the city.

His son, Joseph, John Marquand's great-grandfather, seems to have led the lighthearted life of a man who had just enough money to support a cheerful ease and felt no compulsion to leave anything to future generations. The family rumor was that he had a strong liking for rum and whiskey, and if a mock epitaph by a contemporary is to be credited, for dancing and female company as well:

Here lies our kind Joe
And a handsomer beau
Ne'er danced with a handsomer lady.
He's had his last ball
And he's now left the hall
For a place that is narrow and shady.

Little more was said about the second Joseph Marquand by John Marquand's relatives; he seems to have been a somewhat embarrassing interruption to the Marquand tradition of sober effort. But in his son, John Phillips Marquand, the family traits reasserted themselves. Though he started life as a poor boy he became a rich man. He began self-support at fifteen, shipping before the mast as a common sailor on a voyage to China, though he must have realized that there were better routes to riches in commercial America of the 1850's. On his return to Boston he became a clerk for a shipping firm on India Wharf, and after a couple of years, a clerk for Blake Brothers, the important banking and brokerage house he would eventually head. But still a clerk after four years, he went on to better jobs with a succession of Boston firms, and finally became a member of a prominent company, Hubbard Brothers. In 1873 he was ready for a partnership in Blake Brothers, and a few years later he moved to the Blake Brothers' principal office in New York. When young John Marquand knew his grandfather in the 1890's he was a prominent member of New York banking circles with a handsome brownstone residence on Lexington Avenue.

Even in 1860, when he married Margaret, the youngest of the Curzon sisters, John Phillips was already doing well as a young financier—and this was fortunate indeed, for he was a widower with a daughter as well as his own mother, the gay Joseph II's widow, to support. The Curzon girls were his second cousins, so he could have had no illusions about the conditions of life at the Mill (after the death of John Hoxie, things had taken a downward turn). But he seems not to have blanched at assuming the responsibilities of the Mill property and of a set of Curzon dependents. Besides his mother-in-law and the Hoxie family, he had to take on the sisters' runaway brother George, who was unsuccessfully sheep-farming somewhere in the West. His own good nature amused him afterwards. To his five- or six-year-old grandson, who was walking with him one day down the sandy road to the milldam, he said: "John, when I first came down here everyone was barefoot." Which at the moment the boy saw with a shocking literalness—Great-aunt Mary, for example, whom he could not imagine without her black-kid, high-buttoned shoes, suddenly appeared to his appalled imagination with bare and dirtied feet beneath her gingham skirt. As an adult he still thought he saw the scene as his grandfather went on to describe it: "They were sitting under an apple tree playing 'Quotations,' Margaret was painting a picture and they asked me to stay to supper and then they found there wasn't any supper. I took Margaret down in the carryall and bought some. That was forty years ago. I've been buying everybody's supper ever since. The whole damn family's supper." Very soon, of course, he had six more children of his own. By the time of the walk down the sandy road with his grandson, his wife and one of his sons were invalids and another had died after much illness. His eldest and his youngest daughters were indeed married—but one to an artist and the other to an architect, both of uncertain income, and the other two, Molly and Bessie, had already resigned themselves to spinster dependence on him. As for John Marquand's father, Philip, he had abandoned his profession of civil engineering, having lost several jobs in Wilmington, Delaware, and was trying to get started as a stockbroker in New York—with his father's help.

In looking back at the picture afterwards, Marquand saw the haunted ethereality of Curzon's Mill in a different light. When he too proved himself efficient in earning a living, not only for himself but for a considerable family, and when he too took Curzon's Mill in hand as it was slipping into physical dissolution, he came to identify with his grandfather. He saw there were two viewpoints about the place. Undeniable was the charm of the unworldly and graceful existence that his Curzon aunts led—lives in which an arcadian simplicity was preserved along with an aristocratic high-mindedness and intellectuality that rightly scorned the vulgarities of the modern world. But there was something compelling about his grandfather's realism, his common sense, his unwincing acceptance of the conditions of material life. After all, despite his very impressive expenses, his grandfather had been able to leave an estate of $600,000 at his death in 1900. And this amount, 1900 being a depression year, was somewhat less than he would have left if he had died only a few years later, when his own business calculations, one of his partners later said, would have led to a gratifying increase of his assets. As it was, his annual income was probably about $300,000—a figure that remained in John Marquand's mind. Aunt Bessie told him once that her father had asked a friend if he would not like a partnership in Blake Brothers. When the friend inquired how much could be earned annually from such a partnership her father had said $300,000. "My aunt Bessie, who was somewhat of a romanticist, may, through illusions of past grandeur, have inflated this income, but there always was a universal feeling that my grandfather had a lot of dough. He must have, with trips to Hot Springs and Florida and European tours for the girls and boys."

John Marquand had his theories of how such competence as a provider had affected his grandfather's family: "Now that my grandfather's days are so long over that they begin to assume the romantic aspects of a historical novel, I have sometimes reflected on the effect that his moneymaking capacities may have had upon his children, including my own father and more indirectly upon his grandchildren, myself excluded, due to my father's financial incapacities. The effect, I am afraid, was not always wholesome.

Even in my very early childhood a golden myth began to surround my grandfather, a myth which endowed him with capacities and virtues which perhaps he did not possess. Certainly there was a feeling among his family and among many of his employees that he was a person of inexhaustible wealth and good nature from whom one only had to ask but to receive. His daughter, my aunt Bessie, for example, whose mind was always returning to past glories when I knew her best, was always saying that if Papa were only alive he would buy her this and that. I believe that all my aunts were resentful in some degree when my grandfather, who had acquired the swan farm adjoining Curzon's Mill on the Merrimack River, sold it for a nominal sum to his young friend Mr. Frederick Moseley in order to acquire a good congenial neighbor. My aunts always faced Mr. Moseley's large and increasing wealth with mixed emotions and none of them was ever able to forget that the high bluff upon which Mr. Moseley built his house had once been family property. My great-aunt Mary once acidly addressed a note to Mrs. Moseley as 'Mrs. Moseley high above me,' which was placed in the Newburyport post office and reached its proper destination. My aunt Greta frequently said that all she would ever have needed to do was to have told Papa that she would have liked the swan place and he would have given it to her and would not have sold it to Mr. Moseley. On several occasions I have heard her make this remark to Mr. Moseley personally and I have never thought that Mr. Moseley, who had a banker's blue eye and a measured sense of humor, was ever entirely sympathetic or amused. I have often heard my own mother say that when we were living at 51 East 30th Street in New York all she would have needed to do would have been to ask Papa Marquand to buy her the house and he would have done so. When my grandfather's niece's cousin Nan married a somewhat non-producing farmer named Asa Newhall and produced a large family of children that lived with few visible means of support, my grandfather finally bought his nephew-in-law a large and handsome farm upon the upper Artichoke in the neighborhood of what is known as Turkey Hill. When my grandfather presented Cousin Asa with the farm, I am told that Cousin Asa asked him what good was a farm without stock, and my grandfather bought it for him. When the Newhall's daughter, my cousin Bess, showed scholastic tendencies, my grandfather put her through Radcliffe College. Once my mother visited her there and commented on the expansiveness and beauty of the quarters, and I am told that my cousin Bess admitted they were nice and added that she knew that Cousin John would want her to have the best. Everyone always knew this. When death brought his earning capacities to a sudden halt there was, I am afraid, not only a feeling of consternation but also a slight sense of unfair treatment and a belief that the world was out of joint."

As Marquand's account suggests, his grandfather had no reason to see his own likeness in any of his children; his example of unfailing solvency and attention to practical matters had a quite contrary effect upon those around him. This included, as his grandson clearly realized, Philip Marquand, the only surviving son, Marquand's own father. There is a very special and personal edge to this half-humorous tale of family dependence in the previous generation which John Marquand set down when he too had a large family and felt that his relatives generally assumed themselves entitled to the fruits of his hard-earned success. In the same unpublished reminiscence just quoted from he continued: "I believe that more than anyone else in the family, I have been conscious, perhaps neurotically so, of this collective state of mind, because it happened by sheer fluke that I should be the first one in all the family picture ever to earn any money in substantial amounts after my grandfather, for whom, ironically enough, I was named. When I first began selling stories to the Saturday Evening Post, for two and three thousand dollars apiece, a secret I could never keep, and one that became inflated by gossip, I became aware of a universal feeling that the family was in the chips again. I became amazed by what was expected of my hospitality, and it finally seemed the consensus of opinion among my surviving relatives that it was only socially just that they should live at Curzon's Mill while I supplied them with furniture and paid for upkeep and taxes. As I see it now this expectation was only a part of old tradition and no doubt it is my fault that I did not follow in my grandfather's footsteps, but then I had five children of my own, and he had never heard of an income tax, not even in the Panic of 1891."

The old man could not have known, when he died in 1900, that his eight-year-old grandson and namesake, though soon to show a Curzon propensity for books and ideas, was the one veritable Marquand on the horizon. At some point, perhaps when he first began to suspect the facts about his father's ineffectiveness, the boy's desire for a masculine model may have been satisfied by the memory of his grandfather. It is possible to discern in the remarks just quoted a certain complacency in having brought upon himself, by his superiority of worldly competence, the harassing expectations of others in the family, who looked to him for assistance as their elders had looked to his grandfather. It made the identity more complete. And memory led back towards glimpses he had had for a few brief years of this veritable progenitor. He tried to invoke his grandfather's personality out of stray bits of family history or accidental revelations by those survivors who had known him. "Of course there is no way of knowing now but I imagine he had a sharp tongue and quite a good sense of humor. He also had a capacity for making friends, and his business associates had a deep affection and respect for him. It surprised me to hear my cousin Charles Head say that he was very shy. In the thin and poverty-stricken days of my childhood I have often thought of his kindness and have also thought in a rather mean way of how much money he could have left if he could have been a little more on the ball in Nassau Street. He knew all the great operators of his time. Mr. Pullman was a great friend of his, and I am told that Mr. Russell

Sage liked him, and he despised the morals of Jay Gould." Years later Marquand recalled to a friend the distant memory of an occasion when Jay Gould's son Edwin, who was at grammar school with him in New York, asked John to stay with him on the Gould yacht. When Grandfather Marquand heard of the invitation he exploded. No relative of his, he said, was going "to set foot on anything bought by the money of that thieving rascal."

The elder John Phillips Marquand was on better terms with Harriman and the senior Morgan, Marquand remembered hearing. He ought to have made more of his opportunities to become as rich as they were. "I have often thought he might have given more attention to playing the market, but then I know nothing of his capacities or problems and it is too late to reconstruct them now. I only had one other glimpse into his past and this was a rather strange one. When I was a freshman at Harvard, I happened to call on a house in Weston, Massachusetts, one weekend, and in the family was a very old gentleman sitting by the fire drinking a glass of whiskey. I am sorry that I have entirely forgotten his name. I do remember, however, that he became most effusive when he knew I was the grandson of his old friend John Marquand. They had both been to New Orleans, he said, to buy cotton when that city had been taken over by Union troops during the Civil War. He told me that my grandfather had nerve enough to do anything and that he was brave as all hell, but I do not know what he was brave about. He was a married man with a family and he was trying to get along."

2

Fathers

There is something paradoxical about John Marquand's identification with his grandfather, who, after all, died when the boy was only seven, while his father lived until that boy had become a man of sixty-one, who would live only six years more. For all Philip's persistence upon the scene of his only son's life, he remains a dim figure about whom John would never have much to say.

Philip had been his own father's final hope when, in January 1900, lingeringly dying in Jacksonville, Florida, the old man wrote to his daughter-in-law: "Tell old Phil I want him to cheer up, he is the only boy I have now, and I want him to meet all troubles with pluck and coolness. I hope he is beginning to do a good business now." Successful in everything he had undertaken, John Phillips was now counting his losses. His wife, Margaret Curzon Marquand, had died in 1898, and in October 1899, his invalid oldest son had finally died. Philip's youngest brother, Russell, the family favorite, had already been taken off in 1884 at the age of fifteen; his gay letters written from the Maine woods, where he was vainly thought to be recovering, were shown to John Marquand long afterwards by his still-tearful aunts. So there was only Phil, who responded fatally as it later appeared, to his father's desire to perpetuate his own image. He abandoned the career in engineering for which he had carefully prepared himself and entered the uncertain waters of commerce and finance. "I cannot understand why my grandfather ever thought my father had a head for business," said John Marquand later on, having seen the contrary amply illustrated; "but," he added, "I imagine that emotion and loneliness interfered with his judgment." Buoyed up by John Phillips's wishful thinking and monetary support—which was reinforced by the legacy left at his death—Philip persisted in the pursuit of wealth until the crash of 1907 quite wiped him out. The deflection had become, by then, too profound to be corrected, and though he returned to engineering he could not, it seemed, discover how to get ahead, to seize the next rung and the next until he was able to survey the world of lesser men. Perhaps he was disabled, too, by having seen that fortunes could be made more easily in the gamble of stocks and bonds, for he could never afterwards resist the impulse to plunge into those mysterious depths that had yielded wealth to his father but continued to leave him poor.

No doubt his promise, originally, had been sufficient to his proper destiny. Philip Marquand had been a bright and lively boy, with the gamecock physical quickness and pugnacity that often go with small stature. At Harvard he was not only a competent student who excelled in mathematics and science and was elected to Phi Beta Kappa, but he was also a member of the class tug-of-war team, the shooting club, canoe club, camera club, chess and whist club, and of Hasty Pudding, and he won the university featherweight sparring championship. When he graduated in 1889 he had obviously desired a career based solely on his own abilities and he had gone directly to MIT, emerging two years later with a degree in civil engineering. Then, on March 20, 1892, he was married in Cambridge and shortly afterwards moved to Wilmington to begin life as a construction engineer for the American Bridge Company. He had not chosen the wrong profession, for he had a real love of design and construction problems and the sort of mind that makes either for the tinkering of the gadget maniac or the true inventor. He is supposed, at any rate, to have perfected a new kind of bridge unit called the Marquand span.

Even in Wilmington, however, the powerful presence of John Phillips Marquand must have been felt in the brick house at 1301 Pennsylvania Avenue where the young couple established themselves. When their son was born on November 10, 1893, he was, of course, named for his grandfather. Margaret Fuller Marquand had no memory at all of her own father, Richard Fuller, who had died of inflammatory rheumatism when she was two years old, and she adored her father-in-law as much as his own daughters did. She would often say that he was the only father she had ever had, and when John Marquand was a little boy she constantly strove to bring them into special relation with one another—and perhaps she succeeded—by reminding everyone of the fact that her son was, after all, his only namesake.

And so John was born twice-fathered in a city that would be his home for only a year before the pull of his grandfather's will would draw him and his parents away. Within a year Philip was established with his father's help in Boston in a firm of his own, Marquand and Stearns, which acted as agents for the American Bridge Company. The couple and their baby moved in with Phil's sister Greta and her husband, the architect Herbert Dudley Hale, who were renting a house on Pinckney Street on Beacon Hill. But after a winter of shared quarters the young Marquands moved up to

Curzon's Mill in Newburyport, from which Philip commuted to his office on Kilby Street in downtown Boston. It was during the year 1895, spent mostly in the Brick House at the Mill, that John's earliest memories, already described, began to form. He was never, actually, to "live" at—only to visit—Curzon's Mill, after this year when he was two or three until his sixteenth year, when he moved in with his aunts and entered Newburyport High School. But the Mill remained a rhythmic refrain in the cycle of every year, a place for summer holiday. While his life elsewhere was to prove full of moves and changes, the unchangeableness of the Mill, confirmed with every visit, delighted him. It was even more a kind of Eden because he was forced to leave it at summer's end, and being an Eden, it was the place to which he would strive to return always.

In the earliest years his grandfather's presence occasionally stalked this paradise like an impeccably dressed deity just arrived from Heaven (no doubt a formal and urban place). When he was perhaps no more than four years old, the following incident took place: "I was down at the water trough pushing my boat about in the warmish water and I can remember very well the pleasant slippery feeling of the scum on the trough's sides. I played with the scum out of scientific curiosity until my starched Victorian dress and my long yellow curls were entirely covered with it. At this point I remember that my grandfather appeared, seemingly out of nowhere. He was not a tall or an imposing man. His head was round and partially bald and his mouth was well concealed by a thick, grizzled walrus moustache. His eyes had the same limpid quality as those of his banking friend Mr. Moseley, but they were less glacial and more susceptible to humor. I remember distinctly the elegance of his costume on that lost hot summer's day. Even in the country I imagine the senior partner of Blake Brothers had to keep up his position. He was dressed informally in a greyish sack suit. His waistcoat enclosed his abdomen in a graceful parabolic curve that was emphasized by an enormous watch chain that extended from pocket to pocket (this chain was cut from my own father's waistcoat later by a New York thief when my father fell asleep once in the Third Avenue Elevated). My grandfather's cuffless trousers were exquisitely creased and his black shoes shone in the noonday sun. I remember his telling me to get out of the watering trough, and when I refused and he lifted me out I remember kicking him in the stomach until he set me down and dragged me to the brick house. Then I have a vision of my mother standing in the front door as pretty as a boy's mother ought to be, and I remember my grandfather saying, 'He's stubborn, Margaret, he damn near broke my watch.' I have very little doubt regarding the accuracy of his speech, because I think it was the first time I ever heard the word 'damn' and oaths always stick fast to memory." What must have stuck fast equally with the godlike privilege of cursing reserved for this grandfather was the likeness of character of both man and child. Disturbed in his languorous aesthetic musing at the slimy trough, the little boy did not yield to the will of that immaculate grandparental majesty, but met it with a will as strong, and nearly broke its glittering symbol, the massive gold watch.

Philip Marquand, who would later allow a thief to cut the watch from his person, is absent from the remembered incident, but John Marquand's mother is pleasantly present, almost as the grandfather's spouse, sharing with her father-in-law the responsibility of dealing with the child. She is also, in a way, the son's spouse as well—"as pretty as a boy's mother ought to be." And, as is common enough, she probably was the object of an oedipal devotion the more intense because her husband secured, as the years went on, so little of his only son's regard and affection. She seems to have been one of those mothers whose strong presence in her son's psychic life is demonstrated by the very absence of acknowledgment; he hardly ever referred to his mother in the humorous reminiscences of his early life that became a stock part of his repertoire of monologues; whereas he would tell mocking anecdotes about his father over and over again. She was too sacred, perhaps, to be the subject of a funny story. Or maybe she was too powerful, too threatening. Maybe, on a level not consciously acknowledged, her son suspected that his father's inefficacy was somehow her fault. Margaret Fuller Marquand was, in later years, described as a person of somewhat formidable dignity by those who knew her, a woman who gave the impression of knowing her worth, whatever vicissitudes might overtake her as a result of her husband's vagaries. She was uncomplaining, stoical—and all the more admirable therefore—and she was revered by her son till she died. John Marquand's first wife, Christina, was never entirely at ease with her and in the end would suffer the accusation that is likely to light upon an awkward daughter-in-law: that she had not appreciated this woman whose virtues she could not hope to equal.

In Marquand's fiction a number of characters clearly derive from his father—a recurring image of charm and unreliability. But of his mother there is no direct portrait. Marquand's older female images seem to be modeled upon his Curzon's Mill aunts. His portraits of wives most likely bear a relation to their creator's own experiences in marriage, as will be seen. But they may, on some buried level, also derive from an intuition of his mother's role in his parents' marriage. They are mostly hostile women who destroy their men, dominating women. That he himself chose to marry women who would repeat the pattern of domination, or attempt to, is perhaps an example of the way we tend to create in life our own imitations of early experience, almost as though all adulthood were a species of fiction writing that "imitates" the reality of our childhood.

It is curious, in any case, that his imagination was never drawn to the past of the Fullers, his mother's family, as it was to the Marquands and Curzons. And yet the Fullers were as distinguished an American family. They, too, had had a colonial progenitor, Thomas Fuller, who came to America on a tour of observation in 1638, heard Thomas Shepard of Cambridge preach, and decided to stay in the New World. His great-grandson Timothy was a minister and theologian who preached against the Revolution. He was dismissed from his pastorate in Princeton, Massachusetts, in the year of the Declaration, and he retired from the ministry to his farm, where he worked the land and educated his children. Yet he was not the complete conservative his anti-Revolutionary stand seems to suggest, for he voted against the Constitution because he thought that it recognized slavery, and in his will he freed his own slaves.

Impressive and interesting as Timothy was—Marquand eventually named a son after him—the most famous Fuller ancestor was a woman, Timothy Fuller's granddaughter. Writer, editor, and friend and companion of the great Concord figures of the American Renaissance, Margaret Fuller is the only literary worthy among all Marquand's forebears. And yet he does not seem to have been particularly pleased with the connection. Across the gulf of a hundred years he did not much like Margaret, calling her "that extraordinary Dorothy Thompson of the Transcendentalists," and declaring, "She has never been more than a shadow in my life. She certainly would not have approved of me or have enjoyed anything I ever wrote." Which may have been a way of saying that he did not approve of her. He probably shared Hawthorne's opinion that she "took credit to herself for having been her own Redeemer if not her own Creator." When in 1953, he heard from the biographer Louise Hall Tharp that she was planning to write a life of Margaret Fuller, he replied: "I have often heard her discussed with awe and veneration by older members of the Fuller family, none of whom, however, were old enough to have known her. Though I have a deep respect for her genius, I am afraid that she was a neurotic and aggressive person, and I imagine that had I been one of her contemporaries, I would have reacted to her in much the same manner as Nathaniel Hawthorne. Like many other Fullers including her father, she was an intellectual snob, imbued usually with a puritanical self-righteousness, and utterly devoid of numor. Her view of much of the world around her must have been as myopic as her eyesight, and her frustrations and her attitude toward the male sex would surely fascinate a modern psychiatrist." Clearly, Margaret Fuller seemed to him to be an example of the dangerously aggressive female, and it is significant that these remarks were made at a time when Marquand was experiencing intense conflict with his second wife. Only two months later he suffered a heart attack, which he attributed to the violence of one of their arguments.

Margaret Fuller had been the firstborn of Timothy's nine children and had died in 1850 with her Italian husband and their infant in a shipwreck off Fire Island. Her brother Richard, though fourteen years younger, had been her favorite brother by all accounts; she had tried to turn the lamp of her formidable intelligence upon him and had prepared him for Harvard. In return he named one of his daughters after his famous sister, and this child having perished, he gave the name of Sarah Margaret to another. Whether she resembled her aunt or not, this namesake, Marquand's mother, had grown up in Cambridge in an atmosphere that was full of the Margaret Fuller legend.

As she had told him, her father did not live long enough to be a direct influence; he was gone when she was only two. But his wife lived on in Cambridge and later in Wayland, and was to remain a benevolent, regularly visited, grandmotherly presence into Marquand's college years. This lady's family, the Reeveses, might also have made some contribution to Marquand's sense of family derivation for they had their own store of legends. His fourth grandparental family was, like the other three, descended from a colonial immigrant. John Reeves made the journey from London in 1634 at the age of nineteen and settled in Salem. His grandson Jacob moved in 1740 from Roxbury to West Sudbury, now Wayland, and purchased a house which the Reeves family kept as a tavern for seventy years (it is today one of the historic landmarks of New England). The old kitchen fireplace is ten feet broad, and the tavern bar with its drop gate is thronged with romantic ghosts: men from Burgoyne's defeated army who stopped for refreshment, and refugees from British-held Boston who took shelter there (one of them was a girl who married the son of Jacob Reeves). But they were not Marquand's ghosts. He would never hark back to this scene as he did to Curzon's Mill, and he did not summon it into life in his writing as he would the Newburyport where his boyhood had awakened to its ineluctable dreams.

Two Reeves sisters had married two Fuller brothers: Emma had married a Union chaplain, the Reverend Arthur Buckminster Fuller, who was killed at Fredericksburg—her grandson, Marquand's cousin Bucky, was to become famous as the inventor of the geodesic dome. Adeline married Richard, Marquand's grandfather, a widower who had been practicing law in Wayland. He had, it seems, some desire to impress himself upon posterity, having built a striking stone tower on his property, and in 1860, penned a book of "recollections," which would be privately printed by some of his descendants in 1936. Marquand did not share their regard for his grandfather's literary monument. "In my opinion," he said, "it should never have been printed, for it is a document which displays a man who has few literary attainments and who is unpleasantly conceited, selfish and sanctimonious." And he noted traits which he thought ran in the Fuller line: "I believe he had in him a good deal of his father and not a little of Margaret herself." "The Fullers," he then declared, "are imbued with all that is the worst and little of what is the best in New England."

Quite probably we exclude as well as admit "influences" from an early stage of personal history, and negative choices have as much significance, it may be, as those we embrace. Marquand's rejection of the Fuller–Reeves side of his ancestry seems all the more curious and suggestive because he was so strikingly a man who searched the past for its relationship to himself and traced his connection with his Newburyport ancestors with such keen interest. The act of choice meant an insistence upon Newburyport as his true point of origin. As for Wilmington, his actual birthplace, he had nothing at all to say. Though he developed Wilmington associations in later years, when his parents moved back there while he was at college, his own infant origin in Delaware was simply a baffling fact, unconfirmed by the slightest scrap of remembrance.

But other places were also strangely unmemorable, though he could, if necessary, remember them, having spent as a matter of fact far more time elsewhere than at Curzon's Mill by the time he was sixteen. When he was four his parents again decided to live near Greta and Herbert Dudley Hale, who had meanwhile moved to Concord, Massachusetts. There, he had a playmate, Dudley, less than a year his junior, the oldest of the Hale cousins who would come to spend their summer vacations, as he did, at the Mill. Dudley would be closest to him, and the one whose career would seem to parallel his own—Harvard, the War, newspaper work, and advertising—up to the point where Marquand took the turn into the writing of fiction.

But Concord was to prove another temporary home from which he took along only a few splinters of recollection. He remembered that he had fallen once during his play in the nursery and struck his head against a tin horse that was drawing a toy horsecar, or so he thought he recalled, for his mother told him that the scar on his forehead was made by the sharp metal of the horse's ear. The following year, 1898, the Marquands had again moved, this time to New York City. There Philip was established by his father in a partnership in the brokerage firm of Allen, Sand, and Company, with an office on Pine Street in downtown Manhattan. He rented for his family a dignified red-brick house with a wrought-iron balcony at 51 East Thirtieth Street—one of those cross streets that still preserved, with their high stone "stoops" and tiny gardens and trees at the curb, the vanishing New York of Henry James and Edith Wharton.

It is here that John Marquand became more visible to himself in retrospect, a small New Yorker daily conducted to a Miss Moore's School near Fortieth Street. This "play school" for little boys and girls somehow managed to produce in him a childish first version of the detachment, the skeptical withdrawal, with which he would view the ritualized doings of his kind as a mature adult. With a wide-eyed incredulity, as he remembered, he entered the schoolroom, where he encountered what seems to have been an early version of the "progressive" kindergarten of more recent times: "The piano began to play and I was pushed without wishing it into a game of the imagination. I was a little bird flying around the ring, being instructed how to wave my arms like a little bird. I did not want to be a bird and I have never wished to be one. I did not know then that I was becoming part of a 'group' and taking part in a 'group' game, and that I would be a bird or a football player or a high jumper or an orator—I would be whatever they wanted me to be—until secondary education was over. Curiously I was taught to be a bird but I was not told where the school toilet was until it was too late."

His lack of response to the invitation to accept assigned roles, his resistant self, which would find satisfaction only in the writer's invisibility behind a created world, apparently made a poor impression on Miss Moore. She told Mrs. Marquand that the boy was mentally retarded. The indignant mother hastily withdrew her son and sent him to another, more conventional school, Mr. Simm's School for Boys, where, he recalled, "I learned a little ciphering." There is only one other glimpse of him on East Thirtieth Street. The toddler of five who had walked meekly each day with his nurse to Madison Park to play was now a young backyard adventurer of seven. A friend, Bob Duane, lived in the adjoining house. Fifty years later Marquand could recall, in writing him: "As time goes on, I think more and more about East 30th Street and the policeman with mustaches and a helmet like a London bobby calling to me out of the fish store window to ask why I was throwing a rope ladder over the backyard fence. But when I told him I was simply going to visit some friends he was quite nice about it. Do you remember the big white rabbit I had, who dug a hole all for himself in the yard and once ate the whole hem off our housemaid's apron?"

Surely this is the classic childhood paradise, the excitement-filled backyard where adults—parents or Miss Moore with her presumptuous appropriation of his right to imagine for himself—are blissfully absent except for a distant, benevolent policeman, and one's rabbit performs those assaults upon the oppressor that one dare not make. Yet already the small boy was aware of one adult presence, a little like the policeman in remote benevolence and latent menace. That his grandfather Marquand, for all his distance and intermittence, could hold an awful power over him was again illustrated—as that time by the watering trough at the Mill—on the day he was taken from his home to Lexington Avenue for what was supposed to be a pleasant little visit, and made to lie down on a big four-poster bed for a short nap. While he was lying there, not yet asleep, the family doctor entered the room, thrust a cone of chloroform over his nose, and in due course removed his adenoids. When he awakened, his mother assured him that he would be happier and healthier because they had been taken out, a fact of which the child was not as sure as of who had "paid for the adenoids."

But Grandfather Marquand was more visible during the summer of 1899, when he was living alone, after his wife's death, at his cottage at Seabright, New Jersey, and Philip Marquand and his family spent the season near him in the adjoining cottage. The scene imprinted itself. There was a road that passed the two houses and then a single railroad track and then a rock bulkhead and then the Atlantic Ocean. The sea roared and ravaged along the coast on stormy days, and some of the houses built years previously when the shore had not been eroded so far now stood with their foundations nearly in the water. One of these, a huge turreted castle of wood, was pointed out proudly by John's mother as his grandfather's previous summer dwelling—too large, now that he was alone, but somehow more appropriate to him than his present house.

Only two trains a day passed on the railroad track, but the macadam road presented on Sundays a wonderful spectacle of motion. Sitting on their cottage porch the Marquands watched an endless file of bicycles—singles, tandems, triples, and once, even, a bicycle carrying five riders—the men in tight knickers and checked caps, with high collars and Norfolk jackets, the ladies with leg-of-mutton sleeves and long skirts that seemed bound to tangle in the wheels but never did. One day his grandfather appeared with a man who was dressed like one of the riders and was wheeling along a small bicycle. The bicycle, it turned out, was a present to John, and the man was there to instruct him in its use. It was just like his grandfather, Mrs. Marquand said, to be so generous and thoughtful. Unwillingly, but docilely, therefore, he underwent the course of training prescribed, and at the end of a suitable period, his teacher took him to his grandfather's house, and while Mr. Marquand rocked on the porch John successfully rode three times around the circular drive before the door. "How well he does it!" the old gentleman said, and then the child promptly fell off. His grandfather was amused; it went to show, he said, that if you praise a boy who is doing something well he immediately begins doing it badly. Then he gave the man a crisp new bill and went back into the house without further remark.

And yet, suspecting already that Philip would fail him, the senior John Phillips Marquand had his eye on his grandson. Once, during the same Seabright summer, he spent an entire day alone with him. It was one of those days of small incidents with no special significance that remain gripped in memory as though they contain some clue to subsequent experience. John Marquand later called it "one of the most interesting in my life," and tried to set down an account of it. "I wish I could remember it better," he observed, but he seems to have remembered a good deal of the long-ago occasion when the century was just about to die and he was six. His grandfather "quite suddenly one morning" asked if he could not take the boy with him to New York. "My mother was much more delighted by the idea than I was and I remember asking her what I should do if I wanted to go to the bathroom. She said I only had to tell Grandpa, of course, and then she dressed me in a sailor suit with long trousers, a real navy suit which my nurse Hannah's brother-in-law had had made for me because he was a quartermaster in the Brooklyn Navy Yard. My grandfather was dressed quite differently in the conventional Wall Street attire of the turn of the century—striped trousers, a black Prince Albert coat, a high silk hat, a starched shirt, a wing collar, a pearl-colored cravat decorated by a handsome stick-pin, and a waistcoat showing beneath the Prince Albert adorned again with that massive gold watch chain.

"We took a small commuters' steamboat at Rumson or somewhere and set forth across the harbor to lower Manhattan. There used to be a smell about all sorts of passenger ships which was different from what exists now, or else my olfactory nerves have lost their sensitivity. It lingered once about all ferry boats, about the old Fall River line and later about vessels of the Northeast Shipping Company. It was a coastal smell, not quite like that of an ocean liner. It was more secure and more inviting. I think perhaps it had something to do with horse manure and cuspidors, both more prevalent in those days than now. Tar, rubber and jute matting and woodwork soaked by salt water all formed a part of that symphony. I wish I could see as clearly how New York harbor looked as I can smell that steamboat odor. In spite of the shortness of the voyage my grandfather had his own stateroom, I imagine rented for the season. Once he was inside, a colored steward hastened to relieve him of his silk hat and his Prince Albert coat. Then my grandfather settled himself in an armchair and unbuttoned his vest, and then he told the steward that I was his grandson. I now find myself making the same inane remark about my own children and grandchildren. I can understand why I do it but I still can remember that it is uncomfortable from a child's point of view. Even a child can tell that employees, no matter how they try to seem so, are not especially interested in degrees of relationship. Then my grandfather asked me if I wanted a drink of lemonade, and after this was over I told him I should like to go to the bathroom. I can still remember his struggling with the buttons of my authentic sailor suit, and I can still hear him saying that he did not know there were so many damn buttons in the world. I was surprised, having been told that he went to sea himself in his youth, but I did not take up the matter with him.

"There were still, I think, a few square-rigged ships in New York harbor as well as a great many coastal schooners. Of course there were many ocean liners and tramp steamers in the Narrows, and tugboats and barges glided along the waterfront much as they do today. The great difference, of course, lay in the number of sailing craft. Even the pilot boats off Sandy Hook were under sail, each one bearing its numbers. The waterfront itself, when we docked somewhere near the Battery, had the timeless quality of all waterfronts, but once we were in the street we were in the world of the younger Henry James, of Richard Harding Davis, Sydney Porter and even Robert W. Chambers. It is incredible to think that I saw not a single motor-driven vehicle that day in downtown Manhattan. The streets, I think, were noisier without them. Iron-rimmed wheels and the heavy iron shoes of dray horses made a deafening clatter over cobblestones. Instead of taxis, there was a rank of hansom cabs waiting at the curb, and my grandfather and I rode in one of these peculiar vehicles to the office of Blake Brothers at 5 Nassau Street. The general impression of the New York financial district was about the same as now. People were already writing about the stone canyons and the high buildings but of course they were not as high as they are at present. I rather think, however, that there was a greater sense of noise and confusion, a tangle of horse-drawn traffic and armies of Western Union and bank messengers and more newsboys and more bootblacks. Blake Brothers, I believe, was on the ground floor of 5 Nassau Street. It was furnished, at least to my untutored observation, to exude financial confidence. The customers' room was heavy with cigar smoke, mahogany and leather, and the tickers gave off that hysterical undercurrent of sound which had always had a deleterious effect on people like my father. Clerks and cashiers were all in gilded cages standing up at their desks before the ledgers. My grandfather led me through these outer reaches with civil greetings to everyone until we reached his private office with the massive mahogany roll-top desk, a swivel chair, some easy chairs, a table and a letter press, whose descendant you can see now as a duck press in a good restaurant. My grandfather's secretary, or stenographer as she was called in those days, was waiting with his morning mail. She made enthusiastic cooing sounds of interest when she heard that I was his grandson. I remember that she was very, very beautiful, so beautiful that she sometimes makes me think of my grandfather in a non-ancestral light. Her eyes were blue and her hair was golden, done in the pompadour of a Gibson girl. Her starched shirtwaist had a gold watch pinned upon it and her sleeves billowed like a Monday's washing on a windy day. She did not kiss me but she gave me a gentle squeeze. 'Why,' she said, 'he's a little sailor, isn't he?' My grandfather spoke for me, saying that sailors had a great many buttons. Then he began to read his mail, but it must have been a slack day at the office because he gave me almost his entire attention. He introduced me to two of his partners, Mr. Howland and Mr. Brown, and then he took me with him to the customers' room. 'My grandson wants to buy a hundred shares of Missouri Pacific,' he said, 'and he can countersign the order.' I don't know why he wanted me to buy a hundred shares of Missouri Pacific. It may have been because he thought he was furthering my education. I have never bought any since, and this was sold two hours later at a half a point profit. I can still see that customers' room, and I have been to a few since, but all neatness and majesty had left them years ago."

A sense of historical perspective and the personal changes of sixty years infect Marquand's effort to recall this day. Yet its original impact is still discernible. Just as one voice of the nineteenth century spoke through his great-aunt Mary Russell Curzon, the entire "age of confidence" spoke through his grandfather—a time when the pursuit of wealth could be accompanied by "neatness and majesty." He seems never, though this may have been a laying on of hands, to have considered his grandfather's career a model for his own—and yet, perhaps, again, he did; his was, after all, also a "commercial" success. As for stocks and bonds, he understood them well enough; he had none of the intellectual's vaunted inability to make sense of the financial pages of the newspaper, and when, in time, he had money to invest, he took a firm—sensible and unspeculative—hand in managing his own finances.

His attitude towards money was to be, probably, like that of the hero of his novel *Point of No Return*. If he had not been a novelist he might have been, like Charles Gray, a good investment banker: "He was afraid of money and he never lost that fear, and it was not a bad attitude, either, if you had to deal with investments—caution and contempt held together by respect." Charles Gray's attitude is explained, of course, by his response to the character of his father—"Most of his life was dedicated to being as unlike his father as possible"—a statement that probably applies to his creator. To be in some way, despite obvious differences, like his grandfather was to be exactly unlike Philip Marquand.

And now this countermodel was to be the only one before him. A few months after that Seabright summer he was taken to his grandfather's house in New York and sent into a small sunroom off the old gentleman's bedroom. There, amid potted plants and mysterious medical apparatus, Grandfather Marquand was seated in a wheelchair looking quite well, though the boy had been told that he was very ill. They were alone, and it was his grandfather who made the effort of conversation by asking the name of John's current nursemaid. When told it was Mary, he could not resist the impulse to quip, "Well, Mary has a little lamb," which threw his grandson into a furious silence until he was permitted to leave the room. It was his last sight of the man for whom he was named.

Shortly afterwards the household of Philip Marquand underwent a more transforming transplantation than any of its previous moves and changes. Although his parents said that it was for the sake of his health that they had decided to exchange Manhattan for suburban Rye, it was clear, even to the seven-year-old, that his grandfather's death had brought on a new era of high living for the family. They now lived with a cook and a maid in a large yellow house—curiously a little like the Yellow House at Curzon's Mill—located on the Boston Post Road with a barn behind it that contained a carriage, a horse named Prince, and quarters for a coachman who drove his father grandly to the railroad station every morning and fetched him back each evening on his return from Wall Street. Sometime later his father purchased an automobile—a rare and prideful possession in those days. It was an Orient Buckboard, a shining, high, two-passenger model with a motor behind the seat. On occasional Sundays his father engaged in races with other possessors of horseless carriages, to see who could go furthest on a gallon. On other Sundays he drove with his wife and child to the American Yacht Club on the Sound, where he kept a sailing dory called *The Skidoo* with which he competed in club races. As John's cousin Dudley much later recalled, they lived in "very good style."

In one of his early novels, *Warning Hill*, the narrator remarks, "Is there ever a longer gap than that strangely misty lapse between seven and fourteen?" Surely those vital years of "growing up" often seem without drama. The seasons pass with their changing cycles of outdoor play, and the clothes one wore last spring are too tight in the fall. With no special awareness of growing more sophisticated or knowledgeable, one is inchingly "promoted" to the ranks of the big boys once feared and admired. Marquand's was a boyhood eminently "normal"—that is, it showed no sign of that special bending of personality in a single direction which is so often the sign of genius. His teachers would have said that he was a fine, wholesome lad, who made friends, liked sports, and was proficient in his studies, showing only a mild preference for some over others.

Were there no episodes of any kind to punctuate the flow? The next-door neighbors, the Westervelts, remembered a time when the Marquand house caught fire. It was a snowy winter night, and Philip was still in New York, when Mrs. Marquand discovered the fire, called the fire department, and was told that the fire crew might be unable to come through the deep snow. Mrs. Westervelt, arriving to help a few moments after her husband, discovered Mrs. Marquand and her mother, Mrs. Fuller, young John, and the cook standing at the kitchen door while Mr. Westervelt struggled to move a massive sideboard out into the yard. Mrs. Marquand explained that only that week Phil had stocked it with expensive wines and liquors, "paying more for them, of course, than we can really afford," and so it was easily the most valuable piece of furniture in the house. She then put John in charge of it, commanding him to play a hose over its surface to prevent flying sparks from setting it on fire and to see that no fireman—for the crew had begun to arrive after all—presumed to examine or sample its contents. The Westervelts remembered the small boy with a look of high responsibility on his face as he guarded his father's liquor. Curiously, it was a story that John himself claimed to have forgotten. He remembered that there had been a fire, but his own anxiety, as he recalled, was over his parrot, left behind in its cage in his room. From the chamber of memory the image of himself playing hero to preserve his father's latest extravagance had slipped away. It was, of course, another early scene from which his father was absent and his mother took the active parental role.

On the first of the year, in 1906, when he was twelve, he began a small diary, and kept it intermittently for a few months, the only personal record of his schoolboy days. The childish notes of daily activities are touching in their unremarkableness; what American memory does not include the sweet, callow joys of after-school, when the released small prisoner rushes towards the games of the season—skating, sledding, football and baseball, the inviting outdoors of snow and mud as well as of the grass in spring? He was, of course, wild about animal pets, and their deaths brought tears—there is mention of short-lived pigeons, guinea pigs, hens and fish. And sometimes he went with schoolmates on excursions to New York—to see the circus at the Hippodrome, to buy a tennis racket at Spalding's or a copy of *Julius Caesar* at Macy's. His friendship with his Hale cousins had continued. Dudley came to visit at Rye during the winter holiday, and he went to

Uncle Bert and Aunt Greta's farm in Bernardsville, New Jersey, near Morristown, in June. It was a place he at once compared to Curzon's Mill: "There is a mill, a shed, a barn, a house and two brooks. Dud and I played hide-and-seek in the mill with Margy and Bob. The mill is much more complicated than the mill at Newburyport for it grinds corn either coarse or fine and draws it up to the top floor by elevators. And it sifts the feed. But the Mill at Newburyport is much prettier."

Like most normal children he registered discomfort as the mold of the educative process was pressed down upon him. Coming home from dancing school, with his mother and one of her friends, he was expected to jump out of the carriage and help the lady down, but "just as I jumped out my hat fell off in the mud—it is always that way when I try to be polite." School was the usual alternation of satisfaction, annoyance and humor: "I got a 98% in English. The only mistake I made was hindmost and I put hindest. Have to write a composition. Mr. James reads you a story and you have to write it in your own words. I wrote mine but it is all wrong. Mr. Ayrault makes you sit up straight, put your pen in your hand in a loose position and write *nothing* on a piece of paper. School ended today at the Rye Lyceum. It would have been pretty good if Mr. Kraft did not make us sing some horrid little songs. I got rattled in the first line but luckily someone was making a noise. They thought I was waiting till it stopped. I got the prize for being the head of my form."

The school was a new, private establishment at which he was one of the first pupils when it opened in 1901, the Heathcote Hall School for Boys. He was a day student, for Heathcote Hall was just a short distance down the Post Road from the Marquand house—he could go on the school stage or even walk—or on snowy days hitch his sled to the back of one of the sleighs that glided with a tinkle of harness bells past his door. Of this school he gave a curious, wry account many years later in an address to a graduating class of the Lawrenceville School. Speaking to his privileged young audience he told them that it had been his last experience of private secondary education—for he had gone on after Heathcote to a public high school. It is a question whether his listeners entirely grasped the ironies of his description, which, of course, tells as much about the older Marquand and his view of upper-class education as it does about him as a boy.

"It was not a bad school," Marquand recalled. "It was run by a master who spent his apprenticeship in Groton, which indicates he had the best traditions. Mr. Jones was not an intellectual man, but he believed in his mission of turning out an all-round boy. He gave us talks on honesty and decency and fair play. We were taught school spirit and how to stand up at football without flinching. We were taught table manners and the joys of cleanliness. Granted that there was not much intellectual cultivation, it was a good school, and we were all nice boys malleable to the laudable ideals of Mr. Jones. The world as it came to us through him consisted mostly of uncomplicated examples of manly character, such as the message to Garcia. There was not much music or literature. Art consisted of some photographs of the Acropolis and the Colosseum, and I do not think these things interested Mr. Jones nearly as much as his desire to make us fit usefully into the Grotons and Pomfrets where we would someday be going." Marquand was inclined to take Mr. Jones's word, except for the fact that his teacher's personality and creed contrasted so oddly with that of his father, who cheerfully smoked, drank, called Theodore Roosevelt a lunatic, and generally made it impossible for one to admire both him and Mr. Jones at once. The Heathcote boys came to believe what Mr. Jones taught them—that they were different from the fellows who hung around the stationery shop near the railroad station—and it was something of a shock, Marquand remembered, to meet them at the annual school-townie football game—they swore, bit, gouged and kicked. Marquand and his friends were tempted to respond in kind but Mr. Jones told them they must not.

There was, the Heathcote boys dimly knew, a grim, unlovely outer world from which they were gently sheltered. Occasionally someone was forcibly thrust into this world. Charlie Judd, for instance, who had had to leave the school because his father had gone broke; Charlie was not going back to any school, but was working as a bank messenger. The fate of Charlie Judd would prove, before long, to be like Marquand's own. In the crash of 1907 Philip Marquand lost his shirt, having been trading on margin for years. There was literally nothing left of Grandfather Marquand's legacy—indeed, the whole edifice of life on the Post Road instantly collapsed, along with Philip's position as a Wall Street broker. In no time at all, the house with its servants, its horseless carriage, and the sailing dory at the Yacht Club all vanished into thin air; John left Rye and the Heathcote Hall School in a matter of months. In 1909, while his father was supposed to be job hunting in New York, Mrs. Marquand and her son were living in Cambridge with her cousin Edith Fuller and he had entered a public high school, the Cambridge Latin School. But the next year he was at Newburyport High School, and at last "home" at Curzon's Mill with his great-aunt Mary and his aunts Molly and Bessie Marquand.

With this swift change of fortune, something had happened to John Marquand. All the childhood doubts of his father, a furtive suspicion of his unreliability conveyed by the sighs and headshakings of relatives, the look of forbearance so often on his mother's face even during the reign of prosperity, were confirmed like a hideous prophecy. He could remember, now, the sudden spasms of economy that had seized the household from time to time during those seven golden years on the Post Road. One day, Prince and the coachman might suddenly depart and his father begin using a cab from Mr. Sniffen's Livery Stable to get to the station. But after some weeks of gloom and austerity, his father would come home with an air of triumph and soon a new burst of expenditure would begin—at some such juncture he invited his wife and child to look out the parlor window to behold the just-purchased Orient Buckboard at the curb.

Philip was to prove for a long time, longer than anyone could have imagined, unsuccessful in finding a new foothold. For the next year or two he vainly sought a business or engineering job in New York, Boston or Wilmington, and then, while John stayed on in Newburyport with his aunts, Mr. and Mrs. Marquand went to California, in hope of better prospects. During his senior year in high school and well into his college years, they remained there, living again with a relative, a cousin, Anna Head, who had a house in Berkeley. While Philip looked for "the right kind of employment," he did odd jobs of tutoring, and now and then got some temporary engineering work. It was not until the end of 1913 that he found something substantial, an assignment as foreman of one of Colonel George Goethals's construction crews that were building the Panama Canal. Mr. and Mrs. Marquand went down to Panama together and remained there until the outbreak of the First World War. Then, at last, the upsurge in war production enabled Philip to return, after twenty years, to Wilmington.

It would be a place and a time of reconstitution for John Marquand's father. His new job was with the Edge Moor Iron Company, a sister firm of the American Bridge Company, his former employer. Both firms had been created by the engineer-entrepreneur William Sellers, whose family and friends gave the Marquands a place in their "Old Wilmington" social circle. They now lived in a charming stone cottage on the estate of the Bringhurst family at Edge Moor and were often guests at Ellerslie, a country house on the Delaware River where the Sellerses spent time with their relatives Henry and Anne Bradford. The Marquands and the Bradfords became close friends. Mrs. Marquand, with her stately Boston dignity charmingly relieved by humor, was a considerable success in these surroundings; Philip's jaunty good nature was appreciated, his taste for fast vehicles now satisfied by a motorcycle with a sidecar in which he and his wife arrived at social functions somewhat windblown but exuberant. It was probably the best period of Philip Marquand's career, though far beneath the splendors of Rye. But it came too late to mean much to John Marquand, whose sense of trauma after the collapse of that former life was past mending by 1914, when he was finishing at Harvard and preparing to earn his own living.

Philip's position at Edge Moor remained a modest one, and in 1927, when the company was meeting reverses, he was let go. He was, of course, sixty years old by this time, an age at which it was no longer a disgrace to "retire," though he had not a penny of savings. So he returned to Curzon's Mill to live and now his only child, who had by this time become a successful writer of magazine stories and the author of four published books, helped him to set up a small chicken business, raising Rhode Island Reds and selling eggs to local housewives. It was not exactly the sort of enterprise that would have appealed to John Phillips Marquand, the banker, but it promised a sustenance for Philip, and called upon his old penchant for solving technical problems. And yet, he was still the irrepressible gambler who never lost hope of the Big Killing. One time he received a $1,500 check in payment for a shipment of chicks, and hastily changing from farmer's overalls to his city clothes and taking up his favorite walking stick, he announced that he intended to spend the day in Boston. After two days he returned and the $1,500 was gone. When John Marquand asked about it, he was testily told, "I blew it in, and it's none of your damn business."

His old age at last made him an increasing irritation and burden to his son, for as his faculties weakened he became, like many old persons, even more willfully independent, a menace behind the wheel of a car and utterly undependable as far as money was concerned. It is possible, nevertheless, to sympathize with the cocky, improvident failure who would have his own way to the end, rather than with the son, whose talent and toil and prudence had by this time achieved the success promised to such qualities in the American mythic tradition.

All this later history lay years ahead of John Marquand as he left Rye after his father's failure in 1907. But, already, he had discovered the humiliation that was so painfully mixed with the filial desire to admire. These feelings are reflected in the way he handles characters that have their source in Philip Marquand. There is, to begin with, something faintly autobiographical even in that inconsiderable first work, *The Unspeakable Gentleman*, with its theme of a handsome, suave, apparently unprincipled father who proves to his son, in the closing pages, that he has long been a man of honor. It was at least the autobiography of its writer's dream-life, the youth's wishful dream of a vindication for the man his waking mind despised. Fainter still, but probably related to this dream is the plot of the second novel, *The Black Cargo*, in which an apparent scoundrel also justifies himself to a younger man. But it is *Warning Hill*, the third Marquand novel, that most obviously suggests an origin in personal obsession for all the fact that it seems shaped by the automatic formulas of the magazine market for which it was designed. Tommy Michael, who lives at a sort of Curzon's Mill, has a father who is "out of the ordinary running" for charm and intelligence, but gambles on horses and the stock market. Tommy bears the name of his paternal grandfather, who had made money and become a bank president. He both pities and despises his father as he reflects that his grandfather "had no sympathy, surely, for the curse of facility that lost itself. He had no friendliness for failure. . . . He could imagine his father's adroit irony clashing with the fire of an old man's invectives, though all the while poor Alfred must have known that Thomas was dead right. He was useless—damned useless; not fit to carry a corkscrew in his keyring, by God, or to have a bank account." When Alfred Michael finally loses everything, he shoots himself; in real life, of course, the Philip Marquands do nothing of the sort, their capacity for deceiving themselves outlasting their capacity to deceive others. But here again, romantic convention may express a dream, not of exculpation this time, but of retribution.

The figure of Philip Marquand also appears in his son's maturest writing. In *Point of No Return* the father of Charles Gray is a somewhat spruced-up Philip, another of those men out of the ordinary running who are no good to anybody. "Everyone knew about John Gray, and so did Charles. Charles must have known when he was very young that John Gray was unstable, but he never could get to the bottom of this instability. When he tried to admire his father, even when he was a little boy, there was a gap somewhere." He was a charmer, wittily ironic, debonair and full of promises, but the promises were seldom kept. He explained himself once to his son by saying that he wasn't a man to be satisfied by a small wisp of hay from fortune's bundle—he wanted everything or nothing. There was a certain dash and glamor in such a viewpoint, as there was plenty of personal attractiveness, well illustrated in the novel, in John Gray's personality. He understands his son, Charles Gray—John Marquand—quite well when he says, concerning his ambition to "get on," "You want to because I obviously haven't."

Nevertheless, Marquand did not forget the Philip Marquand that subsisted along with the gambler: the bright boy with a real mechanical flair who was essentially unworldly. In *Sincerely, Willis Wayde* he portrays this alternative man in the father of his successful, self-made businessman, who is the book's rather stupefying hero. This father, Alfred Wayde, is an engineer who has no interest in getting ahead, who changes jobs because he is clever and creative and tires of dullness. And somehow, the tables are turned, the "failure" who failed or at least declined to "advance" by reason of his independence of mind is seen as superior to the son who has made it to the top by talents well applied to a business career and the suppression of other possibilities in his own nature. In this late novel John Marquand may have taken a last considering look at the lifelong problem of his relation to Philip Marquand and expressed his own uncertainty about the success he had made, partly in recoil against his father, and partly in emulation of his grandfather.

3

Newburyport

In September 1909, John Marquand began to attend the Newburyport High School. The school was four miles away from Curzon's Mill. He would walk about a mile along the sand road, often not meeting anyone except a farm wagon on its way to West Newbury, and come at last to the trolley turnout opposite the old fairgrounds in a flat, rather barren region known as the Plains. While he waited for the Haverhill–Newburyport car he could look across the tracks at the empty barns and exhibition halls used for carnivals and cattle shows—it was a place familiar to him as the site of innumerable occasions of entertainment and edification during previous summers. Here he had seen a balloonist hang by his knees from a trapeze swinging crazily underneath the balloon and drink a bottle of soda while doing so. He had also seen a harness race here, won a canary bird for fifteen cents on a wheel of fortune, seen his first shell game, and had his first glimpse of three-card monte behind the trotting stables. But in the fall and winter the place had an empty, shabby look and the tatters of posters announcing past splendors flickered like tongues of multicolored fire in the wind that swept over the level ground.

The trolley car would come jangling and swaying along its uneven track, and after he got on, it would go along Storey Avenue, slanting west through fields and woods, finally intersecting with High Street, down which it turned in the direction of the Bartlet Mall at the center of Newburyport. Drowsing over the schoolbooks on his lap, he did not need to watch out of the window to mark the progress of the car past the procession of High Street houses behind elm-shaded brick pavements. Like most Newburyport residents he knew the names of most of their owners, even though he had gone through only a few of the fanlighted doorways. Along this street lived a good many of the oldest families in town, and some, though not all, of the richest. A few of the houses shone crisply fresh-painted and stood on smooth rises of lawn; others were graying behind overgrown gardens. Yet to live on High Street in any of these houses was to live along a ridge of social as well as physical elevation above others.

The high school at the corner of Green Street, directly opposite the Mall, was a homely brown-stucco building with clumsy square wings, each having an entrance in front, one for the boys and one for the girls. The students would file in each morning, noisily calling greetings and challenges across the graveled space that separated the two groups. In a few moments they would be united, still communicating but only along silent channels of awareness in the high-ceilinged classrooms. At recess time and when school was out they poured from the central door that opened from a vestibule containing a plaster statue of Athene. On the wide porch and along the descending steps, little groups all feminine or all masculine lingered or crossed the street to the grass of the Mall. They walked past the brick box of the old town hall down to the edge of the pond, which lay in a hollow; around it—by the beneficence years ago of William Bartlet—the Mall had been raised and leveled. Or they strolled as far as the statue of William Lloyd Garrison, that poor Newburyport boy whose fame was a reminder that not all history had been made by High Street.

For Newburyport was not only High Street, and the best place in which to learn this was the public high school. John Marquand's fellow students came from all parts of the town. They included the sons and daughters of some of the very poorest families, who lived down along the bank where the harbor widened and was bordered by mud flats at the mouth of the Merrimack, families who subsisted on the earnings of clamdiggers and workers in the shoe factories. Or they were the children of clerks and small retailers, whose small frame houses were closely ranged on the side streets between High Street and the river. There were also—for this was America, and class barriers were not absolute walls of segregation—children from some of the "leading families," a few of whom lived in High Street houses: girls who might later go after all to finishing schools; boys, like himself, who would somehow catch up with their prep-school cousins at an elite college. And dozens of children represented a middle class that was just then beginning to reach for power. They were the offspring of factory managers, successful dealers in coal or building materials, and others who had come up in a generation from the ranks of office functionaries and skilled workers and who lived comfortably in the less fashionable parts of town. Their children were the best dressed in the school. At Newburyport High, too, he came into contact for the first time with demonstration of the cliché that America is a melting pot. Of the sixty-odd students in his class, a majority were still of the older Yankee stock which had populated the town since colonial times, but most of the others were Irish, the forefront of a rising wave of numbers and influence. Scattered throughout the school, moreover, were the pioneer representatives of further additions—French Canadians, Greeks, Armenians, Poles and Italians. Newburyport was already, in the first decade of the century, on the edge of the transfer of power that would give these groups more and more political and social importance, just as in neighboring Boston.

Marquand's attitude towards his public school experience was later curiously ambivalent, a mingling of satisfaction for his unforgettable immersion in the realities of communal life and of a contrary sense of deprivation, which made him insist that all of his own five children attend private schools. His ironic views concerning the limitations of private education have already been noted as he expressed them in middle age at the Lawrenceville School. He had gone on: "I ended my education at high school in a small New England town, scrambling for the meager information dispensed by harassed men and women to a cross section of American society. I scrambled for it in the company of privileged and underprivileged boys and girls, mostly underprivileged. We were thrown together in a drafty, ill-ventilated democracy. There was not much time for 'school spirit' or 'character molding.' We did the latter mostly for ourselves. It seemed that acquisition of knowledge beyond a certain point depended on the efforts of the individual, but the institution offered another sort of education which removed me from the contemporaries with whom I was brought up and with whom I have most often associated since. I cannot speak in favor of the public school system as I knew it. Yet it was part of the world; it was an integral piece of a dismaying, vigorous and crude United States of America into which the accident of birth will rub our noses, whether we like it or not." After he became the Newburyport High School's most famous alumnus, it also pleased him to speak, at the commencement exercises, of the advantages of going to a public school. In 1960, a few weeks before he died, he grasped the hand of fifty-year-old memories by inviting the remnant of his high school class to his Newbury country estate for an afternoon and also spoke to the members of the current graduating class that same week, again of his satisfaction at having once been there where they now were.

It is not probable, however, that he was so complacent in his own high school days. In that interlacing dance, that constant joining and exchanging of pairs and groups that govern the lives of adolescents, he was awkwardly out of step. In the recess periods, when appointments were being made for after-school meetings, he would walk off alone—his head down, his straight, light hair parted carelessly on the side and slipping over his eyes—neither seeking conversation with others nor being sought. In the two years he attended the school he seems never to have had a male chum; he was not unpopular, he was simply, with his own assent apparently, without any special attachments. He joined no clubs, engaged in no team sports, and did not even "go out" for the literary magazine, though he had been on the editorial staff of the student journal at Heathcote Hall in Rye. When the school day was over and his classmates went off to sports and visits or to drop into the drugstore on State Street for sodas, he quietly took the electric car back towards Curzon's Mill and the company of his two elderly aunts.

He came no closer to the girls who passed by him, giggling and flirtatious, and tried to tease him out of his taciturnity or coaxed him, sometimes successfully, into helping them during the chemistry lab periods. He fluttered no pulses; the girls thought him dull and odd with his queer, hesitating, almost stammering way of speaking. He was not at all handsome, and rather short; his adolescent spurt of growth, which took him to five feet ten or eleven inches finally, was delayed until after he entered college. As for his clothes, they were, to critical eyes, nearly sloppy, his whole appearance somewhat negligent. One of the girls, Josephine Little, understood in time why he had insisted on sending his children to boarding schools where all the surfaces of youth are smoothed and trimmed to an agreeable conformity: "If he had gone to Middlesex or Andover he would more nearly have resembled his later, well-groomed, well-polished appearance. He would not have been allowed to wait until his shaggy, unkempt hair reached his collar before having it cut; he would have been urged or commanded, 'Stand up, don't slouch,' as he walked. Some attention might have been paid to his fingernails and his grimy wrists, which emerged from too-short coat sleeves. His hesitant speech might even have been corrected to the point where, willy-nilly, he had to improve it."

Still, one asks, was he not compensatingly interesting in any way? Apparently he showed no sign of that caustic humor for which his adult conversation became memorable. The same schoolmate says: "His school contemporaries, when asked to repeat any witty remarks that they could remember him uttering, wrinkle their brows and shake their heads. 'No, I don't remember anything funny that he ever said,' they admit. He was funny, of course, with that terrible queer walk of his and his voice and his terrible clothes, but he didn't mean to be."

In those later years when his fame made them eager to believe that they had noticed him more vividly or seen something exceptional and promising in John Marquand, his teachers and fellow students tended to gloss over this picture and discover evidences that they had not seemed to notice at the time. It was a progressive improvement of memory that amused Marquand and provided a few pages of irony in his late novel *Sincerely, Willis Wayde*. After the fictional hero became the most successful citizen of Clyde—one of Marquand's several pseudonyms for Newburyport—his aging teachers called to mind forgotten instances of his exceptionalness, which they thought they had been keen enough to observe, and his contemporaries were eager to recall their intimacy with him. The truth was that he had hardly attracted much notice from anyone. Yet it may be that one of John Marquand's classmates actually did respond to something others overlooked, and he, it seems probable, took a special interest in her. Her name was Lillian Simpson. She was the daughter of Judge Simpson, one of the town's important personages, and she lived on High Street in a large, gingerbread Victorian interpolation in the parade of Federalist mansions. Located on the corner where High Street intersects with Newburyport's business thoroughfare, State Street, the house expressed by its overbearing style something of the Simpson self-importance. The first Newburyport Simpson had been hardly as much as the first Marquand, only a shipmaster in a rising time, but Fortune had been kinder to later Simpson generations; the judge was the inheritor of considerable money made by his father, who had invented machinery for combing the burrs out of South American wool and had become the owner of one of the biggest carpet mills in Newburyport. That Lillian had gone to the public high school was probably due to the fact that she was her father's favorite child, an object of such morbid tenderness that she was allowed to go no further from home than the school two blocks away. But though she attended the high school she was not a particularly democratic young person, as she later admitted, but snobbish enough in her own youthful way and likely to be contemptuous, as her High Street girlfriends were, of the Marquand boy from tumbledown Curzon's Mill.

Yet apparently they became friends—by her account because they recognized an intellectuality in each other that marked them off from the rest of their classmates. Literature as it was offered in their English class—Burke's "On Conciliation," "Sohrab and Rustum," *Silas Marner*—fascinated them both, and with aid and suggestion from their favorite teacher, Miss Sullivan, they read other works outside the class assignments—Milton's poetry and Boswell's *Life of Johnson*, she remembered. She also seems to have been, at fifteen, the first girl to be inspired with the kind of half-maternal sexual feeling for Marquand that was to be his inevitable effect upon grown women. She therefore "took him up," did his French and Latin homework for him because he did not like those subjects, and when, as often happened, he came to school having forgotten to bring any lunch along for himself, she ran to her own house and came quickly back with a double lunch to eat with him in some quiet spot on the Mall. But she wasn't altogether proud of her interest—rather the contrary. The true story of youthful romance, no less than of older love, must take account of other factors besides sex and sympathy in a way that would later amuse the social satirist who told again and again in his novels the story of John Marquand and Lillian Simpson.

He did, on one occasion at least, go to dinner at the Simpson house. The episode, which is funny enough, also illustrates just the kind of misadventure that invariably strikes the unconfident. He had set forth in good time, coming his usual way on foot from Curzon's Mill to the trolley stop, but he had taken a short cut across the fields and had tripped and fallen into a muddy spot, completely soiling his clothes. So he had had to go back home again to change, had missed the trolley, and arrived at the Simpson house an hour and a half late. When he came in, it was to find that the family had already eaten—"I will not hold dinner for a Marquand, man or boy," Judge Simpson had said. He was offered some warmed-over food in the kitchen. Despite this disaster his friendship with Lillian continued in strolls and conversations around the school and once or twice she came out on the trolley car to Curzon's Mill for a picnic and was rowed down the Artichoke. Their final meeting was one of ultimate humiliation for him—the classic stand-up. She had accepted his invitation to the "levee," the formal ball of the class, held right after graduation in June. Then, she had apparently regretted her choice and quickly told two other boys that she would go with them. When John arrived at High Street he learned that she was already gone, squired by the first arrival and accompanied also by the second, both of whom she had induced to come early. John followed, but was not accepted as a third escort when he arrived at the hall. Lillian took one look at him and felt confirmed in her behavior: he was wearing clothes that were fatally wrong—white flannel pants and sport coat—while the hall was filled without another exception with young men in tuxedos.

Altogether a ludicrous and banal little story, and one would suppose that it seemed so to Marquand in the perspective of maturity. But this memory lay at the bottom of much of the older Marquand's painful mixture of unmastered sentimentality and mature irony about Newburyport. In one of his novels after another the hero, who comes from a small community consciously modeled on the remembered homeplace, has an early, disappointed infatuation with a girl of superior social position. And the effect of his experience has been to create a lifelong resolution to achieve high dignity in the outer world and to return, laurel-browed, to the place of his former humiliation. The early romance, *Warning Hill*, concerns a boy like John Marquand who attends the public high school, although he comes from a family once powerful and wealthy in the town—the family inheritance mostly gambled away, as already noted, by a father resembling Philip Marquand. He falls in love, of course, with a rich young lady who lives in a grand castle of a house and who teases and eventually spurns him. In another representation of Newburyport, the Bragg of *So Little Time*, the Center Street house of Louella Barnes is a copy of Lillian Simpson's High Street home: "built in the days when people had learned that you could do all sorts of things with turning lathes." Ultimately, long after he leaves Bragg, Jeffrey Wilson, Marquand's autobiographic hero, realizes that "Louella Barnes was responsible for everything"—his resolution to go into newspaper work and writing, his ambition to succeed.

But Lillian Simpson's completest representative is probably Jessica Lovell of *Point of No Return*. High Street in Newburyport is Johnson Street in Clyde this time, and Charles Gray is made to court his highborn lady under her father's disapproving eye. It seems likely that Marquand intended a recollection of Judge Simpson with his neurotic attachment to his daughter. When Lillian did marry, some years after her acquaintance with John Marquand, she and her husband were forced to agree to live with the judge until he died; in the novel Jessica promises her father that, if she and Charles marry, they will never leave him. *Point of No Return*, of course, develops its love story to mutual avowals, lovemaking and engagement, and so goes well beyond the fugitive schoolboy experience upon which it is based. Yet it is all the more revealing of the inward magnitude of that experience. The design of a sixteen-year-old's love-and-loss was present along with the reproduction, the most elaborate in Marquand's fiction, of the Newburyport scene. Spurred by his desire to win Jessica, Charles leaves Clyde for a better job in Boston; spurred even more strongly by her rejection, he leaves Boston for New York, where he succeeds in attaining a height in the world of banking quite beyond the Lovell notion of importance. But the book was not Marquand's final purgation of his early trauma. In *Sincerely, Willis Wayde*, Willis, a young man far beneath the wealthy Bess Harcourt in station, is trapped in the familiar infatuation once again of the Squire of Low Degree for the Princess of Hungary. At a somewhat older age, but no more traumatically than young Marquand, he suffers the unforgettable sting of being "stood up" when she breaks a date with him to go out with a rival from her own group. Willis becomes, in time, wealthy enough to buy out all the Harcourt interests, betraying his role as loyal inferior and becoming the master of those he had once served.

So repetitive a pattern is clearly the reflex in fiction of a life-obsession that made out of the amorphous romance of boyhood the man's recurring dream. It was a dream in which the remembered pain of rejection mingled with the wish-fulfilling fantasy of revenge and recovery. Such dreams are generally delusive obsessions that distract the waking person from the tasks of reality. But Marquand was one of those who prove able to enforce—by will and talent of an extraordinary kind—the realization of their fantasies. The dream became the impetus to a career that enacted just the sort of triumphant recompense and return his fictional heroes strive for. If John Marquand left Newburyport after his graduation from high school as a poor, little-regarded, awkward youth, he was just beginning a journey that would take him back there to live as the most important man the town had ever produced—the famous rich author and Pulitzer Prize winner. Yet it would be a mistake to attach his feelings of humiliation and rejection, his need for compensation and return, simply to the abortive boyhood romance.

Perhaps Lillian Simpson had only become representative of all that he longed to claim as his right. Her house on High Street was as much a part of her significance as she herself. Actually, Jessica Lovell's house is, more than the real Simpson house, the epitome of High Street—more so than Louella's, which is a reproduction of its incongruous Victorianism. The Lovell house is a pure and beautiful Federalist mansion, representative of the specimens on High Street but more particularly resembling one of the best, the Knapp–Healy house with its formal garden and gazebo, its spacious interior, and the French pictorial wallpaper dating from the 1800's. In such a house the refinement and dignity of wealth in Newburyport's Golden Day might still seem heritable. Such a house, indeed, is purchased with this hope by the last of Marquand's fictional self-images, Thomas Harrow, who also returns to Newburyport–Clyde where he lived as a boy, though, as his third wife complains, "It isn't as though he really had roots here. He only came here when he was fifteen."

In Thomas Harrow, of course, John Marquand exaggerated his own misgivings about his claim to a home-source in Newburyport. As we have seen, he, too, was not born there, and it had not been much more than the scene of summer holidays until he came to live with his aunts (just as Thomas Harrow did after the death of his parents) when he also was fifteen. But unlike Thomas Harrow, he was legitimately a Newburyporter by actual lineage, descended from old and honorable local families, however much Judge Simpson might condescend to their modern representative. He had the sense of being a claimant whose ancient right of pride might one day be affirmed before the world. It is no wonder that his interest in his family history became strong, particularly, one guesses, during those two years when he lived at Curzon's Mill before entering college in 1911, lived a withdrawn, dreamy sort of life with those two reclusive aunts who were themselves only partly inhabitants of the present. It was when he was sixteen that he wrote a bit of verse:

It's an old town by the river
Aye, look at it once again,
For its fame has gone forever,
Lost to the minds of men.

There was something personal, probably, in this statement of *sic transit*—not only the town's but the Marquand family's fame had slipped from memory.

Of course, everyone really knew who the Marquands were, that they had a place in the Newburyport picture. When Marquand showed the poem to his mother, who was paying one of her visits to the Mill at the time, she seized upon it at once as evidence of the genius to be expected from the child of a Fuller and a Marquand and immediately asked him to row her down the Merrimack to Deer Island, where they called on the writer Mrs. Harriet Prescott Spofford, who lived in a house that had been a tavern in the Federalist period. What Mrs. Spofford thought of his poem Marquand never knew; he remembered only his acute embarrassment as he sat before the local sibyl, balancing his teacup on his knee. Still, the old Mill on the Artichoke was a lonely dilapidated place that had few visitors, and his aunts were known to be rather queer old ladies who wore dusty old-fashioned clothes on their visits to town. Aunt Molly was quite definitely odd, with lapsing faculties and a fearsome growth of beard, and it did not help that Aunt Bessie was an ordained Unitarian minister, though no one had ever heard her preach, the unnatural achievement Dr. Johnson had compared to a dog standing on its hind legs.

That Marquand had not felt he belonged where he should have belonged had also a simpler explanation. He had come into the high school to do a final year with the class of 1910, his secondary education already nearly completed at Heathcote Hall and the Cambridge Latin School, although he had hoped to enter Harvard directly from Cambridge Latin. He had taken and failed the Harvard entrance exams in June 1909, and again in September 1909, and only then entered the Newburyport High School for a year of further preparation. As it turned out he stayed still another year in Newburyport, taking extra courses with the class of 1911, because he again failed parts of the Harvard exams when he took them in 1910. He was thus only one year with the Newburyport High School class of 1910, and another year with a set of classmates who came up for graduation the following year, probably a stranger and a newcomer, consequently, in the eyes of both groups. Most of his fellow students had not only been together for all of their high school careers but had attended grade school together in Newburyport; theirs was the long familiarity of childhood associations shared not only in school but in the streets of their town.

But the sense of being without a place must have come from within rather than from the attitudes to young John Marquand of the town of Newburyport or of the high school. He felt the ambiguity of his parentless condition because of the continued absence of his father, and of his mother also while his father was supposed to be looking for a new job. Fifteen or sixteen seems rather old for the psychic shock of abandonment, yet something of the sort must help account for his Newburyport obsession, his fantasy of repossession, his resolution to prove that he did indeed belong to a fathering and mothering *place*. So, he was to be driven back to this early scene by more than an expectable degree of nostalgia. When he had become a successful writer and had the money to do so—twenty-four years after he left Newburyport for college—he purchased Kent's Island, a large estate in the Newbury salt marshes near the Parker River. He established himself and his family in a studied squirearchy, keeping farm animals and harvesting the salt hay, and he spent at least a part of every year there for the rest of his life. The place had, after all, once belonged to a family with which he was remotely connected—one of his great-great-great-grandmothers had been a Sarah Kent.

Shortly after the purchase of Kent's Island, *The Late George Apley* was published and Marquand received the Pulitzer Prize. He must have felt that he had returned as he had wanted to. That same year he joined the Newburyport Tuesday Night Club, to whose meetings the incongruously famous man in his London tweeds contributed papers regularly for some years, along with the local doctor, banker, insurance broker, shoe manufacturer, and others with no fame beyond Essex County. And some years later he joined a volunteer firemen's association, the Neptunes, participating more than once in their annual "musters," which featured pumping contests on antique hand tubs with other companies, a midsummer ritual event that drew the whole community.

Of course, the real lost garden was Curzon's Mill, which he craved to own entirely in his own right when he was grown, although others also had claims and titles to the property. Something of the fierceness with which he fought with his relatives in the eventual effort to gain single possession can be explained by his desire to establish himself as the sole and true heir of the Marquand–Curzon heritage. We have seen already how the Mill had become a place of special meaning during his childhood. One memory should be added of a winter night in 1910 when he had just turned seventeen. His mother, who had been at the Mill for a visit, had gone into Boston early in the day and was expected back on the seven o'clock trolley car. The hired man was gone by that hour, and John had offered to go to meet her. A lifetime later he recounted the experience: "The barn in back of my aunts' house had been built in 1902, after the old one had burned down. Thus it was only eight years old that winter evening, a modern functional structure as unremarkable as a two-car garage might be at present. It housed two cows and a heifer, since there was no regular milk delivery so far out of town. In another section was the carriage horse named Pete, standing in a straight stall near the chutes for oats and bran that were stored upstairs in bins beside the hayloft. There was also a harness room, redolent of polished leather, heated by a small coal stove, and finally the carriage room with a buggy, a two-seated buckboard and a light sleigh known as a cutter and a heavier one called a pung. There were, incidentally, three pigs in the barn cellar. Pete the horse, patient, coarse-bred and lazy, was our only means of locomotion.

"It had been snowing hard all day, and by late afternoon the wind had begun to blow hard from the northeast, indicating stormy weather and more snow. I can still remember the order and comfort of the barn when I went in there to harness Pete—carrying a kerosene lantern, for of course there was no electricity. I can also remember the steamy atmosphere and the odor of manure and the stirrings of the dozing animals. . . .

"Pete made no objection to being backed out of his stall or to being harnessed except to shake his head suspiciously at the bit until he found it was warm, and he did walk with unnecessary deliberation into the carriage room. He understood that he was useful and, in consequence, required respect. He was even helpful about backing between the shafts of the pung. I brought out a moth-eaten buffalo robe and the heaviest horseblanket. When I opened the barn door, it made a hollow, solemn sound which one seldom hears today. The horse and sleigh stood quietly in the driving snow while I closed the door again and tied the lantern to the dash. Its warm light shone on the barn for a moment, making it part of a Currier and Ives winter scene. Nothing seemed more permanent or part of that present than the barn. . . .

"The snow had drifted and it was deeper than I had thought. The snowfall was also turning into sleet, so that the horse's plodding steps and the sleigh runners began to make a crackling, tearing sound. We reached the Plains ten minutes before the trolley's estimated time of arrival. . . .

"The trolley was half an hour late and the going was harder getting home than going out. On several occasions, my mother took the reins while I walked ahead of Pete with the lantern to pick up the road, which was becoming obliterated by drifts. We arrived back safely, but we were snowed in by morning. Pete and I were equally pleased to be back in the barn again. He stood happily relaxed while I rubbed him down and put a dry blanket on him and gave him an extra measure of oats."

One may well ask why Marquand remembered this episode with such immediacy for the rest of his life. The details, which read as though set down a day after they were observed, have a warmth that suggests something deeply significant in the experience. There is an immeasurable contentment in the scenes in the barn and in the harmony of the boy and the old horse. In the drive through the snow he appears to have felt a rich excitement, the very reverse of alarm. The wish to reconstitute a past historical atmosphere does not sufficiently account for the strength of his later memory. The security and the harmony of Curzon's Mill provided a special peace that winter night. It no longer mattered that his father was absent on an unpromising search for a way of restoring the vanished splendors of Rye. That night young John had driven home to the Mill through the storm with his mother beside him like a bride.

Another memory, one from the following spring, surfaced afterwards with visionary distinctness. He had undertaken a night walk to Boston from Newburyport in the company of his cousin, John Marquand Walker, then learning the textile business at the Warner Mill, and another boy from the high school. It was the kind of thing one challenges oneself to do when one is young. He remembered that when they got to Salem and sat down to a breakfast of oatmeal, cream and coffee, he momentarily blacked out when the heavy food hit his stomach; he had been teased by his cousin until, at their next stop at a point near Lynn, "Marq" had staggered and collapsed after downing a drink of Moxie. Their friend had given up a mile or two beyond Salem, but the two of them had continued until, a little after noon, they reached the Hotel Lenox, which they had made their destination. But what came back more vividly than any other part of the adventure was the look of Newburyport when they set forth. There had been no moon that night, only the May starlight to aid the few streetlights and the night-lights here and there in some of the stores while they made their way through the streets. Marquand remembered that they could just see the outlines of the houses as they passed and feel the presence of the churches as the bells began to ring the hour not quite at the same moment. "The old buildings looked newer; their antiquity was gone. Although asleep, the town was more alive than in daylight," Marquand would say. He had felt himself a citizen of the old town's past—more powerfully and surely than of its daylight present.

That he "identified" himself with Newburyport is too weak a statement; all his life he struggled to establish an identity in which Newburyport was an essential ingredient. But was he the insider who had not been recognized as one in the beginning or the outsider who had forced his way into the ranks of the Newburyport aristocracy? A clue may lie in his preoccupation with Timothy Dexter, who had tweaked the noses of the respectable and made a mockery of the pretentious by his own parody of high and mighty ways. Marquand was similarly delighted by a modern reincarnation of Dexter who came along in his own time: "Bossy" Gillis, the son of Judge Simpson's cook, who rose in wealth and place, becoming eventually the mayor of Newburyport and buying the Simpson house. When the civic authorities refused him a permit to tear the house down for a gasoline station, he retaliated by ornamenting its proud façade with chamber pots and planting the front lawn with mock tombstones of his enemies. How it must have amused Marquand that the desecrated house was Lillian Simpson's on sacred High Street!

In being amused by Dexter and by Gillis he showed the other face of his nostalgia for Newburyport, his yearning to belong to High Street. He had learned to look with critical skepticism at the very class that had excluded him—for all his claims to membership—when he was young. Perhaps this double attitude was the real making of him as a literary artist; it was the intricate mingling of scorn and tender regard that makes *The Late George Apley* and *H. M. Pulham, Esquire* as interesting as they seem bound to remain. Very early, at any rate, he attained a poise that made his solitariness more the mark of critical detachment than the badge of exclusion; he was more the loner than lonely. No story about his high school days is more significant than the one told by Eleanor Little, who, just a few years older than her pupils, was teaching her first English class at Newburyport High School when Marquand was there. She was a very old lady who had outlived her famous student by a decade when she recalled a moment in her class during a discussion of Hawthorne's story "The Minister's Black Veil." The class was attempting to interpret the behavior of the minister, who had mysteriously elected to wear a concealing black veil on his face despite the suspicion and repugnance aroused in all around him. One boy, she remembered, a bright boy named Ross Campbell, who was the editor of the school literary magazine and a friend of Lillian Simpson's, offered the conventional though not unsophisticated view that the veil worn by the minister was a representation of a Calvinist sense of sin. But John had another explanation to offer. He argued that the minister was a free man who chose to wear the veil because he wanted to be himself and cared for nobody's opinion; the veil was not the indication of a warped nature but of an independent one. It was certainly an original analysis. What seems likely, as one looks back, is that it was one in which young John projected himself as the self-isolated minister.

He had need of any self-sufficiency he could muster when Graduation Day finally arrived in June 1910, a day of bright sunshine and breezy air that expressed for most of his classmates the happy satisfaction of the occasion. The class of 1910, in white dresses and blue serge suits, had been gathered in the basement of the town hall and then marched up to the stage in pairs to stand with their programs in their hands, singing the class ode. It had been written by Lillian Simpson, and it began (to the tune of "Fair Harvard"):

Oh, golden and rosy the dreams of our youth,
And bright are our hopes for success.
We look to the future with wide shining eyes,
And to failure we'll never confess.
Oh, beckoning dreams and confident hopes,
Starry visions your ardor reveals,
In your soft lustrous haze all is beauty and joy,
Every peril the future conceals.

To John Marquand, listening to Lillian's words, there must have seemed less promise of success than of failure. His school grades the past year had been respectably in the 80's and the 90's and some of his teachers had noticed him encouragingly, but he had just received the reports of his performance on the entrance examinations for Harvard, which he had taken for the third time. In June the year before, on leaving Cambridge Latin, he had been graded E in English, elementary Latin, elementary French and advanced French; D in history. Only in plane geometry did he pass—with a C. The following September he had managed to get a C in Latin, but only a D in algebra, and he repeated the E in English. Now, after a year of work at Newburyport High he had brought his English grade up to a D and the Harvard examiners gave him, again, an E in history and advanced French, an F in solid geometry and a D− and C− in elementary German and elementary French respectively. Only in elementary physics had he managed to score a B. He was still short of the required passes for entrance. Certainly it was not a good augury for the future, and it meant, too, that this graduation was a rather hollow ceremony. He would have to stay on at the high school for another year's work before he might hope to tackle the Harvard exams again. And added to these discouragements was the very distinct possibility that even if he should gain admission he might not be able to go to Harvard. There was no money to send him there at the moment and it was doubtful if his parents or aunts would be able to promise him help the following year. Lillian Simpson, meanwhile, was going on to Radcliffe in the fall.

Amid these depressing thoughts he must have been startled by the verses being recited by Gladys Whitson, the class prophet. She had been intoning her doggerel description of a vision of the future for some moments, and as each student recognized the reference to himself an embarrassed or pleased look crossed his face and a slight rustle of amusement swept the hall. Now Marquand heard:

> *Marquand's great dictionary is a marvel to behold.*
> *A day's perusal in its depths should make a boy grow old.*
> *Its prolegomena no exegetical comment*
> *Would ever need to show its clear and plain intent.*
> *He's named it "Stepping Stones for Children to the English Tongue,"*
> *Then speaks in mystic tones of laccolite and vireton,*
> *Defines the harvest spiders, adelarthrosomata,*
> *And designates the human race as archencephala.*

At this distance, Gladys's prescience seems impressive if not precise, based, obviously, on some evidence Marquand had given in school of a liking for rare words. In identifying his future she had singled out the interest in language that serves the writer as well as the lexicographer. Yet to his classmates this penchant may have seemed an eccentric and pointless way of setting himself apart.

A moment later he found himself sitting up in shocked alertness as he heard Gladys follow her stanza about him with:

> *Miss Simpson, famed philanthropist, doth with weighty brow*
> *The lexicographer entrap with definitions wise enow*
> *To wrinkle deep her brain in knotty furrows tight and drawn,*
> *"A Fatal Blunder" is her definition for a yawn.*

Obscure though it may be, the reference—to classroom contests or to their extra-classroom relationship—linked their names in a fashion that sent a titter along the rows of graduates on the platform. He remembered his anguish of embarrassment when he described it again as a feature of the high school graduation Jeffrey Wilson endures. It was comic only in retrospect—that like the hero of *So Little Time* he would have "welcomed death" at that moment does not exaggerate the state of his emotions.

The following fall he was back at Newburyport High School to take more courses in history, chemistry and French, and prepare for the Harvard entrance exams in those subjects and in solid geometry. It still seemed questionable if he could go on, whatever happened. In his best suit, his hair slicked carefully down with a wet comb, he went to visit Mr. Lawrence P. Dodge, one of the town's active Harvardians, in his house on High Street and ask him about his chances of a Harvard Club Scholarship. He received no encouragement. There was a final possibility, however: one of the Wheelwright Scholarships, awarded annually to a number of boys from the high school out of money left for the purpose in 1873 by William Wheelwright, a Newburyporter who had made a great fortune in South America. Mr. Wheelwright, whose original New England prejudices had been reinforced rather than weakened by his life in Catholic countries, had stipulated that winning boys should be Protestant, and also that their proposed courses of study at college should be in a scientific field. After passing the last of his Harvard exams in June 1911, John Marquand was able to inform the college that his fees would be paid by the Wheelwright Fund. He would major in chemistry.

4

Harvard

Harvard Yard is only thirty-five miles away from Newburyport, yet for the freshman who entered it from Newburyport High School in September 1911, it was another country. The feeling of discontinuity must have sharpened his sense of passing out of childhood once and for all. Curzon's Mill and Newburyport were again places to visit on vacations and now and then for weekends. His parents, moreover, had finally removed themselves beyond the reach of any of his memories of life with them; his mother had waited just long enough to see him installed in his boardinghouse on Linden Street before saying goodbye, with tears, and taking the train for California. There she would join his father, who was trying to start a new career working for the Los Angeles Railway. And as though to signify a severed connection with the past, his great-aunt Mary Russell Curzon died at the beginning of November, leaving her nieces, his aunts Molly, Bessie and Greta, to communicate less powerfully the ancestral messages of Curzon's Mill.

Yet because we carry a theater within us where all the struggles of youth continue to repeat themselves, the drama of Marquand's earlier life never stopped. Indeed, as might be expected, he would rediscover in new contexts the plot already formulated in Newburyport; he would adjust the chance stage setting of later occasions to enclose anew the legend of his youth. The suspicion of condescension, the sore sense of a lost title that he must somehow reclaim by his own efforts—all this would translate itself to other scenes. The first of these was Harvard.

He entered feeling obscurely "disadvantaged," as we say today. That he had just managed to achieve admission after four attempts demonstrates, of course, how ill prepared a bright boy from an ordinary public high school could be by Harvard standards. The examination system had been criticized for years, however, not because it was too rigorous but because it made it possible for a dozen or so private schools to devote their programs to intensive coaching of their students with no other educational aim than Harvard entrance. The result was the notorious exclusivism of the Harvard student body—its membership heavily overweighted with upper-class boys from Groton, Middlesex, Exeter, Andover, Milton, Noble and Greenough, St. Mark's, St. George's, and the rest, though there were a few prime public high schools—Newburyport was hardly among them—that did almost as well. At the time Marquand applied for entrance the college had, at last, taken these criticisms to heart and the system was about to change; a year later he would have been able to apply for admission on the basis of his high school record and the recommendations of his teachers, and would have taken only four examinations instead of the fearsome comprehensive series he had sweated through in Sever Hall.

Once in, though, one was in—and certainly a good many of Marquand's classmates cultivated any snobbery before that of intellectual achievement. Still, his poor entrance performance in English must have dampened for the moment any self-esteem kindled in his high school English classes. Probably he simply had not read a sufficient number of classics from the standard list upon which the examinations were based, modest enough but hardly covered adequately at the Newburyport High School. Such a start must have helped him to resign himself to the major in chemistry enforced by the conditions of the Wheelwright Scholarship—after all, he did get a C first time around on the exams in that subject, a D only on the third try in English. Resigned or not, the future writer missed much of what Harvard might have supplied in the way of literary and intellectual stimulus. One contemplates with some astonishment the fact that though he attended Harvard during an era of brilliant teachers in these subjects, he was in the end a case of virtual self-education in the studies that seem most nourishing to literary creativity. He spent only a few college hours in literature and writing classes, and he missed the best teachers of his day. He never sat in Kittredge's Shakespeare classes or F. N. Robinson's Chaucer course or Barrett Wendell's course on the eighteenth century or had Copeland or Baker as writing mentors. Nor did he get a chance to expose himself to the varied challenges of George Santayana or Josiah Royce in philosophy, of E. K. Rand in classics, or of Irving Babbitt in French literature. And though his writing would be notable for its obsession with the relation between past and present American experience and for its almost scientific exactness in the definition of social manners and class relationships, he never heard what Edward Channing or Albert Bushnell Hart or Frederick Jackson Turner or Frank W. Taussig could have told him about history or economics. A somewhat similar experience of educational deprivation was that of his friend Roger Burlingame, who took an engineering program for most of his college course, deterred from the arts by the too-thorough knowledge of the mischances and miseries of writers possessed by his father, the editor of *Scribner's Magazine*. But after several terms of poor performance and a climaxing F in calculus, young Burlingame was permitted to change his major—and he did have both "Copey" and Santayana in his senior year.

For the three years he spent at Harvard, Marquand seems to have taken his scientific vocation seriously enough. Following the advice of his father, who between jobs in California was brushing up his own skills as an engineer, he started towards mining engineering, with courses in geology and metallurgy. He spent the summer of 1913 at the Harvard Engineering Camp at Squam Lake in New Hampshire, studying topographical surveying and map drawing in the field. Here Marquand found, like many of his gently bred classmates, that the hard work in the outdoors could be enjoyable. Burlingame, who was there too, remembered: "At five-thirty each morning we rushed, stark naked, out of our tents to plunge into the icy lake. Then after an enormous breakfast the truly rugged work began and lasted till six. After supper we sweated in the moth-filled, oil-smelling room until ten. On Saturday afternoons we were free till Monday morning. We would paddle five miles down the lake, then walk three to the little town of Center Harbor, which provided drink and dancing. If we could afford it we slept between sheets in the hotel, otherwise we made the long trek back to camp." Marquand must have imagined himself headed for some sort of career in engineering, living as he imagined his father doing that year down in Panama with the Canal diggers.

There is no hint that the theoretical side of science had any particular appeal for him. He might have taken fire, if he had really been ready to kindle into any enthusiasm for chemistry, from Theodore Richards's course in physical chemistry. (Besides being celebrated for his work on the atomic weights of elements, for which he had won a Nobel Prize, Richards was a fine lecturer.) Marquand received a B from him, but he was plainly not a Richards disciple like James B. Conant, a student he had met in the Linden Street boardinghouse. Conant had made such rapid progress in chemistry that he was taking graduate courses in his junior year and assisting in courses taken by his classmates. The two became friends, but already Marquand had begun to regard Conant with a mixture of admiration and envy aroused by the other's ability to learn everything without the slightest damage to his poise and popularity. Conant had been brilliant without being grubby from the time his talents had been noticed by sympathetic teachers at Roxbury Latin School. He would go on to an expectably distinguished career as a chemist, to the presidency of Harvard, and to further authorities and distinctions. His was to prove as "successful" a career, in its way, as Marquand's own, but success had been visible in Conant's case from the start.

Many years after their undergraduate companionship, when Marquand's own fame had put him on an equal footing with the president of Harvard, he enjoyed making wry references to Conant's proficiencies. When he spoke to the Harvard Commencement of 1953, at which he received at last an honorary Doctor of Letters degree, he chuckled with his listeners over the fact that his old friend had been shocked at his proposal to read his remarks, and in a tone that invited all the listening Harvardians to wear the shoe exactly as it fitted, he said: "I realized then what very different mechanical rabbits Dr. Conant and I had been pursuing since we had been Harvard undergraduates. I felt the weight of wasted days upon me. I faced the slowness of my mental processes, and finally I realized how very little I had ever availed myself of what had been taught me at Harvard." Indeed, he confessed he had forgotten most of what he had studied in those very scientific subjects in which he had specialized. He was even unable, he said, to help his thirteen-year-old daughter with her algebra homework, and when engaged with his income-tax form he often needed to remind himself that he "never did have a head for mathematics." As for chemistry, "when I was a Harvard student I specialized in the science of chemistry and spent many hours in several gloomy laboratories coping with various problems of analysis. Yet only the other Christmas, when one of my sons, who had been given a fun-with-chemistry set, asked me how to manufacture chlorine gas, I found myself obliged to turn for assistance to the *Encyclopaedia Britannica*. Curiously enough, someone else has always made my chlorine for me, and frankly I have never objected to the arrangement. In fact I can recall only one small facet of laboratory technique which has been of practical use to me. This is a trick of holding a glass stopper from a bottle in the same hand that pours the bottle's contents—a feat that still commands mild respect when I have occasion to handle a decanter." And so with most of what he had studied at Harvard—his competence in foreign languages was such as to make him glad, when he traveled, of the universality with which foreigners knew English; though he had been told in a philosophy course about Leibniz's theory of monads, he refused to attempt to explain it in 1953; "once I could set up a Wheatstone Bridge with considerable speed and accuracy, but can I now repair the electric bell beneath the dining-room carpet?"—and so on with the terms that distinguish the parts of a Greek temple, the Bill of Rights, the Dred Scott decision, et cetera, et cetera. He went on to assure his somewhat unnerved audience (there were rumors afterwards that Harvard elders thought Mr. Marquand's remarks had been frivolous given the solemnity of the occasion) that of course he had got *something* out of his undergraduate years, even though he remembered practically nothing specific. But President Conant, he admitted, "seems never to have forgotten anything he has learned."

At college Conant was not only the kind of student who exhibited to Marquand what a real vocation in chemistry was, but he succeeded where his interest was slighter, too, and where Marquand might have hoped to find himself—he was elected to the staff of the *Crimson*. The *Crimson* records apparently bear the notation: "Marquand is not being continued in this competition because he does not know how to write," a comment he also later took a certain vengeful pleasure in quoting to a Harvard audience, the Associated Harvard Clubs meeting in Philadelphia in 1948. Conant, after his success on the *Crimson*, was able to join the select company of the Harvard literary club, the Signet Society, around whose lunch table he heard conversation which he found more stimulating, he said, than nearly all his formal courses in the humanities—but that privilege was denied to Marquand. *Wickford Point* records how the snub rankled: Jim Calder and his friend Joe Stowe both fail to get into the Vindex Club. Joe, who goes on to become a famous novelist—and thus also represents his creator along with Jim who writes successful popular magazine stories—says in tones that are surely Marquand's, "You and I are the only people anywhere round who can write, and they didn't take us in. Yes, they'll be sorry someday." And an older Jim Calder, remembering, comments, "The odd thing is I can still feel a twinge of that old bitterness; for the hardest thing to live down is some ancient affront to vanity."

What Conant himself remembered best about their Harvard friendship was the time when, in preparing for a formal social occasion, Marquand came into Conant's room to have his white tie tied for him by the friend whose competence was superior even in this. Socially as well as academically, Marquand must have felt handicapped at Harvard. It was true that he was not exactly a rube from a country farm to be so intimidated by the Boston glitter. As he often reminded himself, he had always known Cambridge, at any rate. His mother's family, the Fullers, had lived there for years past, and generations of Fuller men had gone to Harvard before him. When as a child he had been taken to see his maternal grandmother at her house on Hilliard Street, the atmosphere of family pride had produced frequent reference to the Cambridge Fullers and especially to that famous bluestocking aunt for whom John Marquand's mother had been named. He had lived in that same house during the year when he went to the Cambridge Latin School, and from walking frequently across the Square and into Harvard Yard he had the Cambridge dweller's familiarity with the obtrusive central fact of the locality, the subcity of Harvard. And yet, he afterwards liked to suppose that he had sensed a portentous quality in his earliest glimpse of a Harvard undergraduate—seen him as the gilded youth whose superb easefulness would be forever beyond reach. He was eight years old, and his grandmother had given him a nickel and told him how to get from Hilliard Street to the Square where, at the Billings and Stover apothecary, he might buy himself a sarsaparilla. Once there, he had climbed on a stool at the marble counter and found himself alongside two massive beings dressed in knickerbockers, Norfolk jackets and visor caps, and smoking curved briar pipes. They were, he gathered, discussing the high price of a banana split, then on sale for fifteen cents. "I do not think in all my life," John heard one of them say, "I'll have to bother about fifteen cents because

I'll always have it." Already he understood enough about his own condition of life and his expectations to be awed.

Entering in 1911 he met Harvard Grottlesexism at high tide. There were quite a few among his classmates who would "always have it." They inhabited a very different world from his. Along Mt. Auburn Street were the big new dormitories, the most expensive and well appointed of all the official residences, collectively known as the Gold Coast—Dunster, Claverly, Randolph, and Westmorly—where the affluent students lived. Others lived in less expensive dormitories, like "Thayer Middle" in Lewis Gannett's recollection: "showers on the third floor and toilets in the basement, a coal-grate fire for heating and oil lamps for lighting." But there was a shabbier outer world made up of private rooming houses for students in need of still cheaper accommodations. Into one of these, the gray, wooden structure at 5–7 Linden Street, Marquand had moved—it was called Mrs. Mooney's Pleasure Palace by its tenants because of the notable paucity of its amenities. His Wheelwright Scholarship paid his tuition fees "and railroad season tickets to and from Boston or cash for board not to exceed $100 per annum." Mrs. Mary E. Mooney rented him an unfurnished room on the fourth floor that cost exactly $100 for the school year, which, of course, left him nothing at all for meals, books and other expenses. She asked $50 extra for janitor service and hot water. Some family friends helped out with a small supplement, but there was no question of going much beyond the barely necessary.

Not that he failed to enjoy the raffish Latin Quarter life of the rooming house and the first experience, always intoxicating, of personal freedom. Furnished with a Franklin stove and some mahogany pieces borrowed from the Mill, his room at Mrs. Mooney's took on a certain homely comfort, and just as he had done as a boy in Rye, he kept a green parrot, who impressed visitors by repeating their names or otherwise greeting them ("Laura, Laura," it cried jovially to Aunt Laura Marquand Walker when she came one day for tea; or, "Hello, boys!" it squawked at Marquand's friends as they came through the door). The parrot chewed clothespins for exercise and slept under a blanket in Marquand's closet. Then there were all sorts of jokes among the young men. Jim Conant was a leader and deviser of entertainments. Standing on their respective landings, he and Marquand made themselves helpless with laughter by throwing paper bags of water up and down Mrs. Mooney's staircase. Conant invented a sporting contest known as the Two-Drink Dash. Leaving at intervals during the evening, one after another of the roomers would go by the recently built subway to a bar on Essex Street in downtown Boston, the Holland Wine Company, order and consume two drinks as rapidly as possible, and return to Mrs. Mooney's. The winner of the contest was he whose mastery of subway routes and ability to drink rapidly brought him back to Linden Street in shortest order—generally under twelve minutes, Marquand later claimed.

Marquand lived at Mrs. Mooney's until his junior year, when he and his cousin Dudley Hale rented a pair of rooms in an equally dingy rooming house belonging to a Mrs. Brandon, at 26 Holyoke Street on the corner of Mt. Auburn. As one of his contemporaries recalls it, it was not much different from the Pleasure Palace of Linden Street, though there was the luxury of central heating. "It was a noisy place. Downstairs Sophomore Phil Lowry banged a piano and with a voice as ripe as a yellow squash tortured Gilbert and Sullivan. Down cellar, Franklin, a withered old Negro, rattled the furnace grate at all hours." There was a constant coming and going up and down the stairs and in and out of rooms—shouts, laughter, and probably a good deal of fun.

And yet despite his membership in this lively community of the less privileged, it seems that Marquand was discontented. He knew that a certain group of fellow students regarded him with scorn—and the mere existence of such scorn, however indefensible if one reflected upon it, was enough to recall for him the insupportable condescension of Newburyport's High Street. He knew that to these superior young gentlemen, the successors of the godlike pair he had glimpsed long ago at the Billings and Stover soda fountain, he was a "greaseball." Like Jeffrey Wilson of *So Little Time*, "he was a part of that grim and underprivileged group that appeared in the Yard each morning with small leather bags containing books and papers. He was one of the boys who wore celluloid collars which you could wash off in your room, and who used the reading room in the Library as a resting place because there was no other place to go, and who ate a sandwich there for lunch, and to whom no one spoke unless it was absolutely necessary." Jeffrey understands the exact limits of his acquaintanceship when Louella Barnes mentions some students in his class whom she has met at dances—they are all unknown to him except one or two whose names begin with *W*, these only because they happen to sit near him in the alphabetic ordering of classroom seats. There was only this to explain Marquand's acquaintance with a football star of the class of 1916, Eddie Mahan, the backfield runner. Mahan and Marquand were seated together in Geology I, and "I feel I was of some help to him on occasion," Marquand recalled. But out of the classroom, of course, this BMOC did no more than nod distantly at Marquand if their paths crossed. It was a different matter years later. During the war, the famous novelist touring for the War Department encountered Mahan on duty in Hawaii. "Hello, Johnny! Do you remember the time I picked you out of the gutter at the Woodcock?" Mahan shouted. Marquand had never been to the Woodcock, a Boston dine-and-dance establishment. But, as he would say when he was nearly sixty, "those early snubs rankled all my life."

George Merck, whom he also may have met through the classroom seating system, became a close friend, however, and remained one. A bright and agreeable boy who was to head the family firm of Merck Chemicals, he had entry into the most snobbish circles and was welcome where Marquand was not. There were those dances in the Somerset Hotel, which one attended in full formal dress, with white tie, an attire so far from habitual to Marquand that, as has been seen, he had once needed Conant's help to tie his own white tie (one suspects that the occasion was unique and the costume borrowed). Jeffrey Wilson remembered the humiliation of students like himself one morning after a big dance, when the young "section man," himself elegant and pale as he confronted his subgroup of one of the large elementary courses, invited everyone who had been at the ball last night to leave—and two thirds of the class rose and went out, carrying their distinguished weariness with them from the room. "Those who were left were the plain boys, the last pieces of candy in the box, and Jeffrey was among them."

Of course, Harvard was full of boys who did not mind a bit that they had not been at the dance; many of them proved the best pieces in the box as students and never missed the life that distinguished the true "Harvard Man" of that day from a man who merely "went to Harvard." If not oblivious they were indifferent to the dances and also to the teas in houses on Beacon Street and Commonwealth Avenue that preceded them. But Marquand was the boy from Curzon's Mill, close enough to the background of the Gold Coast to feel a right of membership, invited *occasionally* to a tea or dance at which no one recognized him. As he remembered long afterwards, he was sentenced to lean against the wall, painfully looking for a familiar face and realizing that everyone else knew everyone else.

The key to the superior sphere he stood outside of was, and still is (insofar as it continues to exist), Harvard's ten "final clubs"—Porcellian, A.D., Fly, Spee, Delphic, Owl, Fox, D.U., Phoenix and Iroquois—and it is difficult now to realize how much, to a certain sort of boy, "making" one of these clubs mattered fifty or sixty years ago. In retrospect, one can say that to a future artist, a future dweller in the wide world of men and ideas, it should not have mattered so much. But the fact is that bitterer than the educational handicap of his preparation at Newburyport High School was the discovery that public high school had shut him out of this exclusive club world, which received only the pure stream of Grottlesexism undefiled. The trouble was he had once dwelt in Arcady, he had known these boys, or boys like them, long ago at Heathcote Hall: "When I finally went to college in my late teens, I saw the boys I used to know, finished by their boarding schools. I wanted to join their society again, but I was different and never quite a part of it," he later wrote. "I know now that I was part of the ninety percent of Harvard University, and that these boys I used to know and all their friends were the enviable minority. Something had happened to them in those schools they had left which higher education could not alter. Curiously it did not matter what school; they were all much alike and speaking together in a common idiom. They were the officers of their classes and members of the clubs, but they no more represented the great majority of their classmates than a former member of the Oxford Union represents the type of his constituents in the House of Commons. Their training rather than their knowledge or ability had placed them in a separate class with its own code, with its own dress and manners." And so, he remembered: "I envied them their precocity. They had a philosophy that worked among themselves."

But the older Marquand was also able to say: "I envied it until I saw those of them later who tried to earn their living. They could not understand and thus they found it hard to deal with all the other ninety percent of their countrymen. Furthermore the other ninety percent could not understand them either, and did not want to understand. The net result of their school days, no matter what their advantages may have been, has seemed to me to have been one of ultimate confusion. They had stepped out of an environment which had little or nothing to do with everyday America; their education had set them apart from the world in which they now must live and work." This was the somewhat complacent conclusion of the man who had finally made his way to affluence and acceptance. It was then a satisfaction to see what had happened to the young gods of his Harvard days.

But his attitude remained, in fact, ambivalent, as, to their ultimate gain, his books show. Even the early lighthearted Beverly Witherspoon stories, which he sold to the *Saturday Evening Post* a decade later, tempered scorn with a residual respect. In the first of these, "The Cinderella Motif," Beverly proves capable, at the end, of facing the music, taking the blame for the situation he has created for Professor Hodges' daughter. He says to her: "By this time you must have understood that I don't amount to anything. I am a type that doesn't amount to anything. I am one of the useless elements. There has always got to be someone who is useless, hasn't there? But I never run away." The stories, of course, pleased the *Post* reader precisely because they assuaged without altogether removing his envy of gilded privilege, and the *Post* editors called it "the best story of Harvard any of us recalls reading." And Marquand wrote more happy tales out of the same materials, like "The Harvard Square Student," which dealt with that still-persistent species the complete outsider who hangs about the Square affecting the clothes and manner of a student. Naturally, this imposter turns out to have more dignity—and to be ultimately more successful in the outer world—than those he emulates; Beverly, however, shows some slightly greater grace than others in repenting his own arrogance.

In the same sequestered fraction of the Harvard of the eighties, George Apley had acquired those limiting and yet still functional virtues that Marquand could describe in his first important novel with such mingled derision and regard. H. M. Pulham, a St. Swithin's contemporary who roomed, of course, in Randolph, is a tenderly devastating portrait of the kind of boy Marquand himself had once wanted to be—and grown to see around, his resentment softened by understanding. Bo-jo Brown would seem ludicrous and even contemptible in the end, but Pulham would somehow achieve a species of moral survival despite the handicaps of privilege. In life Marquand would find it possible to catch up at last with the boys who had not elected him to a final club—he would eventually wear the pink and yellow tie of the Myopia Hunt Club on the North Shore; he would entertain his fellow members of the Harvard English Department Visiting Committee, when he was a Harvard Overseer, at the most fashionable club in Boston, the Somerset, of which he had become a member. He would be eager to join these clubs whose memberships were overwhelmingly drawn from that unforgotten Harvard Gold Coast. He would be pleased to be accepted at last by the men these boys had become, for all his ever-ready contempt for the restrictions of personal development that their class training had imposed, their prejudices, their dullness, their emotional timidity. They were always his subject as a writer because he both loved and despised them.

It is probable that even when the sting of exclusion was keenest, in those Harvard years, he was able, as he had in high school, to make isolation look like a chosen aloofness. He is remembered as careless in his dress, with his hair shaggy; he maintained the habit of walking with his eyes on the ground, his hands in his trousers' pockets, giving an appearance of never seeking any company, a "strange, earnest, concentrated boy," Roger Burlingame said. Very different from Dudley Hale, if his cousin's generally supposed caricature as Harry Brill in *Wickford Point* is accurate: "Harry was generally worried about seeing the Right People. It was his opinion that if you just met the Right People everything else would happen automatically. They would ask you to parties and for long visits in the summer. When you were through with college, the Right People would give you a job and the Right People would see that you met the Right Sort of Girl. Harry knew lots of the Right Sort of Girls and he used to go to call on them every Sunday. Harry was always trying to reduce life to a simple formula. He never could get it out of his head that there was an easy way to learn everything and an easy way to do everything." Marquand, even before he was twenty-one, must have realized that nothing was easy, and also that the very things he longed for might not prove altogether worthwhile. Yet not once, but twice, he married the Right Sort of Girl himself.

Perhaps he tended to exaggerate his own exclusion and social failure at college. Jeffrey Wilson, the ultimate Harvard greaseball whom *no one* spoke to, is a nightmare exaggeration of Marquand's case. Marquand may actually have been more like others of his characters—Joe Stowe or Bill King (in *Pulham*), who had had, at Harvard, too much spirit and ability to pine for the dull flaneurs and found better company. Or perhaps, in that endless fitting and refitting to his self-doubt of alternative identities, which is the crisis of young adulthood, he was sometimes one and sometimes the other. He did—as Joe Stowe and Bill King might have—make the *Lampoon* staff, even if he was passed over by Hasty Pudding and the clubs as well as the *Crimson* and the Signet. At the end of his freshman year he began to offer pieces to the *Lampoon* editors, who held open house for would-be contributors on Monday, Wednesday and Friday evenings in the new *Lampoon* building, which stood on its Bow Street triangle—a pastrycook's dream of a medieval Dutch townhouse.

Joining the regular group who brought offerings to the *Lampoon* offices, eating at John's in the basement instead of with the multitude at Memorial Hall, he soon grew to know both the editors and his own classmates who were trying out for membership as he was. A number of them became his friends and to more or less degree remained so in later years. Robert Benchley, an editor during Marquand's freshman year, he would see again in New York after the war, when he tried to start a career there in newspaper work and advertising. Paul Hollister and Roger Burlingame and Edward Streeter became lifetime friends. Burlingame had gone to prep school in Morristown, New Jersey, with Dudley Hale, who also made the *Lampoon* staff. Eventually, Burlingame became an editor at Charles Scribner's Sons and was instrumental in assisting the publication of Marquand's first books by the Scribner firm. Streeter, the future author of *Dere Mable* and *Father of the Bride*, became a bank vice-president and was to be Marquand's near-collaborator in the writing of *Point of No Return*. There was also Richard E. Connell, a classmate who became a writer of *Saturday Evening Post* fiction behind only Marquand's in popularity. And there were others in the group: Neal O'Hara, a future columnist for the Boston *Herald*; and two friends with whom his bonds were to be most personal and enduring, George Merck, already mentioned, and another rich boy of famous personal charm, Gardiner Fiske. Within this company he seems certainly to have been no merely tolerated odd man; that he carried so many of these *Lampoon* friendships into later life proves quite the contrary. Already, apparently, he was distinguished by a gift that could cast a spell, his ability to make an uproarious anecdote out of some trivial real incident. "He would make some simple thing like the crossing of Harvard Square into an adventure. Or caricature his classmates in a way that scared us when we got through laughing," Burlingame reminisced. As the young men lingered on in each other's company and daylight came through the grotesque leaded windows of the *Lampoon* building, Marquand's humor, directed upon objects near and far, held them. "I was not always sure, in his critical moods, whether John was laughing himself or angry. He had a slow, terrific temper: sometimes, when we took him too lightly, he would flare up. John, mad, was something to remember. We all had intervals of being sore at him till he charmed us out of it."

There are several versions of what happened on the night of Marquand's initiation to the staff of the *Lampoon*. One, which he related himself, had him forced to bawl out into the street from a window of the *Lampoon* building—while he was being jovially thwacked from behind—"Yes, my name is John P. Marquand. Stop, stop! I'll marry the woman!" This was, indeed, part of the program of frolicsome ordeal that was traditional for initiates. If it was not Marquand's own trial it was too amusing a tradition not to be assumed to have taken place. Samuel S. Otis, an architecture student who had been drawing cartoons for the *Lampoon*—he was another of Cousin Dudley's Morristown friends—was also initiated that night. He recalled that Roger Burlingame had presided at the ceremony and that he had instructed Marquand and Otis to retrieve a silver coin that was supposed to be clamped in the beak of the carved ibis which perches on the top of the *Lampoon* building. The initiates were stumped, for the ibis seemed inaccessible, but they went outside and stared up at it for a while. Marquand ducked out of sight for a few minutes and returned with a heavy stick, which he quickly threw up at the bird, and when it came down, there was a silver coin wedged into a notch cut into the stick (of course, for Marquand had inserted the coin ahead of time!). The new members were accepted after this with hilarious enthusiasm and till late that evening sat cheerfully singing, among other songs, one composed that night in derision of the *Lampoon*'s despised rival, the *Crimson*. It began:

> *Take a little piece of the crimson*
> *Hang it up beside your "can."*
> *Don't waste your cash on the regular stuff* . . .

Lampoon humor was often just a little above this level and Marquand's contributions, which ranged over the usual topics for the most part, are indistinguishable from the other "quips, cranks, wanton wiles and pictorial jests" that appeared, all unsigned, as the product of "Lampy's" wit. They do reflect, though, some of his responses, his first as a conscious humorist, and Harvard's occasions for satire. His earliest contribution, published in June 1912, was a comic guide to the public transportation system, "Lampy's Key to the Boston Elevated Transfer Rules," which undoubtedly grew out of his special experience with trains and transfers during Two-Drink Dashes from Mrs. Mooney's. He did pieces that showed the encounter of the Freshman with the Stately Senior Adviser, with the college doctor, and with the "automated Dean," who is ready for his visitors with sets of variously appropriate remarks of standardized banality issued on printed slips. He took a sideswipe at the *Crimson* and its treatment of candidates for the staff ("You only handed in 18 scoops last night. What is wrong?"). And he wrote a funny parody of a theme complete with the grader's comments and cabalistic marking symbols ("Cst and Tg. Colloquial lack of adherence"), which probably reflected his experience in English A, the freshman composition course. Did he eat many of his lunches with the vast crowd at Memorial Hall? At least a sufficient number to picture an undergraduate like himself being jostled and conversationally trampled by preoccupied Law School men. After ten of his little compositions had appeared, he was placed on the *Lampoon* masthead in the issue of March 8, 1913. He now was entitled to write some of the rather elegant editorials that distinguished the *Lampoon*—humorous obsequies for Hemenway Gymnasium and an invocation to the vacation period in April (both with George Merck's collaboration).

In his junior year, though his name still appeared on the masthead, his activity on the *Lampoon* slowed down and stopped. He had decided to finish up and get out a year ahead of his class, and he took fourteen semester courses and passed them all with B's and C's and one A, his purpose accomplished, but with little time left for the extracurricular. He had learned the trick of getting through without undue effort or anguish, and now he had had enough of Harvard. His reasons were also probably economic; he was in a hurry to earn his own living at last. So he wound up his major as prescribed by his scholarship, taking in his last year organic and physical chemistry, fire assaying and metallurgy, dynamical and structural geology, and historical geology to follow up the chemistry and mineralogy courses of the previous two years and his summer stint at the engineering camp. His grades in these professional courses had been split between B's and C's, respectable enough to justify the expectation that he would soon be looking for a start in some engineering job. That he never made the slightest move in such a direction—he bolted unhesitatingly for newspaper work as soon as he got out—suggests that far more important than any of his courses was the company he had been keeping in the *Lampoon* office. Most of his young companions there were soon to be found in one of the traditional apprentice occupations of the literary hopeful—newspaper work, advertising, publishing.

They were not all sure that they would be writers, though some of them did become writers of one kind or another. In this they differed from some others. There were, as there have always been, distant worlds that never collided in the small cosmos of Harvard, and the *Lampoon* men did not have much to do with some of their classmates who would become more famous than any of them as writers, if we except Marquand. Around the *Harvard Monthly* and the *Advocate* clustered the "aesthetes." One of these, John Dos Passos, who wrote verses and reviewed Masters, Eliot and Pound for the *Advocate*, was in the class of 1916. He later described *his* college friends: "We were one in our scorn of our poor classmates who were getting ready to go out into the world to sell bonds. We were proclaiming to all and sundry that poetry was more important than submarines or war guilt or brave little Belgium or the Board on the New York Stock Exchange." Another was Marquand's classmate Edward Estlin Cummings (not yet decapitalized). Though Marquand knew him perfectly well from that freshman year in the Cambridge Latin School, the two did not see much of each other. Cummings was easily the most brilliant example on the scene of a young man of distinct and conscious literary genius. He graduated *magna cum laude* and gave the commencement talk in June in the form of an essay titled "The New Art"—

Cubism and Futurism, Ravel, Satie and Debussy, Donald Evans, Gertrude Stein, and President Lowell's sister Amy—in which he accurately identified the modern movement of which he was himself to be a vital part. In contrast, Marquand had, as yet, no real sense of the literary moment and only the vaguest aspirations towards personal achievement in literature. He had merely discovered that he had a certain verbal facility and a sense of humor.

Little time as there had been for courses in literature and writing, he had undoubtedly gained something from his Harvard English classes. In his freshman year there had been English A, which he had spoofed in the *Lampoon*, the famous composition course directed by Dean Briggs. Roger Burlingame remembered it as "an almost unspeakable freshman compulsory designed not for creative writers but for business and professional men who would have to write letters and reports. It was there to prevent any graduate of Harvard College, be he button-maker or bond salesman, from being unable to speak and write his own language coherently. It also was a boon to many Chinese, Japanese, Siamese, Indian, and other foreign students who graced my class in this so-called provincial and snobbish institution. But to the aspiring author it was nearly fatal." But if one came under the direct influence of Briggs, there might be something gained, John Dos Passos thought. He said of Briggs: "He had an old-fashioned schoolmaster's concern for the neatness of the language, a Yankee zest for the shipshape phrase, an old-fashioned gentleman's concern for purity of morals, to use a properly old-fashioned expression, and a sharp nose for sham and pretense which was neither old nor new-fashioned but eternally to the point." There is no telling how much of Briggs's direct attention Marquand ever received—whether indeed his papers were even graded by him. Yet the qualities Dos Passos writes of have a curious aptness in describing Marquand's best prose. We have no more certain a view of his sophomore English composition course, taught that year by a young instructor named Ernest Bernbaum, except that he got a B in it whereas Briggs had only given him a C. But in his last year, along with all the science courses, he managed to take two courses that apparently meant a good deal to him.

One was Comparative Literature 12, "Types of Fiction in the Eighteenth and Nineteenth Centuries," taught by Bliss Perry, formerly editor of the *Atlantic Monthly*. In 1955, when as a member of the Overseers' committee to visit the Harvard English Department Marquand was concerning himself with the teaching program, he wrote a friend: "It meant more to me than most of my Harvard courses, and I only wish there were a comparable successor to Mr. Perry on the Harvard faculty." Just what Perry gave him, again, is elusive, but the subject of the course was the great tradition of the English novel; here, for the first time perhaps, he discovered from Perry's sensitive analysis something of the mystery of technique in the masters of fiction; suddenly it was the business of making stories that seemed, maybe, the most fascinating and admirable thing a man might do. He logically followed Perry's course with "The English Novel from Dickens to the Present Time," which completed his college grounding in the history of the literary form to which he would attach himself.

One other course that seems to have been really memorable was English 12, the more advanced course in composition ordinarily taught by Charles Townsend Copeland in a legendary fashion, with individual conferences with students in his room in Hollis Hall. Copeland was on sabbatical, however, in 1913–1914, and the course was taught by a visiting professor from Colorado, Homer T. Woodbridge. Woodbridge had none, probably, of the famous "Copey" humor, those witty thrusts that suddenly flashed from him as he sat seeming to doze but actually listening to a student read his theme. But Woodbridge taught well. Years later, when Marquand was at the height of his fame, he received a letter of praise for his novel *Point of No Return* and wrote Woodbridge, "You may not know it but if it were not for your kindness to me at Harvard, I might never have found myself involved in this pursuit." Marquand had been amused to discover that Copeland, who really had not known him at all, had become fond over the years of claiming him as one of his students. "C. T. Copeland has definitely convinced himself that he taught me when I was in English 12," he told Woodbridge. "In fact, he can remember in chapter and verse just what he said to me and what I answered, but you and I know the facts." Woodbridge gave him an A, the only A of his college record, and prided himself on having discovered Marquand's talent; the *Saturday Evening Post* would in time publish as a "Perfect Squelch" a story concerning the student who challenged Professor Woodbridge with failing to appreciate "the quality of Marquand's works," and was told, "Perhaps not, but when I had him in Harvard I gave him an A."

Marquand saved some of his college themes—a handful were among his papers when he died. To the accustomed reader of undergraduate writing they seem curiously—and disappointingly—mature. They lack the earnest overambitiousness of the young writer who must tackle only large ideas and deep emotions, who is awkwardly sincere and who emulates only the most profound and difficult masters. Marquand has, on the contrary, his tongue in his cheek; he is writing cheerfully to formula for an imagined market, and he has no particular interest in "saying" anything at all. But he shows some ability to handle the steps and stages, the dialogue and descriptions incident to a well-handled plot of romance or suspense or mystery. The game of effects, the craft and devices, are what obviously interest him. His college writings appear to predict the way he would begin as a professional writer in a few years; one of these stories, indeed, anticipates his early "costume romance," *The Black Cargo*, describing the dramatic reencounter of a wealthy man with the sea companion left on a desert island years before.

Another story had a special history. It was based on an idea he had been given by, of all persons, his faraway father, the never-successful Philip

Marquand, occupied in searching for new opportunity in the Golden West. Between jobs that seemed always unsatisfactory or temporary, Philip had returned to his love of invention—and dreamed of a fortune made by some patentable device; he designed a new kind of tennis racket and hoped to sell his model to Wright and Ditson. And he wrote his son a long account of a German scientist he had heard of who had found a way of predicting the future. Old Marquand's professor had discovered that a newly identified substance would "retard light"—that is, show a delayed reflection of past images; then, by a laboratory accident, he had stumbled upon a way to "reverse" this action so that the substance "reflected" the future. The professor's putative discovery—it enabled him to save the life of his child, who was about to be struck by a passing auto—obviously was the kind of lucky find that the elder Marquand's own daydreams were occupied with. And whether he took his report with waking seriousness or not, Philip also thought that the story might be something that John could use in the way of salable fiction, a lucky find of another sort. "Now John," he wrote, "don't you think with some of your story telling talent you can make a good story of this? You used to be story editor of the school paper [at Heathcote Hall]. You might employ a much better plot and give names to the characters and write it in some shape and send it to some ten cent magazine or the N.Y. American and perhaps get $25 or $50 for it."

How seriously did Marquand respond to this vista of success as a writer for ten-cent magazines and the New York *American*? He may well have sympathized with his father's daydreaming, have hoped to strike it lucky and rich by mining, if nothing else, the vein of a talent he suspected in himself. And so he set at work to remake the story—with improvement of its fictional qualities. He introduced the dramatic situation of a triangular romance and developed the character of the scientist, recast as a young man and an American, and that of his friend, the rival for a woman's love. Immensely improved as narrative over Philip's sketch by the use of dialogue and some scenic elaboration, the story was submitted to his instructor in the sophomore composition course. It failed to make a resounding impression. Then, rewritten, it was submitted again to Woodbridge the next year; he gave it a B+ and called it "an interesting story in the main well told." Perhaps, since Marquand kept both versions of his never-to-be-repeated attempt at science fiction, he had a certain affection for this early effort. It was, if nothing more, his first venture in writing "for the market"—to deliberately produce a marketable product by means of literary skill. That the plot was trite and that the interest depended on mystification and surprise and the fantasy of pseudoscience—all this did not much trouble him. That the thing "went"—that it held a reader's attention by force of sheer curiosity—was something he probably felt proud of. For as he concluded his last jam-packed Harvard year his mind was clearly on the problem of making his way, of securing himself against his father's fate, of which he was kept keenly aware by letters from California. If literature was a means of earning a living he would apply himself to the job of doing it so well that it would make him rich; there is no hint that he had any more ideal conception of the uses to which his talent might be put.

One aspect of his Harvard experience must have contributed to his feelings of handicap, must have strengthened his resolution to make out, to make good, to make them sorry, as Joe Stowe would say, and it is probable that not even his closest friends had any inkling of its embittering pressure. After some months in Los Angeles, Philip Marquand joined his wife at his cousin Annie Head's in Berkeley and began to canvass that area for a job. Months passed, and he found nothing. He did odd jobs for Cousin Annie—built her a birdhouse and painted her fence, four hundred fifty feet long and five feet high—and wrote wryly to his son, "If I got for the job what the Amalgamated Painters get, it would be $75 to $100, but I am not one of the union." He tutored some University of California freshmen in analytic geometry after that, and waited on. The news sent to John was a constant reminder of his father's humiliation and defeat. And in the way of long-suffering moms who place with such unwitting cruelty a moral burden upon their sons, his mother told about her valiant efforts to carry on as the wife of an unemployed man. "I have never done as much housework as in California," she told John. "If Daddy can get anything Aunt Molly could come to us and she would help us out very much, and I could do all the housework except washing and ironing. So far I draw the line at that though I have ironed a good deal here too." Maybe doing one's own housework, including the washing and ironing, was and is the fate of millions of uncomplaining American women but to one of Mrs. Marquand's social origins it was a dramatic fall from dignity. She had probably never lived without servants before. To John, the situation signified a loss of caste that corresponded to his own sense of being déclassé at Harvard. The letters from California must have depressed him with the sense of being helpless to respond to his mother's appeal on behalf of his father, "I know that you will put your shoulder to the wheel and help Daddy pay up his things and get on his feet sometime," she had written. Worse was his inability to remove those unaccustomed burdens from his mother's shoulders.

Partly, one suspects, out of their own sense of guilt for being so far away from *him*, and for contributing so little to *his* well-being at college, his parents' letters were stuffed with instructions, admonitions and advice. He was also burdened with awkward commissions—to go to the Mill and persuade vague-minded Aunt Molly, who was showing reluctance, to come out to join her indigent brother. And he was given lists of his father's Harvard classmates and his mother's Cambridge friends on whom it was deemed proper that he should pay formal calls. It seems unsurprising that sometimes he responded by not responding, that is, by not writing back. And for this numb defiance, his parents' punishment was of an unconscious harshness. In December his mother was writing, "Don't you think you could write Daddy a little oftener—he does care so for his only boy and now all we have is letters." And his father: "Your mother is ready to weep now every day that she does not hear from you. I really think you ought to have some sort of regard for her and write her." As the old often do, they threatened youth with the prospect of their death: "It only takes a few minutes and it will give more pleasure than you have any idea, and you will not realize it until you have a boy and your father and mother are in another world."

But the real armament of reproach was released late in January of his freshman year. He had failed to write for some weeks, probably because he was in the midst of final exams—from which he would just barely emerge above water. His father had sent first one and then another telegram to a relative in Boston and John had responded at last—with indignation. His mother wrote: "John dear, one of the first rules of life is not to hit a man when he is down, and if that man happens to be your father, be even kinder. You will never be sorry. Try to realize if Daddy seems unreasonable it is only because he cares so much. He is just as dear to me now as when he was on top of the world." The effect of this dreadful guilt-inducing appeal, was, of course, to inhibit letter writing all the more, for after three weeks his father had to try another tack. He threatened: "What would you say if I should tell you that you need not stay in college unless you can do better about letter-writing?"

Marquand's parents continued throughout the rest of his freshman year to alternate reproaches and threats. "You will have to make up your mind to spend half an hour a week on your father and mother. You know it is very hard for him to think he is not able to send you to Harvard himself, and when you never write to him he feels even his own son goes back on him." "I think it will be best for you to give up college at Cambridge and perhaps we can arrange for you to go to the University of California where I can see you sometimes." "I do not believe there is anything harder for a man of my age than to be dead broke and out of a job but to add to that to have a son whom he always thought the world of that seems to have lost all regard for his father, that makes it worse still." "Why should you be so absolutely disobedient to me? Is it because I am sort of down and out? Do you not know that besides owing your parents respect and obedience you are legally under their charge? Unless you can obey me to the extent of writing to me once a week and to your mother once a week, I think we will decide to have you nearer to us."

Philip Marquand's own situation did not improve. Early in 1912 he worked for a few weeks on the buildings being started for the 1915 San Francisco World's Fair, then went back to painting trellises for Cousin Annie and tutoring students in elementary mathematics. Somehow a truce must have been achieved between John and his parents—either he wrote with more regularity or they gave over the attempt to force him into compliance. At any rate, in the following year, after much waiting and hoping, Philip heard from the Isthmian Commission in Panama, and he and his wife sailed directly there from California. Some of the pressure exerted upon John across a continent was probably removed, now that they were to be even further away and now that his father had work at last. But it is still likely that his experience at Harvard was constantly underscored in his mind by worry and guilt concerning his parents and his own relation to them. A conscientious only son, he probably felt that he should be helping them. Moreover, he must have viewed with a sort of horror the possibility that he might ever himself be in his father's position.

His attitude towards Harvard was to be a lifelong engagement of yearning and antagonism, very much like his feeling about Newburyport. This, too, was a Home he felt entitled to inherit, one that had somehow treated him like an outsider—and here, too, he vowed to return. He himself became in time aware of these contradictions. For the twenty-fifth anniversary report of his class, in 1940, he wrote: "Harvard is a subject I still face with mixed emotions. I brought away from it a number of frustrations and illusions which have handicapped me through most of my life." He continued to relate to his Alma Mater in later years in the same mingled way. *Wickford Point* made reference not only to his own undergraduate experience but presented a supposed contemporary portrait of a Harvard English professor in Allen Southby, the self-esteeming and affected pundit who sufficiently resembled several real English Department members to set a buzz of speculation going. It was clear that as a successful writer generally ignored by the professors of literature Marquand felt himself still engaged in his old resentful relationship with the college that should have loved him more. A couple of years later he reported on the tempest he had raised: "Wickford Point has got me in very wrong with the Harvard faculty. So much so that President Conant has remonstrated with me at considerable length. Several weeks ago in Washington he even stopped his work of winning the war and asked me what I really thought was the matter with the Harvard English Department. I could only tell him that everything was the matter with it and anything I could say would be destructive and we parted on this note." Towards the end of World War II, when his eldest son was preparing to go back to college after being discharged from the army, Marquand was sufficiently negative about Harvard to suggest the alternative of Columbia: "I do agree with you that two years of hanging around Boston and Cambridge sound a little rugged, unless you have a great intellectual curiosity and a desire to sit at the feet of some great sage like Matthiessen or Theodore Spencer, which I personally would not desire to do. Both Cambridge and Boston are dull backwaters in these days." Some years later, when Conant worried him again with questions about his views, he told him: "You must not really take seriously any remarks of mine about the English Department.

The more writing I do the less I really know about English and I doubt if creative writing can be taught at Harvard or anywhere else, and creative writing is the only subject on which I can speak with any authority." But these slyly half-conciliatory remarks to Conant have a significant date, being written at the end of 1953, the year when his wound, one might say, had finally healed over: he had been awarded the honorary doctor's degree by his Alma Mater that June.

Wickford Point was followed by the full-scale anatomy of the Harvard man in *H. M. Pulham, Esquire*, which was not entirely appreciated by his middle-aged classmates. It also provided an occasion of what seemed, to this distrusting son, an outrageous instance of maternal betrayal: when the book was nearly banned by the Boston police for its alleged impropriety, a top Harvard administrator, then on the City Council of Boston, had failed to dissent. Marquand's hurt, as we shall see, was inordinate, and it probably accounts for his responding favorably in that year, 1941, to a suggestion that he give the manuscript of the novel to Yale. In 1950, Yale awarded him an honorary doctorate and he decided to will all his literary manuscripts to the Yale Library. "Seeing that Yale honored me last year with a Doctor's Degree, I should prefer having my papers end up there rather than at my alma mater Harvard, which takes a dimmer view than Yale regarding my abilities," he wrote James T. Babb, the Yale librarian. Harvard would mend her omission, as just noted, in 1953; later that year he would receive appointment to the Harvard Board of Overseers, and two years after that become chairman of the board's Visiting Committee to the English Department itself, for all his deprecations of the teaching of English there. In 1957 he accepted an invitation to stay at Kirkland House as a "writer in residence," an honored resident sage, an inspiration to the young. He had come back to Harvard, even as to Newburyport, like a hero of fame.

5

The Transcript

Two weeks after he had passed his last examinations at Harvard, John Marquand was working as a reporter on the Boston *Evening Transcript*. He had made not the slightest effort to find a way of putting to use his chemistry or engineering courses, and he would never do so. Indeed, he later forgot altogether that there had been any such possibility, for he wrote a young soldier-admirer in 1945: "I was obliged to earn my living as soon as I left college. I selected writing because it was the only field of lucrative endeavor in which I was in any way qualified, and I started on a Boston newspaper." Actually, there were meager grounds for even this confidence. He owed this first job to the fact that George S. Mandell, the newspaper's owner, had been at Harvard with Philip Marquand; for once Philip's impositions of duty calls on classmates had served his son's own interest. Mandell had probably hired him without taking a glance at the applicant's small bundle of *Lampoon* clippings and college themes. Like the investment broker who had been a classmate of Charles Gray's father in *Point of No Return*, Mandell "had known who he was and had passed on his personal appearance and this was about all that was necessary."

Of course, he was not expected to last; not one in twenty of the young gentlemen who entered via the "front office" stood up to the weather of the city room. Frank Bowker, the city editor, was known for his sea captain's temperament, and he ruled his staff with scowls and tyranny, unbending only to engage in a silent game of dominoes with a subordinate after the page was closed on the late edition. Much later Marquand would say, quite without humor, "I still always think of him as a big bastard." Bowker had the classic city-desk suspicion of college-trained "journalists"—there were derisive invisible quotation marks about the word as he pronounced it. These hopefuls might conceivably find berths writing features, book reviews, or even editorials, but they were no good riding fire wagons, making cronies of precinct captains, and getting all the names spelled right in a society story. He sent Marquand to cover an Orangemen's parade, a local strike, and what he thought of as a particularly suitable assignment for the young Harvard man, a survey of the response of the Morgan Memorial and other Boston charities to war unemployment. In a few weeks Bowker declared that Marquand would never make a reporter and that even when he had collected all the facts the story he made of them was "humdrum." "Indeed it was," an older Marquand admitted. "I was very uncertain as to how to write."

Nevertheless, just as he was about to go down the dusty steps of the *Transcript* office for the last time, another door opened, and Bowker cynically saw him pass into the friendlier Telegraph Department, where he worked under its news editor, Fred Ford, writing leads for foreign cables, and eventually into the Magazine Department. It was here, finally, that he did begin to find a sense of qualification. Burton Kline, a quick-spirited and warmhearted little man, was delighted with Marquand's execution of the assignments he gave him. Marquand's most grateful memory of his *Transcript* days was to be of Editor Kline smiling at him from his rolltop desk near the grimy window that looked over Milk Street, his face full of encouragement and humor. A good deal of the time Kline was at work on potboiler novels with titles like *Struck by Lightning* and *Mrs. Brimstone.* He would happily pause at Marquand's approach to hand him some piece of work, crying, "Here, write these headlines and get the copy up," and quickly return to his labors on his novel. He was probably the first writer of fiction in Marquand's acquaintance—an example that seems to have stirred vague ambitions: Marquand attempted, in collaboration with another young *Transcript* reporter, William A. Macdonald, to write a novel himself. They decided to challenge fortune with an exotic romance located in India—a scene with which both were familiar as a result of reading Kipling—and they assigned themselves alternate chapters, discussing their plans in after-hours in the *Transcript* office while they consumed, Macdonald remembered, many bottles of Sterling Ale, selling then at two quarts for a quarter, and large quantities of Richmond Straight Cut Cigarettes. When the novel was finished the authors packed their bulky manuscript up and sent it hopefully to a succession of publishers until they concluded that they could no longer afford to pay freight charges for shipping it out or pay the collect charges when it was returned. The manuscript subsequently disappeared, and "Yellow Ivory" as it was titled, did not make its authors instantly rich as they had hoped, though long afterwards Macdonald would say that he recognized stretches of Marquand's contributions in some of his successful serial stories.

Kline himself, it would turn out, remained bound to the daily grind of the news press, despite his larger ambitions: he shifted to the New York *Tribune* and then to the Philadelphia *Ledger*, moving from job to job without coming to rest in a permanent post; and during the Depression he was out of a job altogether and on a WPA writers' project. His career must then have seemed just the kind of fate Marquand, remembering his father as well as this later father figure, would strive so strenuously to avoid. He wrote to another old newspaper friend in 1955, "The career of Burton Kline has often surprised and distressed me because he really had great ability with which, unfortunately, he was able to do almost nothing, due, I am afraid, to his never following anything through." In 1915, however, Kline was a man who caused good cheer and optimism to vibrate in the air about him. He enjoyed his own jokes as much as he enjoyed a drink in the barroom down the street, to which he often repaired between editions. One Christmas Eve, after he and his protégé had spent a cheerful hour together, they returned to the office and Kline, uproarious at a story he was telling, stamped in his glee directly into a cuspidor, splashing its contents up and down his person—but he remained undampened in temper.

A newspaper office was, of course, an exciting place in which to work in the fall of 1914. Outside the magazine room and the telegraph room, Marquand remembered, Fred Ford would sit, sorting out the Associated Press dispatches that came popping through a pneumatic tube, and flattening out on his desk the terse announcements of cataclysm on the Western Front. Sometimes the new reporter himself was stationed at the telegraph desk where the dispatches were exploding into a wire basket like light shells in their leather cannisters. As he slipped out the rolled messages and handed them to Mr. Ford, he felt queerly close to the shocking realities of the war, knowing that he was one of the first in America to read the news—and all the time the local atmosphere in the office remained what it had always been, a place full of odd personalities and peculiar legends and the jokes of the newsmen who had grown old together in the six-story granite buildings at 19 Milk and 224 Washington streets. While Ford was scanning the bulletins from the Front his ancient father, also a *Transcript* employee, would sit nearby in a small cubicle unwrapping the exchanges, domestic and foreign. One morning of blizzard weather Marquand observed that Mr. Ford Senior did not appear. His son had successfully left him behind by hiding the old gentleman's trousers.

Marquand also knew William Ralston Balch, "that antiquated but suave London journalist, who had done publicity for Scott's Emulsion of Cod Liver Oil, and who made himself by his own broad knowledge and personality the war expert of the Boston *Transcript*." He recalled: "Mr. Balch would come to the office at four o'clock every morning in order to absorb the situation on the Western Front, having partaken in his Myrtle Street apartment of some cold shrimps and a little tea." Once a week he would compose the paper's "Chronicle"—an account of the week's most harrowing instances of German *Schrecklichkeit* and military disaster rendered in a Carlylean style of resonating doom. Along with Balch's solemn essays, Marquand could describe, a quarter century later, that figure of homely eccentricity: "Once I remember he showed me a photograph of a lightly clad lady in the central square at Brussels and informed me proudly that he had slept with the original. I can remember, too, when Mr. Balch's mind failed gradually and he would tell how as a boy he used to wait in Oliver Wendell Holmes' Beacon Street dining room while the Doctor finished newspaper dispatches, and later still how he believed he was in direct communication with the King of the Belgians over the purchase of a set of valuable postage stamps." It was Balch whom Marquand had in mind when he invented Mr. Jenks in *So Little Time*, the old newspaperman who shows young Walter Newcombe—later a famous foreign correspondent—the picture of a nude marble lady, remarking, "I slept with that girl once." "What? How could you?" asks Walter. "She's a statue, Mr. Jenks"—a comment he would never live down. There is no telling whether a very young Marquand did or did not originally ask the same question.

The foreign newspapers spread over Balch's desk also became a source of feature pieces that the young reporter was encouraged to do for the magazine. There was an anonymous column called "The Cosmopolitan," which pretended to offer readers the reflections of a sophisticated roving correspondent who was on the scene in the Allied capitals. Actually, "The Cosmopolitan"'s observations were culled out of the exchanges by Marquand, who even added an item now and then made up from personal sources—a piece on the Canal Zone laborers who had left the West Indies to work on the construction of the locks, for example, was drawn from his father's Panama letters. Most of the time, "The Cosmopolitan," with the unacknowledged aid of English, French, Belgian and Swedish news writers, turned a pleasant wry humor on minor events abroad—the spy hysteria in Britain, the enlistment into the military service of French men of letters, Sweden's "Amazon Brigade" of female volunteer rifle trainees, a Strand chemist's revelation that eau de cologne is made entirely of non-German ingredients, the exploits of a boy war hero on the Russian side who had unscrewed the breeches of some German guns while their guards slept, the refusal of Scotch Highlander prisoners of war to accept their captors' offer of trousers. The style was distinctly *Lampoon*—the Great War, as seen by "The Cosmopolitan," was a vast seriousness, like Harvard, about the borders of which were many amusing small curiosities. The series must have pleased his superiors, for in December 1914 he appeared in a joint by-line with Balch over a long story featuring extracts from the *Bulletin des Armées*, the French trench newspaper—a mark of conspicuous welcome from the veteran to the cub just a few weeks past his twenty-first birthday.

Friendly encouragement also came from the *Transcript*'s famous drama and music critic, H. T. Parker, whose initials, signed to reviews, dictated the tastes of polite Boston. Legend had it that Parker's erudite analyses were written in Latin and then were translated for the common reader; actually,

Marquand discovered, they were written in pencil in a handwriting so undecipherable that two typesetters were specially assigned to work on them when they reached the composing room. Marquand had also heard the tales of Parker's intimidating presence at openings. An angry thump of his cane or, worse still, a midperformance departure from the hall, might spell the doom of a newly opened show. And there was the tradition of his friendship with Isabella Gardner, whom he had often accompanied to Symphony and polite social gatherings. His short figure topped by a large belligerent face made him resemble a small, ugly bear firmly looped into the arm of the equally homely and unmajestic Princess of Boston. In Marquand's day, however, Parker often took a "lovely lady from the proof room" with him to openings, and sometimes he invited the young reporter to come with him to a play or a musical or even a vaudeville show at Keith's Theater, which he might allow Marquand to review. Parker would take him out to dinner first; then they would go to the theater, where he was warned to sit perfectly quiet and not to talk to the critic between the acts lest he prejudice his judgment.

Writing features under the friendly stimulus of Balch, Parker and Kline, he was quickly educated in the brisk school of newspaper work. As everyone knows, a lot can be learned by a young writer enrolled in the service of a daily newspaper—the quick acquisition of diverse information, the just-as-rapid conversion of information into prose that conveys authority, the habit of deadlines that precludes any cultivation of "blocks." Though his career on the *Transcript* was brief it is likely that Marquand learned these things once and for all while he boiled up his compositions for the newspaper's columns. He became "facile"—a word that would be used against him later, when he turned out stories and even novels with the same quick skill in seizing and shaping materials to a ready form. In any case, he had justified to himself his gamble on capacities barely visible a few months earlier in 1914. He was rewarded by promotion to the post of Kline's principal assistant on the magazine, and then Mr. Mandell, his original welcome now vindicated, returned him to the city room as school and college editor. From this eminence he had the pleasure of looking back at Harvard and her doings, reporting on public lectures and other events, and writing long descriptive articles about those Harvard phenomena he had known particularly well, one on the *Lampoon* and its history, another on the program in field geology offered every year to students in the mountains of Montana. Naturally, he covered the annual *Lampoon* masque in 1915, which included "living caricatures" not only of Theodore Roosevelt and Julia Sanderson, impersonated by Marquand's cousin T. J. Fuller, but of the spirit of the *Transcript* itself, "accurately and conservatively," as he announced, represented by former *Lampoon* staff member Marquand. In addition, there was a burlesque imitation of Professor Hugo Munsterberg, who had come under attack during the preceding weeks for his pro-German remarks; the professor was shown wearing an oversized Iron Cross supposedly presented to him by the Kaiser for his courage in the face of censure from his Harvard colleagues.

Marquand's *Transcript* salary was raised from fifteen to twenty-five dollars a week (which was five dollars more than a former *Transcript* treasurer, William Durant, had decreed maximum for a member of the staff). Towards the end of 1915, moreover, his name—though misspelled as John *Philip* Marquand—did in fact appear on the title page of a published book. *Prince and Boatswain: Sea Tales from the Recollections of Rear Admiral Charles E. Clark as Related to James Morris Morgan and John Philip Marquand* was a project that had grown out of talks during his senior year at college with the admiral, who was his mother's cousin. Clark was a distinguished naval veteran who was full of colorful old-seadog memories. He had come right out of the Naval Academy into the Civil War and had participated in the Battle of Mobile Bay and the capture of Fort Morgan when he was twenty-one; in the Spanish-American War he had commanded the *Oregon*, taking her around the Horn. To James Morris Morgan, a fellow Navy man and Academy classmate, the admiral wrote in May 1915: "When I tell you that Admiral Farragut once ran me out of his cabin; that Prince Pierre d'Orleans bribed me, and that only 'P.J.' [a legendary Navy boatswain] lied to me (he was the boatswain when I was executive of the old *Hartford*), that Cushing was my guest, and that Jones, who followed him as courageously and more intelligently than Porthos did d'Artagnan, was my shipmate, you may allow that I have experiences to tell. One of my auditors was little Margaret Fuller, not the gifted Margaret, Marchioness d'Ossoli, but her niece and namesake. Now her son, John P. Marquand, has been taking down some of my yarns and I hope taking off some of the rough edges at the same time. Now it seems to me you and he could combine or collaborate and get out an interesting volume." So they must have done, for the book was duly put out by a printer in Greenfield, Massachusetts. Marquand was to find it embarrassing to recall this first publication. When an anthologist of naval tales rediscovered it in 1943, Marquand wrote him that it was "written at the insistence of my relative, Admiral Clark, who I imagine had the idea that it would be nice for me to do something useful." He noted on his own copy of the manuscript, which he had nevertheless carefully preserved: "He thought this way I might make some money. He was a better Admiral than a critic." No doubt there was not much more to be gained from this writing venture than from the unlucky "Yellow Ivory," but Marquand is perhaps too severe in his dismissal of this youthful product. His pieces—one on the fabulous "P.J.," one on the Civil War hero William B. Cushing, and one on various bits of nautical romance, gathered together as "Old Salts, Kings, and Heroes"—are written with some professional ease and humor, and they show a kind of zest in the loud and happy sounding of the note of High Romance ("the old sea captains are gone now, gone the way of the old sailing vessels, lost somewhere in a tangle of shrouds and ratlines"), which exhibits the gift for parody that operated, unappreciated by most readers, in the composition of his early romantic fiction.

That winter of 1914–1915 was hard, and, as such hardship can be when one is young, exhilarating. Curzon's Mill with its memories of past Marquand dignity and ease was out of sight; he was in no mood to envy the splendors of High Street or the Gold Coast. He lived in an attic room at 57 Pinckney Street on Beacon Hill. To reach it he climbed five flights of stairs and then another ladderlike flight to the tiny space under a cupola. It had no windows except a skylight, but by first standing on his table and then lifting himself up he could finally climb out on the roof. Precariously perched on the slates he could look out over all of Boston and feel the promise of conquest that his success on the *Transcript* had given him. His room cost $2.50 a week, and before he walked to the office each morning he had breakfast at Thompson's Temperance Spa—oatmeal and coffee—for twenty-five cents. "I don't know how I got on. I was undernourished, I think," Marquand said when looking back somewhat incredulously at the young man who gazed so exultantly out over the roof tiles.

Unquestionably, though his ambitions were hardly yet born and his necessities as small as his ability to meet them, he was happy on the *Transcript*. A letter written years later to a fellow staff member shows how the minutest details remained fondly lodged in his mind: "I can even remember the smell of ink that used to come down from the composing room upstairs and the carbolic smell of the antiseptic that used to be poured into the cuspidors, survivors even then of another age. My mind can even move through that peculiar covered bridge which led into the city room, where the venerable Miss Nancy Bowles did those endless communications about the women's clubs and where a lugubrious gentleman assisted by a former colonel of the militia, neither of whose names I remember, did the popular department of 'The Church Afield.' Then there was the bearded and tobacco-chewing Mr. Shute, who was the expert on real estate transactions, and Elmer Murch, our star reporter. I can recall also Burton Kline's plain, pallid and pure stenographer named Miss Perry, who once turned to Burton when he was dictating letters, using the word 'cooperation,' and stunned us to hysteria by saying, 'Did you say "copulation," Mr. Kline?' I could discourse of Charles Alexander who really understood about the Boston four hundred, and of John Cutler and of Mr. Nickerson in the composing room. Now that I come to think of it I have never had so many friends or such a happy life." So he wrote in 1939, after the publication success of *Apley*, *Pulham*, and, in that year, *Wickford Point*, had intervened. And in *So Little Time*, written next, it was Jeffrey Wilson who kept remembering: "Jeffrey could hear the sound of the linotype machines. He could feel the gentle tremor of the building when the presses began to move. There was that sweetish smell of ink on the freshly pulled proofs that you impaled on sharp hooks upon the wall. He could remember the stacks and stacks of clippings in the morgue, which Mr. Sawyer examined daily as he worked on the page for recent deaths. He could remember the smell of the stairs as you climbed to the telegraph room, and the crowd about the blackboards on the street reading the news about the shifts on the Western Front."

Into the happy sameness of mild daily surprises on the *Transcript*, there came, however, an assignment more startling than usual on March 10, 1916, when Wilson ordered the troops of the National Guard to the Mexican border. The previous day, the bandit Pancho Villa had raided Columbus, New Mexico, killing sixteen Americans—an act of retaliation for our recognition of the Carranza government, which had expelled him from Mexico City. The news bulletin, as it popped into Fred Ford's wire basket and was unfolded for everyone to see, caused a certain amount of excitement in the telegraph room—were we really getting into war down there while all the time real war was crashing and thundering across the ocean? But to John Marquand it was a personal summons; he recalled the nearly forgotten fact that in his freshman year at Harvard he had signed up for Battery A of the First Massachusetts and had engaged in weekly practice with the unit for his three college years. He had joined mostly because everyone he knew seemed to be enrolled. Battery A was a blue-blood Harvard club he could get into, for once; it included a Cabot, an Appleton, a Bradley, an Otis, and two Peabodys from Boston. The Tuesday night drills at the New Riding Club, a dignified Boston institution, and the spring maneuvers near the Brookline Country Club were conducted in an atmosphere of social exclusiveness that fitted well with the character of the membership. He had particularly enjoyed the opportunity the Battery men had to exercise the horses along the beautiful bridle paths that bordered the Fenway and Jamaica Pond. The gentlemen-soldiers were often accompanied by debutantes riding sidesaddle in dark-blue habits and with derbies held to their heads by black elastic chin bands.

Now, he suddenly realized, he was supposed to go where the President had just commanded. Actually, his departure was not immediate. It was June 19 (the day before Harvard Class Day) when the Massachusetts Militia, including Battery A, was called up for duty. It moved to its camp in Framingham two days later. Mothers and sisters and girlfriends in fluttering elegant dresses came down to see the heroes off, riding to Framingham on the open trolley that ran along its tree-lined gravel road—or in Pierce-Arrows and Model T's. On June 26, Battery A was federalized and on the twenty-seventh boarded a train with mules and guns and caissons, horses and tents, the men riding the day coach, for El Paso, where the Battery remained until September. By that time the American army had been politely told by the Mexican government that its intrusion was unwelcome, and the exciting project of Villa's pursuit and capture had been given up. Marquand and the other members of the Battery were kept whiling their time away for three months at Fort Bliss, where they tended their horses, cleared cactus from the desert, and settled into the drudgeries and tedium of camp life without ever seeing a single Mexican.

"Fancy a plain of sand white as that of a sea beach and, unlike a beach, covered with pineapples, unevenly distributed, and interspersed with shrubs and snakes and horned toads. That is the present camping ground of Battery A," he wrote in a special article mailed to the *Transcript* on July 7. The pineapples, he went on to explain, were really cacti, at which "even a pickaxe tends to hesitate—we have picked and scratched and raked under a blistering sun. We've dragged them away in bristling heaps and piles with the dust swirling about them in clouds that settle in the eyes." Upon this painfully cleared terrain they pitched their tents and made their camp, which gradually acquired the amenities of an established post, and they occupied their minds with the multitude of rumors that blew down on them as confusingly as the constant gusts of sand and dust from the desert: "We may go home tomorrow, and again we may not. We may be sworn into the regular army, and stay in for three or four years. Someone has suggested we might be sent to Honolulu and this, too, we all believe with the unreserved innocence which comes of fresh air and simple living. And so we work and watch and look at the tents and the mountains, which glare and shake in the sun and turn purple in the evening and black in the moonlight. The sandstorms that blow out of the mountains sometimes and sweep upon us are growing to seem only a part of the day's work. We sit on the corners of our tents quite stoically now until the storm is over, till we see the mountains again and a little stretch of shining ribbon which someone tells us is the Rio Grande with the roofs of Juárez and the hills of Mexico beyond."

And as the weeks passed, the "boys of Battery A" changed, and Marquand, the detached observer of class behavior, was amused to note: "We are beginning to forget just a little of what we were. Our bankers, our doctors, and our artists and lawyers groom the horses and dig the kitchen sink and to it they drag the refuse from the cook tent. Our conversation is limiting itself more and more to our feet and our stomachs." He later declared that most of his own time had been spent shoveling horse manure into a wagon and then accompanying his load to a site some miles away where Mexican workmen burned it. This took all morning and on the way back he and his driver would stop at the Post Exchange for a beer.

In September, having been relieved by National Guard detachments from Michigan and Georgia, Battery A came home to march like heroes through the streets of Boston, and each man was awarded a medal by Mayor Curley. Marquand, in an article written now from his old desk at the *Transcript*, urged the newspaper's readers not to look on with a skeptical aloofness. Oh, no. "For in those serried ranks famous men are marching, men whose names will ring through the annals of their regiments. Hats off—yonder walks the man who in a fit of blind fury hurled a cake of chocolate at his superior officer and passed resultant weeks in the guard tent. And there's one who while a prisoner embraced the officer of the day at retreat much to the edification of the new guard that should have been right dressing. And there's another who refused to rise from the matitutinal couch at the cheery and inaccurately blown blast of the bugle until his gorge rose to such an extent that his over-insistent corporal fell not to rise till well after the count of ten. And here's the one who told his captain it was right to go lightly clad to the shower bath. Antony and Cleopatra went to church that way." And so, as the brief pseudomilitary occasion dropped from the national consciousness, Marquand was able to conclude that it was farce. He was training himself to identify the ludicrous aspects of human events. War, "especially a bloodless war," could provide comic memories. And he could even express humorous regret at its conclusion: "Now we must labor without being heroes. The tents are struck and the pots and pans have had their final cleansing and with them has gone our fame." Nevertheless, in the *Transcript* office the employees who returned from the border were being rewarded, like real war heroes, with checks for pay lost while in the service. Only Marquand didn't get one. He went to see the business manager to have the oversight corrected, and Louis Hammond, who had been with the paper since 1875, said there had been no oversight. He had not made out a check because he had naturally assumed that young Marquand had ample independent means. It took some minutes to convince him that this was not so. After all, wasn't Marquand a Harvard man?

But now the country was moving closer to involvement in the authentic war raging across the ocean. For many months the sentiments of the *Transcript* staff and of the newspaper's owners had been for the entry of the United States into the conflict. Marquand always could call to mind the spectacle of the *Transcript* office on the day, May 7, 1915, when the *Lusitania* had been sunk. Mr. Mandell himself and half the staff with him went up into the composing room to hurry the printers at their work in putting out an extra. "I can still see him," Marquand would say. "I can see the awe-struck and frightened compositor in his endeavor to put the *Lusitania* column in form dropping the whole thing on the floor. I can still hear Mr. Mandell's high voice—cracked, as gossips had it, by cheering too loudly at a Harvard football game—calling the compositor a damned lunkhead. The *Transcript* was the last extra on the street but Mr. Mandell apologized afterwards to the whole composing room for his loss of temper and bad language." Now, on his return from New Mexico, he noticed that James T. Williams, the editor, had taken to stamping about the telephone switchboard every afternoon at one o'clock, shouting out an editorial denouncing the cowardice of Woodrow Wilson, while Charles Olin, his secretary, followed him around, recording the words in a notebook. One time he saw H. T. Parker rush out of his cubbyhole near the editorial room and in a still-louder voice yell at Mr. Williams to stop his noise, furiously declaring as he often had to lesser authorities, "I will not be disturbed! I will not be disturbed!" But there was no doubt that everyone was due to be disturbed sooner or later. Marquand felt that he had hardly been back on Milk Street at all before the end of his *Transcript* life finally came—though it was not until March 1, 1917, that President Wilson published the intercepted Zimmermann telegram, which promised Mexico three American states in case of a war. On April 2, 1917, Wilson finally committed the nation. For the second, and only other time, Marquand went up to Louis Hammond's office—this time to take his oath before one of the business assistants who was a notary, and sign up for Plattsburg.

He saw it all again, changing only the names, as he wrote on the eve of another war: "In the afternoon the evening war communiqués would come over the A.P., and Mr. Jenks would get out his maps and Mr. Eldridge and Mr. Nichols would come in from the editorial rooms out front and all of them would chat agreeably and perhaps intelligently about the war. They had all read the critiques of Mr. Frank Simonds and other military experts and they read the London *Times* and the Paris *Matin* and the *Spectator* and the London *Evening Post* and the *Chronicle*. They were also familiar with more permanent works on the art of war, so that their conversation was sprinkled with such expressions as 'camouflage' and 'aerial observation' and 'no man's land' and 'creeping barrages' and 'box barrages' and 'primary and secondary objectives.' It was like being in a conference of generals when those elderly men were talking, dispassionately removed from actuality, striving to put order into a confusion that was a very long way off. They talked of the submarine blockade and of attacks without warning on our merchant shipping. The German soldiers were sheep being driven to slaughter, but at the same time possessed barbarous vindictiveness. They cut the hands off little Belgian children and they had crucified British prisoners. It was Mr. Eldridge's opinion that they were inhuman swine. There was even a story that they had rendering plants in which they manufactured soap out of their own dead. There were lots of rumors which you could not set down in print. At such times Mr. Nichols wished fervently that we had a *man* in the White House and not a Presbyterian college professor. . . .

"Those conversations never reached any conclusion. Nevertheless it began to be plain, and Jeffrey felt it vaguely, that those nations known as 'the Allies,' on the other side of an ocean which Jeffrey had never crossed, were not going to defeat the Germans by themselves. There was a dread which lay behind nearly everyone's thoughts and words—a mass emotion—and perhaps this was all that ever caused a war—a mass contagious thought shared by all the people, which the poets, the writers and the artists of the generation would never bring to full expression.

"Later Jeffrey realized that he had been witnessing the phenomenon of a people drifting into war, and that it had been a collective impulse beyond the power of any group to stop. The formation of his own convictions was as imperceptible as the rotation of a planet. You were told on impeccable authority that the world made a complete revolution in space each day, which meant that half the time you must have been walking upside down, like a fly upon the ceiling; but there was nothing you could do about it—everyone else was walking upside down."

6

War

One may forget to count Marquand among the generation of the war—so little does his writing in the immediate postwar years refer to the trenches, to battle, to the never-to-be-repaired break with the "normal" life of peace, jobs and families, careers and ideals, civilian prizes and penalties. He did not write a war novel then. His immediate reaction to his Harvard classmate Cummings's *Enormous Room*, though he later came to admire it, was no doubt like Jeffrey Wilson's in *So Little Time*: it was "an intellectual's artistic whimpering." Dos Passos, who had been in the class after theirs, he always liked, yet when he read his novel about "three maladjusted soldiers," he thought that it merely proved that "war was no place for sensitive, social-minded intellectuals." He watched other contemporaries take a crack at telling about the war in the next decade; he read *Through the Wheat*, *The Spanish Farm*, *No More Parades*, and *Chevrons*, and finally *A Farewell to Arms*, the greatest of them all—and remained convinced that none of these books had got it right because it was a story that could not be told. "They tried to give dramatic significance to something in which significance was utterly lacking. They tried to give an interpretation to something which actually offered nothing for an artist to interpret," he would make Jeffrey say. Yet the experience of war, even its very destruction of the sense of significance, remained with him to be expressed.

In a disguised or subordinate way some of his writing of the twenties and thirties does derive from his early war experience. Among his now-forgotten magazine stories there are a few about the Civil War adventures of a young Confederate officer named Scott Mattaye that deserve to be rediscovered. The romantic plots are nothing—what counts is the existential quality, the exquisite sharpness of detail, the truth to sensation that must derive from the author's personal experience of initiation into war, for there are universals in such experience that are more important than the issues and costumes of particular times. Marquand's own army past is visible, too, in some backward glances taken from a later vantage point in the narratives of *Wickford Point* and *Pulham*, though the main action of these novels is clearly postwar. Finally, however, the Second World War provided him not only with direct new observation but with a stimulus to recall his earlier ordeal. As a civilian he then found himself driven to seek War Department assignments that would bring him close to the "theaters"—as the military so aesthetically term the places where armies meet to kill and be killed. When his son went into uniform, Marquand felt that his own war experience was being reenacted. He wrote four novels—*So Little Time* (1943), *Repent in Haste* (1945), *B. F.'s Daughter* (1946) and *Melville Goodwin, U.S.A.* (1951)—that attempt to come to terms with the subject of war as seen in the later conflict. In *So Little Time*, in particular, he brought the two wars into relation by juxtaposing a father's memories with his participation in his son's war experience—which was, in fact, his own process of memory and projection when the boy became a soldier.

As for many, the First World War was essentially for John Marquand a stripping from the mind and the sensibilities of the presumptions of privilege. It was not merely that those who had been particularly protected, as poor youths had not been, encountered cold, wet, pain and fear in their absolute force. As is often described, the boy who had valued his claim to superiorities of schooling or position or wealth had to realize at last that they counted for nothing at all and might even be handicaps in the encounter. Marquand, who cherished the more—because not quite having—the advantages of class, underwent the same education. He would not abandon the pursuit of these things because of what he had learned, but he would never for a moment, helped in part by the war, be fatuous enough to wholly believe in them. And he *was* thus a part of the famous "postwar disillusion," though less self-pityingly, less dramatically, than most, having suspected the illusions at the very start of his involvement with them. His favorite writer of all the so-called lost generation (he personally found the phrase nauseating) was F. Scott Fitzgerald, whose controlled irony about the rich he could envy and imitate. For, of course, Fitzgerald was not only ironic about the rich; he could never have been a profound writer if his subject had been so limited. He too had sensed the general failure of significance, which made Marquand feel that war could not be written about, and only irony intervened to preserve his desire to write about the peace—and so, indirectly, about the war.

In May 1917, Marquand was at Plattsburg Training Camp. Like Jim Calder of *Wickford Point*, he probably had waited for hours outside a Boston office to get his name down, so as to be sure to be among the first taken. He could not bear to think that he might be left behind while everyone he knew was going. He feared that still he might not have applied early enough.

When he arrived at Lake Champlain, "the American Aldershot" was putting something like three thousand men through a West Point program abbreviated to three months. The candidates were, many of them, older than he—the average age was twenty-eight—and though most were college men, they had had little or no previous military schooling. The ninety-day turn of the crank was being tried for the first time (afterwards, in World War II, the OCS idea would become a familiar one). At the expanding camp new barracks could hardly go up fast enough and equipment was short. John Marquand had been drilling and cramming for over a month when, after transfer to the Second Field Artillery, he discovered that the artillery unit had, as yet, neither guns nor horses. Nevertheless, an atmosphere of hectic eagerness and competitive anxiety hung over the place. In *Wickford Point* he described what it was like: "First we were afraid we would not get there, and when we did, we were afraid of being dropped as of unfit caliber for officers and gentlemen. This was a thought that stalked behind us in the wooden barracks and outside the barracks too, where regular army officers appeared at odd moments with notebooks and pencils, putting down black marks. If you did not listen attentively to the lectures, if you were low in the weekly examinations, if you were found improperly buttoned or if you were caught in the latrine with a cigarette, you might not become an officer and gentleman. The training period at Plattsburg was a curious sort of nightmare." No oversight or error was too small, it appeared, to escape the notice of the flint-faced regulars who had undertaken the dubious task, to their minds, of making officers out of lawyers, young businessmen, or even less plausible types like Marquand. Jim Calder remembered a particular captain: "The perfection of the flare of his breeches and the angle of his shoulders extended to the impassive lines of his deeply tanned face. He made it very clear to us that it was impossible to turn out a soldier in three months, and he often expressed a wonder that we wanted to be officers when the life of an enlisted man was considerably easier." Marquand remembered working at his assignments with a kind of frantic absorption compelled by a near certainty that he would be washed out before the course was over. He found himself at the top of the first lieutenants' list in August. He had lost twenty pounds, and a picture of him taken then showed a pinched, somewhat tense young face beneath his garrison cap.

It would be many months, actually, before he would go overseas with the slowly readying American forces that needed much training before they could become the thirty divisions of battle troops promised the Allies. He was transferred to Camp Devens near Boston during the winter of 1917. The scene came back to mind when his son, at the same reception camp twenty-five years later, wrote of the place, a vast belt-line factory that bit by bit attached a semblance of militarization to the erstwhile civilian. As he read a letter from Johnny, he was back there. "I could smell the burning garbage again. I could see the confused civilians coming in, stripping off their clothes and getting into uniform, and standing lost and homesick in the barracks. I think my feelings at that time were very much like my son's, a mingling of distaste and bewilderment, and simultaneously an intense interest in a new experience. . . . You can never change the general aspects of a camp when recruits are gathering to go to war, any more than you can change the net results of war itself. It might as well be the camp of a Roman legion as Fort Devens. The wheels of war were moving, and the recruits were going into an unknown life." The verbiage of politics, of the war's proponents and opponents was receding: "It was strange how quickly you forgot it, once you were a recruit in camp with the sergeant calling off the roll. We were face to face with something beyond all argument." Many weeks later he was given a confidential military paper to read which set forth a list of reasons for the war. The officers were to impart these to draftees in explanation of the obligation to duty and sacrifice. "Without recalling a single one of them I can still recall that none of these reasons seemed very cogent, and stranger still, that they seemed utterly immaterial at the time. We were in the army and circumstances had made it necessary for us to treat with what simplicity we could why we had got there."

From Devens he soon was sent to the First Army Headquarters Regiment at Fort Greene in North Carolina. Here it was discovered that despite his undistinguished performance in his college course he could speak and read French to some degree and he was about to be assigned to a permanent back-of-the-lines headquarters post as a translator. "After frantic efforts" he got himself attached to the Artillery Brigade Headquarters of the Fourth Division. Major General George W. Cameron, the commander of the Fourth, was a legend at Fort Greene, where his men were being given a strenuous foretaste of the field. The camp was out in rough country with few roads; in the spring of 1918, when Marquand arrived, the clay of the roads turned into streams, and Cameron marched his men with full packs eight hours a day through the mud. The Fourth would arrive overseas toughened by this process and due to be famous for its stamina, but Marquand was rather glad to be a mounted artillery officer. He also discovered that he enjoyed the work of the artilleryman on the range, and even when the reality of battle replaced the make-believe of target practice, the curious pleasure of placing gunfire remained. When his son was assigned to artillery training at Fort Sill, Oklahoma, in 1943, Marquand would write, reminiscently: "I am very glad that you are going out on the range so soon. For the first hour of firing you will be deafened and rather nervous and confused. Then, when you get used to it, I think you will like it very much and be glad for the first time that you are in the Artillery. There is nothing in the world pleasanter than to be a part of a good, quick moving gun crew on one of the lighter guns, where everyone knows just what he is to do and does it automatically. No matter what horrid little squirts your companions may be on this crew you cannot help but getting to like and respect them when you are doing that sort of job together. If they ever let you conduct fire yourself you will get even more of a kick out of it. To stand there and see the bursts around the target and to see them move up and down according to your orders has always seemed to me one of the greatest sensations in the world. I should say as good as piloting an aeroplane. The only thing that I know that is better is directing fire against the enemy, standing alone somewhere by a telephone, not being able to see your guns, but seeing the Germans and watching your shells fall among them and watching trucks and houses blown to pieces. It has all the shooting galleries on Sixth Avenue lashed to the mast."

That sensation still awaiting it, the advanced school detachment to which Marquand had been assigned left to continue its training overseas. It went ahead of its brigade, embarking on April 28, 1918, for France. The voyage in the crowded troopship, a former German liner, was without incident, though the men kept looking for signs of torpedo attack, crying out at porpoises and flying fish under the illusion that they were surfacing submarines. Marquand himself had been on watch one time when he raised the alarm at the sight of a porpoise (it just escaped being blasted by a six-inch gun). On May 12, they landed at Saint-Nazaire, and after a week Marquand's detachment was sent on its way to its appointed place of training, riding straight across the breadth of France by rail to Besançon. Like travelers in peacetime the men were enchanted by their first sight of France. They were far from any rumble of battle. The train followed the peaceful valley of the Loire with its old towns and châteaux, through Nantes, Saumur, and Tours. Besançon, Marquand wrote to his aunt Bessie, "is a splendid old town with houses so old that it hardly seems right to look at them and with an arch of triumph that Marcus Aurelius built when he had a successful game with one of the Gallic tribes and also a Roman bridge and medieval fortifications." The artillery school to which they had been ordered was up in the hills outside Besançon in a romantic wooded area with waterfalls and picturesque perspectives, and they were just settling in contentedly when word came that the brigade had arrived from America and in classic army fashion they were ordered back across France again. Taking a different route from before, their train carried them, still touristically enchanted, west through central France, through Moulins, Bourges, Limoges, to the busy port of Bordeaux, where the war came into view again as they entered streets thronged with the soldiers of three nations and saw the huge docks and warehouses the Americans had constructed at Bassens on the Garonne. Their new camp was appropriately austere—"a sandy, fly-ridden place," he wrote his aunt.

Still, there were compensations. The commander of the brigade had developed a liking for Marquand's conversation, and he was indulgent about passes. Delightedly, Marquand wrote Aunt Bessie: "This business of being on the Brigade staff might be worse. We have two automobiles to take to town, and sometimes, if the general is feeling optimistic, to the beach." And he added, "The General is almost the finest man you ever saw and very, very clever." Brigadier General Edwin B. Babbitt was a fifty-six-year-old West Pointer from New York, the first regular army officer Marquand had been able to study closely; he was impressive precisely because no older man Marquand had known—certainly not his father—had seemed in such easy, unreflective possession of his circumstances, so little given to self-doubt. It was a type he would grow to know well in his association with the military in this and the next war, and finally he would attempt the almost impossible task of making such a man the hero of a novel, *Melville Goodwin, U.S.A.* General Babbitt was his first general—and, somewhat astonished, he found that he liked him. The general, for his part, regarded the twenty-four-year-old lieutenant with a teasing half-respect. Marquand was the only "Harvard man" on his staff, and he had his own notions about *his* type. "Didn't they teach you anything at Harvard?" was, of course, his favorite challenge when the young man stumbled. Yet he was impressed with the way Marquand caught on at the school, the more so because he himself was strictly an ordnance man who had never before had anything to do with the artillery.

The trips into the great French city provided a diversion. The French were in love with the doughboys in a way to dilate one's self-esteem. On the Fourth of July the Americans paraded with French soldiers through Bordeaux, while, as he wrote his father, the people of the city hung out of balconies and stood on the tables of the cafés, "old men and women and little children standing in front waving American flags and shouting, 'Vive l'Amérique.' First there came a French general and then a lot of French class of 1919, looking very young beside the grizzled old sergeants and corporals who herded them along, and very hot in their horizon blue helmets and overcoats. But they marched very well, better, I must confess, than our men, who have the usual artillery man's aversion to walking and who have not all received their horses." Marquand himself neither walked nor rode in the parade, but drove in the staff car to watch it, which he preferred to either way of spending the hot middle of the day. After the parade was over he and his fellow officers went out to lunch, and like all innocents abroad they marveled at the low cost of a bottle of vintage wine in the country of its origin. Then they repaired to a musical show, where the performers flattered the audience by knowing American slang and titillated them by the expected display of Gallic naughtiness.

As soldiers stationed anywhere for more than a few weeks tend to do, they gladly surrendered their awareness of future time and acted as though they would never move from the place. Marquand went to the city kennels, where dogs were being trained for front-line police work and to draw ammunition carts, and purchased a police puppy with a fine pedigree, though he knew perfectly well that he would soon have to leave it.

At the school he was studying artillery orientation. Since it had a great deal to do with maps and surveying, he was glad to find use at last for the summer spent at the Harvard engineering camp. "It rather puts me ahead of some of those fine virile fellows who never cared much about studying anyway and don't see the use of the technical stuff," he wrote his father. His proficiency attracted the attention of the orientation instructor, who recommended that Marquand stay on to teach at the school also. The instructor was a Frenchman who had been injured in a dozen of his country's previous battles in colonial warfare, and he boasted, perhaps with exaggeration, of a wooden leg, a silver skull, and a gold jaw as a result. He was astonished when Marquand protested the order keeping him in the school. "I cannot understand, *mon fils*," he told Marquand, "I simply cannot understand why, after you have looked at me with my gold jaw, my silver skull, and my wooden leg you should still wish to get into action. You can stay here in Bordeaux, teach, and have wine, women, and pleasure. *Quelle folie!*" But everyone knew that the big counteroffensive against Ludendorff was under way, and on July 18 a massive AEF attack was launched against Château-Thierry; Cameron's infantry, whom Marquand had seen slogging in the mud at Fort Greene, were in the assault. He wanted to be there, at the front. He appealed to the general, who had also been especially pleased with Marquand's execution of a large number of maps and tracings for a defense exercise. To his delight, Babbitt had sent through a special request, saying that Marquand's services were needed on the staff. At this point, Marquand was full of *folie*, of faith in his nation's armies and in his own capacities, of ignorance of war. "'What big men the Americans are,' every Frenchman says. It is true. Everyone you see is a perfect physical specimen, anxious and willing to learn in one of the great universities he is attending under the very best of professors, how to make things just as unpleasant for his neighbor in the other yard as his ingenuity coupled with the exact and pitiless methods of modern science can make it." In a few days Marquand was in action.

He would find it difficult, afterwards, to sort out his recollections and attach them to those maps appearing in books describing the battles of the Marne-Aisne, of Saint-Mihiel, and the Meuse-Argonne salient, with lines indicating the succession of fronts, and arrows showing the pressure exerted on those lines by the various military units. There were intervals of complete terror and noise and confusion, but a great many also of a constant bustle, by which one was completely—and not uncheerfully—distracted. The Fourth Artillery Division, with Marquand's brigade, moved up north of Château-Thierry to take up positions along the Vesle River. General Babbitt, Marquand was surprised to discover, now seemed almost as much at sea as everyone else, having never before commanded an artillery brigade. His chief of staff, a major who also wore a West Point ring, had never been more than a battery commander. "The rest of us were just nice bright boys," observed Marquand. Looking back on it, he realized that the sole member of the brigade staff who knew what the score was was a French liaison officer named Boucher. He was the only one who had ever heard a shot fired in anger.

On August 6, Marquand wrote his father from "Fourth Field Artillery Brigade Headquarters, Somewhere in France" and noted, "I am now in a place where they are slinging some pretty hot stuff at us." The locale was probably between Bazoches and Fismes on the bank of the meandering little Vesle, a branch of the Aisne. Behind lay the well-named Bois de Dole, a dry, thorny forest through which the division had worked its way. On August 4 it had reached the riverbank across from Bazoches, which was heavily fortified by the Germans, and the Americans were under fire. Perhaps it was in the little village of Ville-Savoye, from which the Germans had been pushed, that the brigade headquarters was occupying a schoolhouse. The enemy was as close as one's skin—one was aware of him all the time, Marquand remembered. When the shelling of the German guns paused, you could look up at the opposite bank of the Vesle right at the ground he was occupying. "It seems funny," he wrote one night, "that right across a little creek there is another village all smashed beyond recognition like ours with perfectly good roads leading to it. You can see them if you are careful, and yet you cannot get there and live to tell the tale." Their own village "lies out in a little hollow as dark and still as a tomb, very grim and battered. Over the crest of our house you can see the flashes of our guns and hear them rumble now quickly now slowly all night long. Then at regular intervals there is a noise like the wind around a corner of the house and a dull crash and a rending of timbers and you know that they have hit one of the houses near you and it is time to drop down cellar. Sometimes they put in gas and the town wakes up and people go around ringing bells and blowing horns by which you know it is time to put on a gas mask. The Germans have been here before us. You can tell that because everything has been left like a pig-sty—not as bad as usual because they had not long to stay. We are too busy to attend to some of those they left behind, so it is not always pleasant to walk about the country. The fields are strewn with the arms, equipment and dead of four nations."

The country had the unforgettable look of grotesque litter, which he would soon know well as the condition of a recent battlefield. As he had observed to his father, the Germans had had no time to pick up behind themselves. A couple of weeks later, when he had left the sector, he wrote again: "The country around where we were was painfully torn up with dead things all over the fields and woods. All the towns were mashed to a pulp." The landscape would reappear in his imagination when Jeffrey Wilson picks his way over the ground in approximately the same place in *So Little Time*:

"They were near a thicket of saplings, with some taller trees among them, the branches of which were twisted and broken, as though they had been struck by a high wind. He pushed his way through the saplings, looking for a cleared place—which was not hard to find, since the French were neat about their forests. He did not look around him, until he sat Stan down, with his back against a tree. Then he saw that three dead men were lying about ten feet in front of him, two in German field-gray, and one in olive-drab. He had never encountered the dead on a battlefield, and his reaction must have been the same as that of anyone who first saw war dead. . . . He knew at once that they were not asleep. They lay sprawled as though a strong gust of wind had struck them. A number of others had been there, too, who had dropped things and had forgotten to pick them up, but it was no common sort of human forgetfulness. . . . The sunbeams cut through the leaves and branches of the trees, making uneven spots upon that disorder on the ground, and moving with the breeze, erratically centering on new objects. He never forgot the moving light first touching a regulation mess kit, which had burst open, then a roll of toilet paper festooned across the bushes, then a mess tin and a letter stamped into the earth, a muddy blanket, a hand grenade, a torn section of an olive-drab puttee, a rifle with a pair of socks near it, a canteen—a combination that was senseless and indecent; and the dead had collapsed in the same disorder. One lay with his head lower than his heels, with the rim of his helmet jammed against the bridge of his nose, and the mouth gaping. If there were wounds on the two Germans, he did not see them, and he did not care to look, but there was no doubt how the doughboy had died. A fragment of a high explosive shell had blown the top of his head clear off, just above the eyes, leaving all that was left of the head and face turned upward toward the trees. The blasted skull was like a cross section from a book of physiology."

Until two days before they went into action the staff of the Fourth Artillery had not been organized because its table of organization had not arrived. Then, at the last moment it "burst upon our kindly but bewildered general like a clap of thunder. It appeared that the staff had to be organized for supply and operation and what not, and the table called for an intelligence officer." Upon observing this fact the major looked around rather wildly for a moment and then his glance settled on the Harvard man. "I had never heard of intelligence before," Marquand remembered. "And when I asked the Major and the General what I was to do about it, I really doubt they had either. The Major said I was to distribute maps to regimental commanders and to find out all I could regarding the position and intentions of the enemy. When I asked how I could do that, he said he was damned if he knew but he would let me know if he thought of anything."

All anybody seemed to know was that the Germans were on the other side of this little creek about thirty feet wide and three or four deep at the deepest. In the nearby village of Ville-Savoye, two infantrymen of the Fourth had been locating the German emplacements from the top of the church steeple until the enemy detected the cause of the accurate gunfire they were getting and picked off the steeple and the spotters with a direct hit. At this point Marquand began talking to Boucher, the French liaison officer, "and this handsome, cynical, horizon-blue lieutenant, whose only fault was losing his temper when he drank cognac, gave me some very good suggestions. He said, mildly, that it would be nice to know what the Germans were shooting at in our sector and in order to find out, how would it be to ask the captains of all the regimental batteries to give a daily report of the number and location of German shells falling in the neighborhood of their gun positions. Taking these reports together, I might plot the spot where the shells hit upon a map and this might lead to something." Marquand, as he remembered, seized on this idea with avidity and, using his new position, managed to get the battery commanders of their three regiments to report daily where shells were dropping. "I ended by annoying a great many of them since the whole idea seemed nonsensical, and in fact made myself so obnoxious that I was subsequently relieved, but I did find out something about the enemy's intentions." At the end of two weeks, when the Fourth was replaced by the Seventy-seventh Division, Marquand had produced a French 1:20,000 map on which he had drawn the Fourth Division's battery positions, and around each of these, in different colors for different days, a small cloud of dots indicating the landing points of German shells. "At the end of two weeks the sum of these made a significant and sinister pattern. Even I, after three months at Plattsburg and another month at a French artillery school, could see their significance. The Germans had obviously located our batteries, concealed in woods and under camouflage. They had obviously worked out the ranges and had bracketed our position. At any moment they desired they could clearly take us under fire."

On the afternoon of the night they were to be relieved Marquand showed this map to General Babbitt, having first shown it to the major, who had been too busy to pay much attention to it. The general, however, reacted briskly. "He said it was a very interesting map and it showed what a bright civilian officer could do." He intended to show it to the artillery general of the Seventy-seventh who was coming to their headquarters that evening. At 6:30 P.M. Marquand was ordered to report to the general in his room, and he found Babbitt there with the visiting brigadier and three colonels, and they were all looking at Marquand's map, which was spread out on a table. When he entered, their faces all turned towards him, and the looks they bore were not approving. The new general finally asked the lieutenant what he thought the map meant, and Marquand found himself telling him that it was as simple as ABC. The Germans had located our battery positions. It would be safer, sir, not to move batteries into the old positions but to take up new ones. "This remark of mine was what is known in the Army as sticking one's neck out and the new general and his colonels were tired and worried." The general replied to Marquand, "Young man, I am not asking your opinion." He curtly explained that it would take a great deal of labor to dig new gun emplacements and suppose the Germans had been firing at us, did not the lieutenant know that people shot cannons in a war? It would be ridiculous not to move into their positions just because of a map and that was that and that would be all. At midnight the artillery brigade of the Seventy-seventh Division moved into the old positions. Twenty-four hours later "the Germans opened up, causing very heavy casualties and a heavy loss in materiel."

A couple of weeks after the Fourth Division had withdrawn, Marquand found himself transferred to the Seventy-seventh, and back in action in the same area. It was not clear whether this was a reprimand or a compliment following the caper of the map. The command had changed anyhow—the Seventy-seventh had a new division commander, General Robert Alexander, who would lead it to extraordinary exertions and victories, and the artillery general had been replaced also. Marquand was glad, whatever the cause, to be relieved of the burden of being an intelligence officer, and to be in the line. "I am now serving with the regiment," he wrote his father. "Now I am sleeping under a pup tent with all the rest of the soldiers, and do not feel ashamed to look the average individual in the face."

The average American individual was represented in all his variations in the Seventy-seventh. Called the Melting Pot Division because the majority of its men came from New York City, it included speakers of forty-two foreign languages, and the three men from its ranks who received the DSC were a Chinese born in San Francisco, a German born on the Rhine, and a Rumanian Jew whose earliest childhood had been spent in a Bessarabian ghetto. It is quite possible that Marquand was learning from association with these comrades what he had faintly grasped at the Newburyport High School. Harry Pulham would realize that "most of them were braver and more generous than I was."

On August 14 the Seventy-seventh had undertaken to push the Germans beyond the Vesle across the flat plain, which had little natural protection, that lay between it and the Aisne River. Not until September 6 did part of the regiment reach its objective and not until the fifteenth, after a month of battle that cost the lives of seven thousand officers and enlisted men, was it relieved. Then, after a brief bivouac, it moved to the final and most famous of its engagements, the painful conquest of the German forces hidden in the fastness of the Argonne forest—the closest thing to jungle warfare that World War I soldiers knew—a task that occupied them until the middle of October, when they were again relieved.

Marquand, who was now back on the staff as an information officer, remained close to the action during the entire period. He was sent on missions up and down the front. On September 6 he wrote that his commanding officer was a colonel with the zeal for activity "of a fiend," who kept routing his staff out of bed at any hour of the day or night and packing them off to some critical point. On the nineteenth he wrote that he had just returned from a mission during which he saw a large group of Germans surrender in the field while rain poured torrentially, and conquered and conquerors were covered by mud. Then he moved with the regiment forty-five miles west to the Meuse-Argonne sector and saw not only the fighting in the forest but in other areas—as on October 15, when he was at an artillery headquarters representing his regiment. A while later he wrote his father, "For the past month I have been establishing forward information posts and doing liaison with the infantry, both of which are damned ticklish jobs, capable of giving you a definite reaction all the time."

It was on such a mission that he found himself spending an eerie dreamlike moment in a little wood northeast of the town of Septsarges near the Meuse. Here, as in the Argonne a few miles away, the Germans had employed the leisure of a four-year occupancy by building cosy little cottages with gardens and fences and gateways that could remind the relaxed soldier of vacations in the Schwarzwald. There was a motion picture theater in the woods, barracks, stables, and an officers' club with a stove, paneled walls with pictures hanging on them, shelves with books. Best of all, conveniently close to the club was a commodious dugout that one could reach in three bounds—as handy for Marquand and his companions as the Germans had ever intended it to be for themselves. By the time the Americans arrived, the Germans had abandoned this snug retreat and stationed themselves in the valley of the Meuse right outside the woods, in the white-walled, red-tile-roofed town of Brieulles, a crucial point on the river.

In an article on soldier recollections for the New York *Tribune* which he wrote the following spring, Marquand described the sensations of this "quiet" front: "Shells of various dimensions ranging from the 77 to the 150, passing in the majestic curve of their trajectory, used to drop in those woods with lively detonations. Sometimes you would think that the Germans remembered the snug little building with boardwalks and rustic steps, and, remembering, resented our intrusion. If you cared for exercise a brisk walk up one of the twisting little byways would bring you to the northern edge of the trees to a pleasing, rolling bit of ground, ending at the hill from which you could see Brieulles in artistic panorama. You could often get to the top of the hill without much difficulty provided you were careful not to let your head appear above the crest. Sometimes a stray shell or so would splash up brown earth from the greensward, but aside from the noise of the artillery, it was a quiet place."

But a good deal of his time in September and October 1918 was spent at noisier locations. He wrote his father as the period ended: "I've been machine-gunned from land and air, bombed, sniped at with rifles and field pieces, been under three different kinds of gases—mustard, tear, and phosgene. I have been under fire while wrecking some guns captured from the Germans when it was so hot that the pieces bounded off our tin hats. I've seen men smashed into innumerable shapes and pieces; in fact, there isn't much they can send me now that would surprise me a bit." Only the veritable horror of such experiences justifies, of course, the tone of jaunty boasting. He also took a certain pride, it is clear, in having become a boy his mother would have had difficulty in recognizing during those weeks in the field. "If you only knew how long it is since I have brushed my teeth," he cheerfully told her. "I have not bathed for a month, and then only in an incidental way. I have no clothes but those on my back, and have been crawling through mud and dodging things and sleeping on cellar floors so much that my clothes no longer look new and I have not had a chance to clean my boots. I have lost my blankets and found some German ones and also some German socks, thereby getting covered with cooties. Until recently I have been living on what I could find—mostly canned beef and hard tack and, what is worse, no tobacco." There were thousands of others who could have written the same, but the dirt of battlefields, a kind of reverse baptism for fine gentlemen, was, together with physical hardship, a new proof of status under the changed circumstances of war.

More affecting than any personal experience, probably, was the news of the death of a particular friend from his college years. He was Charles Warner Plummer, Harvard '14, a boy who had had no fame in the busy competitive campus world, but who found his vocation, apparently, in heroism. Marquand had been one of his few friends. Plummer was an extreme version of Marquand himself, very solitary instead of being mildly so, shy to the point of morbidity, touchingly sensitive and poetic—and not merely unaccepted by the Harvard snobs but generally ignored by everyone. Yet joining the air force had been the making of him. He became a daredevil of the Eighty-eighth Squadron, and was awarded the Croix de Guerre and the DSC. Finally, on August 11, 1918, when returning from a photographic mission, he was shot down over the Vesle at the same time that Marquand was somewhere along its bank. When his body was recovered "he was still holding the controls of one of those flimsy biplanes that we used to fly in those days," Marquand told his son when Johnny in his turn had lost a friend in another European war. Then he said, "Somehow news of [one's friend's] having been killed is much more of a shock than seeing a lot of nice acquaintances all around you smashed into mincemeat."

Suddenly it was all over. On November 2, he was at a base port waiting for passage to the United States. "When I struck Paris on the way home, I sure was a sight," he told his father. "Fortunately I had stopped on the way and was partially decooterized, but I had lost most of my stuff and had on a tin hat and a trench coat all torn and caked with mud, and I had left a large part of my britches in the barbed wire. It sure gave the Parisians a treat to see me. It took the bellhop at the hotel about three quarters of an hour just scraping off my shoes and when I got to the barber's I didn't get shampooed for fear it would stop up the drain." The mud, the lice, they were the most eloquent testimony that he had been where the war really was.

The joy of having come through—alive, not even wounded, and not more of a coward than most—would pass. In later years he was apt to be self-deprecatory and evasive about his war experiences. Only once had he come close to killing a German, he told Roger Butterfield of *Life*. While scouting some abandoned trenches he had come upon a German straggler; he had fumbled for his .45 but the German had ducked around a corner and got away before he could fire. Naturally, he had come close to getting killed, like so many others, and he had seen plenty of other fellows get it, but he would not make so much of the effects of the experience. "I got frightened to death on a number of occasions and I saw a lot of people get killed, but I don't think it did very much to me," he said to a reporter from *Time*. To Philip Hamburger of the *New Yorker* he gave the impression that "he had no big memories of the war, since he had pushed it deep inside his mind, and only the most inconsequential details remained on the surface."

In the place of war's unbearable melodrama, he preferred to tell about the day he passed through a village on the way to Château-Thierry and stopped to watch a group of soldiers scrambling in a yard for a scattered hoard of antique coins—they had been hidden in a well for a century until a passing shell had bounced them out. He had laughed till he felt weak, at the time. What did it mean? Nothing at all, probably—as some of the grimmest moments of life are beyond accommodation to our sense of pattern. Yet he was irritated, when he got home, by a certain "O.J.F.," who declared in the *New Republic* that the experience of war could only be degrading, without physical or moral benefit. Sententiously, Marquand replied that the soldier had learned something despite his reduction to primitive conditions of existence and his exposure to savagery and waste: "He learned that at times other things are more important than personality. There was fortitude out there in that squalor; he learned it with the mud as his book instead of a tract of social duty. He profited also by frequent examples of generosity and sacrifice that the occasion manufactured more readily than it was fabricated in the regions of the Higher Standard. The life of a Savage, the existence on the marge of the Slough of Despond, had at least the advantage of demonstrating how many superfluous conveniences are wrapped around the Standard. Only a few, I think, learned to look complacently at Death. The cheapness of life added a certain value to living. In the curriculum of the war itself were varied courses in respect, sympathy, and consideration for others." "That guy was never over," would have been, he thought, any veteran's response to the magazine writer's diatribe on the effects of war.

7

After the War Was Over

On the trip home Marquand had been jammed in the steerage along with the other lieutenants on a ship loaded full of casual officers, the colonels, and the majors and captains along with a dozen generals in first class. The lieutenants had cursed the gentlemen overhead with a cheerful abandon. They were not, for the most part, professional soldiers and they were young—but they, not their seniors, had seen the most, after all. Perhaps, as would happen when Melville Goodwin returned from the same battlefields, a major general assembled all the lieutenants on the bow as they prepared to enter New York harbor and ordered them below until the ship docked so that their rush to the side to see the Statue of Liberty might not unbalance the vessel. If so, as in Marquand's novel, a bellow of scorn went up from the throats of the junior officers, who told the general where he could go and what he could do with his Statue of Liberty. They were already civilians.

Yet when they stepped through the barriers at the end of the pier and walked into the streets of New York they were disappointed to find that no one glanced at them in their worn uniforms. The city had seen thousands of them already in the month after the Armistice, had welcomed one marching division after another with cascades of paper, and was back about its business. Marquand found that he, too, was suddenly eager to forget about the war and make up for lost time. "I was full of beans and determined to make a billion dollars," he remembered. The war had done queer things to everyone's idea of wealth. Those who had had money before the war, the rich Bostonians his parents had known, the families of many of his Harvard contemporaries who had drawn incomes effortlessly from bonds and mortgages and rents, were feeling the effects of a shrunken dollar. But there were others who had profited from inflation and the rise in prices, the "new rich," who had bustled and marketed something. What, Marquand asked himself, had he to market? Quite matter-of-factly he studied the possibilities. Even before the war, as we have seen, he had discounted his engineering preparation; there were only his small beginning in newspaper work and the job he had done with Admiral Clark's reminiscences to suggest his skill as a writer. Yet few, after the war, would build a fortune in letters and rise with the postwar tide of moneymaking as surely as Marquand.

Of course he had been changed by the six months he had spent overseas. Like every veteran, he had to figure out just what the war had done to him—the consequences did not always match the descriptions of the "postwar" that multiplied in the literature and the comment of the next decade. Most of the veterans would not have agreed immediately—or even later—that they were "lost." Certainly not John Marquand. For the moment he was one of the millions who would look straight ahead most of the time, though ever and again backwards, "over there," to the experiences that had made them into a generation.

He was determined upon one thing. He would not go back to Boston to work. Jobs were scarce, but New York, that vortex of ambition and talent, that center of every means and manner by which a man might make capital of his wits, his craft, his art, was the place. Less than a month after his discharge he was working there. He went down to Wilmington to see his parents first of all, of course. His father and mother had returned from Panama in 1915 and Philip Marquand was now employed by the Edge Moor Iron Company; they lived in the stone cottage in a maple grove, lent them by one of Wilmington's oldest families, and seemed settled at last in a contented life with a modest footing in society. But Wilmington could not have held twenty-six-year-old John a minute even if there was anything he could possibly have found to do there. After a week he went back to New York to look for a job and found one immediately on the New York *Tribune*. His old friend Burton Kline was now on this newspaper's magazine and able to introduce and recommend him. He had not even taken time to go up to the place that was so much more home than his birthplace. On January 2, 1919, he wrote apologetically to his aunt Bessie at Curzon's Mill (she had continued her wartime habits by sending a package of knitted socks and other gifts to New York, as though he were still overseas): "Well, I'm out of the army and have a job on the New York *Tribune*, paying just twice as much as I was getting on the *Transcript*, which is not so bad considering these hard times. I only hope I can hold it. I wish awfully to see you. Sometime soon when I get on to the work a little better, I'm going to run down on Saturday and Sunday. In a great many ways I'm dreadfully sorry to go away from Boston, especially not to be near the Mill, but the only way to make the *Transcript* appreciate you is apparently to get off it."

He was speaking precisely—his pay was now fifty dollars a week—but it is questionable whether he really wanted to be tempted back to Boston on any terms. Everyone he knew seemed to be trying to succeed in New York. All around him careers were getting started and offering instructive examples. The old *Lampoon* crowd was down in a body trying to make writing pay in one way or another. Robert Benchley had been in New York on and off since 1912. He had begun by taking on the editing of a Curtis Publishing Company house organ and writing advertising copy, and in 1914 had his first story accepted by *Vanity Fair*, to which he continued to contribute even when he was forced to take a job with a Boston paper company. In 1915, he was back in New York as a reporter for the *Tribune*, involved with its new Sunday section for a while, and then, after an interval, with its rotogravure supplement. By 1918, he found that with free-lance writing he was making over five thousand a year, enough to support his wife and child. He had a good idea of how a journalistic literary career might be got under way, when Marquand met up with him again in New York at this time, and he could illuminate the *Tribune* scene particularly well. Benchley himself was about to move on to the managing-editorship of *Vanity Fair*, where, in the company of Dorothy Parker and Robert Sherwood, he would spend the year of 1919. He would then become drama critic for *Life* and, after nine years, for the *New Yorker*.

There was Frederick Lewis Allen, Benchley's classmate and another of the senior *Lampoon* editors of Marquand's time. Allen had got started after graduation by working, as Marquand had done, in Boston, but he had skipped the newspaper stage and gone straight for the magazines, becoming an assistant to Ellery Sedgwick, the editor of the *Atlantic Monthly*. In 1916 he came to New York and took on the managing-editorship of *Century Magazine*, remaining there until, with the entry of the United States into the war, he became involved in war work in Boston and Washington. This led to the post of secretary to the Harvard Corporation, which put him in charge of university publicity. By 1919, Allen was back in New York again, at work for the publishing firm of Harper and Brothers; some years later he would become the editor of *Harper's Magazine*. When the postwar experience was a decade old, Allen wrote a book that would be, perhaps, the most famous summary of the twenties, *Only Yesterday*.

Marquand looked around for other *Lampoon* friends and quickly located them. Roger Burlingame had a right of inheritance in the New York book industry; he had followed his father into the firm of Charles Scribner's Sons after a year on a weekly called the *Independent*. Then, like Marquand, he had found himself on the Texas border, then at Plattsburg, and finally overseas with the artillery in the Meuse-Argonne. On the way home, he had lingered in Paris for four months—acquiring the generational appetite for Europe that was to prove so insatiable in some cases. But after arriving in New York in March 1919, he went directly again to Scribner's. He said at the time: "Now I am back on the job with the publisher, and am one of that restless band of people who cannot get either the war or France out of their systems; I want most of the time to be somewhere else and doing something different. But here I am, tied, strapped, chained, manacled to a desk." He would remain, writing novels on the side but mainly occupied with editing, until 1927, when he would break away, spend four years abroad, and devote the rest of his life to writing books. Marquand saw a good deal of him in 1919 and 1920, and in 1921 Roger encouraged him to submit the manuscript of a novel to Scribner's. Burlingame had published his own first book earlier that year.

Burlingame was to be a lifelong friend and so was Paul Hollister, Harvard '13, who after a long trip in South America had come to New York in November 1915 and started in advertising with H. K. McCann Company. He also produced a book—about German agents in America during the war—but his real destiny was advertising. In 1919, when Marquand caught up with him again, Hollister had come back from the war and assisted in the formation of a new firm soon to be a leading agency—Barton, Durstine and Osborne. He left it only when the Depression had flattened advertising to nothing at all, in 1932—to become a vice-president of Macy's.

Edward Streeter was another friend whose aspirations had been, and remained, partly literary but who went, in the end, into a business career more traditional than Hollister's. He, too, had started on a newspaper, the Buffalo *Express*, before going to the Mexican border and the battlefields of France. In May of 1919 he returned to New York and was working for a newspaper syndicate. By the time Marquand saw him again, he had managed to publish four extremely funny little books using the device of a doughboy's letters to his "Dere Mable," soon to be made into a successful musical comedy. *Lampoon* humor would seem to have issued in a literary or even theatrical career for Streeter, although, by 1921, he was ready to place it to one side. "It suddenly dawned on me that the maintenance of a family was a vast economic enterprise," he later explained wryly. He had joined the staff of the Bankers Trust Company and would eventually be a vice-president of the Fifth Avenue Bank. There would be *Father of the Bride* and other productions from time to time to remind one of Streeter's gift for lighthearted satire, but he would keep faithfully to the job of banker all the while. When Marquand met him in New York in 1919, he seemed far more likely to remain a writer of some kind.

Richard Connell was still another classmate who had turned to newspaper work, but he had gone directly to New York and started with the New York *American*. When Marquand encountered him again, in 1919, he also had just returned from army service and was writing advertising copy for the J. Walter Thompson agency, a job he would soon leave and Marquand would take. Connell was just a step ahead on Marquand's destined course: he would next become a successful writer of magazine fiction, the author of several hundred short stories, mostly published in the *Saturday Evening Post*. Not for some years would it be clear that Marquand's career was to be significantly different from Connell's, that he would labor at letters with more than a Lampooner's intention to spoof the folly of the moment and to entertain.

These *Lampoon* alumni were alike in certain ways. All of them had, in 1919, the idea that they might sometime do "something serious"—but there was no hurry. For the time being the idea was to find a way of making money by the use of their college-proven skills as writers and humorists. None of them pondered much over the high aims of art or attempted to formulate the deeper meanings of their young lives, particularly their recent war experiences. Marquand was aware, perhaps, that they were all living at a moment when the literary arts were about to explode into a new age. Fiction, to which he felt drawn, was full of flashes and detonations no less than poetry. In 1918 Willa Cather had published *My Ántonia*, and in 1919 James Branch Cabell published *Jurgen* and Sherwood Anderson, *Winesburg, Ohio*. Even Edith Wharton, older than any of these three, produced *The Age of Innocence* in 1920—all books he read with excitement, as others did, wondering whether he could ever do anything so fresh and true. In 1920, also, were published two books by writers whom Marquand was to admire more than any others for the rest of his life: one by a man eight years older than himself, Sinclair Lewis, and the other by F. Scott Fitzgerald, who was three years younger. It was some time before he met either author, though *Main Street* and *This Side of Paradise* at once gave him a sense of the direction he might take if he ever got started as a writer. But he was not yet ready to get started in so serious a way.

There were others who already thought of themselves as serious writers. Marquand discovered that in New York, as at Harvard, young literary men might be worlds apart. A few blocks away from West Sixteenth Street, where he was living in 1919, was Greenwich Village, a community of the aesthetic and the revolutionary, not quite yet of bohemian chic. He had friends and acquaintances there whom he saw less often than he did his *Lampoon* companions. For one thing, they never went to the Harvard Club, which Marquand and the Lampooners frequented. John Dos Passos was back from service as an ambulance driver in France and he had already written a book called *One Man's Initiation—1917*, to be published in 1920, his first awkward protest against the stupidity and cruelty of war. In the spring of 1919 he was living in Washington Square and working on his next book, *Three Soldiers*, which would be the most famous antiwar book of their generation. Marquand's classmate Cummings was on West Fourteenth Street, writing, painting, exploring the city from the East Side to the Bronx. He also had already made his contribution to the literature of protest. This was *The Enormous Room*, to be published in 1922, that stunning account of his experiences in a French prison camp. Dos Passos and Cummings had helped to put together a little book in 1917 called *Eight Harvard Poets*, a selection of poems that had appeared in the *Harvard Monthly*. Cummings had then gone down to New York, where he found a job answering readers' letters on *Collier's* weekly; but after three months he had joined the Norton Harjes Ambulance Corps, like Dos Passos. Now, as the twenties began, Scofield Thayer and Sibley Watson, wealthy amateurs who had moved in the circle of the aesthetes at Harvard, had transferred the *Dial* from Chicago to New York, where it would become the most important literary journal of the decade. The editor, formerly editor of the *Harvard Monthly*, was Stewart Mitchell, and to its pages Cummings contributed, together with Dos Passos and others who were at the center of the movement for new expression in the arts. Their circle included many names afterwards famous, and at parties given by the *Dial* music critic Paul Rosenfeld in his apartment on Irving Place one met Edmund Wilson, Marianne Moore, Hart Crane, Alfred Kreymborg, Lewis Mumford, the Stieglitzes and others.

Marquand developed few personal contacts among the greater or lesser originals in the arts who abounded in New York, or even among the numerous young men and women who were said to be "interesting" for one reason or another, though they had produced nothing that anyone could see or would ever see. He did not join any of the little groups at those numerous parties and small restaurants, mostly below Fourteenth Street, where some of the *Harvard Monthly* ex-Harvardians went and where he even found himself from time to time. He realized afterwards that somehow he had never become more than an occasional visitor to the world of the New York intelligentsia. Years later he wrote the wife of the playwright George S. Kaufman, who was planning a book about the period: "With the exception of Sidney Howard, whom I knew before he became intelligentsia, I seem to have had the merest acquaintance with all the others." Shyness, his own sense of having nothing yet to show, no claim he dared make upon the attention of anybody, was certainly a reason why he felt awkward in these circles. And, in truth, he found himself often as bored at the routine Greenwich Village party as if he had not been sitting on the floor and drinking rather sticky Marsala wine, like Bob Tasmin, his character in the late novel *B. F.'s Daughter*. He would never discover the creative uses of *la vie bohème*—though that life had its value for many indubitable as well as bogus artists. As for the famous sensual opportunities—they may have interested him briefly, but before he knew it he was in love with a charming girl of intense respectability who lived in Stockbridge, Massachusetts, which was as far, then if not later on, as one might get from Washington Square.

He was living, anyhow, with relatives who managed to combine in an off-putting way the tradition of New England gentility with an un-Puritan improvidence and eccentricity. Not that he wasn't extremely fond of them, especially of his aunt Greta, his father's youngest sister, who had generously invited him to live with her family in an old brownstone house at 3 West Sixteenth Street. Aunt Greta had originally married Herbert Dudley Hale, a desultorily practicing architect who was the son of Edward Everett Hale, the author of *The Man Without a Country* and a descendant of Nathan Hale, the Revolutionary patriot. Despite his ancestry, there had always been something bohemian about Bert Hale's way of life. He had never quite managed to sustain his family of five growing children without the help of Marquand's grandfather, who left Greta, reputedly his favorite daughter, a generous share of his fortune. After Hale died in 1908, Greta married one of his friends, a fellow architect who was even less of a provider than Bert had been, though he was also, like his predecessor, a man of charm, intelligence and sociability. John Oakman had studied in Paris and lived there with Greta for several years at the start of their marriage. He was a lover of all the arts, a would-be expatriate before the movement became general, for he adored all things French. He was something as well of a political radical. In the eyes of the Newburyport–Boston friends of the Hales and the Marquands he was distinctly a raffish type (he was commonly called "Joke"). The Hale–Oakman family scene, when Marquand joined it in 1919, both fascinated and irritated him. People came and went in the easy casual way of the twenties. Everyone seemed to have time to sit around in the middle of the day to talk, to have visitors, to start a party going—there were always parties and sometimes the Hale parties included artists from the Village or intellectuals they had met abroad who were in New York for a visit; Marquand would meet young Rockwell Kent at his aunt's house, and, one time, Bertrand Russell.

But his own history had made him fiercely determined to be self-sufficient and even to get ahead by sobriety, discipline and hard work. John Oakman, a confirmed if not yet an obnoxious alcoholic, he could dismiss, and Oakman's numerous friends made a cheery intellectual rialto of the Sixteenth Street house. But he felt differently about Aunt Greta, who was simply one of the most entrancing women he had ever known, with an airy refinement that expressed the tradition of the Curzon women of the previous generation. She was still beautiful—Whistler had painted her when she lived in Europe with Hale. She was also infuriatingly vague and impractical—if one could ever be furious with so charming a creature. She managed her children's upbringing, her household routines, her domestic economies, with little visible awareness of necessities and obligations—yet she did manage, miraculously, and there were always those, like Marquand himself, who could not help wanting to help her. Marquand would unforgettably portray her in *Wickford Point*. She is Cousin Clothilde in the novel, just as her husband Jack Oakman is Archie Wright, Clothilde's evasive painter husband. The reader of the fiction discovers soon enough that Clothilde is lovely and kind and that her voice is musical, and finds it as difficult as Jim Calder does to be angry with her because she cannot understand a bank statement and remarks of a clock that has just stopped: "I'd rather not know what time it is. Everything goes on just as well. Clocks only make you later."

What made Greta—or Cousin Clothilde—still delightful was that this disdain for the practical had, after all, a genuine source in the high-minded indifference to mundane things which was part of her tradition. New England idealism, the philosophy of Emerson and Thoreau, the poetry of transcendentalism—all these still tingled a little in the blood when you were in the company of Aunt Greta. But somehow the unworldliness of such ladies as her aunts and her mother was by now ridiculous and parasitic. Maybe it had been so in the nineteenth century, too, but then culture had given a worth and meaning to leisure that were later lacking. And this was the judgment Marquand did, in fact, make, if not of Greta, then of her sons, who considered themselves artists but worked no more devotedly at art than at anything else. The young Dudley and Robert Hale appear in *Wickford Point*, harsh caricatures, the Hales always thought, but unmistakably "like"—Dudley (the novel's Harry Brill) scheming and hoping for a sinecure or a rich marriage; Robert (Sid Brill), eternally lolling on a sofa or musing with infinite leisure upon the curls of cream in his coffee cup; both of them always asking their mother if she had anything in her purse. Time would make more conventional citizens of the two. Dudley would go to work in advertising and end up as a scriptwriter for RKO newsreels and government information agencies; and Robert, though Marquand would once remark, "Bob keeps having a pain in the stomach whenever he thinks of work," would, after some years of art study, teach drawing at the Art Students League and at Columbia, and eventually gain a prestigious and responsible post as curator of American painting at the Metropolitan Museum of Art. But Marquand's dislike of Dudley prosperous and successful was almost as great as for Dudley poor and scheming, as a report in those afteryears to Samuel Otis showed. "Dudley Hale," he wrote his old *Lampoon* friend and Dudley's Morristown schoolmate, "is today a picture of crass prosperity. He has married a rich girl and a very nice one, and waxes his moustache and sometimes alas wears spats, and drives one of those Chrysler cars with a rumble seat in back." Dudley had by then succeeded in advertising and had become "practical" with a vengeance.

What emerges in *Wickford Point*, however, is a judgment Marquand had begun to make well before 1919, when he must have resented the assumption of privileged ease affected by the Hale boys. "Why should anyone do anything if he doesn't have to?" Cousin Clothilde had sweetly asked when Jim Calder called Harry lazy. And before *Wickford Point*, Marquand had also depicted them in a now-forgotten magazine story through the eyes of a resentful, necessity-bound cousin. They were "golden lads" (the story's title) "with that intangible radiant inheritance that makes for carelessness and joy, or that heaven-sent serenity and regardlessness of others' rights which was so beautiful and cruel. It touched me but I did not have it."

And so there were no early risers and workers on Sixteenth Street, and Marquand was amused to discover that he fitted in well with the household since he did not get up until midmorning either—because the *Tribune* was a morning paper and he was not due at the office until eleven. But leaving the somewhat unreal world of Greta's family behind him, he made his way in the rush of New Yorkers going downtown by subway and in the heedless press of the streets to the famous "tall tower," the Tribune Building on Park Row, whose Florentine campanile rising from mansard shoulders twenty stories high did not alter the fact that it was a temple of the gods of reality and practicality. The revelations of subway travel made the subject of one of his first feature pieces for the *Tribune*. An imagined philosophic spokesman is quoted by Marquand as saying: "Strange, that all that is worst in the human race, all the most unpleasant attributes of the individual, seem to be brought out by a journey in the subway. On the street outside mankind is decent and self-respecting. But let him enter a hole in the ground and the Mr. Hyde in his nature breaks forth. He becomes regardless of the comfort of others: he loses his sense of obligation to the community. A feverish, irrational desire to hurry seizes him; be he man or woman he must grab something, push something away. In his haste to leap into the inferno of a car even your friend becomes your enemy." It certainly had to be conceded that at Aunt Greta's nobody was ever in a hurry.

When Marquand joined the *Tribune* staff in 1919, the newspaper had been, for several years, undergoing a somewhat hectic program of rejuvenation. The staid and stately old Republican journal had had a reputation that was the subject of much jibe from its sprightly rival the *Sun*. (When the *Tribune* shop caught fire and was well doused by the fire department, the *Sun* reported: "The *Tribune* came out this morning as dry as ever.") At the beginning of the war, however, the *Tribune* began to add distinctive features that changed this. Franklin Pierce Adams brought his "Conning Tower" over from the *Evening Mail* and remained until he went into the army in 1917, but in 1918 he was back with his famous "colyum," a daily mixed grill served piping hot—poetry, comment, gossip, and contributions from his numerous friends. It was "F.P.A." who had got Robert Benchley onto the paper in 1915, when the Sunday magazine was being revamped with the idea of adding color and humor to its pages. At the time Marquand joined the staff he was likewise assigned to the magazine, probably with the expectation that he, too, would add some of the light "Lampy" touch. Burton Kline had become magazine editor in 1918, succeeding Burton Rascoe, but was to lose his job shortly after Marquand arrived for reasons that give him a certain immortality in literary history. He had accepted some stories by Theodore Dreiser which the newspaper management thought shocking—besides, the *Tribune* had just concluded a hostile campaign against German-Americans.

Nevertheless, there was good company on the *Tribune*, particularly among the younger men. He must have met Heywood Broun, Harvard '10 (who, just like Marquand, had failed to make the *Crimson*). In 1919 Broun had begun his distinctive personal-essay column, later titled "It Seems to Me," after several years as sports reporter, drama critic, war correspondent and literary editor. The paper had also been taking on humorous cartoonists like Clare Briggs, the originator of those commentaries on American life *When a Feller Needs a Friend* and *Mr. and Mrs.*, and Denys Wortman, later the immortalizer of Mopey Dick and the Duke. Marquand liked to think that an assignment jointly undertaken by himself and Wortman had provided the first suggestion of the cartoonist's hobos. He and Wortman had been sent out to do a feature for the Sunday section about the King of the Hobos—Marquand to write the story and Wortman to illustrate it. The "king" turned out to be "a gentle idealist who must have come of good people and from an educated background," a philosopher in ragged clothing. Whether Wortman's famous characters were based on him or not, the experience was memorable to Marquand. Of Denys Wortman he later remarked, "I have never forgotten his intense interest in life around him, an interest which marked the beginning of his career and has never waned since."

Newspaper Row, like Greenwich Village, had its little groupings of the famous and to-be-famous. Broun and F.P.A. were members, along with Benchley, of a sort of informal club that called itself the Round Table. They met at the Algonquin Hotel, with Deems Taylor, the composer, who had worked on the Sunday *Tribune*; Alexander Woollcott, just back from the war to his old job as drama critic of the *Times*; George S. Kaufman, also of the *Times* drama department; and Harold Ross, Dorothy Parker, Robert Sherwood, Marc Connelly, Edna Ferber and others. Marquand was not a Round Table "knight" but he knew these and other bright and ambitious men and women who were trying to make their way in New York, almost all beginning with newspaper or magazine work. It certainly seemed for a while that this would be his own path, one crowded with vivacious comrades and not without its challenges and satisfactions. And yet, after little more than a year, he decided to leave the *Tribune* and journalism altogether. He had done various nicely written feature stories of perishable interest during the year, among them a long, somberly ironic story about Ralph Albert Blakelock, the famous painter who had been for twenty years a patient in a hospital for the insane and believed himself to be the richest man in the world; and a piece about William Waldorf Astor, who might in fact have been the world's richest man, but who was living in somewhat unsatisfactory retirement in England, as Marquand described him. He wrote about the feelings of returned veterans and about the sawdust and spangles of the circus at Madison Square Garden. In all of these and other little efforts Marquand was graceful and witty beyond what he had been capable of for the Boston *Transcript*. But he does not seem to have attracted much notice from his employers: Mrs. Ogden Reid, the wife of the publisher and one of the newspaper's directing intelligences, would admit when he made her acquaintance much later as a famous writer that she had not the slightest recollection of his presence on the staff. He must have decided he was getting nowhere. All around him, along with young hopefuls like himself who were hacking away at obscure newspaper jobs for meager wages, there were good men grown old meeting daily deadlines. Where were they after thirty years? They helped him to a decision: "When I saw men pulled back from important assignments in Berlin and Paris and relegated to minor, poorly paid jobs in the backs of newspaper offices because of advancing years, I was convinced that it was impossible to make a fortune in newspaper writing." He decided to go where the money was—everyone was saying that one could strike it rich in advertising, where a single lucky phrase or well-chosen brand name could be the source of millions in profits to the seller in such boom times as they were witnessing.

One day he was having lunch with Robert Benchley at the Harvard Club. Benchley mentioned that Richard Connell had just left J. Walter Thompson, so, here probably was a vacancy if anyone was interested. Sure enough, when they looked into the newspaper they found it in the "Help Wanted" columns. Marquand remembered that the agency asked for "a sequence of qualifications, none of which I possessed, to fill one of those positions which might lead to almost anything." Perhaps the want ad read like the one spotted by Bill King on behalf of his friend Harry Pulham, just back from France: "The man for whom we are seeking will preferably not have written advertising copy, but will have had a college education and a background of business experience and will possess besides a serious and pleasing personality, combined with a sense of taste and form. For such a man there is a definite opportunity in a large and growing organization which will take every care of his advancement." Marquand checked, and they did need a replacement for Connell in the copy department. The salary was sixty dollars a week, which was ten dollars more than he had been earning on the *Tribune*.

He went for advice to Paul Hollister at the Barton, Durstine and Osborne offices. Hollister could later summon up the moment. Marquand had sat back, looking out of the office window high above Forty-fourth Street in a musing way as he talked. "Look here, what about this ad-ver-tising game," he had slowly, almost drawlingly, asked, pulling out the word as though it were something he had only just learned to pronounce. "It's no game," said Hollister, who felt that he was working pretty hard in his new position. "Why?" "Well, it seems that something called Jay-Walter-Thompson"—again he pronounced the firm's title as though it were an expression in a foreign language—"is where I can get a job." They talked a while about advertising and its future; it was clear that if you could stick it, there was an opportunity now for those who enjoyed stringing words into sentences and paragraphs. They were at the threshold of the age of ballyhoo and promotion, and even the humblest household article was going to be brought to the consumer's attention with an energy never heard of before.

Marquand was put to work on a variety of accounts at J. Walter Thompson. He wrote copy for O'Sullivan rubber heels and Blue Buckle overalls—"big, strong and comfortable—6,000,000 pairs worn a year." But the big campaign of the moment was a soap—Lifebuoy—for which the entire staff was desperately seeking a suitable selling idea. ("It's really too bad I didn't think up B.O.," Marquand observed afterwards. "If I had, all my troubles would have been over.") For weeks the executives challenged the writers at agitated conferences—"What do you use soap for, anyway?"—and on everyone's desk, piles of layouts and texts to go with them extolled the virtues of the soap as cleanser, freshener, germ killer, beautifier. The wastebaskets filled up with discards. One day, a writer brought in what sounded like a winning slogan: "Every day an oily coating lightly forms upon your skin." Marquand, who had been listening distractedly as the slogan was intoned by its proponent, suddenly straightened up and began to intone after him, "Lives of great men all remind us/ We can make our lives sublime,'" and nearly shouted, "It scans, it scans! Don't you hear it? It's trochaic tetrameter. Who says there isn't poetry in advertising?" There was a shocked silence all around the table after this outburst, and Stanley Resor, the president of JWT, was the only person who smiled as he said, "John, I don't think you really have the business instinct." It was distinctly the beginning of the end.

Marquand had not taken very long to come to the conclusion that there was nothing quite so crazy as an advertising agency—all those people, highly intelligent and educated people, too, racking their brains for some idiot phrase that would sell something to an idiot public: "I began to have what might be mildly termed a negative reaction towards the routine of creative selling. All those Phi Beta Kappas sitting around trying to get ideas . . . it seemed to me the most dreadful thing to end your days putting your energy into a campaign for Lifebuoy soap." It pleased his sense of what suited whom when his cousin Dudley Hale eventually achieved a reputation in the advertising business by discovering that "shaving soap does not soften the beard. Water softens it, but the bubbles in the shaving soap hold those small bristles of the beard up so that the razor blade can cut them." Williams Shaving Soap, for whom Hale wrote the account, had more and tougher bubbles than the other shaving soaps. Dudley also went on to discover, in writing the advertising for President Suspenders, that "you grow middle-aged about the waistline if you wear a belt and not suspenders."

In any event, Marquand was in no danger of ending his days in dedication to a soap campaign—he was gently fired soon after the Lifebuoy episode. But his brief interval in advertising stimulated his humor. Never would there be a business as vulnerable to satire as advertising, and long before Madison Avenue became a comic legend in popular novels and movies, such temporary recruits as Marquand went away with stories to tell—stories that managed to illustrate not merely the madness of the advertising business but the obsession with buying and selling, the craze for the multiplication of purchasable satisfactions that was the very essence of the new postwar

America. Marquand wrote a story only a year or so later that would have cost him his job at J. Walter Thompson if he had still had it. It was called "Eight Million Bubbles," and it related the birth of a soap slogan, "Eight Million Bubbles and Every Bubble a Sphere of Health," in an agency closely resembling the one he had recently left. The embodiment of the madness was, as in the actual case, the agency executive, who led his subordinates in the quest for the perfect ad through storms of fury and enthusiasm worthy of the conquest of Rome. The stereotype of the obsessed advertising chief became familiar in the literature of the business. It also made an early appearance in a story written by Marquand's friend Richard Connell, his predecessor at J. Walter Thompson. Connell, too, burlesqued the agency and Stanley Resor, and even Resor's wife, in "Son of a Sloganeer," which Marquand later called "the best advertising story ever written." In this story Connell lightheartedly annihilates agency personalities who are so wedded to advertising that they become—or all but become—sloganized products with trade names. Mr. Bowser's flesh-and-blood baby—for whom a name is being sought at the same time that his daddy's agency is working out an unsurpassable label for soap—is christened through an error, "Smelly Welly: Dirt Devourer."

Roger Burlingame almost joined his friends in the advertising business. He had been writing book ads for Scribner's and growing restless at the dullness and the small pay in this sector of publishing. Marquand would come to see him, invading the genteel Fifth Avenue offices out of which Henry James seemed to just have stepped with Mrs. Wharton in stately tandem after conferences with their editors, and would begin to growl a strange, new language never heard there before—Washo, Spongo, Scouro, Cleano. Marquand told Burlingame about his labors on behalf of a "charm school" that guaranteed to make a social success of anyone. "You, too, Roger," he would say, his eyes glowing, Burlingame thought, with a fanatic salesman's fire, "you, too, can have charm." "You, too" became a favorite greeting—"You, too, can win a million dollars," "You, too, can speak Finnish," "You, too, can play the glockenspiel," or even, "You, too, can get into advertising!" But Burlingame's father managed to dissuade his son from leaving Scribner's. "I promise you as solemnly as I have ever promised anything that if you go into advertising you will never write another word," said Edward L. Burlingame, the wise counselor of many writers.

Young Burlingame did write a novel soon enough. It was all about the advertising business, which Marquand and the others had been describing to him, and it was titled, at Marquand's suggestion, *You Too*. In Burlingame's story, a young agency copywriter is finally driven to the point of suicide after he has composed hundreds of such inanities as the following, inspired by Marquand's reports from J. Walter Thompson: "*You Too Can Dream*: Yet not make dreams your master. You, going about your business and your household tasks can see the visions that these dreamers saw, can make your dreams creative, constructive, real, fundamental, *dividend-producing* dreams, and put yourself and your children, and your children's children on the map of tomorrow. *We will make you a successful dreamer*. Send no money. Simply clip the coupon from this page and you will receive, all charges prepaid, a full set of 'Practical Dreamers of Today' in half morocco." As the author of this persuasion stands on the bank of the river into which he intends to throw himself in disgust he is stopped by the flashing of an enormous electric sign that declares, "It floats."

Marquand was to put a little of his advertising experience into his own fiction, but not so immediately. When Harry Pulham enters the firm where Bill King is working, he discovers that it is headed by a J. T. Bullard, who tells him, "We all go over the top for an idea. . . . First we sell ourselves on the idea and then we go over the top for it"—which was, again, an echo of the inflated tone of Stanley Resor. Pulham is enrolled in the search for an idea to promote, again, a laundry soap called Coza. At Bullard's he encounters something else also: "A girl was bending over [the desk], writing on a yellow sheet of paper with a soft lead pencil. She turned around and looked at us for a second, and then began to write again, arching her back over the desk, displaying a row of pearl buttons that ran down the nape of her neck between her shoulder blades. . . . Her ankles were locked tightly together under her swivel chair, and one of her high-heeled slippers was half off, displaying the heel of a golden-brown stocking." It is Marvin Myles, half flapper, half career-girl, and one of Marquand's most engaging female characters. With her quick intelligence, her practicality and bluntness, her ambition, she is a type to notice now.

Marquand had begun to meet such girls in New York—they worked in advertising agencies, on magazines and newspapers, or they might be, like Pat Leighton, the girlfriend of Jim Calder in *Wickford Point*, directors of advertising programs in New York department stores. They were girls who did not have, did not need to have, "background"—like the girls he had met at dances in college, like the sisters of his college friends. They were distinctly themselves and on their own in the world men inhabited; and they were frequently—his preconceptions about feminine charm went crashing—all the more charming for their independence and their "honesty" about sex, their way of treating a man as no better and no worse than themselves, their ambition, which was exactly like that of the young men. "I'm good. I know I'm good. Someday I'm going to be making thirty thousand a year," Marvin Myles told Harry Pulham. Pat Leighton was pulling down twenty thousand. New York was full of such girls just then, as it was full of young men like John Marquand, and some of his friends were falling in love with them. Roger Burlingame would talk to him enthusiastically about a literary agent who had undertaken to place his novel; she was Ann Watkins, whom he would eventually marry. John Marquand was also, though somewhat later, to make the acquaintance of a lady agent—her name was Carol Hill. She would marry his agent, Carl Brandt, but maintain her own career and direct the important agency of Brandt and Brandt after Carl's death. By that time she would have been Marquand's mistress for years. Her personality would enter into the Marvins and Pats of his fiction.

At J. Walter Thompson there was a girl named Margaret King. In the big open room, like a newspaper city room, where the copywriters sat at their desks, she faced Marquand as they both worked on the agency's campaigns. A low barrier, a "spite fence" as they called it, railed off the desks from one another, but Marquand and Miss King were able to watch each other a good deal as the days passed, and in the badinage that was tossed over the fences between the young men he was sharply aware of the quiet, pretty girl opposite, who rarely paused in her work and turned out better copy than most of her male colleagues. Into just such a copy room, does just such a girl walk one day in "Eight Million Bubbles"—she is the first woman writer to be seen there—and she proves an educative experience for the hero of the story. He begins by being both gallant and condescending, then resents her, and finally falls in love with her. Pretty, clever and self-sufficient, she was also probably the first model for Marvin Myles. The chief episode of Pulham's experience at Bullard's is, anyhow, based on a true one involving Marquand and Miss King during their joint struggles to create a soap campaign. For her part she remembered how Marquand would jump up from his desk and exclaim to the entire room, "Ten thousand tons of city dirt!" Then he would look at her and smile shyly and sit down again. They were laboring on behalf of a laundry soap that was supposed to soak clothes clean without scrubbing. One morning Miss King was sent out with a companion to test the qualities and salability of the new product in a nearby suburb. They would ring a doorbell, and when the housewife came to the door ask her to give them the dirtiest garment she had, then proceed into the house and put it to soak in the sink while the astonished mistress of the house stood by. They came back to the office that evening with stories to tell about the indescribable things they had been given to wash, the apartments they had visited, the encounters they had had with the great American consumer. It was this episode, obviously, that emerged in *H. M. Pulham, Esquire* twenty years later. With a box of Coza Flakes in hand, Harry Pulham and Marvin Myles pay a visit to a Mrs. Frenkel with the request that she permit them to wash the dirtiest item in her clothes hamper. Unforgettable is Harry, removing his tailored coat and rolling up his crisp shirt sleeves as he politely asks to be shown to "the laundry." Mrs. Frenkel, in her housewife's soiled wrapper, conducts him into her kitchen, where she pulls the dishes out of the sink, hands him a pair of Mr. Frenkel's socks. It is the beginning of Pulham's romance with Marvin Myles.

When Marquand left J. Walter Thompson in July 1920, he knew exactly what he wanted to do next. He wanted to write fiction, and he had an idea that he could do the sort of thing that would sell in the popular magazines.

In front of all the rest was the *Saturday Evening Post,* which he had heard made the business of being a popular author really a paying career. They returned or accepted a manuscript within seventy-two hours and paid immediately on acceptance—paid, moreover, with a check for a short story that was likely to be better than his earnings for two months or more on the *Transcript* or at the agency. One afternoon at Aunt Greta's he and Dudley and Bob had been talking about it; a copy of the latest *Post* lay on the table and the young men agreed that it looked as though anyone who could spot the formulas ought to be able to do such stuff—and the formulas were easy to see. Maybe it was not so easy, Marquand had said; if you looked at them carefully, some of the *Post* stories were put together like tight little sailing boats that would take the roughest seas. No careless amateurism had nailed and caulked their seams. Still, he just thought he could do as good a job of work as some of those before them. And in a few days he had done it, half to show the Hales that he meant what he said, half because he wanted to test his own resolution and skill by a definite attempt at the kind of writing which, paltry as it seemed, delighted millions of readers and the editors who served them. His story had a catchy title, "The Right That Failed," and, of course, its subject was boxing, about which, he later admitted, he "knew practically nothing," but he was aware that twenty thousand people had sat in the heat of that Fourth of July afternoon to watch Dempsey knock out Willard in Toledo. He made good his boast to the Hales and sold his story to the *Post*. The first story he had ever written, aside from college class assignments, had landed him securely on the doorstep of commercial success.

Before this had happened, however, he had left J. Walter Thompson and had gone up to Curzon's Mill, where he could find the leisure and atmosphere for a larger project he had in mind. During his first months in New York he had started a novel. As though to deny the validity of the exchange of his earlier attachments for the attractions of New York, his Newburyport home and his dreams of his ancestral past came flooding into his imagination during his lonely evenings. He began a tale about an old American seaport that was a vision of colonial Newburyport: "The houses were as elegant and substantial as any you could find. . . . Our walks were paved with brick. There was not a finer tavern than ours to the north of Boston, or better dressed men frequenting it. Men said in those days that we would be a great seaport; that the world would look more and more to that Northern Massachusetts river mouth. They had spoken thus of many other harbor towns in the centuries that men had gone down to the sea. I think they have been wrong almost as often as they have predicted. The ships have ceased to sail over the bar. No one heeds the rotting planks of the wharves. The clang of hammers and the sailors' songs have gone, and trade and gain and venture have gone with them." What better place to develop a story set in Newburyport's stirring early time than his family home, where Aunt Bessie was at hand to retell again, as she loved to do, the gossip of the Marquands and the Curzons, and where he was so close to the decaying town of the present with its old houses and streets full of reminders of prouder days. That summer and autumn at the Mill were curiously happy. He had saved four hundred dollars from his New York earnings, and because he could live for practically nothing with his aunts, he was able to retreat contentedly into a private world, writing for long hours in the empty loft of the old mill house that hung over the sleepy Artichoke, emerging only to walk over to the Yellow House for meals and at bedtime, and seldom having a visitor.

The result was a strange and secret book, for all its air of lighthearted adventure. The nostalgia for the past that it invited in the reader was actually his own, not just literary make-believe. And the tale had a private meaning for him: the hero believes his father to be a charming scoundrel who has cheated his partners and abandoned his wife—a kind of nightmare exaggeration of Philip Marquand. It was no accident, as has been noted, that John Marquand's first novel is the narrative of a son who feels that he has been let down by his father, and it is touching to observe the contrivance of wish fulfillment in the "trick ending," which vindicates this father and reestablishes the son's thwarted regard. That the theme was obsessive and personal is attested to by his inability, at this early stage, to write anything that did not treat of it. Even "The Right That Failed" describes the childhood of a future boxing champion, spent with a derelict drunkard father who was once a rich gentleman. What Marquand himself longed for in his innermost self—a means of reattaining some height of respectability where he had once belonged—is precisely, it would seem, the motive of the young boxer who shows his stuff in the ring and then, because he "hasn't got a fighter's hands," has to quit. But he wins a rich young lady and a place in her father's business, his real aristocracy coming into its own.

Marquand's instinct for such romance could not have been better timed for the market. The vast public, which supported the *Saturday Evening Post* and its rivals, the *Ladies' Home Journal*, *Cosmopolitan*, *Redbook*, *Delineator*, and the other "slicks," was tired of the realistic literature of the war's aftermath. The editors of the magazines were on the lookout for writing that would soothe and flatter rather than irritate middle-class complacencies, for writing that was either genially humorous or sentimental or frankly escapist. George Horace Lorimer, the editor of the *Post*, wanted to print more fiction that was a counterargument to those writers who, as he said, set out "to prove everybody and everything in America rotten." It was, after all, a time when an Indiana jury took two minutes to acquit a man who had shot an alien for saying "To Hell with the United States." There were strikes in steel and coal, and Attorney General Mitchell Palmer had just ordered his raids on the headquarters of radical organizations and made mass arrests with a view to deporting undesirable aliens. In April 1920, the five Socialist members of the New York State Assembly were expelled on the ground that they belonged to an organization of "perpetual traitors"; in that year Calvin

Coolidge was elected as the man who had broken the Boston police strike, and the Sacco–Vanzetti case was opened. It is not surprising that the magazines were particularly fearful of social critics and radical intellectuals—and particularly eager for material that turned readers' minds into other channels.

Marquand's novel was finished in February 1921. From Cambridge, where he had moved in the winter to live with Fuller relatives, he wrote Roger Burlingame at Scribner's: "It so happens I have finished that damned story. It runs to 40,000. I think it is pretty damned bad, but I wish you would undergo the strain of looking at it, if you can. Bad as it is, I've seen Scribner's use worse." They met and Burlingame took a look and was encouraging and recommended that the manuscript be submitted through his agent, the firm of Brandt and Kirkpatrick, who would also advise Marquand about its possibilities as a magazine serial. Before he knew what had happened, the agency had sent it not only to Scribner's but to the *Saturday Evening Post*, which immediately rejected it. But he had hardly time to feel depressed. Brandt and Kirkpatrick also offered the *Post* the boxing story, "The Right That Failed," which he had written months before, and this was accepted and a check for $500 accompanied the acceptance. Then, to complete his astonished delight, the *Ladies' Home Journal*, to whom Brandt and Kirkpatrick had forwarded the novel, accepted it as a serial and promptly mailed him $500 for each of the four installments into which the novel would be divided. He remembered taking his *Journal* check downtown to the Atlantic Bank of Boston and depositing it, buying himself a pair of new shoes, and getting his pipes fixed on the way from his cousin's house in Cambridge. "I have never felt so good in my life," he later said. There is, after all, only one such moment in a writer's career.

Yet he still had a modest—perhaps too modest—conception of his abilities. When he met the editor of the *Ladies' Home Journal*, Burton W. Currie, he felt impelled to ask him *why* he had taken the serial—and received the answer he often related afterwards with unpretentious acknowledgment of the whimsicality of Fortune: the *Journal* had just gotten new four-color presses, which were able to produce gorgeous illustrations for costume fiction. He did not question that literary success was governed by such accidents as much as by the efforts of genius. Everything that was happening to him just then demonstrated, somehow, the playfulness of fate. The manuscript of *The Unspeakable Gentleman* had got lost, simply lost, the very day he brought it down to New York, on February 22, 1922. This, too, was a story the older Marquand, long used to good luck, still told with a certain wonder. He had been on his way to the University Club to meet his old friend George Merck, and the manuscript, still in the suitcase he had carried from Cambridge, rested next to the driver on the doorless front seat of the cab—and slipped unnoticed into the street. It had taken ten frantic days of search, advertising, and detective work, mostly conducted by the capable George, before the manuscript was recovered. The little interval had given Marquand time to think about the career into which he was so anxious to plunge. He decided that the book he had written was certainly not worth doing over, and he was ready to abandon writing as a profession.

With the acceptance of "The Right That Failed" by the *Post* came one of Mr. Lorimer's famous invitations to come down to Philadelphia and lunch with him in the Curtis Building on Independence Square. Marquand arrived eagerly at the entrance to fame—the great pompous building, rather too grand for a state capitol, with marble colonnade and endless white steps, and the huge lobby inside that contained a fountain and a pool reflecting an enormous Maxfield Parrish mural executed in stained glass by Tiffany. In Lorimer's office on the sixth floor, almost as big as the lobby downstairs, Marquand had his first glimpse of the Editor Enthroned, the cool, imperturbable Lorimer conversing with the visitor at his elbow while subeditors and artists came in and out with cover designs, layouts, editorial problems, which he settled unfalteringly with a word or a gesture, his attention still on the young author who had come to see him. Discovering authors was Lorimer's greatest gift, and he knew better than anyone in the business how to find out what a writer might be able to do next, and to indicate quietly but emphatically the ideas which would be most likely to make *Post* stories.

Since the *Journal* (the *Post*'s unaffectionate sister Curtis publication) had taken Marquand's novel, it was entitled by the etiquette of publishing to first call on his next piece of work. After that, he belonged to the *Post*. The *Journal* paid $500 again for "Different from Other Girls," a bit of fluff about a flapper. Then Brandt and Kirkpatrick set a price of $600 on Marquand's next story, and when the *Journal* editor refused to meet the new price, it was handed over to the waiting Lorimer. Once more, the following year, he might have slipped away when Ray Long, the editor of Hearst's *Cosmopolitan*, as he said, "tried to sew me up on a contract and the Post was obliged to meet their figure." Thus, as early as 1923, John Marquand was getting $1,500 a story from the *Post*, and a few years later, $3,000 or more. There were no greener pastures in American publishing in that time. From 1922 to 1940, he sold the *Post* something like ninety-five stories, while only eight went to other magazines. In the same period it published a dozen of his serials and he gave only one other besides the first to anyone else. Lorimer's *Post* became a shaping influence on Marquand's literary development and paid him more than half a million dollars for his contributions to its pages. After Lorimer's death in 1936 Marquand was writing fewer short stories anyhow, and his serial novels, beginning in 1949, mostly went to the *Ladies' Home Journal*, which had received no further Marquand contribution since "Different from Other Girls."

The story of Lorimer's influence on Marquand's writing is to be seen in the experience of those years as he counseled and cudgeled, in the way he had, to keep Marquand producing what was acceptable to *Post* readers and amenable to the necessary abridging and segmentation of serialization. A conception of acceptability of theme, of accessibility of style, an avoidance of such experimentation as might endanger either, was one obvious result of Marquand's constant awareness of his *Post* audience and of Lorimer as its representative. But a great many literary life histories have been too readily explained by the conditioning forces of the media. Marquand himself, it might be argued, was one of the makers of the *Post* in those twenty years, as much responsible for the character of its pages as his editor.

Nor was Lorimer the only guide and counselor and voice of the market who began to direct the flow of Marquand's talent in 1921. Another was Carl Brandt, his agent. Unlike Lorimer, who always maintained a regal formality even with his favorite writers, Carl Brandt became a close friend whose influence was personal as well as literary. Nothing, of course, is more insidious than the genuine devotion of an author's agent—the more genuine because it is based on the furtherance of the client's success, the augmentation of more lucrative sales of his work. Brandt, an able and experienced agent, had a strong affection for Marquand and bent himself for years to directing Marquand's work into forms that would yield a greater return. Besides, he was a capable editor, one who, like Lorimer, could teach a young writer a great deal about craftsmanship, who studied a manuscript with devoted and intelligent attention and was a skilled critic of details and general impressions—another representative of the needs of the "common reader."

The time would come when Marquand would speak with regret about his early success and about the help and direction he had received from Lorimer and Brandt. To Sergeant Jack Briggs, who corresponded with him from an army base in 1945, he wrote: "For many years I was anxious to do what people told me and I know now that I fell into the hands of the worst possible instructors. I realize now that it was most unfortunate for me that I achieved an immediate and a spectacular success with the Saturday Evening Post. I also found myself associated with a bright and high-powered literary agent. In my callowness I had the greatest respect for his opinion and consequently his influence upon me was enormous. It is only quite recently that I have realized that his mind was on nothing except commercial literary profits and that he never possessed the slightest artistic feeling and was almost wholly devoid of any literary background. I think this is the worst sort of thing that could happen to any young writer. I knew that I had considerable technical skill. I was grateful for the high opinion the Saturday Evening Post had of me and I was only too anxious to continue to write the type of fiction which they wanted. It was a fine school in which to learn technical skills, but no place for thought or art, if you want to call it that. It is a source of wonder to me now that I did not go the way of nearly all my brilliant contemporaries whose names are now almost forgotten, but Clarence Buddington Kelland is a fine example."

But this was the hindsight of twenty-three years. In 1922, Marquand was delighted with his good fortune and with the good counsel of such men as Lorimer and Brandt, and it seems evident that then he wanted *not* to be critical of their advice because he so much wanted what their advice promised—those deplorable big checks that would come so easily if he wrote as they suggested. That they had somehow manipulated him and shaped him into a writer of popular fiction was, perhaps, another legend supplied by the imagination of the legend maker who had already shown his propensity to impose the shape of fairy tale upon the flux of experience. That unacknowledged true heir, that royal son who had gone out into the world to establish his claim, would encounter betrayal and misdirection from apparent friends—yet by some miracle escape their toils. In fact, though, he would, for many years, continue to be grateful that Lorimer's and Brandt's advice had proved sound and that his success as a popular writer had been assured, and he was by no means ashamed of the work he did under their tutelage. He knew that a good deal of imagination and skill had gone into it and that the Village failures who sneered at the fiction he was able to sell were quite unable to master its forms.

He thus found himself engaged in the running battle of the intellectuals versus the popular magazines, which was one of the features of literary life in the twenties. The *Post*, for its part, was aggressive in its disdain for radicals and bohemians as well as for experimentalism in the arts. It recognized that Greenwich Village was the seat of the enemies of the business ethic and the "wholesome" conformities, and inveighed editorially against them while encouraging its writers to ridicule the morals and customs of the Village as a seedbed of personal rebellion and even political radicalism. The young writers and artists of Marquand's generation would, in their turn, tend to speak about "writing for the slicks" in the same way they would a little later talk about "going to Hollywood"—the popular magazines and the films were both forms of selling out: if you had any integrity you wrote only for the little magazines and stayed poor. Only it had to be admitted that the division was never so absolute as all that. The writers who were bitterest about selling out were the ones who had surreptitiously tried to make the *Post* and failed. Lots of good writers had at one time or another been willing to make a living by writing for the slicks, among them Lewis and Fitzgerald, whom Marquand so admired. The ironies of the situation were visible even to critics of the *Post* like Benjamin Stolberg, who wrote, in the *Outlook and Independent* in 1930: "The Saturday Evening Post has done more to develop the technique of the short story as good composition and second-rate literature than any other periodical I know. It is the only magazine where one may find a surprising amount of excellent writing which is not worth reading, except as an index of what the popular mind is allowed for its taste in the best of our mass periodicals." Nevertheless, he added, there were only two classes of writers who did not contribute to the *Post*: "Those who have independent means or make satisfactory incomes from their other writing and those who can't make the grade. Many of the former and practically all of the latter try to write for the Post."

So, for years before he could write so bitterly as he did to Sergeant Briggs in 1945, Marquand refused to bite the hand that so regularly fed him, and he defended the *Post* against its critics. Those critics inevitably involved him in the argument over popular writing when he emerged, in 1937, as the author of a work of "serious" literary pretension which was awarded a Pulitzer Prize. He was called "America's most illustrious literary split-personality" because he continued to produce both "low" and "high" forms of fiction. *Wickford Point*, the next novel that he wrote after that, is marked by this controversy. Its hero-narrator is a popular writer who resents the condescension of those highbrows who really know nothing about the craft of writing—like Allen Southby, the Harvard professor who is trying to write a novel about New England. The assertion that he had written under compulsion and for the money in it was galling to Marquand, all the more because he had had a living to make. He would declare, as he did to Carl Brandt in 1939: "It would be a piece of utter folly for me to sneer at an institution which has supported me for a great many years and, in the second place, I do not feel that way. I have always been proud and pleased to be identified as a writer for the Post and I shall continue to be as long as they want to have me." And to a reader he wrote: "I share the impatience which I imagine every contributor of the Post must feel toward the attitude of the intelligentsia about magazine fiction. The truth is that most of our solemn and sanctimonious artists in the short story haven't the technical skill to write for the Post market, and the critics on the whole have the most abysmal ignorance of the kind of work that is being done there. I really feel that the backlog of any literature we have in America lies in the magazines. Granted a lot of the work there may be second-rate, it is technically very competent and it furnishes a real impetus for literature."

And yet he described the process of preparing a *Post* story with a dry accuracy when he wrote *Wickford Point*, sketching a scene that he had seen many times. In the novel it is played in the office of George Stanhope, the literary agent who is very clearly Carl Brandt, with his versatility, his enthusiasm, his determined concern for the commercial. When Jim Calder calls on the occasion described, Stanhope has been told by one of the "contact editors" of a magazine that "the Chief says there ought to be more boy and girl" in one of Calder's serials, and the agent assures him that the change will be made. "The story is as good as sold. All you and I need is half an hour to fix it up," he tells Calder. And so in a moment Stanhope gets to work, sketching in a new turn to the story, an altered emphasis, an inserted scene or two, in a breathless synopsis from out of an imagination teeming with the clichés of popular romance—even believing in them, and somehow carrying Calder past the barrier of his own skepticism. It was such a constant renewal of will that Marquand received from Carl Brandt: "That enthusiasm of George Stanhope's was what kept us all going. He was in the business and he knew exactly what he wanted, but he had a sense of fitness and creative understanding—admitted that the work he handled was very seldom art. This escapist literature for a hopeless but always hopeful people possessed a quality of artisanship that demanded a very high technique. We both took a pride in our product, not the wild free pride of an artist, but the solid pride of the craftsman. George Stanhope was awakening my interest, as he always did, while he moved among the characters in that half world of the imagination governed by editorial fact." Something similar to the scene in *Wickford Point* may have taken place in 1921, when the manuscript of *The Unspeakable Gentleman* was being sent to the magazines. Marquand wrote Burlingame, who had read the original version: "I have prostituted myself to the extent of adding a certain amount of throbbing, palpitating heart interest here and there in homeopathic doses, to the extent even of adding a clinch, to use the high literary parlance now in vogue, to the end. As a matter of fact I don't think it hurts it much and undoubtedly adds to its marketability." Undoubtedly the new touches had been conceived in Carl Brandt's office at 101 Park Avenue, in the first of many sessions they would spend over Marquand's manuscripts.

Meanwhile, he received still other counsel, for he was about to publish his first book. At Scribner's and at Little, Brown, which later supplanted Scribner's, he would get more editorial direction and advice, still dictated by the need of the market in which literature is a commodity, but a market more sophisticated than that of the magazines. On March 31, Burlingame wrote him that Scribner's wanted to publish *The Unspeakable Gentleman*. To Carl Brandt, Burlingame wrote, "We think it a charming story in many respects and an unusual one and highly promising of the author's future." As for the new "heart interest" ending, Burlingame reported approval, of a dignified sort, in the publishing office: "We are inclined to think that Mr. Marquand's amendments are greatly to the story's advantage; in the first version it ended abruptly and rather unsatisfactorily. Of course the heart of the story is the unspeakable gentleman himself, a very winning gentleman." If less insistent on the final "clinch" than the *Ladies' Home Journal*, the Scribner office was just as excited by the prospect of a revival of historical romance, in which Marquand's book might sail high on the best-seller lists. "Critics say," wrote Burlingame, "that the reading public, many of whom are tired of the sordid realism, cynicism, and propaganda of postwar fiction are ready for a wave of romance." "This sort of romance has not been in fashion for some time," he told Marquand, "but there is no reason why it should not come back and be more than ever popular."

Scribner's planned for publication that fall, but an obstacle immediately presented itself: the serial version in the *Journal* was not scheduled to begin until the following January. It was decided that the book would have to come out in the spring after the magazine run was over. But in July the

Journal informed Brandt and Kirkpatrick that a printer's strike had forced them to put off the serialization until the fall of 1922. It seemed a good time for Marquand to take a holiday. At the end of December 1921, he left a few more stories with the Brandt office, promised Brandt and Roger Burlingame that he would be working on some others, and took some of the money out of his Boston bank to buy himself a steamship ticket to Europe. He was feeling happier than he had ever felt before. He had managed, in a very few months, to carry out Roger's prediction: "You are going to do a lot of writing. You will probably find it more amusing and perhaps eventually almost as profitable as advertising."

"I was Lord Byron on a triumphal tour," he later said, remembering his mood as he got off the boat. Besides, there was a girl he had been seeing on and off during the past year whom he wanted to catch up with—she was traveling in Italy with her parents. He planned to ask her to marry him.

8

The Cinderella Motif

He had found a girl who seemed to promise that complex fulfillment of the psyche, with its unacknowledged cravings for triumph and revenge upon the world which are more powerful determinants of love, perhaps, than sexual desire—if sexual desire is not itself in part the expression of them. Into his first marriage John Marquand would bring his personal myth, already enacted in Newburyport and at college, of resented exclusion. He would bring into it his yearning for restitution and reinstatement among the idle lords of the earth, whom at the same time he would never stop secretly despising. It was thus a marriage profoundly inevitable and profoundly doomed, for what he loved and desired was also, it had to turn out, the object of his most deep-seated hostility. He was really incapable, then, of loving what was not, in a peculiar way, deeply irritating as well as attractive.

Christina Sedgwick seemed at the moment more fitted to be the heroine of one of his own romantic magazine stories than of tragedy. She was a graceful girl with a slender figure, a light, swaying walk, a low "refined" voice, her hair in a light cloud about her delicate face with deep-lidded blue eyes. Her accent clearly marked her type, her class. Her clothes had the slight, not unbecoming unstylishness that identified them as the costume of the New England gentlewoman. She reminded Marquand, of course, of those inaccessible young ladies of High Street, Newburyport, who had once snubbed him, of the girls who had shown no interest in him when he had come on a rare occasion to one of the society dances when he was at college. Yet she was really a complex and divided person, like himself. He would not begin to notice her true individuality until they had begun their married life together.

It would then become plain that his mythmaking unconscious had chosen her both for love and eventual rejection with a terrifying accuracy. That she was fragile and vague would at first delight him. These qualities proved her a true representative of an aristocracy that had no need for efficiency and toughness. Yet before long he was displeased. He suspected, rightly as it happened, that she evaded the obligations of marriage by retaining a childish unworldliness and incompetence, that she criticized his relative poverty by her inability to "cope" with domestic matters without a palace staff. He discovered that her family never ceased to regard him as a mere commoner who had not really raised himself to their level by marrying their daughter.

His vision of himself as excluded and put-upon was thus doomed to repeat itself, for all the triumph over handicap he achieved. Going to Harvard had not reconstituted what had been lost when as a boy he had "rudely had the rug pulled out from under," as he described his sensations at the time of his father's failure. And marriage to a Sedgwick would not remove his—as well as their—feeling that he was not quite good enough for them. These frustrations, by some hidden law of his nature, were as surely chosen as his triumphs. He had, certainly, chosen a wife who would hurt as well as gratify him, and his complaints against her family were perfectly expectable—indeed, in some deep sense, expected.

Marquand, however, was also a mythmaker. He became in time the principal source of legends about himself. It was he who was responsible for the exaggerated account of his sufferings at college, tales his friends accepted literally. He forced the true narrative of experience, which had contained elements of the myth, into a mythic simplicity so that his past could be seen by himself and others as the fable of a young prince brought up as a swineherd. And as his marriage developed its contradictions and tensions the mythmaker in him began to prepare those stories he would tell others about his domestic life, stories so superbly funny that they could be accepted as "mere" humor at which friends laughed without embarrassment. As has been noted, he was becoming a gifted mimic and parodist who could set a scene and take all parts and outrageously and tellingly exaggerate an incident. He told stories about everything that happened to him; and no one, even among his close friends, let alone his family, was immune from his mocking art—he noted weaknesses in behavior and tricks of manner and speech that nailed their possessor down like a squirrel skin stretched on a board to dry. He built a legend of these exaggerations when it came to his account of his private life.

And friends remembered about this marriage anecdotes of which he was the first shaper and disseminator. He told many of them when he was looking back on the marriage and its failure, and rereading his own memories with the bitter scrutiny that searches out the causes of disaster in the mistakes of others. But he told most of them at once, and with a lightness that deceived the hearer, just when something very funny—or deeply irritating—had happened. Marquand's own manner would be a burlesque of pain that made one laugh before one thought to take it seriously. "Do you know what Christina has just done?" he would query a visitor. He would walk up and down in a parody of anguish, talking with a slow deliberateness that was more comically indicative of controlled distress than any outburst of passion would have been, holding a drink or a pipe in one extended and weaving hand and sometimes grasping the back of his own neck with the other as his eyes rolled away from his hearer a little wildly. The story would be told with a sober meticulousness—and mounting signals only from the eyes and arms—of a distress so ridiculous that his auditors, even his subject, who might be present, too, would simply roar. He would tell, for example, how Christina had given a Goodwill Industries collector the trunk that contained *all* his own best winter clothing carefully packed away with mothballs for the summer. Or how she had been seen walking down the street with a leash—but no dog attached—trailing in her hand. And he would tell stories about her parents that were denied, but with chuckles, by them—how Mrs. Sedgwick, when he was desperately at work on his writing in her country house at Stockbridge, had knocked on his door to ask him to take her son's dog for an airing. "Shan's too busy to, poor dear," she had said. "He's trying to write a novel."

Christina Sedgwick had been an attractive and favorite child whose world was sustained at all points by intense family attachments. It was not that the Sedgwicks were "proud," people would say, but that they recognized no community outside the large buzzing hive of relatives and old family friends in which they lived. Their exclusiveness was not overbearing or assertive—after all they were neither New Yorkers nor Bostonians, though they often stayed in those places; they came from Stockbridge in western Massachusetts. But there, it used to be said, the very peepers and katydids chirped "Sedgwick, Sedgwick" all summer long. In Stockbridge the Sedgwicks were everything.

Christina's great-great-grandfather, Theodore Sedgwick, had fought in the Revolution, written the Massachusetts charter of independence, and become a member of the Continental Congress and president of the Senate, as well as speaker of the House in the young republic. He was, it seems, a man of strong opinions as well as personal courage, for he led a resistance party against Shays' Rebellion and also sheltered a runaway slave and defended her rights to freedom. He did not, apparently, crave national honors, for when Washington wanted to make him secretary of the treasury at Hamilton's death, he preferred to return to his home as a judge of the Massachusetts Supreme Court. In the early 1900's his large wooden house on the main street of Stockbridge had come to be called the Sedgwick Mansion on the family notepaper, a pretentiousness which Theodore would probably have disliked. Much added to and redecorated, the house had by that time become a symbol of the Sedgwick sense of importance and continuity.

Still another was the Sedgwicks' genealogical burial plot in the Stockbridge cemetery. Today's visitor will find the Judge buried under an obelisk at the center of what has been described as a huge "pie." Around him, concentrically, like the growth rings of a tree, his descendants are arranged—his own children and their spouses wrapped about him in the first circle, their children layered at the feet of the first generation, in widening pie wedges, each succession fanning out more broadly until the most recent dead are reached on the outer circumference. All are lying with their feet towards the center and their heads outward so that, as tradition has it, they will rise to face their forefather at the Last Judgment. There are 135 graves in the Sedgwick burial plot now, the males mostly marked, like the Judge, with a phallic obelisk, the females with a uterine urn.

None of the Judge's descendants were his equal in achieving posthumous fame except, perhaps, his daughter Catharine, who is remembered rather dimly in literary history as "the first woman novelist in America." Her popular fictions brought her into contact with the world of arts and letters in Boston, New York, and even London. Many distinguished friends came to little Stockbridge to visit her, the actress Fanny Kemble settling by her side, and thus Catharine assisted the development of Stockbridge as a literary colony. In her own family she may have initiated a tradition of genteel cultivation. When John Marquand encountered Christina's living relatives, two uncles were immediately pointed out on the slopes of Parnassus well above his own level as a writer of popular fiction. Henry Dwight Sedgwick was a prolific author of histories, biographies and literary studies, while Ellery Sedgwick was nothing less than the editor of the *Atlantic Monthly*. A third, while not literary, was at least the rector of the fashionable Calvary Church in New York.

Alexander C. Sedgwick, Christina's father, unlike his brothers, had had no formal career. When a child he had been badly scalded by an overturned croup kettle; while still a young boy he had blown off two of his fingers with a shotgun; and he had suffered a mild stroke at seventeen. Prolonged invalidism had put regular school and college out of the question. All that was left for him to do, as Marquand would observe, "was to cultivate charm, whimsy and egocentricity." He had, anyhow, inherited money and had married a wife with more, and he could thus afford to exercise his tastes and play a squirelike role in Stockbridge affairs. He helped to promote the famous Riggs Foundation for the treatment of nervous disorders and Laurel Hill, a beautiful natural preserve, and even served in 1912 in the state legislature. An upholder of life's pleasures, he was inspired to campaign with picturesque vigor against the passage of the Volstead Act in 1919.

He was also an eccentric who diverted a large circle. Marquand would discover his future father-in-law to be a grasshopperish little man with an almost Mediterranean extravagance of speech and gesture and a taste for natty clothes, particularly gay silk cravats and handkerchiefs. His propensities, which he cultivated ("and by God he did!" Marquand observed) were promoted by his wife—his gloom and hypochondria that alternated with enthusiasm, even his tendency to flirt with young girls and his preference for taking holidays abroad without his wife—all were serenely accepted and even encouraged. Marquand would decide that she "used him more and more as a piece of local color for the great house and as a source of amusing anecdotes. He had to live up to his reputation and he always tried to do it. I may say, to a casual visitor he was often perfectly delightful and was refreshingly different from anyone who ever had to face any sort of responsibility."

Lydia Sedgwick was as different from him as possible. She was not a New Englander. In Steuben County, New York, her mother's family, the Davenports, had lived like English gentry, developing, as she once told her daughter, "a feudal state of mind, feeling ourselves to be quality," which prevented her, she admitted, "from caring about Paul Revere's ride." Her father, Sherman Rogers, was a prominent Buffalo lawyer and businessman. She was, like both the Davenports and the Rogerses, practical and executive, and she competently governed her demesne: the Sedgwick household, to which her fortune contributed the larger share; her childish husband; and her children, whom she did not encourage to grow up. Christina, her eldest child and only daughter, did not develop any of her mother's own managing skills—or, indeed, any skills at all.

Perfectly healthy and quite intelligent, Christina suffered the usual educational deprivation of rich girls of her day and received no more formal schooling than had her invalid father. She had nursery governesses, a year in a girls' school in Pittsfield, a year of boarding at Miss May's, a Boston finishing school. Servants, plentiful and cheap before the First World War, were always on hand to do the household tasks that the women of Judge Sedgwick's family had been expected to perform—and her mother was supremely in charge of domestic administration. So, while her two brothers were being prepared at Groton for Harvard, Christina found herself growing up with a vague yearning for a wider life but hedged within the family circle like a sacred rose. Everyone "adored" Pussy or Tissie or Too Too, as she was mawkishly called. Her brothers would write to her in a way that seems today excessively sentimental. But it was her father's attachment that was peculiarly intense; he aroused and demanded an ardent response from the young girl that he could not expect from her mother. Marquand, years later, told his son, "He was in love with your mother in a violent way that would have fascinated Jung and Freud and occasionally caused a shiver to run up the spine of Dr. Austen Riggs," the psychiatric pioneer who was a family friend.

In 1914, when Christina was seventeen, she had an escape from her ferociously sheltered life. She and her best friend, a girl named Harriet Amory, went to France—to learn French—and boarded with a family in

Cerisy-la-Salle in Normandy. The girls had grown enthusiastically fond of their hosts and of the life around them when suddenly they were witness to the somber involvement of the French in the war; they could actually hear the sound of the big guns on the Marne. The young men and even the village horses were being mobilized for the army, and the daughter of the household, their particular friend, left to work at a nearby hospital. This was probably Christina's inspiration, three years later, when America was in the war, for insisting on training as a volunteer hospital nurse in New York. The previous May, the same impulse towards participation had come to her father, who had managed to get abroad, at fifty, as an ambulance driver. He stayed on the Italian Front, and when the American forces arrived, continued with the Red Cross. Probably "Lily" Sedgwick thought him ridiculous and called Christina impetuous. Young Ellery, however, was dissuaded from enlisting.

Though enrolled in her hospital course and living in a rented room in New York, Christina found that a good deal of the time she was lodged with her Uncle Theodore at the Calvary Church Parish House. Once, after being escorted home by him, she wrote her mother: "How I hate this business of being forever dependent on the kindness of others as soon as the 'cover of darkness' falls. It is so humiliating to a young girl!" But soon the war was over and with it Christina's war work. Her family proposed a tour in Europe, perhaps a long stay in England or Italy. She wrote protestingly: "I'm not very enthusiastic about living in Naples, or anywhere in Europe—just living and not doing anything energetic. I can't afford to throw away my time like that and while I want to live with you and Papa, I do not intend to be a colorless girl past her first youth who is waiting around to get married." What then did she intend? Her parents began to worry about what they called "Pussy's unconventionality."

A less conventional *jeune fille* was surfacing in Christina. She now read a good deal and argued about books and ideas with her brothers. Ellery, only two years younger, had discovered Browning, Swinburne and Oscar Wilde while still at Groton, and after he entered Harvard he continued to toss his finds in her direction. He wrote to her: "Do not in your isolation become mousy. Have your own thoughts and keep them—your opinions too. Read—Karl Marx, Morris Hillquit—anything, but read. Beware of mental stagnation." The modernist writers became in particular a medium of communication between Ellery and Christina, and also between them and their younger brother, Alexander or "Shan," a schoolboy aesthete who would visit his sister in her lodgings in New York and read aloud to her *The Picture of Dorian Gray* and the new poets E. A. Robinson and Robert Graves. While Uncle Harry, who called himself an Epicurean, was working on his book about Marcus Aurelius, his niece and nephews were discovering D. H. Lawrence.

They had one ally in the older generation. This was Aunt Nathalie, an unusual woman who was not their aunt but a distant cousin, the daughter of a sister of Christina Sedgwick's grandmother. In the large, tame-feathered flock of Sedgwicks she was an exotic. She had lived in Italy with her mother until the mother died, and, ten years old, the little Nathalie then was sent back to America to be taken in by her relatives in Stockbridge. She was a strange, Europeanized young person who would have interested Henry James. Even as a young girl she was fascinating and somehow dangerous—pretty, clever, prattling of foreign places and in foreign tongues in a way that made the other children feel their country awkwardness and simplicity. The boys, especially Alick, Christina's father, had each in turn suffered a youthful infatuation for her. Their relation with her had that teasing, half-incestuous closeness provoked by her membership in the family as a sister who was not really a sister. She was an instinctive flirt and given to mischievous schemes, it was said—perhaps it was just her foreignness that made this seem so to the Sedgwicks. At any rate she would always be both loved and distrusted—the latter chiefly by the women who married her Sedgwick "brothers," and most of all by Christina's mother.

At the age of twenty Nathalie herself married a young lawyer by the name of Bainbridge Colby, who was to have a remarkable career in law and politics, eventually replacing Lansing as Woodrow Wilson's secretary of state. He was, the Stockbridge Sedgwicks decided, too breezy, vulgar, domineering and two-faced for a Sedgwick, even so dubious a one as Nathalie, but he carried her into an exciting life in New York and Washington, and the Colbys were fun to visit, always seeming to be next door to historical happenings. They had three daughters—Kate, another Nathalie, and Frances—who were to exert upon the children of Alexander Sedgwick something of the same attraction their mother had had for Alick and his brothers in the old days at the Sedgwick Mansion. Young Ellery fell in love with Fanny and Shan with Kate. Kate was Christina's favorite cousin. But it was Aunt Nathalie herself who was the perpetual source of excitement. Her house was where one found daring new books, new ideas. She also proved to be another literary Sedgwick: after she divorced the impossible "Uncle Bain," she wrote novels somewhat in the style of Virginia Woolf—whom she told her young friends to read along with Lawrence. She also told them about the poet Yeats, whom John Quinn brought to her house one day. They felt that she was close to things that mattered—in a better sense than Bainbridge Colby. Certainly she was on their side in their resistance to the assumptions of their elders, for she loved to shock her own generation. Christina remembered how Aunt Nathalie always became more extravagantly risqué at the sight of her old playfellow, the Reverend Theodore. Their elders frowned, but Ellery and Shan and Christina were ravished.

Aunt Nathalie Colby was, it turned out, a model somewhat perilous for the future wife of John P. Marquand. What delighted him in Christina, her whimsicality and poetry, were combined with a fine indifference to duller details, an indifference he would find charming only in the beginner. Yet in Aunt Nathalie this combination had seemed rare and admirable. During visits to the Colbys, Christina's letters home had been full of description that must have irritated her matter-of-fact mother. Once, when she was visiting them in New York, she wrote of their preparation for a vacation: "Aunt Nathalie confided in me that if only going to Lakewood were interesting there would be some point for exertion but this eternal packing seemed hardly worth while. It was a delightful point of view. She asks me if I have ever in my life known such a terrible person as Kate. 'I don't know how I have produced a chambermaid, who measures my personality by the footrule of housekeeping,' laughing all the time, for she adores Kate. Meanwhile time slips by and Nathalie hasn't found the trunk keys, even. I do adore Aunt Nathalie. She rises absolutely above all material complications and preserves her delightful personality in every trial. She does all the essentials of life efficiently. It is only the non-essentials that she leaves messy."

The Colbys were only one corner of the Sedgwick family web. In another, equally important to Christina, was a rather magical place with the strange name of Fasnacloich, in Dublin, New Hampshire. Here, in their handsome, well-appointed summer house set in perfect gardens, the wealthy, good-natured MacVeaghs spent every summer. There were six MacVeagh sons—Rogers, Lincoln, Ewen, Charles, Francis, and Charlton—and Christina had been their darling ever since she was little. Without sisters themselves, her MacVeagh cousins gave her a brotherly affection that was more robust and cheerful—and less intellectual and moody—than that of Ellery and Shan. Fasnacloich was always full of their friends, and all summer long there were outdoor expeditions, hiking and riding parties, swimming and tennis, careless gay evenings. In 1919 and 1920, it seemed a sort of fairy world to the young men, some just back from France, and the girls, some of whom like Christina had been doing hospital work. Of course, Charles MacVeagh, who had married her mother's sister, Fanny Rogers, was not exactly a dweller in fairyland. He was general counsel for U.S. Steel, and the reverberations of the Great Steel Strike, the grim prelude of the decade, must have reached quite clearly through the pines and maples. And in February 1920, a personal disaster touched this cheerful house when twenty-two-year-old Charlie died while snowshoeing on Mount Monadnock, the beautiful mountain that had seemed a benevolent deity looming over their playground for so many years. A sense of the brevity of youth and beauty and the vulnerability even of the privileged was felt at Fasnacloich where, suddenly, everyone was getting engaged.

It was at this time in this place that Christina met John Marquand. He had known the elder MacVeagh brothers, who like himself were "looking around for something" in New York after the war. Lincoln, three years ahead of him at Harvard, had turned up in publishing, like Roger Burlingame, and was about to found the Dial Press, which would print some of the best writing of their generation. But it was Ewen, two years Marquand's junior, who was his particular friend. They had known each other slightly at Harvard, had become close friends in Battery A on the Mexican border, and now saw each other regularly in New York, where Ewen had gone into the safe and sure career for a young man of his kind and connections—business and the law, like his father. He and Marquand used to meet at the Harvard Club, Ewen would recall—they were probably the two youngest members—and amid the smell of leather armchairs and achieved careers they would talk about the war they had just come through—and their futures. Now John was coming to visit at Fasnacloich, something of an anomaly among the MacVeaghs and their friends. Of course—it was the old story—he belonged by right of origins and family connections—his own cousin Sewell Tyng had long been one of Ewen's best friends. And yet he wasn't one of these "golden lads and lasses."

Christina was not obviously available. Ewen himself had been in love with her for years, and then there was another cousin, William Minot, a young partner in the firm of Imbrie and Company, who had been nearly successful in persuading her that businessmen were not necessarily too unenlightened for a Sedgwick. One morning at Fasnacloich—it was August 17, 1920—she found herself riding in the woods with Ewen and the new guest, Marquand, and, she told her mother, "We had an awful argument because they began to curse out business as a career—saying it was deadening and narrowing." Thinking of Minot, she went on to say, "You can imagine where I got material for refutation," and added, "Yesterday, William and I lunched at the Exchange Club, a *businessman's* club. I had a wonderful time." But a few days later she wrote again of guests at Fasnacloich. "The Tyngs were here and are very amusing. John Marquand is one of the most amusing men I have ever known. I had a delightful ride with him yesterday." And again, "John Marquand is one of the most amusing men I know and I like him ever so much. He's mercilessly teased by the other boys but more intelligent than they with more real humor. It's only in brute force—games, etc.—that they have real supremacy." The talent already noted, for inspired persiflage, was serving him well in attracting the attention of the girl who had attracted him. She described his appearance at this time: his clothes somewhat worn-looking and unpressed, his straight hair, parted in the middle, sliding over his forehead: "He's like a ragged terrier—but a pleasant clever person." Then, she ended her letter, "By this Papa will immediately conclude that I am infatuated." And soon her parents got a chance to look John over. One day, on an impulse when Harriet Amory was also visiting the MacVeaghs, the two girls drove with Ewen and John from Dublin to Stockbridge. As they came down the main street of Stockbridge, Marquand saw for the first time the house which had been built by Judge Theodore, and now he met, for the first time, Alexander and Lily Sedgwick.

The Indian summer days passed, and Marquand was again at Fasnacloich. He showed Christina the stories he had written and she was only mildly impressed, but she reported, "His latest story is better than the others. It's about a jockey." And her letters began to point him up to her mother as an exceptional person. "He said everything bored him in college and that he is one of the few people that does what he wants in life." Suddenly, with that detachment that sometimes one proves capable of as life moves to a crisis and change, she added, "It seems like a novel to me, as if we were all characters in it, with our currents and cross-currents." William Minot was still not out of her mind. In November she went to Washington to stay with the Colbys, installed in their splendor and importance in a grand house on K Street. William met her at the station, took her to a play and Delmonico's. She reported: "He is a fearfully hard-headed capitalist. I don't know why I don't hate him." But she did not. The amusing and keenly intelligent young man with the look of a ragged terrier was perhaps nearly forgotten that winter. In the summer of 1921, however, William Minot's status as a suitor was suddenly reduced; Imbrie and Company was bankrupt, and William, the exponent of capitalism, wiped out. John Marquand, on the other hand, was catching up with Christina, seeing her at Fasnacloich, coming up to Stockbridge, and even getting invited together with his cousin Robert Hale to visit the Colbys in Easthampton on Long Island. It was at the Colbys in August that they became very tentatively engaged, Nathalie Colby thought, though the engagement was broken by Christina soon after—a process that became a sort of game between them that year, but also showed clearly how tentative was Christina's conception of the kind of man she could love. It was all summer fun. "I dropped my little emerald ring off the dock into the water. John had to put on a bathing suit and dive in, but Bobby Hale finally got it out with tongs. Since then John watches my jewelry anxiously—especially anxious to know if my pearls would break—a question, as I said, of each pearl a dive!" But Minot was definitely out of the running. She had not even let him know that she was at Easthampton, she told her mother—"It's mean but I can't help it."

In a couple of months the Sedgwicks were in Europe, staying in Rome for the winter, as they had often done before. At the end of December Marquand also went to Rome, his first novel on press, and the *Post*, the *Journal*, and even the dignified *Scribner's Magazine*, to whom he was sending a story about old Newburyport, all waiting for the next thing he would write. He visited the tourist spots with Christina—the Trevi fountain and the graves of Keats and Shelley—and finally, in January, with her parents' consent, they were formally engaged to be married the coming September.

As already remarked, they did not know each other any better than most people do who seek some complement to their needs and dreams, foisting these conceptions upon the delusive surface of that strange world turning upon its own axis that is the other person. Afterwards Christina would say that she had not really been in love with him in the beginning. She had been attracted and repelled. His oddness, his intelligence and humor, his disdain of a commonplace career of "mere" moneymaking had appealed to something rebellious in herself, just as she had warmed to his ineptness at the sports and games in which upper-class youth is trained from infancy. Some of his ineptness she felt in herself, but her rebellions were shallow. She retained the conventional expectation of a moneyed life; she could not really imagine herself living without several servants and cars and "nice" clothes. So she wanted to challenge her upbringing but not to question its foundations. Marquand provided a fulfillment of the paradox she desired—his wit, though she sensed it to be curiously keen, was not, in the Sedgwick sense, "cultured"; his conversation was seldom ornamented with stylish literary or other cultural references. His lack of means, along with his somewhat awkward manner, his indifference to the details of appearance, marked him as a kind of outsider. He was not unlike Minot, the truly unintellectual "capitalist"—he, too, meant to be wealthy. In the inaccurate way of those who have enjoyed but never earned money, she supposed that he was well on the way, after the successes he could boast of, to becoming a rich man by means of his writing. He, of course, would not enjoy the Sedgwick condescension—which Christina also managed to share—to his artistic-commercial labors. And only he knew how much work and time it would take to make him rich. That her parents consented is not so surprising as it may seem. Perhaps too easily but not, after all, incorrectly, they decided he would be a success. He was, also, manly and clever and would probably be able to "settle" Christina, whose ennui worried them.

Marquand stayed on in Europe, traveling sometimes with the Sedgwicks and sometimes alone, and occasionally he ran into the colonies of Americans who would hang on abroad through the twenties. In Paris, some of his contemporaries were already settling into attics on the Left Bank and were discovering, amid much bibulous distraction, that they could or could not write or paint or compose there, now that Prohibition and Puritanism had headlocked their native land. It was possible to live quite an interesting sort of life. Paris was more beautiful than any American city, the French were sensible and tolerant, and you did not need very much to live on because the value of the dollar was favorable. But, of course, you needed something—a correspondent's job or a small income winging its way from home faithfully each month. Marquand knew that his own chances consisted of keeping in close touch with his editors in New York and Philadelphia, without whom he would have no money at all. Anyhow, the life did not really appeal to him, and it would never do for Christina. Those writers he met abroad were all rather mad. Fitzgerald, whom he encountered one day in a Paris café, struck him as driven and morose—he talked obsessively about his fear of losing his eyesight. Marquand did not, at this time, get to meet the other writer he had most admired during the years since the war—Sinclair Lewis. But once, at a party in Rome, he ran into Mrs. Lewis, who offensively referred to her husband as "the white hope of American literature." Lewis was expected to show up but never did. Probably Marquand heard instead the gossip about his idol's unpredictable personality, his philandering, his already crumbling marriage, his heavy drinking. And one afternoon in Taormina in Sicily he was introduced to another writer, an Englishman with wild red beard and hair and burning eyes. Afterwards the friend who introduced them asked Marquand what he thought of the man. "He's a nut," he said. It was D. H. Lawrence (who responded similarly about Marquand—"a perfect madman!"). Fitzgerald, Lewis, Lawrence—geniuses of the first order—but their personalities and lives could never accord with his own, and especially not now that he was marrying Christina.

He was keenly aware, too, that he had a long way to go to achieve either the distinction or success of these three. In Taormina, in a little hotel called the Villa Diodoro, he woke up each morning and looked out his window at the incredible invitation of February sunshine, the air carrying the scent of flowers, Etna holding aloft a small plume of steam like a great tea kettle, and the sea blue enamel at his feet—and he sat down to work on new stories for the magazines. Christina would be pleased—he had just sold "The Ship" to *Scribner's Magazine*.

At the hotel there was an American woman, a Mrs. McKitterick, and her pretty daughter Era, who was being courted by a fervid Italian sculptor. During her free moments the girl gave a little attention to John Marquand, who read some of his stories to her out in the garden of the hotel under blossoming orange and almond trees. Later she would offer this description: "Once, a long time ago, I sat in a beautiful garden and listened to a very young man read to me three stories that he had written. He was a shy, earnest young man, with a perceptive sort of mind and a sort of slow, searching sense of humor. He always went about in very unpressed clothes, that seemed to have been bought for someone a great deal larger or a great deal smaller than himself. In the month we had lived in the hotel we had become good friends and I was very fond of him for he walked and he talked to you with bent head and his eyes on the ground as if searching for something, something I am afraid he never found. These stories were important to him. He had worked for a newspaper and given up the job to become a free lance writer. One of the stories he had sold had been to the Saturday Evening Post. The chief ingredients of these tales were vigorous, large, white-toothed American play-boys, owners of red Stutz racing cars, and sultry, sloe-eyed beauties, complete with mantilla and shawl. The locale: south of the border and then some. They seemed to me dreadful, and when he stopped reading I earnestly wished to be a thousand miles away. I knew how important these stories were to him; he needed the money and much more important he wanted so very much to be a writer, a good writer, but as I looked at him, sitting there, his head, with its uncombable fair hair, bent, and his eyes fixed gloomily on the masses of fuchsia and hyacinth at his feet, I felt I must tell him what I really thought. And I did. I told him I didn't think they were very good at all and that perhaps he had better go back to the newspaper job where he was sure at least of making a living. 'You can always do a little writing in your spare time,' I said. And he answered 'I don't know. They aren't very good, are they? Perhaps when I go home maybe I should go back to the paper. I don't know. I'll have to think about it.' And as I watched him shake away the orange and almond blossoms that had fallen onto his manuscript from the trees above us, I felt very unhappy, and very sorry indeed for Mr. John P. Marquand, who, I felt perfectly sure, would never write anything that anybody would ever want to read."

Marquand still lingered on in Italy, going here and there with the Sedgwicks, trying to write along the way; it was perhaps his first experience of what was to repeat itself throughout his married life—the effort to work in a disciplined fashion while a member of a sort of traveling caravan of family activity in which he and Christina were a minor but securely attached part. "It's an awfully hard job trying to get anything done here," he wrote Roger Burlingame from Florence. However, he was managing something. He wrote a new story—"It's about a crook," he told Roger—which utilized a Sicilian background made up of recent glimpses of Palermo and the mountain country on the road to Segesta where he had gone, like many before him, to see the perfect Greek temple. In the scene—"very south of the border" one might call it—he located again the story of the Princess and the Squire of Low Degree. This time, instead of a boxer, his hero is an American thief who has taken a diamond necklace from a beautiful heiress, but inspired by love and native nobility, he returns it. It was called "How Willie Came Across" and appeared in the *Post* in July 1922. It immediately captivated *Post* readers, who were to be offered more of Willie Lipp's adventures in high society in subsequent months. There was a happy, outrageous banality in all of these stories. They were all versions of what a professor of literature in a later story of Marquand's calls "the Cinderella motif, the commonest basis of plot structure," the story of a hero of inferior social origins who rises through love to royal position. Marquand had perceived that this was his magazine audience's favorite fairy tale; the *Post* was full of stories about the gay life of ease which a lucky careerist could enter, and as already observed, he had his own stake in such dreams. He could now half-sardonically recognize himself in the low fellow who yearned to impress the young lady by revealing, like Willie Lipp, that he was the greatest, truest gentleman she had ever known.

Meanwhile, *The Unspeakable Gentleman* was seen into proof by Roger, and

Scribner's sent Marquand the $500 advance on royalties. It turned out that the *Ladies' Home Journal* was able to run it in February, March, and May, and that publication would not, after all, have to wait till fall. The book would appear on May 5. On April 13, Marquand docked in New York. He found Roger mailing review copies. Some were accompanied by a note urging the reader to recognize the romantic, antirealist chord that had been struck by the new author. To Marquand's *Tribune* friend Heywood Broun, for example, Roger said, "I think you will find it entertaining or at any rate a considerable relief from the realism which has been flowing so freely from youthful writers of late." To Sidney Williams: "Marquand is the first one, I think, of the younger group to break away from realism and plunge so deeply into the good old romance of duels, galloping horses, midnight escapades and lots of good red wine."

And in such terms it was taken. One of the reviewers spoke for nearly all in concluding that Marquand was "a troubadour rather than a crusader." And yet, as one reads the book today one sees that something was overlooked then, something Marquand was sensible enough to keep to himself, maybe. It seems likely that his tongue was in his cheek for the keener reader to discover, that he burlesqued the thing he was doing, betrayed again and again a kind of parodist's exaggeration of costume romance which made a high joke of it. It is the only thing that saves it for us now. Perhaps even so early he was exercising his real gift. Marquand himself made no sign of any covert intent, however, and even permitted himself to be enrolled in Roger's publicizing efforts. "It seems a shame not to give an expert advertising man who has since become an author a chance to get up an advertisement of his own book," Roger had told him, enlisting his help for blurbs and layouts, which the author was pleased to compose, though he wrote back: "I am gagging slightly at this publicity and feel I could do something else with my time." But he observed that the ads might feature quotes from the book that would focus on its high moments. "What I'm suggesting is taking a dozen of these speeches, carefully selected, and making a bold-face headline following it with a few words of copy, and having at the bottom in larger type the title of the book. For instance: 'The hour is growing late. Put down the pistol, Henry.' So spoke the Unspeakable Gentleman on that evening a hundred years ago, as he leaned across a table in the firelight, but his words were not obeyed. Read for yourself etc. etc.'" Surely the *comedy* of it must have been present to Marquand as he composed the ad!

He was paying a visit that May—the lingering last visit of the bachelor only son—to his parents in Wilmington. When he came again he would be thirty years old—and married. Perhaps more keenly than he had for years he felt the tug of their fading lives upon his own. The little home they had made for themselves at Edge Moor, the stone cottage in the park, had a kind of Hansel and Gretel charm that made him feel like a child again. "The place looks like a Monet in the Louvre, if there is one there, and the birds are singing, and you can sit on the grass," he wrote Roger. There was a weeping willow outside the door and two chairs on the small porch. Inside, a Harvard pennant hung in the hall and all the familiar family pictures and his butterfly collection under glass were on the walls of the small pretty rooms. Too late they offered him a Home.

Then he went to Stockbridge to be with Christina and the Sedgwicks. *Her* Old Family Home folded itself more masterfully about him. The Berkshire summer was enchanting and the old house was preparing itself for the ceremonial of a Sedgwick wedding. While Christina and her mother worked on wedding lists and arrangements, John would take walks in the neighborhood with Shan or Ellery or talk to Alick or one of Christina's uncles. He had the impression after a while that however important an event his wedding was in his own life it was far more significant as a moment in the annals of the Sedgwicks. There was a tearful tension in the Sedgwick joy that emanated particularly from the person of Alick. As the weeks went by, he became more extravagant in his rhetoric and expressions. Half comically and half seriously he would say as he came in from doing some errands connected with the wedding: "I feel like a stag pursued by hounds!"

John had, naturally enough, been finding it difficult to seclude himself for work either in Wilmington or Stockbridge. He decided to spend his last month as a bachelor alone. In the wealthy summer resort of York Harbor, Maine, he rented a small cottage belonging to friends and tried to get started on a new novel. Edward Weeks, who was spending that summer as a family tutor in one of the big houses at York, remembers someone pointing out to him a small wooden shack on a rocky promontory: "John Marquand lives there. He's trying to write a novel." Marquand emerged occasionally to go to tea here and there. A young woman named Elizabeth Councilman, who was later to study medicine and settle in Newburyport with her doctor husband, saw him a number of times, and he also met the old novelist Robert Herrick, the reigning literary lion of the place, who was "tweedy and affable," as Marquand remembered, "going out of his way to be agreeable" to the young unknown.

He had hardly got down to work at York Harbor when his father wrote that his mother had had a slight heart attack. It was not disturbing enough to summon him to Wilmington, yet he felt the old anguish of responsibility, as he had often felt it during his school and college years. He wrote to Christina: "Naturally I am all on pins and needles and I guess that about finishes any story for me before the wedding. There is only one comfort I have just now, dear, and that is when a thing like this happens, I have you beside me with all your sweetness and comfort. I know this sounds a little like Harriet Amory, but you'll know the way I mean it. And now that I think of it, there is one other thing which I thank God for almost as much, and that is, no matter what happens, I can, Heaven willing, always see that she, and you too, are both comfortable. Good night my dearest, and for heaven's sake don't you get worn out too—I love you so much I don't think I could bear it on top of this." There are several things to note in this somewhat predictable sample of sentiment. First, one hears the assumption that he—only he—would be ultimately responsible for his mother's comfort "no matter what happens"; implicit is the knowledge that Philip's provision for her was not to be relied upon, a fact curiously gratifying—making him happy, as on that winter night when he drove her from the station to the Mill through a blizzard and his ineffectual father was far away in California. To Christina, of course, the letter meant something else, a promise of the enveloping kind of love and protection that she had always enjoyed from her family. What is also interesting is Marquand 's *self*-assurance. His success was small as yet, but he was sure he would be able to guarantee security to both women.

On September 9, 1922, he was married to Christina in St. Paul's Episcopal Church in Stockbridge, where Sedgwicks had sat in the same pew for four generations. The little church was decorated with blue delphinium and pink gladioli. The bride wore her mother's wedding gown of heavy white satin made over into a modern frock and a tulle veil of old lace attached to a band around her head, and carried a bunch of white orchids. For best man John Marquand had chosen his cousin Dudley Hale, and for ushers, Christina's brothers, Shan and Ellery, his cousin Sewell Tyng, and a little guard of friends—Roger Burlingame and Robert Wood from the Scribner office; Sidney Howard, the future playwright; Ewen MacVeagh; and a Wilmington friend, George Biggs. Aunt Nathalie's daughter Katherine was Christina's maid of honor and two other Sedgwick cousins were bridesmaids. Uncle Theodore Sedgwick officiated.

The ceremony was at four in the afternoon, and then the guests went over to the house that Judge Theodore had built, for the reception. It was 137 years that day since the judge had held a house-warming ball there, the guests and the press were reminded. The newspapers were also told that only a few days previous a long-unopened trunk in the attic had yielded up a treasury of letters from George Washington to the Judge, and others from Philip Schuyler, Samuel Gray Otis, and Jonathan Edwards, and a letter to the patriarchal Sedgwick from Alexander Hamilton, written the day before he was shot. Yes, John Marquand would have agreed as he smiled at his bride, the very peepers and katydids were chirping, "Sedgwick, Sedgwick."

9

Pulled by Strings

A dozen years later, when it was quite over, they could not either of them have said what had been wrong with the marriage. Beneath accusations and counteraccusations, unnameable forces of attraction and repulsion had grappled and recoiled. All language, and especially the language of psychological science—for they sought the help of psychiatrists eventually—seems crude to describe the condition in which love and hate are merely blinking signals of obscure and infinitely complex circuits of feeling. The sexual relation, as already remarked, expresses much else besides technical sex, but it has its own character for every couple. Though Marquand was twenty-nine when he married, his experience with women had been limited. Since his high school crush on Lillian Simpson, such passing flirtations and affairs as had occupied him had not cut very deeply, but women had clearly divided themselves into two types for him—the girls who resembled Lillian and those who were quite different, the prototypes of Pulham's Marvin Myles, who knew what they wanted, not least of all sexually. Christina's fine ethereality, it has been said, was a quality to make him proud of being able to afford it—a mark of class. It also, probably, meant a cultivated distance from sex along with other "low" facts of life. The trouble was that Marquand would expect not only a practical proficiency in this wife but a sexual readiness her upbringing had discouraged. And though she responded to a force, a roughness, that made him different from the men she had known before—and so an ally in her own rebellion against her environment—she remained also slightly repelled by him. In the long run his egotism and sexual exigency threatened her own valuation of herself. It turned out, moreover, that he did not really want to assume the protective-sustaining role, in the place of her father, her mother and the whole Sedgwick family. He himself wanted to be protected and sustained.

Her thoughts turned insistently homeward, as a good daughter's should, no doubt, even on her wedding night, and she wrote her mother: "I know I am going to miss you terribly especially when I know you can't be here, but I hope in time I shall become a little like you. I don't think any girl could be luckier in having their family like their husband than I am." They were spending their honeymoon not far from Stockbridge, driving her father's Dodge into the hills and stopping at vacation hotels, which were now emptying as the summer gently sank into fall. On the first morning of her marriage she woke up remembering to write to her mother and send her love to her family: "I am very happy, and judging from the breakfast John ate this morning John is too. So far our married life has been a complete success. We both think the wedding went off beautifully. John says if I want I can say he is very happy too. Give his love to the family—and mine too, especially to Papa—I think he did very well yesterday." There is perhaps no reason for a more casual generation to question her consideration of those she had left behind, especially her curious, emotional father, who had made something of a scene at the wedding breakfast when he rose to toast the married pair: he burst into tears and threw his emptied champagne glass to the ground.

From the Mount Everett Inn in South Egremont they had gone on until their car stalled in the mud of a country road and they had walked a mile to a farm for help. Then they had had lunch in Pittsfield at the Wendell and had come on to Williamstown for the night at the Greylock, which was rather grand and expensive with a swimming pool, but John, she reported, "says it is a good investment for him as he can study the people for a story." Being the wife of a struggling young writer held no alarms, and she was happy with the sense that nothing had been lost in exchange for married happiness. "I love you just as much as ever and I'm awfully glad I got married," she blithely continued in her letters to her mother. The next day they were at a still fancier hotel, the Equinox House at Manchester-in-the-Mountains in Vermont, after which, she wrote, they planned to drop down from their height of luxury to "cooking for ourselves at Swain's Farm." It was then that domestic reality made its first appearance, according to the story told and retold as comic anecdote in their happy hours, sardonically later. Christina, Marquand would relate, had undertaken to roast a chicken for their supper and had simply placed the uneviscerated fowl in the oven of the farmhouse stove. As she brought it forth, nicely browned and smelling rather queerly, her husband burst into roars that would echo down the years and gently took it from her hands and carried it to the garbage pail. They made a meal of bread and cheese and were very happy afterwards reading by turns from Thackeray's *Vanity Fair*. A *princesse lointaine* might be expected, after all, to be unaware that chickens had entrails!

Then they came home to Curzon's Mill to live, as Marquand had always dreamed he would do, and settled in the Brick House. Christina, with that sensitivity which was her greatest charm, responded to the haunted beauty of the old place. "There is a peculiar poignant loveliness I have never seen so strongly emphasized before," she wrote her mother. She went one day to visit the Marquand graves on Sawyer's Hill nearby, the little graveyard dusky and cool under the pines, and felt the breath of the past gently against her cheek as she saw the old slate headstones sunk crookedly among the brown needles. Next door to the Brick House, in the Yellow House, were the past's living witnesses, Aunt Molly and Aunt Bessie. Aunt Molly came over every morning. "I like her little chestnut burr look," said Christina, referring to the odd round face, bristled with whiskers like a man's. "I like hearing her funny stories and disjointed anecdotes of a more splendid past and her ancestors." Aunt Molly's very mental defects seemed to give her a more direct intimacy with the ghosts of dead Marquands and Curzons.

John and Christina were still, somehow, only playing at married life. "I am not afraid of being in Newburyport a little while without a servant at least while John isn't writing. He cooks very well and is in all senses a perfect wife because he washes the dishes and is so good at all these things," Christina wrote in the first days. Soon her mother and father, her brother Shan and an aunt came for lunch, and Christina asked her mother to bring sandwiches along so that they could have "a picnic in the fields"—the hosts would provide coffee and hard-boiled eggs. So, the omnipresent solicitude of her family sustained the young bride and, for the present, it only amused her husband. It was perhaps symbolical that the very mattress and down quilt of their bed, and blankets he declared to be the fluffiest he had ever seen, had arrived from Stockbridge in time to be used the first night they slept in the Brick House. John, as he went to bed, remarked that "there was a distinct feeling of his mother-in-law about." Mrs. Sedgwick's gifts expressed her desire to cosset them, and Christina wrote her, "You are always a sort of lovely softness to fall back on in my mind."

The Brick House, empty for a long time now since Marquand's parents had been living in Wilmington, underwent renovations and refurbishings, and the wedding gifts and heirlooms found their places. On new shelves in an alcove, Christina placed side by side her own and John's childhood books—she discovered that they each had kept a copy of *A Child's Garden of Verses* from nursery days. She described a fireside scene that might have been drawn by Norman Rockwell for a *Saturday Evening Post* cover: "There is a nice fire in the stove and the comfortable chair is in front of it and John is there smoking a pipe. Aunt Bessie has been over to supper and is just as nice as she can be. I've got John's picture up over my desk and the Newbold Morris desk set on it and a picture of the back of the house [in Stockbridge] right in front of me and also Miss Kobbé's picture of Papa. The Hogarth print is above the mantlepiece and the Crowninshield vases are on each end of it. The antique chest is in front of the front window. It is dear to John's heart and I keep my linen in it. The clock is in the corner directly opposite the door as you enter. The antique table is in the middle of the room. We had tea today off Fisher's tray and it stands all day on the tea wagon with the brass tea kettle on top of it. I am keeping most of the silver upstairs for the time being till we are thoroughly settled."

But John, smoking in his easy chair, knew that everything depended on the hard work that sold the stories printed inside the *Post*. While Christina was fussing in the house, chatting with his aunts or the neighbors who came to call—the Moseleys from just above them, the Misses Amory from across the river, new friends and old ones from Newburyport—he set himself up for work again in the old millhouse hanging over the half-frozen Artichoke. At the end of November he wrote editor Lorimer that he was back at work and finishing a story: "I am sorry not to have completed it sooner, but I never realized the demands put on anyone who has to move into a house four miles away from anywhere. Now, however, that the furnace is running and the garden is covered and the wood is cut and the storm windows are on, and I have a quiet room and a stove here alone in our deserted grist mill, I have every hope of turning out a decently impressive amount of work."

In the bare, familiar loft, furnished only with a single chair and a table, he was contentedly at work on more stories about the adventures abroad of his engaging American thief, Willie Lipp. "Captain of His Soul," just published in the November 4, 1922, issue of the *Post*, found Willie further advanced in his social relations with the royalty of American wealth and stirred to superior nobility of soul by Henley's "Invictus"; in authentic burglar's costume he unwittingly crashes a masked party in his friends' villa and exposes the knavery of some local counts and dukes. Now Marquand was writing another tale of Willie's Italian adventures, "The Sunbeam," in which Willie is inspired again by a piece of high sentiment in verse:

I want to be a sunbeam,
A sunbeam of hope and light,
A jolly little sunbeam
That is always doing right.

Willie is discovered in a little Sicilian town, where he makes his grand gesture of scattering to the populace the money received in exchange for his lady's stolen diamonds. Christina read it and wrote her mother: "I don't think it's so good but just for the situation of Willie in this little town I think it is most delightfully done, and there is a sort of abandon about it that I love. You will have to read it. I think John must have been thinking of his father in law when Willie says, 'All gentlemen are suckers.'"

Christina had ended her letter: "John says life is an unexpurgated hell because he has to finish his story and then put on a dinner coat and go to the Princes for dinner! He says I ought to bear a little red flag as a token of victory." Already he was experiencing the usual problem of the writer who finds the encroachment upon his work-time something that families rarely understand. It was a struggle that would continue through the course of two marriages. To Christina he tried to explain his need for hours of uninterrupted application and she accepted his views: "As long as we lead a quiet, regular life there is no reason why he shouldn't get a great deal of work done and both of us be contented and happy," she wrote her mother. But the Sedgwick understanding of such a program was bound to be different from Marquand's. Naturally, as the Christmas holiday season approached, the newlyweds were expected to make a long visit to Stockbridge and there were discussions and tensions of a kind that would continue to recur for years. On December 18 she wrote her mother: "One thing is a great blow—and I'm afraid you'll be awfully disappointed but I don't see how it can be helped—you see we found that if we went to you this Thursday and didn't get back from Stockbridge till the day after New Year's it would be practically two weeks, and John can't afford being away from his work so long—he is in the middle of a story and Scribner's want the proof of his book immediately and he has to go over that this week. I felt very badly at first, but after all, as John says, if he were in business and had two days off no one would think anything about it. And two weeks is a long time for anyone but college boys to take. I suppose Papa may think it is mean of John but I can't help what he thinks because it isn't really mean." One is suddenly sorry for the young wife with her divided loyalties trying to appease that parental love which is so punishing in its reproachful self-pity.

The book just then in proof was Marquand's second, a quartet of stories that Scribner's was bringing out under the title *Four of a Kind*. Included was his comic takeoff of advertising, "Eight Million Bubbles." But the others also had a certain biographical reference, though they were, like the Willie Lipp stories, basically fairy tales reflecting his own half-romantic, half-mocking feelings about the path to riches and about the rich themselves. The least impressive story is probably "Only a Few of Us Left," which describes a young man from an old "sporting" family. He seems to exemplify some antique virtue of courage that once justified the existence of an aristocracy. He is judged an idler and empty-headed even by the country-club crowd—but it is seen that he is brave and gallant, however anachronously, when he dives from a height because a girl has asked him to, or rides a dangerous course. Many years later in the much more sophisticated pages of his novel *B. F.'s Daughter*, Marquand would depict in Bob Tasmin a character whose outmoded personal honor gains meaning against the background of modern war, making him the superior of more practical men. There was a certain tenderness in Marquand's appreciation of the qualities of old-fashioned "breeding"—it is the sentimental side of his view of Apley and of Pulham.

The other two stories were instances of the Cinderella motif—the boxing story, "The Right That Failed," and "Different from Other Girls" which concerns a modern flapper and a young employee of her father's who proves himself by playing superior golf. Marquand was always to be fascinated by golf, that rich man's sport in which natural ability could match itself against the advantages of class—and he himself tried unsuccessfully all his life to become better than a duffer. In the novel *Warning Hill*, published in the *Post* in 1929, a Marquand-like hero becomes the golf instructor's assistant at the country club and wins a tournament—thereby impressing, again, a rich girl's dad. But with hidden dreams of his own, which gave the Cinderella story a personal significance, went his hardheaded recognition that he was providing a wish-fulfilling fantasy for the millions whose lives would never get far from the grind of the shop and the kitchen sink. He was perhaps not cynical, either, in writing so closely to this prescription. So one may infer from a story written at about the same time as these called "The Land of Bunk." In this lighthearted fable Marquand composed a defense of an artist like himself, a sideshow pitchman who sells an Indian snake-oil soap guaranteed to cure all ills. Launcelot, the soap salesman, tells the born-every-minute suckers: "You know it's bunk! Oh, yes you do! Before you walk up this here track you know it isn't real. You laugh at it before you come, you laugh at it when you go away. But you'll come back again, gents. You know it, and I know it. It's a fake, but you'll come back, even if you have to walk on crutches. And why do you do it, gents—why? You know it's a fake, folks, but you come because you hope it's true. You come back because you want a place where things are different from the things you know. You want to be fooled, folks. And that's what we're here for—just to deliver the goods."

Yet Marquand felt despondent as he worked on the proofs beside his wood stove in the lonely millhouse. "I will be through with the proofs in a day or two and will send them right on. It is cold as hell here, and no small amount of snow. I wish to heaven I could think of something worth writing and I wish I could see you," he wrote Burlingame in the middle of December. The prospect of publishing these stories in book form had brought him sharply to the contemplation of their limitations. The *Ladies' Home Journal* had cut two thousand words from "Different from Other Girls" before publication, and, he thought, "badly mutilated" it—his first experience of the imperial blue pencil that governs magazine writing. He hoped that the book could include his original version. But he knew that ultimate responsibility for the quality of the stories was his own.

He wrote Burlingame: "As I read over the proof I must say in all frankness that my heart sank within me and I could only sit wide-eyed and appalled at the clumsy and rotten [writing] which sticks up from every line. Indeed I blush when I think of any of these stories appearing in book form and wasting the press facilities of the nation." Burlingame replied comfortingly: "The 'reaction' you suffered on reading the stories in proof is one which I find attacks all good authors at some stage in the publication of their books. I am told it never attacks bad ones. It is by far the best thing you have done, in my opinion, and holds within itself the elements of your greatest abilities. 'Different from Other Girls' is quite as good a reflection of the times and the generation as most of Fitzgerald's most popular and widely hailed flapper stories. 'The Right That Failed' was written perhaps before you got quite 'warmed up' in this type of story but it is good stuff all the same. You remember your anxiety about 'The Unspeakable Gentleman.' I can remember your telling me you were glad you had lost it. I am sure you have changed your mind about that." Burlingame was a good friend and a good editor who did what he could to give Marquand heart at the commencement of a long career as a popular author. Yet the doubts that the young writer felt were justified, too. *Four of a Kind* was published on March 24, 1923, and the reviewer for the Boston *Transcript* conceded that Marquand showed mastery of the techniques of short fiction, but found him "markedly less sincere and more artificial" than in his novel. "This is no doubt the result of his writing for one particular magazine," he pointed out. "However good a magazine it may be, there is no doubt that the *Saturday Evening Post* has a tendency to mark its writers." He expressed the hope that Marquand, who clearly knew how to write, would "not allow himself to fall into writing a formula story and doing less well than his best."

Marquand would show in the next decade that he could write many variations upon the formulas of successful magazine fiction and write them with increasing skill and grace. Yet the mood of his letter to Burlingame upon seeing the early stories of *Four of a Kind* into proof would recur often, and ultimately he would be more severe than his critics in dismissing the literary worth of his labors for the magazines. In 1955, when John Mason Brown was putting together an anthology of fiction from the pages of the *Ladies' Home Journal*, Marquand refused to let him consider "Different from Other Girls": "I am convinced that it was never a good story and it would cause me the most acute embarrassment if it were reprinted or even if you were to read it." He would, on the other hand, have moods of irritation at what was simply snobbery in the response of those who, like the *Transcript* reviewer, summarily dismissed anything that had pleased the editors of a popular magazine.

He would, in fact, write a good many magazine stories that had higher claims than these early four. In any case, he was compelled to continue turning them out. "In a short time I found myself supporting my parents. If ever anyone was tied to the chariot wheel, I was. I had to write to pay the bills," he later said. The process had already begun in those first months in the millhouse, for early in 1923 Christina was pregnant. The stories began to multiply, going exclusively to the *Post*, which was now paying him $1,500 apiece for them. In six years he would get twice this amount for each story he sent down to Philadelphia. Meanwhile, Lorimer understood promptly the kind of "property" he had in Marquand, and when the editor of Hearst's *Cosmopolitan* tried to steal the author, he lost no time in raising the price he was willing to pay. Marquand promptly bought a claim on an Alaskan gold mine.

He struck one vein after another that proved pleasing to Lorimer and to the *Post* readers during the next five years. In a mode of sheer make-believe and romance he described persons and situations about which he knew little or nothing. Willie Lipp, the second-story man, continued to figure in adventures that demonstrated his romantic susceptibility, his quaint honor, and even his "artistic touch." In "The Big Guys," Marquand also tried a gangster who had a groping reverence for the unseen governors of the universe. And he invented a coal-barge captain ("The Old Man") who could not forget his greater days as the master of a fine ship. These were clearly enough potboilers.

But if most of the stories were make-believe and formulaic, some had the kind of surface authenticity that makes make-believe most acceptable, for already he showed the realist's and satirist's instinct for dialogue and for backgrounds. He found that a little real observation, well used, went a long way. He remembered, for instance, something about betting and the lure of the racetrack from his glimpses of the gambler in his own father and in a horse-betting townsman who had taken him down to the races a number of times when he was a boy; with "The Educated Money" he began a series of racing stories in which the authentic sense of the paddock matters more than the silly plot. Then there were the stories about the rich and spoiled young—he could write about the Gold Coast undergraduates at Harvard, the young country-club idlers, in the breezy tone of one who knows no world better—which must have delighted those excluded millions who would take his gay burlesques quite literally.

Now and then one catches a genuine reference to personal feeling. "The Last of the Hoopwells" expresses the Curzon–Marquand pride of family: an impoverished family representative holds out against a rich invader who wants his home and his heirlooms—but he gets the rich man's daughter to marry him! And there is "Fun and Neighbors," a rather deft, near-the-bone story about two young couples who are "keeping up" with each other, living beyond their incomes in a rivalry about housefurnishings and servants. More than any other stories Marquand wrote at the time, this one gives a hint of his own realities: when, as seen, he would get up from his writing table and "put on a dinner coat and go to the Princes for dinner." (Morton and Marjorie Prince, a young couple their own age, became their closest friends, but they were like others whose incomes made it unnecessary for them to worry about making money. Morton was the son of a famous and successful Boston psychiatrist; Marjorie was one of those High Street girls, and her wealthy family lived in one of the grand Federalist houses he had passed so often as a boy.) It is doubtful if a process server with a summons to court for unpaid bills ever came to Marquand's door as he comes to the young couples in this story, but Marquand undoubtedly imagined at times that such a visit was imminent. He, too, was working very hard at "keeping up."

Christina, of course, was used to the best, and when little Johnny arrived on October 13, 1923, it was immediately clear that everything from his baby carriage (called "the rolls-royce" by the family because of its cost and splendor) to his nurse would have to be suitable to his station. The Sedgwicks, at any rate, would tolerate no other state for their first grandchild. Not entirely facetiously, Mrs. Sedgwick wrote on one occasion, when the baby was staying with her: "The rolls-royce is in his blood and nothing but silk socks fit him. Johnny has indigestion and nibbles only Huntley and Palmer biscuits. Oh, the precious, cosseted child!" Her desire to provide every advantage to the infant was a major source of irritation to John Marquand. In the late summer of 1924 the tension between Curzon's Mill and Stockbridge became acute. Mrs. Sedgwick urged her daughter and son-in-law to accept her gift of a superior baby nurse named Bridget and John ungenially maintained that they would hire her only when he could pay her wages himself. The banal frictions of domestic disharmony had begun to accumulate between Marquand and his wife as in a million other American marriages. Marquand became convinced that Christina's domestic incompetence was somehow part of the battle. Abetted by her parents, he thought, she made no progress towards assuming the role of the wife of a hard-working man whose income was still modest. And maybe she did resent learning how to cook or to clean or to care for her baby.

A later generation may be inclined to sympathize with Christina's resistance to acquiring domestic skills, with her reluctance to assume the ancient female roles—though she herself was never in any degree a conscious feminist. Shall we say that she might nevertheless have been in unconscious rebellion against the fate that had assigned her from the start a different set of possibilities than her brothers had open to them? A generation more aware of the primacy of the sexual ingredient in marriage may wonder, also, whether there was not something in her rejection of role that had a basis in sexual inhibition. Did Christina resist admitting herself to be a *wife* in the most elementary sense? Most obviously, as many unkindly thought, she was spoiled and snobbish. She had been herself, after all, a "precious, cosseted child" in a well-servanted household: it was natural for her to assume that such conditions would always prevail in her life. Marquand, on the other hand, remembered how his mother, a Fuller, learned to do her own washing and cooking during his father's days of unemployment in California, and he was impatient with Christina's helplessness. Now a note of malice was perceptible where there had been indulgence as he told those funny stories about her incompetence.

Christina's relatives and friends, for their part, continued to take *his* labors lightly, as though they were a gentleman's trivial hobby, which might be expected to give way at any moment to more pressing demands. They found it amusing when, coming up from the millhouse at Christina's request, he greeted her callers with "Christina says I ought to come in and say 'Hello.' So—'Hello'"—and put this down to the odd, acerbic humor that made him a little terrifying and somewhat fascinating to ladies. "What a bear!" they thought, as his blue eyes glinted and he whirled into one of his comic stories about the number of times Christina had already interrupted him that day.

And the serious side of New England gentility was hardly inclined, after all, to take his labors any more gravely. Though Mrs. Sedgwick did read his *Post* stories (it would be later said, untruly, that she never read them at all and advised her daughter not to), she was prone to laugh deprecatingly when someone mentioned one, as though they were an amusing eccentricity of her son-in-law's. Christina sometimes expressed the hope—or so it was said—that he would soon be doing "something nice for Uncle Ellery." "Something nice for Uncle Ellery," Marquand would report himself as having snorted, "and be paid for it $100 or maybe just the gift of a silver inkwell!"—the remuneration he might expect from the editor of the *Atlantic*.

Perhaps it was a desire to detach himself and Christina from such evaluation that led Marquand to try to live in New York after two years at Curzon's Mill. Burlingame had been urging him to make the move. "I think it is a pretty good place to write [in] and I think both you and Christina would enjoy it here," he had written during the first winter at the Mill, when Marquand was particularly oppressed by the problems of maintaining comfort in an old country house and the simplicities of a city apartment must have looked alluring. Thomas B. Costain, the *Post* editor, wrote frankly, "I am hoping that you finally decide to come to New York for a time at least because I believe we could get more work out of you if we had you closer at hand." In New York, Marquand himself felt, there was a world that understood what he was doing, the world he had known when he was writing for the *Tribune* and then for the Thompson agency, and when he wrote his first story—a world that understood that making a living out of writing was hard work. In the winter of 1924–1925, therefore, the Marquands took an apartment at 101 Waverly Place in Greenwich Village.

They saw something of the old *Lampoon* crowd but not so much of their artist neighbors. The experiment was not, in all respects, a success. "My wife, poor girl, lived in perpetual fear that I might drag her into a strange Bohemian world by meeting peculiar people with radical ideas and thus my few feeble adventures in this field were always discouraged," he later remarked. He remained reluctant to make friends among the literati of his generation. In 1924, moreover, he was painfully aware that the rebels and experimenters would not have thought much of his efforts. "I was not doing anything interesting at the time, nothing but short stories for magazines," he noted as a second reason why he made no contact with the Village crowd while living in its midst. The following winter the Marquands were back again in more familiar waters, having rented an apartment in Cambridge at 224 Brattle Street.

And so married life, the conventional "marriage trap" of American experience, closed in with its claims and burdens upon both. Professionally, however, Marquand was really not doing badly. *The Unspeakable Gentleman* had been a moderate success, selling six thousand copies, good enough for a first novel, and Grosset and Dunlap soon would bring out a cheap edition. "The Right That Failed" and "Different from Other Girls" were being made into movies. But *Four of a Kind* did poorly, and Marquand was more than ever confirmed in his feeling that it should not have been published. He began at this point to see himself primarily as a magazine writer: his income came from the magazines for the most part, and it was the expectations of the magazine editors that he felt compelled to pay most attention to. Burlingame warned him that a writer was primarily a writer of books: "You must not be discouraged any more than we, by the small sale of a single book of short stories which have had magazine publication. Of course a writer cannot expect to make a great deal of money through the publication of books of fiction in comparison with what he gets from magazines. But the author gets his work before the critics, gets a recognition, a permanency of name, in short a *succès d'estime* which no amount of magazine publication can give him."

At the moment, Marquand's choice was made easy by the fact that not only Scribner's but the *Post* wanted him to do another novel in the vein of *The Unspeakable Gentleman*. Costain had informed him, "It happens that our list is pretty bare of book-length serials just now." In the fall of 1923, Marquand had completed a novel that again dealt with derring-do in a colonial seaport—and it was enthusiastically received in Philadelphia. In New York *The Black Cargo*, as it would be called, was more critically examined by Scribner's chief editor, Maxwell Perkins, who had begun to take an interest in the new writer. After studying Marquand's manuscript carefully, he wrote him a long letter in which he pointed out that the plot had flaws of carelessness and contrivance. Eliphalet Geer had marooned an enemy, then sent the young hero to kill him—but why hadn't he killed him himself in the first place? Wasn't young Charles too ready to accept the assignment? Perkins saw that such improbabilities might be justified if Marquand stressed motivation, particularly the feelings of psychological connection springing up mysteriously between Geer and Charles, but in the novel as written these were barely hinted at. Then, there was the ending, a matter Perkins considered more important than seeing that all the details "be buttoned up and tucked in." Marquand had wound things up to make a reconciliation possible between Geer and the other man when the chief excellence of the narrative had been its atmosphere of advancing doom. "To me the chief fascination of the narrative was in this theme of something awful to occur. And it did not occur." Thus Marquand's efforts had worked, after all, a kind of fraud by means of portentous stylistic flourishes and hints of tragic outcome that came to nothing.

Perkins, the literary counselor of Fitzgerald, Hemingway and Thomas Wolfe, was making a genuine literary judgment of Marquand's novel, and his criticism was thus rather different from the kind the young writer had received up to that time from Lorimer and his fellow editors, from Carl Brandt or even from Roger Burlingame. Marquand wrote him humbly: "As I glanced over the manuscript the other night a wave of deep gloom swept over me. There are so many parts of it I tried to make good which fall so flat and so much I wanted to do, which I have not done at all, and so much is overdone, and so much is not done enough. I wish I could get far enough away from it to see what the whole general effect is, because if it is as poor as the parts I read, I should be glad to read the burial service over it and consign the whole to the sea. My only consolation is that at least I tried to do *something* which, with all due respect, seems to me over and above what some people do who write better stories, and at least I tried honestly to put a breath of life, however vitiated, into the lungs of the unfortunate characters I endeavored to draw. At least I had a run at the windmill, even if it whirled me into the air and withdrew my feet from all foundations of technique and plausibility. My only hope is that I shall do better, much better, when I begin again."

Marquand had met in Perkins, of course, the ideal editor, whose intelligence, combined with respect for personal talent, would make him unique among American editors through a long career. Personal conferences with him, Marquand later remembered, were even more valuable than the written critiques of one's work. "Without being a writer himself, he could speak the language of writers better than any editor or publisher I ever met. He could make you feel that he understood everything about your individual work and your problems, and what is more he actually did understand. He also gave you a feeling of complete confidence in his suggestions and advice. The best thing about him was that he gave advice seldom and his suggestions were few, but somehow after an hour or two with Max, you went away with more confidence in yourself, and with a feeling that he and you both knew what you were trying to do, and with a burning desire to do it better. Usually only by listening intelligently and putting in a word now and then, he could make you talk and make all your nebulous creative ideas come clear. Without ever pulling a story to pieces, he could make you see what he liked in it, and what was good in it. But aside from this, he was always your friend, whether you wrote well or not. You always knew where you were with him." Perhaps if Perkins's influence had continued, Marquand's career might have progressed more quickly towards the literary self-realization that awaited him. But his writing did not move beyond the indulgences of romance for some years. *The Black Cargo*, it would turn out, would be the last book of Marquand's to be published by Scribner's.

The demands of Lorimer and the *Post* were more immediately significant as the price rose for a short tale Marquand could turn out in a few weeks. As the serial was being readied in the *Post* offices, early in December 1923, Costain called the turn: "Glad to hear that you have a short story under way. You ought to figure on doing short stories for the next five or six months, I would think." The publication of the book was being delayed, anyhow, because the *Post* illustrator, Arthur I. Keller, a favorite and high-priced artist, was behind in his work schedule. As a consequence, *The Black Cargo* could not appear in the *Post* until the following autumn, and book publication would have to wait on that. As a matter of fact, Keller's pictures came in so late that the *Post* serial had to run in the last weeks of October 1924. The book could not even come out for fall publication as Scribner's had planned, but was rescheduled again for the following spring. Book publication had already been announced for the fall list and Burlingame tried to get the *Post* to release the story earlier than the middle of October so that it might have a better chance with reviewers before the holiday season of maximum book sales. Burlingame pleaded that late publication would bring the book to the reviewers "at a time when their minds and columns were crowded to overflowing" and it would also coincide with other, bigger titles that Scribner's was pushing—Galsworthy's *The White Monkey* and Arthur Train's *The Needle's Eye*. "I think it would be a shame to launch so good a book as 'The Black Cargo' into such a maelstrom." But Burlingame's efforts were unavailing, and the book was simply held. It was finally published on February 13, 1925, just about a year after the original date set.

Meanwhile, all Marquand received from Scribner's was his advance of $250, and this was a particular favor since his contract called for payment of the advance on publication. It is not surprising, therefore, that Marquand's energies were chiefly directed towards pleasing Lorimer. Brandt constantly counseled him in shaping stories for the *Post*. "The Big Guys," which had defied the cardinal rule of the happy ending (its gangster-hero dies for his streak of mysticism), was reluctantly taken and Carl's brother and partner, Erdman Brandt, wrote: "Mr. Lorimer did not like this as well as some of your other stories and would prefer not to have any more in this vein. Personally, I was awfully glad that they took it because I was a little afraid of it for them but I think if you keep on the things we were talking about rather than this type, everything will be lovely." And Marquand applied himself industriously to pleasing "the big boss," as they called him. "A Friend of the Family," submitted a few months later, was deemed by the *Post* "the best piece of work you have done so far," and the price paid was raised beyond the rate Marquand had previously received. He was not even thinking in terms of serials that might eventually appear in book form. He had produced only one other to date, "Pozzi of Perugia," an uninspired sequence of episodes involving rich Americans abroad, fake antique jewelry, mystery, surprise, and bogus "atmosphere," which ran in the *Post* in November 1924. As he worked on it in May at Curzon's Mill, Marquand confessed to Burlingame that he was "low in mind," but in July he let him see it as a possibility for another book. In September, Burlingame wrote: "I thought the story 'Renaissance Steel' [a tentative title] was a fine story, with a lot of good suspense and intrigue and color, and that the main character is first rate. Perkins read the story too, and liked it. We are not entirely sure how it will go in a book; whether it is long enough, or substantial enough to make a complete book in itself." But there was no real interest at Scribner's in "Pozzi of Perugia," and the idea was quietly dropped.

So he continued to serve Lorimer, and this appreciative master wrote, finally, "On the strength of 'The Last of the Hoopwells' we are raising your price to $2,250." Marquand responded, "After a long summer's financial drought the news that you like the story fills me with great relief and your raising the price is an unexpected climax from which my head is still spinning in a most welcome way."

This was in October 1925. The preceding "summer of drought" had not been much alleviated by the publication of *The Black Cargo* by Scribner's. There had been good reviews. Donald Douglas wrote an enthusiastic appreciation in three different versions for the Sunday *World*, the *Literary Digest* and the *Nation*, in which he greeted Marquand's novel as an example of "true romance" that had gone beyond Stevenson's "fine avoidance of women and death" and Conrad's "florid mental gestures." Like Marquand's first novel, his second was welcomed particularly by those who disliked the new realism. Douglas wrote: "Many of us would prefer 'The Black Cargo' to a whole mess of midwestern cottages examined and exploited by the industrious realistic garbage men." Nevertheless, sales lagged behind those of the first novel—by September it had sold only three thousand copies. Marquand was grateful, he said, that it had at least done well enough to return Scribner's their investment if not to make money for anyone. Yet Perkins encouraged him to another effort: "'The Black Cargo' did not have as large a sale as it should have had, that is certain, but it is equally certain that it made a most excellent impression." But Marquand wrote from Cambridge at the end of the year that he was "dug in for the winter doing stories." He hoped to be able to attempt a novel again the following spring or summer, but it was clear that he could not, at this juncture, consider any but work that promised to pay. Of writing another novel, he had this to say: "I must say I don't look forward to it with confidence, because my career as a novelist seems damnably slender, and the rather chilly reception of 'The Black Cargo' hardly invites an encore. After looking over a few pages of it the other day I don't blame the public either." Perkins persisted: "The fact is the best writers are not the ones who make a great immediate success as a rule. Such successes are usually made by inferior writers who stand out for the moment and gradually fade away. If you look at the truly important artists you will see that practically every one of them had a more or less gradual advance to a certain point, and then a rapid one. Take Hardy for example." Of course there were exceptions, he admitted. That other Scribner author, Scott Fitzgerald, was conspicuously one of them. But "anyhow there is no use discussing the past. I can only say from the publisher's point of view you have done your part excellently well to date. We hope we will convince you that we can do our part excellently well before so very long." Marquand did not respond to this invitation but continued to grind out stories for Lorimer and put aside any thought of more ambitious fiction. Though some of the stories tended to treat a character or milieu used previously, it was not until 1929 that he found himself doing one after another dealing with certain families in a New England town. Out of these a sort of chronicle-novel emerged, and ten of the stories were published eventually as *Haven's End*. In 1929, at last, he would again produce a deliberately shaped novel, first serialized in the *Post* and then published as a book—*Warning Hill*.

There was one curious book done earlier which seems to have been a gesture of defiance against the coercive forces of the market. Shortly before leaving New York in the spring of 1925, Marquand had met Earl Balch, the publisher, who mentioned that he was interested in nonfiction about early American life. Marquand then told him about Timothy Dexter, the Newburyport colonial eccentric who had always fascinated him, and observed that a short life of Dexter might be an amusing project. The only previous biography had been done in 1838 by a man who disliked Dexter. After moving back to Newburyport for the summer, Marquand did a bit of research in the local library and newspaper files, and decided that he would really enjoy doing such a book, making it about forty thousand words long and illustrating it with old engravings of Dexter and his famous house on High Street with its effigy-studded fence. He told Balch that he did not think Scribner's would be interested in "such a tenuous and doubtful venture," and Balch declared that he would like to try it and he "believed it might go." Then, the project becoming a reality in his mind, Marquand realized that he had perhaps acted too quickly. He wrote Roger: "Now that Balch is clamoring for it to such an extent that I find myself inadvertently between two stools, I don't want to do anything that Scribner's does not like, and I think under all circumstance that it is only fair that you should have the refusal of it. I want very much to write it, solely for diversion, as I think I can do it rapidly, and it will be a pleasant change from fiction."

Burlingame had already had enough experience in publishing to realize that a promising author should not be permitted to wander off the home range. In the contract for *The Black Cargo* the clause which gives the publisher an option or "refusal" of the author's next book had been omitted. And Burlingame had then explained that Scribner's preferred simply "taking it for granted that unless an author has reason to be dissatisfied with our handling of his books he will bring us his next without question. If you should for any reason feel dissatisfied at any time, I hope you will tell me about it and see if we can't fix it up. I think people who know a good deal about the publishing business will tell you (if they are honest) that it is helpful to an author, as a rule, to stay with the same publisher." Of course, he insisted, Scribner's liked the Dexter idea. "We are all very much interested in it and I think a very special sort of book can be made of it which will excite a good deal of interest." Burlingame assumed that the matter was as good as settled—he would be up to Boston soon and they could talk about the "pictures and things" for the Dexter book. But Marquand had got himself in deeper with Balch than he had confessed and Burlingame had to swallow his disappointment. There was clearly some anxiety at Scribner's over Marquand's little detour with Balch, even though he assured his old friend that "it would be only an individual departure." Burlingame sounded more confident than he was when he wrote, "We know that however it may turn out, it will not in any way interfere with our publishing of your books in the future and I can assure you that it will have no effect on our relations."

The fact of the matter was that Marquand had no such view of his own development at this time as Burlingame or Perkins urged upon him. The months went by and he continued working on his magazine stories, though Perkins wrote at the end of the year, "You are in a highly favorable position to go much further in sales with the next novel, and we are looking forward to it." Marquand promised to have something to show him by late summer or early autumn. In October 1926, however, there was still no novel by Marquand in Perkins's hands and he made other suggestions—what about another biography on the order of the Dexter book? He had just heard that there was interesting material available about Silas Talbot, the commander of the sailing ship *Constitution*. Marquand replied, from Brattle Street where he was struggling to meet the bills of resettling and furnishing: "Much as I should like to do the man you suggest, I am out of the market at present, because I simply have to make some money. My plans are to do five short stories and then to finish a novel I have been working on which I shall let you see as soon as I get any of it in shape. This pushes a biography off into such a problematical future that I had better not think of it." Instead he had found new adventures for the irrepressible Willie Lipp—"I always felt Willie Lipp was worthy of further exploitation," declared Costain when "The Artistic Touch" came in to the *Post* offices. "The Cinderella Motif" aroused further enthusiasm when it arrived in January 1927: "The best story you have written in a long time. In fact it is the best story of Harvard any of us recalls reading. Why not do us another Harvard story next—in fact, if you had something about the same people it would be very nice." But in February, Perkins, having seen nothing of a novel manuscript, again suggested a biographical subject, the fascinating Ethan Allen, who "was one of those chaps who was against everything, chiefly because of the intense independence of his character"—not unlikely, he must have thought, to attract an admirer of that curmudgeon Dexter.

But 1927, like 1926, was to prove a year of much personal harassment and financial pressure. In February, when Perkins's suggestion reached him, Marquand was ill with infected tonsils and about to have them removed. He wrote from the hospital: "My plans are to do one more short story—in fact it is largely done now—and then to try a novel, starting, I hope, in the middle of March." March passed without any offering from Marquand, and Perkins, reading some of Marquand's Harvard stories in the *Post* in May, suggested that "if that were one of a group of stories of various kinds, about different types of boys at Harvard, I think you would have an admirable book." It was a somewhat desperate suggestion and Marquand rightly ignored it. In August Perkins hoped that a novel of some sort might be under way in time, at least, for publication the following year, but Marquand replied: "Though I have some of the novel done, 1928 seems a bit dubious, if the thing gets serialized first." Then he tried to reassure Perkins: "I won't let such a time lapse between novels again because they are much more appealing to me than short stories."

It was not until the following year that *Warning Hill* was actually written. In late October 1928, Costain informed Marquand that the masters of Independence Square were delighted to have a serial from him again at last and thought it "by long odds the best thing you have ever done." And a few weeks later Marquand had closed with another publisher, Little, Brown and Company of Boston, for production of the book. Money and nothing else had caused the break with Scribner's: even though Burlingame had left, Perkins continued to impress Marquand as the best of literary guides. But in the place of Scribner's paltry $250 advance, Alfred McIntyre and Herbert Jenkins, head of Little, Brown, offered, as Brandt emphasized to Marquand, "$1,000 and a decent royalty." Brandt, who had swung the deal, was proud of the new conditions. Although Scribner's had finally sold fifty-five hundred copies of *The Black Cargo*, which was better than they had previously thought, Marquand's agent informed him that "Alfred would go ahead on a campaign based on a minimum sale of 10,000 copies. In other words he would plan his publicity and advertising as if there were to be a 10,000 sale of the book." Brandt pointed out, too, that the location of his new publisher was an advantage to Marquand now that he was settled in Boston: "You would have the satisfaction of having your publisher near at hand and he could use you for publicity purposes."

Perkins had a polite, somewhat melancholy conference with Bernice Baumgarten, who had become the editor and agent in charge of Marquand's affairs at the Brandt office. "He was deeply disappointed, of course, that he was to lose your work," she reported to Marquand, "and he told me that it had always been his conviction, and implied it was the firm's, that you would be one of the people who would eventually come out on top, and that they had been publishing your work and supervised promotion to this end. I told him frankly that Scribner's had never given us any indication that this was their attitude, and that I doubted very much whether they had told you about it. I also reminded him that before the publication of 'The Black Cargo' we had definitely told him that if we were not satisfied with the sales on that book, it would mean a change of publishers. I have talked with Carl about this and our joint opinion is that if they had so much belief in you, it is a little strange that they kept it such a secret from us and from the trade in general."

What the change meant, certainly, was that the Brandt agency and Marquand himself did not choose to accept any longer Scribner's idea of simply carrying Marquand along with prestige publication of his fiction until he became an important literary figure. They were convinced that his books, like his magazine stories, could make money then and there. And Marquand, whatever his feelings of attachment to Perkins, must have felt he had no alternative just then. His second child was ill with pneumonia and about to undergo an expensive operation, and he had reached a point of acute exasperation and desperation in his struggle to maintain family life on the basis that he had so cheerfully accepted when he married Christina. For these reasons he had made his break with Scribner's. Towards the end of his life he recollected: "I thought it was fair to make a complete break with Scribner's without telling them I had a higher offer and giving them the opportunity to equal it." In looking back over his subsequent career in a mood of some disenchantment with Little, Brown, whose weakness, he then felt, "had always been its dearth of people who understand writers and writing," he nevertheless told a young friend and fellow Little, Brown author: "I still regret that I took the step. I think continuity in publishing one's books is more valuable than it appears at the time. I have watched Sinclair Lewis and others move from publisher to publisher without, as far as I can see, gaining in the process."

But in 1928, of course, Marquand had already perceived that he was set on the treadmill, and there was no dismounting. He was not encouraged by his progress towards success. Three years earlier, in 1925, he had replied dispiritedly when the secretary of his Harvard class had asked for an autobiographical statement: "Not the longest thoughts in the watches of the night reveal to me any reminiscences either sufficiently startling or different from those of struggling humanity to permit my setting them down without overcoming the casual reader with a horrid species of boredom." Later that year his old *Transcript* friend W. A. Macdonald came down to see him at Curzon's Mill and wrote up his visit in a piece for his paper. He gives us Marquand at thirty-two, a spare young man of medium height bowed a little as he walks back and forth in a room—just as he did years before during their conversation in the turret on Pinckney Street when they tried to write a novel of exotic adventure together. Macdonald's article is accompanied by the pencil sketch of the Stockbridge artist M. O. Kobbé, against which the reader can check his description of a good-looking young American: "His nose is straight, his mouth good, his chin solid"—like the hero of a *Post* story—and he has light parted hair that "strings along his forehead" and somewhat peculiar almond-shaped eyes. He talks in a slow monologue, and is "sparse of gestures," but suddenly grows humorous and animated, and his voice, richer and deeper than when they had first known each other, does not become more rapid but "grows more striking," its measured and genteel tones turning rough, "enriched with forthright words," as Macdonald politely put it. At the end of the most solemn statement he has a way of breaking off with a chuckle. The effect is enigmatic.

When Macdonald visited him late in the fall of 1925, *Lord Timothy Dexter of Newburyport, Mass.* had just been published and caused a little flutter where perhaps it mattered most to Marquand, that is, in Newburyport. The handsomely printed and illustrated book showed up on many parlor tables there, and people began to recall "that Marquand boy," who had managed to make a sort of hero out of an ancient townsman they had regarded as simply ridiculous; and Aunt Molly grew suddenly very sociable and asked her old acquaintances to tea so that she could read out choice passages. But Marquand knew that he was not about to take his place there in the shadows of the old town where Dexter was a legend along with Marquands and Curzons. He and Christina had already been packing furniture for the move to Cambridge, and he had painted over little Johnny's nursery furniture and rocking horse. In fact, most of their own things had already gone to Brattle Street by the time Macdonald arrived, and Christina and the baby had left for a couple of weeks in Stockbridge.

The old house had become again, as it had been in his childhood, a place one visited but did not remain in, a place of passing dreams. As Macdonald sat with Marquand in the old dining room it had, for the moment, a haunted look as the light from the window grew dim along the surface of a blue and white Chinese "amphora" on the sill, a Marquand or Curzon relic of sailing-ship days. Macdonald felt something he could not identify as he watched the light change and candlelight take its place. "The figures on the urn," he wrote, "move in the light of the candles. They seem to move like marching men." But Marquand, laughing in his abrupt way, must have let it be seen that he knew there was something make-believe about his posture there amid the shadows. "I was in love with candlelight and old ships," he said later, but he also added, "I was pulled by economic strings, too." He had just finished "The Last of the Hoopwells" for Lorimer, putting something of the historical nostalgia of the Dexter book into the *Post* story, as the editor had suggested. "I have been loyal to the old home town as you suggest. In fact I think I have worked off a whole life-time of loyalty," he wrote Lorimer when he sent him a copy of the biography. He was not, however, done with the Newburyport subject—he would never be done with it—but somehow

Dexter had helped him to a new, less sentimental view. That quaint, wisecracking old plebeian Newburyporter was, really, a strange ghost for Marquand to cherish. He had brought him to life again, after previous writers had buried him with deprecation, and made him, as Lawrence Stallings noted, the prototype of the self-made man who mocks what he has attained: "half Barnum and half modern captain of industry, whose stunts and follies were worthy of the sage of Bridgeport, whose proclamations and bulls against learning smacked of the philosopher of Dearborn." The reviewers, who had also included Bernard De Voto and Meade Minnegerode, had made it a *succès d'estime*. It was, in fact, the most accomplished piece of writing Marquand had yet done, "a gay and heckling narrative" with a whimsicality and grace in the mode of Laurence Sterne, a unique American mock-epic.

Of course, Marquand had not expected that it would be snatched up by the readers of best sellers. In later years he would mystify others by declaring that this forgotten volume was his own favorite among all his books. This must have been so because, in the first place, he had written it for his own satisfaction at a time when he was also writing desperately to order for others. And the future author of *Apley* and other works of elegant derisiveness had a personal feeling, too, for the leather dresser who became a "Lord" and bought the finest house on High Street, Newburyport—and then proceeded to thumb his nose at the street's other residents.

Meanwhile, as Marquand told Macdonald, he was writing a thousand words a day—a good rate for a writer of fiction who understood, like Dexter, how to make his way.

10

Depression Days

The summer of 1926 was to prove a season of wretchedness, though the Marquands had planned it as a holiday from work and the domestic abrasions of Brattle Street. Roger Burlingame had started the whole thing by talking of his own plans to leave the treadmill life at last; he was resigning his job at Scribner's and going to France, as so many young would-be writers were doing. He urged his friends to go with him, at least for a month or two. They would visit the battle sites both men remembered and the Paris that had embraced them briefly on their way home in 1918. Christina had been depressed; she was somehow less able than ever to cope with small problems in the new apartment. John, grinding out his stories, had felt irritated and driven, and had begun to experience spasms of stomach pain that suggested an incipient ulcer. They both were delighted with the idea of going to Europe again.

The plan was no sooner conceived, as early as January, than it came to the ears of Mr. and Mrs. Sedgwick. Christina's father was at Cannes, having just paid a visit to England, which he loved with the passion peculiar to many older Americans of English stock. He had seen his cousins Basil and Anne de Selincourt, who made him feel loved in return. "They seem to really care for me. I don't know why, because nobody at home likes me any more. Anybody who shows me the slightest affection these days, in whatever form, touches me almost to tears," he wrote his daughter with characteristic self-pity and implied reproach. Then he had heard of John and Christina's contemplated trip, and he declared, "Did I not know John and know that he was like Samuel Taylor Coleridge in so far at least that he is temperamentally incapable of fulfilling his promises, I should be delirious with joy, assuming of course that you would both play around with me a little." He at once made proposals, benignant and engulfing: Mrs. Sedgwick would soon be joining him and would bring with her "one of our, or her, two cars, preferably the big one, in which we can tour England and Scotland." John and Christina could then settle down in Berford, in Oxfordshire, near the de Selincourts, where he had already spotted a lovely cottage which the Sedgwicks might rent for the use of their daughter and son-in-law. In Alick's view it would make a lovely opportunity for John to be thrown into association with the literary de Selincourts—Basil was an established man of letters in England and Anne Douglas Sedgwick de Selincourt was already the author of several successful novels. "It would be an education for him such as he has never had, and the people he might come in contact with might be of inestimable value to him," he wrote with condescension.

One can imagine John Marquand's reaction to these proposals. He and Christina were not going to England and not snuggling up to the de Selincourts, but to France, with Roger—and to this idea they stuck, though it was to prove difficult to elude Mr. Sedgwick's expectation that they would "play around" with him. And it would be difficult to resist the cossetings of Mrs. Sedgwick, who did indeed arrive with her big Citroën and was waiting for them in France when they landed in May accompanied by Roger and three-year-old Johnny. Elaborate plans were made for joint diversion and sightseeing for this incompletely harmonious company, but from the start there was confusion and tension, not alleviated by the efforts of everyone to adapt himself strenuously to the wishes of the others. After a hectic week or two in Paris, Marquand's stomach was so troublesome that he was getting X rays to determine the possibility of an ulcer, and he was put on a wineless diet by the doctor he consulted. Mrs. Sedgwick, to give the livelier members greater freedom, had gone off to Aix-les-Bains with the baby and an English nursemaid, though Christina wrote after her: "John and I agree that with your departure and Johnny's a certain solidity has left the party. We seem all flimsy and at loose ends." While Marquand stayed in his hotel, following a regime "of bed and starvation that is good for everything but his soul," the rest of the group (including also a certain Olga, a particular friend of Mr. Sedgwick's) went out for little drives and dined in restaurants to which Mr. Sedgwick guided them. Soon John was better and the caravan proceeded to its new base at Tours, from whence there would be explorations of the châteaux of the Loire region.

Yet somehow there was the fatal compounding of diverse tastes and temperaments that dooms such enterprises at the start: the desire of Roger and John for some rambling on their own terms, Alexander Sedgwick's somewhat differing ideas of a good time, and Christina's attacks of fatigue and anxiety (in the midst of a girlish eagerness for adventure she had sudden crippling impulses to collapse into the arms of her mother and suffered seizures of guilt in regard to her father's demands). Her conflicts of emotion were conspicuous in the letters she sent her mother. She wrote her from Paris in the middle of June, when they were finally ready to swing out upon their tour before coming back to Brittany for a period of rest: "It would be lovely to go to Aix but I think if we *ever* get off on this trip we ought to benefit ourselves by seeing the châteaux and places of historic France. I feel exactly as if I were in a bad dream where there is time for everything but it is slipping by and nothing is done." She had gone to Tours with her father only to find there a message from John that she return at once to Paris to help him drive the car with Roger, who did not know how; her father, naturally, felt abandoned, and she, guilty; on top of all she had a toothache. On rejoining her father she mentioned that she felt exhausted and "he leapt to the inevitable Sedgwick conclusion from which I was unable to dissuade him."

She wondered if she were really ill, and the Paris doctor she consulted "because I was afraid I might be going to have appendicitis or something" said that she was simply run down and nervous. "I can rest when we get to Brittany," she told her mother. But she continued to feel a sense of collapse more emotional than physical. John showed a surprising inclination to nurse and "mother" her—he had told her that as a little boy he had cried because he couldn't be the mother in games of "house" with his cousins. He made her go to bed and sat in their bedroom with her and Roger and Olga, having an "absurd discussion as to whether it wouldn't be better for all concerned if Olga married John and I married Roger." She was a child again and the discussion had the unreality of childhood fantasy. Meanwhile, "Papa" languished in Tours, and as she tossed about on her play-invalid bed she thought it seemed "so mean to stay in Paris. I think once Papa gets off to Aix, I will be better because trying to combine Papa's idea of a 'party' good time with John when he isn't well is enough to give anyone nervous prostration." Her father's complaints at being left alone in Tours prompted her observation that *she* would love to spend a day alone, "but John tells me he won't leave me anywhere which is very sweet of him—in fact he will give up the trip or anything. But I can be quiet in Brittany and I shall never have another chance to motor when I am comparatively young through the châteaux country." Above all, she longed to be nursed like a child. "I wish the old days were back and that John and I were comfortably ill in bed and you were taking care of us."

Christina herself must have intended to express a certain ludicrous quality in the cross-purposes surrounding her, and only the fact that in a few weeks she was actually prostrated, in what was designated a nervous breakdown by her doctors, gives a sinister tone to her desire to go to bed, along with John, and be nursed by her mother. Seemingly, the Marquands and Burlingame were able to carry out a part of their original plan. They saw the châteaux and went to Bourges and the Midi, and the two men went alone to the old battlefields healed by wheat but still recognizable, and the ruined villages that had hardly been rebuilt at all since they had last seen them. Christina enjoyed their explorations, though she wrote, "The country is lovely but I must say in that respect that the heart contracts in thinking of Cambridge." In the first week of July she was a patient in the American Hospital at Neuilly-sur-Seine and John, expressly forbidden to visit her, was at Saint-Malo with his small son and his parents-in-law.

It is difficult to know what medical reasoning kept Marquand away from his wife's bedside, but as far as one can tell, her condition—apparently of deep depression—seemed to her doctors to be connected with her feelings about her husband. She herself made this connection. After a month in bed in the American Hospital she was judged better enough to move into the Hôtel des Réservoirs at Versailles in the custody of a trained nurse. But even then, though Mrs. Sedgwick was able to visit her, there was still a ban on a visit from Marquand. In a response to a telegram from Saint-Malo early in August, Mrs. Sedgwick wrote that she had asked the doctor how soon John would be allowed to see Christina, "realizing your desperate state," and the doctor had suggested that another week of waiting would be enough—but Christina "wants to be alone for two weeks after I leave."

Meanwhile he went to the beach at Paramé with Johnny. He wrote her: "I am glad to hear that you are doing well, and I hope you are feeling much better every day. This morning I took Johnny bathing in the surf. He is growing so accustomed to the waves and to the water that I think in another year I might teach him to swim a few strokes. It is very pleasant to watch him play with the other children in the sand, for the beach here is a complete nursery from ten in the morning to six at night with little Anglais and Français running about with shovels and pails and balls and nets, building castles in the sand. Johnny has developed a heavy coat of tan and is most cheerful, though he is too young yet to do anything constructive and can only dig aimlessly without achieving any concrete result." And Marquand ended his report with a statement painful in its awkwardness, "I hope you think of me sometimes in a favorable way and don't forget I am very fond of you and love you."

He became that August a familiar figure on the beach among the summer crowds, a bemused young man who looked lonely despite the child's company. Even when accompanied by Mr. and Mrs. Sedgwick he had a way of seeming to be only distantly connected with them. To while away the time they took him for drives in the neighborhood—to Dinard or to Mont-Saint-Michel—and when it was realized that he must wait longer before seeing Christina, Mr. Sedgwick invited him to go to the Channel Islands by the little steamer from Saint-Malo and then spend ten days touring with him in England. Mr. Sedgwick was now able to realize his idea of conducting John through the English scenes he felt so much at home in. Marquand reported their progress to Christina with a certain forced jocularity: "As you can probably perceive by this letter-paper I am at the midway station toward that land of milk and honey where all is bright and fair and where, since my association with you and your family I expect to find a peace past all understanding, shot through with siren's songs, which will rob me of all desire to return home," he wrote from Jersey. "When I said that I could not afford the trip to England but could only do the Channel Islands, your father was as kind and sweet as I have ever seen him and said that he had had no fun of any sort all summer and had been expecting that Ellery would come over to take a trip with him to England. As Ellery's staying in America was a crushing disappointment to him, he asked if I would not come to England for ten days as his guest." Despite his dry note, Marquand seems to have liked the mild little islands—Capri translated into English—from which his own ancestor, Daniel Marquand, had emigrated. The presence of his father-in-law provided him with a certain amusement as they went in a charabanc around the coast of Jersey: "The conductor enlivened the journey with many little jokes which your Papa could not understand until I explained them. For instance we passed a mother goat and her offspring and the conductor said, 'That's a goat and no kid,' and then he said, 'Why are Eden cigarettes like Adam and Eve?' 'Because when you've 'ad 'em you leave.'" They visited a prehistoric burial mound on Jersey which was entered through a long, low gallery at the base. "As it was built by a race of men only 4′9″ high who generally assumed a squatty position, the entrance is horribly low. As your Papa entered he gave his head a terrible crack on a neolithic boulder and shouted, 'Damn these people—why can't they build a place where you don't fracture your skull?'" However, in England Mr. Sedgwick was in better command of the situation and full of informative chatter and reminiscences of previous visits as he took John with him on a six-day tripper coach through the southern counties. In London they "did the town" like conscientious tourists and ate in the most famous eating houses, and her father wrote Christina with complacency, "I have shown John everything it was possible to in the four days we had."

But finally Marquand returned to France and to Versailles. Christina wrote her mother with a kind of humor that might have contained an element of schizophrenic blunting of affect: "I was sitting on the steps in front of the chateau yesterday looking at that wonderful view when on looking around I saw a very nice-looking young man who turned out to be my husband. He spent the night here and I saw him last night and this morning and we had a lovely time." What Marquand saw for his part emerges out of the past in a surviving snapshot of Christina still in her wheelchair on this or perhaps another day in the palace gardens. One sees a delicate-looking, melancholy-faced young woman with a fashionable cloche pulled down over her ears, her long slender legs stretched out before her and her feet, in pretty strapped sandals, crossed at the ankles, her hands laced together in her lap in an attitude of limp resignation. Although the French neurologist pronounced her cured, she did not feel ready to resume normal life just yet. She exclaimed to her mother: "Dr. Claude doesn't want to see me again! In all ways the French are *durs* compared to us. French women are not nearly so high strung as we are." Of her French doctor she said again: "I am consumed with curiosity about what strange cases he treats—I am so banal to him. His entire bill was $24.00." She decided to continue taking the medicines he had prescribed during her illness until she could see Dr. Riggs in Stockbridge on her return.

Marquand was studying patience still, though he declined the Sedgwicks' invitation to go with them to England to meet the de Selincourts. "I am sorry to say John has decided not to go over to England and is going to settle somewhere in the vicinity for the next two weeks," Christina apologized to her mother. And she herself still shrank from taking up her marriage. "John is most considerate about everything and careful. He wanted to stay here but I thought I should want to see him all the time and it would be too much—so he quite understood." Indeed, he wrote, following their meeting after so many weeks: "I can't begin to tell you how glad I was to see you for a few minutes and know that you are real and not a myth. Remember I shall be waiting for you as soon as you are better. Today I did not see you because I was afraid of running a good thing into the ground."

While she stayed on in Versailles till the end of the month, when they were to sail for home, Marquand spent a bit of time at last in Paris—as he had been wanting to since they had come to France—without the Sedgwicks, who had taken Johnny with them to England. He was soon "enmeshed with sculptors and artists of various sorts," as Christina remarked to her mother. Among others he met a young American writer named Drew Hill, who was another of Carl Brandt's clients and whose wife, Carol, had written a flapper novel called "Wild," which she was trying to get published. Nearly ten years younger than he was, carefree and uninhibited, the couple was welcome company to Marquand just then. Carol, in particular, refreshed his weary spirits. She was another of those untrammeled girls he had met in New York before his marriage—girls from nowhere who had slipped from the restraining bonds of family or "background" and who were simply, as he later vainly urged Christina to be, "natural." She was twenty-three years old and the very opposite of the languid Christina—independent, energetic, gay. He did not know and did not care who her people—in Montclair, New Jersey—were, and neither, it seemed, did she. Marquand passed some cheerful hours in the Hills' company, often at parties that sprang up from moment to moment in the large community of young Americans camped in Paris in those days. Carol, who later considered her relation with Marquand the great romance of her life, thought that a seed of mutual interest had been planted on one particular occasion when Marquand and the Hills had been guests at a country house party. John had been struggling to get back to his writing after the disturbances of the summer, and she had carried a typewriter out into the garden and invited him to break through his "block"—a writer's malady from which he had never suffered before and never would again—by dictating directly to her. In the shade of a great mulberry tree, as she liked to recall, he walked up and down as she typed his recital of a new story. Others might later dispute her claims to have been a decisive personal influence upon John Marquand, but she was always to be confident of one thing: she had helped him to discover that he could dictate his fiction, a technique that in time became invariable with him. Anyone might have done this, perhaps, but only some women had Carol's gift for meeting his necessities. His wife had not.

On October 1, the Marquands sailed for New York on the Royal Mail *Orca*. Even aboard ship John carefully respected Christina's reluctance to rejoin him altogether, and she was installed in a three-berth stateroom alone, right next to the ship's doctor, while he had an inside cabin on the deck below. When they landed, there was no question, of course, of going to the Cambridge apartment: Marquand took her directly to the Austen Riggs Foundation in Stockbridge, where the remarkable Dr. Riggs was waiting for her. John then returned to New York and spent most of the next two months uneasily camping at the University Club or visiting his parents in Wilmington when he was not in Stockbridge.

Christina remained at the Riggs Foundation until December. She underwent its famous program for the treatment of neurosis, a pioneer technique of intensive exploration of the patient's history, something like Freudian psychoanalysis combined with an education in self-discipline and activity. The patients studied certain little "green books" or pamphlets, which had such titles as "The Individual," "Sensations and Emotions," "Adaptation," "Daily Living," "Sleep and Its Emotions." They also strove for rehabilitation through a regime of physical exercise, useful work in the "Craft Shop," rest and recreation. Riggs was a tall, dark-eyed, intense man whose personal magnetism was an important ingredient in the process. He had known Christina since 1919, when he had established the foundation against some local opposition but with the fervent support of Alexander Sedgwick, who was one of the first trustees. Riggs was undoubtedly a father figure to most of his patients, and particularly to Christina, who found him more commanding and reassuring than the whimsical, emotionally greedy Alick.

Dr. Riggs, it seems, had no trouble in identifying the root of Christina's troubles in the nature of her upbringing and the conflict produced by her marriage: "Dr. Riggs thinks I am not seriously ill and that my illness is due primarily to what he calls emotional conflicts in my life and my adaptation to it. He says that in some measure a great deal of the difficulty would have arisen with anyone without a certain sort of training which the boys get in boarding school and college." The "special atmosphere" of the Sedgwick family had certainly promoted her emotional and practical dependence on others, most of all on her parents. In pondering Riggs's hortatory tracts Christina observed: "I feel they strike at the root of all my own faults and most of the family's faults. The pamphlet on efficiency, for instance. If I can really get to practicing what they preach I really should be a different person." Riggs fastened on the tendency she had shown to welcome support from her parents in the form of gifts and attentions, even to appeal for it by her demonstrations of helplessness. Such behavior had been a sore point for her husband. It was this tendency that her father had in mind when he remarked sometime later, "You must have a care not to have confidences with [your mother] and then blame her if she reacts to them." After she went home and Mrs. Sedgwick was planning a present of some sort—perhaps the wages of a servant—Christina was forced to explain, referring the matter to Dr. Riggs: "He thinks that your darling presents to me should be regulated. I am very much ashamed that my 'talking poor' as I frequently have done to you has been the cause of your worrying about our finances. I know I wasn't satisfied with my lot but I certainly never meant you to think of making it up to me. I think that is what Papa means when he says I make confidences to you and then blame you for reacting to them. Dr. Riggs's point of view was at first quite a shock to me and I couldn't quite understand what he meant. I do now more and more. I think I have been very weak and childish for a long time now and held to no steady course of action. So that I ended by falling completely between two stools. I am awfully sorry about everything I have said to you about John and me. I had no business to."

Riggs also concluded that the Sedgwick feeling of superiority to others had been no help to Christina and John Marquand's marriage—that it had badly abraded John's nerves in his relations with his in-laws and been even more damaging through Christina's unconscious acceptance of it. There would always afterwards be dispute on this point: the Sedgwicks would insist, sincerely, that they had never condescended, yet John Marquand would insist that they had. "Riggs gathered from you the impression that I and your mother hold [John] lightly," Alexander Sedgwick wrote his daughter shortly after she left the Stockbridge sanatorium. "This is, however, very far from the fact, as I have been very proud of him at times. Neither did your mother hold him lightly, and as far as I know has always, until perhaps quite recently, treated him with genuine affection and consideration. As far as I am concerned I did everything in Europe to make him my friend." But how they really looked on Marquand is indicated by a remark made earlier by Christina's brother Shan. "Personally," he wrote to his father, "I have always felt that what wore on Tissie more than anything else was her constant fear that John was not being appreciated or not given consideration in the measure that his ego demanded it. She has been *too* solicitous of his happiness and has always made allowances for his selfishness."

Shan also opined: "The marriage will become surely a failure if Christina is not taught to be independent and given strength, and John does not learn that Christina is independent and that complaining and teasing and making jokes which are really at her expense are not the part of either a man or a gentleman. I wish he knew how ridiculous he is to dare to take such liberties with such a superior person in every way!" Besides confirming the idea that Christina was deemed her husband's "superior," Shan's remarks suggest that Marquand's comic stories were recognized as an aggressive weapon. He had already formulated the legend about his wife and her family that his storytelling was to establish as truth in the minds of others and in his own mind. Yet it should not be supposed that the legend had no basis. As has just been seen, so expert an analyst as Austen Riggs could identify the substance beneath the stories.

Undoubtedly, Christina's stay at the foundation had been illuminating to her and perhaps corrective. Yet Marquand's distrust and weariness did not vanish with her recovery. He resented, probably, the privileged status of invalid she continued to claim. He too had suffered—or so he must have felt—with no one to wipe his brow. His stomach pains continued to signal his own psychic distress, and when the time came for Christina to leave the foundation he gave her notice of a new sternness in his attitude by advising her that *his* doctor had ordered him to avoid strain and excitement and that he would not be able to drive to Stockbridge for her. She could take the train, which he would meet. He also warned her that he could not promise to remove her worries about the tasks and obligations represented by the apartment in Cambridge, which he had at last opened: "I am sorry that you begin to feel a lack of ability to cope with your situation. Of course I shall be patient and do everything I can to help you, though in the light of the apartment, I am somewhat at a loss as to just where you want to be helped. Much as I love you it seems to me that I have possessed in this whole episode only the limited moves of a king upon the chessboard, and a corresponding lack of power to turn the balance in any direction. It is you that circumstances have endowed with the queen's brisk and energetic powers, upon which I still must wait as I did in France. Otherwise I think you are much better qualified to assume initiative than you have been before, and I have a much greater faith in the accuracy of your judgment. You are receiving professional advice, and I hesitate to add any except this, and this only because I am your senior in age, and know considerably more than you do of life and, I think, of its values: Never lose your sense of proportion to an extent of considering that you and your own affairs are of any vast weight in the world, for then you become an egotist, of whom I could name several in your family. In fact, I believe that egotism is something of a weakness with you and not helped by the Riggs Foundation. If you can get to feeling that your whole problem with me doesn't amount to a particular damn, you will find yourself able to enter your life without nervousness and tension and in a perfectly natural way. For God's sake try to be natural and not make everything you do a strain, and I know you'll be alright. I don't mean my letter to be severe and I love you very much."

And so, neither entirely reassured, they again undertook their life together. Johnny returned to his parents after six months with his grandfather and grandmother, and winter came to Cambridge with mingled cold sunshine and gray skies matched by the dirtied slush in the streets. They went down to the frozen Charles, and Marquand put on his skates and tried to pull the child on his sled while he shrieked and protested until they took him coasting down a little hill. In the evenings the parents resumed the habit of reading aloud to each other, which they had begun on their honeymoon: this time the book was *Pride and Prejudice*. One day they drove to Curzon's Mill to pick up some more things that had been left in the Brick House. The Mill, with its old haunted atmosphere of past lives, mingled its ghosts with the ghost of their own first happiness, and Christina wrote: "I thought of Yeats' line, 'all things lovely and broken, all things worn out and old.' I don't know why I love it so, but I do. When I came to going over the Brick House, now all dismantled of course, I realized we shouldn't be coming back. I felt so much 'the heart-break in the heart of things.'"

Marquand's stomach troubles continued and there were more examinations and X rays. The doctors found "a small spot which may be a very little ulcer," Christina reported to her mother, and he gave up smoking and was placed on a restricted diet. He had trouble with his tonsils, too, which were constantly infected so that he came down with fevers and was in a chronic state of irritability. In the first week of February he went into the hospital to have them removed, and for weeks afterwards suffered; they had been pulled out by the roots, a new technique that left the throat painfully sore. Tensions vibrated between the Marquands again.

They began to argue about summer plans, for naturally the Sedgwicks expected that they would be moving down to Stockbridge. Marquand, working in earnest now on his long-delayed novel, stormed at the idea of living in the midst of the Sedgwick caravansary, with relatives and visitors coming and going and a dozen demands each day for his social participation. Christina still hoped to please both her parents and John: "Do you think you could ask cousin Emily if she will let John use her little house while we're there in August?" she wrote her mother. "I think he'll have to have a place outside the house to work in. He could take some sandwiches and work all day." And even if that could be arranged, there might, she knew, be difficulties: "You see if John goes up the first his book won't be finished so that means he will be pretty busy. And he will simply have to lead an independent life while he is working. If you on consideration think that this will be a source of friction with Papa, perhaps we had better not try the experiment. I could come alone and John could perhaps make some arrangement here. But this seems so unnatural to me. I should think Papa could just accept the fact that he is working and not expect him to go out to dinner or golf club teas all the time. If you seriously think Papa will not understand if John leads his own life, I think we had better not try it."

Probably this tone of reasonable discussion did not persist. There was a mounting hysteria, in fact, behind Christina's words, for John Marquand did not expect to come under any circumstances, while Mrs. Sedgwick protested that "nobody will think it natural" if they did not. Christina was again pregnant, moreover, and the advent of another child presented a challenge of tasks and burdens to come. The depressive gloom to which she had surrendered in France reappeared as winter ended, and she suddenly arrived in Stockbridge one day to see Dr. Riggs. She wept that she wanted a divorce. John, for his part, insisted on the continuance of their marriage in terms that were hardly romantic: "I—whether wisely or unwisely is not the point—have assumed certain responsibilities which cannot be avoided by tears, regrets, or emotion. No matter how sorry either you or I may be for it we have agreed to help in building up the next generation. This involves building up a home environment and by our example doing what we can to make our children see indirectly what is best in life. If you think it over I am sure you will understand that this responsibility is not made any greater because you are about to bear a second child. With the advent of Johnny in the world we both assumed this responsibility. The advent of an addition to our family only clarifies it.

"By living together in a polite society and with the benefits of clergy you and I have evolved an initial responsibility which did not before exist, and it has been necessary to adjust ourselves to it. Please don't think you are the only one who has had to make sacrifices for this adjustment, or who is being obliged to make them. Whether it drags upon our shoulders and whether it causes me ulcer of the stomach and you emotional depression; whether it stifles our intellectual independence—a favorite but inaccurate expression of yours, for I do not believe that you were ever in your life intellectually independent—has nothing to do with the point. As far as I am concerned I know that it would do me no good to shirk or run away from my obligations. Please do not think that you are the only one who has thought of it."

It was a grim and even banal basis for the resumption of their marriage, yet the marriage was resumed. They had been making plans, anyway, for a change that seemed to mark some kind of advance. They had decided in February to buy a house on Beacon Hill at 43 West Cedar Street, a substantial town house that seemed by its very solidity to assert the enduring qualities of their union. They had neither of them enjoyed Cambridge particularly. Christina had been disappointed in finding few friends there besides Jim Conant, Marquand's old college companion, who had stayed on to teach chemistry at Harvard. "The college set with the exception of the Conants are nice but entirely interested in their own world and with no outlook beyond and consequently have no interest in us," she told her mother. Beacon Hill in Boston undoubtedly represented values and associations with which she felt more at home and perhaps for Marquand there was gratification in the fact that he could count on himself to pay the mortgage of $29,000—though it seemed a huge sum, then—for a house as well placed as Dexter's mansion on High Street in Newburyport. Anyhow, Christina was sure they could manage it with only one maid and a three-days-a-week cleaning woman because the kitchen and dining room were on the same floor.

That summer, following Dr. Riggs's advice, they did not go to Stockbridge but rented a house in Weston, a half hour out of town. The house was on a hill and Christina was delighted with it—"palatial, a gentleman's house, with a big drawing and dining room, our bed room and private bath and a room and bath for Johnny and his nurse"—and there was a golf course right beside it where John could play. Gardiner and Conney Fiske lived nearby and frequently visited them, and Christina, seemingly more contented, waited for the birth of her second child.

Was John Marquand happy? No doubt human happiness is a compartmentalized structure. Years later, when he was in love with Carol Brandt, he looked back at one day in that summer when he judged himself totally wretched—and ready to fall in love with someone else. He had seen the Hills from time to time in New York during the past year and when they came up to Weston for a visit, he realized that their marriage, too, was running aground. That day Marquand had taken Carol for a drive in his secondhand Cadillac and stopped at a refreshment pavilion at the edge of Walden Pond in Concord. He recalled: "Here we were sitting in that pavilion, an excrescence which would have turned Thoreau's stomach, and we both ordered ice cream. I was supposed to have a small meal in-between meals. You told me a good deal of what was on your mind. You were obviously very unhappy and confused, and so was I, perhaps even more so, because I had been going through a winter and a spring which still sometimes awakens me in a cold sweat. I tried, I recall, to give you some objective advice. I can think of no one less equipped to give it, but then, no advice has really any current value because in the end no one acts from reason. In any event, I was, and still am deeply touched that you should have come to me in Weston, Mass. and that you should have even thought that I might have been of any help to you. I have often thought afterwards of that scene by Walden Pond, more often than you can imagine. In fact, for years I have not liked much to drive by the place. You see, I was both unhappy and half in love with you, and at the same time I had a number of ideals which I seem to have lost later. I was intensely conscious that I must in no way take advantage of you in your upset condition—I was too fond of you for that—and besides you had told me how peculiarly many married men in their thirties had behaved towards you, if you may remember. I was incensed at the impertinence of these married men, and I greatly wished that you would not think me like them. Besides I was myself a married man in my thirties trying to make a situation work which someone should have told me was patently impossible. Just a month or so before, Christina and I rushed to

Dr. Riggs with the news that she definitely wanted to leave me, and I was told this happened with many pregnant women and that I should stand by and do my best. Somehow my sense of responsibility was far stronger than it seems to be at the present. What would have happened to us, I wonder, if I had said to you what I thought of saying as I ate that wretched ice cream? As it was, on our way back I never ventured so much as to touch your hand, though I cannot say that the idea did not occur to me in a very forceful way. I was afraid that it would have shocked you, which shows how little I understood women and myself—in fact I never did venture to do such a thing until some fifteen years later."

In late August of 1927, however, the Marquands moved into 43 West Cedar Street, and on September 14 the new baby, named for its mother, was born. They began what seems to have been a stretch of tolerable married life, the "compromise" which is supposed to be the basis of most marriages that survive early disenchantment. They were both more contented in the new house and, out of different impulses, gratified by the sense it gave them of an established social position. Christina was able to joke about the sumptuous chaise longue her mother had given her: "It makes me feel that Sacco and Vanzetti will be executed, that the stock-market will be steady and that conservatism will prevail." They did not join the demonstrators massing in those days before the gold-domed statehouse not far away. She was able to have her friends from Boston in to tea more easily than in the Cambridge apartment, and she joined a reading club called The Nucleus and interested herself in charity work, like a proper Beacon Hill matron. Her self-esteem was well sustained in these circles, where her uncle Ellery and his wife were "the peak of the quasi-literary people one sees around here."

John Marquand was not unwilling to take his position in this society. The social defeats of Harvard were now being repaired. His election to the Tavern Club assuaged the old soreness at his failure to make one of the college clubs, for this was truly polite Boston's social-intellectual Parnassus. The Tavern was a genial, exclusive fraternity of men of distinction *and* position whose first president had been William Dean Howells and whose president in 1927 was Marquand's favorite Harvard professor, Bliss Perry. Harvard had always been well represented among the Tavern's 175 members—President Lowell was a member as President Eliot had been, along with such distinguished Harvardians as Charles Eliot Norton (who had married a Sedgwick) and Barrett Wendell, George Santayana and Oliver Wendell Holmes. Since its founding in 1884, the club had included in its membership the city's civic and professional leaders and musical and literary celebrities; even the expatriate Henry James had been an honorary member. A feeling that reparation had been made filled Marquand as he attended the Monday night dinners and other occasions of masculine relaxation at the club's old-fashioned but luxurious quarters at 4 Boylston Place, a hidden alley in downtown Boston. Sixteen years later, he was perhaps less reverent of these surroundings. Fresh from a military tour in the Near East, he used an "Anglo-Saxon monosyllable" in telling a story during the course of a dinner speech. The club's remarkably enduring sense of propriety was offended, and he was formally reproved by Stewart Forbes, the chairman of the House Committee. Though Marquand was by then a famous novelist, and also a man of the world whose horizons had spread far beyond Boston, he quite humbly apologized in writing for his "transgression of etiquette"—evidence of the club's significance and authority in his eyes.

One may be sure that he saw the ridiculous in the situation, too. Already in 1927 he was accumulating observations—predictive of *The Late George Apley*—of that ingrown Beacon Hill social world with its innumerable pieties and prejudices, its convictions and irrationalities, its small rituals of custom and its sacred institutions, as well as of the minutiae of appearances that make the novel a brilliant rendering. Characteristically, Marquand would find in his writing scope for a skeptical detachment that went along with his own involvement, even his own desire to belong to the very world he could hold up to a certain mockery. Among his fellow Taverners and his fellow shareholders in the famous private library, the Boston Athenaeum—for he shortly became that as well—were the models for *Apley* characters in whose company he was so eager to be admitted. Two years later he made the Examiner Club, another bastion of Boston elitism. "Now that I am in it, you may feel definitely that I've made good," he told Christina, but one would need to have seen the snicker flash across his face and heard the dryness in his tone to realize the complexity of his meaning.

The first year of Marquand's membership in the Tavern he became thoroughly involved in its activities and he wrote a funny skit, "The Three Bears," which was presented by some of the members at the annual Christmas dinner. In the club files the script still reposes, to give evidence that it was not meant to be read by those who cannot recall the general hilarity of the occasion or the personal appearance of Taverners dressed in the costumes of Goldilocks and her friends. We may now detect some personal significances—as in the stage direction that describes "Mr. Bear" as being "obviously on the point of going out to one of those functions which husbands must willy-nilly attend in order in some subtle way that the home may be kept together."

Despite his continued wry view of his role as Family Head, Marquand found himself assuming a greater familial authority than ever. He had become the mainstay and director of his parents' fortunes. In the spring of 1928 the Edge Moor Iron Company, in cutting down on staff, dismissed Philip Marquand with nine months' salary. There was little prospect at his age of a new position somewhere else, and the elder Marquands therefore moved up from Wilmington to the Brick House at Curzon's Mill, and with their son's financial help Philip undertook chicken farming. After the salary from Edge Moor stopped, John Marquand accepted the idea that the responsibility for his parents' support was his, though he hoped, of course, that the chicken business would assist. The change, as a matter of fact, agreed with Philip, who had none of his son's fear of losing caste, and stories would be told of his contented chats at the kitchen door with the cooks of old Newburyport friends to whom he delivered eggs when Mrs. Marquand might be having tea in the front parlor. While John was making his ascent into the Tavern Club, his father quite unembarrassedly enjoyed an opportunity to put his practical turn of mind to account in the care and breeding of his Rhode Island Reds. The old man assumed a role somewhat more filial than paternal in relationship with his son. It was John Marquand who was henceforth the worried parent, concerned about the spendthrift and somewhat unreliable, even a little improper, old Phil, who liked to gamble and to drink and to drive his car with a young man's recklessness when his farm chores were done. In 1929 Mrs. Marquand came into a small legacy from a Fuller relative, and John immediately saw to it that she placed it in trust, thus securing it from being spent—on some stock market speculation in that year when the gambling impulse was running high—by the impulsive senior Marquand. It was an act of custodial presumption that Philip Marquand would lastingly resent.

Among the Sedgwicks, also, Marquand gained in dignity, for Christina's two brothers, Ellery and Shan, were giving their parents cause for worry while Christina's husband was proving to be a pillar of security. Shan had been working as a reporter for the New York *Times* with no particular advancement, covering mostly routine police stories, though now and then a big one, like the Hall–Mills murder trial. After a year or so, he left the *Times*, greatly discouraged. His elder brother had already spent a similar year on the Kansas City *Star* and finally had left in disgust, with no prospect elsewhere. In writing to Christina about both his brother and himself, Shan, who had inherited some of his father's penchant for self-dramatization, called them, "a tragic and disgruntled pair." He told her, "It is well, perhaps, that you do not see them, but can only see the hope and success which manifests in your husband."

Shan then proceeded to make a marriage that violently upset his parents. His bride was an English girl he had met abroad, the daughter of a baronet and a friend and informal ward of the family of Alice and Wilfred Meynell. But she was a Catholic and without any money to speak of—and the elder Sedgwicks thought the match highly unsuitable. In January 1929, nevertheless, Shan precipitately married her in Monte Carlo, although his mother had cabled her disapproval from Stockbridge. His father, who was already in Europe, cabled back unforgettably, "Nothing but an act of God can save Shan from gliding into matrimony at 12 noon tomorrow." After "Shan's eccentric marriage," as it was called, Ellery must have gratified his parents by proposing to a Boston Cabot.

It was several years before either son, though married, became self-supporting. Ellery undertook a program of graduate study at Harvard, eventually got a Ph.D., and became a member of the Harvard English faculty; he wrote one truly distinguished book, an appreciation of Herman Melville, which was one of the early studies heralding the modern revival of reputation for the author of *Moby Dick*. But through the years of preparation for his degree he was, of course, sustained by his wife's income. Shan, who eventually established himself as a *Times* correspondent abroad, had at this time given up newspaper work, and he struggled over a novel during the first couple of years of his marriage. Meanwhile, the marriage grew more and more unstable, rendered even more so by the long periods the young couple spent under the family roof in Stockbridge. For some years a remark of six-year-old Johnny's was often repeated in the family circle concerning Shan and his Anne: "Is kissing all their work?" Contemplating her sons' careers and marriages, Mrs. Sedgwick stated her view that they should not have married "until they either had a profession or had found that they could at least support themselves. The only circumstance which could make this conviction of mine unimportant would be the fact that the girl had enough to remove all necessity for immediate support from them, as was the case of your father and me." Ellery had met the second alternative, at least, by marrying Sally Cabot, but that had not been true of Shan. Mrs. Sedgwick announced herself satisfied with Christina's marriage in this fundamental respect. "I did not object to your marriage because John had no money," she declared, "for John had proved his ability to support himself and to meet life on his own and he had the right to marry."

Marquand's solidity as he turned out more and more of his stories was particularly conspicuous to all when the crash of 1929 sent down the incomes of the incomed and even the earnings of most professions, not to speak of wiping out job opportunities for such vaguely qualified persons as Shan and Ellery. Although the legend has persisted that Mrs. Sedgwick always deprecated Marquand's magazine writing, it should be recorded that she wrote Christina in July 1930: "*Don't* urge John to give up the *Evening Post*. I find more and more people read it and I think the fact that John has written exclusively for them gives him a great pull with them. John is so excellent as a short story writer—having such a special gift for that, that I hope you won't urge him to change or trifle with the *Post*." Again, at the end of October 1931, one hears her say: "Several people of late have congratulated John—as it were—on his position on the S.E.P. The financial depression gets worse and worse and anyone who can make money is the object of congratulations." Finally at the very nadir of the Depression, in 1932, she wrote: "I hope that John will stick to the S.E.P. as to a brother! You little realize how the excellence of that periodical increases all the time and in this financial depression John is the object of envy." In the end, it would seem, her Rogers business sense prevailed over Sedgwick genteelism.

He was now a *Post* regular and he had regular characters and scenes that had pleased the readers once and could be made to please them a second, a third, a fourth time. Willie Lipp, the high-principled second-story man, and Beverly Witherspoon, the gilded Harvardian, were back again in stories published in 1928. But new subjects also emerged. Some of these were founded on personal memories, like the encounter of regular army brass and the gentleman-civilian officers who had come out of Plattsburg during the war. He remembered the contrast of the two kinds of aristocracy—military and civilian—from his own service days and wrote about it with a certain humorous alertness that a sentimental plot could not altogether destroy. Resenting—while half admiring—the Beverly Witherspoons before he had joined the army, he could sympathize with the baffled irritation of the regular army officer for the Beverlys in uniform. The first of these stories had come to mind while he was waiting in Paris for Christina to recover from her breakdown—it was the story Carol Hill had taken down on her typewriter during a country house-party. "Good Morning, Major," was chosen by Edward J. O'Brien for inclusion in *The Best Short Stories of 1927* and reappeared in other anthologies for years. Finally, in 1954, Marquand himself culled it for his own collection, *Thirty Years*, apologizing to his readers for this early "commercial" success, yet confessing a fondness for it, the oldest story he had cared to reprint. He had followed up its first success with others suggested by the war years—"Oh, Major, Major," published in 1929, deliberately recalled its title. The theme that had intrigued him was one he continued to think of in a serious way. In 1951 it emerged in *Melville Goodwin, U.S.A.*, an ambitious novel about a West Pointer.

It has been noted that even in his most calculatedly commercial efforts there was nearly always a personal ingredient. Marquand had realized early that the remembered detail always glints forth from a depicted scene with a brighter authenticity than any "worked-up" fact, and his most lighthearted and contrived magazine stories attach themselves to the talisman of actual memory as though to ensure artistic success. In July 1929, the *Post* published another story that mingled the romance of the historical past of Newburyport with his own family history. Beneath the easy manipulation of romantic story there is at times an authentic energy of feeling; and there is a sharp precision of observation in the description of the old town, called Haven's End, its houses and marshy setting along the river, its melancholy history of early splendor and later decline, and the chronicles, based on actual fact, of its old families. "The Powaw's Head" was the first of a series, deliberately conceived as a history linking the colonial time with the present. It introduced the Swales and Scarlets, the two families whose distinguished qualities would recur in later generations. The story also used an early memory of Marquand's great-aunt Mary Curzon: a band of Indians from the upper Merrimack coming down the river to the sea, a strange ceremonial moment in which they seemed to bid farewell to the continent that had been theirs. The following month two more Haven's End stories appeared in the *Post*, and Lorimer was enthusiastic. "Captain Whetstone," he wrote Marquand, "is a fine story—in fact, this series is far away, in my opinion, the best work you have ever done." He added, "I am instructing the treasurer to make your price on this story and on succeeding ones $3,000." The story was in the best romantic manner, indeed—with a pretty girl of mysterious paternity at the center, and piracy and sword play all about, yet it is handled crisply, the details of setting and action are bright and positive, the dialogue neat. Perhaps Marquand's imagination worked surely because he had dreamed something of the story's basis again and again. His own ancestor Samuel Curzon, he had guessed, had loved Marquand's great-great-grandmother without marrying her, had become a sea wanderer, if not a pirate, like Captain Whetstone, before coming back to see the child he had fathered. Marquand had never written so quickly and happily as in these stories with their frank aim to tell a fireside tale of love and danger long ago, and some of the pleasure is still evident, partly because the lights and shadows come out of a personal connection with a past that was truly legendary for him, an authentic sense of the psychic basis of romantic legend. The *Post* had published thirteen stories in the sequence by November of 1930.

As early as February 1930, Carl Brandt had seen that they made a book. Ten stories were selected and given minor reediting. It was Brandt who suggested adding a prologue and an epilogue that would enclose the stories in a frame. Marquand hesitated. *Warning Hill*, which Scribner's had published only a few months earlier, had been a true serial—it had been written as a novel to run in installments in the *Post* during March and April 1929—and Marquand felt that with it he was returning to a more serious effort as a writer. Publication of *Haven's End* was another matter, and in a few years both Marquand and Alfred McIntyre would have agreed that it might be damaging to the reputation he was achieving with book readers. As a book, certainly, its weaknesses are apparent. The too-simple theme of contrasted traits that defines the successive generations of Swales and Scarlets—the symbolism, too often repeated, of steel versus lead—might have sustained a short tale but was "too consistent to be wholly convincing," when extended further, as one reviewer felt. Yet Marquand was persuaded to publish it. Even Mrs. Sedgwick wrote Christina, "I am crazy for his Haven's End stories to be printed in book form."

Warning Hill, though perhaps of no greater literary dimensions, had been more seriously meant, an attempt to write a "real" novel which had hung in his consciousness for years. Unlike his previous books it was *not* costume romance, but a story of modern or near-modern life—the history of a young man who like himself had come of age in time to put on a uniform in the war—and it is more genuinely autobiographical than anything he had written till then. The history of Tommy Michael begins at a sort of Curzon's Mill, a decayed old family home where he lives with his aunt while his father gambles on horses and the stock market, and is altogether, as has been noted, a somewhat glamorized Philip Marquand. The Jelletts, who live on Warning Hill, are, rather obviously, one of those High Street, Newburyport, families whose daughters scorned the young Marquand. Naturally their daughter Marianne becomes the object of young Michael's curiosity and love. Like Marquand, he grows up determined to gain entrance to the front door of the mighty on the hill, and he also bears the name of a successful grandfather. He learns that he is better than the Jelletts, who are only willing to let him in when he is diverting or useful. Marquand clearly recalls himself at Harvard, where Tommy Michael is taken up by a group of wealthy boys, including Marianne's brother, who value him only because he can teach golf expertly. In the end Tommy realizes that some of these boys had been decent chaps—his rival for Marianne dies gallantly beside him in the trenches. But the Jelletts are deglamorized once and for all in a melodramatic finale: the brother is nearly shot for seducing a poor girl, and the father tries to bribe Tommy to marry her. Tommy turns on his heel and gives them up at last, though Marianne still stretches him a siren white arm.

The story is not much different from the fiction Marquand had already written for the magazines despite the turnabout of the ending (boy expressly does not get girl, but rejects her and the money too). Marquand had still to learn that a change of ending alone would not make his fiction serious. But he already had intimations of a better method. Here and there in *Warning Hill* there is a thickening of texture, an atmosphere and psychological suggestiveness, which take over from the crude design. This happens when we are first introduced to the child Tommy Michael playing in the overgrown front yard of his house, trying to grasp the personality of his "different" father, or sailing a skiff across the neck of water beyond which rise the castles of the wealthy. Such moments suggest more deeply the theme of self-development, which must come to terms with longing and pride. But the older Tommy is less realized, and those around him, especially the girl he loves, the coldhearted rich girl Marianne, are mere outline drawings of popular romance again. It is perhaps significant that Marquand could materialize fictionally only the boy he had been. But his ambiguous emotions towards High Street could not yet express themselves and he fell back upon false and trite formulas. He would not deal with these feelings until he had worked out the tensions of his relationship with Christina Sedgwick—to whom, as though in apology, *Warning Hill* is dedicated. The novel is a failure. Marquand was not ready to attempt the cathartic form of literary statement that was to prove his true voice as an artist. But he would come back to the subject dimly proposed in this book and to the scene of his youth: the subject of his romantic infatuation with a girl who was the symbol of place and power.

His later method is already suggested in a story published in the *Post* in 1931. About an eccentric New England family living in a place called Indian

Creek, "Golden Lads" probably did not attract a great deal of response in the *Post* offices: it had a curious poetic quality that might have struck Lorimer as vagueness, and nothing like a discernible story line with satisfactory scenes of action. But though not even Marquand realized it, the story was really a novel in embryo, and that novel was *Wickford Point*, not to surface for eight more years. The old house at Indian Creek and its inhabitants are not, like Tommy Michael's home in *Warning Hill*, merely a free adaptation of some features of Curzon's Mill. For the very first time, Marquand attempted the imaginative transmutation of the home he had known when he was growing up with his aunts and his Hale cousins. The narrator-protagonist is more exactly identifiable with Marquand's inner self than any previous character drawn by him, and bears the same relation as Marquand to the set of relatives that exasperated and fascinated him—the absentminded yet oddly shrewd old aunt, the self-indulgent young cousins who expect the world to treat them as "golden lads and lasses." No character before *Wickford Point*'s Jim Calder will be so close to Marquand as Lee Danzell, the poor relation who is the critic of this family at the same time as he is more haunted than any of them by the ghosts of its past. The story has all the elements of the future novel in it—even the skein of motive upon which they are hung: a plan to marry Cousin Sue, the beauty and the vamp, to a solid citizen who will bail the family out. And it winds in a bit of Marquand legend more hauntingly than ever before—that old story of his great-great-grandfather's death in a duel with his great-great-grandmother's brother. The mixture must have bewildered the *Post* readers, who could not have known how deep in the author's consciousness the connections were made between past legend and present experience, how far from wandering is his narrator's musing and remembering. Marquand, however, recalled the story more tenderly than most of his early writing. As with "Good Morning, Major," he included it in *Thirty Years*, although he sternly censured then its "heavy atmosphere of artificial unreality," somewhat dishonestly declaring, "There was never a family mansion in Massachusetts or anywhere else remotely resembling Indian Creek; and never such preposterous goings on among ancestors in any family whatsoever." And yet, he felt, the story somehow worked: "One of the few things that makes this possible is an enthusiasm in the writing which I certainly could not approximate today."

He did not follow up this start. There were to be several other Danzell stories in the following year: "Ask Him," "The Music," and finally, "Deep Water," which won an O. Henry Memorial Award. But they did not extend "Golden Lads" in the usual way of finding further adventures for the characters. They were as close as possible to exact repetitions of it. "Ask Him" is in some ways one of the most interesting for its reference to Marquand's sense of personal and ancestral history. Not only does it repeat the scheme of a plot to capture a rich suitor as a way of rescuing the family fortunes, already employed in "Golden Lads," it splices into the story a family legend that might have come out of Samuel Curzon's journals: the example of a seafaring ancestor who had been a supercargo on a Yankee ship. But the main plot remains undeveloped from its outline in the earlier tale. There was, in fact, only one way to build upon this family material and the personal theme joined to it, and that was the autobiographical novel which Marquand was not yet able to write.

Meanwhile, he turned back to magazine stories, the real income-producing trade, after all. In 1929 he published twelve, and in 1930, fourteen, all but two in the *Saturday Evening Post*. For the first and only time in his career he resorted to the help of a literary "consultant" who could speed his output, reviewing his drafts and enabling him to produce a satisfactory product even more efficiently than Carl Brandt had been doing. John Gallishaw, to whom Marquand paid one hundred dollars a conference, was not a collaborator, and Marquand warned him, "My position in the magazine field would be weakened if it was thought that I was collaborating with you or anyone else," but he was apparently glad to buy the consultant's help in solving plot difficulties. Ten years later a young writer asked Marquand to recommend a guide to creative writing and was given two titles: *The Only Two Ways to Write a Story* and *Twenty Problems of the Fiction Writer*, published by Gallishaw in 1929. In these Gallishaw provided practical, shrewd counsel such as must have been the basis of his advice to Marquand: how to construct a story as a series of dramatized impressions—"to make one see," as Conrad had said; how to select and control point of view, as James had enjoined; how to differentiate characters; and so on. Marquand later thought that Gallishaw had expressed "certain sound and definite ideas about the form of the short story and about elements which are necessary in every good short story."

To a real writer the Gallishaw books were, of course, "pretty terrible," Marquand had added, "particularly the stories which he has selected, including two very bad ones of my own." The two, quoted in full, were "The Spitting Cat" and "Once and Always," which had been published in the *Post* in 1926 and 1927 respectively. For several years Gallishaw continued to hold his star pupil to the mark of these deftly managed specimens. He characterized himself as "your 'trouble-shooter,' a sort of literary auto-mechanic, who came out and discovered that you were out of gas, or had disconnected a battery wire, showed you how to fix it, and went back to the garage to read the *Saturday Evening Post*." The imagery was apt enough. Marquand had come to think of himself as a kind of motorized vehicle set to go at so many miles per hour when fueled and operated in the right way.

11

Heartbreak House

In January 1929, Tina, the Marquands' daughter, had pneumonia and was operated on for an abscessed lung, and upon her recovery the doctor recommended a summer at the seashore. They moved down at the end of May to a small cottage in Cotuit, on Cape Cod. It belonged to Mark A. DeWolfe Howe whom Marquand had gotten to know at the Tavern Club. The two families—the Howes lived in a larger house alongside—became close friends.

Howe was the quintessential Taverner. At sixty-five, he was a genial gentleman of letters, the author of biographies of Phillips Brooks, George Bancroft, Barrett Wendell, James Ford Rhodes and other Boston worthies. The biographies were old-fashioned and kindly, "commissioned" by the subjects' families and saturated with the spontaneous goodwill of the writer. (Christina reported to her mother one day, "Mr. Howe is going to write a biography of Fred Cabot. He can't find any faults. He went to see some of his friends yesterday in order to find a fault, but none was forthcoming!") They were not, later critics would judge, works of the highest literary and scholarly brilliance—though *Barrett Wendell and His Letters* had received a Pulitzer Prize in 1924. But Howe was a man of both distinction and charm. As he grew older he would seem more and more the genteel ambassador to a ruder world from a vanished Bostonian past. He had been born before the end of the Civil War and died, finally, at ninety-six, a few months after Marquand, in the inconceivable later time of 1960. *The Late George Apley*'s mock-generic design, "A Novel in the Form of a Memoir," was suggested by Howe's biographical memorials. Its narrative voice, one Horatio Willing, echoed that of Howe himself, with the Boston stuffiness amplified and some of the warmth and intelligence removed (and the initials reversed).

Mrs. Howe was a New England female original. Her skepticism and wit, though muffled by her husband's blander personality, were still felt by those who knew her. Her traits were visible in the Howe children, especially the two elder ones: the argumentative, caustic Quincy, seven years younger than Marquand but well able to keep up with him in badinage and debate, and Helen, a shy young woman of twenty-three with a quiet faculty of observation that came out in her talent for enacting mocking dramatic versions of what she had seen or heard. For the Marquands, somewhat weary after seven years of a difficult marriage and the recent anxiety of Tina's illness, the spirited young Howes were refreshing companions. These new friends made them feel that they were rejoining their own younger selves, more unburdened, spontaneous, naive. Christina's own mixture of delicacy and humor was not unlike Helen's, and the Howe way of making fun of things was like Marquand's, though without his bitterness.

The Marquands found Cotuit a place of soothing mildness, like the waters of the sheltered bay in which they swam off the Howes' secluded point. There was no social life to speak of, no golf or yacht club, no dressing for dinner, no cocktail parties. There was sailing, of a gentle, unambitious sort, in the Howe catboat and a small sailboat that Marquand had bought and named (the year, after all, was 1929) *Electric Bond and Share*. But there was conversation, a lively, endless volleying during picnics and Sunday lunches shared by the Howes and the Marquands and occasional visitors. These additions came mostly from Cotuit's summer population of Harvard professors. The modest routines of these gentlemen resembled those of Howe or Marquand himself—long, lucubrating hours spent in some secluded hut where a manuscript was being prepared, then emergence into the dazzle of light-reflecting water and sand and the shouts of small children. Mr. Howe did his writing in a fisherman's shanty or "oyster house" down near the shore. In another, Marquand found a retreat. He was amused to become a member of this little colony, encountering Harvard on a basis of assured membership—as at the Tavern Club—that had been denied him as a student and that he and Christina had not felt when living among the faculty families in Cambridge. Here he met again—but how differently—such awesome figures as Channing of History or Taussig of Economics, and above all, President A. Lawrence Lowell, who made a periodic Sunday afternoon call at the Howes', walking majestically the mile from his house to their oyster-shell drive in his blue-serge suit and white leghorn hat, and leaning on a massive wooden staff.

These visitors and a hundred other objects became material for the private exchanges of mockery between the Marquands and the younger Howes. Helen Howe would recall: "John encouraged us to laugh *at*, not merely with, the world that surrounded us. He and Quincy egged each other on in mordant comments on mutual friends, the national scene, and Cotuit neighbors. The hazy if pleasant blur which had up to then hung like a mesh of scrim over the local scene lifted: outlines became sharper, the light that illuminated them shining from the eye of the beholder, and that beholder, pre-eminently, a satirist." And Marquand would tell his stories, some, indeed, about the Sedgwicks and Christina, but with such apparent good humor that there did not seem, to these young listeners, to be any harm in them. One can imagine him in the summer plus-fours and golf stockings then in fashion, a slender man without the appearance of assurance and solidity that came in later years, his hair rather too long, parted in the middle and combed behind the ears.

Certainly that first Cotuit summer seemed without any tremor of old or new disaster. As far as the Howes could see, "tragedy" and "misery" were only comic masks assumed by Marquand during his entertaining recitals of domestic difficulties. This was so despite the proximity of Christina's parents—a condition against which Austen Riggs had warned expressly. Christina's parents had themselves become fond of recounting, a little scornfully, how Dr. Riggs had expressed his theory that marriage was a "sphere" (they made rounding motions of the hands) which no alien force must impinge upon. They had respected his advice and kept away, and Christina and John had spent the previous two summers at a distance from Stockbridge, first at Weston and then, in 1928, in Wiscasset, Maine, with only brief calls at the Sedgwick Mansion. Now, Christina's parents felt, the time had come to put an end to this "unnatural" separation. They did not propose to live under the same roof as their daughter but they would be right at hand, and they rented a cottage a few miles away in Marston's Mills. It seemed a safe decision, but maybe their presence again promoted their daughter's helplessness. If invited somewhere, the Marquands always arrived late, and their own guests remembered that Christina often forgot to prepare for them—and John was always fuming. Clever Mrs. Howe called them "that ever diverse pair," quoting from a favorite sonnet by Meredith. Yet never after this summer would the Sedgwick influence have the same prominence in their lives. In October 1929, Alexander Sedgwick died suddenly while visiting his wife's old home in Bath, New York.

A month or so earlier, he had bought and generously deeded to his daughter and son-in-law the little cottage in Marston's Mills. The Marquands had been charmed by its mournful, gray-shingled shabbiness, affectionately nicknamed it Heartbreak House (in irritated moods Marquand would also call it Gift Horse). During the winter, renovations were undertaken and the faded trim was painted a rather glaring blue so that, Christina wrote to her mother, "the heartbreak quality of the place has gone, and it seems very cheerful." Still, the name stuck, and proved, in time, to be prophetic. They were to spend the summer there in 1930 and again in 1931, when, by slow degrees, the gears of marriage ground more gratingly. Perhaps without yet fully realizing it, Marquand and Helen Howe had already fallen in love.

Helen had begun by having a delayed adolescent crush on both Christina and John at once—only possible at her age if one has been sheltered psychologically since childhood. She had had a year at Radcliffe, a year of teaching in Boston, a year studying in New York at the Theatre Guild, even a year in Paris living in a French household—and yet her emotional life had never left the bounds of her family. Christina, with her air both melancholy and gay, her changeling remoteness alternating with hoyden humor, fascinated the younger woman, whose personality was open and rational and not, people would say, particularly charming, whereas Christina had charm for both men and women. And John was that masculine mixture that certain kinds of women found appealing. He was at once tough, slightly cynical and egotistic, instinctively tyrannical because he was really interested in no one but himself. But one could also perceive the sensitive and lonely boy in need of sympathy and praise, the boy that he would never cease to be. His achievements and his strength of will, a certain hardness, compelled a woman to admire him and to feel flattered at the same time by the suggestion he communicated that she was needed, that he was a lost child without her. Helen Howe was not the first and would not be the last to feel this appeal. He, for his part, found a combination equally irresistible in her. Her outer primness or appearance of sexual unawareness made his affection for her feel safe to him when it was not. And she adored him uncritically, as young girls tend to adore older men, without realizing at first that her emotions were not the same as those she felt for her clever, domineering elder brother or her impressive father.

And yet the Marquand marriage had not yet reached heartbreak. In the spring of 1931, before going to the Cape, Christina went for a holiday in Europe with her uncle Henry Dwight Sedgwick. That amiable epicurean, globe-trotter, and writer of many books had been a widower for many years. He was fond of young women generally (he would finally astonish the world by marrying at ninety-two a woman in her early forties) and he was particularly fond of his niece. John Marquand made the invitation from Uncle Harry the subject of one of his comic stories. Imitating the fruity tones of this gentleman, he recited an imaginary letter from him written en route with Christina along the byways of France: "We called ourselves Ninon and Ninette. We called our old Ford Sancho Panza." But he did not object when Christina sailed.

She was, no doubt, trying to make up for the wasted weeks in 1926 when she had seen only the alleys and vistas of the gardens at Versailles during her illness, though one may wonder whether she did not long to reattach the silver cord to her father's brother, now that her father was dead. In any case she had a rapturous two-month tour with her experienced guide. Christina, whom touring had so exhausted five years before, was now inexhaustible. They covered a good part of historic France, driving through Gascony, Auvergne, the Dordogne, Burgundy, coming back at last to Paris. Though far from John Marquand, Christina had kept her hand firmly on the Sedgwick cord. In the middle of Auvergne there had been a grand convergence with another of her father's brothers on tour, Ellery Sedgwick and his wife Mabel, along with Shan and his English wife, who were living there. After Paris, Christina and Uncle Harry had run over to England to visit the de Selincourts.

Meanwhile, Marquand was spending most of the time at Stockbridge with his children and Mrs. Sedgwick, writing Christina wry but not unaffectionate letters signed, alternately, "your deserted husband" or "your bereaved husband." "Dear Chrissy," he wrote, "I hope that you are having a lot of fun in the classical reaches of Provence by now, and that you have seen where the French got theirs at Poitiers and where Richard Coeur de Lion got his as he stormed the breach. Between these moments of purely classical ecstasy I hope you will remember that the little group here misses you very much." And in another: "I do wish you'd hurry up and come on home. After your letter from Chinon, I begin to fear that the work of years is being undone, and that you are fast giving way to the more dangerous sides of your nature, and developing a streak of intellectualism akin to the Copley Greenes and to the Little Group which now infests the Harvard Yard. I fully expect that by next year we will be sending out a card at Christmas of a stone figurine of St. Nichole, just attributed, found in the decorations of the organ loft at Loches. When you get back your mind will be set on such high things that you will scarce be able to re-adapt yourself to the semi-barbarism under which your family labors, and you will look with horror upon your intellectually vulgar and besotted husband. Do be careful and keep slightly down to earth, so that you will be glad to see me when you walk the plank at Boston."

His sense of "down to earth" was acute just then as he labored on his stories while some investments he had made went under. "As for me," he wrote, "life, as you so aptly put it, has been in cold storage, complicated by a steady drop in the stock market, which is hard to bear. I wish you'd hurry and come home, but when you do economy must be the watchword." The house at 43 West Cedar Street loomed as a burden of complication and expense. He had spent a day in Tarrytown visiting Carl Brandt's brother and partner Erdman Brandt, and he told her, "I should like you to see how the Brandts live—with less money than we have, fewer servants and infinitely more comfortable. I am never again going to spend a mint as I did last winter and get so little in return." So he drove his pen, feeling resentful of those who were free to cultivate the purely aesthetic, whether in Harvard Yard or at Chinon. Since Lorimer was "stocked up on serials," Marquand still did not dare to think of another novel. He had spent some time in Christina's absence going down to the races in Baltimore with an old Newburyport friend, Joe Hale, and had done a story about a pair of track followers named Jack White and Henry Bledsoe, whose speech had a smack of genuine folk humor. Lorimer was enraptured and wanted more of the same. "I feel badly about it, but with business the way it is there is nothing to do but sit up and look pretty when the big boys tell you to. I wish I could get in a position where I could thumb my nose at the lot of them. When I'm eighty I suppose I can," he wrote Christina.

The Marquands decided against another winter in Boston. They prepared to rent the West Cedar Street house and go to Hawaii—a move that amazed their friends. There were reasons enough to give—it would be an economy and a way of protecting the still-delicate Tina from another Boston winter. Perhaps John and even Christina wanted to get away from Boston and all their circle, the Howes included, after the two summer months in Marston's Mills. Yet it was the Howes of whom they both had the fondest thoughts as they left Boston on October 2. Coming into the city from Stockbridge, their own house already occupied by tenants, they had been sheltered by the Howes in Brimmer Street until it was time to leave for Montreal. From the hotel there, where they rested overnight before taking the train for Vancouver, both John and Christina wrote Helen their notes of appreciation for the warmth of their send-off from Boston, hers signed "ever devotedly, Christina" and his, "affectionately, your friend, John." Helen, for her part, had remarked to John as they parted—if the meaning was ambiguous Christina did not perceive it—that now they were going, she "must try to collect her own personality."

On October 10, 1931, their ship, the *Empress of Japan*, sailed out of Vancouver taking them as far from Boston, in some ways, as it was possible to get, in other ways back to the little universe of the familiar they had left. They rented a bungalow on Kahala Beach outside Honolulu for $150 a month, and Christina at once declared that they were again in Marston's Mills, the bungalow rather resembling Heartbreak House. But the blue water shining at the end of the sand before them had the gloss and color of a piece of Oriental enamel, and across was a view of the island of Molokai where, Christina learned with a shudder (could the germs swim over to them? she wondered), there was a leper colony. The small house had belonged to a Scot who had been "vamped by the beauty of Hawaii," as Christina reported to Boston, and it was stuffed with devices for the employment of tropical idleness—card tables, an enormous Victrola, a stack of popular records, et cetera—while the walls were decorated with pictures made of postage stamps, testimonials of the landlord's achievement of keeping himself occupied in the paradise of leisure. The neighbors, she discovered, were American—mostly army or navy couples. They were a little friendlier than—in her Boston–Stockbridge way—she was used to, dropping in for a casual call if they glimpsed John working at his typewriter on the porch. "A horrid feeling comes over me that the suburb Kahala equals Newton," she wrote her mother.

But on the whole she found herself surrounded by reassuring familiarities. Their real estate agent, Jimmy Wilder, was the son of a friend of Aunt Greta's, a lady of some social prominence who at once asked them to dinner.

Jimmy took Marquand in tow, helping him to buy a new Ford and a linen suit and a pair of rubber-soled shoes. They had been met at the boat by another couple, the Paul Withingtons, who also moved in the upper levels of Hawaiian society—his family had come from Newburyport. Christina noted with pleasure that he had "a splendid football figure," and he reminded her a little of Dr. Riggs. Of course the Marquands had come bearing letters of introduction to the rulers of the island world. As Marquand later remarked, "Any visitor who amounted to anything and a great many more who didn't always had a letter of introduction to Mr. or Mrs. Walter Dillingham when they got off the boat." Indeed, it was said that whenever a Matson boat came in, the Dillinghams would get as many as forty such letters at a time, "so that it would be necessary to deal wholesale with the callers who would all be invited to tea at the Dillinghams' Moorish–Spanish Alhambra on the slopes of Diamond Head." Whether or not they were received in this fashion, the Marquands soon found themselves gently tossed into the social sea, meeting the "missionary families" like the Dillinghams and the Castles at large, casually assembled parties.

Christina was first exhilarated and then somewhat depressed, for the close comfortableness of Boston was absent. She missed friends and intimate gossip in a group where she felt her value, and began to tire of being treated as a visitor. "We *cannot* admire the flowers and trees anymore—we know about the uses the old Hawaiians had for the calabash. We have read the approved history and an awful feeling comes over me, 'That's all there is! There isn't any more!'" she told Helen. From this source she eagerly begged for news of the little circle at home. Quincy Howe's engagement to Mary Post produced pages of comment in the letter she returned to Boston. Marquand noted with more detached amusement the *kamaaina*'s (oldtimer's) condescension to the *malihini*, and the general affectation of interlarding everyday speech with Hawaiian words. "When they say they are through with anything they say they are 'pau.' If they want you to hurry, they say 'wicki-wicki.' If someone is weak in the head, they say he is 'poopooli.' But why go on? You can read it all in the works of Earl Derr Biggers." When visiting Hawaii again during World War II, he would catch Admiral Nimitz working up a vocabulary of such expressions from a pocket dictionary. He found himself recalling then how weary he had become of the Hawaiian host's endless explanations of such expressions, and his repeated instruction in the nomenclature of the Hawaiian flora—as he sat with you on his porch or *lanai*.

In the morning and early afternoon, while the children played in the yard and now and then Christina or Jessie the nurse or the Japanese cook walked past his chair, Marquand sat on *his* porch facing the sea and tried to write. The little house contained no other refuge. There was only a combination living-dining room and two bedrooms besides their own, one for Johnny and one for Tina and Jessie. Yet he was working on a new set of stories suggested by Lorimer that could not have been more remote from his immediate surroundings—the murmuring Pacific in front of him, the palm fronds rattling overhead with a sound like a hundred typewriters mockingly echoing his own. Using research notes he had accumulated before leaving home, as well as recollections of a tour of the Virginia battlefields he had made with Thomas Costain, he was busy imagining the adventures of a young Confederate officer during the Civil War. He groaned over his pages, and Christina reported to her mother: "John is very depressed over his last story. It is terribly difficult to write about the Civil War just through canned information. I wish they had never started him on it." When the first of the series, called "Solid South," was accepted in December, she reported: "John has just sold his Civil War story, which is a relief because neither of us thought that he would. I thought the style excellent but the story lacking in interest. It is, of course, like canned food." And Marquand continued doggedly, producing two more of the stories by March ("all of them poor stuff," he wrote Helen Howe) and finally a fourth in May, when he wrote her: "I got word that I had sold another story about that nice southern boy. Why the deuce they took it, I don't know, but now I suppose I've got to start another."

All in all there were six stories about Scott Mattaye of Deer Bottom in Virginia that Marquand managed to turn out in this mood of distraction and revulsion. They have never been reprinted, and yet they are better than he held them. Here was certainly a case where personal experience had less to contribute than ever before—even the cloak-and-dagger tales of Revolutionary Newburyport had more connection with his real life, it might be supposed. Yet these stories give evidence of intensity of imagining: the details of description are set down with a kind of rightness that comes only from strenuous dramatic testing in the mind's theater; the scenes and dialogue satisfy the reader's own inner eye and ear, and more than ever the contrivance of the plots seems unimportant. What comes through more powerfully than young Mattaye's star-crossed romance or the highly colored portraits of J.E.B. "Beauty" Stuart or Jefferson Davis is a state of mind, a condition of sensation that Marquand did summon out of experience after all. He was writing about war. His months of soldiering in France are the hidden source of the energy with which he sets down, for example, Mattaye's feelings in the story called "High Tide," when the young officer is picking his way alone on a scouting mission through enemy country. Marquand writes well, because authentically, of a soldier's first sight of the grotesque disorder of battlefields and of the dull fatigue after many days. Such effects nearly save the stories from the oblivion to which Marquand cheerfully consigned them.

That his imagination was working on some deep level of personal feeling, even in the composing of these potboilers written to Lorimer's order, may have been due to his feeling that his life with Christina was making a last stand there in the dream-unreality of Hawaii. In December, he wrote to

Helen Howe concerning her brother Quincy's engagement: "If 'Posty' [Quincy's fiancée] just won't start demanding a solid Beacon Street existence, I can't imagine a better marriage. Between you and me I say this with some feeling, because, from my limited experience, a wife, no matter how she may think before matrimony, becomes after the ceremony imbued with all the ideas of her parents, from which she once revolted. Thus, all the Sedgwicks really care for, despite talk to the contrary, is a cosy and regular inherited income and polite round of social functions, attended by the recipients of similar incomes, against a satisfactory environmental background. The idea that a living must be earned by work and the idea that life and luxury depend in any way on personal effort and the vicissitudes of an economic cycle must never be allowed to interfere with true happiness. I hope very much that Quincy will not smash himself or a home against the fat jade-head of capitalism, or if he does, that he will be a 'straight' and not end like me an embittered and hopeless cynic." He did not share Christina's absorption in the progress of their social relationships. Her zest for evening parties had always been greater than his, and here, in this beguiling climate, distracted by the holiday tone of the life around him, and resenting the assumption of all their new acquaintances that he too was on holiday, Marquand felt more prone than ever to condemn Christina's attitude. The lightheartedness and gaiety that had been once part of her charm for him seemed a lack of feeling while he wrestled with his stories, finding them more hateful than they really were, trying to promise himself that he would do something better some day.

It is doubtful if Christina understood the desperation of the mood he found himself in repeatedly as the halcyon Hawaiian days passed, and which he had so frankly expressed to Helen Howe. Yet she must have at least sensed his creative frustration. When Mrs. Sedgwick, who had now become entirely complacent about his magazine success, complimented him on his latest stories, he replied: "Thank you very much for your letter, and for being so kind about my stories. Out here I certainly need encouragement. I have never been to a place where it is so hard to write, or where every method of life seems especially designed to interrupt thought or leisure. Of course the one thing I want to do more than anything else is a novel, but I cannot afford such prodigal gambling of my time at present, unless I could think of one which would make a good serial story first. Otherwise it is a question of taking a year off, and of running the chance of making about the pay of a mediocre chauffeur for one's pains. This is art for art's sake, but if one lives by one's pen this avenue is more or less cut off. If I could once gain a foothold with the novel reading public, as for instance Edna Ferber or my friend Arthur Gibbs has done, who both can be reasonably sure of selling around fifty thousand copies, then I would be all right. I always have the hope of being able to strike through with something of the sort, but I must say this hope grows dimmer as time goes on, and it sometimes seems to me that I must confine myself to doing the best I can in the somewhat narrow requirements of the popular magazines, unless always I can develop some way of turning out a greater quantity of work." Christina, also replying to the same letter of her mother's, innocently had observed: "I am so glad you liked John's stories. I think on the whole they maintain a very high average. I should like however to have him break away now and then from that kind of thing." And with no sense of incongruity she then went on: "I shall miss this place. Here I have an excellent cook for less than I pay Evelyn at home and her husband is an accomplished butler. Last night I had twelve to supper and hardly turned a hair."

In a way rather different from Christina's, Marquand was fascinated by the Hawaiian environment—its exotic natural beauty and the complex social universe which he saw more objectively and comprehensively than she. His eye roamed tirelessly over the landscape, seeking some poetic equivalent in the island's forms and colors for a serenity he longed for. He scented in this midoceanic outpost the breath of that Oriental world which would come to represent to him an order his own civilization had not attained. "I never get tired of looking at the coral reefs and the sea," he wrote Helen. "The trees are so exotic and strange that I still wonder if I am not dreaming. Take the banyan tree for instance. It has not one but twenty trunks so that it is like a house on stilts spreading all over the grass. Another thing I love here is the Chinese temple filled with incense smoke and the odor of cooked food brought to be blest for feasts. A drum is always going and the priest is always chanting and the almond eyed executives are constantly burning paper prayers before the weeping god of business."

Hawaiian society was another matter. He observed the upper-class inhabitants whom he and Christina met socially, but he found himself spending hours elsewhere. Honolulu, he discovered, had become a city of many elements without concourse. As he summarized his impressions years later: "On the upper crust was the decorous and snobbish civilization of the old island families, who had their great houses and their gardens on the mountain slopes outside the city, and their banks and offices with elaborate tropical planting downtown on Queen Street, their beach houses on the windward and their hunting lodges on the other islands." These were such families as the Castles and the Dillinghams and the Cooks. Beneath "this exalted and serious stratum" was another that had brought the traditions of southern California to Hawaii: movie industry people and other "rich maladjusted Americans from all parts of the country" who built extravagant houses along the beach and behaved "in ways they felt tropical visitors should," hiring Hawaiians to sing for them at their moonlight parties. Beneath these, he observed, were the small businessmen who lived in side-street bungalows with their families, the transient Army and Navy population, and "all that strange mass of Americans, who for any one of a number of reasons, most of them not creditable, had been unable to get on at home and wanted something different"; who lived in the area behind Waikiki Beach and patronized the small restaurants and "lived wild and unattractive lives that touched the orbits of the beachcombers and the bums, the stranded sailors, the international drunks." Yet all this was only a surface of a sort. Marquand, who had developed a habit of taking long walks into neighborhoods that Christina did not even know existed, became aware of the other races that had made the island paradise their home. "In the suburban districts and down in the slums around Vineyard Street and the very unsanitary open brook known as Nuuanu Stream, the Japanese market gardener and the Filipino brothel manager and the Cantonese provision merchant all understand what pau, poopooli and aloha mean, and they can all sing the Hawaiian Song of the Islands a good deal more readily than they can sing God Bless America." Most tourists, of course, kept well away from the slums in which these Honolulu citizens were living—but Marquand was curiously drawn to learn more about the mixture of races, native Hawaiian and Asiatic, who lived crowded into wooden tenements around Beretania and King streets—"the slum dwellers and the inhabitants of the slatternly termite-ridden shacks in the regions away from the polite real estate developments," as he would describe them. Thinking back on the Honolulu of 1932, he saw the city "with its veneer of comfort and vulgar luxury, spread over an age-old basis of Oriental poverty—the melting pot of the Pacific which was never hot enough to melt."

Such social observation was doubtless stimulated by the extraordinary events that agitated the Hawaiian scene during the Marquands' stay. In September 1931, shortly before their arrival, a twenty-year-old woman, Thalia Massie, the wife of a naval officer, was raped and thrown into a ditch, her jaw broken, by a gang of five men who had grabbed her in the dark when she left a late party alone. Early in December the islanders charged with the crime were released because the jury could not agree on a conviction, and the large service population—fourteen thousand Army and Navy men and their families—was suddenly catapulted into mass hysteria, during which one of the accused was beaten, and sailors and Marines fought in the streets with civilians. Then, in January, one Joe Kahahawai, identified by the young woman as the most brutal of her attackers, was himself brutally murdered by a party consisting of her husband, her mother, and another Navy officer; they were about to toss the trussed body of their victim over the cliffs at Koko Head when they were caught by the police. The arrest and trial for murder of this posse of avengers produced, as might be expected, the intensest excitement in Hawaii—and even in America, where the case was kept in the headlines for months, despite the greater domestic sensation of the Lindbergh kidnapping. The melodrama of the case was increased by the fact that while Joe Kahahawai was the son of a trolley motorman, his supposed victim was a girl of the most haughty connections. Her mother—who had herself driven the car bearing Kahahawai's corpse towards Koko Head—was Mrs. Grace Bell Fortescue, a wealthy society woman who was a niece of Alexander Graham Bell's and the wife of a friend of Theodore Roosevelt's who had distinguished himself at San Juan Hill.

The case aroused the keenest feeling of racial antagonism that had ever divided Hawaii—where all the races of East and West seemed to have heretofore lived in harmony. At the parties Christina and John Marquand attended as soon as they arrived, there was no more insistent topic of conversation. The Marquands' new friends immediately reminded them that they were members of a racial minority of fifteen thousand in a city of one hundred thousand. There were reports or rumors of multiplying assaults upon white women and an assumption that every American female was in imminent danger from the lust of the nonwhite population. A naval patrol paraded nightly for many weeks in front of the cottages at Kahala and one of the Marquands' neighbors was soon charged with manslaughter because he shot a Hawaiian boy whom he caught—or suspected of—prowling around his house. Christina, going out for lunch one day to a friend's at Lamidai, a little distance along the coast road, and driving alone, took John's pistol in her handbag. This she mentioned with some bravado in a letter to her mother, and Mrs. Sedgwick wrote back anxiously. He replied: "None of us here allows any woman to go out at night without a male escort, but in the daytime there is absolutely no danger, and I do not think you need worry about Christina in the least. It is true that she is careless, but she is much impressed with the folly of running around alone, and no one, wherever she goes, will think of letting her."

The Marquands had a curious sense of closeness to the lurid case because, as they discovered, upper-class Honolulu was a large club. They not only heard innumerable discussions concerning the characters of Thalia Massie and her relatives but they had met these persons at dinner parties. Mrs. Fortescue, Christina wrote her mother, was "very distinguished-looking, very obviously a lady," and it turned out that at home in Washington, D.C., she had been on cordial terms with Christina's relatives, the MacVeaghs. "Frankly," John wrote Helen Howe, "this had been a most amazing winter. I little recked that I should ever be asked to dinner by a murderess, or play water polo with a murderer, or spend all my waking hours discussing the ins and outs of assault with intent to ravish."

One effect, as has been said, was to quicken Marquand's interest in his surroundings and provide some distraction from his toil over his Civil War stories. His instincts as a news reporter were aroused, and he began to assemble information about the complex Hawaiian world and to collect viewpoints from everyone he met. He made himself into something of an expert on the Hawaiian scene at this time and wrote two articles for the North American Newspaper Alliance to be syndicated in mainland newspapers. Later he would use some of this observation as the basis for background in fiction. The interest he found in this troubled exotic world probably also helped to keep him from thinking about his relationship with Christina, which had not improved.

One day towards the end of March, Marquand left her and Honolulu and went, on an impulse, for a week, to the island of Hawaii, staying on the Kona Coast, a stark and beautiful region that moved him strangely. He wrote Helen Howe: "Really I wish I might always stay there. It is the only place I have seen for a long while which seems to have escaped the curse of the tourist bureaus, organized propaganda and modern improvements. This coast was the place where the kings and chiefs of Polynesia gathered. It was once heavily populated. The missionaries came here first in the little bay of Kailua, and the church which the old chief built in 1832 is standing near his palace. Now the Hawaiians have been swept away as though a plague had struck them, leaving only a few isolated families, and a languor has fallen over the place, very like the languor of a deserted seaport town at home."

But it was not only the reminder of Newburyport—where passion and striving were also perhaps a long-ago tale, a faint air barely heard on the wind—that stirred him on the Kona Coast: "The huge volcanoes behind this land, sloping backwards until they rise twelve thousand feet, cut off the perpetual trade winds, so that the sea along this coast is calm for a hundred miles. You cannot imagine a peace as perfect as exists in the still blue of that sea. Nevertheless there is a sort of blood and iron about the place, which I can't help liking. Nearly [all the] slopes going up to the mountains are covered with floes of jagged black lava ancient and modern. Long before the white man came the natives began building stone walls of these lava blocks so that the whole countryside is squared off into diminutive fields surrounded by high stone walls." Summoning again to mind the countryside of his own ancestors, he continued: "The sparseness of the ground and these old walls remind you very much of deserted farms in New England, and when you see the uncompromising outlines of small coral churches, with which the early missionaries dotted the coast, you begin to think you are in a sort of Yankee heaven. You think of a square rigger in the harbor and the church bells ringing, and firm brown bodies emerging from ghostly villages of thatched huts now entirely vanished. You think of the great grass palace of King Kamehameha with seventy war canoes up on the beach beside it, and the tabu sticks planted and the royal spearman at the door and the singers chanting meles to the tune of little drums, and hogs squealing and women beating tappa."

It was a vision of paradise that would linger. A few years later he wrote an essay called "The Road Turns Back," in which he declared that if he were asked to choose from his life's experience a place where he would like to stay it would be the Kona Coast—or perhaps, as a second choice, the city of Peking. Yet he went on to admit that probably he would not be able to stay there—his road would turn back to "a seaport town in Massachusetts with many disadvantages and many limitations. It has no great beauty or no great sources of stimulation but it has the great advantage of being a place where I belong, and probably this definite feeling of belonging is what makes it desirable. What is more, it is inescapable."

Newburyport it was that now summoned him back with unexpected peremptoriness. His mother had suffered a succession of heart attacks, and a dangerous thrombosis made her condition very grave. Marquand left promptly when the news came on May 3, undertaking alone the slow journey by ship and train. But as he traveled there had been an emergency amputation of her leg, and she was dead on May 7 and, indeed, buried by the time he reached home. The shock of her death desolated him. This silent stoical parent, whose care and protection he had mentally assumed as a youth when he realized his father's inadequacy, had slipped away when he was far off. An unreasonable guilt oppressed him, along with a sense that no one, certainly not Christina, who had never liked Mrs. Marquand, could understand what his mother had meant to him. Irrationally, perhaps, he looked back with revulsion at the year in Hawaii and its social frivolities. His parting with Christina—who would follow with the children—had been abrupt. On shipboard, when the cable informing him of his mother's death reached him, his mood was compounded of grief and the feeling that Christina had never tried to emulate his mother's tenderness for him, her life of selflessness. Christina, it is to be feared, must have let him see how much she regretted that his mother's illness was bringing her gay days in Hawaii to an end sooner than she had counted on. As she wrote her mother: "It's been such a joy and I've never been on such familiar terms with admirals and generals before. Really I've never had such a good time from a personal point of view—I mean such a gratifying time. And then this happens. Like a privy paw dragging us back to real life again."

It is not surprising that at this moment of passage Marquand's imagination seized hold of the alternative image it had held in reserve—that of Helen Howe. Christina had reported to Helen when Quincy's engagement was announced, "John has a very melancholy theory that you'll soon be married—and his face drops a mile when I say I agree with him," and in another of her letters she told Helen, simply, "John says he misses you terribly and sends his love." Her own affection for Helen was strong and she was not a jealous woman. She shared Marquand's anxiety that Helen might not be at Cotuit the coming summer when they returned, since the pursuit of her career as a diseuse threatened to take her to New York or even to England. "Stay for one more summer, at least," Marquand begged. Trying to ensure her return to Cotuit he had proffered his interest in her ambition to write as well as to perform on distant stages: "If you are in Cotuit this summer I hope you'll try to write a story because I have a hunch you would be very good at it indeed if you just take the time. You have the interest and the dramatic sense and everything, and it wouldn't hurt to have another string to your bow." Now, as she prepared to follow John to America, Christina wrote to Helen, "I hope you've seen John for it would have cheered him up greatly to have seen you."

She could not have realized how eager he had been, in fact, to reach this friend. Helen had radioed sympathy almost at the moment the news of Mrs. Marquand's death reached him while his ship was in its mid-Pacific passage. Two weeks later, after he had seen her, he wrote: "It has come over me to my great shame in all my selfish complainings at the exigencies of life the other day, that I never said a single word to thank you for the sweetness, the understanding, and the sympathy which you gave me when I was facing the first shock of sorrow and bereavement from the news of my mother's death. I shall never forget the blackness of the day on shipboard the evening I got your radio. If there had been a call to boat stations I should have gone gladly, but then I heard from you and felt your sympathy and affection, which I deserve so little may they never wither." She was the first person he had looked for after he had seen his father and visited the fresh grave on Sawyer's Hill, in the old family burying ground not far from Curzon's Mill. He took her with him for a drive down to Cotuit, where they talked for hours on a day of chill, earliest spring.

His reunion with Christina was strained. Something of the extent of their division can be seen in the letter she sent him from Stockbridge, where she went to visit her mother after they spent two weeks with his father at the Mill. "You have been constantly in my thoughts since saying goodbye to you. There is a great deal I should like to say—but it is all very involved. In the first place, I hate to be away from you now. I don't know why but it's partly because of what I knew you felt about my lack of sympathy with your mother that my being anything to you at this time savored more of side than anything else, and I couldn't think of your needing me. Also, I was unable—tied by a knowledge of what seemed to me at Papa's death the lack of truth which some people seemed unwittingly to fall into—and fearing it would seem the same to you—to tell you of the really profound shock her death was to me, and of how deeply and sincerely I had admired and respected her. She always stood to me as one having supreme courage and a splendid sort of never-failing pride. She never complained. I never heard her 'talk poor,' and her faithful care of the small things in life I always would like to imitate. I have always felt these things and thought of her essentially as one of the pillars of the earth. When she died I felt your father especially needed what in a very poor way I could give. I never felt I could give anything to you. Yet as you once said there is no point going on without sympathy—a physical relation is so little and understanding of that kind only makes one long for a more complete understanding. I have got used to thinking I could never give you more and your reproaches of lack of sympathy seemed something unfair or else something which I could not control. I realize now that we both long for the same thing in the other—a more complete sympathy and understanding of the aims of both. I realize that I have been more to blame than you—not always through fault but through deep difference—but I feel that if it is not too late as far as your feelings go we could grow to be more understanding—and though I could never take her place yet I could be to you in some sort a support."

Was it already too late? Life went on, and the Marquands spent most of the summer of 1932 at Cotuit, and Helen was there as both Christina and John had hoped she would be. By the end of the summer, Helen later remembered: "He had admitted to himself and to me that he had fallen in love with me. I could not pretend that his feeling was not returned. We both saw the situation as impossible *except* that John protested over and over that he was sure that his marriage to Christina could not last." There now began the process in which sincerity and self-deception exchanged places like partners in a dance. Marquand could not admit to himself or to either woman that he did not hope that his marriage was salvageable—it must fall of its own weight—but of course every nerve, now that he was in love with Helen, was alert for failure. There was, probably, nothing Christina could have done to alter the outcome.

Nevertheless, he persuaded her that they should "try" to solve their problems with professional assistance. A Cotuit friend was in the process of getting a divorce and he had found help at the hands of Dr. Irma Putnam, a psychiatrist who had studied with Freud and was interested in the new field of marriage counseling. With the Marquands, she had her work cut out for her. First of all, she advised that he keep Christina in the dark concerning his infatuation with Helen. It was exactly his own preference. Conventional gallantry, reinforced by the insistence also of Helen's brother Quincy, urged that Helen be "kept out of the picture"—she must never figure in Boston gossip as the "other woman" of scandal. Certainly, the deception was an injustice to Christina, who was allowed to struggle for irrecoverable unity while Marquand's attachment to Helen was actually growing more intense. And it was ultimately a disservice to Helen's cause, for his affair with her remained secret, self-accusing and unreal. But only time would sort out these effects.

During the next year Marquand seemed more tolerant and relaxed with Christina. Was he more agreeable because his life was now fed by a secret source of happiness or because he felt a guilty pity for his wife? Whatever the cause, his "better" mood made him perilously passive. He was always ready to write his own myth of the beleaguered and persecuted hero, even collaborating with life's accidents to produce episodes of his own victimization. So he agreed, *now*, when it was most risky, to spend the winter of 1932 at the Sedgwick Mansion with Christina's mother. Economy was the good-enough reason—the Marquands would cut expenses by moving in with Mrs. Sedgwick in this bleakest Depression period. During most of 1932 he had done almost no writing and in 1933 would publish just one story in the *Post* and nothing elsewhere; at the same time *Haven's End* was yielding meager royalties, selling fewer copies than almost any other novel he would ever publish. But it should long since have been obvious that living in Mrs. Sedgwick's household would be the impossibility of impossibilities, the condition most unfavorable to the Marquand marriage. Inevitably he would be writing Helen, as he did just after Christmas: "If you miss me it can't be any more than I miss you. I never missed anyone so much and never will again. Perhaps you'd like to know that, which is the only reason I tell you. This place has been amazing over the holidays. Shan is here with a dog and Ellery is here with that horrid little [dog] of his and the whole conversation seems to get down to an intense sentimentality about dogs. Everyone does his or her best to endow them with personalities which do not exist, discussing their habits and eccentricities by the hour. My mother-in-law keeps saying that Bruno [the Marquands' dog] is a big Swede and you know I often find myself being annoyed by this, which only shows that I am being engulfed in the introversions that have attached themselves to this house like limpets. When we don't discuss dogs, we turn to the personalities of Stockbridge, a ground with which I am not familiar, listening to anecdotes of characters who seem to me either infantile or insufferable snobs or parasites. Now and then I halt this flow by reminding everyone that the New Year will see incomes even more reduced, indeed to a point where there will not be incomes. This has a devastating effect as well it may since everything here hangs on the capitalist system."

More than ever Marquand now resented the inanity and self-centeredness of the Sedgwick way of life and Christina's accommodation to it. More than ever he felt that Christina and her family had no comprehension of his sacrifice in slaving to earn a living by his stories. His letter to Helen had gone on: "This morning I have been sitting working at a blank piece of paper thinking how rotten this thing is I am doing—devoid of any reality and even without skill." He was seated at a corner of the dining table in the big dining room of the house—the one place, it seems, that offered relative seclusion during the day—and that only between meals. In later years he liked to describe these conditions with sardonic humor as part of the cycle of anecdotes he had created about the Sedgwicks. One of these—either a literal episode or a poetic epitome of his situation—has already been mentioned: while he was hard at work on his wretched magazine stories Christina's brother was also trying to write—a novel!—in another room. Mrs. Sedgwick had knocked gently on the dining-room door. Would John mind taking Chou-fleur, Shan's dog, for his afternoon walk?

Yet still, guided by Dr. Putnam, he made no break with Christina but went again to Marston's Mills. They saw little of Helen this summer—her mother had died and she spent most of the time with her father at the Howe family place in Rhode Island. The Marquands did not repair their marriage. Like many another home less dramatically named, Heartbreak House contained all the human mixture of dull persistence, children, visitors, a spoiled dinner, a lost article, an invasion of ants, a breakdown in the plumbing—and the unnameable. Snapshots of the summer's end show the family in poses that have probably a spurious eloquence now. In one, John Marquand, in tweed knickerbockers, cigarette bitten somewhat fiercely, somewhat too jauntily, stands with his wife and children on Cotuit beach, the two children, especially little Tina, with faces somewhat wan. In another, Christina is caught in the act of airing and brushing toys and clothes and bedding on the lawn as they prepare to pack things up for the return to the city. She looks, probably quite characteristically, inept and melancholy as she bends over her task.

In the autumn John Marquand saw more of Helen Howe again on trips to New York, where she was now staying, and he tried to convince himself and her that he was coming to a decision about his marriage independently of this circumstance. "I am trying to make a rational decision and to convince myself that I should do the same thing even if you weren't there," he wrote her. But he admitted, "This has its elements of difficulty and irony because I long for you all the time." His literary sense must have told him that his emotions were falling into banality—perhaps a symptom of insincerity—but he could not help himself. He went on: "It may be that forty is a dangerous age when one makes a last desperate bid for life, but I do not think it is that. I think it is because your attributes were made for me, and I think mine were made for you. When everything else I have known seems to be crashing straight to glory or the reverse, the thought of you makes everything rational and calm and I no longer seem like a bewildered stranger walking in the dark. I only know that everything is better than the life I am living. If it weren't for my promise to Putnam not to be impulsive, I think I should be on my way to Paris this afternoon because this can't go on."

This was October. The following month he had a long conference with Irma Putnam in which he declared that he was at last ready to think of a divorce. As he recorded for Helen's benefit: "I said I might be still shaken by moments of panic at consequences and my qualms of conscience and duty, but that these were growing rarer and of shorter duration. It seemed to me peculiarly indicative that this had occurred after a long period of marital calm, when every effort was being made to keep me in the home. The only honest conclusion that I could reach was that I must get out. I said that, without wishing to exaggerate, I could not recall a day of actual tranquillity or happiness in the past eleven years, because always in the back of my mind there has been a clash between Christina and myself. That, in spite of Christina's protests of how much she cared for me, I could only meet them with an inner feeling of cynicism and disbelief, because there had been an accumulation of incidents over which I am still bitter and indignant. That I could not avoid the conviction that Christina's present efforts, which were inspired only by the knowledge that she was losing me, were continued only through pride, fear of public opinion and fear of losing a certain tangible position. I did not believe, I added, that the general situation had been changed in the last year and a half, except by a certain amount of mutual repression. That Christina's interest in my work and my activities were purely artificial; that she was inherently jealous of my affection for Johnny and of many of my small social successes in Boston; that her real interests are still bound up in herself and in her family; in fact that she is incapable of giving much that could inspire a return of love. Worse than this, I concluded, was a sense of unreality and insecurity, because I could not tell when she might veer to some other angle."

Marquand had told Mrs. Putnam that he was more firm in his new love than ever. His own prosaic phrasing to Helen was to prove characteristic, for he would use the same words some years later to another woman, Carol Brandt: "You were more completely satisfactory to me in every way than anybody I had ever met." For Helen he also produced a statement as sentimental as convention demands: "I seem to love you more and more to an extent that makes me wonder what I ever did before I knew you, and what I could possibly do were you to give me the air. Whenever I think of you, even in my deepest states of gloom, which are quite a few these days, I feel tranquil and almost happy—in most ways happier than I have ever felt. And it hasn't got anything to do with the book on Sexology either, which comes after you have clipped the coupon, in a plain, unmarked wrapper. It is a steadily growing feeling between us and the knowledge that I can rely utterly on your love, companionship and interest that makes me love you so. Everytime I see you I am never disappointed, for I always feel this more strongly, and I think it is the first time I have experienced this phenomenon. At any rate I think in any human relationship one gets back what one gives, and that is why my love goes back a thousand times, because you have given me so much more than I have ever deserved or have a right to ask. Furthermore I really do believe with you and me that this would grow better all the time, ending in something so magnificent that one might well thank God for being allowed a little while on earth."

Except in rare instances, perhaps, most love letters read as stalely as this, even when they are the love letters of a man of letters: love is apt to be a great leveler of expression, reducing the normally inventive to helpless platitude—it is enough, after all, that the letters read like poetry for one person. Helen Howe found them effective under the circumstances. It would have taken an older and more skeptical lover than she to have laughed at passion that concluded: "Remember that when I am dust and in the grave I shall love you." Even Mrs. Putnam, it seems, was impressed by Marquand's feelings. She accepted his severe analysis of Christina, advised him to continue to keep his relationship with Helen secret so that she should carry no burden of responsibility into an eventual marriage with him, and instructed him that he must now quietly tell his wife of his decision—after which he would go away somewhere for a month or so and give her time to assimilate it. Carrying out this plan, he responded immediately to an invitation that had come to him in New York to work in Hollywood on the script of *Naughty Marietta*, which was being converted from musical to film. "A pretty scaly job," it seemed to him, but it would provide a free trip and a recompensed interval away from Christina.

While waiting for the offer to materialize he stayed in the Beekman Place apartment of a Fuller cousin. Lucy Ames was older than he; her marriage with the theatrical producer Winthrop Ames was her second, the outcome of a divorce that had rocked Boston society (she had abandoned a Cabot to run off with Ames). Cousin Lucy had the talents and the inclination of a confidante and go-between, and John, of whom she was very fond, quickened all her impulses to counsel and encourage him to take the path she had done. At times her enthusiasm for recalling her own case got in the way of actual attention to his, as he reported with amusement to Helen: "History, she says, repeats itself. It is the most amazing thing, whenever I try to explain my situation, she will not listen, but instead she wants to tell me about *her* operation which is all that interests her." Nevertheless, he appreciated her provision of a refuge in his troubles, an orderly household where everything ministered to his peace of mind—as contrasted with Christina's helter-skelter regime. And Lucy not only encouraged him to take the direction he desired, but extended her attentions to Helen, often bringing them together with a matchmaker's zeal.

He had other sources of comfort. Carl and Carol Brandt (formerly Carol Hill) made another outpost of the comfortable, well-run life that seemed bliss to Marquand after his years with Christina. His ties of friendly dependence on his agent were strengthened by his old feelings for Carol. The Brandts, too, were in his confidence—and both were also experienced in the toils of marital disunion. Carl had divorced his first wife, and Carol's marriage with Hill had been approaching dissolution when he was accidentally drowned. "They have been awfully sweet to me and have given me a lot of good advice the tenor of which is for God's sake don't compromise, but go ahead as I am going and call off all marital bets," he wrote Helen. The Brandts, like Cousin Lucy, loved to cosset John; at their apartment on Park Avenue, even more than at Lucy Ames's, it could be said that the hostelry services were of the finest order, the food and drink especially excellent, and the company cheerful and flattering. John Marquand was discovering that he had a taste for such things.

Gossip of his distractions in New York must somehow have reached Boston. Christina complained to Dr. Putnam, who promptly passed the complaints along to him. He responded in something of a fury: "The attitude of Christina that she must impose her own ideas of rectitude at all costs, no matter how small the matter may be which is involved, has caused me many humiliations. This is the more true because Christina has discovered that anything she really wants to do involves a moral issue. And when a moral issue is involved she feels it is just for her to gain her point by any immoral method which may pop into her head." She had taken, it seems, to opening his mail. He was beginning to feel that it was no longer possible to pretend to her that he hoped for improvement in their relationship. "I become more and more aware of the impossible situation under which I have been living. I believe it would be better ultimately for us to continue separated. When I said I wanted our situation to turn out all right, my statement was dictated by an agony of soul, rather than by a belief that it ever would." He was tired of the painful and hypocritical game that he and his psychiatrist had connived at. "It seems to me under these circumstances that it does no good to offer Christina too much encouragement. Instead of nursing the belief that everything is a bad dream with no substance of reality, I think she should be made as kindly and gently as possible to face the definite probability that matters will not turn out as she expects. As far as the possibility of a nervous breakdown is concerned, I am prepared to believe that she will have one, as she has had before when she had not been allowed her own way by other means. I do not think that such a recourse, or any pressure from her family will alter my point of view." He realized he was being "hardboiled and unsympathetic," but he had set his course now and the rigor with which he would keep to it was only beginning to be apparent. For the time being, he was tired of Christina's letters, so full of reproaches and appeals, and he asked that the psychiatrist undertake to receive and transmit their messages to each other.

As it turned out, the Hollywood invitation to write the *Naughty Marietta* script did not materialize, but Marquand took his leave of absence from Boston just the same, going for a trip to Bermuda with the Brandts in January 1934. They stayed at the elegant Castle Harbour, then just opened, for two weeks. With his two companions—the vivacious Carol, who continued to charm, and sterling Carl, who told ribald stories and mixed up devilish rum concoctions—he was lapped in cheerful forgetfulness not only of Christina but a little, it is possible, of earnest young Helen as well.

12

Journey to the East

When Marquand got back from his Bermuda holiday with the Brandts in February 1934, his impulse towards flight was by no means spent. And immediately an opportunity presented itself for his taking a longer and more distant leave of absence from all his troubles. The *Post* wanted to send him to China! Earl Derr Biggers, the creator of Charlie Chan, had recently died, and his popular mysteries with Oriental backgrounds—*The Chinese Parrot* and others—were suddenly at an end. Who could continue in this vein? Thomas Costain thought of Ben Ames Williams; but Williams declined—he was well satisfied to be already one of the *Post*'s best-paid writers. A summons was then sent out to John P. Marquand, and when he returned from Philadelphia, he reported to Helen the results of conversations in Independence Square: "I have finally found out—I'm just back from a day in Philadelphia—what the *Post* wants of me. It is one of the most exciting and complimentary things which has come my way. It seems they have an idea that a Chinese character is always popular. Charlie Chan was a big number with them, and John T. Foote's 'Number One Boy,' and Sax Rohmer's 'Fu Manchu' goes big in *Collier's*. They now want a new Chinese character and a Chinese background, particularly as they believe that the Orient will soon be on the front page in the news and will be for a long while. They have hit upon me as the boy to do it, and they want me to pack right off to China—preferably Peking. Aside from all other considerations this excites me a good deal, because it is primarily important business, a part of my profession and an offer which I don't think I'd refuse under any circumstances. Once started I figure the whole jaunt would consume about two and a half months, and they will make a cash advance and raise my rates to pay time and expenses. It means that I shall get a new slant on a lot of things, and they believe it will make me their fiction expert on China."

His sense of his opportunity and of how literary fashions are created was accurate. From his contact with the East, which had hinted its appeal in Hawaii but was now to disclose an authentic and fascinating reality, came greater success as a popular writer. He would outdo Biggers, Foote and the rest in blending the appeals of detective fiction and the Oriental exotic. Indeed, his success in this medium was to be so great that even when he had turned his back on it in favor of serious writing he would remain for large numbers of readers chiefly the creator of the little Japanese agent, Mr. Moto. For millions who would see this character on the screen, Mr. Moto was an unforgettable personality. Marquand came back from China with gold dust in his knapsack. And yet, he would afterwards consider that he had been deflected by this success—as by earlier successes—from a better course.

As he told Helen, he would have as unhesitatingly accepted the assignment "under any circumstances." Still, he also wanted to get as far away as possible from the protracted effort to terminate his relationship with Christina and, also, from the pressure for action and decision that rose out of his relationship with Helen. In the same letter telling Helen about the *Post*'s offer he reiterated the devotion he felt for her in more unreal, pseudoplatonic tones than ever: "There comes a great general impression that we are in some way the same thing, and life doesn't matter and nothing matters, because we are beyond life and death. We are sublimated somewhere into an absolute when we each know all about the other, when there is no need of subterfuge or reticence because we are both the same person." Aboard the *Empress of Japan* on March 4 he could still imagine Louisburg Square, "the cold air and a faint smell of coal smoke," and see Helen's house, "the iron fence and the little white statue, and the windows I have passed so often, like a soul in purgatory." As it turned out, perhaps because of his need for detachment from what lay behind him, the East offered Marquand a surprisingly stirring experience. In everything he wrote in which the Oriental background figures, there are to be found traces of something better than the mere story, a poetry of appreciation for civilizations different from his own. He kept a notebook recording some of the impressions of his travel in Japan, Korea and China. In its entries and a few letters written to Helen Howe one can perceive aesthetic awareness and a note of irony arising out of his realization that the human scene before him was older than any he had known and had seen more changes than he could imagine. It was perhaps in the East that he acquired the observing eye and the ironic reporting voice that would serve him best when, like an archaeologist or a thoughtful traveler from another country, he described Newburyport or Boston or New York. The Orient is absent from his most serious literary undertakings, but not what the Orient had taught him.

His study began immediately. Except for a handful of white officers, the *Empress*'s crew was entirely composed of Chinese, organized efficiently under "number ones," a miniature Chinese society with its hierarchy and customs. Down in the steerage, he recorded, "the culture of China started at once. Lots of the little Canton boys had taken off their pants and were doing washing. A barber had set up a chair in the corner of an alleyway. Bamboo and greens and dried fish and Chinese sweetmeats were for sale in booths. The engineer boys off duty were playing fantan. Some other boys were getting rows of benches together for a Chinese play. They had set up a stage background with very good silk paintings and two chairs with handsome pink silk cushions." From fellow passengers—particularly a Mr. Hart, who proved to be the vice-president of the National City Bank in charge of its Chinese business—he began to collect information about the country he was approaching. He heard stories about the "Young Marshal," who had lost $90 million in silver which had been held in Mukden, and who was finally paid by the Japanese to leave the country for a trip around the world—with eighteen concubines whom the steamship company listed as secretaries.

On the fifteenth he was in Hawaii, approaching again, as though in a dream, the dreamlike outlines of mountain and shore that he had left a little less than a year before. "It seemed to have been waiting," he mused. "The clock seemed to have stopped from the time I had left that island, leaving that world in timelessness and peace, the peace of lotus flowers; the peace of the most languorous day in June. I could swear that the boys had been waiting to dive again for dimes. Their bodies made the same pattern where the mud of the propellers churned up the harbor bottom. The Royal Band in their white suits and orange paper leis had been waiting to play Aloha. The old Hawaiian women and the Japanese with the leis had been waiting, and the hibiscus flowers and the kimonos in the park."

Japan, however, both amazed and repelled him. Like many visitors from the West, he was astonished—and perhaps resentful—of the parody of his own civilization that the Japanese had contrived to achieve in a few years. He was amused by the incongruities of old and new. He had been met at the Yokohama dock by a representative of the Japan Tourist Bureau and whisked through streets crowded with every kind of Eastern and Western vehicle, from oxcart to the latest Detroit model, and pedestrians in all varieties and combinations of the clothing of the two civilizations. He was set down at the Imperial Hotel in Tokyo, but the architectural masterpiece of cultural fusion, Frank Lloyd Wright's great design, apparently made little impression on this visitor, who called it "a swell affair designed by an American who must have gone partially native." It was all part of the queer, out-of-focus sense that everything in Tokyo gave him, and which seemed no more successful than the efforts of the hotel orchestra he could hear as he went up to his room: they were playing oddly stilted jazz melodies while the crooner fitted his song uneasily to Japanese syllables.

After lunch he went out into the modern streets of Tokyo—newer-looking than Chicago and certainly than Boston, since most of it had been built after the 1923 earthquake. The Tourist Bureau guide took him to the largest department store, "a cross between Filene's and Kresge's," where every conceivable consumer article of American type seemed available at a fifth of the price in American stores. In the sporting-goods department he found displays of baseball mitts, golf clubs, fishing tackle, and in the home-furnishing division there were Chippendale suites, the products of the Japanese Grand Rapids. He rode the new, clean subway to the Imperial University with its modern buildings and then looked at the theater district, where a long row of picture palaces with neon signs outside were playing cowboy and gangster movies. Some of the posed blowups showed Charlie Chaplin, or blond Hollywood stars in the clutches of their movie lovers. Still, on the other side of the boulevard where the principal business buildings rose in crisp masonry and glass, the gray tiles of the Imperial Palace were just visible over the edge of a black wall that had been built in the Middle Ages. And at the end of the movie street he came into a narrower alley full of little shops, where he saw a vendor selling medicine made of powdered snake ("Very full of vitamins," the guide said), and this opened up into a great square of Buddhist and Shinto temples. Inside a red lacquer temple a drum was beating.

The slow spring of Japan had not yet arrived and the landscape seen from the train Marquand took north to Nikko looked anciently worn and brown, all divided into little tracts diked and ditched for rice culture or with rows of leafless mulberry bushes tied up with twine, here and there trimmed pines and bamboo. The only uncultivated bits of soil he could see were the small graveyards that appeared every little while, with tall stones surrounded by hedges. Human figures appeared and vanished, caught in the immemorial attitudes of old paintings: men and women bending over mattocks or bearing baskets or walking with the long pole from which two buckets hung. The scattered farmhouses, mostly thatch-roofed, looked as though faintly sketched on an endless faded scroll. Yet electric-light poles and rows of high-tension towers strode over the ageless scene.

At Nikko, where the train emptied itself of several hundred passengers, there were the famous seventeenth-century shrines and temples up in the hills among small waterfalls and streams and bare Cryptomeria trees. Along the single street of the town that was sustained by this tourist attraction were inns and brothels. The ancient buildings disappointed Marquand. He came away with an impression of "a background of elaborate and heavy gold work encased in enormous stretches of fine red lacquer." The richly colored structures seemed to his Puritan tastes gaudy and grotesque. The tourists, who got drunk on sake on the return trip, were noisy and unattractive.

Back in Tokyo, he was taken to meet the puppet premier of Manchukuo, who, it appeared, was just then lodged with his entourage at the Imperial

Hotel. Premier Cheng turned out to be a dignified, refined-seeming aristocrat, "the first great Chinese gentleman I had ever seen," Marquand wrote Helen. He found himself comically exchanging through the translator elaborate declarations of courtesy and national goodwill with the premier, as though, instead of being a touristic journalist of no importance, he had been vested with the responsibility of establishing diplomatic understanding between his own nation and Manchukuo.

On the mainland, on the way to Seoul, the impression of the East that he had already felt in Japan deepened. The earth of Korea seemed older, more submitted to man's usage, than any scene he had yet contemplated. To the American, the New Englander, used to wooded countryside still persistent amid urbanism, there was something almost disturbing in the bare hills from which all vestiges of forest had vanished centuries before, and in the valleys and lower slopes cultivated to the last inch. He had never seen a country, he thought, "where the hand of man had rested so hard," rested, moreover, in exactly the same way for centuries. The look of the village houses with their crudely thatched roofs and mud-and-wattle walls, like the peasants guiding their wooden plows and the women in white robes with bundles on their heads, could not have been much different, he thought, at the time of Christ. "You saw all this like something in a story as the train went by, like something in a story utterly removed," the storyteller told himself. He wanted to get out and touch it, and when he had arrived in Seoul and gone to his hotel—built of English brick—he hired a guide to take him back into the country. The guide could not understand—and charged an exorbitant rate for complying with—Marquand's insistence on returning into the dusty Korean backland by car and even into one of the villages he had passed in the train and into one of the mud-walled houses with their stalls for pigs and oxen under the same single thatch roof as the family, and its storage containers, identical giant earthenware jars containing grain, rice or pickles, or human and animal manure.

Then from Seoul to the Manchurian border by train, rocking companionably along with his Oriental fellow travelers. A few who could speak English were always assuring him that they had met him before, just as he was positive, as falsely, that he had seen some of them somewhere. The landscape held him fascinated through the long hours of travel. The farm buildings, standing oftenest in the midst of fields beside a stream accompanied by a clump of willows, passed him like the fragile groupings on the blue and white ware his great-grandfather had brought back to Curzon's Mill. There was a pleasant air of order and grace about prosperous-looking farmsteads, each surrounded by its mud wall pierced by a wide gate that led into a courtyard with buildings on three sides, and he glimpsed the farm workers, men and women in blue robes or trousers and tunics and black boots, going about their work. It was hard to realize that he was in a country at war except when the train made stops to take on squads of armed soldiers with full field packs.

At Mukden he had a queer sense of being transported out of the East altogether, finding himself in a strange city with Western-looking buildings, streets and parks laid out by the Russians, in a country that seemed "a cross between Nebraska and the moon," as he wrote Helen. The Japanese had moved in and were sending currents of Western—not Eastern—energy into the place, improving the railroads and extending the network of roads into the interior. Here it was, however, that an old Reuters newspaperman gave him a piece of advice that he would remember as the strangeness and variety of his impressions continued to multiply. "Publish your impressions quickly, before you learn to doubt them," he said, "for the things you see will be right, though your conclusions inevitably wrong. Later your conclusions will be right but you will have lost the ability to see." Marquand's own capacity for astonished attention would remain intact, for he would never remain long enough on this or subsequent trips to "get used" to the Orient. His mind was, at present, crowded with unresolvable elements. Behind the spectacle of Japanese expansionism, the old world remained impassive and formidable, he thought, when he visited famous Manchu tombs outside the city—solemn, grand, a complete surprise. It was Easter Sunday, a clear and flawless morning, with a chill that left ice in the puddles on the ground, as he remembered. The wind had a wild, thin purity as though it came from a great distance, blowing over deserted space.

At Hsinking, the capital of the Manchukuoan state, Marquand observed the unease of Japanese authority in this old land. He was given the official tour of the town by a man from the puppet state's Department of Foreign Affairs—mostly through new and muddy streets bordered by vacant lots, where troops, all Japanese, were posted at regular intervals, apparently to guard the path of a visiting Japanese general. But despite the makeshift look of the town he was impressed by the personalities of the Japanese masters of Manchukuo. A Mr. Kawasaki, with whom he lunched, displayed, Marquand thought, that combination of egotism and alertness that made it likely they would manage to remain in power. Back in Mukden he listened to speculations at the International Club: war with Russia in five years, his new acquaintances among the foreign newsmen said.

For some days he had found himself a member of the floating club that springs up in any place in the world, however remote, among the workers of the press. Marquand was always a comfortable member of such groups, a good drinker and a good talker, easy and yet impersonal, interested in everything yet intelligently skeptical. So this night as on others he listened to everything he was told by the old hands—about Manchuria at the moment and in years past under the Old Marshal, and, of course, tales of Chinese torture, of which his informants gave vivid, if secondhand descriptions. But most of the talk was of war. A sound man for Fox Films named Tappan, who had seen the Japanese stopped in Shanghai by the Nineteenth Route Army, doubted the staying power of the invaders. The Manchukuo army, said someone else, was as useless "as another bar boy in this room." The New York *Times* correspondent, Venator, who had covered Russian news for years, offered information on the strength of the Russians: there was a huge new military base east of Lake Baikal; the Trans-Siberian Railroad was double-tracked with bases and airdromes all the way to Vladivostok, which was fortified, and stockpiled with supplies. The conversation turned to Harbin, once called the Paris of Asia. It had been the last of Old Russia until cut off "like some old Roman colony cut off from Rome when she finally fell," Venator said. The impoverished Russian community continued its traditions on thin soup. But in earlier days, he remembered, there had been great cabarets and beautiful girls, and no house detectives interfered with your entertainment of visitors in your room at the Harbin Hotel.

So, as they sat over drinks, Marquand and his friends talked on. "Boy, whiskey *tansan*. This Manchurian air makes everyone nervous and everyone drinks too much," said Venator. The brightly lit bar was filled with diverse specimens of the white population of the city, a strange island in the Oriental world stretching about them in the dark. Nobody had had dinner yet and nobody felt hungry and they had a few more drinks before they went to the Yamato Hotel grillroom and then, after dinner, Venator took Marquand and the two or three other men in his car to the only nightclub. A band was playing American jazz on a platform and Venator introduced Marquand to Sally, the "toast of Mukden," one of the entertainers in the place. She was a Korean girl with sharply slanted eyes, red lips, and a fine figure moving easily beneath the blue silk of her robe. "I felt that I was a swell dancer when we danced," Marquand wrote in his journal the next day. He had felt excited when someone told him that she was not only a hostess in the nightclub, but a spy for the Japanese who specialized in getting information from foreigners. But then, Venator had told him, the Japanese were obsessed with spying; no doubt Marquand's movements were being carefully recorded in some amateur detective's report and the notebook in which he was at that moment writing would be read by someone when he went out of his room.

At three-thirty the cabaret closed, and since Tappan was leaving on the 7 A.M. train for Dairen, nobody thought of bed and the group ended up at Venator's house, where Tappan fell asleep on the sofa. Venator rummaged for more liquor, and Marquand fell into conversation with Mrs. Venator about housekeeping in China. Though they had arrived at four-thirty in the morning, a smiling "number one boy" had let them in and gone silently to the kitchen to make coffee—as no Beacon Hill servant could have been expected to. But Mrs. Venator at once disabused him. "Forget this hooey about soft-footed, perfect Chinese servants," she said. On the contrary, they were dull, lazy, dirty and hard to manage and sometimes made scenes when

Missy was alone in the house. Rather comically, the old American middle-class complaint about servants was the conversational resource of the Californian Mrs. Venator as the dawn lightened the blinds that morning in Mukden. Outside, the air was already smoky from house fires burning soft coal. A rickshaw coolie was squatting between the shafts of his cart waiting for trade, the brasswork on his little vehicle already shined for the day. On a pile of ashes a boy was picking out black bits from the heap of gray. "We gave him twenty sen, a colossal sum," Marquand remembered, "but he kept right on at the coal, and did not seem to consider that his good luck would give him a holiday." Back at the hotel the Venators and Marquand helped Tappan pack and drank some absinthe he had in his room and Mrs. Venator quite forgot the servant problem and was full of fun and song. Marquand found that the night of drinking had left him sober. He attributed it to "the Manchurian air, more invigorating than the air on the Maine coast. A breath of it and your head is clear, two breaths and your nerves are jangling with excitement and unease." He said goodbye to Tappan, whom he would not see again, a descendant, like himself—he had discovered—of an old Newburyport family.

The next morning he went with Venator and a Chinese employee of the American consulate to visit one of the licensed opium shops, an invention of the government which, Venator explained, had been instituted as a source of revenue and as an imperial device to dull the rebelliousness of the Manchurian peasant. They went into the Chinese quarter, a place with its own variety of sights and sounds—of little shops for baskets and brassware, carts with studded wheels, the cries of rickshaw coolies, the clatter of feet in pattens. As they walked along, their guide pointed out here and there a doorway in an old warehouse or store with its windows painted out, but from it they could smell amid the other odors of the street the peculiar acrid smell of opium smoke. Finally they entered one such establishment—it turned out to be a large room—which reminded Marquand of a Mills Hotel or a Salvation Army flophouse. It was divided into cubicles made of white-painted matchboard, each with a black curtain that could be drawn across the front, and inside a thin black quilted mattress and a hard pillow. Behind a counter outside the row of booths hung a supply of wood-and-metal pipes, and a Chinese at the counter was tending a row of little oil lamps with their squat glass chimneys already lighted. The flat pellets of opium, wrapped in paper and looking exactly like sticks of chewing gum, lay on the counter also. For twenty sen one got cubicle, pipe, lamp and stick.

Marquand and Venator explained that they wanted to observe the procedures of the place, and the Chinese manager agreed to sell them a piece of opium which they could watch someone else smoke in their presence—and produced a husky young man who smiled delightedly as the curious fancy of the foreigners was explained to him. He then went into a cubicle and stretched himself on the black mattress. Leaning on his left elbow he proceeded to prepare the opium, unwrapping it carefully and holding the brown lump between two iron needles, one in each hand, over the flame of the lamp, which was set down beside him. The opium began to melt and he turned it expertly about with the needles so that none of it dropped off; then reaching for the pipe he placed opium on the tiny hole, ran the needle through to make a draft and began to smoke. A few minutes later a young girl, rather bleary-eyed, with matted hair, came into the cubicle, lay down beside the man, and also smoked a pipe. For sixty sen you could both smoke opium and have the girl—"rather a bargain for a trifle over eighteen cents," thought Marquand.

The next day, April 5, he was on the train for Peking, each railroad station surrounded by sandbags and barbed wire with a Japanese garrison posted on guard. Now and then officers boarded the train and examined Marquand's papers. Towards sundown, he looked out to see massive watch-towers and the walls of a walled city like an apparition risen upon the level plain—the gray bricks seemed as crisp and fresh as though just laid, the peaked roofs of temples could be seen above, and carts were going through the gates. It was easy to forget that one had come on a chugging train powered by steam along steel tracks laid just yesterday. The town stood as though the empire of ancient China still stretched out beyond the Great Wall. Dark fell before they reached the Wall itself at Shanhaikwan, which had been called "the first gateway of the realm." He changed there for the Peking night train, and the old imperial barrier was an invisible presence. But in the crowded station Marquand noticed the smells that would always seem to him characteristic of China—of dust and of garlic and "cooking bean-fat" and spices, of steaming tea, and of animal and human bodies. The compound odor seemed to express centuries of life in the same place.

In the morning on the train again he looked out now upon the veritable China. It was civilization before the machine, a civilization that revealed itself as having attained the greatest refinement in the use of human labor: "The balance of the baskets at each end of its pole across the shoulders was effective and good, the weave of the baskets, the way they were suspended accurately by thin ropes or by bent willow, the two-wheeled carts with the iron studding in their wheels and the black carriages above them, indestructible and the exact size for draft on the hard roads, the two-wheeled hand carts set at a proper balance, the mattock-shaped hoes." The southward progress of his journey had brought spring closer overnight. In the place of the bareness behind him the landscape was smudged with green. There were yellow willows and poplars in blossom. The winter wheat was coming up in rows eccentrically drawn across the fields, showing the shaping of hand tilling in the place of the straight furrows of Manchuria. And then he saw what everyone expects to find in an Eastern landscape: trains of two-humped camels, with loads between the humps and the driver in front, passing at a leisurely pace beside the tracks.

But finally he was at Peking, outside its immense, gray, battlemented walls. In a few hours he knew that he had had one of the great encounters of a lifetime. As he wrote Helen that evening: "I just got here this morning, but that is long enough to realize, even for a cynic like myself, that Peking is the most beautiful and delightful city in the world, though at last the world is passing it by." He had with some difficulty shaken himself loose from the Japan Tourist Bureau agent who had met him at the station, and after checking in at the Grand Hôtel de Pékin and visiting the ministry and the bank, he launched out, riding airily in the light carriage of a rickshaw "like a baby in a perambulator" behind the jogging coolie whom he had hired for $2.50 weekly. Marquand called out, "Forbidden City!"—and in a few minutes he had exchanged the Europeanized Legation Quarter for "something as strange and dramatically marvelous as anything I have ever seen." He was hardly the first Westerner to have been amazed at a human creation that could only be compared with Versailles or the Escorial for the vastness of its conception, space unfolding into space and ascending from level to level from the first great court, with its marble bridges leaping over the artificial river in its marble channel, to the grand palace of the Manchus. He passed from one empty courtyard to another, glancing at the grimaces of the carved figures, the frozen writhing of dragons on porticoes and balustrades. Here and there a pillar sagged and the brilliant paint peeled from the splitting wood. Grass grew in between the paving stones and between the yellow roof tiles. More than any of Europe's gray ruins this ancient place, gaily painted and ephemeral as a child's toy, was touching in decay. Rebuilt a hundred times by China's emperors, it might never be rebuilt again, Marquand thought, now that empire was at an end in China. Meanwhile, he somewhat guiltily contributed to the looting the monuments were suffering by buying from a guard some dragon medallions taken from the roofs and a figure riding on a horse and two blue dogs from the Temple of Heaven that he promised to bring home to Helen. Then, on his way home, he passed through the Chinese City. It was all alive—as the Forbidden City had been dead—with animated variety. A coal cart went by him pulled by men with ropes over their shoulders spread out fanwise like a dog team, a boy with a wooden bucket strapped on his back scooped up animal droppings with a wooden spoon and tossed them over his shoulder into the bucket.

In the ten days following, Marquand went back again and again to the Forbidden City to explore its maze of temples and courts, and he also visited others of Peking's famous sights, submitting himself to the touristic mood that was irresistible in this ancient city. He went to the Temple of Heaven, outside the southern walls—and compared his sensations to those the visitor feels on entering Chartres Cathedral. He returned daily to the endless variety of the busy street life, and he took the obligatory trips to the imperial summer palaces. For help and advice he called on a few Americans to whom he had introductions. A young sinologist from Boston, George Kates, who had been studying at the University of Peking for a couple of years, was an invaluable if slightly condescending guide to the antiquities, while from Ekins, the United Press man, he got some sense of the complex political reality of China in this crucial spring of 1934. He lacked the confidence, just the same, of another *Saturday Evening Post* writer whom he met, one who was also engaged in "working up" background materials. Frank Packard, author of the Jimmy Dale stories, told Marquand that *his* books had already sold over two million copies. He was full of garnered information and story material—bandit horror tales, descriptions of peculiar methods of torture—and considered himself a specialist in Oriental crime. He had visited many opium dens, he told Marquand; he intimated that his research had gone beyond timid observation. He looked pityingly at his colleague and declared that he thought that the *Post* had given Marquand a tough assignment.

What Marquand wanted most of all was to get out into the Asiatic backcountry, the wild and ancient land beyond the Great Wall. He was lucky to find a guide for such a journey. Walter Bosshard, a Swiss news photographer, took him to see a trader named Larson, who lived in Inner Mongolia four hundred miles north of Kalgan. A big, tough, extremely experienced adventurer, Bosshard spoke English with a German accent and almost no Chinese, but he was so certain of himself in any situation that he could manage what came up with one or two words or gestures rightly chosen. Marquand, who showed up at the train station in Peking in a leather suit lent him by the United Press man and carrying for equipment a flask of whiskey, knew he needed such a companion when he discovered that everything they might require was in the other man's duffel bag—flashlights, medicine for dysentery, iodine, even soap. But Bosshard's competence also saw them through awkward moments on the train, in Kalgan, and on the trip by car from there into Inner Mongolia. Once, when they were stuck in the mud just beyond the border, Bosshard generated a group of Chinese peasants out of the empty landscape and with shouts and cuffs got them to set the car on its way again. He even galvanized Marquand himself to a show of belligerence of which he had not thought himself capable. "Take his stick away and hit him," Bosshard commanded as Marquand found himself colliding with a big, not-so-willing farmer—and Marquand, to his own astonishment, did just that.

It was as close as he got to the kind of dramatic physical danger of which his soon-to-be-written adventure stories were to be full. They met no bandits or secret agents along the way, although Marquand had been hearing plenty of tales about them in Peking. His journey nevertheless provided him with the sensation that he had gone almost as far as it was possible to go away from everything that was part of his familiar world. In recounting the experience some years later to members of the Tuesday Night Club, he was able to convey to these hometown neighbors only a little of the strangeness he had felt in Mongolia. In Kalgan they had been entertained rather austerely by an elderly Methodist missionary, who had arranged that a colleague of his would drive them to Larson in his Model C Ford coupé. Displaying his usual resourcefulness, Bosshard proposed that they also call on a certain Adams Purpiss before leaving. "Will he give us a drink?" asked Marquand. "That is why I suggested it," answered Bosshard. "I do not know him very well but he always has vodka."

And so they went through the mud-brick town of Kalgan, the starting point of the old caravan route across Mongolia to Urga (the modern Ulan Bator), to visit the compound of the last of the old traders, who happened to be a Russian operating under a German charter. They passed through an inconspicuous door in a gray, windowless wall and entered an open yard as big as a parade ground. There, in the center, 750 camels were seated in rows eating hay. The rest of the ten-acre court was filled with camel drivers and workmen who were preparing bales and packages of goods—wrapping bricks of compressed tea in matting, filling boxes of pewter and copperware, packing up bolts of cloth and bundles of leather boots with upcurved pointed toes. In the midst of this spectacle was Mr. Purpiss who, as expected, furnished them with vodka. He was even more cordial when he heard that they were planning to visit Larson—he offered them on the spot the use of his brand-new Buick and the services of his chauffeur in the place of the missionary and his Ford. At a snap of Mr. Purpiss's fingers, a shiny limousine appeared, winding its way towards them between the piles of bricked tea and the camels. It seemed that Mr. Purpiss was quite serious: in fact, he was determined that they borrow his car for the journey. Mystified but delighted, Bosshard and Marquand accepted. Wrapped in bearskin rugs and seated on its fawn upholstery, they set out the next morning.

Marquand remembered his first sight of the plateau which stretched out beyond the Wall north of Kalgan. The undulating buckskin-colored plain was like a frozen sea. Faintly scored was the Urga road over which camels had carried silk on the first leg of a journey to Thebes or Babylon. The Buick produced amazement in each village they passed through—nothing more remarkable had been seen in Mongolia since the days of Genghis Khan. When they stopped they were treated like distinguished strangers and obliged to drink bowls of tea on which rancid butter floated. After fourteen hours, having passed bands of Chinese migrants driven from their homes like victims of the American dust bowl by the exhaustion of the soil, priests in red or yellow robes on a pilgrimage, and a camel caravan, the shaggy animals, each with its five-hundred-pound load of wood and hides, walking in a steady single file, they reached the man they had come to see. Frank August Larson, the fabulous "Duke of Mongolia," had lived among the Mongols in the yurt of a commoner and the palace of the emperor of Mongolia (who had made him a duke), and when Marquand met him he had for some time inhabited an abandoned "Lama temple," on friendly terms with his Mongol neighbors, trading in sheep and camels. He had been in Mongolia for forty years (five years later, however, forced out of business by the Japanese, he would visit Marquand in the United States and offer him his temple for a hundred dollars).

The morning after they arrived they went to see the most distinguished of Larson's neighbors, Teh Wang, the hereditary prince of "West Senurt," a domain stretching hundreds of miles to the Gobi. His palace and court with walls and pavilions was like a miniature of the Forbidden City, populated instead of deserted, with soldiers and courtiers and priests. Bosshard and Marquand were assigned elegant sleeping quarters furnished with red lacquer, and while they ate the Mongol dinner of boiled lamb and rice and rice wine, the prince sat beside them on the raised *tang* and conversed through the medical missionary Larson had sent along as a translator. His Highness was remarkably in and out of touch with the modern world. He was as infatuated as a child with the borrowed Buick and asked that he and his wife be taken for a ride in it. But he understood perfectly the political contest between Russia and Japan, in which he occupied a pivotal position as an independent power. As Marquand said goodbye he was standing in his blue silk gown watching some of his soldiers assemble five up-to-date machine guns that had just arrived by camelback.

Bosshard and Marquand were in the prince's territory for ten days. They were treated with a familiar cordiality; the Mongols took them riding, wrestled with them, fed them lamb and tea-and-butter, and laughed and sang with them before letting them leave. When they got back to Kalgan they returned the Buick, dusty and dented, to Mr. Purpiss, and Marquand, unable to restrain himself any longer, demanded to know the motive of the trader's generosity. No, it had not been for nothing. They had, as Purpiss intended, exhibited the splendid vehicle to the prince, to whom it would soon be presented as a gift in return for rights of caravan passage across the prince's lands.

Marquand took one other journey out of Peking in company rather different from Bosshard's. He had been in the city over a month and was about to return when he met Alan Priest, a curator of Chinese art from the Metropolitan Museum in New York. Priest asked him to join a party going into the interior of Shansi, leaving from the railhead at Taiyuan, the provincial capital. The goal of the trip was the Wutai Shan, which means "five terraced peaks," a mountain range with five peaks each topped by a Buddhist temple. Priest, in search of precious art objects, proposed to visit each of the temples; the trip was also, however, a pleasure safari for several wealthy Americans who had undertaken to foot most of the bills. George Kates, who spoke excellent Chinese, was accompanying the group as an interpreter. Thirty-six years later Kates's recollections were sharp. The Americans, who had an entourage of servants and baggage carriers, "so that they seemed a half-mile train when they were on the road," made, he thought, a ludicrous assortment of disparate personalities. There was Lucy Calhoun, the well-known widow of an American minister to China and sister of Harriet Monroe, the editor of *Poetry* magazine, who for some years had been keeping a sort of boardinghouse in Peking for rich visitors from the United States. Also on the trip was Ray Slater Murphy, the wife of Dr. James Murphy of New York, who had only recently come to China; Kates remembered her as a colorful, good-looking, free-mannered woman in her thirties who "took tranquilizers" and wore a bracelet inscribed "Ricuerdo de Guadalajara." She and Marquand immediately became good friends and remained so; he would later dedicate to her the best of his Chinese spy-adventure stories, *Thank You, Mr. Moto*. In contrast with her was another wealthy lady, Mary Wheelwright of Boston and Bar Harbor, who was the kind of New England spinster jokes are made about; she did not drink and would not even taste the pastries offered in hospitality by the temple priests, "but ate raisins which she brought along in a green Harvard book bag."

The members of the expedition soon found themselves consciously grouped around the polarities of Mrs. Murphy and Miss Wheelwright. One was either a Rake or a Frump. Mrs. Calhoun, a clever, spirited woman with an interest in the arts and a tolerance for the personal behavior of others, belonged with Marquand to the Rakes; Miss Wheelwright had as her companions in propriety a landscape architect by the name of Fletcher Steele and, somewhat unwillingly, Kates himself. As the party jogged along on mule litters Kates decided that he disliked them all—they seemed ignorant, arrogant and distasteful to the serious young scholar, and he hated his assignment of negotiating on their behalf as they made their bickering way among scenes of a beautiful and ancient world beyond their comprehension. Marquand seemed a little more sensitive to what was about him, and Kates remembered some good moments they spent apart from the rest. One day, in particular, the two of them climbed one of the peaks alone. A young priest from the temple on top met them with a picnic lunch; he was staggering under heavy silver plates.

But on the whole Kates thought it an unpleasant journey. Marquand was drinking heavily and flirting with Mrs. Murphy while taking a malicious pleasure in shocking Miss Wheelwright with a display of apparent depravity. Once, when Kates remonstrated at the game, Marquand told him, "You're behaving like a tutor on the North Shore." When the group returned at last to Peking they decided to sink their differences and have a party, renting a palace and a staff of servants and musicians for a grand dinner. It was an absolute fiasco, Kates recalled, and ended with smashed glasses and an overturned table.

Marquand, however, despite his lack of scholarly equipment or perhaps because of it, was, more than Kates knew, aware of something ultimately "mysterious" about the East under Western eyes. As he prepared to leave

Peking for Shanghai and the trip home, he summarized his feelings: "And here is another thing, though I can only look upon the country with the ignorance of a complete stranger, where every sight is strange. In Peking and in any place where the European race lives in numbers, one looks into China in complete comfort and protection, as one looks at a model in a museum case. I do not make it clear, but you have seen fish in an aquarium. You see those fish through glass. But I remember once in Honolulu, when I dove with a spear out on the edge of the coral reef and swam for a little while among the fishes. My body in the water groping through those coral grottoes must have been a shocking, curious sight, but the fishes swam near me unafraid, slow and intent on living in their own world. In a way it is like that in the interior of China. A single foreigner is like a diver in the sea, in an element which is not his own, traveling in a world on the whole as indifferent to him as it is to the misfortunes of its own kind, and in that struggle for survival and in the conventional integration of their lives they are insensitive to misfortune. At any rate you are in the water, not looking through glass. But believe me you are not of that world."

Probably he realized already that he could never write seriously about the Orient, though he would come back again to China the following year and would return on subsequent trips. It was not merely a question of knowing enough, of "working up," of diligent observation, even if he was sometimes tempted to think he could manage it if he had the right resources. Six years later he proposed to Evans Carlson of Carlson's Raiders that they collaborate on a story of Chinese warfare, for he had followed the Japanese war with the greatest attention and Carlson's expertise seemed capable of adding that authority about his subject a writer needs. But the project was never undertaken. Marquand understood that such authority was not transferable. Later still, he told an interviewer: "I remember I thought I'd do a story on China after I'd been there. I've been there a couple of times since. I'm very fond of the East, and I think I have the atmosphere of North China down pretty well. But I can't do it. I've never lived there. I've never worked there. I don't have a stake there."

Yet as the interviewer was well aware, Marquand had made use of his knowledge of the Orient in his half-dozen highly successful novels of mystery and adventure, to which he, like most of his critics, would later deny the title of literature. No doubt *Ming Yellow* and its successors, the Mr. Moto stories, deserve no better verdict now. As fiction they have the merits and deficiencies of their genre—fast-paced, often intricately contrived plots that do not bear close examination from the point of view of probability, characters only occasionally given a depth of interest. Yet the atmosphere of these stories is worthy of more serious purpose; it conveys a sense of place and of history and holds one's attention.

Ming Yellow was started immediately upon Marquand's return in the midsummer of 1934 and was out in the *Post* in December. He had brought home a piece of the rare Ming yellow porcelain and the idea for a story about a group of tenderfoot Americans in quest of such treasure. The plot was probably generated out of secondhand anecdotes of dubious authenticity about the bandits and warlords who did, in fact, abound in the unpoliced countryside. One night in Peking Marquand had sat up listening to a friend of Bosshard's tell one tale after another of bandit adventures. Among other details to be transposed into the book was the story of a courteous bandit chief whose Western guest frowned at one of the host's singing girls—she was promptly tossed off a convenient cliff. But the details of the setting are another matter, for they come out of Marquand's own glimpses of Peking streets or the inns along the country road. Whatever his eye had once rested on appears with a strange vividness behind the paper-thin narrative.

This authenticity, probably unappreciated by readers who gulped down the novel as a thriller, is to be discerned in all of Marquand's writing with an Eastern setting. In the following year he produced *No Hero,* the first of the Mr. Moto stories. It opens in the Imperial Hotel in Tokyo, which had impressed Marquand by its curious blend of East and West. It begins, moreover, precisely on the particular day during his stay when Premier Cheng of Manchukuo was lodged there also. His recollection of the boat trip to Shanghai, which was his last stop in China before his departure in 1934, furnished his description of Shanghai harbor when the hero is brought there. Similarly, his conversation with newsmen about Harbin is the underpinning of the account of her home given by Sonya, the Russian spy. The final scenes are enacted in a North China village—an unlikely place for a secret technical document to be hidden, except that Marquand had seen and could correctly describe one. *Thank You, Mr. Moto* is more meticulously written. Its setting, more elaborated than the settings in the two previous novels, is Peking, in which Marquand could readily situate himself imaginatively. *Think Fast, Mr. Moto* begins in Shanghai but soon shifts to another scene that Marquand had studied well, Hawaii. However improbable its events might be judged, the novel's small references to Honolulu and its suburbs carry conviction. In *Mr. Moto Is So Sorry,* Marquand went back once more to his memories of 1934, and his hero's journey duplicates Marquand's own arrival in China, although there is considerably more melodramatic incident along the fictional journey. The story concludes in Kalgan in a trading compound exactly like that of Adams Purpiss.

The fifth Moto book, *Last Laugh, Mr. Moto,* written late in 1940, is the least effective of the series precisely because that queerly authentic Oriental atmosphere is lacking. Marquand felt the looming of war in the Pacific, for he situated his story this time in other waters—the Caribbean. To make the story more "American" it transpired on a never-never island with little or no local color of its own. All that was left of the Far East was Mr. Moto himself, a somehow less resourceful and charming figure than before. The plot, moreover, hinged upon the contest of Mr. Moto and a German agent for possession of a secret airplane device; this, after the Japanese–German entente, was not merely a bit of melodramatic fantasy but a major improbability. The book had a curious publishing history. Rejected by the *Saturday Evening Post* and the *Ladies' Home Journal* it was finally taken by *Collier's* which sought to remove the once-appetizing Moto label by titling it *Mercator Island*. Marquand was with difficulty persuaded by Carl Brandt to allow book publication, and though a contract was signed, the publisher hesitated to bring out the book after the bombs fell. To everyone's surprise, however, it sold rather better than previous Motos in hard cover. Perhaps the choice of title helped, for it coincided stunningly with the American determination that all the Mr. Motos should soon laugh their last. The title was also prophetic of the fate of Marquand's series, though there would be one last return to the Oriental scene in a postwar revival of Mr. Moto, *Rendezvous in Tokyo*, published in 1957.

Marquand's interest in the politics of the Far East made the best of these tales melodramatic fables of real events. For years China had been the ground of contest among Western states, and now Japanese imperialism was extending its power further and further onto the mainland. China itself was in the midst of a revolution that was also a civil war—only the future would identify the ultimate transformers of the Middle Kingdom. Amid these complexities it was difficult to formulate an appropriate American policy that was both moral and patriotic. It is perhaps significant that Marquand's heroes in most of these stories are somewhat cynical, passive expatriates. They have, as Henry James said of Winterborne in *Daisy Miller*, lived too long in foreign parts—until a spirited American girl stirs up their sluggish blood. The hero of *Ming Yellow* is a newspaperman who tries to mind his own business while quietly admiring the culture of China—but finds himself looking after a wealthy American who falls into the hands of a needy warlord. The American protagonist of *No Hero* is a more extreme case. He is a demoralized flying ace who, now that World War I is over, drinks too much and knocks his own country by pointing out that Japanese aggression is no worse than our take-overs in South America. Hard up and embittered, he lets himself be used by the Japanese agent in a scramble with the Russians and the Chinese for a nuclear bomb design. (Even in 1935 there was talk of the possibility of a weapon that would vastly multiply the power of an ordinary explosion.) The American resident of Peking whose story is told in *Thank You, Mr. Moto* has a characteristic remark, "It doesn't matter, does it?" but his indifference and inertia yield to his feeling for a countrywoman who has been hunting art treasures for a museum, like Alan Priest. Without intending to, she embroils him in a struggle behind the Peking scene involving a bandit plotting to loot the city, an agent of the Japanese war party that supports the bandit, a conservative Mandarin prince, and Mr. Moto, who is in the service of the Japanese moderates. The action of *Think Fast, Mr. Moto* is mostly located in Hawaii, but the intrigue this time is again a melodramatic version of current politics in China: money to support Chinese revolutionaries in Manchukuo is being secretly transferred via an American bank and a gambling house in Honolulu, a matter of interest to the ubiquitous Japanese agent, while the young businessman who figures in the novel has, until romantic emotions sway him, been the servant of an exclusive family loyalty. And in *Mr. Moto Is So Sorry* the American visitor on his way to join a scientific expedition on the border between Inner and Outer Mongolia becomes by accident the carrier of a coded Russian message concerning Japanese plans for military action. It is a message that the jingo generals in Japan wish to intercept, but Mr. Moto, again the moderate, will see it passed on in order that the Russian response can be tested. The American of this last book is still another example of slightly blighted heroism. He is a man under a cloud, whose mission to China is purely personal, and who is so indifferent to politics that he allows himself to be thought a Japanese spy.

It would not be correct to say that Marquand was writing political allegory in these lighthearted entertainments which were purveyed as "escape" reading. Yet their heroes suggest an interpretation of the American role in the Far East in the years before World War II. They are compelled to shake off indifference and passivity, as though to suggest the value of American involvement, American pugnacity in the Far Eastern scene. There is political significance, too, in the calculated appeal to American readers of the ever-resourceful Mr. Moto, the representative of Eastern subtlety combined with Western efficiency, who emerges as a gentleman of wit and charm. Up to 1939 it must have seemed possible to some that Japan would be moderate and reasonable in its expansion in the Far East—that the Mr. Motos would defeat the Japanese military fanatics. Pearl Harbor, of course, put an end to American neutralism as well as to hopes of Japanese moderation—but not before Marquand's Moto series had become one of the most popular fictions ever to be run in an American magazine.

13

Endings and Beginnings and a Persian Interlude

The sense of living in another life, as alien as a distant sea depth from his own, had kept the problem of Marquand's marriage out of his mind for five months. One day in Peking Christina's image rose before him like a reproachful ghost, its garments dripping woe: he heard that her mother had died. Both of her parents, against whom he had so often railed, were gone, and he visualized with discomfort that she "must be utterly alone." But it would make no difference, he assured Helen. He did not join his wife and children at Marston's Mills on his return late in July 1934, but immediately prepared to settle down in New York, where pleasure and work were mixed for him by master hands. Carl and Carol Brandt gave him a room in their apartment and set him going on his new serial, *Ming Yellow*, caring for him like trainers in charge of a racehorse—exercises in the morning, squash at noon, evenings of talk and company framed his hours of work. He had been drinking heavily in China, but now, along with Carl, who was going through one of his periodic attempts to cure himself of a more desperate alcohol habit, he stayed cheerfully sober most of the time. Despite the painful drama of the separation, enacted chiefly over the telephone in talks with Christina and lawyers, life was suddenly very simple. Even Helen, by her own resolution, was not seeing him, and though he declared his undiminished devotion to her he was curiously content in a situation which seemed sufficiently familial. Every afternoon and even on Saturdays and Sundays he dictated to Carol at the typewriter.

With Christina, the painful process of deceiving and self-deceiving, the pretense of an effort towards reconcilement that must inevitably fail, continued for a little while. But after a visit he paid her in August she wrote: "It did not seem to me that you showed either desire or hope of things being better." He stayed away, only picking up the children now and then for a visit elsewhere—to Seal Harbor, Maine, where he was the guest of the interesting Mrs. Murphy he had met in China, or to Cousin Lucy Ames in New York. Christina's letters continued to labor the mystery—equal to that of compatibility—of incompatibility. He reminded her that they had been unable to resolve their differences for two years, which was "proof enough to me that they cannot be resolved now. I have frankly been unable to find anything in either of our attitudes which gives me any certainty that a resumption of our marriage would be any more successful than it was before. There seems to exist the same competition, bitterness and jealousy. I am too tired to have any more strain and battle. The wisest thing, I think, would be to consider this side of our relationship closed." On October 24 they signed a formal agreement of separation. While its details were being negotiated they found relief, as is generally the case, in arranging with bitter care for the protection of their severed interests. Christina would have custody of the children with due allowance for their father's rights to see them and to take part in directing their education; 43 West Cedar Street was to be Marquand's absolute property and Marston's Mills was to belong to Christina, along with their sailboat and the furnishings of both houses—with the exception of those items that even in the legal document speak eloquently of Marquand's symbolic attachments: "two Marquand family portraits, a Sheffield silver teapot, the Atkins spoon, a filigree silver basket, his aunt Greta's lowboy, his mother's console table and butterfly table, two Chippendale chairs, a large blue and white Chinese jar, the Marquand family Bible, the works of Margaret Fuller." The monetary arrangements for Christina and the children seemed, naturally, unfair to both sides. "I'm having most of my fillings removed from my teeth in this settlement," Marquand wrote Helen, while Uncle Ellery Sedgwick was convinced that Christina was being taken advantage of. They argued over the provision for annual payment by Marquand of a percentage of his income over a stipulated minimum—a modest sum at the moment but potentially, as his earnings would increase, one that might be considerable. He would later complain that this clause and the effect of a stepped-up income tax were destroying his incentive to pursue success as a popular author.

Yet as is so often true no finality seems really final to the unwilling party. While their lawyers negotiated the particulars of the settlement, Christina still wrote John letters of anguished regret, to which he replied with implacable sympathy: "Now that we are so rapidly reaching a point when nearly everything between us will be irrevocably ended, it may help you to know that I share your own distress. I know quite well what you are going through, because last January I went through a somewhat similar period of agony." With some hypocrisy, he told her, "Of course I am no more happy about this than you are, and in a way I have a greater loneliness to contend with, but more so I have the perception to see that you and I would be unhappier still in resuming our old life together." Yet as they approached the expected date of the divorce decree, even he wavered, and responded to her appeal for a last effort for the sake of the children: "If you have really had the impulse to come down here to see me, I think you ought to try it and not to feel that you will be considered as vacillating and not be swayed, if you have been, by the advice of other people, however well it may be intended. Our problem in the last analysis is up to you and me; and you and I know more about it than anyone else. It has been ten days now since I received your letter, and what you have said about Johnny, and the piece of paper that Tina wrote on, are like knives in my heart. Why don't you come down to New York, spend a night at a hotel, and spend the day with me here? At any rate I could make myself a good deal clearer about summer plans, vacation, schools and money."

For both, the fear that they were wronging the children was real enough, and it was more generally urged than it is today that couples stay united "for the children's sake." Eleven-year-old Johnny's headmaster at the Indian Mountain School, F. B. Riggs, had even written: "It is not my business to pry into your personal affairs but it is my business to do everything I can do to protect John from what would be little short of disaster for him. Can nothing be done to avert it?" Perhaps, indeed, the son of Austen Riggs was not merely expressing a conventional judgment. Johnny had already suffered the representative deprivations of the offspring of the wealthy and self-indulgent. He had been handed about a good deal, though always with much petting, by his parents and grandmother, and he was already familiar with the shifts of the wind that might send him suddenly away to his grandmother with a governess or leave him with one and not the other of his parents. He understood very little of the drift of events, but he had come to recognize the silent adult language of hostility and anguish as well as its audible expression. The last two years had been full of unexplained matters. "Dear Mom," the bright, suspicious child was writing in January 1934. "Why is my father going to Hollywood?" To Marquand he wrote: "I'm sorry you're going to China. I can't think of anything I want from Honolulu or China. I hope we can go on a camping trip next summer." Yet he was proud of this often-absent parent, and became, that year, aware of his father's writing. For the first time he read *Haven's End* and offered his considered judgment: "I think it is swell at the end." The boy then read the earlier *Warning Hill* and offered his father the tribute: "I think it is the very best or nearly the best I ever read." And when Marquand returned from the East, Johnny wrote from Marston's Mills about his dog Angus, who had developed a craze for pulling out the parrot's tail feathers, but he also added: "We are all very glad to hear that you are back. When are you coming down to see us?"

The Marquands' eleventh-hour impulse to mend their differences for the sake of Johnny and his sister was short-lived, and Christina's visit to her husband in New York was a failure. "I went down determined to be ruled by my head and not my heart and was antagonistic," she later said. He wrote to her, "Our last interview removed my final doubts as to the wisdom of our separating permanently, as I can see now the essential elements of our situation have undergone no change. This being so, I think it will relieve us both of emotional strain, as well as obvious misunderstandings, if we do not have any further interviews or exchanges of notes." They kept to this hard rule until the divorce was granted, on March 19, 1935, in Pittsfield to Christina's formal plea on the usual ground of cruelty. In January Marquand had rented an apartment of his own on East Seventy-fifth Street in Manhattan, and he planned that he would take another long trip out of the country as soon as the divorce proceedings were over. Yet a few days after his interdict on communication Christina made another appeal to him, offering as she had never done before to make efforts to alter herself to his liking, and again he was moved—or temporized—sufficiently to suggest that they reconsider matters once again on his return, before the end of the six months when the decree would be absolute.

Was there a basis for the hope that some change, particularly in Christina, might be the key to reconciliation? In the months that followed she herself decided that she had somehow deserved some of Marquand's charges of selfishness. In a diary she began to keep she wrote: "I suppose I never really loved his nature. I didn't knuckle under. And when he outstripped me I wasn't clever enough to take a back seat. Egotism on my part, I think. Towards John I never showed the consideration I did towards others. I did treat him unconsciously meanly, because I never either liked what he gave me in the beginning or his own nature. His standards did not interest me. I did consider him lower, and low from a worldly point of view. In self-justification I should say that I would have loved had there been inspiration for it. I think had I loved in the beginning we would have merged in a companionship, but I didn't and when I was ready to he lost interest."

As she made this effort at self-inculpation Christina was at no time allowed to suspect the existence—obvious to more vulgar minds—of "another woman," and to identify that woman as Helen Howe. She had heard some vague gossip that he was seeing someone in New York and Helen's name had even been mentioned to her—but she never seriously entertained the belief that this friend, whom she had admired for her "straightness," who seemed to be so much the "old-fashioned girl" in the best New England tradition, was her betrayer. Helen, for her part, claimed later that she pleaded vainly with Marquand for a frank disclosure to Christina. But perhaps hypocrisy is not the just title for a state of mind that grew, as Helen herself realized, out of a desire "to eat his cake and to have it too, to break his marriage because of the flaws in the marriage and *then* to marry me." Probably he could not himself accept the fact that, in violation of his own code as a gentleman, he had got into a guilty relation with his wife's best friend—he feared the plaguings of his "New England" conscience as much as he feared scandal. One escape from guilt was to pretend—indeed to prove—that the marriage had collapsed of its own weakness. But the process that has been described had curious consequences. The pseudoreality of his efforts to save his marriage with Christina took on authenticity. And a certain shadow fell upon his passion for Helen too. He must have seen it as more and more impossible that he would ever really emerge from his troubles and marry her to the resounding comprehension of all of the Boston world that knew them. It was, then, with a sense of welcome escape from the problems presented by both women that he seized the opportunity, exactly as he had the year before, to get as far away as he could for an extended period. Ray Murphy told him about an expedition to Persia she was planning to join, one he might arrange to join also.

Marquand had another reason for wanting to break off and take stock. He had worked with zest and speed on his serials under the Brandts' governance, and *Ming Yellow* was finished a month after he arrived back from China. Even before it appeared in the *Post* at the end of 1934, the first Moto book, *No Hero*, had already been written, bought and scheduled. The *Post* editors were pleased with the results of his Oriental travels. *Ming Yellow* was featured on the cover of the magazine and in full-page newspaper ads, which promised "adventure, mystery, bandits, warlords, romance"—an irresistible package of delights. Lorimer predicted that *No Hero* would be "a second successive smashing hit," which was, as Marquand boasted to Helen, "a good deal, coming from the old gentleman himself." He had added: "I hope you don't mind my telling you these small triumphs. C. either did not understand them, did not believe them, thought they were funny, or did not have time to listen." Little, Brown also contracted to bring both serials out in book form, but Alfred McIntyre was just mildly pleased with them. When *Ming Yellow* came in he told Bernice Baumgarten: "We doubt if the novel will add particularly to John's reputation but it is an excellent story of its kind, and I personally found it good reading; in fact, I read it from beginning to end without laying it down. John has an excellent style which lifts it a bit out of the class of ordinary adventure stories. We shall be glad to take it on moderate terms." Marquand heard about McIntyre's reaction and came to see him to ask point-blank whether he considered that publication of the new story "would injure his reputation." The reply, characteristically cautious, from the president of Little, Brown was that it would not add to his reputation but he "did not see why it should damage it." Marquand had rather enjoyed boiling up his first Far Eastern pot of entertainment, but he was worried. Writing to Roger Scaife, the vice-president of Little, Brown, he confessed, while giving advice on the exact shade of yellow to be used for the jacket: "It is kind of you to take so much trouble with this book, as I am under no great illusions regarding its artistic merit, nor is Alfred. Sometime before too long I hope to give you something better."

Curzon's Mill as seen from the Artichoke River near Newburyport

A Marquand family gathering, August 1888. In dark clothing, seated left to right: J. P. Marquand and his wife Margaret Curzon Marquand (the writer's grandparents) and Philip Marquand (the writer's father). Standing in the dark suit is the writer's uncle, Joe Marquand. The five ladies grouped in the center are (left to right): the writer's aunts Gertrude Fuller and Greta Marquand, a certain Mollie Brown, the writer's aunt Bessie Marquand, and the writer's mother, Margaret Fuller, later to marry Philip Marquand. The lady seated on the grass at the extreme left is the writer's aunt Molly Marquand.

PHOTO BY J. PAUL BROWN

Margaret Fuller Marquand with baby John

Philip Marquand at Newburyport

John at fourteen

John P. Marquand, John's grandfather

John at seventeen

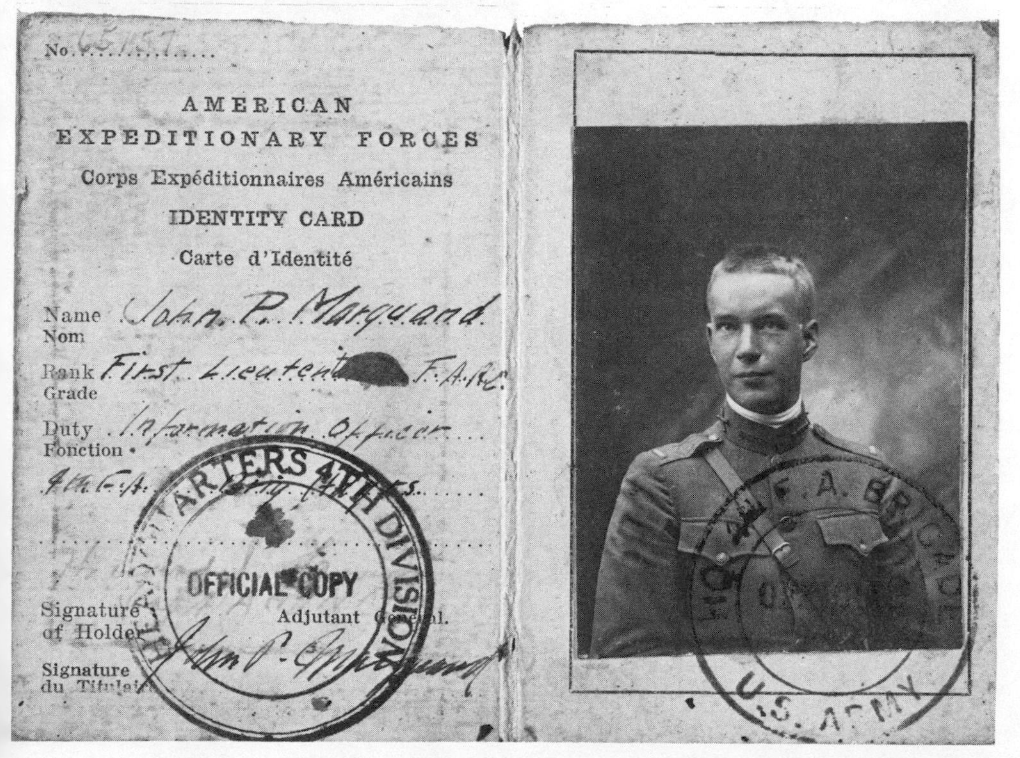

No. 65 1157

AMERICAN
EXPEDITIONARY FORCES
Corps Expéditionnaires Américains
IDENTITY CARD
Carte d'Identité

Name / Nom: John P. Marquand
Rank / Grade: First Lieutent[illegible] F.A.R.C.
Duty / Fonction: Information Officer
4th F.A. [illegible]

Adjutant General.

Signature of Holder / Signature du Titulaire: John P. Marquand

HEADQUARTERS 4TH DIVISION
OFFICIAL COPY

F.A. BRIGADE
U.S. ARMY

As identified by the AEF

DRAWING BY MARIE KOBBÉ

Alexander Sedgwick, John's father-in-law-to-be, 1905

The Marquand family in their West Cedar Street home, late in 1927: the writer, Johnny, Tina and Christina Sedgwick Marquand. The dog is Prince.

PHOTO BY DIONIZY STUDIO

Helen Howe

JPM as travel writer, overlooking the Yangtze, 1935

PHOTOS COURTESY OF CAROL BRANDT

The agents Carl and Carol Brandt

The Wives

PHOTO COURTESY OF JOHN P. MARQUAND, JR.

Christina in Stockbridge

PHOTO COURTESY OF MRS.

Adelaide in Salzburg

PHOTO BY ROBERT GROS

The correspondent in uniform, World War II

On the set of The Late George Apley, *with Ronald Colman and Vanessa Brown, 1947*

PHOTO COURTESY OF MARJORIE DAVIS

The winter season: JPM at Salt Cay, 1950

The second family at Kent's Island, 1951 (left to right): JPM, Lonny, Adelaide, Timmy, Grandmother Hooker, and Ferry

PHOTO COURTESY OF MARJORIE DAVIS

Mr. and Mrs. John P. Marquand at Kent's Island, July 1951

PHOTO COURTESY OF MARJORIE DAVIS

Marjorie Davis on the Spanish Steps, Rome, July 1959 (probably taken by JPM)

PHOTO COURTESY OF A. WATKINS

Roger Burlingame, John P. Marquand's college classmate and first editor

George Horace Lorimer, the fabled editor of the Saturday Evening Post

PHOTO COURTESY OF LITTLE, BROWN AND COMPANY

Alfred M. McIntyre, Marquand's long-time editor and president of Little, Brown and Company

Arthur H. Thornhill, McIntyre's successor, seated in front of a shelf of Marquand's works

PHOTO BY CAMMANN NEWBERRY

The author and his son Lonny just before the publication of Women and Thomas Harrow, *1958*

No Hero was not an artistic advance in McIntyre's eyes, but as he told Bernice Baumgarten, "It is, as Carl says, the Oppenheim type of story and it is well done, and it may be that in this field John's sales can be developed." *Ming Yellow* had not gone over in hard cover—about nineteen hundred copies sold was all the first month showed—but it was hoped that *No Hero* might do better. As it turned out, the sales on the first Moto book were even more disappointing. Initial hard-cover sales of all the books in the series, although they were to pick up for the later novels (and finally, in 1956, make *Stopover Tokyo*, which was a Book-of-the-Month Club selection, a best seller), were never impressive. Yet later they sold extraordinarily well in paperback. *Think Fast, Mr. Moto*, published in 1937, had accumulated by 1972 only 4,354 in sales in the Little, Brown edition—but a total of 848,000 in paperback. Since these quantities were not, of course, initially predictable, the grounds for McIntyre's indifference were not exclusively literary.

But Marquand was disturbed enough to wonder at last about a destiny that seemed to hold him to the magazines by golden fetters. Economically, he was doing so well there—about $40,000 for a serial, now—that he could dispense with success as an author of books. But, as he later summarized: "In spite of the skill I had acquired I knew that nothing I had written had any real value. I saw that I had been writing for years, that I had been writing about places and about people with which I was only superficially familiar. I also developed plots and happy endings which had no reality. I was also getting old and getting nowhere." His self-estimate was perhaps excessively harsh, but it fitted with his mood, in which the need for some total renovation, professional as well as personal, dominated. He decided to write a novel about a life he certainly knew thoroughly, that of the polite upper-class Bostonians, among whom he had been living since his marriage to Christina and to whom he was related himself by ties of family association. He had thought of this vaguely a year or two earlier and mentioned the idea to Christina. As he would later retell—it was one of his Christina stories—she had replied, "That's a good book to write if you want to leave Boston, that's all." Helen Howe, who knew this world even better than he, thought she helped him to discover the form such a novel could take when he spoke of it one day; they were in her father's library in Louisburg Square and she had put her hand out to touch the *Life and Letters of Barrett Wendell* on the shelf of her father's biographies. Why, indeed, not do, as she suggested, a "novel in the form of a memoir" that would use the narrating persona of a genteel biographer who resembled Howe?

In November 1934, he wrote Helen, "'John Apley, Trustee' has reached its eleventh page." He added that "Carl declares it is the best thing he has ever seen me do—and he seems to have snapped quite well out of his late condition—enough at any rate to give his remarks validity." Whether or not Brandt's initial enthusiasm was assisted by his "condition" Marquand was later to prove more cautious. Early in January he sent 104 pages of this new novel, tentatively titled "Journal of a Bostonian," to Bernice Baumgarten in the Brandt office. She did not think much of its possibilities, as she frankly told McIntyre. Suddenly Marquand realized that something very important was at stake for him, and he wrote McIntyre: "The last two months I have been working on a thing which I have often played with in the back of my mind, which is a satire on the life and letters of a Bostonian. I have done some thirty or forty thousand words on it, and the other day showed it to Bernice, who is sending the manuscript on to you to read. Bernice says that the whole thing is too perfect a replica of any actual collection of 'life and letters,' and, as she will probably tell you, she feels it is a great pity for me to waste my time in going ahead with it. I suppose the most damning thing that can be said about the whole business is that I, personally, have enjoyed writing it, and think it is amusing, and think that it is a fairly accurate satire on Boston life. I certainly don't want to go ahead with the thing, however, if you don't think it holds any promise, and is not any good. Besides this, I do not, for purely artistic reasons, feel that the thing can be helped by any great changes such as injecting more plot or making the satire more marked. In other words, if it is not good as it stands, I think I had better ditch the thing and turn my attention to something else. As this is the first time in a good many years that I have been in a position to write something which I really wanted to write, I naturally feel badly about it. I know you will tell me frankly just how it strikes you, and its fate rests largely in your hands. Tell me quickly."

There was, in truth, some ground for Miss Baumgarten's fears. The satire of *The Late George Apley* is indeed so unassertive that the unprepared reader may mistake the parody for the thing it mocks. As keen a reader—but a satirist with a heavier touch—as Upton Sinclair wrote after reading an advance copy of the completed novel: "I started to read it and it appeared to me to be an exact and very detailed picture of a Boston aristocrat, and as I am not especially interested in this type, I began to wonder why you had sent it to me. But finally I began to catch what I thought was a twinkle in the author's eye. (I think this was when the late John L. Sullivan appeared on the scene.) One can never be sure about Boston, and I hope I am not mistaken in my idea that the author is kidding the Boston idea. It is very subtle and clever, and I am not sure that Boston will get it." But Alfred McIntyre took a hopeful view. He told Miss Baumgarten that he was very uncertain about sales possibilities but felt strongly that if the rest to come was as good as the sample the book would deserve publication. To Marquand he wrote: "We think that this may very well be a remarkable book and of great interest in Boston. Whether it will appeal to the novel-reader in other parts of the country we just do not know. It reads like an actual biography but it should be published like a novel." Typesetting style could make it look more like a novel, McIntyre noted: they could put all the quotes, Apley's letters, and the like, in the same size of type, with no distinction in leading or spacing, as the "biographer's" own narrative. One of the Little, Brown editors had suggested the title: "The Late *John* Apley."

McIntyre hoped that Marquand would go ahead and finish the book by the spring of 1935 and that publication could be expected in the fall—and *No Hero* could be postponed until the following year. It was clear where the publisher's preference lay. Yet Brandt and Brandt, with its ten-percent commissions from Marquand's high serial payments in mind, did not then, nor would it ever, concede that the novelist's thrillers and adventure stories should not be promoted and encouraged. Lorimer had already suggested that the little Japanese detective in *No Hero* should be carried on into a sequel, perhaps a series of further yarns in which he would principally figure. From the *Post*'s and the agency's point of view the thing for Marquand to do was to write *another* Moto book. "John Apley" did not seem potential magazine fodder. That Carl Brandt did not strongly urge him to finish the novel shook for the first time Marquand's trust in this friend and guide. Bernice Baumgarten was never forgiven, and eleven years later, when young Johnny was about to take a summer job in the Brandt office, Marquand recalled to him that "when I showed her the first half of 'The Late George Apley' she told me that it was a very stupid effort and that I had better give the whole thing up." In 1935 he was less convinced of the error of this advice, and when the chance to go to Persia came he put the unfinished manuscript of the Boston novel into the Brandt office safe, and on April 6 he sailed from New York. Bernice Baumgarten observed to McIntyre that "privately, Carl thinks there is a chance he may do nothing to it." And in that case, McIntyre decided, they might proceed, after all, to bring out *No Hero*. McIntyre continued to wonder whether Marquand intended to come back to the novel as weeks and months passed without definite word from the absent writer himself, and probably his faith in the projected book also wavered. In August, when Marquand was momentarily expected to show up, McIntyre observed to Miss Baumgarten that "Mr. Scaife feels that he ought to finish it and have it published anonymously, and I am inclined to share this view."

In May Marquand was in Persia. He and Ray Murphy had managed to persuade Dr. Erich Schmidt of the University of Pennsylvania to let them join him in excavations he was directing near Teheran and at Persepolis. His expedition was an elaborate venture supported by the Boston Museum of Fine Arts as well as by the University Museum in Philadelphia, and it included a staff of architects and archaeological specialists, some of whom had been working at the two digs for over a year. There was no provision, really, for supernumerary guests such as had accompanied Alan Priest into Shansi when Marquand was in China the previous year, but Mrs. Murphy had donated two new Buick convertibles to the expedition. She and Marquand took these from Italy, traveling by boat to Cairo, Jaffa and Beirut where they were met by Schmidt and his wife, who drove with them and additional crew and equipment into Persia. The journey had few of the features of a pleasure safari this time. From Beirut they had driven over the mountains of Lebanon to Damascus, and from Damascus there had been a trek of twenty hours of steady driving in convoy through the desert to Baghdad. The trip had been tedious and hot, though they had been lucky to escape the blinding sandstorms frequent in the area. Then it had taken more than three days to go from Baghdad to Teheran, with poor food and depressing hotels along the route. "Personally I should not have missed any of this for the world," Marquand wrote Helen Howe, but Ray Murphy had been miserable, for Schmidt "seemed obsessed with the idea of hurry," and there was little chance for rest, let alone diversion.

Yet Marquand's eye, unrestingly receptive, noted a thousand details. Now and then he dictated some of his observations to Mrs. Murphy, who took them down on her Royal portable typewriter. At Baghdad in the early morning, the Tigris swirled orange mud through the pontoons of the bridge, which farmers with produce and porters "like the porter of Sinbad" were crossing into the city. In the streets were brown-robed Arabs, men in European dress wearing the national Iraqi headgear (which looked like an AEF cap) or the tasseled Turkish fez, Bedouins with cloth headdress bound over the forehead with rope. Their car ground over the cindery desert until they reached the border town of Khanaqin, where Schmidt, smiling determinedly what Marquand called his "skull-like smile," talked with the languid police. Mrs. Schmidt (to whom Marquand took a dislike comparable to that he had felt for Mary Wheelwright during the China trip) stood by, invulnerably the American female traveler with her canvas bag and her divided skirt, and "discussed the beauties of Persia in a way that makes it if possible more deadly than the reality." Of the Persian landscape Marquand himself wrote Helen: "If you picture a lot of jagged hills bare of vegetation ending in a range of snow-capped mountains, then a lot of flat country in between, irrigation ditches with rows of willows or poplars along the way and walled one-story houses, a great many donkeys and loads of straw, now and then a string of camels, a few dusty American automobiles, a lot of dour-faced brown men in ridiculous little visor caps which the present Shah makes them wear, and women completely covered by dirty long black veils, and now and then a bird with the most amazingly brilliant plumage and if you add to all this a lot of very hot sun and swirls of dust and flies—you have a pretty good idea of Persia as I see it."

That first day they made for Kermanshah, hustling through towns that reminded him of hamlets in the neighborhood of Toulouse "all gone wrong," and up into the wild bare hills of the Iranian plateau. At dusk they reached the Hotel Bristol, which, despite its name, was more like a French provincial inn, but infinitely dirtier, though with an air of Oriental luxury—in his room there were rugs everywhere, on the floor and also on the tables and window seat. The town was squalid and uninteresting. Women swathed in black, holding their veils in their teeth, rushed up to the car to beg. But from Kermanshah they went off to see the famous rock carvings at Taq-i-Bustan, caves in cliffs with their bas-reliefs of hunters and warriors. On the way to Ecbatana, the old capital of the Medes, they saw high on the cliff wall, too high for vandals, the inscription of Darius, telling of his victories, and the curly-bearded king with his foot on the enemy's neck. Down the main street of Ecbatana a dirty stream flowed. There were shops with cheap glassware, cloth and pottery, and unsmiling, weary-looking men in vizored hats, and black-cloaked women. In the public garden curdled milk was for sale in blue-glazed bowls. Here the hotel was called the Hôtel de France, but again they ate greasy soup and chicken and leather bread in the dining room carpeted with Persian rugs. Marquand morosely recorded that it was "as comfortless a place as I have ever seen and as uncongenial a town." Only the great mountain ranges gave any glory to the city, whose gold and silver royal citadel had been described by Herodotus.

As they traveled past the bare country villages of mud houses, making tedious police halts and stopping at hotels smelling of mutton tallow, Marquand was reminded of Herodotus' story of Croesus and his adviser who said: "Never let the Persians see Lydia and Sardis. They live in skins—they have nothing in their own country. Once they move to a different place they will not leave." Color and pageantry seemed to have long left the land. Marquand felt dull and bored much of the time and his companions were little help. The learned Schmidt, despite his having traveled in the country many times, seemed unable to answer Marquand's questions about the customs and attitudes of the contemporary Persians. And he did not know the names of plants; nor could he identify for Marquand the jays with blue wings and orange breasts, or a large lizard with raised tail like a question mark. Mary Schmidt, of course, "could speak intelligently of nothing" except what her doctor had told her about dysentery germs on fruit skins: "Even if you cut it with a knife the blade will carry germs inside the fruit." She had been soaking oranges in a basin of permanganate solution. Ray, he wrote Helen, "is about as tough a person to travel with as I have ever seen, because, when she gets tired, she simply loses her temper completely, reminding me a good deal of Johnny and Tina. I may add that she grows tired rather easily." He would write infrequently and listlessly to Helen throughout his Persian travels and in reply at last to a complaint that he seemed to be forgetting her he feebly answered, "The difficulties of existence here make introspection difficult."

Yet travel was bringing out that faculty of taking in things, willy-nilly, as though his eyelids had been pinned open and his mind compelled to register endlessly what was about him. In hot, dry, dusty Teheran, with automobiles and electric lights in the streets but no sewers, he felt the driving personality of the shah, who was bent on modernization, on galvanizing the mystic, melancholy, phlegmatic Persian. Still, there was one aspect of Persia that now revealed its beauty—the art of the garden and the use of the motif of water, so magical in an arid land. Within high walls one discovered the lush shade of poplar and plane trees, mazes of paths in geometrical designs, flower beds, and above all flowing streams of water in artificial ditches lined with tile, pools with carpet patterns in tile on their bottoms, multicolored birds. He could understand the secret of these places, the desire to escape from the immense Persian landscape with its cloudless sky and bare mountains and plains always covered with spiraling dust.

Outside Teheran was the first of the expedition's excavation sites, the ancient city of Ray, that once gathered in the trade routes from the Caspian, now marked by mud-brick walls and mud mounds encircling vacant ground with scorched wheatfields and green ditches and the modern city of Shah Abdul Azim. Ray, as Marquand explained to Helen, "was mopped up by the Mongols in the year 1200 where the boys are now digging for what the Mongols left. As far as I can see, the Mongols did a pretty thorough job, leaving nothing but a few broken pots and a great many mud walls." The archaeological remains that were being uncovered revealed "strata after strata of mud houses, one on top of the other, in all respects the same as those still built, as futile as successive layers of coral on a reef." Marquand was more stimulated by the heedless Persia above ground: a funeral procession carrying the corpse on a shallow carpeted bier; herds of brown, fat-tailed sheep and black goats; a camel train with a bell on the neck of the lead camel and a bell on the neck of the camel at the end, any variation of sound waking the driver sprawled asleep on his camel's single hump. The excavation workers wore the new Pahlevi hat—named for the shah—a schoolboy cap with a vizor that looked incongruous over their bearded, flea-bitten faces.

Schmidt's party had arrived at Ray on May 11 and Marquand and Mrs. Murphy remained at the camp there for nearly three weeks, finding congenial company. With an architect named John Bolles and his wife and a young architecture student whose family had come from Newburyport and who had been at Harvard, they formed a cheerful band that at times had some of the spirit of the Rakes of the Priest expedition in China. Young Eliot Noyes wrote his parents, "Marquand is one of the most entertaining guys I have ever seen." Once, when he was directing some digging in a scorching heat of over a hundred degrees, Marquand dragged out a pair of skis that had been taken along for a later trip to Kashmir and set them before the perspiring Noyes. Noyes wrote home that the two guests were "good company and they kept buying whisky and beer which costs an exorbitant price around here. Obviously we like to have them around." For other diversion the artistically inclined architects and archaeologists did painting and sketching, and even Marquand, for the first time in his life, attempted some small landscapes in oils.

Finally, Schmidt took some of the staff with him to the second dig,

Persepolis, and Marquand and Mrs. Murphy went with them. En route they came to Isfahan. In the middle of a fertile plain of white poppies and ripening melons was a Persian city of the imagination at last, its broad boulevards shaded by plane trees, its great central square and blue-domed mosques supplying the note of grandeur he had missed up till then, its huge hive of a bazaar shaded under a vast vaulted roof restoring his expectations of Arabian Nights mystery. But after a few hours, despite the renewal of the sense of romance, Marquand found also "beggars, fleas, malarial mosquitoes, hard beds, disgusting plumbing, greasy food, undrinkable water, uncomfortable chairs, dirty floors, dirty streets, persistent, undiscouraged Persian flies."

Persepolis was reached after another drive of seven and a half hours through dramatic country with red- and purple-layered mountains that made Noyes think of the American West. The great ruins surged up at last on a vast platform, a bare, wild place for a palace, the last step in an amphitheater of bare hills overlooking an arid plain. It was hard to realize what the great group of palaces and other buildings that had been built by Darius had been like, Marquand said, but the pillars, gates, and niches now left without their connecting walls might be more impressive in their solitude, it seemed to him, than when Xerxes had held audiences in the hall of a hundred columns. The new arrivals were housed in a literal palace, a reconstruction of the old harem of Darius and Xerxes, with immense, well-furnished rooms and bathrooms with hot and cold running water from a tank system and even modern toilets. In a magnificent dining room, quite fit for a Persian prince, they were served superb meals with excellent wine from nearby Shiraz. The Bolleses and Noyes, together with Marquand and Mrs. Murphy, were delighted by the sybaritic surroundings in which they now found themselves. Marquand was stirred by the Persepolis ruins, and he walked around the partly excavated site, where a labyrinth of royal offices with staircases and bas-reliefs was coming into view. He sat down and made a small crude painting in oils of the Hall of Darius. He also made some plaster of Paris casts of two heads from the frieze on Darius's 292-foot staircase by pressing wet toilet paper onto the stone with a nailbrush to make a mold. The whole spectacle, so difficult to summarize in words, was something he wanted to carry away with him. He paid Eliot Noyes a hundred dollars for a more skillful watercolor "in the Joseph Lindon Smith manner" of the figure on the sculptured staircase.

Nevertheless, Marquand now had had enough of Persia. Moreover, there had been a letter from Philadelphia saying that he must show anything he might write on Persia to the director of the University Museum, who wanted to make sure that nothing was said to offend the Persian government. "This means in effect," Marquand told Helen, "that I cannot very well use Persia in a story at the present time, and that so far, from a professional point of view, my trip has not yet yielded much." So he accepted Ray Murphy's suggestion that they both leave the expedition and fly in a KLM plane to Singapore and go to see Angkor Wat in Cambodia, and then take a boat to Hong Kong. On June 17, they took off for the long ride through valleys and mountains and over the plain, which leveled off into desert, till they reached the Gulf—where it was so hot, as an Englishman said to them, that you sweated under water. As the sun rose they found themselves in the rest house at the Bushire field, waiting for the plane. It came out of the whitish blue horizon over the water, "a shining aluminum monstrosity like a meteorite out of nowhere," thought Marquand, who, after his Persian weeks, watched with astonishment as the brisk, immaculate Dutch crew stepped out.

The plane came down for lunch at Jask on the Gulf of Oman, and then at Karachi on the Pakistan shore, where British high tea was served in the lounge, and finally at Jodhpur in India, where they were lodged in a very modern British, "very apple pie" hotel. There he had his Tom Collins at a wicker table on a lawn and turbaned boys came when he clapped his hands, and then he ate dinner in a dining room with fresh napery, shining silver, flowers. Early in the morning they were off again in their plane, flying low over dry, brown country that was waiting for the monsoon and by lunchtime over the suburbs of Calcutta. Then they were over the mouths of the Ganges, the dry India giving place to wet terrain as they flew low in a squall over mangrove swamp and jungle, and down into Burma at Akyab, all green and humid, its flying field bordered by mango and ironwood trees, where again they had an excellent dinner in the style of Kipling's India, in the Government Circuit House. The next morning they were over the Bay of Bengal, passing along the coast with its islands and jungle and river deltas to Rangoon and then to Bangkok, having gone 6,690 kilometers since Persia.

He was suddenly, happily, back in the Orient, among the gentle Siamese, a soft-voiced people, polite and unhurried. In the morning he woke up in his hotel to smell the river, muddy but clean, and walked out along the riverbank where voices murmured and crimson flame trees were in bloom, to see the river shining yellow in the sun. Bare-torsoed crews were squatting around food bowls under matting cabins; small girls paddled dugouts as narrow as thin logs, filled with potted plants; tranquil-faced men in sarongs were unloading yellow grain in baskets upon the verandahs of shops. Beside the river rose a porcelain temple, and behind white walls he discovered a palace with pointed spires and pergolas shining with mosaics of colored glass and porcelain like the Palace of Oz, courts with stunted trees, shadowy throne halls with the royal parasol rising over the throne of gold and jewels supported by gold birds, and in another temple an enormous gold Buddha with diamond-palmed hands and tapering fingers of gold and a placidly smiling face.

Almost twenty years later he would still remember the charm of Bangkok and how he almost forgot to go on to Angkor because a Siamese promoter offered to take him fifty miles outside the city to a place where one might shoot a tiger. The man assured him that there was no danger involved; several of his employees were watching the tiger and all that was necessary was a journey to the spot where the animal, a splendid specimen, was regularly to be seen because it had regularly found a goat tethered to a tree—and to shoot it from a platform conveniently constructed in the branches above the goat. If he missed, someone else would be sure to shoot the tiger for him. The tiger was guaranteed. It would make a fine rug.

But, instead, Marquand and Mrs. Murphy took the train to the Cambodian border. A French-speaking Annamite driver drove them to a village five miles away to be cleared by a customs official who proved to be a rather informal representative of French authority. He was asleep inside his bungalow when Marquand and Mrs. Murphy came to his door, and his Cambodian wife declared that he would certainly be *fâché* if aroused. After a long while, however, he emerged in his pajamas and he was certainly *fâché*, until he saw his guests and at once explained that he had not been told that his callers were Europeans. Shouting to his wife to bring a bottle of wine, he immediately countersigned their passports. In retrospect, the customs official seemed to Marquand to symbolize French colonialism and to explain its failure.

The drive to Angkor took six hours over flat, uninteresting country and Marquand remembered only one sight along the road. They were passing through what seemed to him a cutover forest, such as he had seen in American lumber country—all covered with stumps a few feet high. Looking more closely, though, he discovered that they were in the midst of several square miles of termite colonies. Each stump was a termite city built up out of cementlike material produced by countless generations of the insects, and so indestructible that only a bulldozer could have removed it. The termite cities were as impressive a spectacle, Marquand suspected, as the palaces of the Khmers, and the termite kingdoms, it would appear, might last longer than the kingdoms of the Khmers.

With this image in mind they finally arrived at the ruins, settling themselves first in the brand-new hotel the French had built for the tourist trade. There were tarred motor roads going into the jungle, to take the curious past the ruins, and even two elephants were available for those who wished to ride more exotically. Marquand and Mrs. Murphy made at once for Angkor Thom, the great, jungle-covered ancient city with its many temples, including Angkor Wat, and cloisters, towers, miles of sculptured stone. It would take weeks, he realized, to explore even that single ruin, which seemed to have as much architectural and spatial drama as anything he had ever seen, including even the Forbidden City in Peking. It was all rather clean and swept; the jungle growth that had surged over it had been pushed back by the French, and several other tourists, guidebooks in hand, passed them in their wanderings. Marquand wished he could have seen it all overgrown by the jungle.

He discovered that Angkor Thom was only the first of a series of Khmer cities under excavation: there were four or five others, only partially explored, covering many square miles, and they looked into several of these, seeing the white trunks of gum trees rising in the deserted courts, their aerial roots falling like screens in front of the façades of the buildings, and parrots and black and white monkeys chattering in their branches. He paused before the many enormous stone images of Siva, the god of destruction, especially one at the temple of Angkor Prom with its sandstone cheeks split and small trees growing out of its mouth and nostrils but still as awesome as it must have been to the Khmer worshippers. As he stood looking at the face of the god, Marquand was startled by the appearance of five men in sarongs, each armed with a bow and a quiver of arrows. Speaking in broken French, they informed him that they were hunting the monkeys who inhabited the ruins, and Marquand chatted with them awhile and gave each of them a cigarette. In 1954, Marquand told his Tuesday Night Club friends in Newburyport that he wondered where these descendants of the Khmers were just then. "As I left that face of Siva in the jungle I did not realize as I do now that I was also leaving an impossible era, that era of Western supremacy in the Far East." His remarks would have a curious ring of prophecy some twenty years later, as though he foresaw the intrusion of his own countrymen into Vietnam: "I am not a Communist but I do wish that some of my contemporaries would face a few home truths about Malaya, Burma and Indo-China. Whether we like it or not all these countries with their teeming populations are in revolt. France or England or the United States will never rule the East again. There is something new in the making and when I see what the Khmers achieved at Angkor I sometimes think the East can do quite well without our help."

From Bangkok they traveled to Singapore and Marquand had a sense of return. No other land would ever make him feel that he wanted to absorb all its life into his imagination as did China. Yet Canton was almost another China with its stuccoed modern suburbs for rich Chinese businessmen. He was reminded of Hollywood. It seemed an unattractive forecast of what China might become. In the center of the city a noisy, alert population hurried about its business, more like the inhabitants of New York or Tokyo than like the Pekingese. He walked about the broad new streets past a cotton mill with weave sheds, reminding him of a New England factory. And yet, in sound and smell, in the rich life of the streets, the Chinese quality seemed more vivid than anywhere he had ever sensed it. He made a list of the street signals of the vendors, immemorially constant: the water carrier whose single wheel squeaks its high pitch from his barrow (but the coal barrow does not squeak—the driver has his porcelain vase of oil suspended under the axle tree); the fan mender who carries his workshop on a pole with bells that jingle above his head; the sweetmeat vendor who clanks two brass cups; the ragman with his tom-tom, ticked by a long switch; the charcoal seller with his deeper drum; the tinker with his beaten kettle; the iron vendor with his clanging bits of metal; the barber twanging his tuning fork; the scissors grinder blowing his little brass trumpet. And as he had loved to do in Peking the year before, he wandered into the various districts and found the curio dealer with bandit connections but impeccable taste; the pawnshops in high square towers behind compound walls, like small fortresses; the bathhouses and the food booths in narrow streets; the amusement booths, where acrobats and sword dancers performed. He studied the birds carried in their bamboo cages and the elaborate Chinese culture of bird care, and the traditions of the keepers of singing and fighting crickets.

It was August and time to go home, but he wanted to visit Peking once more, and so, though he had originally planned to sail from Shanghai, he went up to see the great northern city again, this time in its summer aspect. What he noticed immediately was the heightening of sound. Cicadas by day, crickets by night were perpetually in the ear, and the open caves of the shops spilled out the falsetto notes of radios run full blast. The clerks threw buckets of water into the street to lay the dust. The main streets had been recently paved but in the smaller alleys the dust seemed perpetually lifting into the air. Now and then the curtain of dust vanished, the air was miraculously clear, and the western hills seemed to step suddenly close.

He picked up old threads and saw again some of the friends he had made the previous year. One day he came with Mrs. Murphy to a party at Mrs. Calhoun's. The courtyard of her house, which had been a Buddhist temple, was filled with members of the foreign colony, several of the more important Chinese residents of Peking, and some of her boarders, Americans of means, most of whom were seeing Peking for the first time. Looking across the company he saw two young women standing together, and he recognized one of them. She was Helen Hooker, whom he had met at dinner at the Murphys' in New York the past winter. The other turned out to be her sister Adelaide. Both had a quality of vivacious, almost saucy charm that was engaging in its innocence. They made Marquand at once homesick for America, for they were the type Henry James had long ago seen as representative of the American spirit. Helen was the prettier, with the better figure, yet Adelaide, with her fresh pink-and-white skin and golden hair and the flash of mischief in her gray eyes, seemed more strikingly to be another Daisy Miller: one could sense that she would trust in any circumstances to her own good intentions, and she looked about her with a child's avidity for experience.

At the Murphys' in New York Marquand had fascinated Helen with anecdotes of his experiences in the Orient. His manner, witty, rather cynical, that of a man who has experienced much, impressed her; a melancholy mingled with cynicism had its inevitable appeal. She did not fall in love with him because she was already in love, very romantically and in defiance of her wealthy family, with an Irish revolutionary by the name of Ernie O'Malley, whom she had met in New York. But she told Adelaide all about Marquand. He was getting a divorce, she said, and had just hired a Filipino servant with the hope that he would embrace his duties with the ardor he had observed to be part of the Oriental tradition of service. He told her about Chinese servants, their superior sense of anticipation, intuition, solicitude, and remarked that no wife could be expected to devote herself so wholeheartedly to one's comfort. He expected that he would be better off in his recovered bachelorhood than he had ever been in his marriage.

Now, as Adelaide met his glance across Mrs. Calhoun's courtyard, she, for her part, saw a figure with an air of romantic mystery. He was wearing a pith helmet, zippered shirt and shorts, and his skin was tanned from his travels, intensifying the blue glare of his eyes; he looked, she would later say, "like an English officer quietly going to hell in the Orient" or like a character in one of his own adventure stories. When she learned who he was she was only more attracted and wondered whether she might not get to know him. He was planning to leave for America in a few days, while she and her sister were staying on in Peking, but she managed to meet him again before he left. He advised her about some of the places she ought to visit, particularly Mongolia, and gave her the address of his friend Larson. The sisters quarreled over this excursion, upon which Adelaide was instantly determined—for Helen had been chafing to leave for London to join her Irishman. They had planned to leave Peking in a few days and travel to Europe via the Trans-Siberian Railroad. In the end, as was usual in their sisterly tussles, Adelaide had her way and they made the detour to Mongolia before taking the train west.

14

Adelaide, Apley, *Kent's Island*

One day the following March in New York, Alan Priest of the Metropolitan Museum called Adelaide up to invite her to have tea with Christina Marquand. "The old devil!" Adelaide observed to her mother. "Needless to say I couldn't resist and neither could she! She had told him she would like to meet some of John's friends and mentioned me in particular. Well, I nearly dropped dead when I saw her. We look exactly alike, except that I'm fat and she is thin. No wonder John doesn't mind my nose—he's used to it. I found her most attractive and amusing, but she also looked as if she could be mean. The one thing he seems to find eternally attractive in me is my 'kindness.'" Others would afterwards note the resemblance between Marquand's first and second wives. They were both blue-eyed and fair, and had aquiline noses with maybe the same arch. They also had some traits in common and some that were sharply contrasting. But it was not so readily seen how meanness and kindness were divided between them.

Their backgrounds were similar as well. The Hookers, like the Sedgwicks, were part of the myth of New England. The colonial progenitor was Thomas Hooker, a Puritan clergyman who fled the hostility of Archbishop Laud by going first to Holland and then, in 1633, to America. He brought members of his original congregation with him and established a church in Cambridge, but soon found himself opposed to the theocracy of the Bay Colony. Taking his flock with him again, he went through the wilderness to the Connecticut River and founded the city of Hartford. A few years later he drafted the constitution of the state of Connecticut, a model instrument 138 years older than the Declaration of Independence. Hooker's descendants, who abound in the Connecticut Valley to this day, have been able, respectable burghers for the most part, though none has reached the distinction of this formidable ancestor. Still, a certain aggressive independence has been held to be a family characteristic.

Unlike the Sedgwicks, the Hookers made themselves in the twentieth century members of the new aristocracy of industrial wealth. Adelaide's father, the grandson of a Hooker who had left Connecticut to settle in the vicinity of Rochester, New York, in the 1820's, accumulated a fortune in the classic American way by combining an invention—someone else's—and his own gifts as industrial organizer and promoter. He was not rich to begin with, and like Christina's father he married a woman with more money than he had, but while Alexander Sedgwick had utilized his wife's income to cultivate the life of a leisured gentleman, Mrs. Hooker's wealth had helped to launch her husband's business enterprise. Her money was, as the family punned, "seed money," for it had come from the profits of Mrs. Hooker's father's business, the Ferry Seed Company of Detroit. This Dexter M. Ferry had been another example of the fortune builder who applies a single idea to the market at the right moment: he had been the first to think of marketing seeds in five-cent packets to be sold in drugstores and five-and-dime chains.

Elon Huntington Hooker founded the Hooker Electrochemical Company in 1905 to utilize the recently perfected Townsend cell, a device which made it possible to electrolyze a salt solution to produce caustic soda and chlorine gas (and also, as every high school chemistry student knows, hydrogen). Hooker secured the help of two technical geniuses to take the kinks out of the process first conceived by Clinton P. Townsend: Leo Baekeland, the inventor of photographic paper and Bakelite, and Elmer Sperry, the author of four hundred useful inventions including the gyroscope. He also organized a funding company that put up the initial investment. And he chose an ideal site for the new company—Niagara Falls, where electric power, water and salt were all at hand. By the time the First World War enabled American firms to leap into the place vacated by German imports, the Hooker company was well established and able to supply dye intermediates, acids, and other chemicals. In the last year of the war it showed net profits of $1.34 million. The company expanded after the war, built a new plant in Tacoma just before the stock-market crash in 1929, and successfully weathered the Depression. In the late thirties it was already deeply involved in war chemical contracts that would soon multiply its previous profits by a large factor (in 1955 its sales amounted to $75 million), but even in 1938, when Elon Hooker died, he was the head of a hugely successful enterprise and a very wealthy man.

He was also an example of the not-yet-extinct patriarchal American. He had belonged to the generation of young men who thronged behind Teddy Roosevelt, modeling their own personalities on his egregiously masculine example, and supporting him in the Bull Moose campaign. He had been trained as a hydraulic engineer at Rochester and Cornell and was working at the Cornell Dam when Roosevelt, the new governor of New York, appointed him assistant superintendent of public works in Albany. For the rest of his life he remained active in politics. In 1912, when the Progressive party was launched, he was chosen its national treasurer, and he was a candidate—albeit unsuccessful—for the Republican nomination for governor in 1920. He continued to be a "big stick" defender of Big Business, often letting himself be heard loudly rather than softly. In 1924 he proposed to the government that he be permitted to take over Muscle Shoals on a fifty-year lease and use it to power the manufacture of fertilizer. Ten years later he led the New York State Chamber of Commerce fight against the St. Lawrence waterway as an incursion of government into the realm of private enterprise. He was a director of the National Association of Manufacturers and chairman of the National Industrial Conference Board, and, of course, a foe of Teddy's relative, FDR, whom he accused of trying to convert the nation into "a collectivist state."

That such a father had no sons was a matter of keenest disappointment to him, as each of his four daughters was aware from early childhood. He was a big man, with a hard, blue-eyed stare and a bossy manner at home as well as in the office, and his domestic rule was autocratic. To the little girls he forbade such childish gratifications as candy. To all who entered his house he as sternly forbade liquor—yet later his daughters suspected him of being less of a Puritan than he pretended (his masculine friends shared with him the secrets of sexual escapades of which the young ladies heard only vaguely lurid rumors). Lacking suitable male material out of which to make copies of his own imposing image, he contented himself with applying his driving spirit to his daughters, at least to the extent their world permitted. They could not be expected to become businesswomen or politicians like Papa, but if they went in for sports or the arts they must make themselves eminent in these fields as he had done in his. As it happened, Hooker himself had a strong interest in tennis. He had brought Lindley Murray into his company (eventually to become chairman of the board) because Murray was a leading tennis player, winning the National Singles against Nat Niles in 1917 and again against Bill Tilden in 1918. It was not surprising, therefore, that the Hooker girls had tennis lessons nearly from infancy on. They had little choice: Adelaide, who even enjoyed playing tennis in later years, remembered how futilely she had tried to rebel against the daily workout on the court. Helen actually competed in national matches and was ranked among the leading players for some years.

But tennis was hardly a destiny, and after finishing school and college, what future lay ahead for the Hooker girls? Marriage, it is clear, was not quite enough, though it was the only one expected of them. Barbara, the eldest, never married, suffering nervous breakdowns of increasing severity after her late adolescence. Helen and Adelaide, the next in age, did not marry until they were past thirty. The first to marry was the youngest,

Blanchette, on whom the paternal hand had pressed less heavily—she never cared for tennis and was allowed to take up riding instead—but she did marry, of course, in a top-scoring way, having captured a multimillionaire, John D. Rockefeller III. Helen and Adelaide, however, early developed "interests," which they took with great seriousness throughout their lives. Helen studied art and became a competent sculptor, Adelaide had a pleasing voice and was infatuated with opera, and she spent many years training herself for an operatic career. She was, it turned out, to be one of those thousands known to music teachers and music schools who have the longing and the will but not the endowment to make their ambitions realizable. She was thirty-two when this must have become abundantly clear to her after years of fervent application, the misdirection of the same sort of personal ambition and energy that had made her father a business success. It was at this time that she met John Marquand and decided to marry him.

Adelaide had led up till then a life in which personal expressiveness and vivacity, a willfulness that charmed rather than offended others, were abetted by wealth, intelligence and physical vigor. Her childhood had been spent in the Hooker homes in New York City and Greenwich, Connecticut. The Greenwich one was a comfortable country house that had been added to from time to time as the family and its fortunes increased, and on the grounds, running to thirty acres of garden and woods, a tennis court and swimming pool had been laid out. The house was named Chelmsford after the English village where the ancestral Thomas had had his first clerical appointment. Adelaide's oldest friend, Frances McFadden, who also grew up in Greenwich, still remembers a story her mother told of her first sight of the small Adelaide. The Hookers had just moved to town and Mrs. McFadden was wheeling Frances in her baby carriage when she passed a man also wheeling a child, a spirited creature who was climbing out and about to tumble to the pavement. Father and child passed on, he large and serene, she in a characteristic exuberance of self-endangering activity.

As she grew up, Adelaide annoyed some but delighted many at Miss Spence's School and then at Vassar College, where, as throughout her life, it would be said that she had "fifty best friends." She was probably never again so happy as during her college years. To be a Hooker was itself a head start at Vassar, for her grandmother, great-aunt, three aunts and her mother had all been Vassar graduates, and she was welcomed by the faculty with affectionate recognition. But she was popular among the members of the class of 1925 for her own qualities. Gusty and fun-loving, she was the constant inventor of escapades and jokes; like Marquand she had a gift for mimicry and would take off anyone to the great amusement of her friends—a favorite rendition was a parody of a Paderewski performance they had all seen in a movie. She was affectionate and somewhat domineering, the kind of girl who, in a girls' school, is a natural leader and teacher. "What, you don't know?" she would exclaim on discovering some appalling cultural deficiency in a friend—and proceed to an instant reparation, usually a description of a play or an opera of which the other was ignorant. Some of her classmates thought she influenced them more than most of their professors. One of these, a girl from a public high school in Indiana, remembered that Adelaide had brought her to New York to see Eleonora Duse in *Ghosts* and *La città morta* and had taken her to the Metropolitan to hear her first "Cav and Pag" and the Stravinsky ballet *Petrouchka*. It was because of Adelaide's urging, she later declared, that she had gone to England to study lieder with Sir George Herschel and chosen a career as an opera singer. There was always to be something a little imperious about Adelaide's gestures—slightly masculine, resembling her father's. Her classmates nicknamed her "Peter."

She majored in music, but this was only the incidental reflection of a passion for the operatic stage. As a child of about ten, belonging to a group of "Bluebirds," organized by the writer Ernest Thompson Seton in New York, she had ordered a special costume for herself from her mother's dressmaker when the other girls were content to wear a single blue feather in their hair. Adelaide, however, wanted to look like Mary Garden in *Thaïs*. Mary Garden became the special object of her adoration; she saw her in every one of her roles at the Metropolitan. In her sophomore year at college, Mr. and Mrs. Hooker wanted her to make her debut in Society, and Adelaide consented, but she characteristically insisted on shaping the event to her own style: after the Colony Club reception twenty of her friends were to be taken to supper and to the opera to hear Mary Garden in *L'amore dei tre re*. Her college dormitory room had an enlarged picture of Mary Garden on the wall, as well as a shrine, complete with candle, to her favorite tenor, Lucien Muratore. And she was also a fan of Geraldine Farrar's; she was what was known as a "Gerry flapper"—one of the girls who rushed in a band down to the footlights at curtain calls to pay homage to their favorite. In college she had already set herself, with lighthearted impudence, to becoming another Garden or Farrar. Her greeting, when she entered a friend's room, was apt to be a ringing rendition of Brunnhilde's "Hoyo-to-ho!"

Unquestionably, Adelaide Hooker belonged in a Wagnerian spectacle. Her vivid personality, her instinct for self-dramatization, would have served her well on the stage, and with her luxuriant golden hair and her pouter-pigeon figure she really looked like a Wagnerian heroine. She had the performer's impulse towards costume rather than dress; she loved to shock the bourgeois, and one day appeared on campus in a pair of thigh-revealing lederhosen. Another day she cut off her long hair so that curls stood out around her head because she wanted to look like the portraits of Beethoven. Her college friends delighted in all this nonconformism, and only later, when they had become society matrons, looked down on her continued habit of theatrical getup—peasant skirts and sandals fit for *Cavalleria rusticana* that stood out among Worth dresses at a tea.

The summer following her junior year Adelaide went to Europe with the family duenna. It was not her first visit abroad, but it was to be of special importance, for this time she met Lilli Lehmann. The famous singer and teacher agreed to give lessons to the little rich girl from America. These continued throughout the summer and were resumed after her graduation from Vassar. During the following winter and the next as well, she was hard at work with Frau Lehmann, who seems to have grown fond of her pupil, though cherishing, one suspects, no illusions about her talent. At home in New York there followed that familiar phase of the desperate aspirant's career when specialists in the development or manipulation of the throat and larynx succeed one another like medical therapists in a case of chronic illness. The results were not conspicuous. Elon Huntington Hooker's example and precept had ingrained in Adelaide the conviction that industry and ambition inevitably bring reward. It was his daughter's misfortune that she applied his expectations to an enterprise that had to be founded on a natural accident, like finding an oil well on one's property.

But she was an unquenchably hopeful person; she craved some adventure that would justify her qualities, and at the end of the summer of 1928 she really had one. Her sister Helen met her in Salzburg, and together they took on impulse an extraordinary trip into the land of the Russian Communist bogeymen that filled their father's imagination. First they went to Finland and then stopped at the Russian Orthodox monastery on Valamo, an island in Lake Ladoga, north of Leningrad. At the hotel for pilgrims, where the usual stay was three days, they remained five weeks. They studied Russian and made friends with the monks, mostly men between fifty and sixty with long black hair and beards, who had never been out of the monastery since they were boys. They then decided to tour Russia, which few Americans were doing just then, and, in their insouciant way, continued to make friends wherever they went. They stayed mostly in Leningrad and Moscow for the next three months, Helen painting pictures and Adelaide taking notes, some of which were incorporated in colorful accounts published in *Good Housekeeping* on their return. The girls not only made themselves familiar with the great Russian cities, but went into the country, staying at provincial hotels and *traktirs*. They went to see famous cathedrals and convents at Vladimir, Bogolyubovo and Suzdal, crashed a Young Communist ball, and were even arrested for traveling without their passports and taking photographs of a prison building. They were not particularly interested in politics and they knew nothing about the principles of Marxism-Leninism. They enjoyed themselves all the more because the things that caught their fancy—old churches and religious art—were discounted by the

Communists. Adelaide, who had a certain shrewdness in money matters, made a good thing, as it turned out, of collecting priceless antique icons and vestments that were being put on the garbage heap by the Communists and could be bought up for pennies. And they had broken out of their New York–Greenwich society lives. Adelaide wrote in *Good Housekeeping*, "Our reasons for being there at all were curiosity and cussedness." Certainly they enjoyed a plunge into a life in sharpest contrast with their own. At twenty-five Adelaide had had an experience resembling Marquand's in the Far East and Persia.

But, of course, it was all just a girlish fling, and letters from home soon demanded their return. Though Adelaide had gone up to Rochester and enrolled in a program of study at the Eastman School of Music in the spring, she had missed the entire fall semester. To her father, who was then at the height of his career, developing the new electrochemical plant in Tacoma and organizing the chemical industry behind the Hoover campaign, such behavior was incomprehensible. He wrote that he hoped the girls had the "serious purpose to become professional successes in the sense that your Father became a professional success." So Adelaide returned to the Eastman School and eventually received a Bachelor of Music degree and then a Master's degree in 1931. Yet it was pretty well understood that her musical career was to be that of a devoted amateur. She never was to sing in public or teach music or compose (beyond the orchestral exercise that was required for her degree). Shortly after her graduation her sister Blanchette was married, the Hooker family moved into a smaller apartment in New York, and she took an apartment of her own on East Seventy-third Street. She became a member of the Cosmopolitan Club and the Junior League and occupied herself socially and musically. She went to concerts and wrote program notes for the Women's Symphony Orchestra and other musical organizations. She continued to have "fifty best friends." A few of these were now men. She had had several flirtations—with a young man (operatically named Siegfried) in Germany and with others at home, mostly in the world of music, but she was more seriously in love with the composer Howard Hanson, who had been her teacher at the Eastman School. He did not, it is said, offer more in return than a benevolent friendship—a rebuff from which she was still smarting when she met Marquand.

In April 1935 Adelaide and Helen and their mother traveled with a Garden Club of America group to Japan—ninety-five Garden Club members, fourteen of their husbands, five daughters and one son. Chaperoned so abundantly, the sisters were exposed only to the most polite aspects of the foreign scene, being entertained by wealthy Japanese and members of the government and visiting the supreme examples of the formal garden art of Japan. But when the group returned to America they managed to remain behind to go to Peking, and as we have seen, were finishing out the summer at Mrs. Calhoun's. One reason for the China trip had been their enjoyment of an adventure story with a Chinese setting that Helen had packed into her suitcase before leaving home—*Ming Yellow* by John P. Marquand.

After Marquand left Peking the Hooker sisters had gone on to Kalgan, despite reports of worsening war tension in the area, and then had taken the Trans-Siberian across the immense stretch of Soviet territory to Europe. They were once more the harum-scarum girl-explorers among the Red Russians. While traveling across the empty steppes one day, Adelaide had placed her purse containing her passport on the sill of the open window of their compartment and only discovered that it had fallen out some hours and many miles later. They had gotten off and gone back along the tracks and finally found it with the help of some friendly Siberians. In England, Helen climaxed her rebellion against Hooker respectability by marrying Ernie O'Malley. Of course, Mr. and Mrs. Hooker had no use for this Irish radical and poet, though he was a charming and gifted man. Helen did not return to America for fifteen years. Adelaide, who had been the only family member present at the wedding, went back to New York in September to "explain," and to reflect with private admiration on her sister's example.

Almost immediately she got in touch with John Marquand and invited him down for a weekend at Chelmsford together with Negley Farson, whom she had met in Moscow in 1928 and whose book *The Way of a Transgressor* had just been published. They exchanged traveler's tales—of Russia and China and Japan and Persia and Indochina. Marquand was charmed by the freshness and unconventionality of the thirty-two-year-old Adelaide. Behind the quick-glancing eyes and hearty laugh she suggested a capacity for adoration that was intensely flattering to him. He did not discover till later how in Adelaide's paradoxical makeup this was also combined with a desire to rule. For, after all, she was a tycoon's daughter; she was used to seeing how money could buy a great many satisfactions, if not all; she was used to feeling, even in her female veins, the luxury of power. Without realizing all this, however, Marquand was pleased by the fact that the girl who could charm him by being jaunty and original was also very rich and had gilt-edged social credentials. As with Christina he did not foresee that the qualities attracting him were those most dangerous to the future of their relationship. It was as though he had found someone who refuted Christina's timid gentility and yet was even more appealing to his own unconscious desire to belong to the class of privilege and prestige. As with Christina, moreover, even the faults that would later exasperate him were charming at the start. Some of the same faults, in fact, *had* already annoyed him. Adelaide, too, was chronically unpunctual, she lost things, she wasn't altogether neat.

On the first of February, 1936, he sailed with her to Bermuda as her acknowledged beau to spend a vacation with Blanchette and Johnny Rockefeller. She made the sailing by minutes, and Marquand was nearly carried out to sea without her. But then they had simply laughed happily. She wrote her mother of how they strode up and down the decks of the *Monarch* "and never stopped talking for 36 hours." In Bermuda, Marquand impressed her by his gentle, older-man's thoughtfulness. He always made sure to get off his bicycle first on an upgrade, "so that I wasn't shown up as feeble," she reported. He had even condescended to edit and retype for her an article describing her Garden Club tour of Japan which she was sending in to *Harper's Bazaar*. When the Rockefellers left, Marquand and Adelaide stayed on for the next boat, though he had hesitated over the propriety of continuing at her hotel. Adelaide, amused, wrote, "John M. is very conventional—makes me seem like a wild woman—but told me that being divorced is Hell because no matter how stodgy your life, you are immediately considered the rake of all time." The truth was that next to Adelaide's spontaneity Marquand, who had the air of always gravely considering, cautiously choosing, seemed a little dull; and the contrast was noted by fellow guests at the Horizons. "He is shy and can be highly amusing when he wants to be, but he wasn't in a mood to entertain a lot of boarders," Adelaide wrote her mother defensively. But many of her friends would react in the same way. The musician Randall Thompson and his wife, who had known her for years, remembered the occasion, some months later, when she brought Marquand to their house—he seemed so heavy and self-important, so different from the lighthearted young men she had previously known.

She was not quite candid when she assured her mother after getting back from Bermuda: "Don't worry about my getting my fingers burnt. I hate to realize how hard-boiled that Howard [Hanson] business has made me." She was not hard-boiled at all about Marquand, who was rapidly making her feel that the "Howard business" had lost its sting. On one occasion Hanson invited her to come with him to hear the Philadelphia Orchestra play his Merry Mount Suite and courteously asked Marquand to come along. Marquand refused, but turned up in the adjoining box with his friends James and Ray Murphy—and Adelaide had the woman's perfect pleasure of disconcerting the man who had failed to love her by showing him someone else's admiration. The fact is that Marquand and she soon decided that they were in love. She had had "an inferiority complex about Boston cultivation," thinking herself, perhaps rightly, as lacking something that in Christina or Helen Howe was bred in the bone. But he made her feel that her deficiencies were inconsequential. She did not take alarm, either, at his curious compulsion to orderliness, the reverse of her own careless nature, and reported laughingly that when he came to her apartment he loved to straighten out her cupboards containing a collection of pewter and to rearrange the pieces on her mantel.

As he wooed this heiress Marquand found himself clinging more and more to the company of friends who, like her, were wealthy yet easygoing and tolerant—as Christina's Boston circle had not been. The Brandts, of course, were well-off and devoted to him, but their parvenu standards, their apartment with too much of the high-priced interior decorator touch, their conspicuous consumption in pleasures and dress, would always strike him as vulgar. And like himself they had had to work for their money. He preferred in the long run to be with people like his old friends Gardiner and Conney Fiske, whom he began to see more of after his divorce. "Gardi" was a New England aristocrat whose family, unlike the Marquands, had never lost its money; he had been Marquand's best Gold Coast friend at Harvard; he had been a flying ace in World War I; he was now a cotton broker who did not have to work hard at it. Marquand enjoyed the Fiskes whenever he went to Boston to settle his affairs in connection with the divorce or to see his children or to visit his father in Newburyport. On these occasions the Fiskes' Beacon Street house and their accomplished and affectionate hospitality were at his disposal, as well as the country recreations of the Fiske estate, Dudevil, in Weston. To the Fiskes, particularly to Conney, he read parts of *Apley* as the novel progressed; her viewpoint, that of an insider who was able to laugh at Boston, and also her acquaintance with the whole social history of all its First Families, were at his disposal in the development of the novel. As with the Brandts, he formed a kind of familial trio with the Fiskes in which he played the role of a gifted, petted brother for whom every ministering comfort was provided. When, at the end of June 1936, Adelaide went to see Helen in Dublin, he and the Fiskes made a trip to Paris together and then went to London where they joined Adelaide.

It was not until February 1937 that John Marquand and Adelaide Hooker were formally engaged, a year after the Bermuda trip. Somehow he felt that he must make a pause between the old life and the new. Christina would never quite close the cover of their book. When she went down to clean out the house at Marston's Mills she sadly observed to herself: "we are still married in closets and bureau drawers." Helen Howe had, as he might have counted on, made no fuss when she discovered that he would not come back to her after his return from Persia. Unacknowledged publicly, their romance soon seemed to him something that had not really been, but Helen did not marry for ten more years. Marquand, for his part, was busy and happy in 1936. He did two things as important as falling in love. First, he finished *The Late George Apley*. And second, he decided that his life was to be tethered in the New England that was his subject in that book; he settled himself in a new home not far from Curzon's Mill.

As soon as he got back from the East at the beginning of September 1935, he went to see Alfred McIntyre with the announcement that he intended to finish his Boston novel by the following January 1. He also planned to write a new Moto story for the *Post*. For the moment he was full of optimism about the possibility of serving the higher literary aims expressed in *Apley* without relinquishing the returns of popular writing, which seemed to be increasing all the time. *Thank You, Mr. Moto* was finished by December and ran in the February and March issues of the magazine. From Bermuda, Adelaide sent home copies of the six issues. Her Rockefeller brother-in-law, she reported, "was most impressed by the fact that John M.'s name was featured on the cover and rather more impressed when I told him that he had received $30,000 for the bloomin' thing." As she told the Hookers, who were better able to appraise such facts than the Sedgwicks had been: "The advertisement which the Post put in the New York Times about the story sold 250,000 extra copies and they have offered him $40,000 to do a sequel to it." And he was immediately at work on the third in the series, which would be ready in July. It was difficult to relinquish such reapings even if Alfred McIntyre had only a mildest enthusiasm for the thrillers. Having read *Think Fast, Mr. Moto*, the publisher liked it somewhat better than its two predecessors but saw no reason to improve contract terms: "We still have a long way to go before we can say that we have put over the Mr. Moto stories," he insisted. Carl Brandt, on the other hand, had urged upon Marquand the importance of "carrying forward with the Moto book publication. I think you'll be an awful idiot if you don't let these things go [on]. It means things in motion pictures and it's very worthwhile." There was no question that Mr. Moto had been put over in the magazine. He was soon, moreover, to reach his widest public in the movies, as Brandt foresaw: *No Hero* was sold to the movies in October 1935, and the succeeding Moto books followed it into films; Marquand also wrote new scripts with such titles as "Mr. Moto in the Persian Oil Fields," for Hollywood, and there were films that merely used the Moto character in scripts written by others. Peter Lorre would make Mr. Moto an American myth-figure in eight Twentieth Century–Fox films released between 1937 and 1939.

But Marquand had no illusion about the literary merit of these efforts; if anything, as has been said, he underrated them. As Adelaide wrote to her mother, "He is absolutely blah about it all, calls it carpentry work which he has to do in order to buy shoes for the baby, and really likes writing in a completely different style." He had completed the manuscript on the Bermuda trip and shown it to her, and her reaction, like that of other first readers, was a little uncertain. She told her mother: "I have just finished reading the manuscript of a serious novel coming out in the fall—a horrible satire on the bumptiousness of the first families of Boston. It seems like a remarkable work for a very limited public, and so bitter as to be frightening. Also excruciatingly funny if you happen to know that kind of people, but I imagine exceedingly dull if you don't."

In September, McIntyre had put to Marquand the suggestion that the novel be published anonymously; he too may have become uncertain of how such a work would be received within and without Boston. Marquand had at first agreed, but then, when the book was done, opposed the idea. McIntyre's next thought was that the book should be issued at the start as by "Willing," the fictional narrator, the second printing to carry Marquand's name. It is not clear that, as he later claimed, his motive was simply to promote interest by making a mystery of the novel's authorship; he might have wanted to see if the book would first fall flat or not—if it did, there might never be a second edition and Marquand's reputation would be unaffected. "I shall not make any predictions as to its sale, though I feel certain that it will find many readers in this part of the country," was the most encouraging statement McIntyre was able to make even after seeing the completed first draft in March. The question of anonymity was disposed of, however. Carl Brandt sold sections of the novel to the *Saturday Evening Post*, which planned to feature them as Marquand's, and the book, due to come out afterwards, would thus have to be published as by him.

Acceptance by the *Post* had by no means been as sure a thing as a Moto story would have been. Marquand himself as well as Carl Brandt had doubted that it would suit the magazine, and both said as much to Lorimer and to the editor Adelaide Neall at lunch one March day in the citadel on Independence Square. But Lorimer and Miss Neall liked the *Apley* manuscript, though the rest of the *Post* staff were certain that it was of too local a character for their readers. And so the *Post* printed four excerpts rather than the whole and advertised those as though they were a serial, to the annoyance of McIntyre. He held to the view that serial publication was inimical to the sale of books as books, a creaming off of readers who would not bother to buy in hard cover what the magazine had let them have for five cents an installment. In this case he felt that readers would be unaware of the fact that most of the novel hadn't got into the magazine at all; the "articles" had run to only 45,000 words (of a total of 115,000), all, except for a few passages, taken from the last 150 pages of the Little, Brown edition, which came out on January 4, 1937, just as the *Post* series was completing itself.

It was clear that nobody connected with producing *The Late George Apley*, not even its author, had any idea of how it would be received. Reading it forty years after publication, one can realize that its qualities as satire, the species to which it was soon recognized as belonging, were more complicated than many readers understood at the time and had sources in Marquand's own mixed attitudes. What, really, we may now ask, was Marquand's viewpoint in this study of the world he both loved and resented? He had set out to depict with sharpened vision a fictional but representative "Brahmin" who had lived between 1866 and 1933. His truly remarkable faculties of observation and recall were called into play as never before. The travel of the previous two years had increased his capacity for detached scrutiny, for seeing this civilization in the light of human history, like the civilization of China or Persia. Yet not too crudely or oversimply did he depict his specimen Bostonian. He had known the type all his life and in his years in Boston had noted all the Proper Bostonian habits and traditions, from the rites associated with the naming of the young to the burial of the dead. He was thoroughly familiar with all the institutions into which the Bostonian's life was organized: the clubs, each with its separate atmosphere and traditions, the cultural and civic activities, and above all the role of that supreme institution, the family. Those "on the in" could immediately take pleasure in identifying the exact descriptions of certain realities under the designations of the Berkley Club and the Province Club, of Mulberry Beach and Pequod Island, as well as the undisguised account of life on Beacon Street or in Milton.

Marquand would later insist that nothing he described in his story had any specific model and that the only incident he had used that had really happened was the one in which a conservatory was enlarged to accommodate a rubber tree. But as he told an interviewer: "Every incident has repeated itself with small variations in Boston. Plenty of Boston families have had rows over cemetery lots and had trouble with damask roses in Brookline." His disclaimer did not prevent readers from suspecting a still greater degree of actual reproduction nevertheless. Some were misled by the novel's form into supposing that they were reading a true biography, and it is said that for years visitors to the Boston Museum of Fine Arts asked to see the "Apley bronzes" which the novel's hero had donated. Such literalism had another consequence: a Rhode Island lawyer named O'Reilly felt himself calumniated by the portrait in the novel of a dishonest lawyer bearing his name, and sued the *Post* and Little, Brown for libel.

Satire, of course, however mild, must bite, and Marquand surely had a store of hostility, especially in 1936, for the world he had snubbed when he compelled Christina to divorce him. Yet never had a satiric exposure been handled with greater tact, and the objects of derision were at any moment equally capable of being objects of admiration. His narrative method assisted this ambiguity. He chose to tell the story chiefly in terms of letters, thus permitting Apley himself to speak in the first person, generally without the intervention of the narrator-commentator. When he was heard, this commentator was more thoroughly, more uncritically committed to Apley's world and values than Apley himself. In the place of a sharp-witted Marquand spokesman, full of malice, the reader was merely permitted to hear the comments of the dull and conventional Horatio Willing. The very device of an "official biography" as a form for fiction was a happy inspiration, for it gave the reader two related points of view to compare and distinguish, Apley's and Willing's own, while seeming to leave out the voice of the master of effects who had staged the spectacle. Marquand, as has been said, disclaimed an exact model for Willing; he wrote a few years later, when M. A. De Wolfe Howe's own reminiscences were published, "Anyone reading Mr. Howe's wholly delightful autobiography should perceive at once that here is a liberal man of the world who is writing, and one who has escaped all the narrow snobbishness of my fictitious biographer." But the absence of ironic perspective, the reverence for tribal totems and taboos that characterized Willing, were, after all, fundamentally Howe's starting point. Willing (or Howe) was a representative of the system into which Apley had been born and which forever imprisoned him.

The technique of the novel never makes obvious how far Marquand himself might go in subscribing to Apley's own occasional apologues. "For better or worse, we are what we are. Don't try to be different, John," his hero says to his schoolboy son despite his remembered moments of rebellion. We cannot escape the consequences of our training and environment. In his final self-appraisal George Apley confesses: "Everything I have done has amounted almost to nothing." He had hardly ever allowed himself the things that really gave him pleasure. Tradition and obligation had tyrannized over all his hours. And yet he claimed the right to a certain honorable pride in the way he had lived. "The world I have lived in may be in a certain sense restricted but it has been a good world and a just world." Behind this declaration the author remains ambiguously silent, his mixed effects rendering Apley pitiable and ridiculous and sympathetic and noble all at the same time. That Marquand could produce so complex a result was due to the way his own mind contained these contrary views.

Naturally, there was some resentment in Boston. The *Transcript* reviewer, Edw[illegible] Francis Edgett, was expectably snappish, pointing out that Marquand was "not a Bostonian by birth or by long residence" and criticizing the spelling, "unknown either in Boston or London," of the name of the fictitious Berkley Club. On behalf of some readers, no doubt, Edgett seemed to resent Marquand's portrait of the Bostonian traveler who never gets over his assumption that Boston is the Hub—and the Fenway nobler than the Champs-Elysées, Mrs. Gardner's museum more impressive than the Palazzo Vecchio, and the Harvard Stadium as grand as the Colosseum. Marquand's Boston, conceded to exist, was a very minute portion of the whole and "*The Late George Apley*, either as fact or as fiction, is perhaps not so impressively truthful as its author intended to make it when he sought to dissect the flesh and lay bare the bones of Boston." The other Boston papers interviewed Marquand promptly, and the Boston *Sunday Post* got him to admit that "Apley represented not the majority of the Beacon Hill Brahmins, but about 33 percent of them," and to agree with the statement of Porter Sargent that "Boston is one of the few cities in the world where a civilized person can live." And Louis M. Lyons, the *Sunday Globe* interviewer, found Marquand at his publisher's office on Beacon Street rather unhappy over the impression that he had wanted to pan the city. "I have an enormous respect for Boston and a reluctant respect for George Apley. I have a good deal of Apley in myself," he truthfully said. Marquand made another observation to Lyons that would have been appreciated by Henry James, who complained that America lacked the institutions and social traditions necessary for the novelist of society: "Boston is the only city in America you could satirize. No other city has enough solidity, is complete enough. You couldn't write a satire on New York. Nothing is crystallized there. There are really only two things a writer can satirize in the American scene today. One of these is the small town, and Sinclair Lewis has done that in *Main Street* and *Babbitt*. The only other place static enough and finished enough to write a novel about is Boston." If this literary observation was a compliment to Boston, few of Lyons's readers understood it as such.

What happened, in fact, was that Beacon Hill tended to smile at Marquand's critique as applying to that thirty-three percent to which no one recognized himself as belonging. Everyone knew Apleys and no one was one. And the more perceptive readers detected the vein of sympathy, almost of justification, that ran through the book, like Carl Van Doren, who wrote in the *Herald*, "Mr. Marquand, writing satirically as a son, already points forward to another generation which will wonder why the grandfathers were so afraid of life and yet will credit them with their real virtues which could be so irritating at close hand and yet at a distance seem so touching." Privately, from authentic Brahmin sources, there came confessions similar to that of Arthur Pier of St. Paul's School, who wrote Marquand, "I realize of course that you wrote it as a satire on the cold roast Boston type, but I find myself, somewhat to my surprise, growing to like George Apley very much in spite of his ridiculousness and in the end actually admiring him." Yet there was no certainty that Marquand's ambiguous masterpiece had not taken in Apley's admirers as well, and Bliss Perry, Marquand's old professor at Harvard, told Roger Scaife: "I think it is a remarkable achievement of bitter observation and ironically patterned style. I don't see how Marquand could ever have rubbed down his own brilliant phrases into the 'dull finish' appropriate for a Mr. Willing (whom we all know!), but the total satirical effect is all the more masterly. To read this Memoir is to me like stealing a glimpse into the Great Judgment Day Book. I don't mean that it is a personal betrayal of anyone in particular—at least not obviously so—but it does exhibit a whole Boston generation which you and I have known. As a veracious record of certain phases of Boston it ranks with *The Rise of Silas Lapham* and *The Chippendales*, but I doubt if it will be as widely read. The Frog Pond into which such a book splashes is growing relatively smaller with each year." From another novel, *The Dark Horse* by Robert Grant, the author of *The Chippendales*, narrator Willing had drawn a bromidic theme for his narrative: "Everything is certain to swing back." Grant himself read *Apley* with interest, having been, as he observed to Scaife, a spectator of the entire span of time described in the novel. Though he found that he differed with Marquand on occasional details, he declared the portrait of Apley a true one, but he said, "There were plenty of individuals in his set not so futile." He called the story "a very well worked out epitome of the Boston state of mind for three generations, done with much quiet satire but not maliciously. A great many people should be entertained by it."

A great many were, despite the prognostication that it would make no sense to those outside Boston. The New York reviews launched it as a major literary event. Percy Hutchinson perceived the heart of its charm at once—the subtlety with which Marquand, "sympathetic and ironic by turns, now permits his hero to reveal himself as tender husband and father, now as the veriest snob, and of course as unegotistic in the first as he is unconsciously egotistic in the second." Bernard De Voto called it "an essay in a rare and difficult genre. It is satire, but it is satire by indirection only; it is cast in a delicate irony, one that smiles, sympathizes, and almost forgives; it relies for effect entirely on tone, risking the indifference of the hard of hearing." Lucius Beebe, author of *Boston and the Boston Legend*, thought he saw some bitterness: "Before he gets through with him George Apley is a prude, a shuffler, a stuffed shirt and at times not quite bright." But then, he added, "He also appears an honorable and public-spirited citizen (even though some of his concerns may seem trivial to non-Bostonians), a generous and, towards his end, more tolerant man than Mr. Marquand may originally have intended him to be." The book was seen in New York to be, as Lewis Gannett put it, one with "a double edge."

The novel was compared, inevitably, with George Santayana's *Last Puritan*, whose subtitle, "A Memoir in the Form of a Novel," had been deliberately echoed in the inversion "A Novel in the Form of a Memoir," although Marquand had not read Santayana's book until he had finished his own, and the subtitle had been proposed in the Little, Brown offices. Santayana's book had had a remarkable success only months before and the fact that it had been a Book-of-the-Month Club selection had prevented the Club judges from considering what seemed like an attempt at repetition. Superficially, the aims of the two works were similar—to show the effects of the Puritan tradition upon modern generations of New Englanders. But readers discovered that though Santayana had used the conventional novel form, his was a less persuasive fiction than Marquand's "life and letters." The philosopher's elegant narration was, in fact, a coarser imaginative medium—more witty and less realized than the novelist's fiction, lacking Marquand's shadows of human contradiction. Curiously, it was precisely the charge of inferior veracity that Santayana himself made against *Apley* after reading his advance copy in Rome: "In comparing this picture with my memory of Boston society, it seems to me not so much exaggerated as too external, too verbal. Nice Boston people often talked like this, but they had more sense and more heart; they knew and understood everything, while keeping themselves under conventional restraints. Mr. Marquand's hero seems to me not so much Bostonian as provincial. However, the book is a document."

On the whole, as Alfred McIntyre crowed to Bernice Baumgarten, *The Late George Apley* got an enthusiastic press. "It looks," he said, "as though we were right and you and Carl were wrong about it." He took up with renewed energy his contention that Marquand should henceforth serve only one master: "I hope it is going to be so successful that it will lead to John's feeling that he can devote most of his time from now on to serious fiction."

Apley sold. Before it was out a week Little, Brown was rushing a fourth printing and stepping up its advertising. After three weeks, 20,000 copies were printed and it was at the top of the selling list in Boston, ahead of *Gone with the Wind* and *Drums Along the Mohawk.* But, more surprisingly, it was soon among the best sellers everywhere else—in Los Angeles and San Francisco as well as in New York. At the end of the first month, 15,500 copies had been sold and the publisher put more full-page ads into the New York *Times* and the *Herald Tribune.* At the end of April, 25,500 copies had been sold and at the end of the year sales had reached 32,700, far more than the sales of all Marquand's previous books put together. Of course, the following May, there would be a new campaign and further mounting sales when the novel was awarded the Pulitzer Prize.

Yet McIntyre remained convinced that prior publication of portions of the novel in the *Post* had stolen away still other buyers and he was particularly incensed when announcements of the award stated that the novel had been serialized in the *Post* instead of explaining that the *Post* had only carried excerpts. "Now that John has won the Pulitzer Prize I wish he might decide not to have any portion of his next serious novel printed in a magazine," he wrote Miss Baumgarten. In addition, he continued to try to dissuade Marquand as much as possible from writing entertainment fiction—or at least from the idea of publishing such fiction in book form after it had had its magazine appearance.

The difference between Alfred McIntyre and the Brandt agency over the direction Marquand's career should take was henceforth to be a repeated motif of his professional life. It was a contest between two varieties of author building, two kinds of service to the market. That Marquand would now become a considerable literary writer might seem a possibility to him because it was compatible with success in the book market, and from the book publisher's point of view magazine writing was not only a distraction from higher literary achievement but a loss of potential profits from books that could have the success of *Apley.* Also, there might be some reason to suppose that the author of such books must keep his reputation henceforth uncontaminated by the taint of lower kinds of success. Marquand turned out a new serial about the Civil War, *Eight-Three-Eight,* which appeared in the *Post* in April and May 1937, while the *Apley* sales were booming. Brandt sent it in to the Little, Brown office, much to Marquand's annoyance, for he did not want it to be considered for book publication. McIntyre agreed that it would be a mistake to present book readers with such a sequel to *Apley*: "No doubt if John had never written *The Late George Apley* and had no intention of writing more really serious fiction, we should be glad to bring it out, but that is not the case." They were about to publish *Think Fast, Mr. Moto,* but "after that John says no more stories written for the serial market are to appear as books. I can't say that this will be so permanently, of course, but that is his present attitude and I approve of it heartily." The Moto books, as a matter of fact, were to make an exception; they began, after all, to do well enough in book form for McIntyre to decide, when *Mr. Moto Is So Sorry* was offered to him less than a year later, to treat them as a special case. But other magazine serials were less welcome. McIntyre was eagerly waiting for the "three serious works of fiction" which Marquand had said he had in mind in May of 1937. Nor were proposals to make book collections of magazine stories welcome either. Marquand had been publishing a succession of tales in the *Post* about a New England family named March—he was mining the old Newburyport lode again for romantic adventure in colonial days. There were now ten of these out, and Bernice Baumgarten suggested they be collected in a book. McIntyre conceded that "there is just as much reason to publish them as to have published *Haven's End*, although I was hoping that we might follow *The Late George Apley* with another serious novel." He told her: "They are good but they are magazine stories." To his relief, Marquand left the decision to his publisher, who held out for the "very serious" thing that was surely on its way.

Marquand had a reason now for a growing indifference to the lure of profits from writing for the magazines. This was the federal income tax, which, as his earnings increased, left him with less and less of a percentage share of them. He continued to write the stories that came so easily, and the appetite of the public had never been greater. In July, *Collier's* managed to buy into the market for Marquand stories, paying $3,000 for a short one called "Everything Is Fine" and offering to pay handsomely for the serial that Carl Brandt promised from Marquand; he could simultaneously feed his stuff into the *Post* and its rival and double his takings. Yet when, in November, he discovered that Brandt had accepted the *Collier's* advance for the serial—he had expressly instructed that the sale be put off until the next year—he exploded angrily at his agent and notified his lawyer that he wanted to cancel the sale. He began to feel that he was riding a money-making process from which he must—yet dared not yet—dismount. A few years later, when he had pretty much abandoned serials for novels intended primarily for the book market, he commented to Alice Dixon Bond, book editor of the Boston *Herald*, that taxes were working to raise the literary level of American writing: "Taxation may be a good thing for writing in this country. The idea of an author's saving up money so that he can retire from writing is out the window now. I believe that writers will write more what they want to write and less for the popular taste. One of the worst things periodical literature has done is to take brilliant writers and so condition them as regards what they must say and must not say that they have become muscle-bound. The man who made $40,000 a year on a magazine serial will now only get $20,000, so why not do a book?"

He was also consciously aware, now, of the artistic restrictions placed upon his writing by the magazines. In the spring he had written a story that expressed something of his personal life in a genuine way. It was called "Pull, Pull Together," and it related the experience of a father who takes his son for the first time to visit a prestigious boarding school and to be interviewed by the headmaster for admission, just as he had been doing at the time in an effort to place Johnny in a school. The story represented with some sensitivity his own bemused feelings as he had enrolled his son in St. Mark's, his own uncertainty about the way upon which the boy was launched by this step. Johnny had had a difficult last year at the Indian Mountain School; his school reports declared him a "very irregular worker, given to much day-dreaming," and Christina and John deliberated anxiously, almost united in mood, over his next educational step. They had finally decided on Milton Academy, which was closest to Boston and Kent's Island, but as a courtesy to the headmaster of St. Mark's, Francis Parkman, to whom application had also been made, Marquand took his son for an interview there as well. Marquand reported the scene to Adelaide: "For the first time I realized that the little fellow has much of the stubborn and unpleasant disposition of his Papa. The sight of those handsome oak panelled rooms, and of the walls so redolent with tradition and carved with the initials of all the biggest snobs in Christendom, and of the fine turf of the Playing Fields, and of the soft light filtering through the Chapel windows upon the hand carved choir stalls, and of my old friend 'Torchy' Parkman seated in an office as large as Mr. Lorimer's made such an impression on Johnny that he became determined to go to St. Mark's and to hell with anything else." The resulting arguments with his parents were climaxed by Christina's tearful declaration that they had wanted him to be closer rather than further from them in the future because they felt that the divorce had disrupted his life. Johnny's reply was "Then don't disrupt it any more by sending me to a girls' school which is filled with pansies." Johnny's victory in this contest was, for him, no doubt a significant recovery from the feeling of helplessness the divorce had given him, and for his father a warning that he could expect to find his son as determined to mark out his defiance on future occasions. For Marquand the whole matter had a private ambiguity. He had been, in his own day, both contemptuous and envious of the boys who had gone to St. Mark's while he had gone to the Newburyport High School. Though he would send all of his five children to private schools, he would curiously resent what he made it possible for them to have.

The cult of "St. Grottlesex" would, of course, receive its definitive treatment by Marquand in *H. M. Pulham, Esquire*, where Parkman and his boys are given memorable representation. In the modest sketch of the subject in "Pull, Pull Together," the father is suddenly struck with the idea that the school is a static institution where abstractions take the place of a genuine introduction to life, and remembers that he had had to unlearn most of what he had absorbed at this same school. But the boy is desperately anxious to be enrolled; the school, with its rules and traditions, its snobbish conformities, actually appeals to him; he has the adolescent desire to "belong," and the father ends by entering him there after all. This muted ending had not pleased the *Post* editors, though they printed the story in July. As Marquand told the graduates and faculty of the Lawrenceville School whom he was invited to address some months later: "My story had a vague, inconclusive quality which is known to the trade, I suppose for want of a better word, as 'frustration.' Frustration besides being a popular description for any work an editor does not like is now generally applied by the publishers' business office to a story which does not possess a happy ending, nay more than that, a *very* happy ending. My story, in other words, was not sound fiction, although I still maintain that it is the sort of fiction which I should prefer to write."

The issue would not settle itself for some years, however, and in this aspect of his life, as in others, an ambiguous stance was characteristic of Marquand. While he continued to let his work appear in the *Post* or its rivals, he liked to assert himself the prisoner of magazine popularity. But sometimes, perhaps genuinely convinced that honest effort and skill was represented in the weeklies, he upheld the worth of such writing. Even his close friend Conney Fiske, who had undertaken to write a profile of Marquand for the *Saturday Review of Literature* in the fall of 1938, made the mistake of taking Marquand's complaints seriously enough to put them into her article, where they were sure to offend readers who were also part of his faithful *Post* following or even some fans of the Moto films. After Carl Brandt read her article in manuscript, he heatedly wrote George Stevens, editor of the *Saturday Review*: "This article makes it seem as if John only wrote popular fiction with his tongue in his cheek. It also states that John writes only under the compulsion of writing for the money. As it happens neither of these things is the truth. No artist that I know is any more conscientious or capable with any work of his that goes in front of the public. To say that he has written potboiler stuff through the years in order only to write Apley or his new books, I know not to be the truth. He has taken pride, and rightly so, in the work that he has done for the magazines. Out of that work there are things which can stand the test of time to the same extent as 'George Apley' or the forthcoming book. Despite the fact that he like many another writer says he would never write another line except for the money in it he is actively uncomfortable if he does not get an opportunity to do his work."

Brandt went on to insist that Marquand's wide-ranging serial romances had been ignored by Mrs. Fiske: "This article seems to limit Mr. Marquand's work to New England background and to China. This is to ignore the large amount of important work he has done with the Civil War as a background, the South Seas, Hawaii and France. This also ignores the work that he has done with horseracing and horses as a subject matter." How well Carl

Brandt remembered the work *he* had done on these deprecated serials! Mrs. Fiske, plainly, had good reason for setting down views Marquand had often expressed to her. Nevertheless, she was compelled to revise her article. In place of the offending passages the printed version carried the following statement: "Although he cherishes his introduction to a Chinese University gathering—'For those of us who are not ashamed to admit that we read the *Saturday Evening Post*, the name of J. P. Marquand is doubtless familiar'—he has a great respect for that flair and the technical excellence which must be achieved in the writing of successful popular fiction. He feels that any creative writer, even if he is writing for the pulps, is embarked in a far greater effort than any of those who are engaged in producing nonfiction. Above all, he dislikes those writers who take credit for raking in literary dust heaps rather than striking out for themselves. Probably owing to his own experience, he feels that a writer will probably not be great unless forced to earn his own living by his writing."

And this really *was* Marquand's attitude too. When, a year later, after the appearance of *Wickford Point*, the *New Yorker* asked if it was true that during Lorimer's time he had been compelled to write popular stories for the *Post* and only since Lorimer's death in 1937 had been able to write as he wanted to, Marquand was sharply annoyed. To Carl Brandt he said: "You know the way the intelligentsia feel about a popular magazine like the Post. It is their belief that it prostitutes the intellect of everyone who reads it and they take every opportunity to get a crack at the Post when they can. I wish you would tell the editors of the Post that if they ever heard me quoted as running down the magazine or if they ever hear any such stories as the one about Mr. Lorimer, none of this comes from me. In the first place, it would be a piece of utter folly for me to sneer at an institution which has supported me for a great many years and, in the second place, I do not feel that way. I have always been proud and pleased to be identified as a writer for the Post and I shall continue to be as long as they want to have me." He seemed to share the attitude of Wesley Winans Stout, who had succeeded to the editorship of the *Post* after Lorimer's death. When Brandt showed him Marquand's letter he had merely commented, "We are aware of the compulsory attitude of the intelligentsia towards a publication of more than 3,000,000 circulation and we should be insulated against it."

Well, in truth, Marquand had not always been nor would he always be so proud as he claimed of his *Post* connection, and his relationship with the magazine would undergo change. McIntyre's and not Brandt's and the *Post* editors' influence would prevail in the end and there would be no more Marquand serials written expressly for magazines after 1940 except for the last Moto mystery, *Rendezvous in Tokyo*, which appeared in the *Post* in 1956. And despite Brandt's protest that Marquand had not limited himself to the New England subject, he would, in fact, concentrate his artistic attention more and more on it. That he should do so was an idea that had grown in his mind with such strength that almost immediately upon his return from Persia he bought a large piece of rural property in Newbury and began to renovate the old farmhouse for his own use. This seemed, no doubt, an eccentric step to the Brandts, who expected that Marquand would permanently embrace their own writing-publishing world of Manhattan. But Marquand had little taste, as already observed, for the company of his fellow writers, and he had even less use for the milieu of the publishing industry. New York, though he had and would continue to have an apartment there for some years, always seemed bearable for only a few months at a time.

He often described a cocktail party at the Brandts', where he had met Sinclair Lewis. Lewis had arrived already drunk. He was on his way with his editor to a film premiere of *Arrowsmith* and was in one of his moods of hostility towards agents and publishers—all the parasites, as he loudly called them, who were sucking his creative blood. He pulled Marquand off into a corner because, he said, they were the only writers present and he was tired of being pushed around. When the time came to leave for the premiere he waved his editor away and shouted to Marquand, "Come on, John, I want to talk to you; let's get away from these lousy bloodsuckers, these goddam hucksters, these fucking exploiters." Lewis got drunker and drunker as the time passed and more and more obstinate about going on to see the film. He yelled: "Let me alone, let me alone. I want to talk to John here. John and I understand each other, we know what a writer is. Keep these goddam bloodsuckers away from me, will you?" And suddenly, he proposed: "John, listen, come to Detroit with me! We'll disguise ourselves as waiters and get jobs in some joint. Will you, John? What do you say? Detroit! Waiters! How about it? Let's get away from these . . ."

The obvious alternative to New York was Boston, but Marquand had no desire to live in the house he and Christina had occupied on West Cedar Street or to try to find his place, as a divorced man, anywhere in the scene he was depicting in *Apley*. Home, anyhow, was north of Boston, was Curzon's Mill where the Marquands had their pride of past. But at the Mill his father was now living permanently, together with Aunt Bessie and Aunt Greta, and the Hale family were invariably in residence in the summertime. And so, hardly a month back from the Orient, in October 1935, he purchased Kent's Island, to which he would bring his new wife. It must have counted that he was related, though very distantly, to the family which had owned the property from the time they had purchased it from the Indians in 1647 until 1920. Sarah Kent, who died in 1810, had been one of his great-great-great-grandmothers. The place was called an island, though it did not look like one except on the map; it was really a tract of upland and salt marsh bounded by the Parker River and a forking branch, and by streams and ditches. He paid under $5,000 for it, for it was not of great economic value as a farm, the only possible article of produce being the salt hay which had sometimes been cut for fodder. As Marquand discovered soon enough, the fresh-water supply was poor and black flies and mosquitoes were numerous. The original Kent house had been destroyed years before and the farmhouse built in its place needed renovation. He immediately set carpenters to work making improvements and enlargements.

Kent's Island, too, seems to have represented to Marquand an environment where Johnny and Tina could absorb some influence to counteract Sedgwick effeteness. As he prepared to welcome them for a month-long visit in the summer of 1939, he wrote Johnny, "I should like to have you learn to do something useful on a farm and there will be quite a lot of work then in getting in the hay and cultivating the big field." To Christina he explained more precisely: "I should like him to get some idea of how everyone except a privileged few have to earn their living. I think he is gaining a highly distorted picture of the world and his position in it. This is certainly not helped by a summer in Nonquitt with a country club and dancing and sailboats." It is questionable, however, if the kind of gentleman's farm that Kent's Island became ever served to impress on Johnny the virtues of a life of toil.

This country estate would occupy a great amount of Marquand's attention and upon it he lavished money regularly until the end of his life; he would spend almost all his subsequent summers there. Yet when, at his death, an appraisal was made by a realty firm, the appraiser remarked in his report that "only another such as he [Marquand] would be a likely purchaser" of the isolated property. "Such a purchaser must have independent means, and an almost fanatic liking for rural and oftentimes bleak New England. Kent's Island would probably never be suitable for year round living by its owner, because of its remoteness, and the other hardships one would encounter living in the area in the winter." But Marquand's attachment was devoted and in a few years he had transformed it into a "working" homestead with beehives and chickens and sheep and hogs and cows (some of the last named for movie stars—Mae West was an ample Jersey and one of the heifers was called Shirley Temple), and acres under cultivation. The expensive care of all this only justified itself when World War II arrived with its food shortages. The two-story main house gained an addition in 1940, and became, with Adelaide's help, an elegant monument to Marquand's feeling for the American past. A visitor noted in 1942 the living room with its painting of Perry changing flagships in the Battle of Lake Erie, which hung over the Empire sofa; the Hepplewhite chairs and Canton china bowl that had belonged to his great-great-grandfather Curzon; the beautiful colonial secretary with its shelves filled with Crown Derby china; the old copper footbath for fireplace wood; and in the dining room, the dresser filled with old plates and the display of heirloom silver, like the can made by Joseph Hurd for Governor Joseph Dudley, whose grandson Dudley Atkins had married Sarah Kent.

Ten years later another visitor said that the rooms gave him the impression of having been lifted from the American wing of the Metropolitan Museum of Art. In addition to the Gilbert Stuart portrait of Joseph Marquand's sister, Susanna Searle, and the portrait by an unknown colonial painter of Richard Kent's wife Hannah Gookin, he noticed an oil painting of the Bay of Naples dated 1810, with Vesuvius in eruption and an American sloop at anchor in the foreground. Adelaide had also added by then, rather incongruously, an oil by Bouguereau that she had bought, as well as a portrait of Marquand himself which had been painted at her insistence by Alexander James. Where Marquand's study had been in the earlier years, a sort of trophy room had been created. Framed illustrations from the serial versions of *Apley* and *Wickford Point* decorated the walls; and there were other mementos of his career: a wood model of a Yangtze River junk, which Marquand had bought in Shanghai, and a carved "love stick" and a mask that he had picked up on Truk after World War II. This room was to become a home bar, and Adelaide ordered another study constructed in the new wing—a fine, light room with built-in bookshelves. But Marquand never really worked there. By that time he desired nothing so much as immunity from contact with his household—and he would have a third study built into the old carriage house, which was separated from the main house by a gravel walk. Into this room, where he wrote most of his later novels, the sense of the past came in again, despite the modern authors and reference works on the bookshelves and the impression of lively industry. Even here, where fresh pages rose on the work table as Marquand's secretary typed from his dictation, the visitor might note a pair of Queen Anne chairs and a Jacobean rush-seated chair and a clock that had been made on London Bridge, and some fine old blue plates that commemorated the arrival of Lafayette at Castle Garden on August 16, 1824, and an old desk with a secret drawer, an early pine cabinet and pine blanket chest, and finally, a bust of Emerson that Gardiner Fiske had given him.

Marquand's second marriage took place in the Hooker apartment at 620 Park Avenue on April 17, 1937. He had managed to hold out against a big church wedding, but the Hookers arranged to transport most of the ingredients to their own premises. There were two hundred guests. Adelaide wore a magnificent bridal gown and train and carried a bunch of arbutus, and Dr. Harry Emerson Fosdick, pastor of the fashionable Riverside Church, arrived to perform the ceremony. The whole occasion had, for Marquand, a wildly preposterous quality. He often described in later years how the freight elevator of the apartment house was called into service to bring up the masses of guests and debouch them into the Hooker kitchen.

Like all gatherings under Elon Hooker's roof, the occasion was totally dry, even more literally than some of the guests could have expected: no substitute for liquor—like grape juice or punch—was served either, because the bride and groom had vetoed it. Adelaide succeeded in adding some note of her own theatrical taste to the occasion, however. Instead of "Here Comes the Bride," she had arranged for an old musician friend to play the solo horn passage that accompanies the death of Tristan in *Tristan und Isolde*. Marquand would remember best an odd quarter of an hour when he found himself shut up with Dr. Fosdick in the cook's bedroom while they waited for the ceremonial moment. The minister and the groom had a little difficulty in finding something to talk about, and Marquand, after some floundering, heard himself exclaiming upon the wonders of Seeing Eye dogs, a subject to which Fosdick was responding with grateful enthusiasm. When the wedding was over, the guests descended in the elevator in large batches and fled to places where they could toast the happy bride and groom in absentia and the bride and groom went to spend the next day, a Sunday, at Atlantic City. They were not yet on their honeymoon because Adelaide had promised to give a lecture on Japanese gardens—illustrated with her Kodachrome slides—to a local garden club. This done, they finally took off for a couple of weeks in Arizona, after which they began married life immediately at Kent's Island.

As he had warned Adelaide months before, he had "returned to the old town with the reputation of being Lord of the Manor." Old friends of the Marquand family came to call. But not until the following May, when the announcement of the Pulitzer Prize for *Apley* was read by Newburyporters, did he experience the hero's homecoming he had dreamed of since childhood. Now the poor Marquand boy from ramshackle Curzon's Mill was more honored than any of the High Street aristocracy. As sweet, probably, as the occasion of the award—that impressive ceremonial moment when President Nicholas Murray Butler of Columbia intoned Marquand's name at the annual dinner of the Graduate School of Journalism and handed him the thousand-dollar check that meant instant international fame—were certain more obscure occasions in Newburyport. A month later, in June, he gave the annual Ancestors' Day sermon at the Unitarian Church before four hundred fellow townsmen. In the course of a humorous recounting of episodes from colonial Newburyport he reminded his audience that "we are rapidly losing our critical faculties in a period of shifting moral standards where nothing is secure" and that the "intolerance" of the Puritans might be seen as rooted in attachment to principle, an unwillingness to compromise, which was admirable. Among old stories he recalled to his listeners' minds was an occasion out of the past when a certain Joseph Marquand (whom his listeners knew to be his great-great-grandfather) had resigned his membership in the First Religious Society in protest against the minister's politics.

In November Marquand was elected a member of the Tuesday Night

Club. Since 1911 this "literary and social" club had been meeting on alternate Tuesday evenings at one or another member's house for dinner and the reading and discussion of a paper. The membership in 1938 numbered eighteen with the addition of Marquand, all gentlemen of standing in Newburyport society and all well known to him. Among them were several doctors, lawyers and manufacturing men; the Reverend Laurence Hayward, in whose church Marquand had just preached his Ancestors' Day sermon; Marquand's high school physics teacher, Dana Wells; and Laurence P. Dodge, the broker and Harvard Club officer to whom Marquand had unsuccessfully applied for a scholarship when he graduated from the high school. Marquand, the one famous man among these strictly local worthies, would take his place in the club with the greatest seriousness, entertaining it year after year at Kent's Island when his turn came around and offering exotic meals—a Mexican dish and an Indian curry served with at least eight condiments were particularly remembered. On occasion he added to the after-dinner diversions by producing smoke rings of extraordinary size and stability. In regular order, too, he delivered his polished essays, generally accounts of his travels, as though they were on a par with the modest efforts of the rest. They, for their part, thought the famous man a pretty good fellow, adept at masculine badinage, a neighbor to be proud of, who gave himself no airs. Perhaps Marquand alone understood that his desire to be present among them was not a simple matter.

15

The Squire of Newburyport

Marquand's ideal of personal life was, no doubt, monotonous and stodgy: he wanted regular and long hours of uninterrupted work and quiet evenings with early bedtimes. Once settled in Kent's Island he was glad to leave to Adelaide most of the problems of redecoration and to his hired help the care of the livestock he had lightheartedly ordered as bucolic decorations to his new estate. He was forty-five years old in 1938 and already he felt the sense of waning time. He worked day after day on the novels that were to confirm his success with *Apley*—*Wickford Point*, and after it *H. M. Pulham, Esquire*. Now and then the Marquands had a visitor from Boston or New York but mostly the place remained wrapped about by its somber marsh as though it were indeed an island well off the shore of sophisticated society. He took up again, as athletic recreation, his youthful habit of duck hunting, although in November he hurt his back while jumping over a ditch near the Parker River and was in the hospital for two weeks. After his recovery he was glad to yield to Adelaide's impatience for a change, and they joined her mother for a vacation in Jamaica. But when Mrs. Hooker was bitten by a mosquito carrying the severe form of malaria known as blackwater fever and was extremely ill for many weeks, Marquand declared, a little triumphantly, "Perhaps Newburyport has its advantages in the winter."

There was no question that Adelaide took little pleasure in living at that time of the year more or less across the Merrimack from the spot where Whittier had written his *Snow-Bound*. Early in 1939 the Marquands took a New York apartment. It was in the same building as Mrs. Hooker's—One Beekman Place, an address with considerable snob standing. For some years they would stay there until the end of May before moving up to Kent's Island, where they lingered until November. The idea of a tropical winter vacation took hold too, and in 1941 they went for the first time to Sanibel Island off the west coast of Florida and discovered Hobe Sound on the east coast, that paradise of the very, very rich such as Marquand's friend George Merck. But the Beekman Place duplex was hardly austere. Adelaide furnished it with antique pieces lent by her mother—heavy, rather ornate old-fashioned furniture—and her own accumulations of objects, including some of the treasured Russian icons. The apartment had a certain seclusion rare in the city, for the ground floor directly overlooked the East River, a perspective since eliminated by the East River Drive.

Even to Adelaide the idea of a summer home north of Boston seemed attractive enough. Indeed, she conveyed such a sense of the charm of the region that in 1939 Blanchette and John Rockefeller came there in search of a summer house. Marquand was amused by the expectations of his new relatives: "They want to be in a simple place," he wrote Gardiner Fiske, "yet near a lot of rather nice young people with automobiles and motor boats and also near an excellent country club and good tennis. They want to be able to see lots of people but they don't want to go to any place where there are cocktail parties. In other words they envisage a world which doesn't exist." Clearly the Rockefellers did not really want the same sort of life that Marquand was trying to lead at Kent's Island.

For him, there was never to be any question that Newburyport was home. Marquand's renewal of his early ties explains his readiness—despite his preoccupation with his work—to speak on diverse ceremonial occasions, even to the cutting of the tape at the opening of the new A & P store. He was eager to make such affirmations of his connection with the town. In April 1939, the log of the Tuesday Night Club recorded the "maiden effort of our latest member," a talk on his Hawaiian impressions called "Sugar and Soul," which he delivered at Curzon's Mill. His father, a longtime member, was host. The following month he himself entertained the group at the Mill—Kent's Island was still undergoing renovation—and in October he read to the members still another paper, this time on schoolmasters. But, paradoxically, the triumph that had brought him back to Newburyport as a distinguished son tended to keep him from the reconciliation he longed for. In a new sense he was now an outsider to this community. His fame made him an acquaintance, through his books, of many thousands of readers who would never tread Newburyport streets—and somehow removed him from those who did. He was becoming the companion of the famous, one who knew noted writers, generals, foreign dignitaries, and was not so close, consequently, to the average Newburyporter, who would find himself depicted, not always flatteringly, in the writings of this townsman. It was a sort of game he played when he listened dutifully to the offerings of his fellow Tuesday Night Club members. He would not spare them in *Point of No Return* where he described the meetings of the Confessional Club in his fictional Clyde: "There was the gallstone, for instance, which was removed from the interior of Samuel Pepys, the subject of a paper by Gerald Marchby. . . . Then there was 'The Story of the Mammoth,' a paper which had been read by Willard Godfrey. The juvenile quality of this paper had caused John Gray to consult reference books in the public library and to discover that the whole thing had been cribbed from a children's encyclopedia. He might also mention that scholarly work entitled 'Certain Old Teaspoons,' written by Mr. Norton Swing, a retired official of the Wright-Sherwin Company. This was a double-header, because you not only had to hear about the certain old teaspoons but you had to examine them afterwards one by one." John Gray had felt it quite necessary to belong, and when his turn came, to entertain the club just as Marquand had. But only the novelist would ultimately disclose his secret condescension.

The game of coming-home continued to be played out in public view as the years went on. In 1947 Marquand joined the Neptunes, a volunteer fire company, and participated in its musters, during which the antique fire-fighting apparatus of hand-pumped tubs was worked in competition with that of other New England companies. Manning the pumps was, of course, the prerogative of the young and strong-muscled, and Marquand, who had never belonged to the "Neps," was only a courtesy oldtimer as he assisted on these occasions. Still, wearing his fireman's red shirt with the initials N.V.F.A. (for Newburyport Veteran Firemen's Association) printed in white across the chest, he was to be seen among the others when the equipment was set up for the annual contest on a town green or playground on a sunny midsummer day. All of Newburyport, young and old, turned out to cheer and shout, soft drinks were sold from a stand, and stronger refreshment was freely consumed less openly. While a fife and drum corps sounded exuberantly, the firemen would march onto the green with their fire tubs, their equipment, all burnished and new-painted, mounted on a wheeled chassis, and the leaders carrying ancient silver fire trumpets stuffed with flowers. The tubs were placed on a wooden platform and their supply tanks, holding up to five hundred gallons, were filled from a nearby hydrant and moved to an open space covered by brown paper. When the signal to begin was given, the foreman of the company would climb on top of the tub, his assistant taking a position at the nozzle of the hose, and the pumping would begin. The stream of water would arch into the air and descend upon the paper, hopefully beyond the mark cast by the rivals' hoses. The winning company would receive a prize of something like two hundred dollars. In 1950, wearing his red Neptune shirt, Marquand led the Newburyport Fourth of July parade, which started at ten in the morning from the Town Hall and proceeded to the Perkins playground for the muster of fifteen competing hand-tub companies and a daylong program ending with fireworks at 10 P.M.

The occasion was a pagan summer festival that obliterated, for a moment, the old social barriers: a "High Streeter" could, if he wanted to, join with the son of a clam digger in pumping with all his might for the glory of the town. That it was a tribal ritual of masculine solidarity was pretty obvious to Marquand. He did not need the observations that might have been made to him in these terms by the anthropologist W. Lloyd Warner, who visited Newburyport regularly between 1930 and 1935, to conduct a study that would extend to an American community the formulations he had arrived at in the Australian bush. Marquand was both interested in and repelled by Warner's systematic classification of personal types and group behavior which resulted in the massive statistical survey that began to be published in the classic "Yankee City" series (issued by the Yale University Press in 1941). As he applied his attention to his surroundings with the observing interest of the social novelist, he felt at once, probably, his unlikeness and likeness to Warner. "The way to learn about Clyde was to be brought up there," he would reflect in *Point of No Return*. Marquand's description of the muster in this novel is itself a wonderful set piece, a vivid realization of local actuality such as only art could achieve, and it is quite outside the reach of the sociologist with his tables of income, education, and the like, and his caste categories of upper-upper, lower-upper, upper-middle on down to the bottommost lower-lower. Indeed, the whole novel, with its recapitulation of Marquand's own boyhood in Newburyport, is a demonstration of the superiority of the artist's and the old inhabitant's sense of place. Earlier, in *Wickford Point*, Marquand would be as scornful of the attempt to depict his New England home made by another kind of visiting "expert," a literary professor who thinks he can "do" the picturesque natives after a few visits.

And yet he was also, like Warner, working from an emotional outside, the nonbelonging that resulted from his profession. Marching along in his red fireman's shirt he must have known that he was more observer than participant, even a little of a fraud, deliberately preparing himself to write a chapter in a future novel. In that novel, of course, the Clyde pumping company includes John Gray, also, to a degree, an outsider; he is a recruit from what Malcolm Bryant (the Warner of the novel) identified as the "middle-upper" class, which generally did not participate in the plebeian event. But class is not, after all, an insurmountable barrier. John Gray, a charming waster of his family's means and a cheerful eccentric (who is modeled not on Marquand himself but on Philip Marquand), belongs without self-consciousness among his plebeian fellow townsmen.

As Marquand settled in at Kent's Island he kept an eye on Curzon's Mill, where Philip had established himself with complete psychic security after his own wanderings and the long Wilmington exile. The aging man was not without problems: he needed financial help as well as advice, if he would take it, about the conduct of his chicken business. Among the readjustments of relationship that the return to Newburyport entailed was John's assumption of authority over this enfeebled paternal antagonist, whose fecklessness in earlier years had inspired his son's will to achievement. In January 1941,

Philip wrecked his Lincoln Zephyr, driving while intoxicated, and Marquand, then in New York, wrote his father's doctor: "I personally feel that it would be a great deal better if he didn't do much more driving. At his best he is a most erratic driver and lately he seems to have no idea of the speed he is going when he approaches corners and street intersections. I know he will be desolated without a car, but I have an idea that the time has come for him to face it." Since it would be impossible for the elder Marquand to live out at Curzon's Mill without a car, Marquand proposed that he be moved to a small apartment in Newburyport for the winter and stay at the Brick House only in the summer, when there were others on the property; or else he could live at Kent's Island during the Marquands' absence, where their caretaker would see to his needs and even take him into town occasionally. Needless to say, the aging man resentfully resisted these proposals and remained at the Mill. As Marquand had to recognize, he was "inclined to do the opposite of anything I ask." But though Philip was only seventy-four, his son was convinced that senility had compounded a constitutional unreliability to a dangerous point. And, indeed, there were soon other demonstrations: Philip made himself ill eating out of cans in his bachelor fashion and he dangerously set fire to the grass around the Mill while burning leaves. But not until 1947 was he really failing enough for Dr. Snow to agree to recommend what Marquand had asked: the revocation of Philip's driver's license and also a conservatorship that would take the management of money and property out of Philip's hands. As the son coldly observed, "Lapses of memory and a slowing mental process make him utterly incapable of taking care of any sort of business matter—not that he was much good at this even in his heyday."

At Curzon's Mill, too, Marquand watched with his old annoyance the coming and going of the Hale family during the summer months. He would never cease to wish that he could clear them out of what seemed to him, by spiritual right, his own homestead. And when it appeared that he would need a separate working studio apart from the main house at Kent's Island, he talked openly of moving one of the Curzon's Mill buildings twelve miles across land and water to Newbury—a proposal that was practically preposterous, and irritating, to say the least, to his Hale cousins. He was eventually forced to be satisfied with the conversion of the old carriage house at Kent's Island, which was just far enough from the house to reduce Adelaide's impulsive interruptions to a bearable frequency. There continued to be, however, tussles over smaller and more portable portions of Curzon's Mill, such as chairs and candlesticks that both Marquand and his relatives claimed, and there were frequent and disagreeable scenes after one or another object found its way to Kent's Island. The cousins made no secret of their resentment either in Newburyport or New York, and their acquaintance was wide. Renée Oakman, the youngest and least restrained, once commented to other guests at a party at Kent's Island itself that the chairs they were sitting on had been "gotten out of" her mother, their host's aunt Greta. These seizures seem to have had some legal justification. In 1937, Aunt Bessie had died, leaving her money to her sister Greta, half of her share of the real estate at Curzon's Mill to her brother Philip, and the remainder of her personal property to John Marquand, and she had made him also the executor of her will (a fact which his relatives felt he had taken advantage of). In 1941 there was a particularly acrimonious family flare-up over two "Martha Washington" chairs which Aunt Bessie had had in the Brick House and which had been taken into the adjoining Yellow House occupied by the Hales. But Marquand felt that his rights to the chairs—indeed to Curzon's Mill itself—were even more than legal. He told his father at the time: "[Aunt Bessie] left me this property because she was fond of me, and because she felt that I was the only member of the family in my generation who cared about its associations and who was in a position to keep it together." His view of his special responsibility—which was not shared by the Hales—was six years later to result in a court battle with them over the whole of Curzon's Mill.

His mind was very much on the Mill and on the Hales as he set to work on *Wickford Point* in the summer of 1937. In this novel he made claim, more effectively than he would do in the unseemly squabbles over furniture and real estate with his cousins, to the true inheritance of Curzon's Mill, barely disguised as Wickford Point. Representing himself as the narrator, Jim Calder, he depicted the degeneracy of the tradition of New England refinement in Calder's Brill (that is, Hale) relatives.

Calder, like Marquand, was a poor relation who worked at magazine writing for a living while the Brills managed to live in idleness by right of birth. But his own claim on Wickford Point involved an attachment to the past, forgotten by the Brills, a past genuinely connected to the worlds of nature and common life and represented by his great-aunt Sarah exactly in the fashion of Marquand's own great-aunt Mary Curzon. For the younger Brills the past was only the source of a presumption of superiority to others—they had had a famous ancestor, the Wickford Sage (just as the Hales were descended from Edward Everett Hale and Nathan Hale). The New England genteel tradition with its rooting in the sense of the moral and the useful as well as the gracious had become attenuated into the harmless ethereality of Cousin Clothilde and further reduced to neurotic parasitism in her children. Calder preferred, in the long run, the practical honesty of an outsider who could not appreciate the tradition—the self-made business girl from New York with whom he was in love.

The Hales and everyone who knew them immediately identified the originals of these characters. Cousin Clothilde was clearly Aunt Greta—a figure spun more out of the tissue of love than of malice. Aunt Clothilde—like Greta—was as beautiful as she was vague; she was poetic, charming and affectionate; but she could not balance a checkbook, she hated clocks, and she leaned shamelessly on the practical provision of others, first on that unromantic businessman Grandfather Calder (based on Marquand's memories of his own grandfather), later on Calder–Marquand himself. Marquand did not altogether ridicule her late-transcendental scorn of clock time and materiality. There was something exquisite still in the tradition she represented. Its unworldliness was still valid when set against vulgarity, social climbing, ostentation. But her charm was pernicious too. Her hold on her children was an encouragement to helplessness and insipidity. This was clearly visible in Harry, Sid and Mary Brill, the offspring of her first marriage, who were recognizably Dudley, Bob and Laura Hale. Harry, with his snobbery and opportunism, was a particularly unkind portrait of the cousin who had been Marquand's playmate in childhood, his roommate in college. Equally unflattering, yet telling, was the novel's version of Robert Hale as a pseudo-aesthete and idler. And while there was some sympathy in the portrait of Laura as Mary Brill, there was certainly ridicule for her blubbering and helplessness.

Harshest of all, though perhaps the most fascinating of these caricatures, was Marquand's representation of his Hale cousins' half-sister Renée, the daughter of Greta's second husband, the architect John Oakman (lightly sketched in as the alcoholic painter-radical Archie Wright, who could no more stand the atmosphere of his wife's old home than could his real-life twin). Bella Brill—for she is a Brill in the novel rather than Wright's child—is beautiful, unhappy and damned; she is "Bella the Bitch," as Renée herself would put it. Calder is half in love with her, as Marquand may once have been with his youngest cousin. Renée at twenty-six was already a somewhat tarnished siren; but earlier, when he was growing up, Marquand had been captivated by her vivacity and rebelliousness as well as by her astonishing good looks. She would in time bend her endowments towards destruction and, after four marriages, lie down in the self-dug grave of alcoholism. As Marquand began to set her into his story he saw her as committed to the downward path by her very capacity to grasp successfully at mean goals.

Marquand's novel was, without doubt, a roman à clef, and Marquand stoutly lied in saying again and again that he had no basis in real life for his scene and characters. *Wickford Point* is, among all Marquand's books, the most personal. This is not only because it contains innumerable details of description, incident and characterization that are lifted directly from his actual experience, but because its hero's problems were most immediately his own. It has already been suggested that he felt, upon his return to Newburyport, the necessity of coming to terms with the sense of belonging and yet of not-belonging to the traditions of a family and a regional past—the chief of Jim Calder's problems in the novel. Like Calder, he had to explain to himself what drew him back and what held him always off. Then there was a second theme with immediate reference to Marquand's self-questioning. Calder is a writer who has placed himself in the world of literary commerce as an honest craftsman who admits that he writes for the money in it. His mentor is George Stanhope, the Carl Brandt who dispenses expert advice out of a brain crammed to bursting with cheap story ideas, a literary counselor with an infallible sense of the basest cravings of the magazine public. There must always be, for this public, according to Stanhope, a story of "boy and girl" at last united after misunderstanding—it was surefire. The capable writer could exercise his ingenuity in the invention of varieties of misunderstanding between the young couple but in the end they must fall into each others' arms. Calder, as he digests these views, is, needless to say, Marquand, sensing the soundness of the advice yet knowing the inadequacy of the story formula to contain experience. Did it explain how Calder felt about his mistress Pat Leighton? Did it explain why Bella had not made a go of it with her first husband, his friend Joe Stowe? But it was not easy to dismiss the idea of formula altogether. "When one was weary, one thought of this artisanship of popular fiction as slight, a somewhat ghastly parody on life. But then again, perhaps it was not, for was not all human intercourse governed by arbitrary laws of its own? All life was a story, uglier and less perfect than the ones [he] wrote, but with its own grim scheme."

These are the reflections, of course, of the earnest novelist, the Marquand who was writing the very novel of which Calder was a part. Calder's friend Joe Stowe has already made the break into the realm of serious fiction and has become as famous as Marquand became with *Apley*. He is thus not any more a purely invented character than the other personages in *Wickford Point*—he is the alternate Marquand, who has succeeded Jim Calder without rejecting him. There is, besides, one other writer in the book—Allen Southby, the self-esteeming Harvard housemaster from the Middle West who wants to write nothing less, it would seem, than *Wickford Point*, that is, the novel about such a place and its meaning. Marquand's professor is not so certainly identified as some of the representatives of the Hales in the novel, though several members of the Harvard English Department may have contributed features to him: Howard Mumford Jones, or F. O. Matthiessen, whose *American Renaissance* could be referred to by Southby's treatise, *The Transcendent Curve*, or Kenneth Murdock, then master of Leverett House—all notable authorities on American literary traditions. Marquand's hostility to Harvard professors was based, in part, on his old resentment of the successful campus literati, who, like the social elite, had kept him out of their circle. He had never, one recalls, made the Signet Society. "They'll be sorry someday," Joe Stowe had assured Calder after the two of them had been excluded from the Vindex. Were "they" now sorry? There was a distinct smirk behind the appreciation he expressed in hearing that his old classmate President Conant liked the novel. "This cheers me up a great deal because I am weak enough to like kind words from high places," he wrote George Merck, "but in the cold gray light of fact I must remember that Jim

Conant is essentially a research chemist. Although he has one of the greatest minds of his generation, his literary tastes don't keep pace with it. If they did, why does he have such a lousy English Department and why didn't he take some of the things to heart which I said in *Wickford Point* about the English Department at Harvard? The next time you see Jim tell him I said so, but add that I really know nothing about it, because I didn't make the Crimson and he did and, after all, my scholastic record is disheartening."

And Marquand resented, still, the way the door to literary fame was guarded by scholastics, persons who knew nothing, really, about writing. The true writer could owe nothing to schoolroom study of the great models, he said through Calder: "In spite of the dictum of Stevenson on playing the sedulous ape to the great masters, it has never been my observation that education helps this talent. On the contrary, undue familiarity with other writers is too apt to sap the courage and to destroy essential self-belief. . . . Instead, a writer of fiction is usually the happier for his ignorance, and better for having played ducks and drakes with his cultural opportunities. All that he really requires is a dramatic sense and a peculiar eye for detail which he can distort convincingly. He must be an untrustworthy mendacious fellow who can tell a good falsehood and make it stick. It is safer for him to be a self-centered egotist than to have a broad interest in life. He must take in more than he gives out. He must never be complacent, he must never be at peace; in other words, he is a difficult individual and the divorce rate among contemporary literati tells as much." Finally, of course, he resented most of all the assumption of the belles-lettrist, secure in his study and classroom, that those who "wrote for the market" were barred from literary greatness. He thought he knew better, like Jim Calder, how much art went into the achievement of popularity, how much sense of the popular appetite for entertainment the artist needed.

With these convictions he continued pushing his own talent further into the realm of literary possibility—keeping aware all the same of the messages of the market. Even before he had completed *Wickford Point* he had confided to McIntyre his fear that Brandt would see it primarily in terms of the magazines, and McIntyre filed an office memorandum of their conversation, which read: "He is not inclined at present to allow the *Post* or any other magazine to publish any portion of this novel. He urges me whenever I see fit to go over the heads of his agents in connection with all matters concerning his serious fiction. He says as he has said before that he hopes before long to reach the point where he can make a living from his serious novels and not have to write anything especially for the magazines." The publisher offered Marquand an advance of $5,000 (the advance on *Apley* had been $500), but this was to be payable at the beginning of 1940 so that Marquand could escape the tax gouge out of his year of maximum sales after the book was published in March 1939. When it seemed likely that the book might prove a success like *Apley*, the publisher offered a plan whereby the royalties could be paid out in monthly payments of $2,000, beginning in 1940 and continuing until all the earnings were disbursed—for as long as that might be.

But Carl Brandt was successful, after all, in his persuasions on behalf of magazine publication also, and the *Post* did publish a version of *Wickford Point* just before the book came out. It had been cut from its full length of 190,000 words in the Little, Brown edition to 70,000. The quantitative reduction was only part of the alteration. As *Time* observed, "The *Post*'s seven installments accented the Brill foibles, heightened the picturesqueness of the story, toned down the dialogue ('so damn screwy' to 'so queer'), cut out narrator Calder's cynical reflections on love ('all lovers are consummate bores'), on writing popular fiction for the big mags ('a somewhat ghastly parody on life'), blotted out one character (the narrator's mistress) entirely." Carl Brandt had done the cutting and altering, and he had encouraged Marquand to concern himself as little as possible with the operation; Marquand did not even look at the copy that went to the *Post*, and probably, until his attention was drawn to their peculiarities, did not even look at the installments as they appeared in print. But Alfred McIntyre, who had opposed serial publication to begin with, was aroused, certain that they would damage the book's chances. He decided to inform the book trade that "the book and the serial are two different things." Circulars and posters were sent out which reproduced the first thirty-two pages of the book with the deleted portions scored, and a banner heading over the display reading, "The black spots mark the blind spots in the new serial version of *Wickford Point*." The public was to be told: "You won't really have read 'Wickford Point' as the author wrote it unless you read it in book form."

Despite his fears the book seemed bound to make a success. The Book-of-the-Month Club judges at their February meeting made it an "A" choice and by the end of the year over 51,000 copies had left the publisher's warehouses, nearly 20,000 more copies than the bookstores had taken of *Apley* for the same period. But then something seems to have happened. The books began to come back to roost as unsold "returns" from the disappointed booksellers, and as a consequence, in the second year of sales the publisher's accounts actually showed negative sales of several hundred copies. In contrast, *Apley* had continued to press forward, adding 8,350 sales by the end of three years while its successor only reached the miserable mark of 106 copies in the same length of time. Of course, the economy was at a low level, in the spring of 1939; but McIntyre was convinced that the serial had deprived the book of sales it had rightfully deserved. The public had not known "the difference between a serial and a book." Brandt for his part blamed the publisher for failing to spend enough on advertising—to which McIntyre responded that they had by the end of August spent over twenty percent of the book's receipts on advertising: "Isn't this liberal on a book that pays the author a royalty of fifteen percent of the list price?" Once again, Marquand's opposed advisers squared off.

Brandt continued to see only expanding opportunities for Marquand as a provisioner for the magazines. If Marquand was unhappy with the way the *Post* had handled *Wickford Point*, Ken Littauer of the *Woman's Home Companion* was begging for a serial, offering $40,000 for 50,000 to 70,000 words. And, characteristically, as though he had not grasped the nature of Marquand's present ambitions, Brandt went on sending him story ideas as he had always done. "What about this situation?" he was writing in July. "Suppose a guy was deeply in love with a gal that had all the oomph possible—who queened it in her particular circle. He's gotta make his own way and his chance for a quick advance is only possible if he leaves the girl and goes far off—China say. The girl probably loves him as much as possible for her to love anyone but with him over the edge of the world she succumbs to the money and prestige of a very kindly but pretty dumb being of a man who has been in her circle. It's a brilliant match in terms of the society in which she moves. This news comes to him when he is already on his way home to say he can modestly take care of her." The scenario bubbled along. "The gal" has "a sister or cousin or sompin of the sort who has already been in the group but who has been overshadowed by the force, vitality and glamor of the first girl. She moves in and by attrition marries our hero. The first girl is caught in a trap; when she sees what's going on she is amazed at her jealousy, shocked by it probably. Yet she cannot protest—possibly has to forward the so-called romance. Yet the mouse girl knows she's fighting a battle and her hatred for the glamor gal is intensified to a horrid degree." And, "comes a turn of the wheel, and the rich young man by good natured stupidity loses his money and he, his wife and their children become largely dependent upon our hero. This, it is easy to see, gives Miss Mouse the most exquisite revenge."

But Marquand at that very moment was thinking about another kind of novel; he was already conceiving the story that would become *H. M. Pulham, Esquire*. To Brandt's suggestions he simply replied, "I think the best thing for me to do at the present time is to start on another novel which I intend to write without any idea of serialization. I don't want to write the type of serial which you suggest because it is so close in form to a novel that I am afraid I should find it confusing. I should prefer for the time being to confine my magazine work to adventure-mystery serials and to short stories so that I can keep the two types widely separated." And so Brandt went out shopping again. *Cosmopolitan* offered $5,000 for a short story, but, he warned Marquand, "they want a story which has a certain romantic element—that is not a completely ironic one. It should have a gal in it, in other words." An even better deal was offered by the women's magazines, who would pay $10,000 for a 20,000-word "one-shot." But on the last day of August Marquand wrote Brandt that he had begun work on a new novel. He was at Kent's Island, where he hoped to keep quietly at it into December. And, indeed, on October 10, 1939, he announced that he had written about two hundred pages, which he invited Carl to come up to Newbury to read.

As the new novel grew, Brandt failed to give it enthusiastic support. "After struggling through the first draft," Marquand recalled to a friend a year later, "Carl besought me not to have it published because he said that it missed out all along the line." Brandt advised him against working on it any further, and taking the first-draft manuscript in hand proceeded to "salvage" what he could for a short serial. By May 1940 his work was finished and the serial, called *Gone Tomorrow*, had been sold to *McCall's*. The agent was proud of his accomplishment. "It has been as difficult a job as any I have ever tackled, and I do think you know the amount of extra work I have put in on the cutting. It truly would have been an awful disappointment if we hadn't pulled something out of the fire," he told Marquand. Again, he advised him not to read the altered, abbreviated adaptation of what he had written: "My feeling is that a version of the story so radically different from the way you had written it would, undoubtedly, cause you to have qualms, but I can assure you that it has been done with care and care. This is not a job of a magazine cutting simply to space but it has been a collaboration on this final stretch between Connie Smith [the *McCall's* editor] and myself, and I do think you know how jealous I am of your work. The simplest and most peacemaking attitude for you to take would be never to look at the McCall's version."

Marquand probably followed this instruction and was, in fact, so grateful to Brandt that he suggested that the agent take a thousand dollars above his regular commission because he had done so much work in cutting and revising. Still, he rejected the advice about going on with the novel. Again, as with *Apley*, Alfred McIntyre had seen a promising book in what had aroused misgivings in the Brandt office. At the end of November it was finished, and the judges of the Book-of-the-Month Club chose *H. M. Pulham, Esquire* as their March selection. Brandt wired his congratulations to Marquand, and complimented McIntyre on his "influence at the Book-of-the-Month Club," seemingly unaware that he had come to what was almost a breaking point with the novelist for the most mistaken counsel he had ever offered. "I hope Carl may be as wrong about 'Pulham' as he was about 'Apley,'" Marquand said shortly after the book-club choice had been announced. To Carl himself he wrote reminding him of the thousand dollars above commission that he had let him take on *Gone Tomorrow* because of the extra work in quarrying it out of the first draft. "It seems to me that things have been somewhat the other way as far as the novel is concerned, seeing that you advised against my finishing it for the book version," Marquand said. "Naturally I could not adopt your suggestion under these circumstances and what I have done was done over your head and against your professional judgment. Under these circumstances I wonder if you don't think that 'Gone Tomorrow' and 'H. M. Pulham, Esq.' together should net only ten percent commission. As you know, Little, Brown & Company are paying fifteen thousand cash advance on the book because of its acceptance by The Book-of-the-Month Club, and personally I should feel happier about the whole arrangement if you would agree to take only five hundred dollars instead of fifteen hundred as your commission on this amount." The suggestion was meant as a humiliating reproof, and felt as one. Brandt replied: "As to your feelings regarding commission on the book contract for 'H. M. Pulham, Esquire,' I accept at once your wishes in the matter. I am fully aware that my judgment was faulty in regard to this book but it was given in an honest, if alcoholic, effort to advise you to your best advantage. That I think you'll allow me. Also, I think it is fair to restate the situation regarding your books from Apley on in view of your bringing up figures in your letter. You wrote Apley with no thought of serial and so expressed yourself to me. It was on my enthusiasm and belief that we collected on that $7500 gross; $6750 net to you. 'Wickford Point' also you felt was no serial. After I'd read it at Kent's Island I thought there was a chance despite your conviction to the contrary. Stout [the *Post* editor] gave me only the barest of encouragement and I, with your consent, put in many weekends and nights in cutting the novel on the sheerest speculation of my time and energy. Luckily he came through and we again collected, $35,000 gross this time, $31,500 net to you. On 'Gone Tomorrow' the same procedure took place and we failed at the Post but we again collected $25,000, $21,500 net to you because you, on your own generous initiative, cut me in on an extra payment of $1,000 for the work I'd put into it, but out of which came $161 in typing charges. This means that from the serial rights in these three books you've snagged from the editors $59,750 net. And in writing these three books you had, of your own volition, chosen to disregard serial and would not have been surprised if you'd not gotten a penny." Brandt felt he had demonstrated loyalty and usefulness; in his view it did not matter that he had failed to appreciate such successes as *Apley* and *Pulham* (judged by many to be the most notable of Marquand's achievements) since, after all, he had helped him to make nearly $60,000. "I am jealous of my professional advice and constructive work, particularly as it applies to you because I count you as the closest friend I have. I therefore want this record clear in your mind as I think it proves that I have judged correctly and worked and acted under that judgment in most instances. Well, let's now forget it all and get on with our war with the editors," he blandly concluded his letter.

H. M. Pulham, Esquire, which was published in February 1941, was again a personal coming-to-terms with Marquand's past—in this instance the four unforgettable and galling Harvard years. The suggestion for the novel came out of his feelings as his Harvard class prepared to celebrate its twenty-fifth reunion in 1940. His reaction to the reunion plans was caustically expressed to George Merck: "The one silver lining I can see in the European situation is that we may not have a twenty-fifth reunion. I can think of nothing more incredible than a body of supposedly intelligent people, endowed with the gifts of a higher education, who should have some responsibilities of leadership, spending forty thousand dollars—that was the amount that Brother Parker told me they were going to spend, forty thousand dollars—to get wives and kiddies and indigent classmates together and to have champagne cocktails and bus rides and dinners and a happy day at the Swampscott Country Club. My idea is to spend that forty thousand in keeping America out of the European war."

Pulham opens with a chapter in which the narrator-hero finds himself being roped into the twenty-fifth reunion preparations of his Harvard class, and the year is 1939. It was a scene that could almost have been written as it was happening, in this or another form, for in the fall of that year, precisely as Marquand got to work on the novel, he was being solicited to "play up—and play the game," as his chapter heading put it, by his own classmates. Dr. Joseph Garland, a Beacon Street pediatrician, asked him to serve on the reunion Publicity Committee, to help prepare bulletins with "some real heart interest such as only you can supply," and Marquand repeated to him what he had said to Merck: "I hope the steering committee is giving serious consideration to just where in the international situation we are likely to find ourselves in June 1940. Frankly, even today I have no inclination to support and cheer while the sons of my friends by the dozens have gone forth from Canada, England, France—and Germany too—to be shot up." It hardly befitted the class of 1915, many of whose members had vivid recollections of their own war service, to proceed to the usual jollification. Nevertheless, the jollification went forward of its own momentum, and Marquand, like Pulham, was unable to resist the pressure to contribute his bit. The Reunion Committee, headed by "Wally" Trumbull, who was director of admissions for the Middlesex School, continued on the assumption that not even another war should be allowed to deflect the class from its illusion of return to school and college yesterdays. So, by the beginning of the year, they had even prevailed upon Marquand to write the theatrical show to be staged in Sanders Theater. "A favorable reply is not only expected but required," said "Eddie" Thayer, chairman of the Entertainment Committee, exactly in the jovial bulldozing accents of Marquand's fictional Bo-jo Brown. Early in February, his script was ready, and the following month the members of the cast were assembled and production started.

Marquand's literary reputation will not gain by bringing to light his script for the reunion play, though it was no worse, probably, than most such compositions. From the typescript in the Harvard alumni archives the hilarity it generated can just be suspected; most of the fun was due to the ludicrous personal references communicated between actors and audience. Marquand himself played the part of Peavey, the 1915 man who has been visiting his psychiatrist in order to "integrate" his past and present experiences—and the show consisted of a "March of Time" sequence of flashbacks induced by the doctor. The recollected scenes were mostly comic embarrassment and disaster—a drunk collegiate Peavey collapsing on the floor during a Boston society ball; a sad-sack Peavey at Plattsburg with his tunic buttoned wrong; Peavey uneasily greeting fatherhood in a hospital maternity ward; Peavey fatuously living high in 1929, then, as the banks closed, listening lugubriously to FDR assure his radio listeners that they had nothing to fear but fear. The hero was permitted some fantasies of wish fulfillment—and was seen arriving home from a world tour after reconciling the leaders of the warring states. To the shouting multitudes he offers a few superb banalities: "I owe my success, my record in the world, my record in business and finance to two things—to my dear mother and that other greater mother, Harvard University. I thank God I am a Harvard man and a member of the class of 1915." But, as June approached, the European situation grew steadily more serious, and Marquand felt only a renewal of the misgivings he had had at the start about the whole thing. To his friend Merck he wrote again, in the middle of May: "It may be too late to do anything about it, but do you think that any influence could possibly be brought on the committee to make some change in the reunion plans to conform in some small way with the gravity of world events?" He suggested that the class celebration be abbreviated to a single day and the money saved donated to the Red Cross for the relief of Dutch, Belgian and French refugees. Still, the show went on.

After the publication of *Pulham*, Brooks Atkinson wrote Marquand about his own twenty-fifth reunion forebodings, and Marquand recalled, in replying, "I just went through mine last June, but before that time my mental pattern, my doubts and the artificial sense of moral obligation aroused in me by high pressure were as like yours as two peas in a pod." Like Atkinson, he remembered, he hadn't known the class leaders, the big athletes and the club men, when he was at Harvard. Robert Nathan had once told him that he knew no one in his college class for "obvious reasons." But "mine were just as obvious," observed Marquand. "If you went there from high school no nice boys ever spoke to you." In 1940, to Marquand's ironical amusement, they all did. As he told Atkinson about his reunion, "I went to mine because I didn't want to be a heel or a sorehead." He had taken Adelaide and Johnny and Tina along and they had been housed in a dormitory in the Yard. They all wore badges inscribed with their names. "I can't say the thing was a success. My children didn't want to join any of the organized group games and I kept trying to get to the bar in order to work myself into a more extrovert mood. I kept feeling that if I only had a few quick ones I might remember everything about all these people. The trouble was that the bar was always closed when I wanted to go there most. The management of these functions is always careful that the classmates shall not exceed themselves in front of the wives and kiddies. I left the reunion with the same feeling a male Alice might have in a masculine wonderland."

H. M. Pulham, Esquire had in an earlier draft been titled "Reunion," but the final novel was far more than a satiric vision of the festivities of the class of 1915. The central personality of Pulham had been developed with loving care by Marquand into a life history, more intimate and contemporary than *Apley*, of another Proper Bostonian. Like the hero of the earlier novel, Pulham appeared in the mingled light of Marquand's qualified satire: something of a fool and a stuffed shirt, and yet a better man, when all was said and done, than his cleverer, more liberated friend Bill King. As in *Apley*, a romantic plot tension was created by the Bostonian's one departure from the mold, his love affair outside the tribe. But whereas Apley's love for the South Boston Mary Moynahan had been drawn in dim pastels and the girl had never emerged into the novel as a character at all, Marvin Myles was the triumph of *Pulham*. She had come out of Marquand's observation of the type that would continue to fascinate him: the woman represented already by Carol Brandt—a self-made girl, ambitious, full of energy and will as well as charm and good looks, and free of the restraints of conventional morality. In Harry Pulham Marquand had set out to depict a fictional classmate who was his own opposite, a man who *did* know everyone when he was at college, who made a club and fell heir to wealth as well as family position. Yet he had identified with his hero more than with Bill King, who had always made fun of Harry and in the end betrayed him. As Marquand wrote in his real class report, "I still observe that one of [Harvard's] best known products is a type with which I find myself identified." He had given Pulham many of his own experiences in the war and in an advertising agency, and like Pulham, he had, after all, married the "right" kind of girl, and not once, but twice. But in being both outside and in, both Pulham and his skeptical biographer, he had written a novel that was another demonstration of his ambiguous style. He had achieved a similar subtlety in the portrait of Kay Motford, whom Pulham married. Perhaps because his own second marriage still seemed a success, he was able to depict the prototypical American wife with a good nature and insight never equaled again in his work. Despite the reader's predispositions for romantic favoritism, she is, in the end, a figure even more distinct and just as sympathetic as Marvin Myles.

Pulham was more objective, less directly autobiographical than *Wickford Point*, and none of the chief characters—Pulham, Bill King, Kay or Marvin—was a direct rendition of an actual person, though both Christina and Adelaide recognized aspects of their marriages in Pulham's domestic life. Bill King, like Jim Calder in *Wickford*, was a sort of imagined alternate Marquand—what he might have been if he had stayed in advertising. Yet the minor details of the novel, as in all Marquand's fiction, grew recognizably out of his experience to such an extent that identifications were sure to be made by knowing readers. As always, Marquand abounded in disclaimers.

To Stanley Resor, for whom he had worked in his own advertising days, he wrote: "The office of J. T. Bullard turns out, I hope, as I intended—a very fictitious advertising organization, far far removed from the J. Walter Thompson Company." With some justification, this was not accepted as entirely candid. As was to be expected, the frame-story of the Harvard reunion (which sets Pulham remembering as he composes his biography for the class report) attracted a good deal of attention, and most remarked upon was the egregious figure of Bo-jo Brown, whom everyone thought he could identify as one of Harvard's famous football figures. After all, Wally Trumbull, one of the star members of The Team, *was* just like Bo-jo, head of the Reunion Committee of Marquand's class. And Eddie Thayer, if not as prominent in football, *had* twisted Marquand's arm in true Bo-jo fashion in connection with the undertaking of the reunion play. To Thayer, Marquand wrote, "As you will see, solely for the purposes of time, Mr. H. M. Pulham must be a member of the class of Harvard 1915, but I do not think that he or any of his classmates are much like the boys we know and this includes Bo-jo Brown." To Frederick Bradlee, who had been, like Trumbull, a "football hero," he wrote: "I hope Bo-jo Brown does not sound like any football player of our time at Harvard. He certainly does not seem to me like you or Tack Hardwick or Wally Trumbull or Mal Logan or any of the others. Of course he has certain football characteristics, but he is meant to be only a symbol." As time passed Marquand believed—or liked to pretend—that he had got no hint at all from the actual details of his own twenty-fifth but that he had completed the novel before the festive drums had begun to beat. In 1956, he spoke of his gratification upon discovering at his reunion that he "had made no mistakes in [his] preview." The first draft, he then thought he recalled, had been completed in "the late summer of 1939 many months before June, 1940," and he had, he said, "indulged in none of the festivities or social preliminaries that surround a twenty-fifth reunion when I wrote the book." This, as we have seen, was not true at all: in August 1939 Marquand *began* his first draft of the novel and by December had written only its opening chapters; not until November of the following year was the novel actually ready for publication by Little, Brown.

Symbol or not, to those who regarded football as a heroic tournament of collegiate knights, Marquand's sketch of Bo-jo Brown seemed something of an affront. But Bo-jo is not an easily dismissable takeoff of the type he represents—upper-class overbearing strengthened by the prestige of athletic stardom in the schoolboy and college years, insensitivity and cant, suspicion of intellect and of liberalism. There is all this behind the comedy of his portrait in *Pulham*, though the tone is not mordant. Bo-jo is given no private life in Marquand's novel, but one can imagine it only in terms such as those Fitzgerald gave Tom Buchanan in *The Great Gatsby*. What Marquand held up to view, however, was a side that does not appear in Fitzgerald's characterization, though one might easily presuppose its presence: the sentimentality about Alma Mater which Marquand found so nauseating in middle-aged men. And yet, and yet, he compels the reader to respect Pulham's persistent school-tie loyalty; in the makeup of this other kind of gentleman it was still honorable.

In *Pulham*, probably, Marquand felt he had finally laid his hostilities towards Harvard to rest; he was only half in jest when he suggested to his old friend President Conant that now perhaps she would recognize this son with an honorary degree. Sending an advance copy to the president's office he wrote: "I thought perhaps, if executive cares are not weighing too heavily upon you, that you and Mrs. Conant might be amused by the mythical life of Henry Pulham, who must have wandered about the Harvard Yard and have lived and loved in Boston and its vicinity about the same time we did. I remember when I saw you last that you expressed the hope that I would cease making fun of the show you were trying to run. Although you will find Harvard mentioned here, I hope you will see that it is dealt with through Mr. Pulham's eyes in a serious and constructive manner and that all through the book Mr. Pulham recognizes the gifts which Harvard gave him. Needless to say, I hope that the effort will so impress you that I may be on your list for one of the honorary degrees next June, although I fear that long experience with the academic world may have narrowed your good judgment."

His ambivalent feelings about Harvard were sharply revived in a curious aftermath to the book's publication. Shortly after it came out in March, the Catholic cardinal of Boston, William O'Connell, expressed his disapproval of the novel because of the adulterous relationship intimated between Bill King and Kay Pulham. "Of course my experience is limited," the cardinal had said, "but I sincerely hope that Bostonians, especially the women, have not degenerated into the type he describes." In response, one of the city councillors, Maurice H. Sullivan, offered an order in the Council that the book be condemned as "disrespectful to Boston womanhood." The measure was passed without dissent, and the police of Boston were asked to halt sale. As always, a proposed Boston banning was national news and an aid to publicity for the book everywhere. In a week, while the Police Department dallied, local booksellers reported that sales in Boston had doubled. But as it turned out, the ban did not take place. On April 3 the deputy police superintendent of the city announced to the press that he had examined the novel and failed to find anything objectionable in it.

The whole event would hardly have disturbed Marquand except for one thing. Sitting on the City Council was Henry Lee Shattuck, a wealthy Boston lawyer and Republican party leader, who had been president of the Harvard Board of Fellows and was serving as acting president of the university while Conant was in Europe on a mission for President Roosevelt. Shattuck had passed the condemnation order along with his fellow councillors. His explanation to news reporters—that he had not really read *Pulham* and so "did not rise to object"—only increased the offense, Marquand felt, and he wrote Shattuck, the latter thought, "an indignant and humorless letter": "I gather that you voted for this suppression when you were Acting President of Harvard University, whose head has taken such a definite stand against intellectual tyranny. I can understand the motives of Mr. Sullivan and other members of the Boston City Council, but I am frankly both hurt and bewildered by your vote." Shattuck replied with the explanation that the City Council customarily made such rulings (the police actually did the banning) in a nonchalant way, on the suggestion of a member and on a voice vote without a roll call. "This shocked me very much when I first entered the Council nearly eight years ago, but I have become used to it." But Marquand was not at all mollified by this explanation, and did not accept Shattuck's invitation to observe the Council "as a human-nature study." Circumstances, moreover, had just then placed in his hand a means of rebuke to Harvard, the treacherous mother who had failed to protect her own child. Keyes Metcalf, head of the Harvard library, had just asked Marquand for the manuscript of *Pulham*, to be placed in its new Treasure Room. Simultaneously, as it happened, Yale's distinguished collector, Wilmarth Lewis, had been reading the new best seller, and had stopped, inspired, at the point where Bill King remarks to Pulham, "Harry, you should have gone to Yale." Although Pulham had confessed that the idea of going to Yale "made me wince," his creator responded to Lewis's suggestion that the manuscript go to the Yale library. Yale would, eventually, receive almost all of Marquand's literary manuscripts, for he kept to a promise he had made even when his anger against Harvard had cooled. Harvard still got the bequest of his correspondence. But Yale nevertheless gave him an honorary doctorate before Harvard did. Just the same (though perhaps with a certain rancorous humor), in December 1941 Marquand presented Harvard with the manuscript of the *movie script* of *Pulham*—an "atonement," he said at the time, for the gesture which had sent Harry Pulham to New Haven.

With the success of his three novels of Boston and New England, Marquand had established himself as the most conspicuous representative and analyst of the regional traditions to which he belonged with conscious assertion and secret unease. Later he would complain that the regionalist tag had cramped his reputation, that he had written about other places and kinds of persons: "It seems since Pulham that no matter what my efforts may be I am always writing about Boston. Self-consciously and often with hopeful determination I have moved my characters to Hollywood, Washington, New York and Paris, and also to the New York suburbs and Palm Beach, but I am still a regionalist," he wrote in 1956. He would, by then, have wandered some, though his imagination returned regularly to familiar ground. But the popular error had accomplished something he really longed for, after all; it had established the identity he had always craved, the authenticity of willed belonging. *Life* magazine, the final arbiter of identities, now, in 1941, published a big picture story called "Marquand's Boston: A Trip with America's Foremost Satirist." Boston was, henceforth, his. "John Marquand's family has been living near Boston for 200 years," the story began. *Life*'s reader was taken on a tour of what was termed "Marquand country," where Marquand was glimpsed in various poses—feeding pigeons on the Common, walking through Louisburg Square on Beacon Hill and standing opposite a house "once occupied by his grandfather" on Mount Vernon Street, reading at a table in the Athenaeum.

The *Life* story was accompanied by a piece by Marquand himself: "My Boston: A Note on the City by Its Best Critic." In it he set forth some of the tiredest local jokes—that the old houses on the Hill have windowpanes of glass turned purple with age "and the proud owners replace these panes with new purple ones whenever they are broken"; the story about "two men from the *Post* and the *Globe*, sir, and a gentleman from the *Transcript*"; some lines he imperfectly recalled from an old Hasty Pudding Show; and other such random cullings from the Boston legend. An editorial writer from the *Herald* remarked that none of these were new to other Bostonians—and finished off the fragment of Hasty Pudding verse over which Marquand had stumbled. Boston shipping firms complained that Marquand had exaggerated when he said that the shipping business had vanished (it had merely sunk from first or second to tenth place among U.S. ports). It was curiously true that outside of his fiction, which called upon unconscious, personal creativity, Marquand's report on Boston was shockingly banal. In 1953 he was asked by *Holiday* to write a long article on "his" city for a series that included essays by E. B. White on New York City and by Faulkner on Mississippi. Marquand would disappoint the *Holiday* editors by a piece that sounded "written off the top of [his] head," though it was eventually published. Still, early and late, the impression remained that Boston's most articulate representative had been identified as John P. Marquand.

Harry Pulham, like George Apley, became, for some years, as familiar a designation of type as Sinclair Lewis's Babbitt. The book was to be read by many Americans, not only in the serial that had run in *McCall's* and in a *Reader's Digest* condensation, but in printing after printing—fourteen by 1949—as well as in the separate Book-of-the-Month Club edition, a cheaper Dollar Book reprint and later paperback reprints. And yet, this popular success did not leave Marquand wholly satisfied. True, when *Harper's Magazine* asked the questions "Is the 'best seller' the best book? Is a book's popularity a measure of its quality or as some acidulously contend, exactly the contrary?" its poll of twenty prominent reviewers showed more of them ready to place *Pulham* among the ten "best" novels of the spring of 1941 than any other choice. Marquand's got the vote not only of Clifton Fadiman of the *New Yorker* and J. Donald Adams of the New York *Times* but also of reviewers in Atlanta, Chicago, Galveston, New Orleans, Nashville and Salt Lake City. Even reviewers in Boston were pleased with Marquand's account of their world. With *Pulham*, thought the *Transcript*, Marquand had "completed a trilogy that should explain the essence of Bostonianism to dwellers in the most savage hinterland." Harry Pulham, it said complacently, "is undoubtedly reading the *Transcript* at this moment." Nothing could have been more touchingly apt than the *Transcript*'s sense of identification with Pulham and other readers who, as Thayer Donovan Bisbee wrote in the *Saturday Review*, "once swayed in the wind like a field of ripe corn as their births, marriages and deaths were recorded in that unique journal," for as their day dimmed the *Transcript* itself slipped under the horizon in 1941. In the "savage hinterland," pleasure in Marquand's account of the Boston essence was also high—it had been this outsider fascination with the country's still-prestigious Hub that had been underestimated by Marquand's agent and even by his publisher. As Van Wyck Brooks wrote in his *New England: Indian Summer*: "The nation could not forget New England, could not let the subject drop—Americans could do anything but leave it alone. They liked to tease New England, but they were never indifferent to it. They could not have enough of Henry Adams, Santayana's *The Last Puritan*, the novels of Marquand."

But the arbiters of more sophisticated literary taste who wrote for the weeklies, mostly published in New York, gave Marquand only qualified praise. Fadiman, for example, had actually written for his *New Yorker* readers that the book was a "smooth inside job" performed with the sympathetic gentleness that would prevent it "from reaching a level higher than that of extremely intelligent entertainment." He found that in order to enjoy the novel you had to practice a "willing suspension of indifference" to its characters, and he didn't find *Pulham* as sharp and interesting as *Apley* or *Wickford Point* had been. A little more acridity, he said, might turn Marquand into the American Aldous Huxley, but Marquand wouldn't want that. "He's just too darned nice to his friends." Malcolm Cowley, in the *New Republic*, praised the social observation of the novel. It was precise anthropology, as good as that of Robert Lynd, the author of *Middletown*, turned through the gears of a highly efficient plot mechanism and style. "Mr. Marquand still writes novels, and purely as fiction they are all right, which is to say all wrong. As social history they are marvellous." Even *Time* condescended with "Marquand's writing puts the ideas of T. S. Eliot's 'Love Song of J. Alfred Prufrock' into the language of a *Saturday Evening Post* serial"—somehow an uncertain compliment. Margaret Marshall of the *Nation* had a single-sentence notice: "For those who read and liked *The Late George Apley*, *H. M. Pulham, Esquire*, which exploits the same New England world of dullness and stability, is a deftly written but rather long-winded demonstration of the fact that even a clever writer can't do the same thing twice."

It is not clear how much Marquand minded that the "literary establishment" denied him the title of greatness. He would feel to the end of his career that he was penalized for achieving too supremely the identity of popularity for which he had worked so hard at the beginning. The change of character he subsequently struggled for—from the writer of magazine fodder "for the millions" to that of serious artist—was never to be completed as far as these critics were concerned: he would never join his contemporaries Hemingway and Fitzgerald and Faulkner—even Sinclair Lewis—in the literary histories. He would be bound—this aspirant for social restitution—to resent this exclusion from the very best company, as he knew it to be, the company of the immortals. He was sure that *Pulham* was a better not a worse book than *Apley* and that the critics were unfair to him. He wrote his teen-age son: "There does seem to be a tendency among critics to point out that I am really not much good anyway and that my smooth technique is deceptive. I am encouraged by this general attitude, because when they start doing this it seems that they are taking you quite seriously. Although most of them liked it, it seemed to me that a great many of them have no conception of what the book was about. This doesn't surprise me either, because book critics with one or two exceptions have always seemed to me to be the lowest form of animal life and I can think of no sadder profession to devote your existence to than hashing over other people's work." But he took comfort, one may be certain, from the private judgment of an imaginative writer he admired before all others. Sinclair Lewis wrote, after finishing *Pulham*, that he had gone back to *Apley* and *Wickford Point* and it seemed to him that "the beginning, middle age and old age with the suggestion of new youth of a culture have never been better expressed, I think. You have no idea what elevated congratulations I send you."

The story of the Bostonian Pulham was about to entertain a vaster if less critical audience when it became the first of his serious novels to make a big success as a movie. Shortly after the contract was signed with MGM, Marquand, concerned about Hollywood's interpretation of the Boston scene, sent King Vidor a list of suggestions for characteristic background details: the row of ash cans outside the service-entrance doors on the brick sidewalks of Beacon Hill each "ash morning"; the giant teapot with steam coming out of its spout that hung outside a restaurant near Scollay Square; single sculls being put into the water from the Union Boat Club on the Charles River; and other such. As a result, Vidor summoned Marquand to Hollywood to work on the script with him and with his wife Betty Hill. Marquand arrived in April and stayed a month to see the film cast with Hedy Lamarr as Marvin Myles, Robert Young as Pulham and Van Heflin as Bill King. Of course, Kay's defection from the path of wifely propriety had been cut out of the story by Vidor, but Marquand did not seem to mind this censorship, even though he spoke with some bitterness about Henry Shattuck and the Boston City Council to Louella Parsons, who caught him working at the studio at the end of May. To another columnist he had more to say about minor points of interpretation—Pulham's dog should have been a fat cocker spaniel instead of a spry Sealyham, and the Harvard students shown in the film shouldn't have been wearing big *H*'s on their sweaters. The scene in which Bo-jo's sweatered teammates marched into Hollywood's version of a Harvard undergraduate's room had made him cringe. "We were all carefully dressed in Brooks Brothers suits," he said. He also deplored Robert Young's mustache as "not Bostonian."

At moments, Marquand was almost as dazzled as the average moviegoer by his stay in the manufacturing capital of "glamor." The gorgeous Hedy quite overcame his original feeling that she was unsuited to the part of Marvin Myles (he had at the outset suggested Rosalind Russell), and he told her gallantly that she seemed exactly right. He wrote to Adelaide about an occasion when he had dinner with Miss Russell, Mr. Zanuck, the Vidors *and* Dolores Del Rio and Charlie Chaplin, "who is by now quite a friend of mine." Chaplin had beguiled the table by improvising his version of Harry Pulham in Boston. But by December, in Newburyport, reminiscing to the members of the Tuesday Night Club, he had recovered his satiric poise, and his experiences took on the sharp light and shade of his best fictional descriptions. His memory of the details of his visit had the clarity of a camera making the most of perfect shooting weather. And, indeed, the weather, from his arrival at the Los Angeles airport to his departure, was true to its reputation—unfailingly flawless, or, as he would later hear Samuel Goldwyn say, "a beautiful day to spend Sunday" every day of the week. But, Marquand remarked, "no one I ever saw in Hollywood ever spent Sunday. We were never in one place long enough on Sunday. We were motoring across country or swimming in someone's pool or getting seasick on someone's yacht on the way to Catalina." Even as he drove from the airport with the MGM publicity man he saw the well-advertised spectacle in his own peculiar way, like the traveler he had been in China and Persia, with the eye of the perfect stranger so chaste in its unpreparedness. Along Hollywood Boulevard there were the open-air markets and popcorn stands, and bars and Seventh-Day Adventist missions and roadstands with curb service, where the girl carhops, dressed like the sailors in *Pinafore* or else like bullfighters, "hand you Orange Crush and hope to get into the movies," and he passed the famous Brown Derby and Ciro's, where the autograph hunters waited with their alphabetized files of Kresge glossies, ready to snatch out the star's picture in the twinkling of an eye and obtain her autograph—the complete job to be sold for fifty cents as soon as she had vanished.

Soon, he and the MGM man were driving past the Beautiful Homes of the Important People, the older ones Mission Spanish, the newer ones Georgian, all planted about with an astonishing variety of flora from the far corners of the earth—monkey puzzle trees from Africa, eucalyptus from Australia, "grotesque and sportive" specimens from Japan or Egypt or elsewhere, cohabiting with rambler roses in something of the same preposterous and unnatural conjunction as the human inhabitants of Hollywood. During the course of his stay he became familiar with the interiors of such houses. All, he reported back to the distant civilization of Newburyport, contained "bars" equipped with comic signs like "Ladies with Escorts Only" or "Don't Hog the Free Lunch." Your host would hurry you to this room and get behind the brass-railed counter to hand you a drink, his hands sheathed in "cocktail mittens" with other wisecracks printed on them and bells on the fingers that tinkled as he shook the cocktail shaker.

Charlie Chaplin, like the rest, had a swimming pool and a tennis court, as well as a "game room where he likes to sit and talk about Spengler, which is easy because Charlie has never read Spengler." His house was in rather poor repair, which was all right with him, he told Marquand, because he had once been a poor cockney in the slums of London. But Ginger Rogers had something special in her house: a fully equipped *ice-cream* bar or soda fountain which she had had put in because she had never had all the sodas she wanted when *she* was little (although she now in fact ate no ice cream at all because she was dieting). Vidor's own home, where Marquand was often entertained, was set upon the summit of a small mountain, the top of which had been sliced off to make room for the house itself (half Swedish and half Swiss) and its appurtenances of lawn and swimming pool and terrace. Slapped about by the winds from the sea, you could see Los Angeles beneath you and the fog rolling by Wilmington, where Vidor kept his yacht. Vidor had a touching story to confide about the house: "You see, my life has always run in a sort of pattern, and I'm trying to break that pattern. First I fall in love with some star in some picture out here, then we get married, and I build a house and swimming pool and plant trees. Then somehow or other it never works and we get divorced and I leave her the house. Then I fall in love with another star and we get married and I build another house. This time I'm breaking the pattern. I've married my script writer and by God, I'm going to stay here until the trees grow up." Marquand had a vision of the Hollywood hillsides covered by the houses that had contained Vidor's former marriages.

When Vidor appeared at the Beverly Hills Hotel to meet Marquand, he looked a little like Jack Dempsey and was wearing a plum-colored suit. He cast a swift look of pity at Marquand's worn tweeds and took him in hand on the spot. "You see," he said, "you've got to work with me in the studio. Of course you're here as a literary figure but you'd better come with me and get some clothes first, or they won't understand you." So, in no time at all Marquand was at Vidor's haberdasher being fitted for a plum-colored suit and the new kind of shoes without laces called casuals. He asked Vidor if he could buy one of those shirts with the tails that hung out, a blue one, but Vidor thought he had better not.

Down on the fifty-acre MGM lot Marquand was to discover a world within a world, a hierarchical compound no less intricate in structure than the population of Peking's Forbidden City in its days of splendor. At the top of the scale of authority, above Vidor, were the executives like Louis B. Mayer and Ben Goetz, who wore spats and had their clothes made in London. Each had a dressing room and a valet to attend to his changes of costume, which were as important in their way as the proper dressing of the stars. Many levels below were the poor drudges who wore what looked like bright-colored beach pajamas. They worked away at scripts in sweaty cubicles while those in the higher rank, like Marquand, were assigned detached bungalows; he shared his with Anita Loos.

Yes, the world of the lot was stranger than any exotic society to whose customs he had applied the perspectives of the Bostonian Traveler. Occasionally he would take walks in the evening through the lighted streets of the lots and in the great barns of the indoor stages where ruined castles, slums, battlefield dugouts and English country houses were receiving their finishing touches. Once he met an old man walking around blowing something that looked like a Flit gun here and there in corners. He was the cobweb man; he was squirting cellulose threads into cobweb patterns for the spots on the set that must look as though they had been undisturbed for years.

In between work sessions on the script he observed the way another successful novel, Marjorie Kinnan Rawlings's *The Yearling*, was making its way into celluloid. "The word came down to go all out on it, to make it cost at least three million dollars and not to crap it up. It had to be real and artistic, in technicolor, long shots of sunsets, plain simple southern folk with dialect and overalls. It was good for the Academy Award." The main thing, the brains of MGM agreed, was to make it "absolutely real," and so the whole immense machinery of production was moved down to the St. Johns River in Florida, where there had been, fifty years ago, an actual Baxter's Island, the original of the novel's setting. Little Jody Baxter had long ago grown up, aged and died, but his eighty-five-year-old brother was discovered. His help was enlisted in the reconstruction of the old farm, which had reverted to palmetto wilderness. The slab cabin, the corncrib, the back-house, were all faithfully re-created by the building crews; in order to get a split-rail fence, authentically worn and weathered, another farm some distance away had been purchased that had one—the farmer had refused to sell his fence by itself. Then there was the problem of adjusting nature's clock to the production schedules—the corn in the field would have to be three inches high in some scenes, two feet in others, full grown in later shots—and plants were grown in pots in a greenhouse. A baby raccoon three weeks old had to be available at any time they would get to the scene he would figure in. And the fawn! There had to be fawns in five stages of growth from three months to a year ready at any time—a problem complicated by the somewhat fixed rutting season of deer—and they all had to have the right number of spots and be properly trained to romp with Jody. The little boy, of course, was the real problem. Talent scouts looked at hundreds of little boys until they found the right one, "just a nice unspoiled kid whose accent you could cut with a knife." They sent him up to Hollywood to have his teeth straightened but he was not allowed to meet any of the other child actors for fear he might lose his naturalness.

Nevertheless, there were difficulties. Spencer Tracy, who was playing the part of Jody's father, "the big strong kindly man whom you see so often giving up his last drop of water for a pal," took one look at little Jody and balked. "He said he was God damned if he would act with any little boy with an accent like that and that it was too hot anyway and the whole thing was corny and would ruin his reputation." And everyone else's nerves were pretty frazzled by then. So the whole show took train and plane back home to Hollywood, a million dollars down the drain into the St. Johns River. "All right, King," said Louis B. Mayer, "we will build Baxter's Island for you on the indoor stages."

Vidor was not very enthusiastic about the script, though: "It's all about a boy falling in love with a fawn, isn't it? That sounds to me pretty corny for a three-hour show." Of course, he hadn't read the book. Mr. Goetz hadn't read the book. None of the other MGM executives had. When Marquand admitted that *he* had really read it, and even reread it aloud to his children, Vidor called a meeting so they could listen to him tell them what it was all about. "Wait a minute," Marquand said, "haven't any of you read *The Yearling*?" King Vidor smiled at him. "You know," he said, "you want to get it out of your head that any of us read any of those books."

16

So Little Time

At Newburyport High School Marquand had memorized "The Chambered Nautilus" and at odd moments throughout his life he would roll out its stately verses; his children remembered his solemnly chanted "Build thee more stately mansions, O my soul," and ordered Holmes's lines set on his gravestone. But Marquand was often filled with an irony they did not perceive; he had come to think that like the poet's shellfish one moved through life as through a series of compartments. Jeffrey Wilson, the hero of *So Little Time*, Marquand's novel of what historians would call the period of the "undeclared war," quotes the poem to a girl at a cocktail party and tries to explain the likeness and difference between his own history and that of the nautilus. "Most of my compartments," he said, "aren't lined with pearl"; moreover, there was no reason to suppose that each was "nobler than the last." You simply moved on; suddenly you were somewhere else and the past was sealed off. So it seemed to Jeffrey—as it had to Marquand himself—in 1940. He was in a new compartment, the era of the coming war. Adelaide's first child, a girl, given the family name of her maternal grandmother, Ferry, was born in February; Marquand was elected a member of the National Institute of Arts and Letters; in June his Harvard class reunion took place, and in August, after two weeks on a trip west with Adelaide, he went, as he had the year before, to the Bread Loaf Writers' Conference; finally, he published *Pulham*. But suddenly his life contained another element.

Like most Americans, Marquand had underestimated the threat of the Nazi program of conquest until Poland was invaded and France and England had declared war on Germany, but his sense of the outcome of events in the Far East was prescient. "It seems to me," he told Lester Walker, the editor of *Commentator*, which had published an article on the subject in July 1939, "that matters there, from the long range standpoint, are vastly more important than anything which is happening in Europe. We are going to see in the next eighteen months whether or not the United States is going to end in our lifetime by being an isolated nation whose best days are over. I do not believe in Jingoism, but I do believe that the only way to treat an arrogant nation like Japan is by showing that we are not afraid of her and by showing a willingness in the last analysis to resort to force. I believe if we do not do it now we shall have to do it sometime if we are going to protect Alaska and our western coast and our position in South America. It may be an open question whether or not these things are worth fighting for, but I imagine that they may be." Yet the air was full of the rumble of caissons from over the Atlantic as well as the Pacific. On the radio and in the news columns the voices spoke of disaster, sacrifice, the "little people" of the embattled countries who were holding the dike against a tide that ultimately threatened our shores. The Foreign Correspondent had come into his own, a new species of oracle, naive and yet mysteriously intimate with the forces of history. Everyone had read such works as *The Way of a Transgressor* by Adelaide's friend Negley Farson, and also Walter Duranty's *I Write as I Please*, Vincent Sheean's *Personal History*, Eugene Lyons's *Assignment in Utopia*, and John Gunther's *Inside Europe* and his more recent *Inside Asia*. In his novel, Marquand neatly defined the type in the character Walter Newcombe, which some people thought had been based on Gunther. He had become particularly skeptical of the new breed of radio commentators who were manipulating public opinion by chastising the American public for escaping the privations of England—and he protested to one of them, Helen Howe's brother Quincy, concerning Howe's colleagues Trout and Murrow: "We have been told for about three years that we should be ashamed of ourselves for not coming into this war, and now that we are in it, we are still told that we should be ashamed of ourselves. We may be having it easy, but a lot of people who are suffering extortionate taxes and whose sons have gone to fight and whose sons have been killed already, don't like to be scolded at 8:45 every evening."

The European war, formally declared in September 1939, filled Marquand with a fear of American involvement along with a readiness, common to many veterans of the First World War, to aid the French against the Germans once again. He was perfectly serious when, on September 22, he declared to George Merck that the class reunion funds should be dedicated to "keeping America out of the European war." Johnny, just sixteen, "isn't quite ready to get shot up, but he is coming right along," he observed, reminding his friend that young George and Albert Merck "ought to be right in the front when the first wave of the A.E.F. goes over the top." But proponents of greater commitment to the fight against Hitler were lining up their forces. He had just read in the morning papers Roosevelt's message to Congress urging repeal of the embargo on arms and the substitution of a "cash and carry" plan to get war materials to the Allies. In a few days the Non-partisan Committee for Peace through Revision of the Neutrality Law was organized, with the Emporia sage, William Allen White, as chairman—soon to be replaced by the Committee to Defend America by Aiding the Allies. And as at the start of the First World War the American Field Service set up local committees of volunteers for ambulance companies in France. At the Tavern Club in Boston in October a group of Marquand's friends organized a New England committee; many of them, like his Harvard classmate Charlie Codman, had been ambulance drivers in the earlier war. Marquand seems to have agreed impulsively to have his name put down for the first section to go over, but after some reflection withdrew.

In April, Hitler's new wave of conquests got under way—Norway and Denmark followed by Holland, Belgium and Luxembourg, and in the middle of May, the invasion of France; in June, Italy was in the war. As the Nazi timetable was inexorably fulfilled, sentiment in the United States to aid the democracies increased and the White Committee and other rapidly formed groups engaged the support of prominent Americans—college presidents, business and labor leaders, and intellectuals. Soon there were over three hundred chapters of the Committee to Defend America. Marquand sympathized with these groups and yet hung back from direct participation. When the Writers Anti-War Bureau asked him to join their national committee in April, he refused: "I believe if a novelist's work is to be of any value he must, even against his will, stand on the sidelines. I do not think this sort of writer helps himself or any cause by proclaiming his opinions." Still, the national election, for him, as for most of his countrymen, hinged upon the issue of the European conflict. A longtime Republican voter, he wanted the party to choose Willkie at the nominating convention in June because of his stand to give "all aid, short of war," and wrote Colonel Theodore Roosevelt, who was expected to support the isolationist Dewey, that he ought to "swing over to the only good man in the running who has the brains and the ability to debate the issues with your cousin Franklin."

At the Republican convention, which did choose Willkie, the first steps were taken by a number of those on the losing side to form the America First Committee, which formally announced its existence in September 1940. Like the White Committee, this organization of influential proponents of isolationism won support in every major city in short order—a strange alliance of those traditionally fearful of "foreign entanglements" with political radicals and pacifists, and with others who covertly if not openly were profascist. Among the recruits to the very active New York Chapter was Adelaide Marquand. Until Pearl Harbor abruptly terminated the isolationist movement, she was caught up in daily work for this cause. Most of those who knew Adelaide at the time refuse, now, to convict her of sympathy with Hitlerism. She was sentimentally pro-German, however, for the happiest years of her early life had been spent in Germany when she had studied with Lilli Lehmann and had had a romance with her young Siegfried—and she did not share with Marquand the hostility for the Boche he had retained from his combat experience. She was also influenced, undoubtedly, by the fact that many of her old New York friends—like Anne Morrow Lindbergh, a Chapin School classmate of her sister Helen's—were enrolled among the noninterventionists. Of course, Charles Lindbergh seemed then the most incorruptible of figures, the very symbol and representative of the heroic American spirit, his isolationism a natural outgrowth of his identification with traditional American attitudes, particularly in the populist West where he had been nurtured. His personal charm was that of an archetypal American innocent, the unspoiled boy. Only later would the image of the Lone Eagle be tainted for Americans by the revelation of his anti-Semitism—or what seemed like anti-Semitism—in the famous Des Moines speech of September 14, 1941.

Whatever Adelaide's reasons for attachment to the cause of America First, the Hooker drive for achievement and authority, which had not found successful outlet in her life, now made her a valuable partisan. She became a conspicuous figure, a member of the National Committee with her name on America First stationery. The Marquands were in constant touch for over a year, consequently, with leading noninterventionists of every stripe. One of these was Verne Marshall, the Iowa newspaper publisher who organized the No Foreign Wars Committee; early in 1941 he appealed to Marquand to join his group. But Marquand replied: "Although I feel that our involvement in a European war may very well prove fatal to this country, it may be that an unavoidable situation will arise when we must take this chance. I certainly do not believe that the German government, as it is now constituted, can be trusted to adhere either to the letter or the spirit of negotiated peace. I am still hesitant about coming out whole-heartedly against all foreign wars." He was under particular pressure just then from some of Adelaide's friends and his tone was defensive and querulous: "My refusal to join you may mean that I am unenlightened, as indeed I am, but, believe me, it does not mean I am either a physical or a moral coward. I am actually as patriotic, though perhaps not as forceful or well-integrated an American, as you are and I have proved my patriotism by serving for some two years in the armed forces of the United States and by risking my neck in three major offensives with the American Expeditionary Force in France. When the cause arises which I feel involves the best interest of my country I shall take the same risk for it again." And yet, he was not ready, either, to join up with the other side. He wrote, at about the same time, to Robert Littell of the *Reader's Digest*: "I find myself in the uncomfortable position of not being able to decide what the United States ought to do in this war, because I don't know the facts, and maybe no one knows them."

His main quarrel with the White Committee, he told Littell, was that it did not itself seem to know how far it wanted the United States to go. This was indeed the case—one group of important New Yorkers, members, like Herbert Agar, of the prestigious Century Club, to which Marquand now belonged, was in favor of the repeal of the Neutrality Act and the use of American convoys to aid the Allies. While White held back from this position, Lindbergh, Verne Marshall and others had been calling upon him to clarify his stand. As Marquand observed, "Where are we going to get if all our molders of public opinion are in such a mental fog? The same fog, I may say, seems to be over the minds of the isolationist groups also. I do not even believe that the President himself knows definitely how far he would want us to go." What did seem obvious, he thought, was the need for a great step-up in industrial production, and "damn fast." Mr. Roosevelt had declared that we would supply England with twenty-six thousand planes, but where in hell were they?

He gave the same sort of answer to Henry Seidel Canby, who was also urging him to join other writers in support of the White Committee. Marquand probably spoke for a great many of his bewildered countrymen in early February 1941, when he said, "Right now this business of joining a committee seems to me a good deal like signing up with the church and accepting the whole creed. While I have great emotional sympathy for England and the deepest admiration for the fight she is waging, including the conviction that she is fighting indirectly for our own traditions as well as hers, I do not feel that this country is in any condition right now to go to war to help her. I may feel differently at the end of three months, provided England has been able to take what Hitler is preparing to dish out. In the meanwhile we shall be doing about all we can for her, particularly with the passage of the lend-lease bill. Anything further may involve this country quite disastrously." However, despite the fact that he concluded "I seem to be in the unhappy position of falling somewhere between the America First and the White Committee in that I can not see either a negotiated peace or war," he was constantly embarrassed by the assumption that he had chosen to attach himself to one side or the other. Many of his friends continued to assume his approval of America First because of Adelaide, and he would have to state, as he did in March to fellow *Post* writer Walter Edmonds: "Don't bother about Adelaide's America First stuff—an activity with which I have never been wholly in sympathy, and less now than ever before. If there is any chance that our aid to England—and not short of war either—can decisively defeat Hitler, I am all for it, and the only thing that makes me hesitate is the possibility of a stalemate." But some of his interventionist friends tended to assume that he was entirely with them, and he was startled at almost the same moment that he wrote to Edmonds to find that his name was actually listed as a member on the stationery of the Committee to Defend America by Aiding the Allies, though he had expressly withheld his permission.

Adelaide's America First activities, however, gave her greater prominence in the public eye when, on April 23, she opened the public meeting held by the committee in Manhattan Center in New York. Senator Walter George, Lindbergh, and the writer Kathleen Norris were the speakers at the meeting which was presided over by John T. Flynn of the National Committee before an audience of fifty-five hundred jammed into the flag-decked hall and two thousand more in an overflow room upstairs, a crowd of fifteen thousand to twenty thousand outside in Thirty-fourth Street. The next day the Marquands gave a cocktail party in their apartment at One Beekman Place for the Lindberghs, the Flynns, the Archibald Roosevelts and the principal guest, General Frank Aiken, the anti-British Irish minister of war, which was followed by dinner upstairs in the apartment of Adelaide's mother. A month later a still larger meeting was held in Madison Square Garden. Adelaide, who had advanced the committee on the occasion $4,500 to pay for ads in the New York papers, spoke on the same platform again, with Lindbergh, Kathleen Norris and Flynn, and also Senator Burton K. Wheeler and the Socialist Norman Thomas. This time the audience numbered twenty thousand, the Garden's capacity, and a crowd of ten thousand or more was said to be outside, listening to the speeches broadcast by loudspeaker. Considerable excitement was contributed by the presence in one of the front rows of Joe McWilliams, the leader of the fascist American Destiny party—Flynn found it necessary to make a public statement disclaiming any connection of McWilliams with America First, and when he was finished with his remarks the crowd surged furiously at McWilliams until stopped by the police who formed a protective wall around him. Then, to the still tense and heaving audience, Adelaide spoke briefly, followed by Thomas, Kathleen Norris, Lindbergh and Senator Wheeler.

Marquand, who had left for Hollywood, was probably glad to be off the scene, though his wife sent him long letters detailing her activities and representing, in a quite disturbing way, the hysterical state of mind she shared with many at the moment. She wrote him just before the Madison Square Garden meeting that the President, who had postponed until the twenty-seventh the speech he had planned to make earlier, had done so in order that he might assess public opinion—as evidenced by the meeting—before making "what would probably amount to a declaration of war." She also told her husband: "The William Allen White Committee has launched a huge financial campaign which includes, I have heard from two people who have received them, chain letters and telegrams, which are, I believe, illegal. Amos Pinchot told me last night that he had been advised by a very reliable source in Washington that the White Committee is receiving liberal support under fronts from the British government and also that the British secret service has spies in every peace organization in this country."

Meanwhile, Marquand sent his rather contrasting reports from Hollywood, and only added laconically, "I'm sorry you can't get out—I can't see how you can stop us from getting into war." In June he left New York for

Ecuador, not returning until the middle of August; from this further distance he responded in a still more decisive way to Adelaide's continued bulletins of her activities. "I think America First ought to be about through now. Let the President run the country and you run Butch." ("Butch" was baby Ferry, now a year and a half old. Marquand's "sexist" instruction could not have pleased Adelaide. She was again pregnant.) He recommended that she pick up William L. Shirer's recent book. "It might change some of your ideas. You must get it into your head that we are going to get into this war eventually—and don't get yourself so far out on a limb that you can't line up with anyone you have always known when we do. It isn't worth it." He concluded a long description of his travels with a note of his reaction to a recent advertisement of America First entitled "No Red Allies": "It puts me finally out of sympathy with your organization—and indeed it seems to me that you have finally worked yourselves into a position of being pro-German. You do not seem to realize that the Nazi menace is vastly more important to our future than Communism. If Russia can only be kept in the war, there is a slim hope that Hitler may be defeated without our being further involved. Certainly this is not a time for you or anyone else to be giving comfort to Germany, and I hate to think of your being involved in such a cause. Things are moving so fast, and we are now so deeply involved that I think it is better for you not to do any more back seat driving. There is nothing more that you can do to change destiny, and all you do in the future will be increasingly unpatriotic, because we are now at a stage where it is my country right or wrong." His tone was disagreeably overbearing, but events soon sustained his views.

Yet on his return to New York he would find Adelaide still engaged in the same activities as before, and though she was now in her eighth month of pregnancy, on October 30 the Marquands gave a dinner for about fifty members of America First, including Lindbergh, Thomas, Oswald Garrison Villard, Senators Clark and Nye, and former ambassador to Ireland Cudahy, preceding another big Madison Square Garden meeting where Lindbergh, the ambassador, and Wheeler spoke. Marquand's reaction to it all expressed itself in a characteristic style of humor. "New York this winter," he said to the cartoonist Gluyas Williams, "seems to me particularly poisonous with everybody steamed up about some cause to the point of acute hysteria. My wife is for America First and personally I feel that when everything is said and done we are going to get into the war anyway and we might as well get ahead with it, but even simple views like these split themselves like amoebas. You can either do Bundles for Britain or Fight for Freedom or Feed French Babies or Keep the Chinese from Getting Parasitic Diseases or Love the Communists or Hate the Communists or Entertain a Soldier or a Sailor Every Sunday." To a reporter who interviewed him at about the same time in anticipation of the opening of the movie of *Pulham*, he again was called upon to explain Adelaide. He declared himself: "Mrs. Marquand has been an active and prominent member of the America First Committee. Her public activities have been rather curtailed lately by the fact that she is about to go to the hospital to have another baby, but she still thinks the same thoughts. There has never been any isolationist sentiment to speak of in New England—that is among those who are in the New England tradition. But as I have explained to Mrs. Marquand, she comes from Greenwich, Connecticut, and that is very close to the line. In any case there has been no chance for me to escape the tradition. Anyway, I was in the last war, and never have been able to get over the feeling that there is an open season on Germans." Marquand's anti-German feeling was a deeply persistent attitude, finding expression in the same language, again and again in his conversation, and in sharp contrast to Adelaide's pro-German sentimentality. As late as 1956, when he was asked to consider a book about the crew of a World War II German surface raider for the Book-of-the-Month Club, he responded in "fury"—his own word—and repeated: "I hate the guts of all Germans. When I hear their foul language spoken in Europe and see their sweating stinking bodies, I always reach instinctively for a Tommy gun or a hand grenade. Being conditioned to trouble with the Germans, I feel there is still an open season on all the race."

When the United States entered the Second World War Marquand's emotions, like those of many men of his generation, had a doubled intensity, a reliving of his own past of twenty-five years earlier and a participation in the experience that the war might bring to the next service-age generation. He had been thinking a good deal during the year before Pearl Harbor about Johnny, and it was perhaps with a feeling that they had "so little time" in the face of the probable future that he dropped everything in June 1941 to take him on a trip to Ecuador.

They had had a not unusual father-son relationship since the divorce from Christina. His eldest child aroused in him both a deep sense of identification and a resentment of the fact that by being *his* son and not Philip's, Johnny was born to the advantages Marquand had missed. Johnny was able to go to St. Mark's and to open charge accounts at Saks Fifth Avenue, Brooks Brothers and Abercrombie and Fitch, whereas Johnny's father had minded his shabby clothes at the high school in Newburyport. Marquand would never entirely suppress a scorn, and an envy also, of the boy who took all his comforts and privileges with the easy assumption that they were his natural due. The fact, too, that Johnny was also Christina's child, and now much under her influence, made him think of the boy as threatening to turn out to be like, for example, her brother Shan—and made him rage against the "Sedgwick strain" in his son. He sometimes expressed a fussy suspiciousness of youthful masculinity that may have had its roots in his own cynicism, but was also, if one wishes to put it this way, oedipal, growing out of the feeling that this son was now more than ever the possessor and possession of his mother, even though the father did not love her. Yet they resembled one another strongly, not merely in appearance but in intelligence and temperament. The boy showed a literary flair—to his father's delight—in stories written for the St. Mark's *Vindex*, and beneath an outer love of fun he was, like his father, secretive, stubborn, inclined towards brooding resentment and irascible bursts of anger. Marquand's own private dourness was clothed, in his adulthood, with a glittering wit which the boy could hardly hope to match, but Marquand was startled to hear from a father who had taken Johnny along with his own son to a football game that the seventeen-year-old had developed "a dry and acid humor." He wrote him a caution: "Even I who am sour and bitter now do not always get away with it. Certainly I should have more friends and be more sought after today if I were more cheerful, less malicious and saw more silver linings instead of clouds."

Johnny, for his part, was of two minds about his father as much as the father was of two minds about him. Marquand's literary achievements and fame stirred his admiration. Also, it was hard to be indifferent to the prestige gained when everyone in his form was reading Marquand's adventure-tale "Castle Sinister" in *Collier's*, as well as when they tried to read *Wickford Point*, which they had to confess they could not understand; Johnny himself wrote a book report on the novel and sent his father some suggestions for its improvement. His father was a famous man who was often interviewed in the newspapers and in *Time* and *Newsweek* and who even appeared on "Information Please." Reading Byrd's *Alone*, Johnny was thrilled to discover that the heroic admiral had taken his father's early book about Timothy Dexter with him to the South Pole. But in various ways during his school years Johnny showed his desire to assert his independence of this formidable parent. In the spring of 1939 he surprised Marquand as well as Christina by joining the Episcopal Church without asking their consent or opinion. His father distrustfully guessed that the boy had taken the step only because it was the "thing to do"; more likely it was an action that appealed because it was the most important step, he had been assured, that a person of his age could take, and it was entirely at his own disposal. It was in the same spirit that he went into a Bowery tattoo shop a year later and acquired an American eagle as permanent decoration on his left forearm, to be followed, in his freshman year at Harvard, by a formidable snake over the bicep—somewhat to his father's derision and his mother's horror—but, after all, what one did with one's body as with one's own soul was exclusively one's own affair.

By the time Johnny reached fifteen Marquand had begun to worry about the young man's way with money. He adopted devices, which the boy thought rather mean, to impress upon him the value of the dollar. Johnny was required to render an itemized account of his past expenditures to Marquand's law firm before the allowance check for the following month could be mailed to him, and such firms as Brooks Brothers were instructed to inform the parent if his son's charges ran over fifty dollars. Marquand also fretted about the "habits" to be acquired from the cowhands at the western ranch to which Johnny was sent in his sixteenth and seventeenth summers, though earlier he had considered the ranch a desirable corrective to the "country-club dances and yachting at Nonquitt" offered by Christina. It was clear to him that when Johnny had a chance to get away from the school he was eager to see and do as much as possible—an attitude which reminded him of his own feelings on military leave in Paris during the war but which in someone his son's age "leads naturally to bizarre adventure." Johnny and his friends apparently liked to go to the Central Park Zoo after dances and wake up the seals and blow cigarette smoke at the zebra, which made Marquand declare that he would punish him severely if he ever caught him "smoking a cigarette in public or in the company of older people"—a restriction not of the act itself but of the performance of it under the eyes of society. Marquand had been alarmed at learning that some of the St. Mark's fifth formers had got themselves expelled by becoming soused at the Ritz bar after a Yale game. He saw the same fate threatening Johnny who, he was positive, was on the brink of discovering the special pleasures of adults, especially when consumed freely. Yet he was wise enough to realize that repression does not encourage restraint and he advised Headmaster Parkman that the boys should be given occasional weekend liberty to prevent such violent discharges of energy during their rare holidays.

During his last two years at St. Mark's, Johnny seemed to fall afoul of his father's temper rather frequently. There was an occasion during Christmas vacation in his junior year. Young John, by delaying his departure from New York for personal reasons of his own, embarrassed his mother, who had expected him at a dinner party in Boston. He had also left behind him in New York certain messes in the way of unpaid bills, the price of a dance ticket and of his carfare back to Boston, and a charge to Marquand's telephone bill of a fifty-two-minute long-distance call, all of which was not only "sloppy," Marquand scolded, but "on the verge of dishonesty and a breach of hospitality in any house, even mine, and what is even more, it shows you are not well brought up."

Johnny's junior year at St. Mark's was apparently a difficult one. He had become so indifferent to his schoolwork that there was talk of transferring him elsewhere for his last year—to Exeter, perhaps—where his interest might be better stimulated. He had begun to drink, and not merely the wine and beer to which Marquand had ordered him to restrict himself (Marquand demanded a "written promise" that he would do so before he came to Beekman Place for the 1941 Christmas vacation). As for money, Marquand had written Christina with heavy contempt: "I am very sorry that Johnny's mind seems so preoccupied with money at the present time, particularly as he probably won't ever have any. He certainly does not exhibit any of those acquisitive capacities that go with making money." At St. Mark's the following year his teachers reported Johnny's boredom despite evident intelligence, and his poor social adjustment as evidenced in his tendency to nervous clowning. "He may think," his adviser said, "that if he went out of his way to be a bit more pleasant it would be an acknowledgment that the so-called powers are correct and he is wrong, which is not his conception of himself. Speaking very frankly I feel there is little more that can be offered to make up this personality blank space. It is now up to him to stop feeling sorry for himself for real or imagined wrongs of the past and to take a constructive outlook on what he has to do for himself."

But Marquand blamed the school for failing with his son. Now, when Johnny had been giving trouble in so many irritating ways, he felt a surge of paternal feeling, a desire to achieve a bond before it was too late. In the spring of 1941, convinced that the country was on the brink of inevitable entry into the war, he began to plan a trip for both of them to South America. He wanted to share with Johnny the kind of travel experience that he had found deeply meaningful. In the Far East and in Persia he had spent months amid scenes so different from anything he had known before that they helped him to acquire a perspective upon human affairs and upon his own life in particular. During the interval between his marriages, the trips had enabled him to withdraw from his involvements with Christina and Helen Howe. It was fortunate that Adelaide's pregnancy and her America First commitments made a journey of this sort out of the question for her, for with Johnny he hoped to have the masculine rapport which, he probably believed, is spoiled by women.

He discovered several ways of working the trip as a sponsored safari. The *American Magazine* had asked him to write a three- or four-part serial of the mystery-adventure type with a South American background and had offered to foot the bill for a trip up the Magdalena River into the jungles of Colombia in search of backgrounds. Then, the Standard Oil Company, at the instigation of his brother-in-law Johnny Rockefeller, had offered him a trip through the back country of Venezuela in the Lake Maracaibo region in order that he might be inspired to write about oil developments there. He finally decided to go with his cousin Sewell Tyng, who was president of a mining and development company in Ecuador, to visit two gold mines—one at Portovelo in the Andes and the other at Macuchi in the southern part of the country; at both places they would arrive in time to witness the fiestas in the neighboring villages and they would travel through a great deal of wild country. Besides Tyng they would have for company two other young males of about Johnny's age: Henry Luce III, the son of the publisher of *Time*, and another friend.

They sailed on the *Santa Clara*, a Grace Line vessel, on June 20, and arrived ten days later at Guayaquil, which turned out to be a hot, humid town on the edge of a muddy river. "All day long," Marquand reported dispiritedly to Adelaide, "the inhabitants blow motor horns or sit in small sidewalk cafes or walk by the statue of Bolivar." The streets were lined with large balconied buildings of wood; underneath the balconies there were arcades of shops displaying Arrow shirts and Kotex. No one spoke English, and while Tyng was about his business, Marquand and the boys wandered around trying to explore the city with the aid of some feeble Spanish out of their phrase books. Some months later, on a radio show, Marquand depicted, with retrospective self-contempt, the helpless tourist: "The souvenir dealer marks me as the man who will buy his worst panama hat and perhaps a pair of boa constrictor suspenders and a wallet from an alligator's epidermis. I am the man you see in the arcade trying to buy a copy of *Life* or the New York *Times*, or searching through a pocket dictionary for some Spanish way of saying 'Do you sell Bromo-Seltzer here?'"

They thought with eagerness of the dry, cool Andes, "hidden somewhere in the murk that hangs over the town," as they left the next day for the first of Tyng's mines. The journey was extraordinary, involving a night on a riverboat, a seventy-five-mile trip on a narrow gauge, single-track railway, a six-hour mule ride and finally several hours further by car. The mining camp of Portovelo was accessible only over mule trails that led into the mountains. Marquand and Johnny saw villages of mud and thatched houses in front of which companionably at play were dogs, thin pigs and goats, mud-smeared small children, and roosters kept for the Sunday cockfights.

The poverty of the Ecuadorian back country was certainly a revelation to the young St. Mark's boy, and even his father found it difficult to describe, though it was not worse, really, than the life led by Chinese peasants. But in China, he remembered, there had always been, under conditions the most rudimentary, the sense of an immemorial culture and of a rhythm of methodical industry that seemed to guarantee human continuance. The life of the Indians in these villages seemed without hope; the technology of survival was almost infantile compared with that of the Chinese. The houses, framed with logs and with sides of split bamboo or wattle and daub, usually consisted of two rooms, the front room an open porch where a fire could be built on a heap of mud, and an inner room without windows where the family slept on a few rugs. The Indians looked depressed and sickly to Marquand; they suffered, he heard, from malaria, dysentery, tuberculosis and hookworm.

Leaving Portovelo they mounted mules with all their baggage and then followed a trail through tropical jungle so wet that the mules constantly slipped into sloughs, and steam rose from the watery hollows. Then it was back along the little railroad through the jungle of the coastal plain for four hours to a miserable little place called Puerto Bolívar, where they boarded the steamboat and finally crossed the Gulf of Guayaquil. Certainly the comforts of an advanced civilization, which the three youngsters had always taken for granted, seemed remote. The little hotel at Guayaquil, which had earned their contempt at the start of the journey, now seemed like the Ritz, and Guayaquil itself assumed the splendor of a metropolis. After a trip to Quito and Macuchi they took the Grace Line *Santa Lucia* home. They were back with a jolt in the world they had left behind. Adelaide had sent them her best wishes that the "good will tour" might be successful.

After Pearl Harbor, Marquand wrote Johnny: "You mustn't get too excited about the events of the last few days because we are going to have a lot more and perhaps a lot worse for the next three or four years." He was probably more excited himself than he admitted. He had been having tea with friends in Beekman Place when the news of the assault was announced on the radio and, it was later said, he picked up a nice Japanese teapot from the table and tossed it into the fireplace. When a *Life* reporter asked him three years later about the story Marquand said that his reaction had actually been less spectacular. He had simply picked up the teapot and put it down again, remarking, "I ought to bust the damn thing, but what good would it do?"

But he had not been as surprised as a great many other people—and he wrote Johnny that American failure to estimate correctly Japanese strength and the Japanese frame of mind was a case, really, of St. Mark's mentality—which, as he had been saying to Johnny all along, was no preparation at all for real life. "As far as I can gather from the few bits of gossip that are filtering in, the Navy at Pearl Harbor was just St. Mark's on a larger scale. Being brought up to what is, alas, only an Anglo-Saxon code of decency and honor, it was evidently not conceivable to the officers of the naval base that Japan would attack beneath a cloak of peace negotiations, yet every one of those officers has been taught from his earliest days in Annapolis that war in the Pacific would begin with a treacherous surprise attack by Japan upon the main body of the American fleet and upon the Pacific coast." The St. Mark's mentality, he declared with some grim satisfaction, "has been smashed into a cocked hat now, I hope, for good and all. We must forget all this talk about the Japanese being funny little people and about their being rotten aviators because their eyes don't focus. The fact is that the Japanese bombers have shown themselves vastly superior to the German. Japan is now the dominant sea power in the Pacific and I think may be for a long while to come. There is another possibility worth considering, for I think it is well to face the worst, and that is that France throws her fleet in with Germany and Italy. This naval power, plus that of Japan and Germany, will very nearly equal, if it does not exceed, the combined naval forces of England and America. There is no reason to be frightened by this possibility, but it does mean that the world you were brought up to think was reasonably stable has been finished forever with Pearl Harbor, and something new is coming. We are in for a very long and very dangerous war."

In *So Little Time*, Jeffrey Wilson would jibe at his friend Minot, who had said: "People with Mongoloid eyes can't focus the way we can. Everybody knows they can't fly." Minot, of course, was a perfect St. Mark's product, which also meant that once the United States went into a war he was filled with happy fury and the desire that everyone else's son—he had only daughters himself—get into battle as soon as possible. But Marquand, like his fictional representative, had a more complex feeling, and when Johnny decided that the problem of entering Harvard in 1942 was now settled for him, he replied: "Before long you are certain to be either in the Army or the Navy. This isn't such a bad thing either for in the end it will teach you more than you ever learned in college and if you live through it you will have the satisfaction that you will never lose that you were young enough and strong enough to fight for your country. I can understand what you must be thinking quite clearly because I went through it all myself, though on a smaller scale, back in 1917 when I was not much older than you. The main thing right now is for you to keep your shirt on and try to learn all you can which will help you to be a good soldier and probably a good officer because of your educational background. I have no doubt that in a day or two the Boston Draft Board will call you up, but I don't think that your age group will be put into service for some time. In the meantime I should like you to join some sort of officer's course in Harvard until you are called. If you are interested and able to meet the mental and physical requirements, I think I might be able to get you into West Point or Annapolis."

And that June Johnny graduated from St. Mark's and was admitted to Harvard. Interviewed by a reporter from the Boston *Globe* he acknowledged that his father had wanted him to be at Harvard but added that there was "little danger of my emerging as H. M. Pulham." He planned, he said, to join the Harvard Unit of the Army ROTC, which would probably mean, the reporter noted, that he would emerge as a lieutenant, the rank held by his father in the First World War. As it turned out, this reenactment would not take place. Johnny, despite his own efforts and Marquand's to get him into an officer training program, remained in the ranks until his discharge. Marquand himself realized immediately that Johnny would probably not stay at college much beyond his freshman year if the war continued, as he was convinced it must. That fall of 1942, Johnny, like most college students, was at loose ends, expecting that sooner or later the draft would reach him. To Christina, Marquand admitted: "I am naturally appalled, as you must be, at Johnny's future prospects, but then every parent is also. This war is going to be much worse before it gets better. The casualty lists will run into millions, and in the end there is not much use trying to plan, but this may be the wisest course when destiny has removed everything so completely from any sort of plans."

Johnny stayed at Harvard through the fall term of his sophomore year, but then the enlisted reserves were called up. Marquand wrote his son, "I imagine you are not going to have the problem you thought you had as to what to do with yourself." He was pleased that Johnny was going in as an enlistee: "It is a prejudice of mine, no doubt, but I did not like waiting around to be drafted in the last war, and I am glad that you are not waiting around to be drafted in this." And the pattern of identification continued when Johnny's orders arrived—they were for Fort Devens, where Marquand also had started out. Johnny's first letter detailed with some vividness and humor the assembly-plant routines of the huge reception center, and Marquand was so proud of its reportorial quality that he quoted from it at length the following month in an address he gave at the Lawrenceville School. He read his son's letters with extreme empathy. "Do write him as often as possible because he gets a terrific vicarious thrill out of it," Adelaide told Johnny. Marquand was also pleased that the rookie's test scores had qualified him for OCS and that he was being sent for basic training to Field Artillery Headquarters at Fort Sill, Oklahoma—the replication was eerily continuing, for not only had he himself been attached to the artillery, but, in *So Little Time*, just then completed, he had sent Jeffrey Wilson's son Jim to Sill. He wrote Johnny enthusiastically: "Fort Sill and the School of Fire is the best thing of its kind in the United States Army. In army circles anyone from Fort Sill has the same sort of prestige that a graduate from Harvard or Oxford has in a more intellectual life. The best military teachers in the country are there and the best equipment and the most thorough training." It was a decided compliment to Johnny to have been selected. Johnny described his barracks-mates at Sill—the bright, four-year men from Duke, always up on all technical points; the dull fraternity boys from Bowdoin and Amherst, clean-living and without ideas—and confessed that he found himself seeking out his own kind: boys from "St. Grottlesex" and from Harvard, Yale and Princeton, all of whom, like himself, were taking a beating as they saw their assumed superiorities crumbling under the challenges of the program. He felt more at ease with Tennessee and Kentucky backwoodsmen and Italian and Portuguese boys from Fall River who were in the group than with the upwardly mobile achievers from the less elite colleges. Again, Marquand remembered a similar revelation of the meaning of class in his own Army experience. He too had found the bright boys from the small colleges "small-minded, limited and noisy, selfish and pushing, and not worth talking to." He, who had reason to resent the snobbery of the representative Harvard man of his day, curiously identified, now, with his son's instinctive snobbery and only cautioned him to study these rivals well, learning their strengths and weaknesses, for he could expect to compete with them not merely in the Army but for the rest of his life. And, after all, "as they get older some of them grow mellower and really turn out to be nice people. If you are patient and not intolerant of them you will find that they will get rather to like you." Marquand himself, after trips to the war areas during the next two years, yielded up much of his residual snobbery in the contemplation of American servicemen. Just such a man as his son was now encountering was to be the hero of *Repent in Haste*, the short novel Marquand wrote in 1945.

Despite his identification with Johnny's military career, Marquand was not entirely willing to see the burden of the war assumed by his son's generation. His mood, and that of thousands of men of his age, was well expressed in the chapter of *So Little Time* in which Jeffrey Wilson goes to Washington to see if he cannot get back in. He discovers that he can, but only as a swivel-chair soldier in public relations. The novelist probably did not bolt down to Washington the day after Pearl Harbor as Jeffrey does, but he understood the impulse. He spent a gloomy winter in Beekman Place awkwardly adjusting to the realization that he was middle-aged in a time when the youngest were doing most. He also found it difficult to adjust to becoming the overage father of another infant—Timothy Fuller, born November 16, 1941. His renewed experience of fatherhood was a source of astonished dismay. He was not, he found, willing now to meet the demands upon his tolerance and time that babies impose. The distractions and irritations of life with small children, from which Adelaide and hired nurses seemed unable to shield him sufficiently, became another favorite subject of comic complaint. As he had done when Christina's children were young, he would dilate with only half-humorous exaggeration upon the difficulty of carrying on a writer's job in a noisy, numerous household dominated by the needs—somehow never met with dispatch or efficiency—of infancy; he would refer frequently with snarling humor to the "patter of little feet."

In such moods his recourse was, as many times before, the company of Carl and Carol Brandt. For the Brandts, though they too had a son approaching military age, the war did not exist with the same inescapability that it did for Marquand. Carol was thrilled—there is no other word appropriate—by Johnny's metamorphosis into a soldier, and wrote him gay letters. "As part of her war effort she is going to see that you get a letter once a week from her. Doubtless with perfume on it," Marquand informed Johnny. Indeed, the letters did come—if not weekly, at least full of offers of books and cookies, addresses of conveniently located friends in the military or out of it, and, finally, the offer of the use, when the Brandts were not occupying it themselves, of their apartment in the St. Regis in New York should he be able to get away from camp for a weekend. Their conception of the soldier's state of mind was of a piece with their general formula for existence: they lived industrious but quite unreflective lives in which pleasure was successfully maximized whenever possible. Their competence in the management of the comfortable—they would say the good—life had served Marquand himself many times. Now, again, as he found his home scene more oppressive, the air filled with the bawling of dissatisfied infants, they offered refuge. There *he* was treated as a child whose needs were always effectively met.

In February 1942, having left Adelaide at home with Ferry and the new baby, Marquand went on a trip to Cuba with the Brandts. After arriving in Havana, he wrote ruefully home, "I have a shrewd suspicion that everything is going much easier in my absence." But at the luxury hotel, the Nacional, it was easy to forget both the war and his family life in an environment of extravagant hedonism. "They have crabs here with black claws which are almost as good as the San Francisco ones and the bar downstairs is full of people drinking the native rum and selling themselves to each other, including women," he reported. From the hotel the trio went to a beach resort where the sun and the sea and the little thatched cabanas were delightful, even though, Marquand observed, man was vile: "There are some of the worst bums and tramps here I have ever encountered anywhere. To see the way they behave after dinner around the little tables in the darling little coral stone bar with its juke box which has records of loud Cuban singers shouting about the Rhumba and Let's Spend the Weekend in Havana has made me turn into almost a complete prohibitionist." So, in search of purer pleasures in a more authentic Cuba, they drove for seven hours to a town on the southern side of the island. There they ate a meal cooked in heavy oil in the dining room of their hotel, which opened onto a square resounding with noise, and then withdrawing to their rooms found that the noise continued to penetrate (though the rooms were windowless) far into the night; Marquand needed two Luminals to achieve unconsciousness. After this it was pleasant to return to the beach resort to "witness the more appalling phases of dipsomania." The three friends groused and sneered and enjoyed themselves, especially Carl, in whom the condition of dipsomania was well entrenched. "I have great qualms of conscience in my selfishness in going off this way but I dare say things are more peaceful at home," Marquand wrote Adelaide again.

But that spring, at Kent's Island, his mood did not improve as he tried to make progress on the first draft of *So Little Time.* The house on its rise above the salt marshes was close enough to the sea to make a nightly blackout necessary—another irritating reminder of the war in which he could not participate. "I only hope it makes it as tough for the [enemy] as it does for us," he told a friend. His middle-aged disgruntledness was only exacerbated by Adelaide's vivacity; bouncing back into her usual energetic fitness after the birth of her second child she persuaded her husband to go with her on another vacation quite unlike the one he had spent with the sybarites and dipsomaniacs in Cuba. She took him on a hiking trip in New Hampshire—than which nothing could have been less calculated to cheer him up—or so he gave the impression. As he told another friend: "I have been and still am worried about the war. I have been trying to write a novel which is fast giving me nervous indigestion and also Adelaide recently took me for a tramp above the timber line of the White Mountains and we spent the night in places known as 'Appalachian Mountain Club Huts.' If you have never done anything like this, I advise you never to attempt it. For me, the physical suffering was intense, as a cold north wind blew steadily for three days and I was thinly clad and the footing on the trail consisted merely of round boulders which gave way beneath me. What pained me more, however, was the mental anguish caused by the merriment and the good clean fun of all the college boys and girls who congregated in the huts and who made tea and cocoa and romped and laughed. I never realized how old I was until I encountered them, and I must say I did not look back wistfully on youth." The style of such talk is recognizably Marquand at his burlesque best—but there was, as usual, a current of real misery in his tone. And indeed, he was not feeling well. His middle-aged stomach was giving him trouble.

The summer was climaxed by the discovery that Adelaide was pregnant once again. His response to becoming a father for the *fifth* time was expressed in comments and complaints still more comically frantic than ever. In the following winter also, he was intermittently ill, once even in the hospital with what was diagnosed as virus pneumonia, and more and more depressed at the prospect of hearing the first squalls of an additional member of what he had come to refer to as the "anvil chorus" of his household. The remedy, again, was for the Brandts to take him off somewhere for a holiday—this time just as soon as Adelaide's delivery was over. During the weeks of waiting, Marquand and his two friends made plans for a visit to New Orleans and to the Homestead at Hot Springs, with a stop "on route" to see Johnny at Fort Sill. The baby, Elon Huntington (after his maternal grandfather), was over two weeks late, and the last moments of impatience were acute, not merely for the mother who bore him finally on March 28, but for the father, who complained to Johnny: "I have been planning to go with the Brandts a week ago to Hot Springs and I have been doing nothing but making reservations and breaking them. The time has come when I have just got to get away somewhere for a few days and I hope that maybe I can leave this Sunday. I had planned to go with them to Hot Springs for two weeks and then go with them for a quick visit to New Orleans, but I am in no mood for New Orleans now as I would die of indigestion eating pressed duck, rare wines, shrimp and other shell fish without having some sort of a rest first." He was certainly in bad shape, and when the baby arrived the next day it was Adelaide herself, not Marquand, who sent the telegram to Johnny announcing the arrival of his little half brother.

Immediately, Marquand and the Brandts took off, though now, more than during his flight to Cuba the year before, he felt the preposterousness of their blithe escapism. However guiltily, he enjoyed himself, but he wrote Johnny on his return: "I was away for two weeks to Hot Springs trying to recover from the effects of parenthood, and all the good it did me was to catch cold again riding and walking in the mountains. It was very queer staying at the Homestead because all that place seemed to be going about the way it always has, completely removed from any trace of war. There were moving pictures every night and kiddies from school were spending their vacations with their parents and there was ping pong and all sorts of other games in the big corridor and saddle horses and golf and people with gout. I kept thinking of the time when you and Tina and I were there seven years ago."

His sense of his oldest child as participant in the sternest trials of the day was, as we have seen, acute. His awareness of Johnny's sister as another member of the same generation was unexpectedly aroused that March of 1943 when she staged as dramatic a youthful revolt as was possible for a fifteen-year-old at a well-regulated girls' boarding school. Tina, too, in her way, was responding to the times. Yet she had been, since infancy, so shy and unassertive as to seem actually dull. As a very little girl she had been silent and withdrawn, baffling her parents by her appearance of living in a private world and chary of her responses to adults. When she was about twelve her teachers at the Beaver School had still not been able to make her very proficient at arithmetic or spelling, and her IQ on a test they gave her was only 100. Marquand and Christina had hired a special tutor, who assured the worried parents that despite her poor performance on tests Tina's "logical processes" were good and he was able to coach her with some success. But her IQ score three years later was still 100, and by then Tina herself was convinced that she was a stupid girl.

Yet the tests and the teachers were quite wrong, for her childish letters, saved by her father, reveal an odd, noticing, wryly witty young mind of an unconventional sort. At Westover, which she herself described as "a feminine equivalent of St. Mark's," she looked about her at the ranks and orders of the miniature society of rich schoolgirls and found them contemptible. Still spelling quaintly, she wrote her father in 1942, "The war news and the war that darkens the earth never is heard in the years of the pure Westover girls." She described these girls in some detail with a tiny echo of his own capacity for satiric derision—particularly her roommates, one a pretentious New York miss, the other a "small town glamor babe," and with a little mockery thanked her father for the $3,000 he had plunked down for the year's tuition. In his answer he showed that he had not taken the measure of her critique: "There are several things in your letter that make me very pleased—one is that your handwriting and spelling are definitely improving and another is that you and all the girls are living a quiet life, away from the increasing mess and discomfort which this war is causing everyone. It gives me a very pleasant feeling to think of you safely tucked away in a nice little world with nice little Park Avenue creams and nice little girls from Dayton."

She continued to write to him about the inanities of the Westover world: how the girls were divided into "Wests" and "Overs" and Seniors and how there were apple trees in the quadrangle belonging to the respective divisions; one was allowed to stroll only underneath the tree belonging to one's own group—and there were gatherings of the respective athletic teams under the respective apple trees for group singing. Years later, a grown and married

Tina with children of her own recalled the peculiar "dating system" at Westover with the mixture of fear and repugnance it had once stirred in her. "Old girls" invited "new girls" for lunch or dinner or Saturday night dances where they danced with each other; she remembered hiding under a bed reading a book with the help of a flashlight so that she might escape attending one of these dances. The quiet freshman, hardly noticed by anyone, had thoroughly hated the place, which seemed a brown stucco prison with walls appropriately matching the ugly brown uniforms the girls were required to wear, and she made not a single friend that fall and did poorly in her classes. At Christmas she had not been able to tell her troubles to her father, who was ill with the flu and nervously irritable ("one instinctively knew he was not to be bothered"), and so he was quite unprepared when he learned that she had run away.

She had written her mother for money—giving the excuse that she needed it to pay for a chair she had broken—and in the middle of a cold February night had silently put on her clothes and climbed out of a window with the aid of a knotted bedsheet like a heroine in a juvenile adventure story. She walked along the highway four miles to the nearest bus station and took the bus for New Haven. She was about to board the train for Boston when she was stopped by a detective. She did not have to go back to Westover, but her mother was distressed, her father dumbfounded, and only her old grandfather, Philip, said to his son as he put his arm around her, "Tina is a brave girl. Aren't you proud of her?" Some weeks later Marquand had recovered his poise and wrote her: "I have been impressed for a long while by the big act you put on at Westover. I think you did exactly what I would have done if I had been in your place. I know that I had the virus pneumonia when you were here but honestly, if you had told me how much you hated Westover, and hated it so much that you were thinking of running out on it, I should have got you out of there myself." With some self-pity he complained: "Johnny tells me that you are afraid of me and this hurts me quite a lot since I have made frantic efforts ever since you were two years old to give you the idea that I am a nice person. I hope if you ever have any further impulses and your existence gets you down to such a point that you will make a big effort and try to talk to me about it instead of sitting around with a dead pan."

The bolt from Westover proved, for Christina, a literal self-liberation, and at Winsor, the following year, she was a changed girl—popular, concerned with clothes, an editor of the literary magazine. In characteristic fashion, meanwhile, Marquand summarized his condition of fatherhood in June of 1943 (for John Bolles, whom he now heard from, eight years after their time together in Persia): "Everybody assures me that children are a great blessing, but I am still open to conviction on this score. But having two litters of children rather gets me down in this hot weather. My eldest son is now fighting for his country in a place called Stillwater, Oklahoma, where for some reason known I hope to the Army but not to me, he is being classified in a scholarly way so that he may go to some college for 20 or 30 weeks perhaps to study some subject—he does not know what. My eldest daughter, sixteen, ran away this winter from a very expensive boarding school and now wants to be a glamour girl, and would like to join the Waves but her tender age does not permit her. This, however, is far from all. My second marriage, which I believe was in prospect the last time I saw you, has been blessed in such a big way that sometimes I am surprised. I have one daughter a little over three who spends most of her time cleaning out the toilet bowl with my shaving brushes. I have a son one and a half, who tears the palings out of his play-pen and pulls things from the table to the floor. Besides this I have another son whose age is practically zero. All three of them are in the apartment now and joined together frequently in an infantile anvil chorus, each screaming out its individual woe in an unmistakable manner." And then he added with only seeming irrelevance, "I don't seem to have done much about the war either, except to make a few empty patriotic gestures in the vicinity of Washington and the finishing of a novel which I hope will come out this Fall."

Johnny's war career did not eventually satisfy the craving of the World War I combat veteran to reenact his own past. Johnny did not get into OCS but was sent back to college under the ASTP program at Texas A. & M. and then at the University of Maryland, where he was set to the intensive study of Spanish. It was all very well, and as Marquand wrote Christina after seeing Johnny in Washington, "I think the army has done him a great deal of good, particularly from the point of view of posture and from the immaculate neatness of his uniform." It had become obvious, however, that he was destined for a noncombatant service. His father expressed his own disappointment as much as Johnny's when he told Christina, "He realizes that this is not going to be a happy situation with so many of his friends in the air corps or on their way overseas in combat units." After a few months at Maryland there seemed a possibility of his being sent to a Caribbean base, and it was Marquand who only half-jokingly remarked, "I would not feel too badly about it because life there is just as strange and due to malaria and other tropical diseases just about as dangerous as it is at the front." Marquand tried to get help from the top brass he was then meeting in Washington so that Johnny might be transferred to officer training, but he had no success, and the young soldier himself was advised by one of these military friends to try to get into the Office of Special Services—"the only remaining branch of the service where attention is paid to influence and proper connections, to the tradition of the old school tie or whatever remains of it today." Perhaps this effort was successful, for it was as a member of this branch of the Army that Johnny finally, after a stop at Camp Crowder, Missouri, was transferred to the European theater.

Before leaving, he had engaged his father's attention in quite another way by proposing to get married. After several romances in his final years at St. Mark's, Johnny had fallen in love with a "dizzy little blonde" (Marquand's words) whom he had met at the Chevy Chase Country Club. Marquand had objected to the union as tactfully as possible but his grounds were very conventional ones such as might have concerned the Apleys—Jhan English's family was Catholic and "not suitable." He was glad when the girl's parents decided not to announce the engagement; he told Johnny that he would be making a great mistake if he rushed into marriage before he had enough education to fit him for some sort of work. He brought up his favorite warning example of effete improvidence, Shan Sedgwick—who had married "for love" and then depended on his parents for support—whose marriage had not stood up. He did not mention the obvious fact that Sedgwick's bride had also been a Catholic, but his prejudices soon became evident. He gathered—rightly or not—that Jhan's parents had gone back on their promise of approval and had sent a rude letter to Christina concerning their objections to Catholic–Protestant marriages, and seized the opportunity of declaring to Johnny: "It is completely characteristic of the way Catholics do things and explains why they are seldom liked or trusted by persons not of their faith, particularly in matters of business or of honorable understanding. There is a belief in the best of them that the end justifies almost any means, and you must expect them to act accordingly. Fine though Jhan is, and I like her more everytime I see her, you must remember that they are her parents and that even if Jhan is not like them, she cannot help but be deeply influenced by their ideas and manners." Adelaide added in a letter of her own, "Catholic families are in my experience a great deal more closely bound to each other than Protestant families, and if they resent you and suspect you as a Protestant you yourself will suffer much unhappiness and so will Jhan."

In this case Marquand reversed the model he had provided in the novel just then on the best-seller lists. Because Jeffrey Wilson had realized that *his* son had "so little time," he had urged him to marry his sweetheart at once, before being shipped over. He had even given the young couple some funds to make their brief domesticity at Fort Sill possible. Still, Marquand insisted that Jhan was a "swell kid" and he took her out to lunch in Washington and gave her tickets to the opening of the play just made out of *The Late George Apley*. In the end, the engagement gave way—perhaps merely as a result of distance and time. Before Johnny returned from Europe Jhan had married someone else. And hearing of this, Marquand declared that all was for the best—he knew boys among his son's contemporaries who *had* got married just before going overseas and then quite forgot what their young wives looked like. "I know a B-17 pilot from the Italian Front who came back to New York a while ago wounded. Three months before he went overseas he got married. When he got back he had a daughter two years old. When he returned his wife couldn't understand him nor he her. Inside of two months they were separated and she is in Reno getting a divorce." This revised view of war marriages was soon expressed in Marquand's postwar work of fiction, titled so pointedly *Repent in Haste*.

17

War Again

In the end, despite his feelings of frustration, Marquand accepted the precept, which he often quoted, "Old men for counsel, young men for war," and unlike Jeffrey Wilson was glad to find a desk job in Washington that enrolled him in the war effort. A good many writers were making contributions to the activities of the Writers' War Board, such as the promotion of war-bond sales by writing advertising copy and special articles and even fiction on subjects related to the progress of the war; but Marquand, after desultory participation early in 1942 (he prepared lists of topics for essays and suggested authors) asked that his name be dropped from the War Board list. He wanted more direct involvement in the military struggle, even if it meant the sacrifice of time from his literary work. So he responded eagerly to a telephone call from his friend George Merck, which reached him at Kent's Island that summer. Merck was in Washington setting up a research unit concerned with the highly confidential subject of biological warfare, and he asked Marquand to take on the job of director of intelligence and information.

Although his activity in this capacity was probably as important a war-connected responsibility as any assumed by a major American writer, the nature of Marquand's official war work has never been publicly known. The reason, of course, is that biological warfare was the most hush-hush area of our military preparation. The use of germs as weapons had been outlawed by the Geneva Protocol of 1925, although all belligerent nations in 1942 were seriously contemplating such use as well as the defenses that could be mustered against it. As early as 1940, Army intelligence reports had suggested that the Axis was already engaged in the preparation of biological agents as a secret weapon, and in the fall of 1941 Secretary Stimson, with the help of the National Academy of Sciences, convoked a panel of leading bacteriologists to investigate the possibilities of using disease germs against men, animals and plants. The panel reported that such weaponry could be developed and also that defensive techniques were rudimentary. When the unit for development in this field was organized, it was so secret that it was not even designated as a War Department project but placed under the administration of the Federal Security Agency, and a civilian, Merck, was put in charge instead of an Army officer. As Marquand later would remark, "The armed services characteristically did not want to be held responsible for any such dirty business as spreading disease germs and toxic poisons, but at the same time they would informally render every aid and assistance." The unit's advisory committee of scientists was known cryptically as the ABC, and then as the DEF, committee.

Marquand went to work with Merck and the committee at the end of the summer of 1942, and it was he who suggested the unit's innocuous official name, the War Research Service. As the director of intelligence in this "strange and starry-eyed effort," Marquand was immediately occupied with collecting information from all branches of the armed services and from the FBI and the OSS concerning evidence of German and Japanese use of biological killers. As in all high-secrecy procedures, this investigation had its comic aspects. "For many months I found myself chatting in sound-proof rooms in guarded buildings about all sorts of things which nice people avoided discussing." After intensive screening he was admitted, he found, to an "antiseptic little club" of individuals at the highest levels who were able to talk freely about such subjects with one another. And he discovered that "I was a repository, but there were no secrets. The truth was that nobody knew anything about biological warfare." It was so secret in fact that it was extremely difficult for the information officer to find out anything.

In November 1942, the Service's activities had begun in earnest with its request to the chemical warfare branch of the Army that a major installation be created for research, and in April 1943 construction of the mysterious Camp Detrick began at an Army airfield outside of Frederick, Maryland. There, behind heavily guarded fences, several hundred scientists and their assistants would work on ways of propagating as well as suppressing the agents of such human diseases as cholera, tularemia, anthrax, brucellosis, yellow fever, bubonic plague and pneumonic plague. They would also investigate in their laboratories the use and control of such diseases of domestic animals as rinderpest, foot-and-mouth disease, the Newcastle disease and various rusts, blights and plant inhibitors that could be used against crops. Marquand, who went back and forth frequently between his office in the Academy of Sciences Building on Constitution Avenue in Washington and Camp Detrick, recalled vividly the impression made on him by the new installation: "There were, of course, other secret camps around the capital, among them the camp for the education of code experts and camps installed by the Office of Strategic Services for the moral, physical and mental education of saboteurs and agents behind the lines, but I doubt whether any of these were either as grim in their implications or in parts as hospitably comfortable as our own pet installation. This consisted of a large acreage outside a pretty Maryland market town not far from the meadows rich with corn that Whittier described in 'Barbara Fritchie.' The entire area was surrounded by impassable riot fences, guarded by watchtowers and searchlights, and the interior area was again divided by other guarded zones open only to authorized personnel. No one was admitted, in the services or in civilian life, whose past and present had not been exhaustively checked by security offices, and no visitor was allowed to walk alone even in the more innocuous areas. Furthermore, the habits of personnel stopping at the nearby town and the townspeople themselves were unobtrusively checked by visiting agents of the F.B.I."

Inside, he had been surprised, somehow, to find that the post had exceptionally attractive facilities, particularly a commodious club with a bar. "It had to be a good club because many people working there stayed for long periods without stepping outside the pearly gates." Standing on the club steps Marquand often looked with a certain awe at the laboratories and animal buildings, each with a separate crew of day and night guards where the experiments on viruses and rickettsia were taking place. Once he even went into the precincts of the typhus project, dressed in an entire suit of special clothing that had been handed to him outside along with a respirator and gloves. He also visited an old airplane hangar which had been remodeled to house projects that had passed the test-tube stage and were ready for the pilot-plant stage. "Here were more guards and decontamination chambers, huge air compressors, and honeycombs of little rooms and laboratories opening out to huge walled rooms filled with valves and vats and tanks." It was a relief to him to leave this building, to be cleaned and cleared, and to return to the fine club to discuss with the scientists the work being done.

They were preoccupied in a perfectly abstract fashion, he found, with a satanic dream—the mass production of a long-lived virus, capable of maintaining its virulence when distributed from the air over a population center. The virus would create a disease that would spread like the historic plagues of old. Typhus and encephalitis were the favorite candidates for this possibility, but the technical problems were as yet prohibitive. On the other hand, it was already possible that spores of anthrax, a gray powder that could be dropped in quantity in spring bombs or sprayed from the air, could do a devastating job. But its use was not practicable for a conqueror who expected to occupy the conquered territory since the spores could survive in the ground for forty or fifty years. Another available agent was botulinus toxin, which could be stored in the form of a dry, rustlike powder; absorbed through the mouth or lungs in very minute quantities it was deadly. Marquand heard one of the scientists say that one pinch of it tossed from his thumbnail within the room in which they were sitting would kill everyone within its four walls (this might have been Dr. Carl Lamanna, who later published the estimate that the killing dose of the toxin for a 165-pound man was .15 gamma—a gamma being a millionth of a gram). The whole spectacle of Camp Detrick was curious and horrifying at the same time. Nothing, perhaps, was stranger, Marquand thought, than the scientists themselves—pleasant, friendly people intensely interested in their work, not obsessed at all with a vision of its effects—though of course they were intelligent men who understood what the diseases were like and how effectively they could torture and destroy human beings. "Disease to them was a delightfully impersonal subject. They were pleased at the fine opportunities offered them to experiment with disease and viruses in an atmosphere where no expense was spared and there was priority one for everything."

Marquand himself found a certain, hardly admissible satisfaction in his visits to Detrick. It was like the compensation he had seen for Johnny in assignment to a Caribbean Army post. At Detrick, also, the danger of infection by dreadful diseases, even for an occasional visitor like himself, gave him the sensation of being a little closer to the fighting front—for there had been instances, one heard, of brucellosis, tularemia and psittacosis contracted by persons who had merely walked past a container of virulent culture.

But where he really was, a good deal of the time, was wartime Washington, a place exceeding Hollywood for improbability yet one where the most important matters in the world were being decided every moment. He grew to know the offices of the men who wielded the power that directed the war from a long way off—the civilian government chiefs and the generals. In the winter of 1942 he was down in Washington for two or three days of every week and though he felt that he was not, personally, accomplishing much, he was impressed by "the terrific activity and the drive and the waste of energy" all around him. Miraculously, despite the enormous amount of superfluous motion, the most complicated operations in military history were being organized and directed there. The entire North African expedition, as he gathered, had been planned in Washington, and over a thousand persons had known what was going on. Marquand himself found out about it almost six weeks before the expedition sailed. He had been having lunch with two Army officers and the editor of the New York *Herald Tribune* and had idly remarked that the only way to win the war was to get control of the Mediterranean by an invasion of North Africa—and had seen the faces of the officers freeze as he rattled on.

There were other astonishing moments during the many lunches he had with high officials, one of whom was Harvey Bundy, special assistant to the secretary of war. Marquand wrote: "Mr. Bundy has a large office right next to Mr. Stimson's and a green light flashes upon the wall whenever Mr. Stimson leaves his desk, even, I presume, to go to the bathroom. Mr. Bundy has three secretaries, only four less than Julius Caesar kept busy, and there are maps and maps and maps and every time he presses the button, in comes a Major General." But then they went to lunch. As they sat down in a small paneled dining room across the hall and a mess sergeant inquired in a whisper whether he would like the clear consommé or cream of asparagus soup, Marquand's eyes encountered great figures: "There was, for example, Mr. Stimson, and my old acquaintance Robert Lovett, now Secretary for Air. General Marshall was toying with a second cup of coffee and General Hap Arnold was eating his chipped beef, and there was General Surles, and lots of other generals I should have known but didn't. By far the most remarkable of all these generals, however, and at whom everyone stared, was General Kenney, who had commanded the bombing and fighting planes which had completely wiped out the big Jap convoy in the Bismarck Sea. It shows what a small place the world is now to think that General Kenney should have been right there in the dining room when it seems to me that the Bismarck battle did not occur very much earlier than the day before yesterday."

Of course, like everyone, Marquand groused about the minor but multitudinous discomforts of wartime. At the Mayflower, where he put up regularly during his days in Washington, everything was changed for the worse. The hotel, he wrote Johnny in April 1943, "now smells very distinctly because they are never able to air it out or thoroughly clean it since it is always jammed full of guests at every hour of the day or night. The elevator boys are now all gentlemen of over seventy and upwards and so are the bellhops and so are the waiters, except for the girls in the Coffee Shop." Still, he went down to the capital regularly on the train, which would be two hours late getting back to New York and crowded with servicemen, and it was impossible to get anything to eat before nine o'clock and then the food was lousy. In New York rationing was now a fact of life. "Meat," he observed to Johnny, "is almost an unknown quantity and the one useful thing your little brother has done for me is to produce a ration card of his own with points for shoes, coffee, and everything, none of which, thank heavens, he consumes as yet." Going out to dinner was not what it had once been—the martini at Longchamps was so nauseating that the taste lingered in his mouth for a day, he declared, grieving particularly at the degeneration of his favorite drink.

Yet by the summer of 1943 he felt a craving to get a closer view of the war than this. In June he suggested to the War Department that he might be useful if he got a chance to gather impressions of the fighting. "I asked them why they sent a lot of newspaper punks overseas instead of a real novelist who could do an artistic job for them. I said you didn't need to be in a fox hole being shot at, but if you were somewhere behind the lines with a chance to talk to the boys you could do all sorts of stuff about the war." He also approached the State Department and said, "On the basis of my China experience how about sending me to Chungking?" But it was impossible for him to consider taking off for long from his work for the War Research Service. And it was this work that produced just then the opportunity he wanted, after all. As a result of his reports concerning the inadequacy of front-line information about biological warfare, he was sent on a tour of some of the principal world theaters.

As he later recalled with amazement, "I was placed upon a plane, hanging on to the coattails of a general from the Surgeon General's Office with a priority that could bump off anyone except the President, the Secretaries of War and the Navy, and General Marshall and Admiral King." The general to whom he was attached was James S. Simmons, a former dean of the Harvard School of Public Health and an expert on tropical diseases. Simmons was surveying the disease potential at a number of points, including French Morocco, Algeria, Tunisia, Sicily, Egypt, Iraq, Iran, Palestine, India, West Africa, Brazil and the Caribbean. Marquand did not get back until October 25. He had enjoyed an extraordinary renewal of his taste for travel to faraway parts of the world, but on a basis of momentous urgency that gave an odd perspective to everything in ancient and primitive lands that had not changed for a thousand years. As they bounced from place to place the only constants were the aluminum bucket seats in the aircraft in which they moved, and the Army airfields where "machine shops, plumbing, air conditioning, outdoor movies, ping-pong tables, boxing rings, *Time*, *Newsweek*, the weekly comics, Pocket Books, Gillette razors, Williams' Aqua Velva, Rheingold beer, Johnson's baby powder, Spam and Planter's Peanuts, all followed our army into the war for the edification of dark-skinned men in G-strings and for the shocked amazement of the French and the British." The meals, when they touched down, consisted, whether breakfast or lunch, of pineapple juice, powdered eggs, Spam, canned pineapple, and coffee. General Simmons was chiefly interested in the observation of disease conditions in the places they visited but Marquand was occasionally able to get him to linger here or there for touristic reasons—and together they gaped at the Taj Mahal or visited bazaars where the general invariably bought a piece of brassware or a tablecloth to take home.

Perhaps the most remarkable episode of the trip, as far as Marquand was concerned, was his meeting with General George Patton immediately after the successful Allied invasion of Sicily. Marquand arrived with Simmons in Algiers on September 1, and some days later, coming down into the lobby of the Hotel Aletti, he had run into his Harvard classmate Charlie Codman, who was wearing a lieutenant colonel's silver leaf on his shoulder and the ribbon of the Legion of Honor. Codman, it turned out, was General Patton's aide-de-camp, and he was in Algiers at the moment on an important mission—he was trying to hunt down a hundred cases of whiskey the general wished to present as a gesture of his satisfaction to the officers of the Seventh Army. Marquand spent the day with his old friend helping him look for the whiskey, driving about in his own general's car. They talked about Patton.

Codman could not have been more different from Old Blood and Guts. He was a Boston aristocrat, a sort of Pulham, of refined manners and delicate scruples. With income drawn from family interests in real estate he had cultivated his tastes for gracious living and for travel during the period between the wars by becoming an expert on foods and wines. When World War II started he was wine consultant to the old Boston fancy-grocery firm of S. S. Pierce. He had been assigned to Patton's staff after the French surrender at Casablanca because of his perfect command of French and his familiarity with the French army.

His life with Patton had been an education. He had found himself a member of a trio which included also the general's chief of staff—a West Pointer who distrusted the morals of anyone who spoke with a broad *a*—and a simpleminded second aide whom, according to Codman, the general kept "in case he wants a trigger man" (the aide carried two guns in shoulder holsters at all times). Codman was constantly at work doing errands for Patton and his subordinate generals. "I know everything about generals," he told Marquand. "All my life is spent bringing them drinks and pocket handkerchiefs." It was hard working for generals, he observed, because they always wanted everything on the double, even the impossible. Patton would have no idea, for example, of how much the hundred cases of whiskey weighed and no idea that they couldn't be carried on the plane he had assigned to Codman—but he would be very angry if Codman did not manage somehow to lay his hands on another plane and get the whiskey right up to Palermo.

Two days later General Simmons and Marquand took off in a C-47 transport with bucket seats, changed planes at Bizerte, and sat on bucket seats again until they arrived at the Palermo airport. They drove along the coast road and came into the old city, whose waterfront was a shambles of sunken ships and rubble but otherwise much as Marquand remembered it from his visit in 1921—the year when he was courting Christina—full of ornate baroque buildings, the streets at midday silent and hot. Patton's troops were to be seen here and there, all very neatly uniformed in winter wool with the sleeves rolled down, prepared, by the general's command, for instant amphibious action.

The general's headquarters were in the Palazzo Reale, an immense palace whose central portions went back to the twelfth century. In a stateroom with crystal chandeliers they were finally ushered into the general's presence. He sat behind a rosewood desk on which lay the two famous pearl-handled revolvers and the steel helmet with three stars denoting his rank painted on it. Marquand noticed that his eyes under the sandy lashes were slate blue, and as he smiled, his lean, freckled face crinkled and his teeth between his thin lips were even and white. General Simmons said politely that they had just wanted to pay their respects. "Hell," said Patton with energy, "sit down. You know what's happened to me now. I've just had my ears pinned back. All they do is to pin my ears back. You know what they've pinned them back for? It seems I haven't given the Italian prisoners enough latrines. God damn it, they didn't know what a latrine was until I built one for them."

That afternoon Simmons and Marquand got a chance to see the rest of the palace. Behind the cloister off the courtyard there was the royal chapel, the Cappella Palatina, with its mosaics that had been described in Marquand's Baedeker. A huge marble staircase led to the royal apartment, and in a private reception room that had been used by kings, Patton and a large group of high-ranking officers were gathered around the fireplace, less important officers at the end of the room; a long table was covered with bottles and glasses. Marquand, the only civilian present, was acutely aware that his clothing was not *comme il faut*. "I had been riding on bucket seats so long that I had finally purchased an officer's khaki pants and shirt, but I had not thought to buy a necktie. The rest of my costume consisted of a greasy gray felt hat and tennis shoes." Contemplating him from the fireplace group were all the important brass of the Seventh Army—one-star and two-star generals, and several colonels, and, of course, Patton, immaculate in his unregulation tailored uniform and shining boots.

Dinner was served in the royal dining room. The generals filed in and seated themselves according to rank at one table, the entourage at another. They ate clear soup, steak, salad and ice cream off the royal china and used the royal silver. As Codman had previously described, they talked and laughed very carefully according to rank. (Codman had told Marquand: "Two-star generals laugh at three-star generals' jokes and if a four-star general says anything amusing, everyone rolls on the floor.") Then the two groups returned to the apartment of kings, where Codman passed out liqueurs and cigars and the generals occupied all the available chairs while the other officers stood against the wall. As he had done previously, Marquand tried to join the inferior group, but Patton, who had made him sit with the generals at dinner, cried out, "No, no, God damn it, come over here. Get him a chair. I want to talk with you about the war."

The general asked what he thought of the war from the account he had read in the newspapers and Marquand told him: "I had gathered the impression from the speed of the American advances across the island that the Americans had been engaged principally with disaffected Italian troops and that the British had met the real opposition around Catania." The general's response to this praise of his rival Montgomery and lack of recognition for his own achievements was startling; a sore spot had been struck. "God damn it," he said, "you can see what we were up against on the way to Messina. Where's Codman? Get four cub planes tomorrow morning and take this party up the line toward Messina. Have them met and take them inland. I'll tell you why we moved and why the British didn't. We fought them day and night and hit them on the flank. All the British know is artillery preparation and frontal attack and that's why they stopped at Catania. This is a damn fine war," he ended almost with a sob. "I hope to God I get killed up front somewhere. This is a damn fine war."

And then the general went on in a sort of personal expatiation while the other generals and the rest of the officers in the room listened respectfully. He said things like "There is only one thing a leader of an army is good for, to be everywhere at once, to look troops over and know how much they can take." Or, "We've got the best God-damned army in the world. You give me any thousand Americans and put them against any thousand Germans and we'll lick them anywhere." Or, "All this God-damn tripe about the four freedoms! Why don't they understand what makes troops fight? By God! They fight for just three reasons: to make an impression back home, particularly on their best girls, and because of their outfit, and because of their officers. Every officer has got to inspire hero worship. God damn it, they've got to love their officers." At this point Marquand somewhat tactlessly interrupted with the observation that the troops didn't always love their officers. "No," said the general, "but they love them when they're fighting, or else the officers aren't worth a damn. They even love me, by God, when I'm in the front lines." Why, there was that time in front of Troina when they said the road was mined. "I got so damned emotional that I drove the car right over it." And then he burst out again: "I don't give a damn who the man is. He can be a nigger or a Jew, but if he has the stuff and does his duty, he can have everything I've got. By God! I love him. You've got to love them. You've got to be proud of them. You've got to give them loyalty when they give you loyalty."

It was altogether an unforgettable performance. Two days later, just after the Italian armistice, Marquand saw Patton again and he was still talking about loyalty. He waved at a pile of letters he was signing on his rosewood desk, letters of thanks to individual soldiers whom he had noticed. But who ever noticed *him* that way? When did he ever get a letter of thanks from someone still higher up? "I only get my ears pinned back by some little squirt from the Inspector General's office." It did not occur to Marquand to wonder particularly at the general's tone, both defensive and belligerent. Patton's state of nerves was, of course, explicable if one knew, as Marquand did not, that he was then at the moment of greatest crisis in his career. Only days before, on August 3 and then again on August 10, he had slapped and insulted hospitalized soldiers whom he considered cowards and malingerers because they were not visibly injured. Although on the seventeenth he had entered Messina in triumph, a detailed report of one of the slapping incidents reached Eisenhower that same day and in a personal letter to Patton he ordered the general to apologize to the patient he had abused by his "despicable" conduct, and to the doctors and nurses and other patients who had been present and to the Seventh Army as a whole. The entire press camp had buzzed with the scandal and only suppressed the story under the plea from Eisenhower that Patton was too essential to the winning of the war to be sacrificed to the fury of public reaction. On August 22 Patton had carried out the ceremony of apology in the grand Spanzadi Ruggero, the opulent stateroom of the Norman ruler Roger II; against the glittering background of its mosaic walls depicting hunting scenes in gold and colored tiles, groups from the two hospitals were brought up to the general to hear him make his apology. Then he retired for a couple of weeks behind the gates of the palace. It was during this interval that Marquand had visited him, unaware of the secret that was to become worldwide knowledge when Drew Pearson broke the story on November 21—after which the storm of public reaction nearly led to Patton's removal.

Marquand saw Patton only once again, when he watched the general's car roll down one of the main streets of Palermo. Across the radiator of the olive-drab vehicle, a red flag with his three stars was draped, and also an American flag, and on the front seat beside the chauffeur were two orderlies dressed in winter wool and wearing helmets although the day was hot, each holding a Garand rifle at the ready. The general sat staring straight ahead of him "like Washington crossing the Delaware," Marquand said to himself. "He had," this witness reflected afterwards, "a sentimental streak. He wanted his men to admire him as much as he admired himself. And furthermore, God damn it, he wanted to be loved!" The following spring, when Patton was in England to take part in the invasion of the Continent, there were pictures of him in the newspapers and Marquand noticed once again the combination of showmanship and vanity that was a functional part, it had to be admitted, of a commander's personality. In the news photos he looked, Marquand thought, "more like a polo player than a general." He was wearing the three-starred helmet and "something which looked like a monkey or mess jacket" and "circular, elaborate britches only the best Bond Street tailor could possibly have created, and high riding boots that fitted his symmetrical calves to absolute perfection, and even in that dingy photograph, it was obvious that his orderly had sat up all night to give those boots the hand-polished lustre of a Steinway piano." By this time Marquand, along with everyone else, knew the story of the slappings, and he would summarize his impression of Patton harshly: "a tactless, high-strung, profane officer with a one-cell juvenile mind. No one has been able to teach him the amenities and now it appears he is at it again."

For though Patton did not go on slapping shell-shocked soldiers he would make speeches like the one he had just delivered at the opening of a United Kingdom service club in London: "The only welcoming I've done for some time has been welcoming Germans and Italians into hell. I've got about 177,000 there." He approved of the service clubs because "the sooner our soldiers write home and say how lovely the English ladies are, the sooner the American dames will get jealous and force the war to a successful conclusion, and then I shall have a chance to go and kill Japanese." Still,

Marquand had to admit, such talk probably would sound well at the front where "they don't think much about ideology or the world of tomorrow." Patton would be with the troops on the beach, "where no one cares much about tact or clean language or democracy." And Marquand was held—repelled but fascinated—by the mystery of military command.

The other experience of the journey with Simmons that impressed itself deeply on Marquand's memory was the stop, on the flight home over the Atlantic, at Ascension Island. Simmons and Marquand had, by then, seen a lifetime's worth of spectacles. They regretted missing only one—flying the Hump to Chungking—but they had been balked by windstorms over the valley of Assam. Calcutta, where they lingered, was then suffering from a severe famine. The general was exasperated with the irrationality of the Hindu religion, which prevented its adherents from eating the hundred thousand sacred cows that were supposed to be in the city. The river was full of human corpses and the trees of vultures and there wasn't enough firewood at the burning ghats to burn up the dead. When the weather over Assam was still bad the third time they went to the Dumdum airport, the general said: "That tears it. We'll get the hell out of here. We'll take the Karachi plane."

So, once again they were in the bucket seats of a C-47 flying across the subcontinent. At Karachi there was a plane for Khartoum in which, for the first time since they had crossed the Atlantic, there were actually fine reclining seats like those in a commercial passenger airplane. At Khartoum, Marquand wanted to get a ride into Central Africa, where they could see lions and giraffes on the range, but the general said the only lions he wanted to see were the lions in the zoo in New York. So they were up and on, over plains and rivers and jungles and Lake Chad until they reached Accra on the west coast. There they spent a day and visited the bazaars, and the general, with a last clutch at the world behind them, fell in love with a coffee table in the shape of a mahogany elephant which weighed about a hundred and fifty pounds. He would have sent it to the plane if Marquand had not dissuaded him.

But now, ahead of them until they got to Natal on the bulge of Brazil was nothing but trackless ocean except, after ten hours, Ascension Island. First, they saw only clouds hovering over a small land mass, and then, suddenly, the whole island, its single peak, faintly green, rising out of black lava and pumice rocks and a ring of surf. The plane came down onto a field cut out of black rock that looked, Marquand thought, like the portals to Dante's hell, "a gash in a region of volcanic desolation as cheerless as the surface of the moon." The field resembled all the other American military airfields they had landed on, and the lieutenant colonel who greeted them—he had been a football hero at West Point—was familiar. But for the first time in weeks Marquand felt relaxed. All about them, even in the dust-free air, there was a benignant emptiness: "no starving natives worshipping strange gods, no danger of air attack, no poisonous snakes, no bloodsucking leeches, no Baghdad boils, dysentery or cholera, no sand flies or malarial mosquitoes, not even a poisonous plant, nothing but weirdly shaped lava rocks and pumice stone and the sea." Marquand felt that everything they had seen of the war in Europe and everything in Asia and Africa where men still lived contentious, afflicted lives had been left behind, and for an interval they were standing "in the innocent beginnings of creation."

Most visitors to Ascension Island stayed at the field while the planes were being gassed, but the general and Marquand, with their top priorities, rated a little more, and they were taken for a jeep ride to the top of the mountain at the general's request. As they went up, the lieutenant colonel recited some of Ascension's history—how it had been discovered on the day of the Feast of the Ascension by a Portuguese vessel in the sixteenth century. It was, of course, uninhabited, for there was no water except the rainfall that now and then burst out of the clouds that snagged on the mountain, and no European had wanted to live there until the British took it over two centuries later; a few homesick English families and their servants stayed when it became a station of the South Atlantic cable. These settlers had tried to soften its stony austerity by planting every kind of seed where something might take root—and the mountain was curiously decorated with small stunted groves of firs or eucalyptus; on one slope wisteria had prospered beyond all expectation and grown like a weed. The jeep passed through a belt of lush green growth, the region where the rain from the passing clouds fell, and then, suddenly, at the top, they reached a kind of moor where some sheep grazed. On a neat lawn stood the house of the British governor and nearby a radar tower. Ascension was a queer place, the lieutenant colonel said. They had only been able to get a little water by piping to the springs on the mountain, and the rest had to be distilled from the sea. Then there were the rats, brought long ago by some visiting vessel, which had multiplied in the absence of predators until they populated the honeycombed volcanic cliffs of the island in enormous numbers. The seabirds would come back to their nests at nightfall in overwhelming numbers, too, sometimes obstructing a pilot's vision and stalling the engine with their bodies.

When they returned to the field they met the commanding officer, a full colonel with the only waxed mustache Marquand had seen on the entire journey, who told them that the installation was about to get a real treat: Frederic March had landed with a USO show. After watching it a few minutes, Marquand walked out into the night over Ascension. A breeze was blowing in the clear air and the sky was blacker than he ever remembered having seen it among the familiar constellations. He had, again, the sensation of being somewhere out in space. Later on, he found that he could not fix his mind on Ascension Island. When, finally, Simmons and he sat drinking Scotch at the American base near Belem in Brazil, the last stop before

Miami, they talked about the places they had seen—"of Iceland and London, of the English country inn where the waiter explained to us that hare was game but rabbit was vermin, of the Arabs in Tunis, of the German raid at Bizerte, of the Jews in Jerusalem, of the heat at Basra and of the Indian Untouchables." Marquand tried to remember Ascension. "They ought to be able to control those flies in the governor's hogpen," the general said. And then in a moment they forgot it.

Marquand experienced a feeling of letdown on his return to New York and Washington. Other writers he knew were getting assignments as war correspondents and visiting the various fronts for continuous stretches. "Kipper" (Christopher) La Farge had been on such a trip in the spring—he had flown to New Caledonia, gone out on a shakedown cruise, and was writing a series of stories as a result. Marquand found a letter waiting for him at Beekman Place from Frederick Lewis Allen, editor of *Harper's Magazine*, who proposed to send him as a correspondent to the Pacific, where military action would soon be stepping up. He could be accredited by the Navy for a three-month tour of duty. The offer was tempting, and Marquand held off until December before regretfully turning it down, hoping that somehow he would find a way of accepting it without deserting his responsibilities at the War Research Service. The Washington job had after all given him the long trip with Simmons and it would be poor grace to drop it now. As he summarized to Carl Brandt: "It is a difficult, tedious task, trying to cooperate with government bureaus, particularly the Army. Still, they gave me a swell trip in an airplane and George Merck is one of my oldest friends and he seems to be very dependent upon me at the present time. Also the sheer element of patriotism enters into it. Therefore, I think I had better stay with it for this winter at least." But he was definitely fed up with shuttling back and forth on the train, particularly in cold weather, and he had got so that he would "wince from a conditioned reflex every time I check in at the Mayflower." There was nothing for it but to move the whole family down to Washington for the winter. In February, Adelaide, the babies, the various housemaids and nursemaids, were in a house at 1902 R Street. Still, he was getting tired. In March he was in the Walter Reed Hospital with gravel in his kidneys. He was the only civilian patient, and he talked a good deal while he was there to many of the soldiers from the various fronts, and felt, more than ever, a desire to be where they had been. As he wrote Helen Howe, "After this tour of duty I hope to see my job so well established that I can hand it over to some nice red-cheeked little boy, and let it run itself."

That spring, however, the situation of the biological warfare agency altered completely. As the massive Allied invasion of Europe was being prepared, the Joint Chiefs began to take apprehensive account of some of the intelligence that Marquand's office had accumulated. There were reliable reports now that the Germans were about to use certain deadly poisons in their guided cross-channel missiles. The War Department decided that the time for diffidence was over. Biological warfare was put directly into the hands of the Chemical Warfare Service in June 1944, days before the invasion. The civilian officers of the old WRS were invited to put on uniforms, but both Merck and Marquand declined. Merck was made special consultant for biological warfare to the secretary of war, instead, and continued actively as chairman of the United States Biological Warfare Committee, which advised the secretary on policy matters. But Marquand, who was also named special consultant to the secretary, was freed from the burden of regular duties: his function as intelligence chief was absorbed by the Army command. He continued to assist Merck until the end of the war in the preparation of major reports on biological warfare, particularly the historic report, released on January 3, 1946, which first divulged publicly some of the biological warfare story.

The public relations problem involved in "declassifying" the subject of biological warfare was, of course, of the greatest touchiness. Merck and the War Department people had first wanted to admit publicly only to our defensive efforts, but Marquand had advised that there would be an inescapable implication that offensive preparation had also been made—and to conceal the latter would be obvious prevarication. If the story were to be told it would have to be told more frankly. The Merck report, while reviewing the intelligence on Japanese and German biological warfare plans, released the basic facts concerning the large-scale weapons development the United States had conducted at Camp Detrick and other projects. The report's admission was still somewhat evasively put: "While the main object in all these endeavors was to develop methods for defending ourselves against all possible enemy use of biological warfare agents, it was necessary to investigate offensive possibilities in order to learn what measures could be used for defense." Still, Marquand's advice had been heeded.

In July 1944 he was arranging to go to the Pacific. The Navy Office of Public Relations, which had been corresponding with *Harper's* for months over the matter, was delighted to have caught the big fish at last. Walter Karig, commander of the book and magazine section of the OPR (who had once, under the pseudonym of Carolyn Keene, written the Nancy Drew books for girls) sent his appreciative compliments to the *Harper's* editor in the form of a drawing of a fisherman walking up a beach tugging at an enormous fish with a little typewriter attached to its tail. The fish was labeled Marquand and the fisherman was editor Allen, and ahead of him, waiting with outspread arms, was a tiny, grinning person, Commander Karig. But Marquand was himself pleased to have the chance to look at the Pacific war theater, which he had failed to reach on his previous trip. *Harper's* was advancing him $1,000 for expenses and paying him a retainer of $250 a month, while the Navy was charging him a dollar a day for all living costs and transportation. The magazine would pay ten cents a word for the writing he would produce—the editors expected about ten thousand words.

He did not, as it turned out, leave for Pearl Harbor and the waters beyond until January 1945, for he found himself occupied all that fall working with George S. Kaufman on the play version of *The Late George Apley* and seeing it through rehearsals and tryouts until it opened in New York. When he crossed to the Coast by train the country was locked in blizzard weather and the train was ten hours late getting to Sacramento. But immediately, at San Francisco, he was in the Navy's tender care, and, as he had found when traveling on a general's priority with Simmons, nothing was too good for a VIP in wartime. The attention he received at the hands of the Navy was to be augmented, part of the way during this trip, by the fact that he was a member of a celebrity junket that included Gene Tunney and other noted persons. The Navy behaved towards them very much as the porters, taxi drivers, hotel clerks and other civilian functionaries had done when he and Tunney were together at the outset in San Francisco. "Traveling with him is wonderful," Marquand had reported home. "They all want to carry our bags and he gets lots of priority." As Marquand would later recall, "Those were the days for a Navy correspondent! Did you want a date with a base hospital nurse? Did you want to see natives in raffia skirts? Did you want to visit the interior of New Guinea, take a trip to Australia by air or by submarine, or have a friendly chat with an admiral who had other things to do? Did you want to go with a troop of marines who were flushing out Japs in the back country jungle? Did you by any chance want a drink? It was retailing for five cents a jigger at the officers club and when the bar was not open you always had your private supply beneath your bunk. Did you want a rescued flyer to tell you what it felt to be ten days on a raft? Public Relations would be glad to arrange for private, exclusive conversations. Or would you like a marine combat knife to open your beer cans with, a new pair of shoes, a combat overall, a flying jacket or maybe a Japanese Samurai sword? No wonder the Navy made friends and influenced people."

Certainly Marquand did not take advantage of all these opportunities, but, on the record, he did enjoy a number of them. The Navy "flying boat" Mars, then the biggest airplane in the world, brought him to Honolulu, where he and Tunney were installed in the Moana Hotel in a room on Waikiki Beach. The city was jammed by a streaming population of servicemen moving in and out of the Pacific war zone, everyone of them trying hard to have a good time at the end or the beginning of something, to have a good drunk and get photographed, at the least, with a hula girl who obligingly smiled and threw her arms around his neck while the picture was taken. For Marquand, on a more privileged level, entertainment was also available. He wrote Adelaide: "I've seen a lot of gold braid and really been having a time. The public relations boys have taken a lot of care of me—almost too much."

As he had had an interview with Patton, so he now got a chance to sit chatting one afternoon with Chester Nimitz. The admiral was about to leave for his headquarters on Guam, but when Marquand found him in his office he was conning a little dictionary of Hawaiian expressions. "Do you know what *poopooli* means?" Nimitz had asked him. And answered his own question, "It means crazy." He continued, "*Hoomalimili* means roughly to kid someone along," and so on. When Marquand left the presence of the great naval strategist, he found in the anteroom Major General Kirk, surgeon general, U.S. Army, who was waiting with the quartermaster general of the Army and a number of lesser generals. Kirk, whom Marquand had known in Washington, asked him what he had been doing in there with Nimitz. "I told him he was teaching me Hawaiian words," Marquand recalled. The waiting generals were baffled but Marquand understood the effect that, even in wartime, Hawaii was having on the admiral. He remembered how its white society loved to sprinkle its conversation with native words—it marked the difference between the newcomers or *malihinis* and themselves, the oldtimers, *kamaainas.* In the story "Lunch at Honolulu," which Marquand wrote immediately upon his return from this trip, an Admiral Smedley is seen visiting one of these *kamaainas*, and is heard to remark, "In my spare time I've been making a little study of the Polynesians. I've got a dictionary of Hawaiian words. . . . Do you know the word for 'cat'?"

While he was in Honolulu the Navy did arrange for him to get, also, the "first-hand story" of the rescue of men from three sunken destroyers by the crew of the *Tabberer*, which had accidentally spotted them floating in their kapok jackets in the midst of a storm. The press conference probably took a form very much like that Marquand used for the scene near the opening of *Repent in Haste* in which a Marquand-like correspondent, William Briggs, first meets Lieutenant Boyden; Boyden, a Navy pilot, has just been found floating with his crew on a rubber raft. Briggs listens to the men spell out their names and addresses and tell their story into the recorder microphone—as Marquand had that day in Honolulu. Briggs "wondered at the time whether it might not all have been different if that interview had not been so artificially contrived." But no amount of PR contrivance could obscure the reality of the men's experience, after all. "I know a bit more about the war than I've ever known before," Marquand wrote Adelaide from Honolulu.

He already perceived that Honolulu was America's war city, a city which like Berlin or Paris or London had felt the impact of enemy bombs and been engulfed by the tidal wave of fighting armies in their transit, a city which would never be the same afterwards. He could not help taking note of the alterations that the war had brought to the Honolulu he remembered from his 1931 visit with Christina and the children. The war had not only swamped the streets with uniforms so that it was nearly impossible to walk except at a snail's pace. All the hotels, once caravansaries for rich vacationing Americans, were now filled up with Navy men; they were four in a room at the Moana. Sailors had cleaned out the shops, looking for souvenirs and paying whatever was asked. Boys from the submarines were watching boxing matches at the Royal Hawaiian Hotel, and the palazzo of Doris Duke on Diamond Head was an Army officers' club. The road from Honolulu to Pearl Harbor was the busiest highway on American soil, gorged with tanks and self-propelled guns, buses with Navy Yard workers, and soldiers and sailors on pass. Steam shovels were frantically at work widening it, though the added inches would make little difference in accommodating the flow. The fields of sugar cane that he remembered on either side of the road had been replaced by camps, hospitals, supply dumps. There were new airfields everywhere on Oahu, crowded with planes being readied for carriers, and there were amphibious- and jungle-warfare schools, rest camps and embarkation camps. When Marquand described the scene later that year for his Newburyport friends, he concluded: "The only peace that occurs in Honolulu is the ten o'clock curfew when all unauthorized Army or Navy personnel are arrested if they are caught out on the streets. This peace, however, does not extend indoors. Though the bars are open only for limited periods and though the liquor they dispense is also limited, you can still get a bottle to take to your hotel room or to the house of a friend, if your friend has a house. There is always someone who is just going to the Pacific or someone who is just back. There is still ice in the Moana Hotel."

Hawaii was in the middle of a boom that fed upon this extravagance and chaos caused by the war. Marquand's civilian friends described how at first, after Pearl Harbor, there had been panic: it was clear that the Japanese could have seized the islands; for months the United States did not have the force to stop them, though pillboxes and barbed wire were set up along the shoreline. People began to prepare for living under Japanese rule or else getting out. Real estate was going for a song, mostly to Chinese businessmen who bought up some of the largest estates. Then the Battle of Midway turned the tide, and if, like the Chinese merchants, you had had faith in America, you were rich. Marquand went out to Kahala Beach to take a look at the house he had occupied with Christina and Johnny and Tina. He wrote Johnny: "The coral reef off the beach was still covered with barbed wire. Everyone says the Japs could have taken the island any time they wanted after the Pearl Harbor strike. It is different now. Real estate is sky high and that place of ours recently sold for $125,000. I wish I had bought it back in 1931 and maybe I wouldn't be worried so much about finances."

On February 11 Marquand left Hawaii on a trip that took him into the

Central Pacific past Wake and the Marshalls, with a stop at Kwajalein, to the Marianas. He arrived at Guam in the company of Tunney and the newspaper publisher Roy Howard, thereby creating a dilemma for the Navy public relations staff on the island. Which one of these VIP's was to be given the only extra bed currently available in Admiral Nimitz's quarters? William Brinkley later recalled his conversation with his fellow officers. Perhaps the bed should go to Tunney since he was the biggest, but what if Marquand was offended and wouldn't write that "favorable Navy novel"? If Howard felt slighted wouldn't it have dire effects upon the handling of Navy news in his chain of papers? They finally decided that the bed should go to Howard, whose power to express his resentment seemed capable of finding most immediate expression, and Marquand and Tunney were provided with the most comfortable nonadmiral beds the station could offer. Guam was the Pacific theater headquarters, and impressions of this post were later to appear in the pages of *B. F.'s Daughter*, particularly the atmosphere of "the Room," where "Operation Vanity" against Japan is being planned by a conference of Army and Navy intelligence chiefs. In the correspondents' area, Bob Tasmin meets his old friend Milton Ouerbach, now a radio commentator and a visiting celebrity. Like Marquand, no doubt, Ouerbach has a room to himself in a Quonset that is part of the BOQ (so unnecessarily named when the officers could not help but be bachelors).

But even Guam, staging headquarters for the Pacific theater, was "behind the lines," as, in a sense, Marquand had been all along in his travels. Now he was going to find himself right on top of a battle scene, closer than he had bargained for, and the battle was one of the roughest of all, the taking of Iwo Jima. He was on Saipan when he got the chance to go out on the battleship *Nevada*, which was steaming into action. He had as yet only a vague conception of what was to happen. But from the time he climbed with middle-aged difficulty onto the main deck he realized he was a part of a vast, awesome operation. On board, nothing was secret any longer. In the junior officers' wardroom there was a complete collection of all the intelligence that had been gathered about the island, the latest aerophotographs, the target areas assigned to every unit in the attacking force. The landing forces would find black sand under their feet, then a soft soil of volcanic ash, almost barren of vegetation, then cliffs of brown volcanic stone and patches of coarse grass full of mites that probably carried scrub typhus. To aid the imagination in anticipating the situation there was a large rubber contour map of the entire island with everything in scale—the cliffs, the roads, the airstrips, the volcanic cone of Mount Suribachi on the southern tip. Piles of secret orders assigned to hundreds of vessels large and small their exact position at every moment of the invasion. A scenario for an hour of action was spelled out in thousands of pages, a kind of literary realization of actuality all the more impressive to a reportorial mind like Marquand's.

As its enactment approached, the radio loudspeakers on the open bridge broadcast in clearly articulated accents the cryptic poetry of code, the conversations of ships and planes scattered invisibly over a vast area.

The *Nevada* was part of a task force of battleships, cruisers and destroyers scheduled to bombard Iwo Jima for three days before the amphibious craft moved in. Marquand remembered his first sight of the island just at sunrise, a silent, reptilian silhouette of rock with its crest of volcanic cone, looking incongruously delicate in the pink light, like a painting on silk. Then the ship's guns went into action. The concussions at each firing seemed to grab your chest, and everyone crowded forward to watch for the cloud of smoke that rose from the land. The process was almost boring in its repetitiousness, "a slow, careful probing for almost invisible targets with long dull intervals between the firing." You could see puffs of smoke from other ships and then a sound of explosion would come "almost languidly" over the water, and then another geyser of smoke and rubble was visible on the island. The island, otherwise, was silent.

But that silence was one of the intensest watchfulness; he was aware of hundreds of eyes and ears monitoring the sky and the land—on the ships and in the "air cover" above them and in the underwater listening devices of the destroyers that were screening them. The enemy's eyes and ears were, one knew, fastened upon the vessel and its companions, though giving no sign—there were perhaps twenty-three thousand Japanese soldiers on Iwo. As the day wore on and the ships came slowly closer to the island one could see the details studied on the maps: the black beach, the gray terraces above it, the airstrip with a tangle of smashed planes. But though the Americans continued to hit the pillboxes and antiaircraft emplacements there was, by the end of the day, no return fire. On the second morning the LCI's were there, accompanied by small launches that reconnoitered along the beach, and then, as the landing craft approached the beach, the silent watchers on the island suddenly fired on them. One of the vessels near the *Nevada* was hit and the battleship commander, Captain Groshopf, disregarding the order to withdraw, pushed her to what looked to Marquand like something less than a mile offshore and started his guns firing. He used the *Nevada* as though she were a destroyer, Marquand later told the wife of one of the *Nevada* officers: "It seemed to me, though an amateur, like a very courageous and brilliant decision. He was able to quiet down the Japanese fire and save a number of the LCI's and a great many lives." But nevertheless there were wounded and dead being strapped on wire stretchers and passed up over the side of the battleship. In the LCI that lay near them were twenty-two dead out of a crew of sixty.

The next day, D-day minus one, the pounding of the island continued while again the Japanese held their fire, though their gun emplacements now lay exposed by the explosions of the shells; they were waiting, clearly, for the assault upon the beach. Then, D-day, February 19, dawned. The waters of Iwo Jima looked to Marquand "like New York harbor on a busy morning": the transports were there with three divisions of Marines, the fleets of LST's filled with tanks and alligators, the LSM's and LCI's—perhaps eight hundred different ships spreading out in a seven-mile arc. It looked, Marquand thought, "like a Hollywood production, except that it was a three-billion, not a three-million-dollar extravaganza." And now, from the air lookout station on the bridge of the *Nevada*, Marquand tried to follow what was happening: the shells and the bombs dropping from the carrier planes and finally the Marines coming down the landing nets into the small craft and the LST's letting down their ramps. Marquand felt incapable of unravelling the threads of the events about him. All his study of the documents and maps did not help him when he was confronted by the reality. He felt himself laughing at the descriptions that occurred to him. When the tanks splashed out of the LST's he remarked to a chief petty officer, "It's like all the cats in the world having kittens!" But now the first wave had hit the beach. The bloody struggle for the island was about to begin.

Marquand remained on the *Nevada* during the four days that followed before the flag was planted on Suribachi. Sensibly, he decided that his function as a correspondent did not require him to step out into the murderous cross fire that rained over the beach, unlike Ernie Pyle who was killed by a Japanese machine-gun bullet a few weeks later on the nearby island of Ie Shima. He returned to write one of the best descriptions of an amphibious landing, in the opinion of the naval historian Samuel Eliot Morison, who quoted from it at length in his definitive *Victory in the Pacific*. Marquand's account, published in *Harper's*, ended with the first landings on the beach. This was not merely because he had only been able to watch the ensuing events from the ship—he had seen it all clearly through the eight-diameter artillery glasses—or because there were soon many reports of this outstanding Marine victory.

He was critical of the way the battle had been conducted and was reluctant to say so. The carnage had horrified him. "The boys were dropping like flies after a spray of DDT," he told Johnny. In a letter marked "personal" he explained to editor Allen: "The fighting on Iwo Jima had nothing to recommend it except the amount of blood spilled and the almost universally high courage of the wounded and the dying. The fighting was a simple frontal attack on a fixed position. There was nothing new about it and nothing to describe except death and destruction. I have certain strong personal reservations about the way the whole operation was conducted. I may start by saying that the Marines are an elite corps of very superior men. Their morale and their pride are tremendous. Their combat leadership is good, but I personally feel that their higher leaders from field rank up do not compare with the Army. I honestly believe that if a good Army general had planned the operation instead of leaving the job to General Smith or the Marines and admirals, the island would have been taken with considerably lower casualties. Anyone with military experience knows that a three-day shelling of an enemy in a well-entrenched strongpoint does little towards softening him up before infantry attack. Anyone familiar with land artillery observing the fire on Iwo Jima could see that we were doing nothing except wasting ammunition. A heavy two-hour fire preparation before the landing would have done as much as the three-day search for the targets. After that, I think, the barrage should have been lifted for the beach but every other part of that small island should have been kept under steady fire, particularly smoke and phosphorus, so that our troops might land and establish themselves while the enemy was kept underground."

Marquand got back from the Pacific early in March, touching again at Guam and Hawaii and flying back to San Francisco in the Mars. On May 8, V-E Day, he was in Newburyport, where he read the Tuesday Night Club his paper describing the Hawaii he had just seen. By July—although he could not have anticipated the dramatic ending of Hiroshima and Nagasaki the following month—he was able to perceive, as did other close observers of the military situation, that the war was reaching its terminus. As he wrote Johnny on July 19: "I am rather inclined to believe that you may not see the Pacific or the CBI theater in a military capacity in this war, as it really begins to look in the last few days that it may be over by the end of this year or very early in the next, if the civilians over here will stand the shortages and keep on pushing. Certainly when Halsey can move his fleet a few miles off the Japanese coast only twenty-five miles off Tokyo and bombard the shoreline, even disregarding radio silence, it must mean that the Japanese are pretty well through. Also, when I note the military personalities who are attending the Berlin conference, it is hard not to gather a hint that Russia is about to intervene in Manchuria. If she does, this ought pretty well to tear it. Thus, I should not be surprised at all to see the end come rather unexpectedly." Then, indeed, with horrifying suddenness, it *was* all over.

Marquand's "war work" was over, too. Though he continued for some months his function as a special consultant in the War Department, both he and Merck shut up shop and submitted their resignations at the end of October. Yet the war and Marquand's association with the armed forces produced one more trip into the Pacific almost two years later. On April 16, 1947, he was again in Pearl Harbor taking off with a small naval group aboard a C-54 in the company of Admiral Louis Denfield, commander in chief of the Pacific Fleet, on an inspection trip of the recent battle areas. Their two-week trip took them to Kwajalein, to Truk, to Guam, to Nanking, to Peking, to Tsingtao, to Tokyo, to Manila, and back to Hawaii. It was another VIP junket of the very finest order—no bucket seats anywhere along the way. Marquand, as he frankly admitted to Johnny, owed the opportunity as much to accident as to his merits as an authority on the Pacific: he had become good friends with Denfield's chief of staff, Captain Howard Yeager, aboard the *Nevada*, and Yeager had fixed it up—"an invitation which I just do not want to refuse, riding plush all the way and meeting all the great figures, including the Generalissimo and MacArthur."

Whether or not he got to meet Chiang or MacArthur is not certain. His stop in Peking, the city he had always thought the most beautiful in the world, was only a quick twenty-four-hour layover, but he found the city hardly changed; the Peking Club was still running full blast and several of his old Peking friends, like Walter Bosshard, were still, unbelievably, just where he had left them in 1935. "The Peking Man has got lost, but everything else seemed to be in place. I don't believe that the Communists can ever change it much," he later told a friend. He also brought home an anecdote to tell at the next meeting of the Associated Harvard Clubs. The mayor of Peking had given a small, elegant dinner for Admiral Denfield and his companions, and among those present was General Li, the commander of the North China Army, known to his countrymen as the Tiger General. Several other Chinese officials were present, in black silk gowns, but besides Marquand only one other guest wore European civilian dress—the English-speaking Chinese interpreter. The meal was elaborate and formal; they ate bird's-nest soup and thirty-year-old eggs, and quantities of warm rice wine were drunk in toasts, but there was little conversation. Marquand was delighted, therefore, to hear the interpreter say that he was a Harvard man and told him that he was one too, a fact which was conveyed in Mandarin to the Tiger General and to the mayor. The latter then declared, by way of the interpreter, that this made Marquand and the interpreter brothers—in China all who study together are brothers. More toasts were drunk to the brothers—until Marquand was checked by a growl from a Marine colonel seated beside him. "If it's all the same to you let's get off this Harvard man angle," he said. "I'm just a poor boy from Iowa and I personally cannot stand much more of it."

But the Navy had a serious motive in taking him about in the Pacific: it was hoped that he might be able to see—and present—the Navy's side in the current controversy over the rule of the scattered lands and peoples that had come under its control since the war. Critics like Harold Ickes of the Department of the Interior and the columnist Drew Pearson had been charging that Navy government of Micronesia had been insensitive, even oppressive, and slipshod. Marquand was not exactly under compulsion but he did feel that the Navy was doing a pretty good job, considering the difficulties, and he wrote an article that appeared in *Harper's* in August called "Why the Navy Needs Aspirin." He suggested that the Navy be allowed to assimilate justified criticism and continue on the job: "Certainly, at the present moment, if I were a Marshallese or a Trukese, a Guamian or a dweller on Yap or some other Micronesian rock—and in many ways with the world the way it is I should rather like to be one—I think I should prefer the protection and errors of the Navy to the problematical rule of Mr. Ickes or Mr. Krug. I should rather have things settled, find a means of livelihood, have a good school for my children, before worrying too much about 'democracy' and my right to strike and other privileges contained in the Bill of Rights. . . . I should prefer, in short, the Navy mind to the political mind, and to stick close to nurse in case I find something worse."

His 1947 trip to the Pacific, with its vision of tiny human settlements scattered over the vast oceanic waste, continued to reverberate in his mind. He would always remember Truk. They had reached it after a stop at Kwajalein, which had turned into a ghost town in two years: the temporary barracks buildings, which had been crowded into nearly every inch of space outside of the roads and airplane runways, were already rotting and every bit of metal was crumbling into rust. It was clear that the only kind of building that could stand up for long there was the pandanus-thatched house of the Marshall Islanders. "It all looked much better from the air," he recalled, remembering the sight of the island in the sea, and the succession, as they passed over Marshalls and Carolines, of those unbelievably perfect atoll circles, each set in a shimmering gradation of purples and blues. Truk was the largest of all, its lagoon having room for ten world navies, and rising from the center of this clear circular bay were five ancient volcanic peaks covered with thick growth. One had the sense of looking down upon the emerging back of a whole continent. On the principal island in the Truk group, Moen, he met the chief of the atoll, a man named Moses Arkana, who could speak English. Marquand and his companions talked with him awhile and asked him what his people needed. He replied that they wanted nothing, except, perhaps, some fishhooks; his people had almost forgotten how to fish because the Japanese, before the war, had deprived them of their canoes and other fishing equipment and commercial fishermen from Okinawa had taken over. The Trukese had health problems, of course—yaws and tuberculosis were common—but a small hospital run by a naval doctor was doing rather well in bringing these diseases under control. There was still a shortage of food for the islands, largely because a giant snail, imported for food by the Japanese, was devouring the leaves of the breadfruit trees and the yam plants.

Sitting in the island commander's bungalow the group discussed the fate of Truk, and wondered what the world could do with it. Truk had no natural resources that the white man would want. It had its beautiful lagoon, but the powerful nations and their ships had no use for it. It was too bad, an officer was saying, that this magnificent anchorage, large enough for adequate dispersal in case of air bombing, could not be towed six hundred miles north, for then it would make a better base than Guam. The only Truk product that had interested visitors during the war had been a sort of carved wand called a love stick, which the Trukese suitor used in wooing the girl of his choice—it had been a popular souvenir among servicemen and the Trukese were now making them in quantities and selling them for a quarter apiece.

As they flew off for Manila, Marquand decided that the kindest thing the rest of the world could do for Truk, after helping a little with its medical problems, was to let it alone. Perhaps, because of its remoteness and utter uselessness, Truk might be lucky enough to vanish again from the sight of nations.

18

Writing the War

"If you write this thing just the way you see it," one of the officers on the *Nevada* had said to him, "maybe it might mean something to people back home." But Marquand was daunted by the task of conveying the reality of the war to those who had not seen it themselves. War was a foreign country and there were too few common values between what was felt aboard the battleship off Iwo Jima beach and the sensations of peacetime or of civilian life as it persisted even in time of war. When he came back from the various fronts and tried to think of putting what he had seen into fiction he felt very much as he had on his return from the Orient years before. Or as Sidney Skelton, the narrator of *Melville Goodwin, U.S.A.*, is made to say: "When I boarded one of the Empress ships bound for Vancouver, and when we began moving in the dark down the Hwang Pu River to the sea, I left many intangibles behind me on the Shanghai Bund, among them a glittering assortment of enthusiasms and illusions. I had gone to China for a news syndicate, imbued with the idea so prevalent among newspapermen that some day I would write fiction and that all I required was experience with exotic backgrounds. I was leaving this idea behind me and carrying away in its place the disturbing discovery that the more I saw of the Orient the less equipped I was to reach conclusions. You could not simply board somewhere. You had to have a permanent stake in a land before you really knew any part of that land's meaning. I faced much the same series of reactions when I left the European Theater of Operations a few months after the German collapse."

He was able to do a good job of reporting—as his essay on Iwo Jima showed—and he could get down travel impressions better than anyone; he could have been one of the great travel writers if he had bothered to put into print more than one or two of the faraway places he had seen. But travel writing as such always struck him as sterile; he could not "use" his memories unless he could make them part of a story or a novel. As he wrote in 1949: "I have never been able to make any use of travel experience, although I have been to a number of interesting and out-of-the-way places. I have seen the Assam Valley, Bushire in Persia, the Gobi Desert, the Sahara Desert, the Andes, Iceland, Ascension Island, Lake Chad, the Amazon, the Nile, the Ganges, the Colosseum and the Taj Mahal, and a few volcanoes, and yet I have brought back no photographs, no notes, no material for a book or travelogue—and no stuffed animals. Of course I have collected a few memories, because you can't avoid bringing back assortments of impressions from thousands of miles of travel, but there is a catch here also. If you have moved about long enough, these memories and impressions, once so vivid and indelible, begin merging into each other, until it becomes difficult to recollect whether it happened in Peking, Tokyo, Cairo or Lima. And finally, all that is left, at least from my own experience, is a spirit of restlessness, an impatience with all travel literature and a passionate desire to see it all and do it all again. This sense of confusion is greatly intensified by air transportation. A few long trips and everything about them becomes so indelibly blurred by the shrinkage of distance that all that is really left is a recollection of airfields, each approximately the same as the other. At a conventional cruising altitude of eight or nine thousand feet, most mountains are inclined to level out, and most terrain, even unexplored Arabia, Central Africa and the Amazon Valley, has only a map-like appearance. About all one finally learns from extended air travel is that there is a very great deal more water than land on the planet." The way air travel reduced the earth to a map and blurred differences was only a maximization of the effect of travel generally. He had lingered in one spot or another before the war—Hawaii and Peking, for example, had made a detailed and vivid impression on him. But he had used these scenes only as background for his light fiction. However deeply he had been moved by the Orient, the Moto stories were destined to be their chief literary consequence. And even that outlet for his travel impressions was closed off now.

Yet despite the difficulty of translating the experience of war into literary art Marquand wrote more than any of the novelists of his generation about the period between 1940 and 1946. He registered his impressions of those changing days in four novels: *So Little Time* (1943), *Repent in Haste* (1945), *B. F.'s Daughter* (1946) and *Melville Goodwin, U.S.A.* (1951). And these books were mostly written, as has been seen, when he was actively engaged in nonliterary work as at no other time in his career, and doubt about the possibility of writing at all was, in fact, always present to him. Having finished *So Little Time*, a work that required enormous effort and was longer than anything he had previously done, he remarked to Johnny: "Lord knows when I shall ever write another book. I don't believe until the war is over because times are changing so fast that it is very hard to write anything long." And after the short *Repent in Haste*, he said again, "This is a pretty tough period for novel-writing because superficially backgrounds and equations seem to change about once a month." But he added this time, "However, I am going to try to write a novel this summer," and in the summer of 1945 he did get started on *B. F.'s Daughter*. Only with *Melville Goodwin, U.S.A.*, begun early in 1950, had he the advantage of looking back upon the war period as a finished whole, and even this novel reached into the incalculable dynamics of the postwar period in which it was written. Between *B. F.'s Daughter* and *Melville Goodwin* Marquand wrote his true novel of the postwar period, *Point of No Return*.

Marquand's coping with the subject of the war years involved no attempt to render directly its intense center—there are few battle scenes in the books. Instead he preferred to use the viewpoint of some outsider at a distance from the war's deadliest trials; it was his own position, after all, and he had always written best when he wrote autobiographically. Thus, in *So Little Time* his perceiving consciousness is that of Jeffrey Wilson, who fought in the last war but is too old for this one. It is Jeffrey who successfully represents the drift of America over the brink from 1940 into our first year of involvement. His is a civilian drama (which was exactly Marquand's own), that of frustrated participation in his son Jim's experience. *Repent in Haste* locates the reader's awareness in the sensations of a war correspondent a generation older than the young Air Force officer in the Pacific theater whose story he tries to understand. *B. F.'s Daughter*'s primary focus is a woman, Polly Fulton, who is married to a civilian PR man in wartime Washington; its other center, for only a few chapters, is Bob Tasmin, who *is* in the Army but nearly always at a command post out of the danger area. The narrator of *Melville Goodwin, U.S.A.* is a man who has been in the Army, but as a public relations officer. And it is from the vantage point of his civilian perspective after the war that he tries to understand the career of a regular Army general, a man of combat, whose character must somehow explain the course of history.

Marquand had begun work on *So Little Time* during the summer of 1942, when he fidgeted miserably at Kent's Island as the great machine in Washington spun faster, drawing so many towards it. In August he complained that the effort to get the book going was giving him his old nervous indigestion, but he soon discovered that precisely his own situation was the key to a connection with the queerly contradictory condition of the national consciousness—at once sentimentally moved by the melodramatics of journalism, particularly radio newscasting, and at the same time unaware of the harrowing necessities towards which the nation was rapidly moving. A central figure became Walter Newcombe, the foreign correspondent and author of *World Assignment*, who refers to heads of state by their first names and is always telling touching little stories about his conversation with a cockney taxi driver or a skirted Greek soldier—but whose conception of the reality of the conflict is all shallow formula. Jeffrey finds himself surrounded by persons who in one way or another exhibit their essential unawareness: his wife, Madge, who keeps telling him to "stop worrying" about the war, and their affluent friends who, in one way or another, exhibit their unshaken self-preoccupation. Marquand's comedy of manners is at work in the characterization of Fred and Beckie, their expensively quaint Connecticut farm and the company they gather there on weekends, as much as it is in the sketch of Jeffrey's sister, a grass-roots America Firster with an enamel flag pinned to her blouse. His best friend, Minot, is a World War I flying ace and clubman—surely modeled on Gardiner Fiske—who has never really grown up, to whom war is an escapade out of a boys' adventure book; it is appropriate that Minot affirms himself as a man after the war by his willingness to risk his neck taking his horse through jumps. Then, there is the world of theatrical and Hollywood personalities, which are a part of Jeffrey's professional life—persons whose imaginations, for the most part, have become subdued to the medium they work in. If Marianna Miller, with whom Jeffrey is in love, is offered as an exception to this effect, it must be said that Marquand's own intelligence sees through her, too, as someone moved by shadows on a screen, the fantasy of the supremacy of true love over what life is and what one is. Marquand may have sought, like Hemingway, a way of distinguishing truth from illusion and those who know—like Jake Barnes—from those who are deceived by their own fatuousness and pretension—like Robert Cohn. But Marquand's cynicism is really more thoroughgoing, and by refusing to exempt Minot or Marianna he leaves Jeffrey isolated in his recognition of the paltriness of human opportunities.

So Little Time is crowded with minor characters and includes, besides its foreground of present time, recollective interpolation of Jeffrey's past, his boyhood in Newburyport-like Bragg, his newspaper days, his World War I experiences, his gradual drift from journalism to lucrative play-doctoring. Jeffrey thus recapitulates once more, as previous Marquand heroes had, the career of his creator, though he is not permitted Marquand's emergence into literary fulfillment, theatrical rewriting being an analogue of Marquand's activity as a popular magazine writer. Jeffrey's life with his rich wife may be indebted to the experience Marquand had in both his first and second marriages. Unwillingness to depend on his wife's money, even at the price of artistic self-sacrifice, was a continuing motif in both Marquand unions, though Madge seen in her New York apartment is more clearly Adelaide in Beekman Place and the Wilson country estate is Kent's Island. The novel was, as this summary barely indicates, ambitiously inclusive. When the first draft was finished on December 14, 1942, it was 1,040 pages long. After it was cut and rewritten it was still, in March, 675 pages or 260,000 words long compared to the 175,000 that *Pulham* had been. Alfred McIntyre, still opposed to serial publication of novels before their appearance in book form, was emphatic that the size and design of the book forbade reproportioning into magazine installments. "I don't see how a novel of this length, where it is so hard to determine what can be spared from it, can be cut down to serial length without weakening it greatly, though I can see where two or three lengthy episodes could be lifted and with some slight revision printed as short stories," he said. Brandt, as usual, did not agree, but thought the novel could be cut to about 80,000 words for magazine use. The manuscript was sent to the *Post* over Marquand's protest and McIntyre's standard warning that book sales would be hurt if it were printed there first. In June, however, the Book-of-the-Month Club judges, having studied the galleys, approved the new novel for their September selection, and the expected financial reward must have strengthened Marquand's decision that *So Little Time* should be subjected to no form of digest or condensation for magazine publication.

McIntyre's objection on aesthetic grounds—that the book *could* not be adapted to the magazine without the severest violation of its form—was legitimate. The novel's structure did not lend itself at all to the formula of brisk dramatic progression with well-placed climaxes at the end of installments; it was notably nonprogressive, to the point of seeming to have no plot at all. Henry Seidel Canby, who wrote the puff review for the *Book-of-the-Month Club News*, privately remarked to Marquand, "John, you know this is in no sense a novel." But Marquand felt that those who thought the work formless had failed to appreciate its aims: "Most of them have a preconceived and highly crystallized idea as to the purpose, scope and structure of a novel. I still believe that there is only one test for a novel and that is whether or not it holds the attention of the reader and whether or not it contains some ideas about life and about our times which are presented entirely by indirection." The fact of the matter was that the form of this novel was a subtle one. Marcia Davenport thought, as she told Marquand, that "the most remarkable quality is the calm, subtle development in a constant minor key. Your view of all our grim fate through the eyes of so undramatic a man is infinitely wise. You have bent your gift for satire into a peculiar quality of steady understatement which makes trash of the calculated bullseyes that most of us attempt." The narrative proceeded not linearly but in a spiral that caught up successive levels of Jeffrey's past at the same time that it moved slowly forward a short distance. Of course, there was a plot in that span: young Jim's enlistment and marriage (despite the obstructive efforts of Minot and Madge), Jeffrey's affair in Hollywood with Marianna, his unsuccessful attempt to return to playwriting, his futile effort to get into the Army, and his final acceptance of his inability to do very much about anything—a sequence of about a year and a half which is distributed over the much larger pattern of scattered incidents and vignettes from past and present. The obvious way of cutting such a work would be to reduce digression and retain progression—but the trouble was that digression was its essential method. It did not go forward because its mood was one of uncertainty and drift. Its most striking scenic moments—the house party in Connecticut, the publisher's cocktail party in Manhattan, the visit to Jeffrey's brother Alf in Rednow ("wonder" backwards), California, and the scenes with Walter Newcombe, not to speak of the flashbacks into Jeffrey's past—have nothing to do with plot.

Yet the apparent looseness and diversity of the book made it seem to lack a focus and a sharply defined theme, and this was made evident by some of the difficulties Marquand encountered as he tried to shape it to a close. And there was the greatest trouble in finding a title that would suitably sum up what the book was about. In December, Marquand and McIntyre and Brandt were discussing "Where Everything Is Bright," "Looking for a Happy Land" or "The Happy Land" (from a song Minot is always humming), and "The Flag Was Still There," "The Thirteenth Hour," "Not So Long Now," "We Haven't Much Time," and "Too Little Time." To these were added in the following months, "In That Last Year," "No Time for Laughter," "The Fifes Will Play" (from Whitman), "Young Men for War," and "Time and Jeffrey Wilson," until, finally, as the novel was going into type, they settled on "So Little Time." Marquand's ending for the novel dissatisfied some of its first readers—not only Adelaide, who had worked closely over the manuscript, but also Edward Sheldon, the veteran playwright and adviser to Broadway's most famous stars who dispensed his counsel now from an invalid's wheelchair. Sheldon read it in galley proof and he wrote Marquand: "I am afraid that I agree with Mrs. Marquand about the last pages. As I read your long, absorbing novel I felt it mounting slowly but inevitably to great, shattering and illuminating events in the personal lives of that family—especially Jeff and Madge—and I hoped they would reflect the great, shattering and illuminating events to which the country as a whole was moving slowly but so inevitably. However, nothing of this nature took place in your story and thus the ending seemed to me somewhat inconclusive and lacking in significance. It just sort of trails off. I don't doubt that this is exactly what you wanted it to do—life can trail off or go on in desultory fashion regardless of world catastrophe—but it seems too bad to have this happen in a novel. Especially when the novel has indicated throughout a slowly increasing, almost suffocating pressure on the lives of the individuals concerned. I found myself wanting a great big catharsis of something or other and I did not get it and I felt let down."

Marquand, however, refused to change the last chapter. Unquestionably it ends on a diminuendo, Jeffrey walking out along Fifth Avenue with the bemused sense that everything has been changing in ways he cannot identify. "A girl with yellow hair and with one of those small hats which women were wearing then was walking half a block ahead of him, and her figure and the way she walked made him think of Marianna Miller, but it was not Marianna Miller. You knew someone, you loved and laughed, and then it was all different. Nothing in the world ever stayed quite the same." He realizes that it could not have turned out differently with Marianna—he had already given most of what he had to give away. He had done something for Jim, but now there was nothing more that Jim would need from him. Maybe Madge, dumb, snobbish Madge, was the only one for whom he would be able to do something. This was hardly a windup for the sentimental, certainly not the happy ending expected by magazine readers. Jeffrey stumbles almost by accident into St. Patrick's Cathedral and murmurs, "Forgive us our trespasses, as we forgive those who trespass against us." The sense of the unresolved that was conveyed by the ending was, after all, of a piece with the irresolution visible throughout the book in the very style. Marquand had carried the effect of a balancing of appearance and doubt into his sentences in a way that made an easy mark for a parodist like Geoffrey Hellman in a *New Yorker* piece, "How to Take the War in Your Stride." His comic imitation of *So Little Time* began, "It was very hard for Roger to remember what he had been thinking about on Tuesday, now that it was Wednesday. It was one of those weeks that passed like a dream, and you could not tell, from the flowers at Schling's, the mansard roof of the Union Club, or the barred windows of the old George Blumenthal house across the Avenue, that the Russians were entering Kiev, that Tom Dewey was back from Mackinac, and that the Pope was in the hands of the Germans."

So, when the book appeared on August 20, 1943, some of the reviewers were annoyed by its open form and by the hero's lack of positive conviction about anything which matched this absence of formal closure. Lewis Gannett compared the novel unfavorably to H. G. Wells's World War I novel of the little man adjusting to the onset of a war, *Mr. Britling Sees It Through*, because, unlike Jeffrey, Mr. Britling "finally made up his mind." Harry Hansen disliked that last-minute episode in St. Patrick's—it looked like but clearly wasn't conversion; Jeffrey's detached and secular vision, his *un*forgiveness of others, had been all along the basis of Marquand's satire in the book and there seemed not to be any change of mind to replace it. Dawn Powell in *Mademoiselle* showed a feminist perceptiveness that would not be conspicuous for another generation. She, too, disliked the hero—and recognized that he was a Heel who sacrificed others all along while telling himself that it was "kinder that way"; she thought that by exempting Jeffrey from the overt scorn visited on all the other characters Marquand had really brought reader hostility down on him the more.

Still, the unresolved quality in the book made for its peculiar appeal for many readers. The novelist had not waited to come to conclusions about the changes under way and his book had an immediacy that was felt by those as bemused about the future as the hero—or author. John Chamberlain in *Harper's* had objected that Marquand's satire was too wholesale but then decided that the satire was only one aspect; the work was a success because true to its time and place. It was, as Joseph Warren Beach said in the *New*

York Times Book Review, "the first of the American novels to make something of the present war," even if that was exactly nothing. All that had been proved was that daily life, so little altered for the average American at home, was trembling beneath the surface as though on the way to irreversible changes caused by the faraway clash of arms. "Although its background is New York and Connecticut and Hollywood, *So Little Time* is a war novel," wrote Rose Feld, the New York *Herald Tribune* reviewer.

Of course, there were extremes of distaste and approbation. The harshest response ("hysterical," Marquand called it when he read it) came from George Mayberry of the *New Republic*. Under the heading "Book-of-the-Month Club Dud," he declared that the latest Marquand confirmed what he had always thought: the novelist was merely competent as he laughed at his upper-class arrivistes and bores "oh so easily, and oh God, at such length," with "tedious documentation of what people said, wore, sang, filled their stomachs, minds and houses with"—all in prose that was "so unaggressively unassuming." The *Saturday Review of Literature*, on the other hand, exhibited a collection of quotations from its past reviews to show how it had always recognized Marquand's genius since its first notice of the book on Timothy Dexter in 1925, and Ben Ray Redman now wrote of Marquand's "literary wizardry." In daily newspapers up and down the land the reviews were largely favorable. Many took their cue from Canby's essay, which called Marquand the "Sinclair Lewis of a slightly younger generation" who applied the sweet-sour of irony to his subjects in the place of the vinegar of satire, and the announcement that Marquand had replaced Lewis was picked up repeatedly. What probably accounted for the widespread enthusiasm in the nation's daily press was that the book did not seem, despite Jeffrey's New England background, to be about a regional species, and the cosmopolitan critic of the *American Mercury*, Philip Rahv, decided that it was the best of Marquand's novels to date because it was concerned with the national scene as a whole. Or as the Omaha *World Herald* put it, "Marquand writes for you and me." A lady named Madonna Todd, in the Houston *Press*, represented these numerous common readers: "While the academic ladies and gentlemen are wrangling about Mr. Marquand's standing in American letters, disputing whether he is the reincarnation of Thackeray or just another *Saturday Evening Post* hack, the public goes on reading him. So what are the odds if the *New Republic* calls him a 'Book of the Month Club Dud' while the *Saturday Review* goes overboard in two issues with fulsome praise of his latest novel? This is a democratic country and Mr. Marquand has the votes."

And the vote was a landslide. The advance printing in response to booksellers' orders and expected Book-of-the-Month Club sales totaled 450,000, a figure *Esquire* called "astronomic." The book went immediately to the top of the best-seller lists. The New York *Times* compilation of reports from leading bookstores in fourteen American cities showed that the sales for *So Little Time* led those of all rivals (including *The Robe* by Lloyd Douglas, *A*

Tree Grows in Brooklyn by Betty Smith, *The Valley of Decision* by Marcia Davenport, *Hungry Hill* by Daphne du Maurier, *The Apostle* by Sholem Asch and *Kate Fennigate* by Booth Tarkington—all remarkably successful novels) from early in September until the end of the year. It was evident from the start that Marquand's success with *So Little Time* was going to be something beyond even his previous popular triumphs. He was at last about to fulfill the classic native dream, having arrived from humble beginnings to the very summit by industry, talent and the breaks, having outdistanced all rivals. *Life*, which had already given him his title as the voice of Boston, now was about to attach a still more significant identity. Early in the new year, Roger Butterfield and his research assistants went to work interviewing Marquand for a full-length profile which, when it appeared in July, led off with the declaration: "Marquand is now the most successful novelist in the U.S."

Yet he was properly skeptical of the way the winds of popular favor were being made to fill his sails, particularly of the role of the Book-of-the-Month Club. He had already tasted the advantages of its sponsorship when *Pulham* had been made a choice and over 76,000 copies had been sent out to its members, but the sales guaranteed for this next novel by the Club's favor would be far greater. He cast a cold eye, despite the fact that it was making him richer, upon the process, and wrote to Johnny, when the judges announced that *So Little Time* would be the September selection offered its subscribers: "This, as you may know, is one of the things which we boys in our profession strive for, and I am told that I am peculiarly honored since I am one of the few novelists who have had two novels selected by this august money-making organization, and nearly the only one who has had two in succession. Aside from this I am not deeply moved. I think the Book-of-the-Month Club is a racket that is spoiling the general sale of books by concentrating on the few that it sends to its customers. It is really another of these organizations which exploits our writers as do agents and the publishers themselves, as well as the damn movies. Due to the literary stupidity of the general public, the Book-of-the-Month Club has about 300,000 subscribers and Alfred McIntyre estimates that at least 275,000 of these will buy my book. Under the Club regulations the publisher and the author divide evenly on royalties since the publisher sells the Club the books very cheap, so that the Club can make money too. Even so, with all this division it looks as though I'll get about fifty thousand dollars out of the deal and this does not include any copies which will be sold through the ordinary channels of book stores. Added to this the chances are that the movies will buy it, even if they did not want it before, because of its wide circulation, and even now the boys in Hollywood are beginning to make quite definite motions with their check books. It is even possible to conceive, when all the figures are finally totted up that I may make as much as a hundred thousand dollars out of the thing."

These expectations would be more than realized. Book-of-the-Month Club sales of *So Little Time* ran to over 469,000 copies, and two months after publication date Little, Brown announced that 501,409 copies had already been sold and that this exceeded the number of copies of any other book of fiction or nonfiction sold in a similar length of time by the firm in all its history. By the end of the next month, the novel had earned its author $90,000, and though his contract with the publisher provided that payment would be spread along with continuing earnings over a three-year period, he still would be making more money than he had ever made before, even if he did not write another line for the whole of the period. *So Little Time*'s success continued. There would be twenty-four printings in its first three years of life. In addition, Marquand would soon have, of course, the fat extra of $25,000, which David O. Selznick paid for the movie rights, reputedly the highest price ever paid till then for the privilege of making a film out of a work of fiction. Probably the sale was made with even less preconsideration of the movie possibilities of the story than Hollywood generally exercises. The long, static, low-keyed book was no doubt a puzzler to the studios when they actually tried to do something with it. After three years no acceptable script had been worked out and Vanguard Films handed it over to MGM in a swap for rights to "The Paradise Case." But it fared no better with MGM—and no film was, in fact, ever made of it. For Marquand this must have made little difference. His income was bounding upwards not only from the current book and movie sale but from the reprints of his other works. *Apley* had appeared already in Modern Library and Grosset and Dunlap editions, *Pulham* had come out again under a Garden City imprint, and *Think Fast, Mr. Moto*, the most durable of the Moto series, was available in Pocket Books and Mercury editions. These were only the beginning of the paperback boom in which Marquand's novels would participate.

Tritely enough, the top, when one got there, was not such a contenting place. The criticism of some of the reviewers had reminded Marquand that he had not thrown off the stigma of popularity earned in his work for the magazines, but had fastened it on himself more securely than ever. For these critics, he was still not a real artist—simply the maker of a commodity that sold. In *Harper's Magazine* Diana Trilling launched an onslaught upon popular fiction in general which she titled, "What Has Happened To Our Novels?" She noted that, despite paper shortages, America was in the midst of a book-buying boom at the same time that it was in a creative depression. She charged that the current best sellers had fallen from the glory that American fiction had exhibited after the First World War and through the twenties. No one was coming up in this later time to the level of Sherwood Anderson, Lewis, Cather, Fitzgerald, Hemingway and Dos Passos—not even these writers themselves. The cause, she thought, was the lack in current fiction of the energy of rebellion and criticism that had fired the earlier group; the novelist had "put himself at the service of established institutions" and heroism had left his writing. *So Little Time* seemed to her one of the best examples of all this. Marquand had himself, as we have seen, spoken caustically to Johnny about popular taste and the influence upon it of the book clubs. But now he read in Harry Hansen's column in the New York *World-Telegram* that the editor of a midwestern book periodical had accused the Book-of-the-Month Club and Little, Brown of using promotional tactics to force *So Little Time*, an inferior book by a "hard working" author, upon the public. Marquand felt outraged enough to tell Alfred McIntyre that the book firm and the Club should buy advertising space to answer such a charge. "The truth," he protested, "is that the Book-of-the-Month Club selection is apt to prejudice many critics against it." Hansen's own original review as well as those in other important places had been unfavorable. Marquand's attitude towards the Book-of-the-Month Club was certainly ambiguous—it could help to make his fortune, apparently, or it could ruin him critically. And the paradox of his contrary feeling was deepened by his decision, that very spring, in 1944, to accept the invitation of the Club to become one of its judges. For fifteen years he would be its most prominent representative in the public eye, closely identified with the process he had deplored to his son. Perhaps Marquand made, by this step, a commitment, finally, to a definition of literary self that he had resisted; he allied himself more firmly than ever with the middlebrow literary establishment—the *Saturday Review* and the Book-of-the-Month Club crowd—and once and for all renounced any expectations from the literary avant-garde, the small and exclusive band of the elite whose reputations were made in little magazines of small circulation, in the liberal *New Yorker*, *Nation*, and *New Republic*, and among college professors of English.

He remained, probably, distrustful of the effects of success—the satirist in him was too watchful to permit his absolute surrender to the hoopla that made him, suddenly, a hostess's prize and produced, overnight, a multitude of would-be friends and also of enemies. To Helen Howe, to whom he liked to appear a purer spirit, he said in December 1943: "I don't like at all the social and professional position that my last book has put me in. Except for a few friends of mine, it has divided all others I know, even remotely, and a great many whom I don't know, into two sharply defined categories. One category sucks up to me with the motive, I suspect, of trying to get something out of me, and the other is out to get me, simply because I have achieved a certain amount of success. This is probably all a psychosis, but you realize yourself in a measure how it works, and it is difficult to strike any sort of balance." He had never liked the social side of the book industry—the author-publisher-agent merry-go-round, which was always awhirl in New York and which he had represented in his literary cocktail-party scene in *So Little Time.* Now, more than ever, he cultivated his curmudgeon side to avoid such occasions, and was happy to claim the press of his war work in Washington as a protection. As he told Helen, "The best escape I have found is to play around with the officers of the U.S. Army, particularly those in the Pentagon Building, few of whom have ever read a book, and most of whom recognize me only as the writer of detective fiction." His interest in the kind of men who were running the war without much assistance from the intellectuals was sharpened by the actual refuge he found in their company.

The assured monetary returns from his performance as a writer of books raised, again, of course, the old question of whether he should continue to take any interest in the popular magazine market. Two years earlier, when Brandt had pressed Marquand to publish *Last Laugh, Mr. Moto,* even posting his office boy outside the Beekman Place apartment to collect the contract as soon as it was signed, Marquand had complained that the agent had "the most amazing attitude about book publication. He seems to feel that a publishing house is a kind of sausage machine to which the author-agent throws a lot of manuscripts, the use of which has been exhausted elsewhere." Now he wrote McIntyre in November 1943, with a more certain sense of his ability to change the picture: "It seems to me that government taxation combined with the success of *So Little Time* has done a great deal to change my literary future. Certainly my status as a contributor to the popular magazines will undergo considerable revision for the next three years; at any rate I don't seem to be under the old compulsion of earning so much money by writing. Between you and me, Carl Brandt, fond though I am of him, is of no help to me in this regard. I don't think he has ever had a client in this position and I don't think he is able to revise his ideas in terms of the future."

To Brandt he had written on the same day that he was finishing a story for magazine publication: "And after that I don't really know what to do with myself. It hardly seems worthwhile doing any magazine writing unless the spirit moves me very deeply since with taxes the way they are the net return I get from it is not much greater than ten percent." And while the short novel *Repent in Haste* did emerge in two magazine installments, the magazine was *Harper's,* where Marquand deliberately sought a new audience. When, in 1945, he heard that Norman Cousins was starting a magazine that would print "adult fiction in which the boy does not have to win the girl, win the job and a million dollars, and also solve his ideological, religious and other spiritual problems in such a nice way that the subway reader is very, very happy," Marquand told Cousins, "Personally, I have made a resolution some time ago that I would never put a clothespin on my nose again and write any more of those magazine stories." *B. F.'s Daughter,* like *So Little Time,* did not get into the magazines. The three years were more than up when *Point of No Return* began its run in the *Ladies' Home Journal* in 1948. As for short stories, he would publish just three more in the magazines after 1944.

He was finishing in November 1943 "The End Game," which was to appear in *Good Housekeeping* the following March, heralded by full-page ads taken by the magazine in the *Times*, the *Herald Tribune*, and other important papers throughout the country. As though to refute Marquand's new policy, this story had grown out of a suggestion from the editor, Herbert Mayes, and turned out to be one of Marquand's most accomplished performances, and it was reprinted in anthologies. Yet its weaknesses, taken with its virtues, only confirm the thought that in writing it Marquand's literary aims had been fatally mixed. Mayes had talked to Marquand in the summer of 1943 about developing a tale about a dropout from the tradition of a strict Army family who is discovered playing chess for a quarter a game in a penny arcade in Manhattan. Marquand saw immediate possibilities in the idea, for it gave him a way of expressing some of his views about Army traditions. Before he actually sat down to write the story that fall he would have collected further impressions of the regular Army during his trip with General Simmons. The story wrote itself with a silken fluency, probably because Marquand felt no compulsion to give it the wider-ranging scope of a novel; in contrast with the expansion of *So Little Time*, "The End Game" exploited the advantages of compression. It was about the same length, Marquand later observed, as Henry James's *Daisy Miller*, which, he added, "I hasten to say is the better work of the two." In writing this sort of brief fiction, Marquand found a way of utilizing settings provided by his travel observations just as James had needed only his own visitor's impressions of Rome for his tale of an American girl in a foreign city. Marquand could locate some of his scenes in Honolulu, where the Army family is temporarily stationed, and then confine himself to the impressions of young Joe, who falls in love there with the daughter of a slightly disreputable beachcomber. He could preface the story, on the other hand, with a scene provided by his current New York—a party in a Park Avenue apartment, where the hostess has put together out of the ingredients of wartime a general, a somebody from the British embassy, several friends who were doing hush-hush things in Washington, and Henry Ide, who had been too young for the First World War and was too old for this one, but who had been caught in Hong Kong after Pearl Harbor and sent to a Japanese concentration camp.

Henry Ide's consciousness made a perfect register of the story he learned from the mysterious chess player; he had suffered from the war but he had never been a soldier; he had returned after his year's imprisonment to a New York grown enigmatic: "There was a disturbing blandness about the afternoon sunlight on Park Avenue; there was a deceitful sort of glitter in the shops, reflecting the effort he, and everyone else, was making to prove that everything was going on as usual." Ide had made the right choice because he too, as the chess player discerns, wouldn't have liked the Army, isn't the Army type. The Army type is unflatteringly represented in the story by Joe's father, known to his family as "the C.O.," who expected all four of his boys to go to the Point and ran his home like an Army post. They all played chess—that was another family tradition—but Joe discovered one time that he could beat his father. And when the old man marched up to the bungalow where Joe was visiting his girlfriend and hauled him home like an AWOL soldier, he simply ran away, from the family, from the Army, forever.

Maybe the story should have ended there, but Henry wants to know what happens next. The chess player tells him, "It doesn't matter. . . . You think it over and you'll see the beginning is all that matters. The middle and the end are always mixed up in the beginning." Exactly as in a game of chess. And we do get, finally, the end game—how the runaway married the girl and lived in the Orient and got mixed up in the China war, becoming, in time, the aide of a Nationalist general. It turns out that he outranks his military brothers and that Johnny, the one Henry met at the Park Avenue party, is about to be assigned to work under the Chinese Republican army. It seems, after all, that "if you are born in the army you are always in it." Joe has fulfilled, though he has defied, his father's intention for him. The ending, of course, was Marquand's concession to formulas he had accepted uncritically too well from his years of magazine work. The turnabout not only provided a diverting surprise but also assuaged the moral disturbance the story had aroused. Marquand had written it nine tenths of the way as a challenge to the narrowness of a spit-and-polish martinet and the system that creates one, and then, by making his rebel a military man *malgré lui*, had seemed to justify that tradition after all. Later Marquand wished he had done without the artifice of the ending—as his hero had seemed to advise. Its weakness, however, was more than a matter of structure—it was really ethical. That Mayes "demanded" it may be doubted: Marquand himself declared ten years after it was first published that "the ridiculously contrived ending would not have been necessary even for *Good Housekeeping Magazine*." It was a case, probably, of Marquand himself having learned too well the lessons of popular authorship.

Repent in Haste was a more consistent denial of platitude. Marquand was determined that it not be offered to his old magazine audience. This short novel carried the mood—wry, ironic, bemused—of *So Little Time* into the further stage of the war itself. It took a standard sentimental situation of the magazines—the young flyer torn between the hometown girlfriend and a new wartime infatuation—and handled it totally without a vestige of romance. As William Briggs, the correspondent, gets to know more about Lieutenant Boyden's background in East Orange, New Jersey, and about the "cute little trick" whom he met at Pensacola just before he got his wings, he is brought into sympathetic connection with that ordinary stuff of life out of which even heroes are made. The satiric notation is mild but unremitting as Marquand sees, through Briggs's eyes, the home that nurtured the typical American boy: his mother, a member of the Women's Club and the Altar Guild of the Episcopal Church; the minor executive–commuter father; and Verna May, who lived not next door but down the block. The war bride, Daisy, goes back to live with Boyden's parents, but soon she is two-timing her husband, or, as she would say, she is "engaged" again, even though she is married. It is all just "one of those things," and only Briggs invests the situation with tragedy. When he finally brings his report of it to Boyden it is the latter who has to do the comforting for the collapse of old meanings: "Just remember it's happening all the time. Kids get mixed up in a war, I guess—particularly around an airstrip."

The character of "Boysie," as Daisy nicknamed him, is what really challenges the understanding of Briggs and of Marquand, who identifies with this representative of an older generation. Indubitably a hero by the conventional requirements of bravery, honesty, good nature, he is quite without heroic concepts. He is scornful of a broadcast which asked, "Do our boys know what we are fighting for?" and says to Briggs, "I mean why the heck should it bother them, if we're in here pitching. We're in here pitching, aren't we?" And when Briggs himself asks, "But why do you do it?" Boysie says to him, "What d'you think I am, Pops, emotionally unstable? . . . The thing is not to think too much. I've seen a lot of kids thinking, especially the new kids, and it isn't normal." Marquand's combat man is not Hemingway's Lieutenant Henry, who learned painfully in the chaos and futility of war to distrust all those fine words. He has almost instinctively *begun* with an aversion for the talk which belongs behind the front but not at it—as Patton, Marquand remembered, had told him ("All this God-damn tripe about the four freedoms!").

The short novel was not one of Marquand's most ambitious efforts, but he took it seriously enough to insist that it might deserve a serious reading. It had not been written to make money, and although Brandt was indignant Marquand refused to let him send it to *Good Housekeeping*, where Herbert Mayes was willing to pay handsomely for a successor to "The End Game." In 1945, as before, he was wearily repeating to his agent: "It is honestly very puzzling to me that you do not seem to understand my literary problems from a tax angle, both with stories and motion picture rights, and also books. All of my literary business has gone through your hands and surely you can see that my income for this year and probably for the next means simply that any work I do is about as good as given away—in fact I get 8% and the Brandt office gets 10%." There was no longer any use, he went on, "in my building up a magazine market," and so he planned to give the story to *Harper's* "if they will take it." If *Harper's* printed it, it might at least "add something to my literary prestige, more I think than *Good Housekeeping*."

Yet the book did not do much for Marquand's literary reputation. A good many of the reviewers were puzzled by it. What was Marquand about? Was he issuing a warning against hasty war marriages, making the point in this fictional case history that he had already made to Johnny when he became engaged to Jhan English? If so, the book was bound to seem dated almost as soon as it appeared in *Harper's* in October and November: the war was over. As Charles Lee of the Philadelphia *Record* said, "With the war and its abnormal compulsions gone its point is dulled." Harry Hansen in the New York *World-Telegram* thought Marquand had not been quite fair in his implication that such a marriage was representative, anyhow: "Actually the evidence is probably the other way. I know of a number of marriages in which the short honeymoon and subsequent absence of the husband have made the young wives all the more eager to guard their new status." Many reviewers were dissatisfied with the portrait of Boyden. Sterling North in his widely syndicated column said testily, "Everything Marquand says or implies about Lieutenant Boyden is probably true—his virtues are few and rather nebulous, while his emotional immaturity, his middle class bigotries, his social astigmatism, all come through with appalling clarity." But Marquand had been guilty of snobbery and paternal condescension towards those who deserved a nation's gratitude, North thought. "Marquand should also perhaps have pointed out that Ulysses, Roland and Paul Bunyan were similar oafs (from his own aloof and cultured point of view)." A. C. Spectorsky, speaking to younger readers in *Junior Bazaar*, was in turn supercilious of the author: "It is entirely likely that readers of this page will know more about his subject than does John P. Marquand as he reveals himself in *Repent in Haste*. The subject is what goes on inside a young carrier pilot's mind and heart, and it should be explained at once that Marquand is not deficient in describing the outward manifestations. But the chronological and philosophic gap between him and his young hero is too great for him to fulfill the function of social analyst which we have come to expect of him, and for once he is reduced to the status of efficient, readable reporter." Even the loyal *Saturday Review* critic, Theodore Purdy, found Boyden an "unconvincing" figure, "though he talks a recognizable if expurgated Navy jargon and is a thousand times more real than most pilots of fiction."

Though the rebuff was not universal, most of the critics had given Marquand a clear negative vote, quite different from their reception of *So Little Time*. The sales of the book were unimpressive, and MGM decided not to exercise its option to purchase screen rights. But Marquand was probably correct in observing to a friend, "I can only repeat what every writer does when a book of his has an unfavorable reception—that it is over the reviewers' heads." Most of the reviews did give the impression that the writers did not appreciate Marquand's subject and viewpoint—they and the general reader, too, would have preferred the sentimentalities he had deliberately refuted.

One critic, however, who understood Marquand's point quite well, took the occasion of this slight production to write the most devastating judgment that Marquand's work would ever receive. This was Edmund Wilson of the *New Yorker.* Wilson wrote: "The story creates suspense; it has point; it is based on first-hand observation and conscientiously accurate reporting; and it says something rather intelligent about the difference between the older generation of Americans and the young generation of the war. The only trouble is that, here, as elsewhere, Mr. Marquand hasn't the literary vocation—or maybe métier is the better word. A novel by Sinclair Lewis, however much it may be open to objection, is at least a book by a writer—that is, a work of the imagination that imposes its atmosphere, a creation that shows the color and modelling of a particular artist's hand. But a novel by J. P. Marquand is simply a neat pile of typewritten manuscript. Mr. Marquand, as a fiction-writing journalist, is a not unsympathetic figure. He sees through certain kinds of fraud and he does not hesitate to make fun of them; unlike some other highly successful novelists, he does his work in complete good faith and is not pretentious about it. It was not he but an excited reviewer, quoted on the jacket of 'Repent in Haste,' who shouted, 'Let's face it—John P. Marquand is the major American novelist writing today.' But, fortunately, we do not have to face it. We have plenty of novelists in America who make Mr. Marquand's abilities seem as modest as his pretensions. And a book like 'Repent in Haste' cannot be called anything better than a thirty-five-thousand-word job that is Grade B but does not let you down."

Wilson's was indeed the kind of judgment that gave success the taste of ashes. *Life* might have identified Marquand as the most successful novelist in America, but Edmund Wilson, for whom he had some respect, had said that his novels were only neat piles of typewritten manuscript. As Wilson had realized, Marquand was not pretentious about his gifts, but he hoped he was better than that. He took refuge from the impact of the review in the knowledge that *he* had never claimed what the jacket blurb had so unfortunately declared, that *Repent in Haste* was never intended to be a major performance, and that Wilson had tipped his hand, anyhow, by unfavorably comparing the book to an inferior one by Christopher Isherwood. "Bunny Wilson has as much right to his opinion of me as a writer as I have of him as a critic," he wrote Brandt. "If we both take dim views of each other, after all, this is a free country, and Wilson, you must admit, has a lot of interesting ideas. I notice on his book page he rates a little work by Mr. Isherwood, called 'Prater Violet,' very highly and decides it is on a higher plane than mine. In my opinion this story of Isherwood's is a nauseatingly lousy and meaningless effort, and I am glad to let the whole debate stand or fall by Wilson's comparison. Actually, I have never considered 'Repent in Haste' as much more than Wilson makes it—a competent piece of reporting with perhaps a few implications. I think Little Brown made a mistake in quoting that Chicago Sun statement about let's face it, I am the best novelist in the country. This sort of thing is naturally calculated to arouse the opposition. I haven't any idea whether I am a good novelist or not, and it may very well be that Mr. Wilson is right. Certainly I have never implied that I am as good as Red Lewis at his best."

B. F.'s Daughter, which was a more ambitious piece of work, received just slightly better verdicts from the critics who had already labeled Marquand as the middlebrow master. In the *New Yorker*, following the severe dismissal of its predecessor by Edmund Wilson, John Lardner could only write: "*B. F.'s Daughter* is a readable book. Most all of Mr. Marquand's books are readable. Thanks, however, to the school of reviewers including jacket writers, which holds that they are also 'significant,' 'provocative,' and 'bitter satire on a mentally decadent society,' you sometimes feel it necessary to mention that Mr. Marquand's talent in his novels is exactly the same he applied in his earlier potboiling, highly successful *Saturday Evening Post* stories about Mr. Moto, the Japanese solver of crimes. That is a talent for finding and using over and over again a formula that will entertain a public accustomed to formulas." James McBride of the *New York Times Book Review* appeared to praise, but when read closely, was revealed as praising Marquand chiefly for his "competence": "*B. F.'s Daughter* is another major Marquand product. To say it is up to snuff is merely to endorse the inevitable rush to the bookstores. To say that it is always entertaining (and sometimes brilliant) is only to reaffirm the virtues of craftsmanship that has proved itself abundantly. To say that it goes no deeper than its own multicolored surface—and produces its effects with a strictly limited frame—is only to repeat that competence is praised above riches in the fiction field today." It was obvious that the lines were drawn and fixed between Marquand and the intelligentsia.

The critical "right" stood up for him, however. Edward Weeks could declare in the *Atlantic*: "I think it is time to take off our hats to John Marquand. I think it is time we acknowledged the increasing skill he brings to his fiction; his shrewd observation, his true ear for dialogue, his humor, his mimicry and his satire. I think it is time that people stopped disparaging his books because they are so darned easy to read." Marquand found comfort in the remarks of Orville Prescott, who outrightly accused his fellow critics of looking "a gift horse in the mouth" and called the deprecators of *B. F.'s Daughter* "supercilious" and "condescending." Writing in the *Yale Review*, he said: "It has long been plain to the most obtuse, or it should have been, that Mr. Marquand is one of the most accomplished of living American novelists, a brilliant craftsman, a superb social reporter, a man blessed with a thoughtfully comic mind and an unrivalled gift for adroit satire. But Mr. Marquand writes about our 'upper classes.' He does not crusade for particular political or economic nostrums. His books are very entertaining and they sell prodigiously. These sins are hard to forgive in certain dogma-ridden quarters." But the division between Marquand's popular audiences and the elite tastemakers would continue to the end.

B. F.'s Daughter deepened this division, moreover, because it seemed to find virtue among the conservative and wealthy and unintellectual, while the one liberal in its cast, the heroine's New Dealer, ex-academic husband, is the object of the novelist's derision. The leading reviewers who identified with Tom Brett were offended by Marquand's portrait of a New Dealer who was always telling others to remember that there was a "war going on." Brett self-importantly "experted" in Washington and suffered the strains of wartime along with the alleviations the capital provided, which included a small affair with his secretary in Georgetown. As for the heroine, Marquand remembered a remark someone had once made to him: "No one ever feels sorry for a girl on a yacht." Polly Fulton had always been a girl on a yacht, and she had always had everything. Marquand tries, nevertheless, to make us like her and feel sorry for her—and he succeeds. Like her tycoon father, though fond of her own way she is honest and incapable of cant. Marquand's discovery in this novel, as in *Repent in Haste*, was one the critics did not appreciate in a time of overblown highmindedness: that one of the effects of war is the increasing cheapness of ideas and ideals. Nobility, on the other hand, is more likely to persist as a matter of character, of instinct. He spiked the reverse snobbery that denied such an instinct to a boy who had all the advantages of an upper-class upbringing—like Bob Tasmin—as positively as he had wanted to refute the opposite notion that a rather ordinary guy without any "views," like Boyden, was incapable of the beau geste.

Marquand had written about the rich before, but only in terms of the special Bostonian problems of caste as they molded the lives of George Apley and Harry Pulham. In Burton Fulton he sketched a more forceful figure, someone who had become rich by exercising superior qualities of energy and mind. Now that he himself had become an example of how such qualities do sometimes really fulfill the American success myth, the self-made businessman interested him; he would come back to the subject in the later novels *Point of No Return* and *Sincerely, Willis Wade*. Fulton is gently handled, perhaps because of this personal sense of kinship—his qualities of affection and humor charm Bob Tasmin, the Pulham of the story. We see "B. F." almost entirely through the eyes of either Tasmin or of Polly, his beloved daughter, and so he is shielded from what might be a reader's distrust of powerful, power-loving millionaires, and comes off rather well. Of course, Polly, who is very much like him, is apt herself to apply the clichés of rebel youth to her old man. She married Tom, the brain truster and social critic, because she wanted someone as unlike her father as possible. The novel is about her education, through marital disillusion and the war, in the truth about the things that count most—kindness and courage—and the discovery that she, in marrying Tom, had tried to "run" him no less bossily than her father had run his own affairs.

The book ends weakly. It satisfied neither sentimentalists nor realists. Polly, aware of the failure of her marriage, becomes convinced that Bob Tasmin, whom she had long before rejected, is really her true love, and flings herself at him upon his return from a dangerous Pacific mission—only to be gently rejected and told the truth about herself. The sentimentalists felt balked of the chance to finally see the boy-at-last-gets-the-right-girl ending, while the realists felt that Marquand had made Tasmin too improbably honorable. What few noticed or appreciated was Marquand's truthful setting down of his observations of the war. Better than the plot is the atmosphere Marquand accurately conveyed out of his own experience. There is the headquarters on Guam, where the officers and their aides as well as the civilian correspondents are sharply seen and heard out of Marquand's film-reel and tape-recorder memory. And once again, as in *So Little Time*, he depicts with humorous distaste the type of the world-swinging newsman-pundit: Milton Ouerbach is almost another Walter Newcombe. There is the prefatory episode in New York, when Polly finds herself out on a date with an Air Force colonel on leave and nearly goes to bed with him out of depression and good nature. And there is Marquand's evocation of wartime Washington—the soiled and overcrowded Mayflower bursting with civilians and servicemen.

Marquand seems to have believed that this sense of the way things felt in wartime was the real subject of his novel, and for *Wings*, the newsletter of the Literary Guild, he said so in a piece titled, "Why I Wrote *B. F.'s Daughter*." The blurb with which the Guild presented the book to its members called it "the story of a marriage, the story of a love that ripened too late." The novelist himself said merely: "I must have felt a need to describe that past and set down certain details of it for my own satisfaction before it was too late to remember. During the war I had lived as a civilian. I had also spent much of my time in and out of Washington, and besides I had been to the war theaters. I have tried to translate some of these experiences which we all have shared into fictional terms in this book. The result is perhaps a novel of manners, if it is possible to put any novel into any category."

B. F.'s Daughter had been started in the last months of the war and written rapidly; in August 1945, McIntyre was reading the early parts of the first draft, and the following March the long manuscript of 280,000 words was being worked over by McIntyre and Brandt and Marquand himself for cuts. Since Marquand was now a Book-of-the-Month Club judge, it seemed inappropriate to offer it there, but the Literary Guild promptly agreed in May to make it its November selection, and John Beecroft of the Guild also sent suggestions for cuts. Beecroft, though he was glad to get a chance to sponsor a Marquand selection, was uncertain about the shape and meaning of the novel. He disliked the inconclusive ending; Marquand's vagueness about Polly's future bothered him. "Does she finally give up both Bob and Tom?" he asked, judging the story, as most of the reviewers had, in terms of its romantic plot alone. Although Marquand had refused to let the story go to the magazines—where the same question would have been asked by the editors—there seemed little chance that he would be perceived in terms other than as a writer of boy-meets-girl stories.

Of course, the book would sell, as everyone agreed in predicting, and Little, Brown and the Guild were optimistic enough to have printed 980,000 copies by the beginning of the year, including the Guild edition. In fact, it did not do as well as *So Little Time* and eventually 771,000 copies would be sold, this figure to be achieved slowly by the addition of four different paperback editions from 1947 to 1963. Loew's bought the screen rights for $90,000 in 1946, which was then an impressive price even if somewhat below the amount Selznick had paid for *So Little Time.* This movie, at any rate, went into production and was released in 1948, and the cast featured some of Hollywood's most expensive stars—Barbara Stanwyck, Van Heflin, Charles Coburn and Keenan Wynn.

The moviemakers had no difficulty in deciding what Marquand's story was about. As one reviewer summarized the revised plot: "Polly Fulton's marriage to Tom Brett, the New Deal disciple, founders when he learns that she has been financing his climb to success as an economic expert, and that B. F.'s money has bought an ornate mansion for them near Washington. An erroneous but heartbreaking incident involving 'another woman' guides the self-sufficient Polly down the only path to reunion. It comes when she is willing to tell her husband, 'Tom, I need you so much.'" The important movie reviewers were as deprecating as some of the reviewers of the novel had been and thought, like Howard Barnes of the New York *Herald Tribune* and Bosley Crowther of the *Times,* that its original weaknesses had been magnified and its interest destroyed in the film version, which was not even a satisfactory vehicle for the minimal talents of Miss Stanwyck. Marquand took a wry amusement in the spectacle of Hollywood at work on his book. He had observed to a friend in March 1947: "The other day in New York I had lunch with a very nice boy who is doing the screen play of 'B. F.'s Daughter.' He is somewhat perplexed at a meeting of B. F.'s daughter with her husband's secretary, with whom her husband has been having an affair. For reasons of censorship, it is impossible to deal with adultery on the screen unless one or both of the parties gets killed or poisoned or something. As this is impossible in the picture, it has been decided the secretary must wear a brace on her leg to show that there could have been nothing wrong in the friendship. There is a lot of fun dealing with problems like this, but on the whole I think it is much nicer to starve quietly and to write for 'Good Housekeeping.'"

Clearly, Hollywood had no interest in Marquand's attempt to make a record of the mood of wartime. In fact, there was a tendency to suspect that war-connected subjects were beginning to lose audience appeal. Early in 1948 Marquand even heard that MGM was still trying to wring a script out of *So Little Time* by rewriting the story "without any reference to the war." In fact, the generation that had most acutely felt the experience of World War II was still involved with the memories that were becoming myth. In 1952 it would put its favorite general into the White House. Yet even then Marquand's newly published novel about a general would not readily find a welcome in Hollywood. Marquand asked for $200,000 for the screen rights in 1951 but found no takers, and the book was offered to one studio after another until, in 1955, the rights were sold for $46,500, and Melville Goodwin finally reached the screen in the person of Kirk Douglas in *Top Secret Affair* in 1956.

Marquand had been thinking hard about the military personality ever since his own close view of it during World War II. He had been fascinated by the enigma of leadership, not only in a flamboyant character like Patton but in the more standardized officer types he encountered in the Pentagon and during his military tours. After the 1947 trip with Admiral Denfield he proposed to *Life* that he try to make a sort of novelist's sense of Denfield, who was rumored to be in line for appointment as the next CNO. The profile-writing process got under way and Marquand began to supplement his recollections of the admiral with research into his personal history and a program of intensive interviewing before word came down that Denfield had been passed over for the appointment—and the project was no longer appealing to the magazine. Now, four years later, Marquand wrote a novel that was a fictional profile of a commander, *Melville Goodwin, U.S.A.* It would never have served General Goodwin as an election-campaign biography.

Marquand set out to discover the explanation for military effectiveness at the upper levels and elaborated his investigation in one of his longest works of fiction—and the hero turned out to be only another Boyden, a brave and able fellow with just a few ideas, and those of the most routine sort, ordinary in his virtues and ordinary in his failings. Marquand's problem in making an interesting story out of the life of such a man is represented within the novel by the difficulties of an interviewing team that is at work on the general's profile for a national magazine. Marquand drew upon his experience with such undertakings—he had been subjected to the operations of a profile team himself in 1944, when Roger Butterfield of *Life* had directed the research and written a story about him, and in 1949, when teams from both *Time* and *Newsweek* had developed cover stories on him. He himself had considered writing profiles on others, among them President Conant of Harvard, as well as Denfield. The uncompleted Denfield project, however, was the most significant in the composition of *Melville Goodwin.*

Marquand remembered complaining to Yeager, the Navy PR aide who was helping him dig up biographical materials on Denfield: "Up to date, with the exception of his mess boy, all the people I have seen are careful only to speak in enthusiastic and general terms. All I can gather is that the Admiral has always been a perfectly swell guy, a wonderful officer, efficient, kind, and brave as a lion, and with the genius of a Nelson. I know all this already and it doesn't make any sort of a profile. Can't you find me some people who will loosen up and tell a few stories which will make the Admiral more like the rest of us? He must have got sore at somebody sometime, and maybe Mrs. Denfield doesn't like the way he leaves his shaving soap in the washbasin, or something like that." As General Goodwin narrates his history for the interviewers, they, too, cannot help but notice the conventionality of the authentic life of the small-town boy who went to West Point, married his school-days sweetheart, was a good soldier during the First World War and waited out the period until the next by keeping his buttons bright and his wits alert at one post or another. He feeds the reporters little anecdotes about the places and persons he has met and he can tell a joke on himself becomingly—and it is all expectable, as true to formula as—well, as a magazine serial. But the demand for individuality that serious writing makes of its characters may, Marquand seems to argue, betray reality, which is so often more banal than fiction. Melville Goodwin, therefore, does not resemble any of the more colorful chiefs whom Marquand had met or read about. Yet, as his PR officer says, "he's got a few of the Patton traits" besides his faith in tanks. And the book's narrator replies, thinking of generals as a class, "They've got to be the same piece of goods because they all have to do the same thing." Marquand himself wrote an article for the *New York Times Magazine* during the election campaign of 1952, "An Inquiry into the Military Mind," in which he remarked: "Any general, past or present, is very much like any other general. All professional soldiers have similar attitudes and reactions, unavoidably, because they have the military mind."

In the novel, consequently, Marquand worked to define a type by means of close notation of representative details, and his instinct for telling detail was still operative. His working-up of the whole fabric of regular-army life—in the war theaters and at the Pentagon—was careful and full. The result was not quite as satiric as he could have made it—perhaps, like the narrator, Sidney Skelton, he is really of two minds about Goodwin, not certain at times whether to find him laughable or admirable, equally convinced of his limitations and his capacity of heroism. Yet exactly such a division of mind had functioned well in his previous successes with Apley and Pulham. With secondary figures like Mrs. Goodwin, the general's general, he was more lightheartedly comic. Where the book went awry was in the handling of the central story, the general's romantic entanglement with a rich publisher's widow, Dottie Peale, and the narrator's efforts to keep the general from ruining his life on her account. Somehow, the general's naiveté seems unbelievable, and, moreover, ludicrous.

How accurate the picture of military life was, from the expert's point of view, may be questioned, despite Marquand's abilities as an observer. Colonel Joseph I. Greene of the Association of the U.S. Army had been asked by Marquand's publishers to look at the manuscript and he responded with twenty-four pages of comments, largely critical. Principally, he objected to the portrait of Goodwin as a man who hated desk work, the occupation of the staff officer. He pointed out that to become a combat-division commander Goodwin would have had to have already spent half his service "at desks and at various staffs" and that the distinction between line officer and staff officer went out with World War I. The so-called field-soldier types never became generals in the Second World War, for staff ability would have been necessary even to a captain commanding a battalion. Altogether, Marquand had romanticized Goodwin into a simple-soldier type who could never have got his two stars in the modern army. In reality, such a man would, Greene objected, have become far more sophisticated in a hundred small ways than Mel Goodwin—would never have been uncertain about how to buy civilian clothes, for example. Marquand shrugged most of these objections away. He felt that his portrait was a true one.

If Marquand had failed, he had not failed as badly, anyhow, as the greater novelist of his own generation who had reared up with more false romantics the flabby image of Robert Cantwell in *Across the River and into the Trees,* a regular Army colonel once a breveted brigadier. Goodwin's prosaic likelihood and even his digression into a foolish love affair might be preferred to the exaltations and despairs of Hemingway's hero. But Marquand's book was in no sense a reply to Hemingway's, which had come out only months before his own. It seemed, on the other hand, to be an intended reply to the work of a younger generation of soldier-writers, like Norman Mailer, whose *The Naked and the Dead* had appeared in 1948 and offered still another image of a general. Mailer's General Cummings was a disturbingly meaningful figure, a representation of the ambiguous nature of power, both in the Army and in society at large. Yet it was not Marquand, but the younger Herman Wouk, in *The Caine Mutiny* published earlier in 1951, who wrote an explicit defense of authority—in this case of naval discipline and the Annapolis graduate. Though Marquand's novel was widely felt to be a similar defense of the Army product (the *Combat Forces Journal* claimed that Marquand deserved a special award from the Defense Department for showing "the armed forces as they actually are"), his novel is subtly deglamorizing; it is the banality rather than the evil *or* the virtue that clings to the figure of his military man. Marquand's general might even seem more frightening to the liberal spirit than a tyrannical reactionary in uniform because he is so innocent of emotions larger than a desire to be used for the special purpose for which he has been trained. His lifelong hope is that the world will continue to provide him with wars in which he can show what he can do. Leftist critics did not generally perceive this, however, probably because they read the novel exactly as the *Combat Forces Journal* had. Perhaps an extreme of miscomprehension was reached by a Soviet critic who broadcast on the Moscow radio concerning "America's Reactionary Literature in the Service of the Warmongers": "The widely advertised book written by John Marquand fully conforms to this program. His hero's thoughts are permeated with sorrow at the ending of the war and the alarm that a new war may not break out. The author stresses more than once that his hero, General Goodwin, is happy only on the battlefield or when expecting new bloodshed. The great success of this book bears witness to the fact that the author has managed to please the ruling circles."

The year 1951 was a year for war novels—the Pulitzer Prize for fiction went to *The Caine Mutiny* and the National Book Award to James Jones's *From Here to Eternity*; sales for the year were led by the Jones book, which sold 240,000 copies, closely followed by the Wouk novel, which sold 236,000. *Melville Goodwin* was linked in everyone's mind with these two, for it was an open secret that the Book Award judges had split five to seven between it and *The Caine Mutiny*, and Jones's popular success had been a compromise choice. (Discarded choices had been Faulkner's *Requiem for a Nun*, Styron's *Lie Down in Darkness*, Salinger's *Catcher in the Rye*, and Capote's *The Grass Harp*—none a war novel and each having some claim as a lasting work of fiction that was perhaps better than those three that were.) *Melville Goodwin*, though it had missed the prizes, did capture that guarantee of sales, selection by the Book-of-the-Month Club for December 1951 (scruples concerning Marquand's judgeship having been set aside).

And yet the middlebrow readership that had sustained Marquand's success in the past seemed to waver over *Melville Goodwin*. Booksellers found that they had overestimated the public reception of it and the sales were so low that the returns the next year were higher than they had ever been for a Marquand novel. In the long run there would be many copies sold—four paperback editions between 1951 and 1967 would rack up sales to 934,000, beyond the total for *So Little Time*. But its immediate impact was disappointing. Perhaps the theory that a serial publication damaged immediate book sales was substantiated this time, for the version of the novel that appeared in the *Ladies' Home Journal* was, as Marquand exclaimed when he saw proofs for the first installment, "the most God-awful hodge-podge you can imagine." But to Stanley Salmen of Little, Brown, he admitted, "I must accept this because I was paid an enormous sum for the prostitution." That sum had been $80,000, advanced even before the book had been written. One way or another he could not help continuing to make money.

Yet the critical reception of his book did not rejoice him. The *Time* reviewer said: "Novelist Marquand's stock does not plummet, but it passes a dividend. His effort to show that Army folk are somehow different from civilians, and stronger on the simpler virtues, falls flat because his examination of Mel never gets beyond his surface manner. The old Marquand narrative skill is still there, with its painless transitions and smooth flashbacks. The talk is easy and natural, whether the talkers are Pentagon brass or radio tinhorns. But they all seem to be saying the things that better Marquand characters have said before." Maxwell Geismar, in the usually genial *Saturday Review*, decided that this was "one of the poorer Marquand novels" and described—but failed to define—the thing that had been going wrong, as he saw it, in Marquand's more recent books: "They are marvelous entertainment, but somewhere along the line there has been an 'upward twist,' a cunning piece of literary magic through which the real story has disappeared and something else—a white rabbit, a handkerchief, an empty box—has been handed to us." And even the reviews in daily newspapers were more severe than they had generally been in the past. If Edmund Fuller in his syndicated column said that Marquand was "at the top of his form as a story teller and subtle satirist," the Kansas City *Star* reviewer declared, "I don't see how a man can have so little to say and say it so well." *Newsweek* had said that the novel "never seems overexpanded," but Anna Hunter, the astute reviewer for the Savannah *Journal*, declared, "It should not take 600 pages to prove that some generals are dull." The Minneapolis *Tribune* said likewise: "A novel that is not as important as *The Brothers Karamazov* should not be as long as *The Brothers Karamazov*." On the whole, Marquand's final attempt to register in fiction what the war years had taught him was less of a critical success than anything he had written since he had begun, with *Apley*, his effort to ascend the heights beyond magazine popularity. Such newspaper praise as the book received was apt to be animated by quite unliterary and unattractive prejudices, as the comment made by the New York *Daily News* showed: "In this warlike age it is a prime necessity for the United States to have such officers. Thanks to Mr. Marquand for a book (obviously the product of tremendous research) which is most reassuring—and a valuable contribution to American Literature, we'd say, than any half-dozen recent war books by soreheads whose gripes against the Army blind them to its many virtues. These are our generals—and we're lucky to have them."

19

The Second Postwar

One project of the war years had escaped the claims of the present and given Marquand a chance to return to the mood of his first literary success. In January 1944, on a day filled with the conferences at the Pentagon, he had lunch with Max Gordon, the producer, and the playwright George Kaufman to discuss a dramatization of *The Late George Apley.* Marquand went to work on it immediately in the R Street apartment amid domestic distractions tuned to an even higher pitch than usual by the tension of Washington, and continued his efforts to recast the novel into dramatic form at Kent's Island that summer. Edward Sheldon had told him, after criticizing the structure of *So Little Time,* "I think it would be a good idea if you wrote a play. That medium would force you to feel acutely responsible for movement, climax, and drama." Now Marquand seized the opportunity for disciplining his craft by submitting to the stringent requirements of the stage. Collaboration with Kaufman seemed to promise instruction as they blocked out the dramatic design and composed the dialogue of the play, though Marquand felt frequently that he was making sacrifices both aesthetic and thematic to Kaufman's practical judgment. He wrote Johnny in September: "I feel just too old to learn the technique of what the boys call 'theatre,' which seems to me a tortured and limited piece of business, consisting of one tenth writing and nine tenths arguing with and placating a lot of fuzzy-headed impresarios. George Kaufman, needless to say, knows 'theatre' backwards and forwards, but alas he is lacking in that attribute which St. Mark's boys like you and me would call background and taste. Now these things are not so important in the AEF as they are in the creative arts, and you can do 'You Can't Take It with You' and 'The Man Who Came to Dinner' without them, but they are necessary if you do anything but farce comedy. Frankly this whole collaboration has taught me two things. The first is that

I know nothing of play construction or how to gauge the effect of a line going over the footlights. The second is that I know how to write. At least I have some sense of the use of words in revealing character and thought, and George Kaufman hasn't. The net result is to me a painful piece of collaboration, good theatre, maybe, but intellectually lousy. The Gordon office, though, does not think it is bad."

Marquand's conferences with Kaufman took place, oftenest, during visits with Adelaide to Barley Sheaf Farm near Holicong, Pennsylvania. There Marquand found himself in a world he liked to describe aloud to others. Kaufman, he would relate, "had a swimming pool 600 yards long," four or five cars and an indeterminate number of bathrooms. In the elegant seclusion of this Bucks County estate the war seemed remote—until an occasion, never to be forgotten in the Marquand oral legend, when Mrs. Charles Lindbergh tried to telephone her friend Adelaide there. Mrs. Kaufman received the call from the wife of the man who had been decorated by Hermann Göring and refused to summon her guest. "You may call her back if you wish," she told Adelaide afterwards, "but not from this house."

Despite such reminders of present reality the work on the play about a vanished Boston continued, and it opened on the road in October. Marquand was suddenly swept up into the gypsy life of show business for which, as he told Johnny, "you must be born and not made, sitting up all hours, fussing, worrying and conversing." He became infected with the ever more constricting anxiety that afflicts theater people before an opening: "It is well enough for me to say to myself that Kaufman did most of the general planning of the play and that therefore when the critics pan it, as I think they will next Tuesday, the blame rests largely with him. It is also not enough to console myself with the thought that had I worked with a more literate playwright, it would have been a much better job. The fact of the matter is that there it is, and when you see something which is even only partly yours, played in front of an audience, you have a nervous naked feeling which cannot be compared with anything else." Marquand was present when the play opened in Wilmington for three nights and was well received but showed the need of some cutting, and he came along when it went to Washington for a week, after which the final scene was rewritten. Then he was in Baltimore for a week and in Boston for two more, while the actors continued to rehearse and the authors to alter and polish the lines. Despite the adjustments made in the script he was still unhappy about the play when it opened in New York at the Lyceum on November 21. "Though the customers think it funny, I don't think it is a good play. It is not a farce like 'Life with Father' and yet it has not the depth of good comedy, but falls unconvincingly somewhere in between, and this I feel is more my collaborator's fault than mine, since I have never been in a position to argue with him, knowing nothing of the theatre."

But the play was a success and ran for a full year. The audiences in New

York generally found what they had come to see—a somewhat broad comic treatment of a scene they did not know very exactly—and they loved best those farcical moments when Apley scolded a servant for placing Emerson on the bookshelf beside *The Scarlet Letter*, or, having looked into Freud, remarked that sex "very largely governs the lives of people . . . in other parts of the country." A high moment of stage comedy was reached in the episode of Cousin Hattie's invasion of the Apley burial plot and Apley's threat to have her dug up. Kaufman's dramatic instinct had reduced a life-saga to a single action-packed year in Apley's middle age—and eliminated, consequently, the effect of Apley's slow accommodation to the mold which Marquand had achieved in the book.

Leo G. Carroll, an experienced English actor, was generally held to have done an excellent job of interpretation. He had worked hard at getting into the spirit of the part of George Apley. Before rehearsals began he went up to Boston with Marquand, who introduced him to the St. Botolph's Club. He hung around at the club for several days, listening to the accents and observing the mannerisms of the gentlemen who came there. From time to time someone would come up to him and point to a member dozing in a corner. "That," the man would tell him, "is the real George Apley." The Boston Brahmin accent gave Carroll trouble, for he discovered that there was not one but a whole scale of accents, even among the select speakers of the St. Botolph's, who pronounced their native city in every gradation ranging from Bawston to Bastin. Marquand remained convinced that Carroll gave Apley's speech an Irish quality, and Kaufman communicated this to the actor who admitted only that his aspirated "*What* is it now, Margaret," projected energetically above the rustle of the programs as the curtain rose, might, misleadingly, have *sounded* Irish.

And yet, the play had, in the eyes of some discerning viewers, failed, just as Marquand feared it would. John Mason Brown conceded that the play was entertaining, but added, "especially if Mr. Marquand's novel is forgotten." But maybe, he seemed to acknowledge, the fault was not that of the writers of the play but simply of Time. In 1937 the novel had performed a daring feat by exhuming the vanishing concept of the "gentleman." Now, only seven years later, in the midst of war, it was clear that nobody, not even in Boston, was sure any longer of what that person had been. Though the Proper Bostonians were still a fit subject for comedy, the serious value of their standards was bound to be lost upon the audiences that applauded the play.

When the play became a film three years later, its lingering reference to a significant American past had vanished altogether. The movie opened with fanfare as part of the Easter holiday offering at Radio City Music Hall. It was framed by a lavish stage spectacle, and despite the elaborate scenic reconstruction by the director Joseph Mankiewicz, it bore little relation to the Boston of 1912. The integrity and pathos of the original character of

George Apley, somehow admirable despite his rigidities, had been altered out of recognition. Ronald Colman was a spruce charmer in pearl-gray spats and wing collar, who delivered his lines in a lilting tone and with flourishing gestures that, as Bosley Crowther, the New York *Times* reviewer said, gave "a Hollywood bedside manner to the role." The change was not really the actor's fault alone. Apley had been reconceived by the scriptwriter, Philip Dunne, as a fuddy-duddy who is converted to geniality. Whereas the original George Apley had prohibited his daughter's unconventional marriage, Apley–Colman literally winked at the marriage of the delectable Peggy Cummins. The film got lavish publicity, with picture spreads in both *Life* and *Look*, and it did well at the box office. But Marquand, who was in Nassau when it opened in March 1947, had taken very little interest in its progress. The price paid in 1944 for film rights to the play had been of consoling proportions—$275,000, reputedly the most ever put down for film rights by a Hollywood producer and more than twice as much as the payment, previously record-breaking, for the rights to *So Little Time*.

Even Marquand's own sense of Proper Bostonianism doubtless had been slipping since the war. There was the incident—already referred to—that occurred in the fall of 1943 after Marquand came back from his trip to the war theaters with General Simmons. He had apologized formally to the Tavern Club for using "ungentlemanly" language. But he had written Stewart Forbes with an irony that the House Committee chairman may have overlooked: "It was most thoughtless of me not to have given this consideration before I spoke, and this makes me realize that I have picked up bad habits and language from certain sections of the Army with whom I consorted while abroad. Further I can see that the whole story may be more amusing to someone who has been pushed about recently by the natives of Cairo than to someone who has not."

The Apley play closed on November 17, 1945, a little over a month after V-J Day, and the postwar era, with all its uncertainties, immediately arrived. Marquand, as an experienced world watcher, saw the future as highly problematical. A lifelong Republican, he voted for Roosevelt in 1944. "I am relieved that Roosevelt was elected the other day rather than Dewey," he told Johnny, still overseas. "The Old Man, whatever his faults may be, is able to sense the trend of world events, and is able to cut policy to conform to these trends, instead of trying to pour trends into the mould of fixed ideas, as the Old Guard Republicans over here are still trying to." He did not vote for Truman in the next election, but he remained convinced that Roosevelt had properly understood the strategic necessities of the war. Although he classified himself as a "non–New Dealer" he accepted membership on the FDR Birthday Memorial Committee in 1952 because, he said to Robert E. Sherwood, he could not "forget his courage or the high quality of leadership he gave us." Yet he still felt that Roosevelt's "intellectual dishonesty" had been evident in the methods by which he had brought the country to take the necessary step of war. "When Sherwood makes his deceits and contrivances seem noble and Christ-like, as one of the palace guard should," he confided to someone else, "I get a little sick to my stomach."

Realizing that the national economy and political temper had undergone a permanent change as a result of Roosevelt's leadership, he betrayed the self-contradictions that arose from his attitudes towards established privilege and wealth. "When you get back home I don't believe you will know the old place," he told Johnny in 1944. A year later he had a further report on economic trends to give: "The *rentier* class, which includes most little St. Mark's boys, is on the ropes and getting slugged with lefts and rights, and I imagine that the standard of living in the upper brackets is going to be permanently pushed down." His tone was curiously complacent; it sounded as though he took satisfaction in the unsettling of the *rentiers*, the St. Mark's boys. Yet his observations about the discomfiture of the rich took off from the rising cost of household help under his own roof. Chambermaids were now getting thirty-five dollars a week, including their board and keep, and "the other day the waitress left and we let the cook go largely because they were not worth the money we were paying them. It is tough enough now to get someone to do odd jobs or to get the washing done."

He foresaw even more transforming developments in Europe. "When this show is over, I have no idea and I don't think anyone else has of what will happen in Europe. The way things have been smashed up there makes it all a problem." A good many people were throwing around the word *communism*. But Marquand showed a prescient sense of the complexities in the term: "I think it is employed very loosely, and covers a hundred ideas regarding the relation of property to the common weal. Knowing little about it, I am willing to bet that the communism which you see in France is more akin to the ideology of the French revolution than it is to the doctrines of Marx. Communism in China again is something different, and so again in Greece. Russian communism is undergoing radical changes. The most old-fashioned and confused doctrinaires are the communists here in America—theorists who are miles from reality. We are living in a chaos of political and social thought and I don't know what the ultimate development may be, except that things will never be what they once were, and that we will all be shifting somehow in a leftist direction—maybe not such a bad idea either, when you read of life in America and England in the early days of this century." He was to be proved wrong, of course, about the direction this country would take in the Eisenhower period—the road of national politics would swerve to the right rather than to the left—but his long-range sense of the multiform potentialities of the communist idea was to prove remarkably correct.

Marquand became aware that since 1941 his private life, too, had traveled a distance difficult to estimate. His eldest son and daughter were now adults launched upon separate lives. Tina, since her bolt from Westover in 1943, had ceased to give him cause for worry. Two years later, when she had graduated from Winsor and was about to enter Bennington College, Marquand remarked with complacency that she was "now a very attractive girl and quite a number in the debutante world." He expressed anxiety because her current boyfriend suffered from migraine headaches and was making her read Schopenhauer, but he was never to be seriously troubled about her; she would prove to be the most stable of his children, the one on whom, in the end, he felt he could most certainly rely. In 1948 she married a very respectable young college professor who was working for his Harvard doctorate in history, Richard Welch. His family came from Newburyport.

Johnny, still in Europe in the fall of 1945, began to worry Marquand by showing an inclination to linger abroad like some of those veterans of the First World War. "I once had such an idea myself, and I love the civilization there, and both the simple and the complicated pleasures, and the sophisticated and esthetic qualities of France," he told his son. "However, I am very glad I did not. If you are not born a Frenchman, you can never wholly identify yourself with the life there. You are always something of an outsider, and furthermore, as time goes on you cannot adjust yourself to things at home either. You end by becoming an expatriate which is a very unhappy and unsatisfactory status." Johnny undoubtedly was thinking that the lives of such expatriates as Hemingway and Gertrude Stein had contained some satisfaction, but Marquand offered cautionary examples. There was Aunt Greta's second husband, Jack Oakman, "born in Pittsfield, Massachusetts and educated at Williams College, who went to the Beaux Arts, went nuts about France and knows the language better than he does English, and has been unhappy ever since because nothing here is like France and nothing in France is like America." Another family example often cited with high derision was, of course, Christina's brother Shan, who had lived abroad for many years as a New York *Times* correspondent. "His career, though glamorous, seems to me basically unsatisfactory," Marquand flatly declared. Oakman and Sedgwick and others like them were "all playing a little game and are all out of touch with reality." As for writers—and Johnny had shown some indications of wanting to be a writer—"there is Louis Bromfield, who might have been a good writer if he had not elected to settle on the Riviera where he lived until what we call 'the fall.' Now he is unable to write anything deserving serious attention. His background is American and his instincts are continental. He has a split personality." And he added without going into details, "So, likewise, has Hemingway." He went on to pour this overeasy scorn on expatriates in general, insisting that he did not want Johnny to be an isolationist, but hoped that he would be at home anywhere in the world. "But I don't think you can get away from being a U.S. citizen. Of all the people I know, only Americans, because of some sort of inferiority complex, keep attempting the impossible and keep trying to get away from their environment. This seems particularly true with women, not to mention Lesbians and homosexuals. The American colony in Paris, Rome and Peking, and anywhere else, is a pretty sad group on the whole." Johnny had protested that he had no desire to "go to pot on the Côte d'Azur"; he simply wanted to get some kind of government job that would keep him on to watch the European spectacle unfold for a while—and the prospect of going back to Harvard "and putting about there, minus a few very dear friends, for a couple of years in order to get a degree," did not appeal to him. But Marquand was only slightly reassured. He urged his son to come back to finish out his college program: "Your educational background, though vivid, is somewhat spotty, and I think you should give up a couple of years, dull though they may be, in order to get a degree from an institution of higher learning." He did not at all insist on Harvard. "I suggest that you consider some sort of compromise such as going to Columbia or going out to the Middle West where the future of America lies, if we have any future, and attending the University of Wisconsin." On the issue of expatriation he was again reliving, in his identification with Johnny, the choices of his own past.

If Johnny did not become an expatriate there was the other danger, to be feared by a conservative American parent at the war's end, that he might become a Red. Though Marquand had himself the openness to ideas of change that had made him vote for Roosevelt in 1944 and even declare that a shift to the left might be a good thing for the country, he began to be alarmed at the way war experience was altering the viewpoint of many of Johnny's friends. One was Alfred McIntyre's son Harry, back in the States having finished fifty-five missions with the Fifteenth Air Force and emerging as a captain with a DSC. Marquand encountered him in the summer of 1945, and expressed himself in characteristic ironic mode: "It appears that Harry had led a sheltered life in Boston and Milton, and then over in Italy he met a lot of people who were not Harvard boys or Milton graduates. He saw a lot of tough plane mechanics and a lot of simple peasants. It seems to have surprised Harry very much that all these people were basically good Joes, simple, kind and generous, and more hep to the great verities than most of his privileged friends. While Harry was doing some ferry work at Casablanca, he even found himself playing about with a Negro pilot and this boy, in spite of his pigmentation, he discovered, was just as good or better than the average member of the Porcellian Club. All this has always seemed to me very obvious but to Harry it was a revelation, and now he wants the social order changed. He believes that everyone in his age group should work towards Communism, and he has piles of paper-covered books from the International Press, such as 'The Dialectics' of Karl Marx, and 'The Social Fundamentals of History' by Stalin. Personally, when I tried to read some of these works, the sentences were so long and involved that I could extract no meaning from them, and I don't believe that Harry can either." He added the warning to Johnny: "Maybe it is just as well to let ideas and great discoveries simmer for a while, particularly as there are going to be a lot of queer ideas and discoveries in the next few years."

Johnny did not, as it turned out, take either dreaded course. If Marquand tended to see a replication of himself in his son it was also true that Johnny, despite a show of resistance, had a deep, if hardly conscious wish to be like his father. Harry McIntyre went to Columbia to finish his college studies, but for Marquand's son there appeared to be no question, after all, about returning to Harvard. He also wanted to be a writer, and the summer of 1946 he was trying to find a place for himself in the slick-magazine world, where his father's career had first flourished. Marquand's old friend Herbert Mayes, the editor of *Good Housekeeping*, was glad to give the young man a start as a manuscript reader in his office. In June 1947, twenty-three-year-old Johnny graduated from Harvard. He had even gone beyond replication of the paternal actuality and eliminated one of the flaws in his father's college career by being duly elected a member of the Fly Club. Immediately after graduation he was married to a pretty Sarah Lawrence student, Rita Delafield Kip, who was described in the newspapers as a "New York socialite." Marquand's only objection to Johnny's choice seems to have been the color of her hair, a frankly artificial blond, which, however, she pleased him by dyeing back to its natural hue shortly before the wedding.

Marquand's own domestic life, meanwhile, had been growing more and more difficult in many ways. It was "a humdrum world not quite of diapers," he told a friend, "but of children recently removed from them." He had three youngsters living with him who had become distinct personalities ready to make new and difficult emotional demands yet still irresponsibly noise-making and distracting. He had never found the company of small children supportable for very long, had been an irritable father even to Johnny and Tina; now he was in his fifties, and Adelaide's efforts to protect him from the incursions of his younger offspring seemed as ineffectual as Christina's had been. Ferry from the first had been a bright child; Marquand, who was intelligent enough to recognize signs of superior quality in her endless enterprise and curiosity, would find himself quite exhausted by an afternoon of her company. "Take her," he would say to the children's nurse, Miss Malquinn, "for God's sake, take her away. I'm much too old for this sort of thing." Her young brothers, Timmy and Lonny, added to his impression that his home was filled with clamor. He had a way of snarling the phrase "the patter of little feet" which was well remembered by many to whom he mock-woefully described his domesticity. When he gave over the effort to concentrate on some reading or writing of his own he was "obliged to read 'The Swiss Family Robinson' and listen to the adventures of the Hardy boys," an activity for which he had little taste. To be the father of young children did not, as sometimes happens, make the middle-aged father feel younger. For the thirty-fifth anniversary report of his Harvard class he wrote, after summarizing some of his war work: "Aside from these activities I have been involved in raising a large family, a difficult and distracting process." In response to the demand for his thoughts on Life and History he had added with his usual exaggeration, "These and other matters during the past decade have so occupied my attention that I have no fixed ideas on anything and so abstain from giving any."

Kent's Island, the homestead where he had hoped to lead the simple, quiet, country life, was a scene neither simple nor quiet when Frances Alexander, a writer for *Vogue*, visited it in 1944. She more or less transcribed Marquand's own seriocomic complaints. "The Marquand farm in Massachusetts looks peaceful and remote. It stands on a hummock in the middle of the salt marshes—a sprawling house with large screen porches—a surrounding cluster of white clapboard buildings—a cow pasture—an orchard—a few fields of hay—a large vegetable garden. The nearest town, Newburyport, is almost four miles away, so it should be quiet. But it isn't. From sunup to sundown it's the scene of violent skirmishes, the battleground of a war, which, in its intensity, makes Thurber's most sanguinary drawings look positively anemic." Like most wars, she observed, this one was a battle for peace. Marquand told her that he just "damn well wants to be let alone," but with his three children, all under four years old, and a household of servants who came and went so fast that it was "impossible to call anyone by name," peace was elusive. "If the farmer's dog hasn't bitten the baby, then the hard water filter's on the blink—and if it isn't the filter, the nurse and the cook have come to blows, or the man from Boston has come to hang the new curtains, and John, dear, don't you think they're much yellower than the samples?" The journalist had accurately caught the note of Marquand's voice, including the wicked mimicry of Adelaide's whining interruption of his "peace" with some trivial inquiry. He had located his studio in the old barn, adjoining the tool and tractor shed, a pleasant sunny room with an open fireplace, maps and prints on the walls, a big maple table in the center. There he generally worked, dictating to a secretary until lunch or until, as he would relate it, there was heard a faint scratching on the screen door. It would be Adelaide, "her solid figure wrapped in a cotton tennis dress, her bushy blond hair on end, her eyes alight with humor and enthusiasm." Something Had Happened. Marquand would stop in midsentence. "What is it, Adelaide?" he would growl. There would be a quite legitimate reason for her interruption, of course. It would require that he knock off for the rest of the morning, and stamp out to investigate a problem that had arisen in the house or on the farm. Still fuming, he would finally arrive at the lunch table and offer any chance visitor a vivid analysis of the fragility of newborn pigs or the cost per potato of the homegrown vegetable on the plates, all with the slightly hysterical exaggeration of his customary rhetoric.

Marquand relished the complications, too. In the fall it was haying time—and salt hay, the only marketable crop on the place, had to be harvested with enormous effort by everyone. Marquand would strip to the waist and spend the afternoon tossing the mown hay onto the wagon or unloading it into the barn. He complained, but he took an intense interest in his stock animals, though it seemed to the friends to whom he would relate his woes that his sheep were always suffering from worms or eating him out of house and home. In 1944 he would declare to the novelist Kenneth Roberts that he would have to leave Washington in the midst of his war activities "either to milk my cows myself or to watch someone milk them who is not sufficiently responsible to be allowed to milk them alone." His hired help, like the household servants, were constantly providing more cause for distressed outcries. The manager he put in charge of things would run up bills without consulting him and he would feel as helpless in handling the man's ingenious excuses as had Jeffrey Wilson in *So Little Time* in asserting himself to his Mr. Gorman. To Roger Butterfield of *Life* he would offer an account on a return from Kent's Island to New York: "I have been in the country looking at the crops and at the peasants and sniffing the rich smell of manure until I felt very much like a character in a Tolstoy novel and now, thank God, I am out of it for a little while and wish that I might be relieved from ever again seeing either the front or rear end of a cow or any part of a tractor. We have a new man who, for some odd reason, is called a 'farmer.' No sooner did he arrive than his wife began to have hemorrhages and he began to develop strange complexes, the most important of them an intense fear of the draft horse, a fear which has grown to such proportions that he has been unable to clean the manure out of the stall. He has also become so frightened of the ram that he is unable to clean out the sheep barn and I am sure in another week he will become so frightened of the world that he will be unable to do any work whatsoever." Nothing thrived at Kent's Island. Even the police puppy, Moto, caught distemper.

Humorous exaggeration allowed for, Kent's Island *had* proved less of an arcadian retreat than expected. In the summer the black flies were a scourge (in 1945 he appealed to his friend General Simmons for War Department DDT with which to fight them), and when the flies departed in the autumn the mice and rats would infest the house in surprising numbers. But, above all, the water at Kent's Island had been unsatisfactory from the beginning. When he had first moved there he discovered that there were five or six wells on the property, all dry. He had hired engineers, who put a pump into the most promising of these and forced up a thick brown liquid at seven gallons a minute. More elaborate and costly machinery and filtering devices were installed, but still the water contained so much iron and manganese that Marquand's whiskey highball had an ominous dark color and a peculiar smell. After an expensive new well failed, Kenneth Roberts brought over a man named Harry Gross, who claimed to be able to locate hidden water sources with a dowsing rod. Roberts and Gross studied the Kent's Island terrain together, producing a map that indicated a splendid dome at one end of the property. From it a vein of fine drinking water supposedly flowed at twenty-two gallons a minute, and Marquand was persuaded to get a hole dug with an air compressor. After forty-eight hours a small amount of water was indeed apparent in the bottom of the hole—but not enough for another costly go at well digging. "I don't know what has happened to Kent's Island," Marquand said to Johnny. "Seven or eight years ago it used to be a simple place with only the Ricketts [the caretakers] living in one end of the house, but it has assumed such monumental proportions that I should like to give it all back to the Indians." Certainly the mere mechanics of daily life had become more complex. It should be observed also that the humdrum householder problems which might have figured as minor annoyance to someone else became for Marquand one of Fate's assaults upon his effort to achieve a tranquil and productive middle age. He added the chronicles of the Kent's Island water battle to his dramatic monologues. They would seem comic in his stylized narration, yet they voiced his feeling of being crowded to the wall by petty distresses and distractions.

His aging father also increasingly presented a problem. Philip Marquand had an income of a little over $3,000 a year but contributed very little of it to the expense of supporting himself at Curzon's Mill (he still loved to gamble and was reputed to play the local slot machines regularly). He had been living for some years in the Brick House with his niece Laura Hale and her husband Pat, to whom Marquand made a regular allowance for his father's care. Early in 1947, however, Laura suffered a mental breakdown and Philip was left to fend for himself, a situation, his son decided, that was absolutely untenable. Philip had, indeed, become unreliable in financial matters. Marquand had tried for some time to persuade him to agree to a conservatorship, whereby his money would be put into someone else's hands—and this step was finally taken in November. But it was even doubtful if the eighty-two-year-old man could look after his daily needs alone. He could no longer drive. After several accidents—in one a bicyclist had been injured—Marquand had had his father's license revoked. If Philip were to stay on at the Mill—as he strongly desired—he would need caretaking company.

The situation at the Mill had other aspects. The property—forty-seven acres, the fourteen-room Yellow House, the eleven-room Brick House, and the seventeenth-century grist mill—had been allowed to deteriorate, for neither the Hales nor Philip had done much towards keeping the buildings in repair. Left vacant during the winter, they had even been vandalized. As Marquand struggled with Kent's Island he had also begun to worry about this ancestral estate on the other side of Newburyport. It was owned in a very complicated way by his father, himself, and Aunt Greta through varieties of joint and common possession of its different parcels, which had been added together through the inheritances of four generations. He conceived the idea of making an appeal to the courts for a division—a plea that could be made on the grounds that under the existing forms of ownership the property was losing value through neglect. In the usual course, such an action would lead to a public auction. If this were done, he could probably bid successfully for the entire place. Thus, he would not only bring the whole of Curzon's Mill under his management, but be able to realize the dream he had once cherished and relinquished: to make this home of his youth his own, establishing himself in affluence and fame in the hereditary seat of the Curzons, which he had left long ago as a poor boy. He would sell troublesome Kent's Island—he could never feel the same sentiment for it—and move his family to the Yellow House, which would be repaired and improved. His father would stay at the adjoining Brick House, to be looked after by the year-round caretaker when the Marquands were away. The old Mill building, where he had written his first magazine story, would make an excellent studio. So he launched in 1947 upon one of the most curious episodes of his life.

Marquand had asked his aunt to sell her share of the property to him ten years earlier, but she had refused—and he had bought Kent's Island. Now, he renewed his efforts, though it was apparent that he would again meet with opposition and even resentment from her and from her children. They also regarded Curzon's Mill as their ancient home and came and went there during the summertime. They were, in fact, bound to resent the presumption that their cousin John had a superior claim of family pride. Yet Marquand insensitively declared that he was moved to try to get it all into his own hands, not only to make an arrangement that would keep his father in his own house but because "I have a deep affection for the place itself. I have lived on it off and on since I was two years old, and I believe I have been there for a longer period of time than any of your own children. Furthermore, I feel a deep sense of personal responsibility regarding the future of the place, as Aunt Bessie and Aunt Molly both asked me, in the last years of their lives, to take care of it and not let it go to pieces, as it is in the process of doing now." When his offer was not accepted, he advanced other proposals, perhaps not with entire sincerity—that Greta buy his and his father's share of the property so that the whole could come under one ownership and so be better cared for (she could not have afforded to do this even if she wanted to, and Marquand refused to accept a mortgage from her as payment); or that she sell to him at half value and retain the right to use the property when she liked for her lifetime. None of these suggestions engaged the interest of Greta and her children to any serious degree and were probably not expected to.

The Hales felt, in fact, that they were being harassed as John's proposals began to come to them insistently—and in the course of repeated and heated arguments—in the fall of 1947. The anxiety aroused in Greta was, her children were convinced, a threat to her health. Dudley Hale wrote to Marquand: "You see, so many people are involved, and so many degrees of need and feeling, that it is very hard to treat this affair as a simple transaction. It is, when you come right down to it, the only place that any of us Hales owns—or feels that it is owned by his family—and one hates to give up the last vestige of what, in however distant and inaccessible a degree it may be, nevertheless represents what one feels as 'home.' This must be particularly so in Greta's case and I rather feel that the spiritual wrench of selling her mother's place would take so much out of her as to perhaps result in serious consequences. Then there is the question of who has what. You have a place to live in and you have achieved a capacity to earn money enough to buy us out. But we are a scattered lot, with small and scattered incomes—all harried by the same tax and dependency problems which make the money seem like so little when we finally approach the net." He felt that the issue had reached a perilous acuteness for Greta. Robert Hale complained to his lawyer that his mother had suffered a number of heart attacks "brought on by arguments concerning property with John and Adelaide. You understand how she might feel as a mere tenant on the land she loves so much—and always intended to hand on to her children. I am not exaggerating when I say that the loss of her sense of ownership in the property might be the cause of her death. Why cannot John and Adelaide understand this?" His prediction seemed to be realized when Greta Hale did die suddenly at the end of January. Three days earlier she had received still another proposal from Marquand of a division of the property. He threatened her politely with an appeal to the courts that could result in the sale of everything to him if she did not agree to this plan—or could not afford to meet his terms.

The cable announcing Greta's death came to him so late, while he was away in the Bahamas, that he had been unable to attend her funeral. He felt defensive about the probable attitudes of the Hales and observed to his lawyer, Murray Forbes: "Needless to say, had I been able to look into the future last summer and autumn I would not have endeavored to have settled the ownership of Curzon's Mill, and I can only hope that our efforts in that direction did not disturb her last month too much. Although in all practical ways Aunt Greta was unrealistic to the point of exasperation, I have always been deeply fond of her and most grateful to her for her kindness to me when I was a child and an adolescent and when my parents were away as they were for years in California and Panama. Looking back, however, I cannot violently reproach myself for the efforts I made in trying to get her to buy the place or sell it, especially in view of my father's increasing dependence on me. I can only hope that her children will appreciate this side of the question but, knowing them, I don't suppose they will." Greta's children—Herbert, Margaret, Robert, Edward, Laura and Renée—now owned 38 percent of the property and Marquand 19 percent, while the remaining 43 percent still belonged to Philip.

With the death of Greta Hale all pretense of a desire for continued co-ownership with the Hales was over. "Difficult as co-ownership of the place has been with my aunt and my father, it will be impossible with my cousins," he observed. He withdrew his offer to sell to them and put himself on record as being averse to any arrangement that would result in their occupying any of the three buildings on the property. He suggested that they use the money he would pay them for their share—he subtracted the cost of making repairs and offered $12,000—to buy another piece of land nearby on which to build themselves a new house. He needed it all, he insisted, for his wife and children, his father, a caretaker couple, a studio for himself. His further reasons were admitted to his lawyer and to friends. The Brick House was only two hundred feet from the Yellow House, and across that brief distance the offensive qualities of the Hales would be felt as a corrupting infection. He refused, he said, "to face the problem of having my small children exposed to the mode of certain individuals." His cousins knew what he meant, having, since they had read *Wickford Point* in 1939, a pretty good idea of Marquand's opinion of their personalities and habits. Time had not improved his view of Renée, in particular, by now three times divorced, who was often heard to identify herself frankly with Marquand's satirical picture of Bella Brill.

About his father's attitude as co-owner he was by no means sure, and the fact that part of the property held jointly by Greta and her brother now reverted to Philip, who had already possessed the largest of the shares, made Marquand and his lawyer uneasy, for the unpredictable old man might do anything, even making a will that would disinherit his son. Marquand pressed his father's conservator, Ralph Webb, to arrange to sell the elder Marquand's shares to him before that might happen. "He may very well do this as he is much incensed about the conservatorship," Marquand observed. So this was applied for, though Marquand's lawyer pointed out that such a sale by a conservator would simply increase the money in Philip's bank account, and that this sum could itself be willed away. It was decided nonetheless that in case this should happen the old man's generally acknowledged feebleness made it likely that any change of his will would be ruled invalid.

Such, in the spring and summer of 1948, was the state of Marquand's relations with his close relatives in Newburyport. It was a condition that soon became a local scandal, with sympathy high on the side of the Hales. Marquand, who had labored so strenuously to establish himself as the town's first citizen, was now seen by his fellow townsmen as a rich man who was trying to drive his poor kin from their home, and despite his claim that his chief motive was provision for Philip, the word got around that the old fellow was being callously manipulated. "I now feel that my rights in the place not only equal but exceed those of my cousins," John Marquand was heard to say, but most of his neighbors did not agree. Nevertheless, on July 22 he took the final step. A petition for partition, expected to result in public auction, was filed, and on October 21 the hearings opened in the Salem Probate Court.

The case at once became a national news story, full of color. Present in the court were the famous novelist, tweedy and confident, little old Philip, looking rather morose, and the "embattled Hales." Reporters took note of Edward Hale, an Actors' Equity executive; of Robert Hale, a director of the Metropolitan Museum; and, particularly, of Renée Oakman Bradbury, still handsome at thirty-seven, who, they were reminded, was a former Powers model. Before the hearing she was photographed at her home on Long Island with her pet dogs and birds, including a talking blue jay, and she showed up in the staid Salem courtroom in a stylish gown and hat. But the principal note struck by the Hales was to be that of innocence abused. Visible on the counsel table were copies of *Wickford Point*. The Hales would use the novel in making a claim that they were being persecuted by their cousin, who had already made literary profit out of their idiosyncrasies and was now trying to rob them of their patrimony. The Hales spoke at length of their attachment to Curzon's Mill. Robert Hale said: "I should hate to see it leave the family. It is full of family legends. Our mother was married in the mill and she and my father rowed up the Artichoke River in a rowboat. It is the only place we have ever owned." Margaret Hale Thorne, who had come up from her home in San Antonio for the trial, recalled that she had spent twenty-one summers at Curzon's Mill, which she called "our last link with our mother and father and our childhood." Robert Hale was also quoted as saying: "We want it because it has been a part of us for so long and when you get old you want to go back to the beginning. The family has always lived there. The weddings are always there. The family has always gone back there to die—and be buried on the hill. We still like John. He has as much right there now as we have. He has relatives buried up on the hill. But we judge everything on the heart, John on the dollar. He is using the proceeds of 'Wickford Point,' indirectly perhaps, to put us out as characters, to kick out his cousins."

The Hale attorney, a local lawyer named James Connolly, was inspired to end his argument with a peroration that reminded the court that the Hales were the great-grandchildren of Edward Everett Hale, author of *The Man Without a Country*. He solemnly said, "Requiring sale of the land would subject his heirs to the cruel punishment of the man without a country. Their roots are here." Some of the reporters got the impression that Curzon's Mill had actually once belonged to Edward Everett Hale, which was, of course, not true at all—but in the general inflation of sentiment one exaggeration more or less was unimportant. Marquand found himself quite swamped by the wash of indignation that the Hales had aroused against him. His own lawyer, Albert Wolff, made an unsuccessful protest that "sentiment has no place here; it is a question of the greatest profit to all concerned. But if you are going to weigh sentiment at the bar, the petitioner has sentiment for the place too." Wolff, who was an outsider, a member of a big Boston firm, had struck precisely the note that offended the local people in the gallery. They had responded to Connolly's rhetoric.

And it was local sentiment that won. Marquand, expecting an order for sale, had let the court know he was ready to pay up to $40,000 to buy out his cousins, but Judge Phelan decided to decree a division "by metes and bounds." This meant, first, that the various parcels were taken apart so that Marquand got three twenty-fourths of one, three twelfths of another; his father fifteen twenty-fourths of one and three twelfths of another, and each of the six cousins one twenty-fourth of one parcel and one twelfth of another. The fragmentation left them all dissatisfied and was reviewed again, resulting in a new division the following July by which the Marquands, father and son, got both the Yellow House and the Brick House and some land, and the Hales the Mill and the rest of the land. Marquand's hope that they would be required to sell anything to him was definitely defeated, though he was able to reach an agreement with them by which he got the Mill in exchange for the Brick House. He was never to have the undivided demesne he had longed for and would not be able to exchange Kent's Island for the Mill property since a part of the latter would always be in the hands, as he put it, of "six families who intend to turn it into a summer resort." For some years he rented out the Yellow House. Only when Johnny and Tina were grown and married did he encourage them to use it and the old Mill building for summer vacations. He himself never lived there again. In 1951 he told his daughter that although Adelaide wanted to move to Curzon's Mill, "I don't think I shall ever want to live there with my relatives next door, the sight of whom always increases my blood pressure and makes me very ugly."

The struggle had been deeply defeating and humiliating, for there could have been no Marquand reader who missed the conspicuous stories in every daily newspaper that carried reports of the trial, and the accounts in *Time*, the *New Yorker* and *Life*. The *Life* picture story, which showed views of Curzon's Mill and the contestants as well as a genealogical chart of the Marquand–Hale relation, had been titled "Trouble at Wickford Point," giving a new view of the writer the same magazine had called the most successful in America. In the neighborhood of Newburyport the impression remained strong that Marquand had tried to take—had even taken—what was not his. "Did you filch it?" asked a visitor there one day in the summer of 1952 as she contemplated the portrait of Mary Russell that had previously hung in the Yellow House. "How's that again?" Marquand had responded. "I said, 'Did you filch it?'" the lady had repeated. Marquand, after counting ten, as he remembered, told her that the picture had been left him by his aunt Molly, together with all her personal property at Curzon's Mill. It would have been futile to try to explain to anyone that he had not been urged into his curious battle over land and things by greed, that he was a haunted man who craved a fullness of coming-home, final authentication as the true heir to a kingdom from which he had once been sent out to make his way friendless and unrecognized.

Meanwhile, "home" for the Marquand family continued to be something more like a caravan journey across rough terrain with a noisy, ill-organized company than a settled, stable existence. "Home" was always at least three places in every year—sometimes more. Though Marquand had enjoyed foreign travel, his trips had been the more welcome because they were intervals of freedom from the trammels of personal relationship. Shuttling from one habitation to another with Adelaide and the children was another story. During the war they had given up the apartment at One Beekman Place in New York but moved into a house in Washington so that Marquand could be close to his War Department office. Then, when the work on the *Apley* play got under way, it was obvious that he would have to be nearer New York for a period, and in the fall of 1944 they were all in a cottage on the Hooker estate in Greenwich. Stays long and short with Adelaide's mother soon became a regular part of their yearly program. As soon as the children were old enough for school it was decided that Greenwich provided better educational opportunities for them than Newbury, and the family spent at least part of several winters there. Marquand, however, increasingly found the situation at his mother-in-law's establishment impossible for work. In 1949, he took an apartment on Sixty-seventh Street in Manhattan, where he would remain during the week.

In the summer of 1944 Timmy came down with a severe case of asthma and received a series of tests to determine whether, as Adelaide said, "it was due to ragweed or Sandy [the children's dog] or just the general atmosphere of hypertension in the family." The last factor might have been considerable, it now seems. When Timmy got out of his teens he was somehow no longer an asthma sufferer, but he was seriously afflicted throughout his childhood, subject to sudden attacks of near suffocation which could terrify the household. The doctors, at any rate, decided that a warm climate might help, and that winter, after the month in Greenwich, the Marquands moved down to Hobe Sound in Florida to remain until May. Hobe Sound had proposed itself naturally because George Merck and his wife were regularly there in the winter; the Marquands had visited them several times and found the climate delicious. Besides, there was excellent tennis for Adelaide.

Towards this playground of the very rich Marquand would develop an attitude of mingled distaste and fascination. After his long trip to the war theaters he was glad to be among civilians again and, to Adelaide's surprise, went to a lot of parties. Soon, however, the zest began to wear off. One day at a luncheon at Palm Beach he looked about him and realized that he had never seen so many dull people. Not even his old friends on West Cedar and Beacon streets could compare with the denizens of Chicago, St. Louis and St. Paul who sat at the tables all around him. To Tina he described the rituals at Hobe Sound: "At noon everyone foregathers, as they say in books, at the Beach Club—a sort of semi-enclosed pavilion beside the surf. Here drinks are dispensed from a little bar to tired executives, most of them in their sixties, dressed in schoolboy clothes, and to their women who are either their daughters about your age or reformed chorus girls. Then there is a cafeteria lunch, which means that you have to take your own tray and bring it all by yourself to the table. Lots of women get their diamond bracelets mixed up in the potato salad and break their pearls as they lean over for a piece of black market roast beef. The noise is terrific because everybody is having lots and lots of fun, and thank God, here we all are in the divine Florida sunshine." Johnny, still in the Army and far from such fleshpots, got a similar report at the same time: "It is too bad you can't see this place because it would suit you fine. Dinner dances at the Beach Club, a bar, ocean bathing, music and merriment every minute and nice, nice people—everyone of whom would cut up for $10,000,000. For instance, Vincent Astor is here, and, for example, we are dining tonight with Ernest Weir, the cruel industrialist without social conscience who crushes the workingman. It is all quite different from Guam and Iwo Jima."

He must have concealed, beneath the scorn he liked to express in certain quarters, a secret satisfaction that he now "belonged" amid the bloated millionaires. Their vulgarity and their snobbery, their social and racial prejudices, were derided to other friends, but it was not clear that he did not derive some satisfaction from the fact that they had let *him* in. For Marquand, to belong to such a set, however deadly, was to have mounted to a position beyond mere literary fame. That spring of 1945, the Marquands bought a house in Hobe Sound to which they would return the following winter, "a terrific-looking house with funny stuffy old grounds but right on the most beautiful beach you ever saw and very near the club," Adelaide described it.

Even she, to whom the spectacle of the wealthy at their ease was quite familiar, echoed Marquand in describing with humorous repulsion the atmosphere of "entrenched greed" in which they had located themselves. The seven-year-old set, she reported, was spending its out-of-school hours playing Oklahoma for high stakes, and Timmy could be expected to run up gambling debts in short order. But they would remodel the house after the war to suit their tastes, she resolved, and "try to step up the intellectual percentage by persuading some of our queer friends to migrate." There is no record that the Marquands brought any remarkably queer or intellectual visitors to the scene. The Gene Tunneys were there, and in April 1946 the

Lindberghs came for a visit, but it is doubtful if Marquand felt the atmosphere to be enlivened to any degree. "I find the Lone Eagle pretty tough to converse with as he does not understand the light approach to anything," he reported to Alfred McIntyre.

By the winter of 1948 they were ready to try alternatives. The Hobe Sound house was finally sold in 1952. Three years after that, while visiting George Merck there, Marquand found that the few sprightly people he had managed to meet had either died or moved away from the resort. Going around again to cocktail parties with the Mercks he met only monumental tycoons. The hostess would explain that the fat gentleman over there was a very remarkable man, the president of Cincinnati Bolt and Glue, and that the thin man who was trying to pinch the blonde was the president of Minnesota Can, Tank and Toys. Everybody except himself at these functions seemed to be the president of something, and he was welcome only because he was the guest of the president of Merck and Company. The Marquands' old house now belonged to a former president of Allied Chemical and Dye who had redecorated its interior in "Louis XIV French" and added two powder rooms. The old scruffy grounds full of bushes and fallen coconuts, which the Marquands had never managed to get into shape, had been primped up to look like all the other grounds at Hobe Sound belonging to the presidents and vice-presidents of major corporations.

Timmy's asthma, a summer as well as a winter problem, promoted the addition of still another outpost. In the autumn of 1948 John and Adelaide took a trip with their children to the West for a visit to a camp on the Rogue River in Oregon that Adelaide had inherited. They stopped along the way at Aspen, Colorado, where she found herself among mountains and music, a combination that reminded her, probably, of the Salzburg of her happy girlhood visits. Aspen's establishment as a cultural resort was just getting under way then, under the impetus of the Aspen Institute and the Aspen Music Festival established by the millionaire Walter Paepke, and Adelaide longed to throw her energies into these projects while providing the children with a healthful environment. The following June she was there again, and purchased some property which she envisaged as a summer home that might eventually replace Kent's Island. In August the family came for a month. But Marquand was not attracted by Aspen at first sight or upon further acquaintance. To friends he reiterated his distaste for all aspects of the place. He did not like being up eight thousand feet instead of at sea level, and he did not care either for horseback riding or concerts, and he positively disliked the new Aspen intelligentsia. "Adelaide loves the tall mountains and the cowboys and those corny roundups and that phoney nostalgia of the Old West. I would rather be on the beach looking out to sea," he said at once. After a couple of visits he pretty much made up his mind that he would stop behind when she and the children went there during subsequent summers. "Though Adelaide has offered me many inducements to accompany her, including a promise to take up golf if I would do so, I am going to sweat it out here in Newbury," he reported to King Vidor the next summer. And in 1952 he was still saying: "My wife spends a while in Aspen, Colorado, each summer. I have told her that I cannot bear the Rocky Mountains or the rarefied air or equally rarefied intellectual atmosphere of Aspen." Aspen was to prove a striking symbol, in fact, of the widening distance between John and Adelaide Marquand. She seemed unable to accept his refusal to think favorably of Aspen, she could not accept the fact that he did not want to live in the picturesque old house on the shore of Hallam Lake which she had found, and she even attempted to persuade his acceptance by building a separate studio on the edge of the lake where he could do his work—which he would never use. Marquand, who simply hated everything there, got in the habit of calling it "My Ass-pain."

For the winter of 1948 they let the house at Hobe Sound and paid a visit to Nassau at the suggestion of Kenneth Roberts. Nassau, Marquand soon realized, was nearly as full of appalling American millionaires as Hobe Sound had been, and the atmosphere of British stuffiness at Government House was not alleviating. At the Porcupine Club he continued his observations of U.S. coupon clippers and their wives. When he got back to Kent's Island he wrote two stories about an imaginary West Indian "Mulligatawny Club" which expressed his peculiar mixture of satirical condescension and indulgence towards the last untouchable, the bloated escapist in his tropical paradise. "Sun, Sea and Sand" and "King of the Sea" are narrated by a man who at first arouses only the reader's contempt—a middle-aged, retired stockbroker who is married to a tycoon's daughter. He rather innocently loves the good-fellowship of his friends, the infantile rituals of their club, and even the gross foolery of one Epsom Felch, a pincher of female bottoms and an ingenuous practical joker. The narrator's "unreliability," betrayed in banal thought and phrase without auctorial comment, is as cleverly employed in these stories as Horatio Willing's had been in *The Late George Apley*. And yet, in the end, we are astonished to discover that we have been drawn into complicity with him. He is better than his wife, whose snobberies are not so innocent, whose propriety is steeled by the arrogance of her money-power. In the second story as in the first the most trivial of tempests in this teapot results in the husband's unlikely victory over his wife—this time in the issue of the "unsuitable" romance of a younger rich man's daughter. In both stories Marquand showed his willingness to discover moral themes where one would think them unavailable by demonstrating that even among the members of an idle class with no stake whatsoever in ideas there might be some slight opportunity for grace. The point was probably too subtle for most of the readers of either *Cosmopolitan*, which had published one of the stories, or *McCall's*, which had published the other. To his old *Lampoon* friend Paul Hollister, Marquand remarked, at least half-seriously, after "Sun, Sea and Sand" was published: "I doubt if I will be well received at the Porcupine, the Hobe Sound Club, the Bath and Tennis of Palm Beach or the Surf Club of Miami. However, now that Boca Raton is no longer anti-Semitic I might get in there." These rather lighthearted stories had irritated a good many people. "I have even been reproved by some of my acquaintances who have told me that these stories are malicious and that I have Gone Back On My Class." On the other hand, the Left was equally unappreciative. "Instead of saying I had, at long last, developed a social conscience it ended by calling me that worst name in its lexicon—an aristocrat." Marquand had been pleased himself: "I thought when I wrote these stories that at last, after thirty and more years of endeavor, I had solved the problem of writing a story that the readers of a popular magazine might enjoy and yet a story that a few critics might take seriously." But their successful artistry had not struck anyone else, and their thematic exploration, the fruit of his own bemused involvement with the very rich, had not been understood. Convinced that he could not any longer bring his insights to bear through the medium of short fiction, Marquand wrote no more short stories after these two. But he continued to regard them affectionately, including them in his selection of his own short pieces, titled *Thirty Years*, which was published in 1954. By now he had nearly completed his retreat into the pose of an unenlightened middlebrow. From Nassau he wrote Cedric Gibbons, the MGM executive, thanking him for his company during a visit from John Dos Passos, "a nice guy but hard for me to talk to, due to my mental limitations." He took exactly the same tone of mock humility when, a month later, he addressed the Associated Harvard Clubs meeting in Philadelphia. "I am not intellectually equipped to discuss what Harvard means. I only know that I have been there and have obviously brought something of it away with me," he told the assembled alumni, having in the course of the ten preceding minutes gently debunked the notion of that cultural aristocrat, the "Harvard man."

One day during the 1948 Nassau winter a friend took Marquand to a small island called Salt Cay, four miles off New Providence. As they approached it from the west they saw a tall stone watchtower and steep stone steps which led down to the water. A sort of drawbridge was lowered for the tender that took them ashore from their anchored boat. The effect of a seclusion broken only at the will of the island's proprietor charmed Marquand immediately. And the place pleased him further as he walked down the palm-shaded walk that led to the Great House with its high terrace overlooking the sea on one side, and its sheltered, vine-covered dining terrace on the other, with ship's lanterns swinging over a long wooden table. There were no other houses on the island besides quarters for the servants and a small guesthouse. The whole place belonged to the widow of the Chicago *Tribune* cartoonist John T. McCutcheon, who was willing to rent it for the succeeding winter. In January 1950, the Marquands were established for three months on what was nearly the blessed tropical isle of everyone's dreams.

Salt Cay was four miles long, with high coral cliffs and white sandy beaches on two sides. Included in the rental was a fifty-foot yawl with a crew of three, and a caretaker. In addition to this staff the Marquands hired a nurse for the children, a cook, and the cook's husband, who did odd jobs; Marquand's new secretary, Marjorie Davis, was installed in a tent. Although there was neither electricity nor telephone and not even a horse and buggy, and they depended for water on the rain collected in an ancient cistern and on bottled water, Marquand felt that life with his family was more tolerable than he had found it for years. Every day the yawl, the *Windrift*, came out from Nassau where it had stayed for the night—the island had no real harbor—and entered the little lagoon through a cut in the coral rock. The yawl went back with Adelaide's shopping lists and brought the provisions she had ordered, anchoring for the night again in Nassau. Unless they chose themselves to pay visits they could keep the rest of the world quite at arm's length. "Don't forget the bastards can swim," Kenneth Roberts had facetiously warned Marquand, and it was really true that occasionally uninvited guests did arrive in speed launches and scramble ashore. But on the whole the Marquands were able to achieve the relaxed seclusion Marquand had been looking for. "I wish you could be here to see the life—beautiful swimming and nothing to do except that I am trying to write a novel and trying not to drink too much Scotch, which is now selling for $2.80 a bottle due to the devaluation of the pound. Honest to goodness I wish I could live here permanently," he wrote a friend. Even Marquand's ever-festering temper seemed to relax into good humor at Salt Cay, or Treasure Island as they came to call it. The children, with irresistible outdoor diversions occupying them all day, were never under foot, and Adelaide was cut off from the "projects" that ordinarily filled the Marquand homes with frenetic activity. In the evening, rejoining one another after their happily separated preoccupations, the members of the family gathered on the sheltered terrace for dinner, often a special chowder concocted out of fish caught that day. Then Josephas, the elderly black caretaker, would sing "Hoist Up the John B Sails," as well as various ballads of his own composition, while Marquand sat under a wooden sign that had been put up on the terrace by the former tenant and that read, "I am monarch of all I survey." Indeed Marquand felt he was. Though Salt Cay had its various inconveniences, and though he soon developed a satiric recital of woes that included diverting accounts of the servants' skulduggery, Marquand was nearly as content there, visitors thought, as he had ever seemed to be, and his mood seemed to relax into true geniality. "Not for a great many years have I had such a complete sense of leisure because nobody can possibly ask you to do anything. We swim every morning and fish every afternoon," he told Harry Scherman, the busy president of the Book-of-the-Month Club in New York. To his elderly cousin Elizabeth Hoxie he wrote, after the first month there: "The days pass as they used to in my childhood when there were none of these efficient means of communication. Yesterday I went to Nassau for the second time, only because I had to call up New York and get a haircut." After that first winter the Marquands came back again for the next three years.

20

Point of No Return

Out of the mingled moods of the postwar time Marquand wrote *Point of No Return*. It drew its peculiar quality from the fact that it brought into one design both his personal sense of passing into a new condition of life and the realization that American society as a whole was changing. The technique, which he had used before, of interlacing past and present by means of the flashback, here functioned meaningfully, for the reader was compelled to set against one another the alternating qualities of the early and late experience of Charles Gray and make a complex series of contrasts. They were contrasts not merely of personal history but of History. Gray had left the stable, old-fashioned society of his youth in Clyde, so closely modeled on Marquand's own Newburyport background, in order to become a success in New York and an inhabitant of the commuter suburbia, where the corporation hierarchy had taken the place of the ordered distinctions of the older American life, the tribal society categorized, at the very moment it was about to vanish, in the social studies of W. Lloyd Warner. Gray's later life was, of course, postwar America as it was fast becoming, even though there had survived such pockets of the past as Clyde—or Newburyport.

That Charles Gray of *Point of No Return* was a man striving for advancement as a banking executive was not so surprising a choice of subject for Marquand. He could identify with Gray and give him his own past. Gray would possess as well his own impulse to make a success in a world that was becoming the whole American world. The phenomenon of a rise to the summit in literary popularity was not so different from the banker's ascent in its impulse and in its rewards. Marquand had become a member of a new success society without fixed geographic or social boundaries. Reentry into the old Newburyport order was an unrealizable, fairy-tale ending to a personal dream. He knew that he belonged to a new American time, when writing was one way of rising into a stratum defined only by income. He had not so much reached the top elevation of a graduated older America as floated to the surface of a liquid and changing society in which money alone was the principle of buoyancy. So he could well understand why he was acceptable to the tycoons of Hobe Sound and Nassau. It was not only because he was a friend of George Merck's. It was because he himself had "made it" in terms that were quite clear to them, though they never read books. He was "the most successful novelist in America," after all. Long before, Adelaide's father, who had built his fortune by the inspired exploitation of a chemical process, had seen in Marquand a similar capacity and approved of Adelaide's choice.

Marquand had become familiar with the new American aristocracy of Big Business during the war, when his work in Washington brought him into regular contact with the executives who crowded the Pentagon or visited the Merck and Company suite at the Mayflower. But the Hookers, though they were as aristocratically descended as any modern Americans, were part of the aggressive, money-making class of wealth. Hooker Electrochemical got seven Army–Navy "E" awards for producing lubricant additives and the synthetic rubber essential dodecyl mercaptan, having supplied nearly half the entire industrial need for that substance. Along with other products these brought Hooker's wartime output of chemicals to two and a half billion pounds. Hooker's postwar expansion was spectacular, its investment in plant and equipment rising from $15 million in 1945 to $87 million ten years later. Adelaide inherited a good deal of Hooker Electrochemical stock when her father died in 1938, and by virtue of her holdings as well as his own, Marquand was elected a member of the board of directors in 1941. When attending the board's regular meetings in Niagara Falls, he was exposed to the personalities of industrial chieftains as few literary men have been. *B. F.'s Daughter* offered his first portrait of a successful industrialist in Burton Fulton, who owed something to Elon Huntington Hooker, as well as to others who governed the company in later years, and, of course, to George Merck. The new rich who had succeeded to the authority of the Apleys and Pulhams and the thin-veined Brills of *Wickford Point* were to be the subjects of much of his late fiction.

Point of No Return deals with the career of a man who works himself up into the top ranks of banking, a subject previously unexplored by American writers. *Sincerely, Willis Wayde*, published in 1955, describes a self-made king of manufacture. Both heroes succeed by surrendering rather than by retaining any local attachment and tradition. Born in Clyde, Charles Gray leaves it forever once he has set forth upon his upward path. Wayde, who comes to the same Clyde from some unspecified midwestern birthplace, likewise puts it behind him once he has decided to move into the world of unlocalized Big Corporation power. It is symbolically apt that the novel's climax arrives when he betrays Clyde by destroying the old company which had given him his start.

After the war Marquand began to encounter the businessman at leisure. The country-club world, where older and more prestigious wealth now mingled with the new, interested him as his own success made these resorts accessible. In 1948, he became a member of the Myopia Hunt Club on the North Shore and seriously took up golf. He had regular lessons from a professional in the hope of mastering the sport that had become the medium of contact for social and business ambition. The phenomenon of the country club in upper-class American life was to figure in the evolving history of the hero of *Point of No Return*. He once takes his Clyde girlfriend to the "Shore Club" (clearly Myopia) for dinner during his father's boomtime spell of prosperity, and in Connecticut commuter country, later, joins the Oak Knoll Country Club, aspiring to the more exclusive Hawthorne Hill Club in the course of his rise to the vice-presidency of a New York bank. The modern subculture of the country club was put on exhibition in Marquand's new novel with his accustomed precision of observation, and subsequently in the humorous sketches for *Sports Illustrated*, which were collected as *Life at Happy Knoll* in 1957. He had also, as has been noted, become familiar with such winter playgrounds of the rich as Hobe Sound and Nassau, and used this background in the Mulligatawny stories. Such recreations lie ahead for Charles Gray, no doubt, after his attainment of higher rungs on the ladder of banking. Willis Wayde, who becomes an authentic rich man and not merely a well-paid custodian of wealth, spends his honeymoon at a luxury hotel in the Adirondacks. Its main purpose was "to be expensive. . . . A symbolic prize for industry and endeavor, a happy resting place only for those who have made good"—and there he makes an invaluable "contact" that assists his advancement in the belting industry. Later he learns to stop at the Ritz when in Boston—the Ritz was Marquand's own favorite Boston hotel, no doubt for similar symbolic value as well as for its authentic comforts. The final step upward to the very summit, to becoming the king of the belting industry, is achieved by Wayde during a convention at the famous Hotel Carolina in Pinehurst, North Carolina—in the late fifties, Marquand's regular winter resort. But Wayde, like his creator, never entirely overcomes certain initial disadvantages and remains a duffer at tennis and golf, having gone in for these games too late.

The Stuyvesant Bank, scene of Charles Gray's contest for success, was a brilliant conception. Such a conservative institution could be shown to have its own traditions of absolute reliability as the servant of its depositors, and Gray's inheritance of old-fashioned virtues might still be pertinent there, as it might not have been in manufacturing or commerce. In the end it is those residual virtues and a lingering distaste for money, an unwillingness to buck too hard, that gain him the promotion he wants, and eliminate his rival, Roger Blakesley. Marquand had found the model of this enclave of business refinement in the Fifth Avenue Bank, then housed in a converted pair of brownstone residences on the corner of Forty-fourth Street in Manhattan. Marquand was a depositor; he had been there often enough to be able to describe in his novel its open first floor, where light from stained glass in the windows painted golden fleur-de-lis on the high brown walls and the officers sat at their rolltop desks in full view of the customers.

Marquand's *Lampoon* friend Edward Streeter, one of the vice-presidents, was able, moreover, to enlighten him on the conditions of a banking career. Streeter himself was almost what Marquand might have been if he had become a banker. His gift for humorous observation of social life had produced, as the by-product of his leisure hours, some lightly satirical books early in his career, and now, in the year Marquand produced *Point of No Return*, he wrote his best seller and Book-of-the-Month Club choice, *Father of the Bride*. In the spring of 1947, Marquand had a talk with Streeter at the Century Club about his idea for a novel about banking, and that September he showed him chapters that were about to appear in the *Atlantic* as a serial under the title *Banking Is an Art*. Streeter, the nearly professional writer, was more than a technical collaborator, for he was greatly excited by the literary importance of Marquand's project. He said: "I would like to see a book done by a novelist with a wide audience which directly interprets the emotional life of those who work in large corporations. It has literally never been done to my knowledge because no writer has ever been fool enough to work for a corporation long enough to know what it is all about."

During the course of their conferences Streeter prepared for Marquand a log of a "typical day of a vice-president" taken from his own calendar. None of the various telephone calls and conferences listed by Streeter exactly duplicated Gray's. But the day so carefully elaborated for Marquand's hero from the time he leaves his house for the eight-thirty at Stamford until he returns home again that evening has the same kind of successive detail. Streeter had probably conveyed to Marquand the way his profession ultimately made the dignified banker into a sort of lackey of the very rich. Marquand began Gray's day with a telephone conversation with a large depositor, Mrs. Whitaker, and ended it with a command call at her apartment before he went to Grand Central. Probably the characters of Tony Burton, the president, and his subordinates in the Stuyvesant Bank were not so much based on the Fifth Avenue's personnel as on Streeter's general description of banking types, but when the novel appeared, everyone, down to the doorman, thought he recognized himself in it. As a matter of fact, Marquand was not wholly loyal to the particular actualities of the bank, even on the technical side. He insisted on locating a staff conference in the vault, where conferences were never held, because he thought the background of the shining steelwork, smelling of banana oil, was perfect for his purposes, and Streeter conceded that it was the best fictional use of a bank-vault scene since *Alias Jimmy Valentine*.

More important than the specific details Streeter supplied was the assistance he gave Marquand by personally exemplifying the kind of man needed for the novel's central figure. Streeter somehow brought with him into the very temple of money the loyalties and scrupulosities that Marquand identified with the tradition out of which he and his friend had come. As members of the last prewar Harvard classes, they shared the moral illusions that the war did not entirely erase. Charles Gray gets his vice-presidency in the end without any flagrant surrender of his inherited code, as has been noted. And yet the title is well justified. The reader realizes that Gray's struggle for advancement, with the amount of petty jockeying for advantage it has entailed, has nearly exhausted both his integrity and his capacity for disinterested friendship and love. He is, nevertheless, a far more attractive figure, when all is said and done, than Willis Wayde, who sets forth from Clyde upon his own energetic climb in the novel published six years later. Willis Wayde's chosen field is almost symbolically industrial—the manufacture of conveyer-idler systems. His career turns out to require less of whatever the older tradition might have taught him about fixed obligations and principles. Willis is contrasted with his father, an eccentric man of talent who loves knowing how something works and inventing a new machine or process for the sake of the knowledge and the achievement themselves—and despises those who merely exploit other men's knowledge or ingenuity.

The central character of *Sincerely, Willis Wayde* is a little uncertainly defined—or perhaps Marquand intended the reader to feel surprise as he slowly learns to dislike him. Willis begins as a reasonably attractive boy, very much a self-portrait of the young Marquand, even to such a physical detail as the longish straight hair that slides over his eyes. His early crush on a rich young miss who humiliates him by standing him up, her ultimate rejection of him, and his resulting determination to get ahead come out of the old autobiographical story which once again makes its claim on the reader's sympathy as it had in Marquand's earlier fiction. Soon, as the chapters succeed one another, one finds oneself admiring Willis Wayde's ability and grit while wincing at his vulgarity. There is something innocent in his conviction that conspicuous consumption of more and more is a good thing—it stands up better as an attitude, in its simplicity, than the refinement of the professor's daughter he has married: she, too, despite her cultural and ethical pretensions, really wants all that his success brings her. And so we are led, barely prepared, towards the book's ending as Willis shows his ability to shuck off old attachments—to the Harcourt Mill in Clyde and the Harcourt family who helped him upward (and who also had known how to use him), to the management firm who had given him a chance to enter a wider sphere of opportunity, to the ailing firm that gratefully accepted him as its manager after he pulled it out of difficulties, to the aging top-man-in-the-business who takes him into a trust merger with the clear prospect of yielding place to the new leader. Willis Wayde is the freely moving careerist, the modern unattached man. It is only he, not the reader, who is surprised that Bess Harcourt, snarling, "Uriah Heep!" should snub him when they meet again by accident on a Paris sidewalk. Yet it was his infatuation with Bess that had started it all! The reader may well be quite sick of Willis now, a millionaire who speaks and thinks in clichés.

What is oddly revealing is that, even at the end, he is a portrait of the writer, who knows exactly the course he has come in a lifetime and mocks himself in this grossest self-version for vainly yearning to belong to the natural inheritors of the world—and is still frustrated by his poor game of golf. The old, never-forgotten Sedgwick presumptions of superiority are resented still in the Harcourts. And Christina's covert desire to have, unearned, all the rewards of riches is remembered in Sylvia Wayde's acquiescence in luxury. Through his fictional fable Marquand became able to see his personal history, finally, as the dispossession of a succession of fathers. Wayde discards his own biological father (a somewhat improved version of old Philip), discards old Henry Harcourt (the paternalistic head of the Harcourt Mill, who taps him for advancement and sends him to the Harvard Business School), discards Joe McKitterick (who gives him his break in New York), and discards Mr. and Mrs. Manley Jacoby who, childless, virtually adopt him as he takes over their mill. Finally he is ready for the last act of oedipal aggression against his idol and model, P. L. Nagel. All along he is damned and haunted by guilt—as Marquand himself was for his own rejections and progressions.

The backward glance at Newburyport represented in the Clyde chapters of *Point of No Return* is probably the best among Marquand's many fictional representatives of his early environment, done with the intensity of direct recollection. It amused him to counterpoint his re-created reality with the viewpoint of Malcolm Bryant, the spokesman of sociological perception in the style of W. Lloyd Warner. *The Social Life of a Modern Community*, the first volume of Warner's Yankee City series, which had resulted from his study of Newburyport, does not contain the passage Charles Gray read in the novel's *Yankee Persepolis—A Social Study*, in which his own "lower-upper" family is described. But the real-life sociologist's Chapter VIII, "Profiles from Yankee City," was an attempt at a kind of fiction in which conventionalized representatives of the six classes in Warner's scheme are described and allowed to speak about their lives. Marquand's categories could be fitted into Warner's system, though his treatment, obviously, had more art than the social scientist's. The Lovells, whose daughter Jessica is Charles's first love, are specimen "upper-upper" types like the Breckenridge family of Warner's feeble drama, and properly live in a square white Federalist house on "Johnson Street," the "Hill Street" of the study, even though Lillian Simpson and her father (upon whom the characters are based) had, it will be recalled, really lived in a gingerbread Victorian mansion. (Marquand modeled the Lovells' house on the Knapp-Healy house at 47 High Street with its famous French wallpaper and beautiful boxwood garden.)

Curiously, Marquand's remembered youthful romance conforms to Warner's profile of Elizabeth Breckenridge. Though the sociologist's young woman does not suffer from the effects of her father's excessive and possessive attachment as Jessica or the real Lillian Simpson (or Christina Sedgwick) did, she is also threatened with spinsterhood because "there's just no one in this town for a person like me to marry." In Marquand's novel Jessica Lovell does not marry until many years after Charles Gray leaves Clyde—not, in fact, until the novel's present, when he discovers that she is engaged to his old "upper-middle" friend Jackie Mason. As though Marquand wanted to illustrate Warner's thesis of the "upward mobility" of certain types, he showed how Jackie attained all those marks of social rank that had once been beyond the reach of "lower-upper" Charles Gray. He became a director of the Dock Street Bank, a trustee of the library, a member of the Tuesday Club—and even married a Lovell.

Thus, *Point of No Return* showed how, after the Second World War, a man's social identity became something achieved in his own lifetime rather than prepared before he was born. "Equal opportunity" had come to mean that all men were equally entitled to compete in the often unequal scramble for advantage, equally entitled to the social regard due their degree of success in achieving the money prize. The process is further advanced in *Sincerely, Willis Wayde*. Though Marquand does not, in this novel, return again to a depiction of the town life of Clyde, he correctly identifies the essential economic forces that made for change there. He shows the passing of an old "family" enterprise, and the decay of a younger generation that does not really have the ability or the sense of responsibility to rule. The small kingdom of the Harcourts is swallowed up by a national corporation with headquarters in Chicago. The process was not one over which Marquand had ever wasted sentiment. The Lovells and the Harcourts, snobbish, even arrogant, in their social and familial pretension, deserved that power should pass from their hands, not only outside Newburyport but inside it. Not only "side-streeters" of the old stock, like Charles Gray's friend Mason, but the representatives of new ethnic strains—Irish, Greek, Italian, Jewish—would be running the town in a few years. Marquand, an outsider in an inner psychic sense if not in a social one, could take an ironic satisfaction in the displacement of the envied and resented "High Street gang."

Marquand first thought of *Sincerely, Willis Wayde* as a novel that would firmly put behind him the lost world of early twentieth century America. He planned to depict a hero "swatting it out with life, strictly in the urban world of today—somebody on the down-wind side of the point of no return." The book had been begun with some thought of using a flashback technique. He had then changed his mind, decided not to "give away" his outcome but to order his story in straightforward chronological sequence with as little foreshadowing as possible. Partly, this was a response to the critics' frequent comment that he had settled into a single way of telling a story, but the flashback method was no longer useful to describe a man who had no past that counted. As Arthur Mizener observed when he reviewed the novel, "Harry Pulham and Charley Gray can put past and present side by side and see the values and defects of each by contrast with the other. They have the true sense of the past. Willis Wayde never possesses his past, however many pieces of it he picks up [by collecting antiques] at the Parke-Bernet Gallery." Before writing *Sincerely, Willis Wayde*, however, Marquand wrote one other novel, which resorted to the technique of interleaving a brief span of present time with a history extending back to small-town boyhood.

But in *Melville Goodwin, U.S.A.* the hero's birthplace plays only a minor part in his reminiscences. After the general leaves it for West Point he seems to enter a timeless world. The fixed code of the military in peace as well as in war brings him to the present relatively unchanged. Marquand seems to say that only such constricting continuities as that of the Army provide anything that looks like a persistent tradition in our time. In contrast with the general is the novel's bemused narrator. Sidney Skelton has achieved his success by accident; he is a man who just happened to have a perfect radio announcer's voice. All about him, in the frenetic world of radio and advertising, are examples of the new formula for success, the hustling, jostling, free-swimmers who are making it rich without regard to any code whatsoever.

The publication of *Point of No Return* in March 1949 identified Marquand once again as the country's leading popular author and confirmed his own fulfillment of the Alger myth. Marquand's previous six novels, from *The Late George Apley* to *B. F.'s Daughter*, had now sold 2,600,000 copies, three of them had been book-club choices, and three had been made into movies. Whatever critics would say about this newest Marquand, a large public was pretty certain to buy it. It seemed to mark the summit of Marquand's career. *Time* and *Newsweek*, with almost unprecedented simultaneity, carried his picture on their covers and ran long life-stories (that same week, too, the *Saturday Review* and *Books* both had Marquand covers). The *Time* piece was a full-scale, no-expense-spared effort, which had begun with lengthy interviews in the magazine's Manhattan offices the previous winter. The book editor of *Time*, Max Gissen, and his researcher, Ruth Mehrtens, had followed their subject to Nassau. Marquand, who had recently discovered Salt Cay, took them to the island in a hired sloop for a day of further discussion in complete solitude. The resulting twelve-column story was embellished with pictures of the Marquands against a background of tropical foliage; they looked tanned and contented, he in a Bahamian open shirt and she in a gingham island dress.

But the story not unexpectedly viewed Marquand's life in terms of the question behind his latest novel: "Are the rewards of all your efforts worth the effort?" *Time* recalled the "27 years of unbroken writing success" that had led to the present moment, and noted that, with a well-engineered economy of effort, he had finished every book and story he had started and sold everything he had written with the exception of one story. The magazine reviewed the fruits of success to date: after the *Satevepost* had paid out something like half a million dollars for one hundred and ten serials and stories, he had won the Pulitzer Prize for *Apley*, which had spun off a play and a movie that "settled him even more firmly on Easy Street." "Practical, a lover of comfort and the good things of life (including among others, three cars, two scotches before dinner)," the story said, "Marquand is by no means contemptuous of money and is mightily pleased that he has made the financial grade." And then the writers explicitly identified him with his hero, with perhaps little warrant from Marquand: "Like Charley Gray, he knows that something is missing. He wishes there were something more at the finish than an annuity and a new station wagon. And he is no more sure than Charley Gray what that something is." Marquand told them, according to Miss Mehrtens's shorthand notes, "I've been so warped and conditioned by life that I haven't found anything that will satisfy me." The profile concluded: "At 55, Novelist Marquand is still trying to win repose for himself but finds it a continuing and perhaps useless process, with daily ups & downs. He is 5 ft. 11 in., with gray hair that is white about the temples, physically alert, and dieting to reduce a slight paunchiness."

Marquand's expressions of discontent with life, reflected in the *Time* profile, apparently aroused protests from readers who liked to think of their favorite authors as offering some reconciling wisdom in the face of the human condition. In June he told the graduating class of the Governor Dummer Academy in South Byfield, Massachusetts, of receiving a deluge of mail from many parts of the country. The writers were aroused by his admission that he was not entirely satisfied with life—he had even said, "carried away by [his] own eloquence" that "life for most people . . . was pretty much of a rat-race." He praised the virtues of discontent as a general attitude and urged his young listeners to cultivate discontent with themselves and their society. He was, however, secretly irritated by the *Time* article, perhaps for its too-pat and yet not altogether inaccurate discovery that, like the man in his novel, he had reached a point of no return. To an English friend he explained that the *Time* and *Newsweek* stories "are the distillation of hundreds of pages of notes taken from interviews with the subject, his family, his friends and his enemies." He contented himself with pointing out minor inaccuracies. Gissen had written that the household in Rye during Marquand's boyhood had included two maids and a footman, when "the truth was that we had an Irishman who lived out in the barn who looked after our one horse, looked after the furnace and mowed the lawn." He added: "I am quite sure that the writer of the article although he is an eminent literary critic does not know what a footman is but did know that it sounded well in the context."

Probably it was the viewpoint of Gissen's whole essay that disturbed him more than such lapses. Five years later he may have expressed his resentment, unknown to Gissen, by blackballing him when he was being considered for membership in a prestigious New York club. Although Marquand admitted that he did not know the *Time*-man very well, he wrote to the Committee on Admissions: "Much as I dislike writing a so-called 'red letter' about anyone, I must tell you that I consider Mr. Gissen emotionally unstable and a highly inaccurate and malicious gossip. I do not think he is the sort of person who will recommend himself to most members." Nevertheless, in *Melville Goodwin, U.S.A.*, which utilizes the news-magazine profile mission as the technical excuse for the general's reminiscing flashbacks, Gissen and Miss Mehrtens contributed to his characterization of Phil Bentley, the writer, and his researcher, Miss Fineholt. When Marquand reencountered Gissen in 1952 he told him, "All the time you were using me I was using you," and conveyed particular apologies to Miss Mehrtens for her unflattering portrait. Gissen had also supplied an important small detail of the plot. Sidney Skelton had bumped into General Goodwin in a ditch at Saint-Lô (they both had dived into it at the same moment during a bombardment). Gissen, it seemed, had had just such a meeting with Eisenhower.

Although Marquand may have resented the presumption in the *Time* article that, like his hero, he had reached a point of no return, this perception again underlay the more sensitive, more deftly composed profile done for the *New Yorker* in 1952 by Philip Hamburger. Hamburger adopted the device of writing his story in the form of a Marquand novel, making the novelist one of his own representative heroes. The title of the profile was a reminder of both *Apley* and *Pulham*: *J. P. Marquand, Esquire: A Portrait in the Form of a Novel.* Hamburger's narrative made use of the Marquandian flashback to bring to the surface of his Marquand-character's mind bits of his past history provoked by a profile writer, much as Melville Goodwin's recollections had been. He had deliberately imitated the opening of *Point of No Return* in a scene whose use of small telling details ("the orange chintz draperies that framed the small, partitioned window that cranked in and out but not up and down") was exactly in Marquand's manner. Allison Craig, Hamburger's reporter, is both double and contrast to the fictional "Marquand," a sort of Horatio Willing whose perceptions are hedged by the same conventions but who exhibits himself as shallower than his subject. He is not a Bostonian but a New York striver like Charles Gray, who feels, as he sets out upon his day, that "things might have been different but there's no turning back." In Hamburger's fiction Marquand is said to have attained something of what he has heard the Chinese call "the balance of things," and yet, it is suggested, to have remained haunted by past and early frustrations never quite assuaged by success—like Charles Gray or even Willis Wayde. It was the best portrait of Marquand anyone would do during his lifetime. Hamburger had spent the day of talk with Marquand that his persona is depicted as doing, traveling down to Newburyport on May 22, 1951, and accompanying him to the meeting of the Tuesday Night Club at the High Street home of the same Lawrence P. Dodge who had refused the boy Marquand a Harvard scholarship. Hamburger heard Marquand deliver a paper about his 1947 visit to the Orient with Admiral Denfield, "The Last American Plane from Peking."

The 1949 *Newsweek* story had not been as ambitious as either the *Time* or *New Yorker* profiles, but it had opened with the reminder that Marquand's success was firmly tagged as popular rather than highbrow: "Over the years the more erudite literary critics have ignored the writings of John Phillips Marquand. Although he started writing shortly after the first world war and his latest novel, *Point of No Return* is the eighteenth book to bear his name, the editors of the *Literary History of the United States* have seen fit to mention him but three casual times in their massive opus" (the "*LHUS*" had appeared the year before). Marquand had complained to the reporters about the snubbing he had received at the hands of the editors, Professors Robert Spiller, Willard Thorp and their colleagues. He would often mention this slight in the course of his diatribes against the critical conspiracy, as he felt it to be, which had placed him outside the pale of high seriousness. And *Point of No Return* encountered the same divided critical response as had *So Little Time, Repent in Haste* and *B. F.'s Daughter*. There was the usual praise from daily-newspaper reviewers across the land, exemplified by Joseph Henry Jackson of the San Francisco *Chronicle*. He was quite aware of the judgment of the other camp when he concluded, "If his technical brilliance has deceived many of the intellectuals into putting him down as just another 'smooth' fictioneer, then so much the worse for them." But many reviewers found that the low-keyed narrative and the commonplace personality of the hero made for a book without excitement. The New York *World-Telegram* reviewer complained: "Charlie Gray, though a nice guy, is frightfully dull. It takes real artistry to make dull people fascinating in fiction. Flaubert could do it with Madame Bovary, for example. But Mr. Marquand's very dull hero makes for very dull reading." Many, like Louis Zara in the Philadelphia *Inquirer*, thought Marquand had lost ground in this novel: "Alongside *The Late George Apley* Marquand's *Point of No Return* can only be regarded, despite its great length, as a polite little story."

Among the major reviewers Marquand found support from old friends like Edward Weeks of the *Atlantic* and Orville Prescott of the New York *Times*. John Woodburn in the *Saturday Review*, which generally supported him warmly, called the novel Marquand's best since *Apley*. In the Herald Tribune *Book Review*, James Hilton, the author of *Goodbye, Mr. Chips*, was charmed by its mood of gentle melancholy; by the Christmas season he decided it was the best novel of the year (John Chamberlain made the same choice for the *Information Please Almanac*). But there were the usual deprecations. Brendan Gill in the *New Yorker* even challenged the assumption that Marquand had written satire—his tone, Gill said, was more like that of Booth Tarkington, too benignant. *Point of No Return* struck him as just the kind of book Charles Gray and his wife Nancy, themselves so fearful of rocking the boat, so anxious to get on, would have liked. He imagined Charley saying, "I read a book to be entertained; I don't read it to see what's biting the author. One thing's sure—Marquand's no radical. He may grumble a bit but he knows which side his bread is buttered on." Once again, Marquand's own ambivalence, which tended to elicit both sympathy and deprecation from the reader, gave his best fictional moments a peculiar quality, like moiréed silk that changes its pattern with the light or the angle from which it is viewed. In the case of Charles Gray, however, some thought that the writer's mingled effect was simply a way of backing off from his own insights. Maxwell Geismar, writing in the *New York Times Book Review*, praised Marquand for his understanding of the central importance of money as the motive force behind modern American lives. But he thought Marquand had evaded the proper conclusions of his story. Charles Gray had succeeded at the bank, and despite his acrid knowledge of his loss of freedom, he accepted his bargain without protest. In the end, Geismar thought, Marquand tended to dignify the life he pretended to satirize, and there was no poignance in Gray's submission to benevolently coercive forces.

As often happens, the stage or screen versions of the novel could later be seen not as making adjustments that violated the essential spirit of the original but simply as making its real intent more unequivocal: vulgarization was sometimes a clarifying process. The version of *Point of No Return* prepared for Broadway by Paul Osborn did not betray Marquand's message, it might be argued, although it imposed some notable changes upon the novel and tampered with its original ending. In Osborn's version, as the play went into production, Gray concluded that the game had not been worth the candle after all—almost as in the novel. But a small touch had somehow restored his honor. He had refused to join the Hawthorne Hill Club even though he accepted the vice-presidency of the bank. This seemingly minor revision, as Marquand said, "makes the play seem to mean 'the game may be worth the candle if you learn to walk erect.'" But the producer Leland Hayward had pushed the final scene further in this new direction when Tony Burton, the president of the bank, virtually begs Charles to accept the job and declares, "I *never* thought I could dictate to you." Gray is thereby able to convince himself that it has come as a deserved reward for which he has *not* made demeaning compromises. Hayward explained during the Boston tryout: "You can't charge people a lot of money for seats, get them involved emotionally in the struggle of the Grays for the job and then at the end when Charley's won, tell them, ugh, the job wasn't worth having, and poor Charley's hooked." Marquand seems to have accepted the changes unprotestingly, even telling Henry Hawes of the *Saturday Review* that the play was "the most successful job of adapting since Sidney Howard's job on 'Dodsworth.'" But, during the last week of the New York run, after the play had been going for close to a year, Osborn again rewrote the ending, partly in response to the wishes of the actor Henry Fonda. In this version, although Gray still accepted his promotion and also turned down membership in the country club, he was given lines to show that he realized he no longer had freedom of choice in any significant sense. Perhaps even this rectification did not alter the drift of the original Marquand story towards the acquiescence Geismar had detected in it.

If this was the hidden inclination of Marquand's own feelings about success, he may not have been too distressed by the way the play came out. The theatrical production was a superior one. Fonda, despite an occasional midwestern twang, managed a fine, low-keyed interpretation of Charles Gray. Osborn, the scriptwriter of *A Bell for Adano* and other hits, had created a smoothly working theatrical vehicle. Jo Mielziner had devised ingenious sets that made the flashback structure presentable on the stage, as he had done for *Death of a Salesman*, a previous Hayward production. (One critic called *Point of No Return* "a rich man's *Death of a Salesman*.") Hayward, who had for some years been a producer of hits, had three others on Broadway when *Point of No Return* opened, including *South Pacific* and *Call Me Madam*. It was clear that this would be another. The play ran from December 1951 until December 1952, when it went on a national tour until the following June.

Unlike the earlier version of the American rise-to-riches story, *Sincerely, Willis Wayde* (1955) left the reader no possibility of supposing that one could still get there with enough gas in the tank for a moral return. The sacrifice of the ambiguity that had guaranteed popularity to *Point of No Return* made for comparative failure. The 1955 novel sold less than half as well as its thematic predecessor (62,500 copies in the first year to *Point of No Return*'s 128,200), and it received no bids from stage or screen for a further lease of life, though in 1956 "Playhouse 90" offered a TV version with Peter Lawford that was forgotten as quickly as it was seen.

The inherent artistic difficulties of the novel were, as Marquand knew, considerable. As he told Helen Howe, "I really had to face quite a hard problem in it—that is, to draw a picture fairly of a rather dull, disintegrating character who still seems to me to represent a large segment of American private enterprise." Outright burlesque would have been easy, but he aimed for a measured understanding, even some pity. "If I had started throwing custard pies at him, he would only have been a caricature, which most writers achieve when they try to put a businessman into fiction," he said. In the opinion of most of the critics he had not enabled the reader to feel very strongly about his protagonist. The hero was duller than good, dull

Charley Gray, the details of his career more uninteresting. There was still some praise, here and there, for Marquand's skill, but even Edward Weeks in the *Atlantic* was, as Marquand himself remarked to Henry Canby, "flatulently condescending." "Only a craftsman as assured and practiced as Mr. Marquand could provoke and maintain interest in this hero," said the *New Yorker* in the "brief mention" that was all it afforded this Marquand novel. The *Nation*, in its equally brief notice, headed "Discerning but Dull," felt that Marquand had failed to deal sympathetically or imaginatively with a central figure who was "essentially unimaginative and unsympathetic" himself, and that Marquand's realistic method had resulted in a nagging water-faucet drip of continual and uninteresting small details. William Barrett, in the *Saturday Review*, complained that this novel was all cold machinery, the absolute zero of a writer who had always tended to be "cool." "Up to now the coolness never froze into ice because Marquand had, and was able to communicate, a real feeling for the pathos of the American male trapped in all the entanglements of middle-class life. . . . But the pathos has all gone out of Willis; where the great American business of getting ahead and being successful exacted all sorts of human conflicts within Charlie Gray, Willis has long ago sold his soul to the apparatus." Barrett, who announced himself a Marquand fan (though Marquand found his review "savage"), thought that this time the novelist was simply going through the motions, so well practiced and facile by now. Marquand had succeeded in arousing *neither* sympathy nor indignation. And yet the book's dull honesty might have involved an important personal statement. The theme of success, as already observed, was the most intimate possible for him. Perhaps, on some unconscious level, it was his veritable self that he now dismissed along with his disappointing hero.

He may have had, in the years that drew him closer to the end of his career, an increasing sensation of unsuccess, though he was still selling at the top of the competitive book market and the favorite of many thousands of American readers. He continued to be oddly alone in the literary world. He had always avoided the company of fellow writers; their jealousies and neuroses were a bore, he often said. He had never cared for literary cocktail parties. He advised his son to avoid the members of the New York literary crowd in his own efforts to become a writer: "You will find, like other writers, that most of them are dull, and very few, simply because of their own preoccupations, will be able to share your particular interests, or to understand in the least your modes and habits of work. The truth is, if you are a writer—and by that I mean a really good one—you will always live a life apart, and you can never have an integral place in any community; and in this regard I do not believe that artistic and writing colonies are any help." He had never made much effort to meet even the writers for whom he had a particular respect—Hemingway, Fitzgerald, and Lewis, who had somehow managed to win both popular fame and its material fruits along with a place in the literary histories. For Lewis in particular he felt an affinity not only artistic but personal; yet their occasional encounters had not established a relationship. For Faulkner, the turgid and powerful rival who pleased academic critics, and, after *Sanctuary*, a certain number of general readers, he felt only middlebrow hostility. He observed to his daughter Tina in 1958 that the master creator of Yoknapatawpha County would be "recognized for some time in academic circles but his work will never be known or understood by most people, and I do not think that he even will be known as a literary influence." He found few among younger writers, particularly those who seemed to have lost "faith in our society and institutions," to applaud or befriend, either—though he made some exception of Herman Wouk and James Jones, whose work had come before him when he was a Book-of-the-Month Club judge. To a Club subscriber who complained about the selections offered in 1952 he wrote explaining that current fiction showed "general pessimism and lack of morale." His own essentially pessimistic and social-critical tendency was suppressed from consciousness when he declared, "I wish some of them would get the idea that this is a pretty good country and that it still offers greater opportunities for ordinary individuals than any other country in the world and that in spite of inequities and race discrimination, people are still better off here than anywhere else." After all had not *he* proved the persistence of the rise-to-success formula? He would not confess, except through his fiction, the sad failure of success. To a reporter in Boston, who was interviewing him after the publication of *Sincerely, Willis Wayde*, he spoke as though his own novel had conveyed a reply to youthful pessimism. "You would think," he said of the younger writers of the moment, "that they never had a good time in their lives—that they never had a good time in school, in the army, in business, or in love. . . . It would be very nice if [they] would try to do a little 'positive thinking'—to borrow from Norman Vincent Peale—about the land that gave them birth and opportunity." But how positive was his own deepest thought? Among all the possible literary friendships, Marquand's only visiting-and-visited writer-friend was Kenneth Roberts, who had also become successful as a middlebrow master, a writer who had no doubts about the present of America, his best books being journeys into a vanished past. Visits were exchanged over the years at Roberts's home in Maine and at Kent's Island, and on Nassau. A favorite topic between the two was their shared dislike of William Faulkner.

When Alfred McIntyre died suddenly at the end of 1948 after seeing *Point of No Return* into print, Marquand lost the most prized of his readers. Under McIntyre's encouraging supervision he had made the transition from popular magazine stories to *Apley*, and McIntyre had helped him through each of his novels thereafter. In publishing circles, where the relationship of Marquand to the Little, Brown president was well known, there were immediate rumors that he would leave the firm—and solicitations. But Marquand refused these and later invitations to make a change and remained attached to the same house with a fidelity grown rare in modern author-publisher relations. The new president, Arthur Thornhill, became a friend without difficulty, although he was not an editor like McIntyre. Thornhill had come up in the company through the sales division; he had started as a messenger boy in the shipping department and become a supersalesman. Later, his contribution to Little, Brown's maintenance of a prime place in the publishing world was due to his keen sense of the importance of new distributing formulas and the use of secondary rights in paperback publication. But Thornhill was also a man of considerable force and charm, with a robust, blunt practicality, good-natured and shrewd, who gave authors a strong sense of support. And for Marquand, the intimate intellectual participation of a McIntyre was, perhaps, no longer necessary. He could take or leave the solicitous attentiveness of the editors who attempted to continue McIntyre's role—Stanley Salmen, Cammann Newberry, Alexander Williams. Thornhill, who took no editorial role towards Marquand, offered him something else, a friendship more equal, fraternally sustaining. They would form the habit of prolonged monthly luncheons together in Boston during which, over drinks and the best of meals at the Copley Plaza or at Locke-Ober, they would talk on and on about matters ranging from the state of publishing to the nature of marriage. To Thornhill Marquand spoke as frankly as he would ever speak to anyone about the rocky course of his second marriage. Thornhill sought Marquand's advice about other authors.

The fact was that Marquand's relationship with his publishers now rested on a different basis. His peculiar contracts with Little, Brown had resulted in the accumulation of greater and greater amounts of earnings. To reduce the income-tax loss that would have resulted if they had been paid promptly, they were disbursed in fixed annual payments for a period that would outlast the earner's lifetime and continue to enrich his heirs. He thus became, after a while, as these sums increased with the yield from one book contract after another, no longer merely an author but a major creditor of the firm. In June 1955, Little, Brown held $250,000 of Marquand's royalties, out of which he was receiving by contract $20,000 a year, the balance to be taxed only when paid. Three years later, about $600,000 of Marquand royalties were in the hands of Little, Brown, being paid out at the rate of $40,000 yearly. The situation in Marquand's last years did, indeed, reach such proportions that his lawyer, Brooks Potter, became seriously concerned about the nature of his contribution to the company's working capital: he received "not one red cent" in the way of interest—though this loss was less than he would have suffered if he had been required to pay taxes on the full amount at once. Crucial was the question of Little, Brown's own future solvency. Marquand's involvement in the firm now exacted a permanent devotion on his part as the producer of future best sellers. Not personal sentiment but ineluctable economic interest bound him to Little, Brown.

There was a change, also, in Marquand's relationship with his agent, Carl Brandt. In September 1948, Marquand decided to end at last the costly pretense that Brandt was any longer useful to him in the development of his books. He arranged to negotiate his book contracts directly with his publisher, leaving to Brandt only the handling of magazine and film rights. The step was financially advantageous—Marquand no longer needed to surrender to the agent the commission on his books that had for years been Brandt's large stake in Marquand's career as an author. To Brandt this must have been a considerable blow, especially since the magazines were to get only a few stories and serials in Marquand's remaining years, and just two more Marquand films would be made, a belated version of *Melville Goodwin* (titled *Top Secret Affair*) in 1956 and a final screen appearance of Mr. Moto the following year. But probably even more important than this monetary alteration in the relationship between the two was the understanding, now openly admitted between them, that Brandt's role as representative of popular taste was over. Marquand had ceased to care very much what the magazines did to his novels when they serialized them, and took comfort from the checks that plastered the wound. When the *Ladies' Home Journal* carried *Sincerely, Willis Wayde*, it cut the book by forty percent, making it, as Marquand said, "a very mutilated piece of work." He would have refused to allow such an abridgment were the magazine not paying him "enormously large sums for the serial rights," the amount being in fact $56,000 after Brandt's commission was deducted. His friendship with Brandt continued, and when the latter died of alcoholism and emphysema in 1957, Marquand remarked, "He had been my literary agent ever since I started writing which, I am appalled to say, was about thirty-five years ago. Like most of his clients I was deeply devoted to him personally and even the bad literary advice he sometimes gave me never disturbed our friendship." But clearly the friendship of the last years had its ambiguities, not only on intellectual and professional grounds, but, as will be seen, on personal grounds as well.

To the general eye, Marquand was an eminent Man of Letters, a guide to popular taste to whom thousands looked for direction. The Book-of-the-Month Club board was, in a way, an academy of letters for the common standard of taste. He had joined it in September 1944, it will be recalled, even though he had just the previous year termed the Club "a racket that is spoiling the general sales of books by concentrating on the few that it sends to its customers, another of those organizations which exploits our writers as do agents and the publishers themselves, as well as the damn movies." But for the rest of his life he was to be one of the panel of five who selected the works of fiction or nonfiction that were mailed monthly to the subscribers of the largest book club in the world, significantly affecting the careers of writers and influencing the reading tastes and the opinions on politics and other general issues of its numerous subscribers and their families. Since its inception in 1926 the Club had become a phenomenon that disturbed many observers. When it reached its quarter-century mark in 1950 it had distributed 112 million copies of 15,000 titles; in 1950 alone it sent out 7,011,936 selections and dividends. In 1951 it had 600,000 members, whose tastes and views were, to some extent, in its keeping. Yet Marquand seems never to have had second thoughts about his role once he had assumed the judgeship, for which he was paid $20,000 annually.

The judges themselves constituted a sort of five-member club. They met thirteen times a year to discuss the forthcoming books which had been culled out of the mass by a staff of preliminary readers and sent to them in page proof or galley proof during the preceding weeks. The burden of reading on each judge was often considerable. He would be expected to read a dozen or more volumes each month, some indicated as "A" books, which the other judges read also, some as "B" books, which he was expected to designate for oblivion or presentation to the whole board. Yet Marquand, though he often complained about the time he spent on this task and the inexorably recurrent obligation to get to New York for the meetings summer and winter, maintained his membership until his death and only in the last months of his life arranged to reduce his participation. Unquestionably he enjoyed the meetings; his fellow judges were congenial middlebrow literati who respected his judgment, understood his point of view, reveled in his humor. The board was remarkably constant over the years, and the members who constituted it in 1944—Marquand himself, Henry Seidel Canby, Dorothy Canfield Fisher, Clifton Fadiman, and Christopher Morley—continued to serve throughout the forties (one by one Mrs. Fisher, Morley and Canby retired, but in 1960 Marquand and Fadiman were still members, along with John Mason Brown, Gilbert Highet and Basil Davenport). Present also at board meetings were the Club's president and vice-president, Harry Scherman and Meredith Wood, who were supposed to refrain from active participation, though they succeeded in doing so at times only with the greatest difficulty. The meetings, by all accounts, were spirited, and personalities came into play as the members talked together over lunch served at the big conference table in Scherman's office. In the present Club offices in Manhattan there still hangs a striking painting by Joseph Hirsch representing one of Marquand's early meetings: according to legend, Meredith Wood, with his napkin to his mouth, is supposed to be suffering spasms because the judges have just selected *The Goebbels Diaries*.

Perhaps the impression of a real conflict of viewpoint among the five or seven who were responsible for the Club's imperial decisions was illusory. On the whole the members of the board, including Marquand, seem to have been pretty much agreed on the social and literary conservatism that characterized their choices. Politics hung over their deliberations, although they were constantly reminding themselves of the importance of avoiding partisan positions. In 1947, they aroused considerable criticism by choosing *Why*

They Behave Like Russians by John Fischer, which was based on a tour of the Ukraine he had made as part of a UNRRA mission. The book was angrily denounced for its anti-Soviet bias by the chief of the mission, Marshall MacDuffie, who had read portions published in *Harper's*, and MacDuffie made a strenuous effort to prevent its adoption by the Club. But Marquand and the other judges decided to distribute it, even though, as Lewis Gannett remarked in his review, it was an obvious "quickie," based on slight observation and a good deal of hearsay. Yet the Club rejected other "political" books, such as *The American Democracy* by the socialist Harold Laski. Marquand had said of Laski: "At times his penetration and his general view of the American scene is better than anything I have ever read." Nevertheless he voted to reject it: "I don't think the Book-of-the-Month Club should be in the position of tacitly supporting his views by sending out his book, at least until things in America are a little worse off than they are." In 1953 he responded to Elmer Davis's anti-McCarthy *But We Were Born Free* with the remark that it had a "political slant and bias, and consequently if it were ever sent out it would indicate that the Book-of-the-Month Club subscribed to a political stand."

When, in 1948, John King Fairbank's *United States and China* came to Marquand for review he admitted that he shared the author's judgment of the Chinese situation. "I believe," Marquand said, "that most of the key men in the Chinese Nationalist government are incompetents or rascals or a combination of both and that the situation is now out of the grasp of even the best of them." But he felt constrained to remind his fellow judges that the book's sponsors, Theodore H. White and Owen Lattimore, were supported in their views by "Communists and fellow-travelers, and I hate to be in their company." Yet Whittaker Chambers' *Witness* seemed to him an inescapable choice, during the national paranoia over the "Communist threat" in 1951. His knowledge of Chinese affairs made him critical of Chambers' attack on White, whom Chambers had described as one of the writers most responsible for our Chinese failure. "This implies," Marquand warned, "that White is a Communist and a traitor to his country. It will probably mean, if published, that Mr. White will be deprived of his means of livelihood"—and he recommended that the book be carefully revised, but accepted. The question of bias continued to trouble the judges. Marquand's last review for the *Book-of-the-Month Club News* presented *The Politics of Upheaval*, Arthur Schlesinger, Jr.'s third volume of his history of the Roosevelt era (the other two had been previously sent out to the members) with the observation that the Club had been accused of leftist leanings, but Marquand now, in 1960, reflected that Thucydides, Gibbon and Motley had had each his bias, and "no historian, no matter how he tries, can be neutral." It was a case, clearly, of changed times, changed manners.

When it came to literature Marquand understood very well the Club's role as the representative of the great American middle-class book-consumer—had he not responded to this public himself in all his writing? When his old *Saturday Evening Post* colleague, Thomas Costain, presented the board with *The Moneyman* in 1947, Marquand reminded his colleagues that it was "a darn good story," and added, "It seems to me about time that we gave the customers something with entertainment value, and never mind the art and implications." The board saw what he meant, although when Gilbert Highet joined it in 1953 Marquand expressed fear "that we might have to reconcile ourselves to the tastes and aspirations of a university critic" and the next year complained that he was having difficulty in reaching agreement with Highet as well as with Clifton Fadiman and Amy Loveman, "who stick together like the Pharisees and like those interesting people, have the same holier than thou tastes." At the same time he resented the charge made by J. Donald Adams in the *New York Times Book Review* that the book clubs were all making more and more mediocre choices, pointing out that the Book-of-the-Month had stuck its neck out for distinguished works—*Animal Farm* and *Aurora Dawn*. But there was no question, he would admit, that the Club had let some good ones get by—*The Caine Mutiny*, *The Grapes of Wrath*, and Faulkner's *Intruder in the Dust*, the last because it made one of the members of the board (it was probably Dorothy Canfield Fisher) "nervous." He wrote Amy Loveman that the Faulkner novel "for some peculiar reason held my attention although he does not approve of sentences or paragraphs. Why he doesn't is something I can't understand. It really would be easier to read if he adopted a few printer's conventions, but perhaps its being hard to read makes it great literature."

Nevertheless he would often express his literary responses with a witty irascibility. John Mason Brown would remember the style of his diatribes, a variant of that performance which the exasperations of private life could stimulate: "John would moan with outrage. His right hand would reach for his chin and swing his head to one side in agony. His blue eyes would freeze in mock anguish. He would howl to the deity. These were outbursts of which W. C. Fields would have been proud." He might say: "*Prater Violet* is a very sloppy piece of work and one which I do not think would be tolerated here if it were written by an American instead of a Britisher named Isherwood, because the British can write 'oh, so beautifully!'" Or: "J. B. Priestley's novel sits on my mind as an indigestible dinner might upon my stomach, giving me mental cramps and gas pains." Or: "Robert Penn Warren writes with his genitals and all his characters can scarce keep their minds off theirs for a single moment. His women are nymphomaniacs. All his men seem to take two tablespoonfuls of Spanish fly before breakfast. There is more dirty talk in this book, *The Cave*, about private parts and fornication than in almost any I have been privileged to read while a member of the Book-of-the-Month Club board. However, this is what we now term 'lusty' and maybe I am undersexed. Take the book. My objections are old-fashioned and maybe all this thrown-away potency makes me jealous." Or: "James

Michener has always been a lousy writer, and, worse, a literary exhibitionist. By word-of-mouth advertising he has made himself literary ruler of the Pacific and interpreter of all the primitive and not-so-primitive people dwelling in that area. This is too much for him. This grandiose book on Hawaii is too much for me as well; it is like eating a piece of dough without even a sugar plum in it."

Not all his energy was reserved for an assault. When he liked a book, he could summon up the kind of enthusiasm he gave Alan Paton's *Cry the Beloved Country*—"one novel in ten thousand." There had been some hesitation over James Jones's *From Here to Eternity*, but Marquand urged that "in spite of the foulness of its language and the unsavory realism of its situations and its occasional artistic clumsiness it will probably be recognized by the critics as one of the best novels that has been published for years. I feel personally that every bit of the foul language has an artistic purpose and that without it he could not have created such magnificent characters or have done such a really outstanding piece of work." When this opinion was expressed again in Marquand's review for the *Book-of-the-Month Club News*, Jones wrote that this praise from someone whose work he had studied helped him believe that he had written the book he had dreamed of.

But Marquand did not like to be pushed. When the vote had gone against *The Young Lions* by Irwin Shaw he had been annoyed to receive a letter sent by Bennett Cerf urging the board to reconsider because others had expressed extreme enthusiasm for the novel and because ONE MILLION DOLLARS (capitalized in Cerf's letter) was being asked for the motion picture rights. Marquand's reply had the full titer of his characteristic acid: "I do not agree with Mr. Thomas Heggen that reading this book is one of the most devastating experiences in one's life and I do not think it is the finest novel yet written by an American. If Mr. Leland Hayward wishes to ask one million dollars for the moving pictures rights, a figure which Mr. Bennett Cerf capitalizes, it is all right for Mr. Hayward to do so, and it is all right, too, for some psychopathic movie magnate to pay this price if he wants to, but I doubt if it is one of the finest properties in years. I think that Bennett Cerf has got himself unduly steamed up because he too sees dollar signs in the sky, and I wish you hadn't sent me the copy of the letter because it prejudices me against the book, which I liked for itself without being faced by the cloying and undignified experience of seeing Bennett Cerf jump overboard for it with all his clothes on." Surely Marquand was the last person anyone should try to impress with "success." He had just written *Point of No Return*—which in a little while would be produced as a supersuccessful play by the same Leland Hayward.

21

Women and John P. Marquand

Marquand's last novel, published two years before his death, was called *Women and Thomas Harrow*, a title which suggested that his final vision of self in the ever-autobiographical hero was of a man whose life could be defined by his engagements with those loving antagonists, his wives and mistresses. His fiction had always drawn upon his own experience with women. Although his wives were never certain which of them he might have intended to depict—the truth being that their personalities were often fused in one image and mingled with invented traits—marriage as he had learned to understand it was one of the chief subjects of his art. From *Apley* onward, he showed an interest in the special nature of female authority in the institution of the middle- or upper-class American marriage. Out of the frustrations imposed upon them by a sex-discriminatory yet mom-worshipping tradition, women in America, he appeared to say, had turned to the contests of the marital sphere. As guardians of tradition and conformity they had become the gentle jailers of their husbands.

The Late George Apley, conceived in the dusky last days of his marriage to Christina, had defined the role of Catherine Apley, chosen for her husband by his family, as one of these conservators of order. Proper Bostonianism had been threatened by Apley's infatuation with a Boston Irish girl, and perhaps potentially by other impulses towards liberalism or individuality. His old-fashioned friendship with Clara Goodrich, a thing of bird walks and elevated conversation, was later the permitted outlet that offered no threat to the structure of things. Marquand's relationship with Helen Howe had begun by being just such a sanctioned relationship, and though it surmounted the traditional restraints, it could never quite liberate itself from the conditions of this Boston sanction, could never, in itself, become a new marriage. *Wickford Point* seems the exception in Marquand's continuous study of American marriage. Its primary female images are an eccentric spinster remembered out of the past, Jim Calder's Aunt Sarah, and his cousin Clothilde, whose husband is a hardly noticeable presence. Jim himself is unmarried, though he has a mistress who would like to marry him. Yet Clothilde, in her way, is also a matriarch and a conservator, not so much of Proper Bostonianism as of the idealist cult of the nonpractical, which has become in the generation of her children the *im*practical. To such a woman, to whom in a sense Calder is wed by his attachment to Wickford Point, is opposed the new woman whom he loves but cannot unite with: the self-made, traditionless female professional like Marquand's friend Carol Brandt. This alternate type had emerged more distinctly as Marvin Myles in *H. M. Pulham, Esquire.* Efficient in the working world of men, bright, free, frank about sex, she unsuccessfully threatens Pulham's foreordained marriage to Kay Motford. But Marquand makes Kay a formidable, occasionally sympathetic figure, whose sense of reality is stronger than her husband's, and it is she, in fact, who can lay aside the conventional code (without disturbing the conventional marriage) sufficiently for a love affair, making her husband's loss of power in the domestic realm absolute.

The war altered the terms of many human arrangements, marriage included, as Marquand showed in *Repent in Haste*; but in his longer and more important novel *So Little Time*, he again described the American wife as the unforgettable Madge Wilson, always complaining, as Adelaide Marquand did, that her husband shut her out of his thoughts. Shallow, manipulative, preoccupied with social position, she is a more contemporary example of the wife who makes herself the family watchdog of class. She contrives to send her son into the Army, against her husband's wishes, in order to prevent an "unsuitable" marriage. She does not scruple at this exercise of her dominance, this violation of the myth of equal parental partnership. Jeffrey, inevitably, is drawn to another—*the* other sort of woman, the actress who inhabits his own world of work and understands his agonies of frustrated masculinity and stalled creativity. But he cannot marry her; he must accept his life and even accept and comfort Madge, who obscurely understands that she has lost some of his love as the price of her power.

The outcome changes in *B. F.'s Daughter*, which places the American wife at the center of the story. Marquand is sympathetic yet critical of Polly Fulton, as he must then have been of his own wife. Like Adelaide, Polly is a rich man's daughter; she has inherited her father's executive ability and his enjoyment of power and so she runs her home and her husband with well-meaning authority, being too good at the job. In the end, he prefers a worshipping secretary. Marquand would later say that the only woman who understands the American man is his secretary, and in *Women and Thomas Harrow* he would finally adumbrate the ideal, self-effacing, yet completely sympathetic and understanding helpmeet, the woman paid to serve. At the very end of his life he may have even fancied himself in love with such a girl.

Perhaps the subtlest portrait of the American woman in Marquand's fiction is Nancy Gray of *Point of No Return*. She is a *former* secretary, and she has brought into her marriage her competence in handling details and managing schedules and her awareness of the politics governing business careers. But, like Polly Fulton, she tends to run her husband a little too masterfully, all for his own good and out of perfect devotion. Like her upper-class counterparts in *Apley* and *Pulham* she has acted as a brake upon his feeble impulse to rebellion, helped him to accept the conditions of his advancement to success. She is the essential policeman of the family, the guardian of the status quo. More than Charles she has been aware of every play of the game and, like an anxious coach, has directed from the sidelines. Marquand is not without regard for Nancy—she is an idealized version of his second wife, who was executive *without* being efficient. And Nancy is redeemed by the fact that *her* intelligence is accompanied by an awareness of what she may be doing to the man she loves, and what the cost is.

Sincerely, Willis Wayde may be, as has been suggested, the bitterest chastisement that Marquand ever inflicted upon himself in the process of writing fiction. Unlike all his other heroes Willis is made to bear the entire burden of guilt for what he is and does. Sylvia Hodges, the professor's daughter who wants a dress out of the Bergdorf Goodman window, is only a passive accomplice in Willis's rise, not a manager like Nancy Gray. Willis himself, whose ambitions even invade the housekeeping, home-building sphere, is the one who purchases, without consulting Sylvia, grander and still more grand establishments that will represent the augmentation of his wealth. Marquand himself had had a desire for houses as symbols of his own achievements—the recovered homestead of Curzon's Mill, the gentleman's farm of Kent's Island—but in this Adelaide had more than abetted him, and it would be she who would buy, finally, houses that he had not even seen. In his total lack of self-knowledge and his vulgarity, Willis is, of course, most unlike his creator. Only the secret consonance of spirit—for which no woman was to blame—linked the author to the character. In this way, perhaps, his ultimate self-criticism dispensed with Adam's excuse that the woman had persuaded him.

But finally there are the three wives of Thomas Harrow in Marquand's last and most misogynist book, which emerged after the destruction of both his marriages. Each wife, in her way, has failed Harrow: Rhoda, the hometown girl who turned out to be a socially ambitious main-chancer; Hoopdale, the actress who caught him on the rebound, but, unlike Jeffrey Wilson's actress girlfriend, had more personal ambition than amorous devotion; and, finally, Emily. Emily is not successfully executive, only bossy and rather stupid, yet she has helped him to sell out his talent in the service of a comfortable success. She is quite incapable of coping with his failure, much less sympathizing with it. So the book ends in Tom's aborted attempt at suicide—a reflection of Marquand's last mood. As this terminal Marquand self, Tom drives away from the cliff over which he has almost plunged. He reflects that "in the end, no matter how many were in the car, you always drove alone." It was Marquand's final word on the subject of marriage.

In Marquand's second marriage, as in his first, it was probably impossible for him to say at what point the irritations and conflicts operating between two demanding, differing personalities began to seem insupportable. The bond, whether of love or sexual attachment or affectionate dependence or even the comfortable partnership of domesticity and social relations, can, as everyone knows, take a good deal of strain—but no causes are too trivial to seem the breaking weight once a connection has grown brittle. In viewing Marquand's marriages, witnesses were always to be baffled by his comic inflation of complaint, which had the effect of making his stories about Adelaide's shortcomings seem two things at once: harmless because so obviously exaggerations done in affectionate humor, and revelations, masked as comedy, of the quite terrifying truth that the speaker was frantic with rage and despair. Since Marquand *always* told such stories—even at the beginning of the marriage, when he could not have really meant to proclaim the relationship impossible—it was quite difficult for a listener to judge how much he was driven beyond bearing early or late.

Unquestionably, like Christina, Adelaide had peculiarities that could be made the subject of a tale, and the tales that linger were not always Marquand's. She did not have the usual vanity of women well able to afford maids and hairdressers and expensive clothes—and to some of her conventional acquaintances this seemed a defect. She was often positively frowsy, blowsy. Her thick, somewhat frizzy light hair might stand out about her head as though she had started the day without combing it, and she wore full dirndl skirts of European peasant embroideries or Indian prints that emphasized her heavy figure, and sandals (such an appearance, which startled the Cambridge ladies she knew in the fifties, would not have seemed so eccentric in the neighborhood of Harvard Square ten years later). Marquand had obviously found her attractive when they married, and many of her friends declared that she was always the fresh-complexioned, "zippy" Vassar girl, with a ringing laugh, a wonderful spirit of fun, even in her saddest days. But unhappiness must have increased her appearance of self-abandon and disorder. If the Cambridge ladies are to be trusted she finally became positively sloppy—the peasant blouses and medieval robes were noted to be split under the arms and stained, her hair, now graying, was wilder than ever, the laugh became strident. Even earlier she had begun to seem to Marquand a striking opposite to another type of woman whose appearance of studied, stylish attractiveness was the index of her awareness of others.

Adelaide's *un*-awareness was a root quality—and perhaps the result of a kind of vanity of another sort. Though intelligent, she could not imagine an attitude in someone else that she might not alter to her liking or, for that matter, an objective situation not to be remade to her pleasure. She was energetic, affectionate, generous—and had lifelong friends who felt themselves the beneficiaries of these qualities. Yet some of those who knew her best found her very virtues to be instruments of her will; she tried to *buy* people with her affection and her generosity, they would complain; she was ready to do anything to get her way, but get her way she must. She retained, perhaps, the rich person's fatuity that everything is for sale, if not for money then for some other gift less material—affection being one. She could not understand a refusal. The Harvard classics professor Mason Hammond remembered how baffled she was when he refused to arrange that teen-age Ferry be taken on an archaeological dig—after all, were not the Hammonds friends to whom she had been devoted for years? So she blithely nagged—surely there was something he could do. It was only a trivial example of a nature that insisted and insisted on persuading a reluctant husband to spend his summers in Colorado rather than in Newburyport. She was unable to believe that she would not eventually succeed in making him agree with her. Even more fatally, at the end, she would not believe that nothing would change his mind about separation and divorce. Her gestures in defiance of fact had a certain grandeur. She built and furnished in Aspen the studio Marquand refused to use. In 1953 she bought and furnished the huge old-fashioned house in Cambridge, which she proposed as a home for her family at the very moment it was ceasing to be one.

One of her personal assets might have been her abundant energy. Into whatever she had in hand—work for some public cause she identified as her own or some personal or family plan—she poured the strength of twenty. But the projects often ran counter to the feelings of those others they involved. Marquand had disliked her America First activity, but she had offended him more in carrying out plans for family living that were products of her fancy—particularly in the arrangements of their various residences and the disposition of the lives of their children. Aspen and the Cambridge house were only conspicuous examples. There would be, in time, a craziness, a mistaken overplus of effort and motion as she complicated her own and others' days. She would not let life say no. And so, as might be expected, she failed to get many things done well.

She was always missing appointments and arriving late. In this last respect, one is reminded of Christina, who often arrived late at other people's parties and was sometimes unprepared for her own invited guests. When Marquand would tell an "amusing" story of Adelaide's chronic lateness those who had known him in earlier years had an eerie feeling that a reel of old recorder tape was being played again. Making trains or planes with Adelaide was always a frantic near-miss, sometimes a miss, and Marquand would rage as he had in the past, his own precise and punctual nature irritated immeasurably. On a deeper level, his own ego may have been wounded by the egoism that makes others wait. Forgetfulness of this sort became more grotesque in Adelaide's last solitary years, and was probably complicated by depression and alcoholism. The Cambridge witnesses remember that it was then risky to invite her to a dinner party because she might not come, or, if she did, would come disordered and tipsy when one had given up waiting for her. Or she would herself arrange a party; the guests would arrive, only to be served by the confused servants while she was unaccountably delayed, and when she did come home at last, during dessert, she would go directly upstairs and fall asleep. But these are the pitiful marks of a terminal condition in a character that must once have appeared just charmingly absentminded.

It was already late in the day, sixteen years after their marriage, that Marquand would offer such a description as the following: "This winter has been unusually hectic. This business of trying to live in three or four places at once and shuttling madly from spot to spot has finally got terribly on my nerves. Timmy and Lonny are staying at the cottage at Greenwich with the governess so that they can attend the Greenwich Country Day School. Ferry has been in the apartment with Adelaide and me in New York so that she could attend Miss Chapin's. The result of this arrangement has been that I never see much of the children and they are of an age now when I might be of some help to them. Over the weekends, when we are together, Adelaide has such a round of activities—movies, operas, philharmonics, skating lessons and so forth—that the apartment is a madhouse. In order to keep the show going Adelaide shuttles about like a beetle on a hot stove, with no time to read the newspapers, no time to sew the strap on her slip, no time to get her hair washed, no time for anything. Somehow or other I am caught in the contagion and I seem to have no time either to write, to think, or even to get a haircut, though I don't know what I have been doing." It is only one of Marquand's funny stories, one may say—one suspects exaggeration, one is ready to ask how different is what he describes from typical, uncatastrophic family life in the upper middle class. But as a matter of fact, his description could have been properly taken at its most alarming value at this moment. Just two months later Marquand suffered a severe heart attack, which he was convinced had been brought on by an argument with Adelaide. He was almost decided that he could never resume married life with her again. And though they were not actually divorced for another five years, the point of no return had probably been reached.

And yet the rule that it takes two to make a marital disaster is clearly demonstrated. The bossiness and presumption with which he charged Adelaide was partly the fruit, anyone could see, of his own willingness to surrender responsibilities. He complained that he did not know his children, yet he had always demanded that they be kept out of his way. He hated making arrangements for his own living situation or for his movements, so that others—his agent, his publisher, his secretary, or his wife—took on the managing of these things. With one side of his nature he loved to be managed, to be taken care of. It is perhaps significant that he disliked driving a car—he preferred to be chauffeured by wife or secretary, or, when these were not available, in a hired limousine. When he traveled, logistics and reservations were the concern of someone else—his agent, his secretary, his lawyer. Like royalty, he sometimes did not even carry money with him—friends like the Fiskes were surprised to find that they had to lend him small change for tips when he went out visiting or traveling in their company. Adelaide's lapses and inefficiency as a caretaker constituted an annoyance. But he also resented the surrenders of power involved when she was of genuine help to him.

An important example was the role he permitted her to play in the area where his own authority was most precious. In 1951, when Christina was dying, Marquand told Johnny, "I used to complain that your mother never took enough interest in my work." He gave his son a message for his first wife: "Tell her that I am now on the other horn of the dilemma." Indeed, Adelaide "took an interest!" She insisted on the preservation of his early work, digging out the old magazine stories he preferred to forget and planning with the help of the Brandt office several collections of them; she kept scrapbooks of reviews of his novels and even of the plays and films made from them; she had complete sets of first editions of each of his books specially bound for her children. All this was harmless enough

In addition, however, Adelaide was for some years of major assistance to her husband in the preparation of his manuscripts. Marquand had become accustomed to the practice of dictating directly to a typist and then reworking the prepared copy, which was apt to be not only repetitious but full of solecisms more apparent to the eye than to the ear. Severe cutting and textual correction were necessary. Adelaide, with her Spence School–Vassar training was, it soon appeared, a competent copyeditor. During the war, when Marquand's working time was reduced by his war work, she became a part of the team—along with the Brandt office and the Little, Brown staff—which helped to prepare his manuscripts for the press. *So Little Time* was, in 1943, corrected for grammar, spelling, repetitions, and the like by Adelaide. Marquand both permitted and resented this participation in typically ambiguous fashion.

He wrote Johnny: "Adelaide and I are still having the dreadful time we always have whenever I finish a novel. She has been over the first draft with a fine tooth comb and I thought that perhaps she would let the second draft go, but now she is going over that and we fight over it page by page—675 of them, double-spaced. The other night Adelaide and I had dinner with Mr. and Mrs. Robert Nathan and Mr. Nathan had just finished a novel. I told them that Adelaide was working on my grammatical mistakes. The next day I saw Mr. Nathan who said a terrible thing had happened. His wife had gotten after his novel and made him rewrite the whole last chapter and found one page where he had used the word 'sometimes' fifteen times." Adelaide, besides, had views, which she pressed, about the still more important matters of composition. When Marquand consulted Edward Sheldon about the way he had brought his novel to its indeterminate close, he asked permission to bring Adelaide to their conference: "She would love to hear what you have to say because she had been over the manuscript twice with a fine tooth comb trying to pick up bad pieces of diction and split infinitives and she is very much against the last five or six pages at the very end. She would love it if you also did not like them." She did not win this argument—though, as has been seen, Sheldon supported her about the ending—but she would later claim that she deserved credit for finding the title, which was chosen, as she told Johnny, "after battles" between the publisher, agent, author and wife. It was that autumn, when Marquand was overseas, moreover, that Adelaide took on other burdens. It was she who cut the book for the armed services edition and assumed a certain amount of business management and correspondence and discussions of film contracts and commissions with Brandt and Little, Brown on his behalf. After the war, her participation in the Marquand workshop continued, obviously valued yet at the same time resented more and more as time went on. He would miss few opportunities to express publicly his gratitude with a clear ironic emphasis, a snicker at the schoolmistress authority that she exercised over his woodnotes. Eventually he came to believe that this authority had been forced upon him, that it was the ultimate demonstration of her desire to make him an appurtenance of herself. There was rumored to be a double portrait of the Marquands by the painter Gardner Cox, which Adelaide's husband professed always to dislike because it showed them together, he standing, she sitting at a desk with papers before her, as though she were "writing his books for him."

It is possible to see, in a mood of sympathy for a female condition so representative, that Adelaide was someone who had not sufficiently discovered how to live in herself. Her excess of egotism was a perversion growing out of an incapacity to be distinct to herself other than as the invaluable wife and amanuensis. To this she applied all the force she possessed, in this she strove for an importance and power that she had not found elsewhere. Her motherhood, too, it would turn out, became a further function of her craving to do, to make, to *be*. She was insensitive to her children's actual needs, to their separate desires to be each what they were, to have their own being. Yet she was "devoted" in her efforts and schemes on their behalf. She wanted to give them everything—except free choice.

Again, as in the collapse of his first marriage, Marquand's complaints were not the whole story. "Another woman" had once more become the focus of his secret life. This time it was a very old friend, Carol Brandt. As early as 1927, during his troubles with Christina, it will be remembered, he had discovered the appeal of the woman who later became his agent's wife. Over the years Marquand depended upon both the Brandts for innumerable acts of advice and aid well outside their professional relation. They provided a constant personal refuge during the difficulties of his first marriage, Carol as well as Carl giving him more effective caretaking than either Christina or Adelaide ever had. His affection for the Brandts never lost, it should be noted, a certain measure of skepticism, and it was probably a lasting attitude that he expressed to Johnny in 1946, when, urging him to know them better, he said: "I think you might be amused by Carl and Carol Brandt, who, as you know, are old friends of mine. They live in a strange, and to me, an unreal world—the world of the entrepreneur which is based largely on a ten percent commission. They are very anxious to have shiny automobiles, excellent clothes, gold cigarette lighters and to be known affectionately by headwaiters in all the hot spots. Though I am very fond of them, these ambitions of theirs seem to me to lack what I might call validity, and as their advice in general is based upon these attainments, I should listen to it but not follow it too carefully. They are people you ought to know because they represent a very definite aspect of society, but do not take them too seriously." But this cool intellectual apprehension did not preclude a certain indulgence, especially towards Carol. In 1934, when attending a party with both of the Brandts, he had felt their superiority, he told Helen Howe, to Christina's friends. Carol, "despite flowing dresses, cars and perfumes made more sense than all the women put together." To Helen, who was helping him to reject his first wife—as in time Carol would help him to reject his second—he added, "There is something in being down to actualities in life—and there is no substitute for that something—no travel, tennis, intelligence, reading the latest novel or looking at new pictures or anything."

Carol, it continued to be always obvious to him, was close to actuality, practical-minded and even vulgar, as befitted a marketeer in the rough world of buying and selling literature, a world which his wives could never understand. Carol was not subtle. Her taste for the expensive luxuries that came out of her own and her husband's toil was frank. The style in which she dressed and the style in which she decorated her apartment on Park Avenue were both emphatically expensive; not for her the genteel shabbiness of Beacon Hill. Her brunette good looks were boldly emphasized by elegant clothes and furs and showy jewelry, her hair was stylishly "done," her long, manicured fingernails were bright red, and she used liberally the heavy perfume called Shalimar. Even when Marquand was deeply in love with her, in 1949, he would still write, with humorous reproach: "There are things about you, of course, of which I do not approve, my darling, and yet it is wonderful that I can recognize them so clearly. I do not especially applaud, for example, many phases of your literary taste. You enjoy certain elements of power that I am willing to skip. You have a materialistic approach toward a good deal of life which I cannot wholly share. You are more concerned than I can ever be with phases of 'gracious living.' You put too much wax on your furniture and too much polish on your silver, and your theories of interior decoration have a Chippendale sumptuousness with which I am not at home, because unlike Leslie Ford and Marcia Davenport I like worn carpets and frayed upholstery. I do not much care for your fox and mink and sable jobs either, although I think they have a definite comedy value. Nor do I like large pieces of costume jewelry, especially large bracelets and brooches which scratch and have combination locks on them. I am very definitely against the excessive use of lipstick and long sang de boeuf fingernails, and I don't like girdles either."

Clever, worldly, attractive, fashionable, Carol pleased Marquand most by the clarity with which she grasped external situations—it made her a successful agent in a competitive world dominated by men—and with the same clarity she understood his and her own feelings. She was as realistic about sex as about everything else. She would later say quite openly to others that Carl Brandt, increasingly alcoholic, had gradually become incapable of offering her sexual satisfaction. Marquand, more and more out of love with Adelaide, in flight from a crowded, noisy, problem-filled domesticity, responded to Carol's need and his own. It was not until 1942 that he "ventured so much as to touch [her] hand," he later recalled, with some wonder at his own restraint. Somewhere during the coming-and-going war years they began the affair which, she related long afterwards, was suspended by their own resolution for a year, then resumed. He got into the habit of seeing her regularly on trips to New York for the monthly Book-of-the-Month Club meetings. He would come down from Kent's Island or fly in from Hobe Sound or Nassau. Carol, alerted by a note or a wire, would have made his reservation at the St. Regis, where the Brandts themselves also had a suite. She would arrange to have a leisurely dinner with him alone on the evening before the meeting.

In the last years of his life Marquand seems to have felt drawn, besides, to still another type of woman. When waiting for his divorce to be consummated in Reno in 1958, he told Ruth Whitman that the only women who had ever been good to him or understood him were his secretaries, the women who could share his work. "Perhaps this is because they were in another stratum of society and I felt more relaxed with them. Certainly they were easier to get along with," he said. "H. M. Pulham's mistake was thinking he had to stick to his class." In *Women and Thomas Harrow* he had given his unhappy hero only one source, neither wife nor mistress, of female sympathy and understanding. Harrow's secretary, Nancy Mulford, is defined as selfless, devoted and undemanding. She has put her own fulfillment in love aside and served Tom, understood him, advised him, without ever inviting the slightest violation of their professional relationship. Marquand may have received such support from more than one of his secretaries, and he dedicated the last of his novels to his current assistant, Dorothy Brisson. But another secretary, her predecessor and her successor (for she came back to Marquand at the very last) probably fulfilled this ideal of subservient handmaiden less austerely.

This was Marjorie Davis, who began to work for Marquand as his secretary in the fall of 1949. She was, unlike any woman he had been close to before, a girl of modest background, the daughter of a Scituate dentist, who had only had a business school education before going out to earn her own living. Katharine Gibbs, her school, had referred her to Marquand because she had last been employed in an overseas government agency on confidential work, and he had asked for someone of proved discretion. She was twenty-six years old, shy and rather plain, at first glance a very commonplace small-town girl. But she had a quick intelligence and a sense of humor, and she was one of those persons capable of choosing, for life, a fixed devotion. Marquand was probably unaware of these qualities when he hired her, but she seemed able and willing and she amused him by having a liking for two things that he had loved in his youth—sailing and tropical fish.

It was only gradually, probably, that their working relationship deepened into friendship and only at the very last briefly became love. For her it was the old story of the famous, immensely experienced and cultivated man arousing the admiration of a young person, a kind of hero-worship. It no doubt amused him to talk with this perfectly uncritical companion who was not at all stupid, to educate her in a thousand small ways during their conversations when they relaxed from their work. He discovered that she had wanted to be a writer herself and had edited her high school newspaper; and the great man suggested books for her to read and several times went over a few stories she had written, blue-penciling them with humorous comments.

Then, bit by bit, as his relationship with Adelaide became filled with quarreling and distress, Marjorie became aware of the domestic situation from which he fled when he walked down the path to the studio in the old carriage house at Kent's Island. Adelaide would frequently follow, uninvited, to continue some argument, indifferent to the presence of the silent secretary. On some occasions she would openly voice her troubles to Marjorie, trying to win her support, but after a while she quite correctly sensed the younger woman's coolness, her criticism; eventually she suspected her of being a sexual rival. In this she was, or eventually became, justified, although Marquand's passion for Marjorie Davis was not, probably, anything powerful enough to account for the progress towards divorce after 1953. She left Marquand's employ in April 1954, and did not return for four years. Though they occasionally met in Boston or New York, she remained on the outskirts of his life until she came to work for him again after the divorce in 1958. Their January and May romance flared briefly before he died two years later. Thereafter, like his Miss Mulford, she remained unmarried.

Carol Brandt had become Marquand's mistress well before he wrote the cautionary description of the Brandts to Johnny in 1946. But then, and for some time, the relationship was not exigent. The marriage went on; the lives of Marquand and his wife were interwoven by connections of habit and mutuality. After finishing *B. F.'s Daughter* that spring with the usual help from her on the manuscript, he arranged to assign twenty-five percent of the royalties to Adelaide. Although his motives were predominantly connected with his effort to ease his income tax situation, the copyrights listing her as co-author did not entirely lie. When a contract was signed with Loew's for the script of the novel in July, the Marquands made a trip west, stopped for a few days in Hollywood, and spent two and a half months vacationing together. They visited Yosemite, Tahoe, Lassen and the Mother Lode region as well as two of the Big Sierra power plants of the Pacific Gas and Electric Company. They then went up to Oregon for a month's fishing for steelhead trout on the Rogue River, where Adelaide owned a camp, and they were joined there by King Vidor and his wife whom Marquand, despite his tendency to laugh at Hollywood, had always liked. He seems to have had a good time even if he occasionally protested against Adelaide's "campfire girl" enthusiasms. Quite uncharacteristically he told George Merck upon his return, "After observing life in the Northwest, maybe it would be a good idea if we stopped all this business of trying to live in New England and went out and got a ranch there where everything grows all the time and where there are no insects and very few troublesome people."

The following year Marquand and Adelaide took another vacation trip. She met him in Honolulu on the first of May and they went for a few days to visit the Kona Coast, which had seemed to him in 1932 one of the most beautiful places in the world. Then they flew back to San Francisco and motored north—in a car with a driver sent down by Adelaide's cousin Albert Hooker—to the Rogue River. They arrived home just in time to give a cocktail party at the Cosmopolitan Club in New York for Johnny and Rita Kip, who were about to be married. And yet, with all the pleasure-seeking—or perhaps because of it—the strain that always characterized Marquand family life had intensified. Since Laura Hale's illness had left old Phil adrift, the Marquands now took him down with them to Hobe Sound. He wandered, confused and unhappy, among the sun-bathing and cocktailing tycoons, a visible image of Marquand's private sense of misplacement. Hobe Sound, that year, "had been *anything* but a vacation," even Adelaide admitted to Newburyport friends.

In the fall and winter of 1947, Marquand stayed on at Kent's Island, already engaged in those arguments with the Hales over the Mill that have been described. He was reluctant to go to Nassau, though Adelaide kept insisting on the importance of a tropical winter for Timmy. He had been working on *Point of No Return* on and off since the beginning of the year and managed, rather remarkably considering the distractions, to finish the first draft by September, but the slow work of cutting and revising this novel with its melancholy personal resonance occupied the following months. As he dug into his work *Time* extracted from him the observation that he did not believe "a writer's apt to evolve very much after he's 40," and noted that he was fifty-three. Something of his own longing at the end of a busy year for peace, immobility and silence crept into the essay he gave to the *Atlantic* about the island of Truk, of which he said, "the kindest thing the outer world could do would be to leave it alone." In December, when Adelaide went down to Hobe Sound, he may have felt glad to be left by himself while snow drifted upon the Newbury salt marshes. He wrote Carol Brandt, who had been abroad that winter on a government-sponsored trip: "I have often wondered how you got on during your patriotic and cultural vacation tour—better than I, I hope. Adelaide left on the 27th in the midst of a blizzard for Florida, again, to get the house ready for tenants. Since then I have scarce moved off this upland. Drifts were heavy on the road and the selectmen were so confused that we were all snowed in here for four days during which the only way one could travel was on snowshoes, and I mean snowshoes. In fact it was lucky indeed that in my more romantic youth I had learned to operate on them with considerable speed and skill. Even so I had not been on a pair for years and I was stiff, weary and wind-burned. Yesterday again the wind lashed up into as bad a northwester as I have ever seen, but thank goodness it rained part of the time and nothing drifted. There is one lesson I have learned from all this. I shall never, unless obliged by personal or political accident or financial necessity, stay in this neck of the woods after December 10 at the latest, and then only if you will agree to join me in a cabin further north entirely cut off from everything, but completely equipped with all luxuries and necessities to cover a six months' period. These supplies would include a few books, not one of which will be one of those goddamned Modern Library nightmares—namely Shakespeare, the Bible, an early translation of Tacitus, a good Thucydides, Plato's Republic, one Fielding, one Austen, one Balzac, Paradise Lost, a good Iliad and Odyssey, Walton, one Thoreau, one Emerson, and not a single goddam Russian, but perhaps a little Euripides. The perusal of the volumes, which you will read aloud to me in front of the primus stove while I repair the rabbit snares or jerk venison, will do you a lot of good. For one thing they will round out your literary background so that, if you will continue to be a didactic writer's huckster, at least when you return to civilization you can be didactic and you can draw generalities too from what I think is a firmer basis of pronouncements than a smattering of Thomas Mann—I'll bet you've never read more than two of his short stories and nothing more—the works of your old pansy Maugham, and God help us, the complete opuses of your clients, Ford, Davenport, Sheean and Fischer. In the meanwhile, if I am not stricken with pneumonia, I plan to abandon this place before the next snowfall taking the five o'clock to New York on Monday the fifth of the bright new year. If you can see your way clear to dining with me quietly on the sixth, it would be nice from my point of view, I think. At any rate the luncheon on the eighth will still be possible, and I shall save 12:30 to 4:30 and I'll call you on the sixth anyway. Love."

It is not exactly a love letter, for Marquand has undercut his imagined winter idyll with Carol by a tone of teasing condescension, a suggestion that whatever there was between them was still a light matter, held very well in hand. It was not until a year and a half later that he wrote her the further declaration from which quotation has already been made. After pointing to her deficiencies he had then gone on: "Still, I find myself able to put up with these defects. You have qualities which offset them, but I haven't the time to name them now. The main thing is that you have never let me down, and I don't think you ever will. This I find a very valuable quality and a very rare one, darling. I can't tell you now how much I appreciate it, but please come home soon from Claridge's."

The hectic round of family life had continued through 1949. After an unsatisfactory stay at Nassau, the Marquands had returned to the battle over Curzon's Mill, which poisoned the spring and summer at Kent's Island. In September they went west once again, again going to the Rogue River, but perhaps this trip did not give them the needed recovery of spirits. They had stopped at Aspen on the way out; it delighted Adelaide, but not her husband, on this first visit. The trip to Colorado was not an escape from an overpopulated family life, for the party included also Johnny, and eight-year-old Ferry, "an interesting combination of age groups and generations," as Marquand would recall. There had been the usual change of trains at Chicago and a stop for dinner at the Blackstone Hotel, during which occurred the incident that became one of his funny-bitter recitals. "Our group of four sat at a round table and our orders were taken by a friendly and attentive waiter. In the midst of the meal my daughter Ferry began fussing about her spinach, and her mother remonstrated with her until the whole scene became domestic. Finally my daughter asked me whether or not she might skip her spinach, and at this point the waiter patted her on the head and smiled at me in a friendly way. I have always noted that Chicago waiters are kind to their customers. I could see that he was making an intelligent estimate of the whole situation, and finally he said two words to me that proved it. He said, 'Grandpa's girl.'" In recalling the incident two years later, he observed to the Harvard classmates gathered for their thirty-fifth reunion dinner: "I do not suppose I should have been shocked but at the same time I was. There comes a time when you stare at the hourglass. My time arrived in that unexpected way in Chicago." Whether or not his awareness of encroaching age could be so precisely dated, he henceforth became fond of observing, as the children remembered, that he was too old to be their father. "What am I doing with little monsters like you; I'm old enough to be your grandfather," he would say.

The following year had begun with the publication of *Point of No Return* and the fanfare of the *Time* and *Newsweek* cover stories. But on his return from Nassau, Marquand experienced the severest ulcer attack he had ever known. He was hospitalized in the Presbyterian Hospital in New York for two weeks of tests and probes. As he told Carol, he had suffered "digestive" episodes for years, and since 1942 he had had them at the rate of three a year, but the last time he had experienced anything comparable to this crisis of 1949 was in 1927, when his marriage with Christina had reached an acute stage of breakdown. For a while the Presbyterian doctors thought that his troubles this time might be due to an infection picked up in China during his 1947 visit, but Dana Atchley, Marquand's physician, finally decided that his condition was psychosomatic or, as Marquand translated, "a nervous condition due to certain environmental stresses."

What these were that summer and fall can only be guessed. In June, Adelaide was again in Aspen with Anne Lindbergh, enjoying the cultural scene and furnishing the home she had bought. Marquand wrote the Aspen writer Carl Jonas, who had just put Marquand into a novel about the Paepcke paradise: "You may have heard that Adelaide has bought Mrs. Morgenthau's place in Aspen consisting, as I remember, of a few lots, a small shack and a privy. What she is going to do with it is somewhat beyond me." Marquand remained at Kent's Island. He supervised the search for a better well site on his property. He told the Governor Dummer boys at South Byfield about the value of discontent. He saw Ferry off to camp and stayed on with his two small sons and the nurse, reading *Hiawatha* to them in the evening, "a gruesome occupation," he told Adelaide, "but better I think than listening to the odes and speeches at the Aspen Convocation." The "patter of little feet" seemed to make necessary a small slug of whiskey just before dinner, but otherwise he was managing. He even played some golf and went trolling for striped bass with a local friend and spent the Fourth of July in Framingham with Gardi and Conney Fiske; later in the month he went to a writer's conference in Vermont, where he lectured on the novel. Only, one morning, when he had taken the boys into Boston and stopped at the Somerset Club to let them use the plumbing facilities, old John, the doorman, had remarked that it was nice that he had two such large, strong grandsons. With reluctance, at the end of August, he went to join Adelaide for a month at Aspen, "a great extravagance and one which I do not care much about. I wish she did not like those mountains so much," he told George Merck.

Upon their return on the first of October, Marquand stayed long enough at Kent's Island to enter a last futile legal plea against the estate division of Curzon's Mill that had been decided upon in the Salem courthouse months before. Then he moved down to his new apartment on Sixty-seventh Street in New York while the children and the governess (and sometimes Adelaide and even sometimes he himself) were established in the cottage on his mother-in-law's estate at Greenwich. It was from Greenwich in the autumn of 1949 that he wrote to Carol far away in London at the Hotel Claridge the letter relating the beginning of his feelings for her long before, when he and Christina had been living in Weston. He had not then expressed those feelings. "I wonder what was the matter with you and me," he now said. "Were we afraid of each other, or were we afraid that something would spoil what we had? Well never mind. It is now nine o'clock in London and I am thinking of you in Greenwich, Conn. I am thinking that I am older and wiser (I think) but not a bit sadder than I was that afternoon at Walden. I have known a few more women since then—not as many as I should perhaps, because I have never been either gregarious or promiscuous, and certainly not as many as perhaps you think I know. I may have told you, but here I am telling you again in case you have forgotten that you are the only one who has been completely satisfactory in every way. I know that this is an unpoetic way of putting it, and that it sounds like an automobile or a washing machine but one of the beauties of all that lies between us is that I do not feel under the slightest compulsion to use words which are not like myself or to behave toward you in any sort of artificial way. I know pretty well that nothing I may say or do will in any great measure alter the opinion you may hold of me, and I imagine this is much the same with you. There is no need to create a good impression. We neither of us have many cards left up our sleeves, and most of the deck is face up on the table, and I find myself glad to take a card—any card. At least this is the way I always feel about you, and this is why I prefer your company to that of anyone else."

And what, the story reader asks, happened then? The answer, a defiance of romantic plot, is—nothing. As far as Carol and John were concerned their relation was exactly what they wanted it to be and did not call for any changes in the established design of their marriages. They were—it was Carol's expression more than his—"civilized" persons who had no desire to disrupt the lives of their children or even of their spouses. Carl Brandt appears to have acquiesced in a triangular arrangement by which he acknowledged Marquand as his wife's lover and his own old friend and client without ceasing, in his way, to remain attached to Carol. Marquand continued to be the favorite family visitor at the Brandt apartment; the Brandt children, Denny and Vicky, perceiving or not perceiving the exact state of things, regarded Marquand as a fond uncle. He was never better, never more genial and less acerb than at the Brandts. Probably it was not as easy as it looked. Carl's drinking became steadily heavier; he periodically committed himself to establishments for drying out alcoholics, but after a time was again on the bottle. No doubt "environmental stresses" were as much responsible for his addiction as for Marquand's ulcer. Yet his marriage, whatever its curious compromises, remained acceptable to him, and he made no move toward change. "I shall not—in fact I cannot—do anything to try and crack that weld," he would pathetically write Carol. "I, very simply, would not know how to envision life without you. Make up your mind what you want most. You are the arch priestess of that religion. I'll help you get it when you're sure. I love you that much, no matter what it does to me. But remember there's this to be said, that few people love you as I do or want you so consistently. I know you better than anyone else. We've more together than can be jettisoned with a 'skip it.'"

No such acceptance of the situation could be expected from Adelaide. Long before she had actual knowledge of the liaison, she resented Carol's managing intervention in her husband's life. When the divorce was imminent, she would recall a statement made by Marquand in 1943: "The Brandts can't stand to have any of their clients married because they can't push them around. The wives get in the way." Adelaide observed, "He only likes bossy women—Brandt, Cousin Lucy, Fiske, Howe"—and she could have included herself, one "bossy" woman competing with the others. But her very resistance to reality, the reverse of Carl's acceptance, had a similar effect. She might suspect the nature of her husband's relationship with Carol, even have it plainly spelled out to her, and yet not believe that irreparable change and division was taking place.

And in the winter of 1950, at Salt Cay, the Marquand pendulum did swing towards comparative peace. Isolated with their three young children on the beautiful island, the Marquands enjoyed a degree of harmony that had for some time been absent from their days. Marjorie Davis, not yet a player in the emotional game of the marriage, worked peacefully in her tent-studio taking Marquand's dictation. "There is a dreamy sort of solitude about the place and an unworldly mood that is best stated by 'The Tempest,'" Marquand observed on his return in the spring. That summer at Kent's Island the long tug-of-war over Curzon's Mill was finally over, and the family's belongings were moved out of the Brick House into the Yellow House, which was now Marquand's by the court's decision, and Philip was installed there with a housekeeping couple. Marquand was more cheerfully engaged with his neighbors as he led the Fourth of July parade and participated in the Neptune's muster, and he erected a forty-foot steel flagpole from which Old Glory waved near the house at Kent's Island. "I have seen more of life in Newburyport than I have for many years and I have enjoyed it," he reported in September.

Adelaide, of course, was then in Aspen, having left behind Ferry as well as two young beagles she had purchased (and which Marquand abominated) but taking the two boys with her. The little girl, alone with Marquand and a new governess, enjoyed a good deal of undivided attention from her father for almost the first time in her life, and was happier and better behaved than she had ever been. For the first time since infancy, he said, she had fingernails, "grown under compulsion of bribery and persuasion." But Marquand felt curiously tired. He did not sleep well at night and toiled day after day at *Melville Goodwin* with an oppressive sense of haste, feeling overworked and weary. "I know what you will say," he wrote Adelaide. "Why not take Ferry out in the plane to Denver and you will meet me in that 1942 jeep and we will have barrels of fun going over two mountain passes and ending in that beauty spot just in time to hear a lecture on the Little Flowers of St. Francis. Though I would love to see you and the boys, honest to God this is not my idea of a rest. I would immediately get a headache from the altitude and severe intestinal spasms from seeing pictures painted on silk and from meeting Gary Cooper and Clare Boothe Luce and from burning the garbage in the morning."

The Marquand calendar for 1951 was much like that of the preceding two years. They were at Salt Cay for January and February, then back to New York, then at Kent's Island for the summer (with Adelaide in Colorado in August), and in the fall, once more in New York and Greenwich. But nothing stands still, and despite the resolutions of everyone concerned, the Marquand marriage, like a car without a driver, seemed sometimes to careen down the slope above which it had been uneasily poised, and all the jests began to sound earnest. The small explosions that were a regular feature of Marquand family life now seemed capable of blowing the whole into bits. That October, Marquand was invited by the Navy to go on maneuvers in the Caribbean for nearly a month, and he eagerly accepted the invitation as an opportunity to escape from his domestic scene, particularly in its Greenwich–New York phase, though there was, as he told Carol, "opposition on the home front" to his absenting himself. The last afternoon in New York before his departure Marquand's irritability mounted over Adelaide's complicated program: Timmy and Lonny were first conducted to tennis lessons and then picked up for a luncheon visit, after which there was a stop at a bar before the desperate dash for La Guardia, where Marquand nearly missed the plane for Washington and boarded it, finally, in a state of fury. Adelaide admitted that "the trouble was (to quote Marquand) we hurried in the wrong places and were slow in the wrong places," and she posted him a long letter from the Hooker cottage. He may have felt contrite as he read her account of her activities after his departure; she had returned to Kent's Island to organize her clippings and discovered with horror that the boxes of reviews of *Repent in Haste* and *B. F.'s Daughter* had been misplaced. Then she had organized several parties of their friends to attend the pre-Broadway openings of the Osborn *Point of No Return* in New Haven and Boston and the New York opening. Marquand must have been amused to hear about her struggles to get the group together for the Boston opening: Marquand's lawyer Murray Forbes and his wife, the Fiskes, Dr. Howard Rogers and his wife Dr. Elizabeth Councilman from Newburyport, and a few others, including Tina and Dick Welch—but not Ken Roberts, who, hearing the rest of the list, refused to come: "Who am I going to get fried with?" he had shouted over the long-distance telephone from Kennebunkport. When Marquand was safely aboard his vessel and traveling with the task force out of Norfolk, he took a moment to write Adelaide that he was sorry to have been so difficult, and that it had really been great fun being in town with the boys—"the children are turning nice—except for their faults—and I love them." But he added, warningly: "Really I do think if we were not faced with so many possibilities of where to live and what to do, we might be happier. It is in the end better to try to do without than to try to do with everything—and I hope you'll try to eliminate instead of trying to make everything work."

He greatly enjoyed the drama of the war games he had been given a chance to witness. The ship he was on was cruising as part of a large task force under attack by planes and subs with two carriers, the *Tarawa* and the *Midway*, three fast cruisers and destroyers, mine sweepers, transports and tankers. "It is really something," he wrote to Carol. "The other day I left this ship by helicopter and had lunch aboard the Midway to see the new Jets take off—making the passage while the whole force was cruising at twenty-five knots in a twenty-mile breeze. You have never seen anything like those helicopters. They can land right on a postage stamp, the only danger being a sudden down-draft from the ship's bridge and funnels." But the games were soon over and the real war resumed in New York. He wrote to Carol: "Please try to leave some time open, because I feel rather distracted about life. I wish I didn't feel so dependent on you because I'm afraid I'm becoming a burden."

The following spring, however, after Salt Cay had again worked its magic, he agreed to go to Europe with Adelaide for a holiday without the children, an attempt at a "second honeymoon" upon which Adelaide, at least, counted for the recovery of the irrecoverable. On board the ship to England she was rudely reminded of how little even this was of her own making. A telegram from Marquand's travel agent saying that their accommodations at Claridge's and elsewhere had been reserved in accordance with Mrs. Brandt's instructions came to her hand and, as Marquand later said to Carol, "caused a cyclone. O tempora, O mores!" Nevertheless, the trip was a full draft of the travel cure; they were gone for seven weeks, stopping in London, Paris, and Rome, and making an extended tour of Greece.

Rome must have had curious reverberations. The last time Marquand had been there had been in 1921, when he had come to propose to Christina, his first novel having just been accepted for publication by Scribner's. Now, in 1952, she was dead. She had died of cancer the previous fall after a brief and apparently happy second marriage to an old Boston friend, Harford Powel. Marquand had perhaps already come to the point of thinking that his first divorce had been a mistake, that he might have been able to make of his union with Christina something better than his second marriage. As

Christina was dying, Powel had written: "I've had a truly wonderful time for two years now, the happiest in my life. You can guess why. A mature and experienced Christina, wonderful about money, but still extremely good-looking and gay. The old Stockbridge situation has evaporated, and the old uncles and aunts are so widely scattered one almost never sees them." Marquand would later admit to Johnny that his second marriage had proved "vastly worse" than his first, "which I see now might have been salvaged had I been more mature, and consequently better able to deal with the Sedgwicks and the great Stockbridge myth."

In Rome, Adelaide and Marquand did the antiquities with assiduity, and Marquand wrote to Ferry, who was beginning to develop a passion for archaeology, about his rummagings in the greatest of historic rubbish heaps. Mason Hammond, who was doing research in the Roman Forum, spent four hours wandering with Marquand among its venerable rubble. Hammond had been the Marquands' well-qualified guide on the Palatine Hill as well, and to other sites. One day, at Hadrian's villa, he amazed them by picking up a bit of old brick from the ground and identifying the consular seal marked on it. But, like many an earnest tourist before him, Marquand began after a while to grow impatient with travel-as-education. "I'm having a pretty good time, but I grow weary of art and ruins," he wrote Carol. He loved the flower shops and the beautiful gardens and fountains and the restaurants where he could just manage to order a meal with his smattering of Italian.

Adelaide, however, had an insatiable appetite for cultural tourism and was never more her characteristic self than when she strolled up to—and unseeingly past—a foreign monument, reading aloud from her guidebook. Marquand told stories later to illustrate how *little*, sometimes, she seemed to care for the thing itself, as when, outside Chartres, she had spent precious moments bickering with a vendor over the purchase of some lace gloves while the great interior spectacle of the cathedral waited. Her peculiar shortcomings as a traveling companion became even more evident in Greece, where they next went in the company of the composer Randall Thompson and his wife.

Thompson was one of Adelaide's oldest friends; he had known her and her sisters in New York when she was a young girl just out of Vassar. He was at the American Academy in Rome that spring, and he responded warmly to the invitation to accompany the Marquands for a tour in Greece and Crete. They had gone first to Athens, where Shan Sedgwick, the old resentments forgotten, welcomed and entertained them. One day the Marquands and the Thompsons and Shan and his Greek wife Roxanne had gone in two cars for a trip to the temple at Sounion, "where Byron wrote his name." They had breakfasted at a Greek inn and then motored to Delphi. Marquand and Adelaide were shown the spot where the sibyl once sat over the inspiring fumes and with much laughter they took snapshots of each other sitting in the seat of the oracle. But Thompson remembered also the moments when Marquand's temper had given way. Adelaide was always irritating him, somehow; she was never ready on time for anything the group planned; she was always lecturing to them out of her *Guide Bleu*, translating aloud with irritating slowness as they rode in the car and even when they stopped to look at something. And it was just as Marquand had remarked it at Chartres. She did not see, Thompson felt. He would later reflect, rather severely, that she illustrated the same aesthetic insensibility—combined with pedanticism—in his own field of music. She had taken all those courses at Eastman and studied voice for so many years and gone to so many concerts—and yet, he would ruefully declare—she did not *hear*. But was not this blindness and deafness to beautiful sight and sound, though her mind eagerly seized upon the fact of their existence, only another side of that general insensibility that made her relations with others something she believed in rather than felt, the unawareness that was the flaw of her nature? "Poor Adelaide," the Thompsons said to one another. She believed so touchingly in the *idea* that she and Marquand were recovering Romance together. She insisted so fatuously that he see the Parthenon with her by moonlight—as well as at sunrise and at sunset.

Marquand's own wry amusement at Adelaide's cultural enthusiasms found outlet in his letters to a new feminine sympathizer, his daughter Ferry. With the divisive instinct of the warring parent he would invite the twelve-year-old to join him in mockery of Hooker "queerness": "Although we were in Greece for eleven days and saw all the places where the gods and nymphs did all those queer things, and even the place where Theseus killed the Minotaur, I don't think it will make Mummy as queer as it did Auntie Helen—but even so maybe she won't be quite the same again." And when they had returned to Rome he observed: "The other day in Rome she started buying pictures, and I could not make her stop. She almost bought a lot of queer, and I think, rather crappy pieces of wood made by a blind shepherd from the island of Sardinia, but I told her that she must forget them and finally she did." Now she wanted to hire a car and drive north, though "I dread it, because I would rather have a chauffeur and Mummy thinks that is sissy."

Chauffeured or not, they were soon in Salzburg, which, Marquand told Ferry, was "the place where Mummy spent five years learning how to sing. It is way up in the mountains and I think would be very beautiful if it did not keep raining all the time, but Mummy is *nuts* for it. She can speak the German language and she tells everyone in the shops and everywhere that she has not been here '*für fünf und zwanzig Jahren*' which means to you and me 'for twenty-five years.' Everyone is very polite, but not as interested in this fact as Mummy is, but then why should they be. This morning and most of the afternoon we have been climbing up a big mountain to a perfectly enormous old castle like something in a fairy story. It had a big room in it all filled with things they tortured people with. I kept wishing that you had been there to see these implements, because I really think that you would have felt that school is not so bad, and even baseball might be better than being roasted alive or being squeezed to death. I am back from the walk feeling perfectly exhausted, but Mummy is still outside buying things. In fact Mummy is in what you might call a buying jag." In the end, he left Adelaide in Germany—he had never been able to overcome his repugnance for the Germans—and went to England to wait for her to join him for their departure home. In London, the *Daily Express* columnist Eve Perrick interviewed "author Marquand, a smooth, silky-looking man whose fresh complexion has a rose-copper glow and whose silver hair and moustache have a golden gleam. . . . At 58, with fifteen novels behind him, [he is] an established success." She asked him the question that now dogged him publicly and privately all the time: "Are you happy?" And he countered: "Who is? . . . Tell me, have you ever met a successful man who was happy?"

So they sailed back on the *Queen Elizabeth* at the beginning of June, Adelaide perhaps enjoying the voyage but Marquand feeling that the great liner was "a little overpowering for my taste, the number of passengers enormous, the dining room as large and noisy as Waterloo Station, and the ship attendants suffering from a bad attack of itching palm." Soon he was at Kent's Island, quite alone, for Adelaide had taken all the children with her to Aspen. Marquand was writing Ferry with his usual mixture of self-pity and wife-mockery that he was glad he was *not* there to be compelled, as the child was, to take horseback rides before breakfast: "The truth is I am too old for Aspen. My back is too stiff to ride in those wonderful western saddles, not having been a cowhand all my life, and I am peculiarly aware of my debilitics right now because I wrenched my back the other day and have been strapped until yesterday in adhesive tape. Personally nothing gripes me more than getting up at six-fifteen in the morning and going somewhere on an empty stomach, but I always feel cross if I don't have a cup of coffee or something. However there is one thing about a breakfast ride that you must not forget. It gives you a real reason—albeit an artificial one—to climb out of that valley and up one of those mountains. Please let me know how you found it and whether or not your appetite was whetted by the good clean exercise and the fine clear mountain air. Perhaps even a good clean drink of water from a mountain brook—provided sheep had not misbehaved or died in it—might taste better than giggle water, but I doubt it."

The young recipient of this letter responded with a little bravery that the breakfast rides had proved not so bad after all; breakfast had tasted surprisingly good after them. But Marquand's paternal seduction had worked enough for her to feel that she could complain that Adelaide had arranged for the three children to take swimming lessons from a former Olympic-team member: "I do wish Mummy would stop trying to make me learn things from a lot of snazzy experts. I'd like to take swimming lessons, but I know this famous personage will get bored stiff with my feeble attempts. Do you remember that French tennis champion at Nassau? Oh, that was a ghastly experience." Already the girl understood her father's annoyance with Adelaide's appetite for parties, and his implicit invitation to treachery yielded: "Mummy is 'flourishing' in the high altitude and goes to dinner parties every night. She is giving a sort of kiddie festival tomorrow night with a lot of boys and girls about my age. I'm dreading it. I hate things like that." She also reported that she now had a permanent wave and looked just like any other "dime store" girl, as her mother put it, "but that is just the way I've always *wanted* to look. I hate being different." Marquand must have understood the reference to Adelaide's attempts to dress Ferry in her own exotic style; Ferry would later suffer agonies at the Winsor School when she arrived decked out in Russian peasant costume to meet the future debs in their uniforms of safety-pinned kilt, round-collared blouse and cashmere sweater.

Soon the autumn was upon them, and the family was reunited, if that is the correct word, in New York, "to be engaged again," as Marquand told Philip Hamburger, "in that eroding process of trying to give the children a few educational advantages." Deliberately or inadvertently he then miswrote: "It seems that these little grandchildren of mine must learn more than my elder children—the Australian crawl, the figure eight backwards on the ice, the rumba, the forehand drive in tennis, the forward seat, the backward seat, and musical appreciation, and also take a quick look at the creative efforts at the Museum of Modern Art, and a smattering of the opera and the drama. This on top of their ordinary schooling, I fear, will keep Adelaide and me very busy indeed, seemingly to the exclusion of everything else." This Christmas was perhaps "less painful" than some Marquand could remember. The children were growing up—"fewer screams, fewer vomitings"—and the activities of Adelaide were somewhat circumscribed in winterbound Kent's Island, where it was almost impossible, he remarked to Tina, "to take the children to adagio dancing lessons, declamation classes, operas, hunt balls, lectures or yogis."

But it was all no use. Adelaide would later remind him, bitterly, that during the winter of 1951–1952 he had already withdrawn his interest from her with a resolution she had not been able to alter. The trip to Europe she had so much counted on "took place too late for its purpose as far as I was concerned. When we returned from Europe the pattern of your life of the winter before was resumed and all my efforts to establish our previous camaraderie seemed to meet a stone wall." She had desperately offered, the following spring, to alter their living arrangements in New York and Greenwich by renting a house for them all in the city, and she even secured acceptances for the children in New York schools so that they might be together, and proposed that Timmy be sent alone to Aspen the coming summer. But Marquand shrugged these suggestions off. Their days were now full of dispute and distraction. Marquand began to have talks with a psychiatrist, and Adelaide consulted one of her own. Marquand took the step, finally, of renting an office in the neighborhood of the Sixty-seventh Street apartment where he might work free of interruptions; he refused to let Adelaide have its address.

Nor did Salt Cay offer any balm. Somehow there were more houseguests than ever, or there seemed to be. Adelaide was continually discovering old friends at Bay Street parties and inviting them to the island. Marquand added some new lines to Josephas's calypso repertoire:

> *Madam, madam, don't go to Bay Street no more*
> *Madam, madam, don't go to Bay Street no more*
> *Madam, madam, you've got lots of knowledge*
> *Don't bring friends from Vassar College*
> *Madam, madam, don't go to Bay Street no more.*

Anne Lindbergh, after visiting the Happy Isle at this time was to remember the message of silent misery she read in Marquand's eyes. She wrote him: "I realize this time that you were going through quite a lot of pain—of one kind or another. And I felt quite badly that we should be there and not be able to do anything for you. I also wanted you to know (for when one is in pain one does not know how much one gets through to other people. One is locked away in a secret muffled place) how much you gave to us even out of this."

He complained of feeling tired all the time that spring of 1953. He went without any lift of spirits to the Harvard exercises in June to receive his honorary Doctor of Letters degree and his speech of acceptance had an odd, offhand quality that offended some of the academic listeners. At Kent's Island the daily arguments between husband and wife seemed more intense and frequent than ever—they argued about their living plans and schooling for the children, but also over the most inconsiderable trifles, as though no issue could really contain the whole of their difference. At the end of June the general tension had become so unremitting that Marquand moved in with his cousin Lucy Ames at North Easton, Massachusetts, and from there sent Adelaide his proposals for the next few years, a program to simplify their lives and make them more stable: "I have decided we will move to Boston for the winter months, rent a house there, furnished or unfurnished, and send Ferry to the Winsor School and the boys to Browne and Nichols or the River School or to Shady Hill. Living in Boston, it will be possible to use Kent's Island—which we all consider as our home—for weekends and for school vacations. I have decided on Boston because life is simpler there and less expensive, and I believe that in the end it affords a sensible environment and background for the children. If the climate there should prove too hard for Timmy, I think he should be sent to some place like the Desert School in Arizona." For the time being he wanted to work on his new novel (he had begun *Sincerely, Willis Wayde*) and thought it best to remain in North Easton during the week, coming over to Newbury only on weekends for the rest of the summer.

Nevertheless, one weekend in mid-July must have proved particularly trying and he collapsed the following Monday under the impact of a coronary attack. Adelaide was not in the house, and Miss Davis called her only after several hours because the prostrated Marquand begged that his wife be kept from approaching him. Lying in his four-poster as the days passed he stared at the statue of Kwan Yin, the Goddess of Mercy and Peace, that stood against the wall in front of him, and saw only Dr. Rogers, the trained nurse who had been called in, Marjorie Davis, Ferry, and Murray Forbes, his lawyer. Ferry now found herself burdened with the painful privilege of bearing her father company in his depression, which seemed extreme, and taking tear-stained notes from her mother past the closed door. In a few days, after Marquand rallied, he staged a little scene of melodramatic bravado for Ferry's benefit. He sent her down to the pantry to sneak up a glass of Scotch for him, and then, as he was sipping it, he ordered her to bring him his samurai sword, which hung on a wall of the room, and his copy of Marcus Aurelius. Ferry sat on the bed and read to him from the famous *Meditations* as he lay with the sword lying on the coverlet by his side. Presently, Marquand was moved to the Anna Jacques Hospital in Newburyport, where he remained for nearly a month, steadily refusing to see Adelaide. As is so often the case, his collapse had made death the reality he had spent sixty years denying. He had been close to being killed several times in his life, as he later remarked to Helen Howe, but these occasions had not touched that inner confidence in his own survival, which now disappeared before the prospect of "death upon a Beautyrest mattress." He was convinced that the preceding weekend of strife had brought on his heart attack that Monday of July 13, and that another such emotional ordeal might be fatal to him. Adelaide was to blame. The hatred and fear born of this conviction would never really leave him, and henceforth all her expectations of their future together were quite vain.

He was not candid when he wrote her from the hospital that it was the orders of Dr. Rogers and Dr. Atchley and his psychiatrist, Dr. Powdermaker, that prohibited her visits; he himself had demanded that she be kept away. But Adelaide's own willingness to be deceived coalesced with his own doubt or dishonesty to maintain her illusion that their life was soon to be resumed as before. While he lay secluded she flung herself with energy into efforts to carry out the program he had previously seemed to desire. After investigating the local schools she secured the children's admission to Shady Hill for September. And in a few weeks, she found One Reservoir Street in Cambridge. This was an old house whose grandiose style and monstrous proportions did not keep it from being a bargain at $25,000. It was located on a valuable lot, and she had a right to feel that its architectural preposterousness might prove, for a happy family, more amusing than oppressive. She began to furnish it with odd pieces of furniture picked up at auctions and some shipped up from her mother's house in Greenwich. For laughs, she kept some of the Victorian bric-a-brac that had been left behind by the previous owners, including a quantity of stuffed and mounted animal heads that decorated the walls. In front of the stately living-room fireplace there stood a pair of rather comic, stuffed leather pigs. Eventually, the house would be a strange mixture of the personal and the accidental, half museum, half rummage-shop. Several very valuable works of art, Adelaide's own purchases during her marriage, would survey the scenes enacted there: in a boudoirlike room lined with mirrors at the left of the entrance hall, the Bougereau that had never really fitted among the colonial portraits at Kent's Island; against the wall of the central staircase, the famous Grant Wood *Parson Weems' Fable*; and in the library, between two windows, the beautiful Rossetti panel *Proserpina*. The house was situated conveniently, and was potentially comfortable as a temporary home. For Marquand she planned a study in one of the drawing rooms off the central hall.

And yet she had to accept the fact that even when Marquand came out of the hospital he did not feel up to confronting her, and she must hie herself off to Aspen before he arrived at Kent's Island. There had been some dispute about Ferry, whom he wanted to keep with him in Newburyport—Adelaide had begun to resent the alliance that had formed between father and daughter and had appealed to the psychiatrist for support—but he was glad to have her take away the boys without his having seem them for more than a few moments at a time. He wrote Carl Brandt: "On Saturday night Adelaide and the boys leave for Aspen and I return to the Island with, I hope, Ferry to keep me company. The doctor said that if I had Ferry with me it might give her a Father Image which would prevent her marrying in later life. I said balls I would take the risk and I expect my directions to be obeyed. Adelaide, whom I have not seen since my attack at my personal request, tells me that she has purchased a house in Cambridge and will have it all ready for the family in autumn and has entered the children in the Shady Hill School. I shall not be able to join the group for many months—if ever. I plan to spend the autumn and maybe early winter at Kent's Island and then either go south or to New York or both." He hoped that the Brandts would be able soon to come up to see him and take him off for a holiday at "Wentworth-by-the-Sea or some such quiet spot."

A month later, as Adelaide prepared to come east again with expectations of joining him, he was still putting her off with the plea that he was not yet up to the discussion "which I know would occur if you and I were to start going over our plans and problems. In going over the matters with the doctors I have concluded the best thing for me is to stay quietly alone at

Kent's Island for quite an extended period." He promised that he would try to come to Cambridge to see her after a while and hoped to be able to receive the children on weekends. He had begun to embrace the idea of two separate Marquand establishments. "Now that you have a house in Cambridge," he would begin a message to Adelaide (who steadfastly ignored his hint that the house was exclusively hers), he wanted to help by sending over some furniture *he* did not need at Kent's Island. He was particular about the things he would send, though—he suggested she take the valuable Thomas Benton landscape she had bought with her own money some years before, but not any of his family heirlooms, furniture or silver, or portraits of the Marquands and Curzons that she wanted in Reservoir Street as reminders of unity for the children. To this distinction he kept even a year later, after they seemed to have resumed some measure of joint living. Adelaide bought some pieces at an auction of furnishings from an old estate near Curzon's Mill and left them at the Mill, where they fitted in well with the Marquand–Curzon relics. Marquand asked his daughter Tina to try to buy them from her. "I shall secretly underwrite the expense," he confided to Tina, "because I am most anxious to have the Mill and the Yellow House entirely my property and my project."

It was not until October, three months after his attack, that he came up to Cambridge and at last stopped in for an hour to see Adelaide, the children, and the house. He was on his way back with George Merck from lunch in Framingham at the Fiskes. With vast distaste that he did not hesitate to communicate later to his friends, he viewed "Adelaide's Folly"—the huge, white-pillared housefront with porte-cochère, like an overblown Southern plantation house, and inside, the rococo woodwork in the great hollow of the entrance hall with its ornate double staircase. He glanced with some amusement at the side parlor, open to the winds of traffic, which Adelaide imagined suitable for his study, and the bedroom on the second floor that she expected to occupy connubially. Adjoining the "master bedroom" was an ornate marble bathroom with a sunken tub of veined marble ornamented by a frieze of dolphins leaping from stylized wavelets. Ferry would later remark, after she had seen Knossos, that the motifs had been borrowed from the palace of Minos. Marquand was never to know, of course, the final scene to be enacted in this bathroom. In a plain small tub that she had had mounted above the marble one Adelaide would be found by a visiting friend in 1963. She was floating face down, drowned, perhaps after an evening of lonely drinking. For the moment, however, the bathroom, like the rest of the house, testified to her optimism. As they went up to the third floor, she explained to Marquand that the top of the house would be turned over completely to the children, segregating their basketball-heaving, chemistry set–exploding, and trombone-playing from the adults below. Then he went back alone to Kent's Island.

He was really quite over his attack as far as the electrocardiogram and X rays indicated. But he was tired and afraid still. "I have been trying to work an hour a day on my novel for the last few days, and I seem to have completely lost my capacity for invention, not to mention my enthusiasm. I begin to be terribly afraid that I shall never get these things back," he told a friend at this time. To Dorothy Canfield Fisher he confided the mood which she, as an aging writer, could share: "You and I have lived with writing so long that perhaps it seems more to us than anything else." The resumption of family life was only an obstacle that interfered with this single devotion, as, indeed, it threatened life itself, he felt. But Adelaide, as the months passed, continued to send him appeals. She was becoming desperate because she could no longer successfully sustain the tale by which she covered the fact of their division to outsiders. Going out a good deal in Cambridge she found that others knew more about her husband's current activities than she did. She quarreled with Miss Davis, whom she suspected of promoting her exclusion, and she voiced her well-founded suspicions about Carol Brandt. Carol's opinions about Adelaide, particularly criticism of her methods of child rearing, had come back to her via New York friends. Miss Davis had discussed their mother with the children in a tone of "good, clean fun" that covered damaging deprecation. With Marjorie there were some unpleasant occasions when Adelaide paid flying visits to Kent's Island during Marquand's absence. She found that the secretary had taken over and reorganized the files, including Adelaide's clippings and her collection of Marquand magazine stories which had been prepared for publication. She had taken it upon herself to express open objection to the children's governess, Miss Malquinn. And when Adelaide made some appeal for sympathy, observing that "the Boss" had been taking an odd attitude about possessions since his illness, the young woman, as the much-repeated tale went, had calmly said, "Why don't you take your possessions and go back to Greenwich?" Adelaide wrote her husband, "It seemed to me that sooner or later you would realize that the juxtaposition of two women in your life which reaches this point could not continue." Mrs. Brandt, she was sure, was also continuing to play a malign role. "To speak brutally, the distaff side of my home at present seems to me to be directed by two other women in varying proportions, as you see fit. To me they appear as a Quisling and a Gauleiter, however indispensable they are to you."

And still she refused to recognize that her husband was simply in terror of her. As the children's winter vacation period approached, she grew frantic and sent him letter after letter with proposals and demands. Would they not have a family reunion in Kent's Island for the holiday and then return to Cambridge together? Perhaps she and he could take a trip alone to Yucatán to see the Mayan ruins. Would they not all be going soon to Salt Cay? The children, she warned, were suffering from the pattern of visits to him without her. Ferry, especially, was now taking refuge in her obsession with archaeology, "retreating more and more into Egypt," as her mother put it, and was also unwilling to have much to do with other children. She might be helped by a trip to the real Egypt—what if they all went for a tour in Egypt and Greece? She made sailing reservations for five and was planning to get a young history or fine arts professor to come along for the sake of the children, who would miss some weeks of school. She became enchanted with the idea of celebrating Christmas in Bethlehem.

Marquand had, naturally, no interest in any of these proposals and even dreaded Christmas with the family at Kent's Island unless Johnny or Tina and Dick could be present as buffers. When neither of his older children proved able to come, he wrote Tina, "According to my present plans I believe I shall go away leaving no address. This, incidentally, has been one of my dreams for the last quarter century." What he finally did was visit Reservoir Street for a few hours on Christmas Day, returning alone to Kent's Island in the evening. Yet as he achieved this seclusion he became suddenly alarmed at Adelaide's inspiration to take the children to the Near East herself. He remembered that her sister, Helen Hooker, had abducted her own children when she left her husband, Ernie O'Malley, in Ireland, and he conceived that Adelaide would do the same. His suspicion of her now reached back to the recollection of other actions of manipulation and instances of "deviousness" in the past. Only the previous January Adelaide had telephoned Nassau and attempted to engage a secretary to take Marjorie's place. Now she was "slandering" Marjorie in an effort to get her to leave. He was ready to take any steps to prevent her taking his children out of the country and he demanded that their passports be turned over to him; he instructed his lawyer, John G. Jackson, to file a custody petition if they were not. To Ferry, Marquand crisply wired, "Deeply sympathize with your predicament but suggest you complete your Algebra assignment before leaving for Cairo." Then he made plans to go with his Book-of-the-Month Club friend Henry Canby to spend the rest of the winter in Grenada in the British West Indies. Marjorie Davis, having found her continued role in his household untenable, was preparing to leave his employ and go to Europe, and he took with him as companion and secretary the young daughter of his cousin Marquand Walker.

Grenada proved an odd, not entirely satisfactory interlude. Marquand and Jacqueline Walker were housed with the Canbys in the home of a woman who had worked for the Canby family in the United States. It was a cheerful establishment, bustling with the human and animal activity of the Grenadian family and servants, and of hens, cats and pigs. As Marquand conceded to George Merck, "I ought to be having a fine time if I were not full of error." But he had continued to feel miserable with a wrenched or arthritic shoulder and then a cold and then intestinal flu, and he reacted badly to the "wonder drug" administered by the local doctor. In February he got news from the nursing home in Concord where his father had been living for several years that the old man was failing. He made no plans to leave but wrote Adelaide elaborate instructions on what should be done in the event of his father's death—the funeral home to be selected and the services arranged for, the old friends to be notified, and so on. Adelaide willingly undertook the task of attending to her father-in-law's last hours, which were shortly at hand, and his burial. Philip hardly recognized her, but she remained with him during his last day until he sank into a coma, and when he was dead she handled everything until he was placed in a grave in the old Marquand burying ground on Sawyer's Hill, beside Marquand's mother. She arranged for the service and the flowers, called and telegraphed friends and relatives, including some of the Hales to whom Marquand was still not speaking, and selected the pallbearers. Probably she felt some renewed sense of indispensability to her unfathomable husband, who preferred with almost parricidic indifference to stay so distant from his father's passing, and she took off for Aspen with the children more cheerful than she had been for some time. She expected him to join them there on the first of April.

Of course he did not, but when he was back in Kent's Island and the family had returned to Cambridge, he began to spend occasional weekends at Reservoir Street, often with Johnny for company and protection. Reservoir Street began to supply him with new material for those terrifyingly funny descriptions. "Well, the house in Cambridge is very large and I still am so physically feeble that it seems like a very long walk from any one of the numerous sitting rooms to the dining room," he told Tina. "In a small house you have children falling all over you, in one the size of the Poe cottage you can never find them and have to shout for them all day long except during school hours. Adelaide's shouts reverberate through the halls causing even the moths to fly out of the mooseheads."

Adelaide could also offer Tina description in the same style—she had learned it from her husband: "The Boss and Johnny were here for the weekend, and while the children shrieked among the mooseheads, the Boss and Johnny and I lived in ease on philosophical remarks and alcohol, and both domestics gave notice Monday morning. Johnny and I made a pact about the fiction rights of the weekend. I said if he wrote it up I would sue him and he said that if I wrote it up he would sue me. This all came up because I let drop that Ann Watkins, my former agent, had written an urgent letter asking me to write my autobiography. When I told this to the Boss he hit the ceiling and said he would sue me if I mentioned his name and I said I would sue him for the seven books he had written about dull wives since we had been married. You should have been with us! Johnny was a great leavening influence, and, in the middle of it, all three children were marched out and given an explicit talk on Anglo-Saxon monosyllables, with definitions and descriptions of appropriate moments to use them. This all came up because there had been an outbreak at Shady Hill School in which three girls from the ninth grade wrote in large letters all over the bathroom that Ferry Marquand was pregnant because she had been 'blanked' by the English teacher. This was done in red paint and even the bottom sides of the toilet seats were decorated with hearts and initials. I still don't know whether life in Cambridge has been worse for the Marquands or whether we have ruined Cambridge by coming here. I think it is a toss-up."

And so, gradually through 1954, the Marquands settled back into some degree of intermittent family connection. In August, Adelaide was permitted to take Ferry on a very short trip abroad while Marquand went with Johnny, Timmy and Lonny to Crawford Notch, New Hampshire. Marquand even consented to a Christmas family reunion in Greenwich. Aside from his personal feelings about the multiplied efforts, forced joviality, and tribal confusion at his mother-in-law's, the season seemed to him, in general, an increasingly baleful manifestation of contemporary society. He reported: "Every year the sugary sentiment reaches a near hysterical pitch. Every year the Christmas cards are more horrible and this year the Hooker Electrochemical Company sent to its friends a record of 'Holy Night' gift-wrapped. This seems to me a fair example of carrying a good thing a little bit too far."

His heart attack began to recede from the foreground of his consciousness, and he could think more detachedly about death. An autumn hurricane had done considerable damage at Curzon's Mill. With a show of philosophic acceptance he wrote to Tina: "The damage is really pretty bad but there is one strange thing about these things which I have observed since the hurricanes of 1938 and 1944. The trees go down and you think the place will never be the same again. Yet, when you remove the wreckage, there always seem to be plenty of other trees, and in a year or two you finally forget about the old ones. This, I might say, taking a gloomy view, is equally true with human beings unless they are Washingtons or Lincolns."

22

All My Children

In April 1955, Marquand invited Johnny to accompany him around the world. His impulse, when his personal life became insupportable, was always to take off for distant lands. In 1934 he had escaped from the terminal anguish of his marriage with Christina by going to the Orient; now his relationship with Adelaide had reached the same stage of dissolution. The *Saturday Evening Post* had paid for the earlier trip which had resulted in his first Moto story. The *Post* would be happy to pay for a journey to the East again if he would revive the little Japanese agent for the many thousands who had not forgotten him since he had bowed out, smiling and saying, "so sorry," during the war.

And he wanted to draw closer to Johnny. He had been similarly impelled in 1941, when at the brink of the war he had taken the boy with him to South America, realizing that there might then be "so little time." Now his eldest child was thirty-one and it might well be altogether too late. They had, since the end of the war, continued the classically close and distant, loving and hostile, relationship of fathers and sons. Johnny had shown his desire to emulate and challenge his father by resolving to become a novelist. In the summer of 1946 Carl Brandt had helped him to get a job with Herbert Mayes on the staff of *Cosmopolitan*. Perhaps he thought of entering the literary profession by the familiar door of popular magazine writing. He then married a society girl who, like Christina Sedgwick, had the habits of unearned wealth, but more quickly than his father's first marriage, Johnny's ended in divorce—in 1949, when he was launched upon a novel. In the spring of 1950 he had a third of it finished and showed it to his father. Marquand thought it good enough to ask Paul Brooks of Houghton Mifflin to take a look. "I really think he may have a literary future," he told Brooks. And Johnny quit *Cosmopolitan*.

He was still at work on his book the following spring when, during Christina's final illness he stayed at his aunt Sally Sedgwick's in Boston. Marquand sent Christina a message well designed to give her cheer: "Please give her my love and tell her that Johnny spent the other day reading me the section of his novel that he has been writing since he has been down here. It seems to me astonishingly good, and I think he is going to end up being a writer of outstanding ability. Tell her that his book is about fifty times better than the first book I wrote."

When the first draft was finished in July 1952, Marquand encouraged his son: "As the book stands it is a balanced and impressive novel, with authority and feeling. In fact it has all the elements a good novel ought to have, and this is remarkable for a first book." But he was anxious to give Johnny the benefit of both his literary experience and his position in the literary marketplace. He went over the whole manuscript carefully, recommending specific changes for its first revision and after it had been at the publisher. Johnny accepted some but not all of his father's suggestions. Like Marquand himself, who had refused to make the alterations in the ending of *So Little Time* urged by Adelaide, he insisted on retaining a final scene of postlude which his father had thought unnecessary. And Johnny himself eventually found his publisher, Harper and Brothers, whose board chairman, Cass Canfield, was the father of his own friend Michael Canfield. Still, he must have felt that he was incorporated altogether too thoroughly into the well-oiled Marquand machine for literary success. Brandt, whom he had accepted as his agent, declared that the novel was "a valuable piece of property," and it was forwarded with dispatch to Marquand's friends on the board of judges of the Book-of-the-Month Club. It would be a Book-of-the-Month, although Marquand properly absented himself from the board meeting. The judges felt that it was in need of cutting by as much as twenty percent, which seemed excessive to Marquand. He urged that it be sent to the rival Literary Guild as a way of needling the board into favorable action. Meanwhile, the *Saturday Evening Post* offered the young author $25,000 for the right to run it as an eight-part serial.

The *Post* made one proviso. Johnny must sign his own name, John Phillips Marquand, so familiar to *Post* readers, to his novel. With a resolution that his father found impressive considering the sum of money involved ("I wonder whether I should have had the intestinal fortitude to do the same thing if I had been in his shoes") Johnny went down to Philadelphia to withdraw his manuscript. He succeeded, actually, in convincing the editor Ben Hibbs that the serial should be run under the name he had assumed for writing, John Phillips. He hoped, despite his father's formidable assistance, to make his own reputation.

But the victory was really compromised. The *Post* had insisted that although the installments would bear the pen name, the magazine must feel free to reveal the author's real identity in advertising and publicity. As soon as he agreed, Johnny realized that the battle for integrity and independence had been lost. To Marquand the issue seemed somewhat unreal. He was aware that the reviewers would know, in any case, that John Phillips was his son—in fact the identification had already been made in the *Saturday Review*'s advance notice of the book. He dryly remarked, "Johnny acts like an outraged virgin and gives the feeling that he has been wrongly seduced for money." Remembering with resentment his own long years of artistic servitude he bared the teeth and claws hidden by paternal indulgence: "I pointed out to him that he might change his artistic attitude, since the Saturday Evening Post had paid for his birth and education, without which it would have been impossible for him to become a person of finer clay than other Post contributors."

Johnny had been having a hectic year for other reasons as well—he had been engaged in a prolonged on-again, off-again romance with a young lady who finally married his rival—and he decided, in familiar Marquand fashion, to put his troubles out of mind by going abroad. He went to Europe, staying through the winter as the publishers prepared to bring out his novel. His father wrote to Paris: "I am glad in many ways that you won't be around here when your book comes out, because all the publisher's promotion and so on always turns the head of a young writer. Writers now seem to me to be divided into two classes. One are the young gentlemen like Mr. Styron who are saying to themselves, 'Can it be true that I am the greatest writer in America? I think perhaps I am.' Then there are the others in the class of Louis Bromfield and Edna Ferber who simply say, 'It is a definite and established fact that I am the greatest writer in America.' I don't know which group I find more disturbing."

The Second Happiest Day was published in February. And every reviewer mentioned the real identity of the author. They also pointed out that the book in many ways was another Marquand novel. Actually, it was a quite creditable one, but it had the familiar features—it told the story of a member of that privileged group (like Harry Pulham) bred in the New England church schools and the Harvard clubs, and it utilized the point of view of an outsider from a small New England town who stands observingly outside this world of privilege (like Charles Gray of *Point of No Return*). Its style showed that the author had, like the senior Marquand, the satirist's adhesive memory for details of dress and decor, of behavior and speech. He had even put to use his father's favorite device of the flashback. Sterling North spoke for all the reviewers when he said: "It is no secret that John Phillips is actually John P. Marquand, Jr. writing under a pseudonym to avoid confusing his novels with those written by his famous father. It is just as well because the Marquands are at least as akin in literary style as Dumas père and Dumas fils."

Of course, Johnny had written of his own generation. His observation had been applied with considerable wit to the lives of the boys he had known at St. Mark's and Harvard and in the Army and afterwards. The critics quickly saw an analogy to Fitzgerald's rich boys; they seemed to embody a new "lost" generation. For his rendering of their own kind of postwar scene young Marquand deserved credit. What the reviewers could not have discerned, however, was the personal meaning of this exercise. Indeed, he had rewritten his father—he had blatantly "imitated" if only to show that he could do the older man's kind of novel, replicate his achievement. And he had used this imitative form with perhaps unconscious irony to represent the generational contest itself. His narrator—for it was a first-person story—stands not only removed from the *jeunesse dorée*, somewhat tarnished, of his own age, but looks with bemused contempt at the remnants of the generation before—the aging flappers and bloated sports who are shown mingling with their offspring in the extended description of a wedding at the Water Club in New York: "They were all there, the survivors of Aiken and Tuxedo Park. Why did they call out to us? Why did they wave?"

Some of the reviews that reached Johnny in Athens could not have surprised him. He had found Arthur Mizener's piece in the *Saturday Review* more flattering than he deserved; Mizener had concluded that *The Second Happiest Day* was a significant novel that would "give shape to a generation by providing it with a way to understand its unique experience." But *Harper's Magazine*, despite the book's Harper imprint, had been "dense and uncharitable," and *Time* had sneeringly said that the author had told his story "at just above the level of fashionable young folks' gossip and at that something less than the depth of a good college bull session." The *Time* piece, written by the book editor Max Gissen, was perhaps intended to arouse reader suspicion by its statement that Marquand had discreetly stayed away from the meeting of the Book-of-the-Month Club judges during which his son's book was discussed and that the book had enough "pace and surface savvy . . . to turn the nodding heads of the Book-of-the-Month judges, John Marquand Sr. abstaining." The headline of the *Time* story was "Marquand j.g." In addition to the review, reports of bookland gossip reached Johnny.

He wrote his father an emotional letter: "One thing I have heard enrages me. That is, briefly, that Max Gissen of Time and some others in that charmed circle have developed an *on dit* to this effect: That you wrote my book for me, that you were instrumental in getting the Book-of-the-Month to take it, that, in one way or another, most of the proceeds are going to revert to you." Painfully, Johnny conceded that reviewers were justified in saying "that the book is saturated by your influence, style, tone, etc. Though I can't expect anyone to believe me and therefore shall never attempt to tell anyone, it's my opinion that if this is so, then it's because of genes and chromosomes. What I mean is that I cannot control unconscious characteristics, even if I must be accountable for them, any more than I can control the color of my eyes or the way I speak or walk. As you may have sensed, I made a particular effort to avoid imitating you whenever I consciously could. I purposely declined quite a few of your suggestions when I was writing the book, not because they weren't good, but because they didn't originate in me. And, when I took four extra months rewriting the last half of the book—an operation which you found perplexing and pointless—I did so with the definite purpose, though I didn't have the gall to tell you at the time, of satisfying myself that it would be, good or bad, for better or worse, my own book. On the other hand, I did quite brazenly imitate the three-section organization of *Point of No Return*, and I did accept minor suggestions from you and suggestions as to cutting, though, as it turned out, the final cuts were vastly more devastating than anyone anticipated. Furthermore, you traced after me through every state in the book's preparation and were the only person, frankly, to whose editorial comment I paid the slightest attention. But more than any of that, your contribution to the book was encouragement. For if you hadn't originally encouraged me and if you hadn't continued to in the times I was most discouraged, the book would never have been written at all. I am indebted to you above all for that. And you certainly would have refused to write a line of the book, if I had asked you, which fact, when I think of it, makes me more than ever anxious to fly back to Greenwich Village, find Max Gissen, and either emasculate him there or take him back to Beirut and let the Arabs loose on him."

And after this outburst of gratitude, humiliation, and inescapable identification with the father-model against whom he struggled—and the unattractive anger against Gissen—Johnny let loose a piteous appeal, full of buried resentments: "In the future, if you are asked to comment on this business, remember that it is deadly serious to me, and bear that fact in mind, even in the most jocose moments, among the most intimate of your friends. I am quite resigned at this juncture to absorbing all kinds of low blows about Marquand, J.G., and Junior, but if I am unfortunate enough to be able to go on writing, I shall become increasingly more intolerant of that. I do not think of myself as Junior, and do not intend either to behave or write as Junior. If I did, it would have disastrous effects upon my psyche. Either I'd become a hashish smoker or you'd have to ship me out to Dr. Menninger's. So it's probably just as well I took the pseudonym (for this real reason and not just to avoid confusion in bookstores which was never my real reason for the pseudonym) and that I continue writing under it in my own way, even if I fall on my face. It's very easy for me to mention this glibly, as I do now, but if I am to try to be a writer, I'm going to have to be allowed my share of writer's vanity, which is quite different from swelled-headedness, and this junior business is going to be more and more of a red flag before a bull, I know damned well."

Marquand's reaction to this anguished appeal was not entirely comprehending or sympathetic. To Tina he gave a grossly simplified report when he had heard no further from her brother after two months: "I wonder when Johnny is returning. The last news I had of him was a very upset letter from Athens, complaining of the bad notices of his book. He was especially burned up because many of the reviewers compared his work with mine and noted some similarities in style and delineation of character. This seems to have filled Johnny with resentment. He was annoyed that he was named after me and apparently annoyed, too, that I gave him some assistance with his novel—assistance which I still feel was very necessary. If his mood persists, I have fears that in trying to be different and in pursuing his neurosis of making an independent name for himself, he may write something that is so utterly different from anything that he can do well that it will be a flop."

Shortly thereafter Marquand did hear from Johnny that he had decided to stay on longer in Europe. His reply, which opened with the salutation, "Dear Junior," voiced the viewpoint he had expressed before, when Johnny had thought of staying in Europe right after the war: "Whether you like it or not you had better accept the fact that you are an American born and brought up in this country and that you want to be a writer and not a diplomat or an ambassador of good will. If you can learn about America and the life that people live here and can get a mature point of view about it, maybe you will be a good writer some day. You will not accomplish this by living in Greece in order to get a new perspective of America. Neither will you do so by living in Paris, motoring through France, or seeing bullfights in Spain. You will be a second rate Hemingway or worse unless, of course, you want to be a John Gunther and comment on the European scene, which I believe is somewhat out of your line. Who the hell cares whether the French love us or not? And the fact that you who are approaching 30 should be impressed by this psychopathic nation is to me alarming and rather sad. I had made up my mind after reading your previous letter never to offer you further advice, either of a literary or practical nature. However I can not refrain from suggesting that you come home and allow your adolescent emotions to subside, and if you have any coherent ideas perhaps do a little serious work, preferably in surroundings that are less disturbing to you than Paris, St. Jean de Luz, Madrid, Rhodes, Cairo, or even dear old Baghdad. I would also suggest, by the way, if you do go to Spain, that you read Don Quixote in the original and observe how sadly a rather admirable man lost his intellectual balance. I know you won't do any of this but there is one thing you need not fear. I shall not show your letter to the Atchleys, Mrs. Brandt, or in fact anyone because I honestly don't think it would interest them except as a case history." Probably after this there was no further communication until Johnny, who was now living in a cottage in the Basque country, saw the *Time* item reporting Marquand's heart attack. He then wrote reassuringly to his father that he had been studying boat schedules and expected to be back in the United States in September. The Basque country had been a quiet place for work except for the presence of a few Hollywood notables like Gary Cooper and John

Huston: with the latter he had had "a long talk about dads and lads, his dad having been Walter Huston." The Marquand dad-and-lad relationship had received a severe strain in the upsurge of feelings caused by Johnny's book.

Yet Marquand called upon his son now more than ever in the distracted days that followed his collapse and repeatedly solicited Johnny's company during his solitude at Kent's Island, for a trip to Virginia to see Tina and her family, or for a little holiday with his younger sons at Crawford Notch in the White Mountains the following year, and always at Reservoir Street. Johnny's stay at the Crawford House ended during a hurricane, and Marquand had to drive him back to the train station some twenty miles away while trees, as he recalled, were crashing across the road. "Johnny," he told Tina, "did not seem impressed. He wanted me to go an additional six miles to North Conway so that he might get a little whiskey at a package store, and he seemed surprised when I refused." Under the bantering tone there was the irrepressible paternal condescension—it was another of Marquand's funny, not-so-funny stories. After this episode he did not hear from Johnny for a number of months.

The young writer was trying to get started on a second novel, always a daunting challenge, and for Johnny destined, possibly, to be permanently daunting. In the spring of 1955 he had written some parts of it, which he showed to his father. Marquand thought them pretty good, though, as he told Tina, "he is making a prodigious effort to have it much better than the first one and written in a style which no one can compare with mine." When he had seen a little more he reported, "I frankly think it is rather unprepossessing and I feel I have made him unhappy by telling him that his characters are so unpleasant that I doubt if anyone will want to publish it. What really concerns me more than this is that after working on the thing for over a year he seems to have been able to produce only 149 pages. This might be all right if he were Mr. Auden writing poetry, but not for a young man who wishes to make fiction his career." He lied stoutly to a Boston *Globe* reporter who interviewed him about this time when he declared: "People said I had a hand in his first book which is completely untrue. I haven't seen a word of the new one and probably won't until it is ready for publication." Johnny continued to elicit not only literary but personal comment from his father. In uneasy progress was his love affair with Sue Coward, whom he would eventually marry; Marquand had decided that she was by far the most promising of Johnny's girls. His comment to Tina on his son's hesitations was, "Each year he grows more egocentric, more set in his ways, and pretty soon he will find it impossible to make up his mind to marry anyone. This may all change if he can once finish his book."

That winter, 1955, Marquand stayed on in New York while Adelaide and the children went to Salt Cay. "I kept thinking," he told Henry Canby, "what would happen if I got sick and the vision of dying in Josephas's arms while he sang, 'Goodbye Boss, you're going home' was more than I could really face with equanimity. Also, Adelaide with her perennial spirit of hospitality, has got the whole place filled to overflowing with disparate personalities including some physically ugly adolescent girls who are friends of Ferry, a doctor from Johns Hopkins who induces nervous breakdowns in dogs à la Pavlov, a musical composer from Harvard and perhaps, for good measure, John Dos Passos and his new wife." He had discovered for himself, instead, a new wintering place. This was Pinehurst in North Carolina, which he visited in March as the guest of a Boston friend, Donald Pearson, and which pleased him so much that at the end of his stay he decided to rent a cottage for the coming year. Though there would be provision for guests—three master bedrooms and two baths—Adelaide would not be invited to accompany him there.

Pinehurst might seem, again, a curious refuge for a writer—another rich person's Great Good Place, the resort of retired corporation executives. Marquand had protested the bloated inanities of Hobe Sound and Nassau, yet that something pleased him about his anomalous situation among such companions was more evident, now that he chose it for himself without regard to Adelaide's inclinations. He, the irredeemable duffer, was happy in the paradise of golfers, where four superb eighteen-hole courses started and ended at the Pinehurst Country Club. He had hardly ridden since his Army days, yet he found congenial the company of those who came to witness the training of pacers and trotters at the Pinehurst tracks or the even more thoroughly horsy set of neighboring Southern Pines, where his old friend Conney Fiske had established her own winter home. As he explained to Henry Canby, Pinehurst was "a place devoid of intellect and concerned only with bridge and golf, but a place which I find pleasant because on the whole people let me alone and I can write in the morning and play golf in the afternoon." But perhaps he also enjoyed the ironies of being accepted by these rulers of American society, for whom he might nourish, as he had at Hobe Sound, a private disdain; perhaps he enjoyed the desert-island solitude, in which he could work far from the challenge of the literary mainland, where writers live in acute awareness of each other. Whatever the causes for his satisfactions at Pinehurst, they continued to hold until his death. In the winter of 1955–1956 it seemed the ideal place to finish a new mystery novel, his return to entertainment fiction. The following year he was back in Pinehurst again. He had made the acquaintance of General and Mrs. Marshall, whom he would entertain at dinner together with Carl Brandt and Conney Fiske. The winter after that he occupied a new brick house of impressive proportions which he described to his daughter Tina as a modester version of the governor's palace at Williamsburg, and he rented still another house before he decided to purchase one for $30,000 in the spring of 1959. Apparently he did not object to the restrictive covenant in his deed: "the party of the second part, his heirs, assigns, or lessees shall not permit said premises to be occupied by a Jew or a Negro or any person affected by tuberculosis or consumption."

There was an unreality about Pinehurst. It had been conceived in 1895 by the Bostonian James Walker Tufts, who bought some thousands of acres of cutover pine woods and set upon them an amazing village laid out according to plans by the great landscape artist Frederick Law Olmsted. Along artfully winding streets cottages with a gentled New England air had been located, and imported and domestic shrubs and trees had been planted. The trees and shrubs were now of giant size. In the spring the dogwoods and the jasmine and the Cherokee roses and Judas trees burst into extravagant blossom all together. In the winter the thousands of holly trees gleamed with red berries. The winter climate was marvelously dry and yet bracing, like the best Indian summer day in New England, Marquand thought. Some absorbent quality in the sandy soil, an ancient sea bottom it was said, seized the moisture out of the air. About all these charms of the locality as well as its limited program of diversions, Marquand would write a voluntary booster's piece for *Ford Times* in 1959 (he received a handsome golfmobile as an honorarium for it).

Now, in the spring of 1955, with his family about to return to Cambridge, he was ready to go much further away than Kent's Island. It didn't seem he could wangle another Navy trip. "All the big brass I know is retired, nobody realizes what a contribution I could make to the Navy if they would only send me to the Riviera to go out and watch a few manoeuvers on the 'Med.'" But there was always the *Saturday Evening Post.* Johnny agreed to leave with him in the last week of June and they proposed to fly to the West Coast and on to Honolulu, then Japan, Hong Kong, Bangkok and Cambodia, and over to Karachi, to Cairo, then to Rome and to London. From the first there was tension between father and son. The father, of course, was paying the bills, but the boy had become a man by now and would resent the authority presumed by the father. Marquand decided against including India—which Johnny had longed to see. "I told him I was old and tired and had seen it twice, and that the Hindus and Pandit Nehru, too, can get along without me. I really believe if I ever see another piece of cow dung plastered against an Indian village wall to dry for fuel over which they can boil their wretched rice, I could not recover from the shock," he complained irritably to Tina. And India remained off the itinerary, though they did, as a compromise, stop in Ceylon.

Once they were on their way it became obvious that they wanted very different rewards from the trip. Marquand had seen most of it before and he was inclined to skip one thing or another if he happened to feel tired; Johnny was seeing the Orient for the first time. "I was thirty years younger and quite selfish and willful: I wasn't going to miss out on anything if I could help it," he remembered afterwards. And Marquand's preferred mode of travel, more so than ever now because of his anxiety about his health, was different from his son's. He liked big hotels and embassy limousines; he had planned to take advantage of connections in high places wherever they went and had armed himself with letters of introduction to ambassadors in Bangkok, Tokyo and Cairo; to New York *Times* correspondents in Hong Kong and Tokyo; to American public health officials in Tokyo, Hong Kong, Bangkok and Beirut. Weariness also no doubt increased his tendency to treat the menials who served him with a testiness that Johnny found embarrassing. "I had a sort of postadolescent 'liberal' conception of my father as a Kiplingesque traveler among 'lesser breeds without the law,'" the younger man admitted later on.

When they got to Japan, Marquand chose to stay in Tokyo. Cabot Sedgwick, a son of Christina's Uncle Ellery, was, as it happened, an officer of the United States Embassy, and this rather distant ex-relative was delighted to make a fuss over Marquand, placing a chauffeured embassy limousine and an interpreter-guide at his disposal. For nearly three weeks they were entertained in style in the city. Johnny, who broke away when he could to see some of the old Japanese towns and shrines in the countryside, remembered that they were taken, once, to a restaurant, run by an Anglophile Japanese, which was supposed to be a replica of Anne Hathaway's cottage in Stratford-on-Avon. From Tokyo, they went to Hong Kong and were escorted by colonial police up the Kowloon Peninsula to the border with Red China. They took the ferry for a day in Macao, after which Marquand decided to skip the excursion planned next for Singapore. Johnny, with the reservations already made and paid for, could not bear to forgo the opportunity. He went to Singapore alone and caught up with his father again in Bangkok. There they were again lavishly entertained, floating upon the glossy surface of a political situation about which they had no comprehension (the American ambassador who had them to dinner, along with Perle Mesta, was "Jack" Peurifoy, who was assassinated in Thailand only a few months later).

Marquand decided that he liked Ceylon, which he was seeing for the first time, "a neater, sweeter India in a neater, cleaner way with lots of wild elephants trumpeting in the jungle that covers the ruins of ancient cities, and a number of kindly black face monkeys with very long tails that would come out of the trees and sit by the side of the road as the sun was going down," but he was content to stay in Colombo and Kandi while Johnny hired a car and took a three-day tour of the interior. And the same thing happened in Egypt. Marquand preferred to stay in the Semiramis Hotel and tour Cairo while Johnny visited Thebes and Luxor as he had anticipated doing. At Marquand's insistence they skipped Beirut.

They had some unforgettable moments together, nonetheless. At Angkor Wat they had shared each other's awe in contemplating the famous ruins. They went with a dragoman to see the sun set upon Giza behind the great pyramids, taking food and blankets and waiting in the desert for the moment when the yellow and pink light streamed about the monstrous shapes. But the moment of bitter personal revelation came in Cairo, when they had less than a week more to spend together. (They were to part in the Milan airport. Marquand would spend some time with Carol Brandt and her son Denny at Marcia Davenport's villa at Lake Como, at the Hôtel Trianon in Versailles and at the Savoy in London.) "It came out," as Johnny remembered it, that his father had expected Johnny to look after him all those weeks—that was why he had taken him along. Johnny realized that every time he had noticed his father's sullen air when he returned from one of his side trips he should have understood that something was wrong. He had failed to function as he had been expected to—"as a sort of factotum" more or less hired for the job. Marquand had first planned to take Jacqueline Walker along with him for this purpose, he revealed. His sense of not having been well served by Johnny was so strong that after they had parted he did not communicate with his son for two and a half months. Then he wrote: "I should have told you long ago as I tell you now that I greatly enjoyed your company to the Orient, and that I appreciate your kindness in going with me and thus dragging out the time that you'll need to finish your novel. I only hope that you got enough out of our rather hasty trip so that you do not feel that it was all time wasted, and I also hope that my age and infirmities and marital preoccupations, did not bear on you too heavily."

Of course, Marquand had wanted something more than service, had hoped during the trip for a loving attentiveness that would not only have served him practically but might assuage the bitterness of age and loneliness. As it was, he continued to refer to his son as "Junior" in letters he sent along the way to Marjorie Davis. His sentimental longing reached towards a woman younger than his son yet capable of giving him love. He told her at each stop of the journey how he wished she could be at his side and mentioned his disabilities, knowing that she would sympathize. "I wish you could see the hot springs and the 100 year old goldfish that are beginning, like me, to get a little sprung in the spine. The heat is very tough, but I have a good time if I take it easy in the middle of the day," he wrote from Tokyo and Hong Kong. When her letter caught up with him in Bangkok, he said, "You are the only link with any sort of past I have had. Junior is very active but I sit around a good deal."

Again, Johnny felt the desire to linger in Europe. After parting from his father in Italy he went back to Greece, spent two months there, and made a visit to Cyprus to prepare an article on the political situation for *Harper's Magazine*. On going back to Italy, he came down, in Venice, with typhoid, recuperated in a clinic in Milan, and then went to London, where he laid out six months' rent for an apartment. His father, meanwhile, having run into Sue Coward's father at the Century Club, was quizzed about Johnny's future plans, and now wrote him, remonstrating against his "protracted stay" in foreign parts, as he had done before. He suggested that writing travel articles for *Harper's* was a mistake. Six months later, when the article on Cyprus appeared, he told Sue that he was impressed by Johnny's piece of reportage but "I do hope this praise will not go to his head. I think he has a chance of being an excellent fiction writer and this in the end should be far more useful to him than trying to be a John Gunther or a Vincent Sheehan or a Quentin Reynolds or a lot of other bright and shining lights who have travelled madly over the globe." He would always identify this appetite for travel in Johnny as a sign of the pernicious Sedgwick inheritance: "Your grandmother Sedgwick, I recall, once told me that frequent visits to Europe were a part of the Sedgwick tradition. In my opinion she might better have said that they were part of a perpetual Sedgwick effort to escape from reality, which I fear is still a Sedgwick trait." Johnny, who insisted that he agreed completely with his father about Sedgwickism, also insisted that he was hard at work on the new novel in London. He thought he could concentrate more *un*distractedly there than in New York, where he found himself splitting his idle hours among polite young people on the East Side, angry "young maladjusts" in the Village and the comfortable, valueless denizens of the Knickerbocker Club.

As for his marital plans, he admitted that once burned he was twice shy, and that his father's past and current problems did not encourage a faith in the permanence of marital compacts. To which Marquand could only respond: "I do not blame you for having a trauma when marriage is mentioned when you have been swimming for many years among the debris of partially wrecked lives. I personally think the institution of the American marriage is barbarous. I have been through two of them myself with a marked lack of success." And yet, he urged, "gruesome as marriage is in America, and frightful as the matriarchal sentimentalisms are that surround it, it is better to be married and make a mess of it than to be calcified and single." In fact, Johnny and Sue were married in London the following February, though as Sue confessed, the younger Marquand was still apt to express an aversion to matrimony which, his father told her, "does not stem from me. It comes from Lord Byron, model 56, who lives restively in Athens with your Aunt Roxanne and a poodle"—another thrust at Shan Sedgwick.

Johnny's novel did not seem to get itself written. Marquand, the professional who knew that the habit of constant productivity was at least as important as talent, worried at the slowness of its progress. He reminded Johnny that a second novel was rarely as successful as a first and that his state of mind would be improved if he would start thinking about his *third* novel instead of agonizing over this one. He kept insisting that Johnny and Sue ought to come home from Europe, and invited them to Pinehurst or to the Yellow House at Curzon's Mill for the summer, hinting that he would give the old Marquand home to them permanently if they committed themselves to it in some way. The offer was deeply significant. Johnny understood that his father was now thinking of passing on to the next generation his poignant attachment to this ancestral place. "The place has me almost as much as you in its ineradicable spell," Johnny responded. He could foresee that he might, in his own declining years, even want to live there, but for the present he was hardly inclined to settle in Newburyport. He had all sorts of plans—he even thought of getting a job in the Far East so that he could live *there* until he could write a better novel about it than Michener. He had no intention yet of filling his ears with the "patter of little feet"—he actually used his father's phrase—as his sister Tina and her husband had already done. So, Marquand continued to worry about the future of Curzon's Mill. The thought that in the event of his death Adelaide might take over his ancestral premises (for she shared title to the property) filled him with dread. On the eve of his divorce in 1958, however, she was persuaded to sign the joint deed of gift which made Johnny and Tina the owners of it.

By 1956 it was already four years since Johnny's first novel, and Marquand knew that this was too long a time for "Dumas fils" (as he now began to call him in letters to Tina and even to Sue) to delay in catching up with Dumas père. The young Marquands left London for France and Spain and he continued to write letters repeating his warning that Johnny was showing signs of becoming like "your Uncle Shan" and "the tiresome band of escapists who sit in the 'Dome' and grow beards and try to act like Graham Greene."

And so time passed. The younger John Marquands returned to the United States in the fall of 1956 with the still-unfinished manuscript in their luggage. Johnny continued to labor at his project, holing up at a cottage on the Sedgwick property in Stockbridge for the winter. In May 1957, Marquand remarked again to Tina, "Johnny works and works but cannot finish his novel," and soon after, when his son and daughter-in-law came to see him at Kent's Island: "Johnny, I fear, is by way of becoming a man of letters in the best Stockbridge tradition, an excellent pursuit, but one which will not buy shoes for the baby, but then, there isn't any baby." They had not got along very well during the visit, having fallen into argument over politics. Johnny, at least, recognized that their quarrel was not really over anything so objective: "What happens is that, not always realistically, I sense that you are riding me and trying to demolish with ridicule certain notions that I have developed by myself," he wrote when he was back in Stockbridge. "This makes me very defensive and when it occurs in the presence of others, particularly of Sue, I tend not just to draw a line and make a stand but to attack you back so as to prove that I'm not afraid. As we both must have known, that ugly lunch we had was not caused by divergent views on the care and feeding of Asiatics, but by more basic things. I don't suppose I ever confessed to you that as I grow older I perceive with some alarm that I have my share of that Marquand aberration, of which you used to tell me, which causes one to imagine that he's beleaguered by everyone about him.

And, like you, I find myself striking out in a needless wrath against shadows." His feelings about the external political world were not, however, irrelevant to his personal problems, he thought. He felt that the members of his generation "were born out on a limb, and the limb was sawed off by the cold war and World War II." Their problem was conviction, and they were still struggling with it, which was why there were, he thought, really no good writers among them, and this "explains in part why it's taking me so long to do one insignificant novel." So Johnny "worked and worked." It was nearly done, perhaps, early in 1959, when Marquand observed to his lawyer Brooks Potter: "The seven years he has spent trying to write a novel which in its present unfinished form in my opinion is so bad that it may not even be published, have tended to erode his character. He has lost the system and responsibility he once possessed when he was younger and I don't know whether he will be able to find it again."

By then he was drawing up his accounts with a grim pessimism. Not only Johnny seemed to have disappointed him, but his connection with his three younger children had become seriously compromised during the three years it had taken him to achieve a legal severance from their mother. In November 1958, when his divorce from Adelaide was at last approaching finality in Reno, he told Tina, "Of all my children you are the only one I can count on for loyalty, affection and understanding." The excruciating steps and stages by which the divorce had been achieved had involved more than the usual wear and tear on Ferry, Timmy, and Lonny, and on their bond with their father. Leaving for the Orient with Johnny in 1955, Marquand had already laid his plans for achieving some kind of permanent separation from his second wife. A long talk with his new lawyer, Brooks Potter, just before his departure, had settled his resolution upon divorce. John Jackson, an attorney with whom Marquand had discussed the possibility of a custody suit in 1953, observed to Potter, however: "You are going to deal with a man who, I am sorry to say, runs away from rather than faces difficult problems. He is an artist and not a business man in any sense. His wife is an eccentric, overpowering woman, of whom he is literally scared. I think he is fond of his children but would be inclined to let her have them, if he can obtain his freedom, which is a complete escape from her. This, I doubt he will ever be able to obtain, with the result that a separation agreement, or even a divorce decree will benefit him very little and possibly hurt his children."

Marquand had not notified Adelaide of his decision when he left with Johnny in June 1955, perhaps still fearing that she might run off somewhere with the children. Back in Kent's Island in September, he prepared a letter with Potter's help which she found at Reservoir Street when she herself returned from the West a few days later. It was flagrantly toneless. "During my trip abroad I have given long and serious thought to our personal difficulties with the result that I have finally been forced, reluctantly, to the conclusion that you and the children and I will all benefit more by a complete separation than by further periods of dissension. It is my hope that such arrangements as are necessary can be made with as little disturbance and unpleasantness as is possible for the benefit of all of us, and I am most anxious to help as much as I am able towards achieving this result. Therefore I am asking my friend Mr. Brooks Potter of the firm of Choate, Hall and Stewart to forward this letter to you, and I hope that when you receive it, you will get in touch with him. Personally, I do not feel that anything can be gained at this time by further discussions between us. Instead I suggest that we communicate through our lawyers until they have made arrangements that we both consider satisfactory." Predictably, she refused to recognize that this numb formality exactly represented the state of mind Marquand was striving to achieve in regard to her. "My dearest, I received your lawyer's letter while going through piles of mail looking for some word from you on my return Monday," she replied. "Because the tone does not suggest you in any way whatsoever—at least the you of seven years ago when we were a married couple—I therefore am still able to write to you. I think we should stick together. John, you are a complete stranger to me now but I love you from past associations." She recalled a conversation they had had before he left for the trip, when he had told her that she should be satisfied with "half a loaf." "Twelve years ago in May I told you that I wouldn't survive in a split-level marriage." She wanted the whole loaf. "I want you to come back this year, complete without the Brandts. Total marriage at 52 and 62 must be better than total divorce."

The process by which she was to be brought to the point of accepting the idea of separation or divorce was not going to be easy. Her husband's determination only stiffened with time. His hostility increased with her resistance, expressed to the end in tearful appeals for reunion, for their beginning again. She would from time to time besiege him by letter—despite his prohibition of direct communication—or, more painfully and exasperatingly, via Ferry or Timmy or even young Lonny, who were the bemused bearers of her messages. Marquand refused to take these sentimentally. He was convinced, as was his lawyer, that Adelaide was an obstinate opponent who would manipulate every factor in her power. He adopted with Potter, and Potter with him, a tone of bitter jocularity as he made his own countermoves. "I do not feel that appeasement has ever helped with the Russians, North Koreans, Hitler or American women, and in this respect I shall put Adelaide at the forefront of her sex," he said to Potter. Writing about "topic A" at the end of November, he declared that he was more convinced than ever that she had not the slightest intention of seriously discussing any kind of separation agreement with him. "Unfortunately I know the way her mind works. She always loves to talk; she loves new audiences, but in the end she does what she wants, and this time she wants to do nothing. Under these circumstances I believe that placation and appeasement as we have practiced it to date will get us nowhere."

Probably any divorce lawyer can testify that the behavior of the Marquands was typical. As their legal representatives skirmished between the parties there was a degradation of tone and a preoccupation with trivia, as well as a contest of two reality systems. Marquand began to hear that Adelaide was bruiting her woes all over Cambridge and New York. She was bitter over his insistence on barring her from Kent's Island, the home she had helped to create, as all her friends knew. She felt it mean of him to cut off her use of some of the minor courtesies and privileges she enjoyed as his wife—the use of the Somerset Club, his Harvard Coop account, the advantage of discounts on book purchases made through the Book-of-the-Month Club. Of course, dismembering their joint finances and real estate holdings was more than usually complicated, and nothing galled Marquand more, probably, than Adelaide's participation in the copyrights on his books. Then, the children, who had inherited Hooker stock and other securities from their grandparents, had incomes of their own, and Marquand was constantly insisting that their expenses—including high medical fees—come out of their own funds, while Adelaide argued that the cost of their upbringing was a parental responsibility. Particularly in the case of the bills from psychoanalysts it was "tawdry," she would say, to make the children pay for the troubles brought upon them by their elders.

But the major contention was over parental rights to the children's company. Their visits to their father (who was in Pinehurst or elsewhere during their Cambridge school year, while their mother planned to continue the Aspen removal during the summer months that he spent at Kent's Island) were to be continuous sources of disagreement. Each accused the other of trying to alienate the affections of their offspring during their stop under the enemy's roof. Adelaide's lawyer, George Naylor, was probably correct in saying that there was an "armament race" going on between Marquand and his wife, the familiar one in which the love children bear their parents becomes the parents' weapon.

For some years, moreover, the three children had already been developing into individuals with difficult temperaments of their own. Even in their Greenwich phase they already showed the effects of tense family life. They suffered from the continual, arbitrary shifts prescribed for them from one year to the next. The best or most expensive governesses and tutors could not, naturally, compensate for their sense of being furiously shoved off or snatched at by distracted, unhappy adults. Marquand, for his part, had always blamed Adelaide for the children's intrusion upon his needed quiet and privacy; she would explain her complex arrangements as her effort to meet his requirements. But now that they were separated and were fighting for their shares of authority, it was not always clear that the children were genuinely wanted by either. Marquand himself declared at the end of 1955 that the contest over the children had reached such a point that he was ready to consider "the advisability of not seeing any of them or communicating with any of them for an indefinite period, since I believe this contingency would be better for them than having them between the millstones." And he added honestly, "This is not such a difficult matter for me to achieve since the children were born when I was late in life and their activities and interests are very far removed from mine."

His mood that Christmas was one of release and content as he stayed alone at Pinehurst. To Ferry, now nearly sixteen, he wrote: "I have never been able to think so many thoughts through consecutively for many years. And now comes the best of it—I am, God willing, going to be here all by myself for Christmas, no holly, no mistletoe, no pattering of little feet, no eggnogs, no candles, no jollifications whatsoever." Instead, he was playing golf daily with the new friends he had made in Pinehurst. The dry, mild atmosphere agreed with him. He was finishing the new 90,000-word Moto serial for the *Post*; "It may not be art but it is not bad cabinetmaking," he wrote to Johnny. *Stopover, Tokyo* was, in fact, written as much for his own amusement as for any other reason. Despite the objections of the magazine—which had paid him $75,000 for the story—it would come out lacking the once-obligatory "happy ending," and the heroine, murdered by Russian agents, was not "brought to life in the last installment." Marquand remarked that "for some reason, literary hack though I am, the frayed vestiges of my artistic integrity made me refuse to make the change." Every day at noon his new secretary, Dorothy Brisson, would mix him a dry martini, and after lunch, a nap and an hour or two more of work he would walk down the street under the red-berried hollies to the little bridge club made up of retired businessmen who called themselves The Wolves. They were such excellent players that he was content, a good deal of the time, simply to watch them as he sipped whiskey from the sideboard. Then he would go home to a good supper cooked by his black maid, and read for an hour before bed.

But, in the battle with Adelaide, he considered himself bilked when, at the end of the winter, he found that the children had not been able to come to see him: "She wanted them for Christmas; she wanted them for the midterm vacation. Now for the Easter vacation Lonny is not able to come because of his Shady Hill School extracurricular activities; and Ferry will only be here for five days. Tim will be here for seven. In other words I will have had the children for considerably less than one-third of their vacation time." An elaborate calendar was set up for the rest of the year so that both parents would be satisfied that they had their proper share of the three youngsters. From the end of school to the first of July they would be at Salt Cay with Adelaide, who had rented the island on her own. For the whole of the next month they would find themselves at Kent's Island, and then

Ferry would leave to join her mother at Aspen. There she would attend the Aspen Music School (she had turned out to have, like her mother, a pleasing singing voice). The boys would stay on with their father a couple of weeks more, then follow their sister to Aspen. Before coming back East to Boston for the opening of the Winsor School, Ferry was scheduled to visit her father for another week.

He was particularly anxious to retain his connection with his younger daughter, to keep hold of that vibrating cord he had flung across the gulf of family dissension by appealing to her juvenile tenderness. From Pinehurst, on Christmas day, 1955, he wrote her: "Here in America we live in a matriarchy and as far as I can see daddies have no control over their kiddies when the chips are down. They can only say please they would like to see them some time and hope for the best. Well I hope." When he came up to Boston in March he confessed to her, over a lunch during which he was wistfully gallant, that he had not been quite as happy among the golfers and bridge players as he had made out—he had really been dreadfully lonely. "Oh, Daddy, if you are so lonely, I would love to come and live with you," the girl had then exclaimed. Marquand proposed that she live with him in Boston the following winter. But things did not work out as smoothly as the lawyers' schedules had promised. Ferry, though ready at one moment to give up her mother altogether and stay with her father, felt herself betrayed by him in ways that he seems not to have properly understood.

She had looked to him for support in her continued struggle against her mother's efforts to make her a well turned out subdeb. Even at the Greenwich Country Day School, Ferry, at eleven and twelve, had been nagged to make more "social efforts." Adelaide, who had had so many "best friends" when at school and college, did not understand the temperament of this pretty blond child of lively charm who preferred to be a solitary or else to have a single, generally "undesirable" comrade. Ferry's early interest in archaeology, particularly the civilization of ancient Egypt, seemed to her mother a symptom of morbidity. No doubt the girl's imagination had reached ardently towards a dead past of unimaginable beauty and stateliness precisely because her immediate world contained neither dignity nor grace. But such a bent was more than a mere psychic refuge and deserved respect and encouragement instead of uncomprehending deprecation. Adelaide could not, herself, appreciate the mental cast of a youngster who would refuse to accompany her mother to the opera in order to attend a lecture on hieroglyphics. She had gone so far as to take her daughter for a brief visit to the Near East, but this was more in the hope of "getting Egypt out of her system" than of endorsing her absorption in Egyptian studies.

At Winsor, Ferry's exclusive interest in the ancient world had continued; she scorned everything in the curriculum with the exception of ancient history, Greek and Latin. Marquand frowned no less than Adelaide on such perverse exclusiveness, though in his usual self-contradicting and seducing way, he had seemed to give his approval: he returned from his own visit to Egypt in 1955 with the gift of a genuine piece of sculpture from the sixth century B.C., a scrap of relief showing Queen Nefertiti receiving her marriage scroll from a priest, recognizable by his shaven head. But it was his reception of complaints against the stifling social atmosphere of the Winsor School that was most severely disappointing to Ferry. He would respond dryly (as he had done at the time his older daughter had castigated Westover) when Ferry satirically "ripped the epidermis off the lares and penates of Winsor's." He told her with crushing banality, "Let's face it—life is only what we make it up to a certain point, while for the rest you must learn to roll with the punches like a good lightweight boxer." He quoted to her, as he had to his two older children each in turn, his old saw about holding still when you are the anvil, and when you are the hammer—but not before—striking your fill. This intelligent child had read his own books and listened to his own conversational satire of social ritual, and she expected the author of *The Late George Apley* to share her scorn and support her rebellion. But Marquand blandly attended Father's Day at the school, pleased that she seemed to enjoy handing him a lamp of knowledge cut out of cardboard in a ceremony with her schoolmates. He lightly observed to George Merck that she apparently had "refused to be a citizen of Winsor City, and thus like Philip Noland in 'A Man Without a Country,' is alone in her communal group [and] appears to be quite a character." But he did not interpret her lack of the proper social instincts any more tolerantly than Adelaide did, and wrote to the Winsor headmistress that in his opinion Ferry "took a contemptuous attitude regarding the mores and attitudes of her contemporaries doubtless out of latent envy." He hoped that the school would try to make her less difficult. Perhaps they could do something also about her continual fingernail chewing and bad posture.

Ferry's sense of her father's betrayal was more than an adolescent kicking up of heels. Much later she still bitterly remembered: "My father trained me to be a rebel, but when I got to Winsor he wanted me to shape up and be like the others. But by that time it was too late to be like the others—forget it. I was just an oddball." Shrewdly, the older Ferry could then analyze: "He wanted it both ways. He had encouraged me to be critical, but he wanted me to conform. I think the same conflict existed in him, and he reproduced it in me." At sixteen, however, she was not capable of such objectivity, and became depressed, convinced that her mother was someone whom her father was right to reject. Yet her parents were leagued to force her into a conventional mold, and she felt guilty for not fulfilling their expectations. She did not write to her father that spring and summer. Once only, she telephoned an appeal that he "bail her out" of going to a summer camp, and he refused. In September Marquand wrote her, "You will not hear from me again either directly or indirectly until the spirit moves you, if it ever does, to communicate with me," and then he took off with the

Brandts for a three-week trip to France and Spain. After a while she wrote, and with her brothers she spent Thanksgiving at Kent's Island before Marquand went down to Pinehurst. But by December the psychiatrist who had been treating her since the summer declared that she was on the verge of a breakdown, and she was all the more in revolt against Winsor. Paradoxically, she was then persuaded by both her parents to "come out" like a good little debutante; Marquand had got the idea that she wanted to go to the cotillion, and she, in a mood of repentant humility, yielded to what she took to be his wish. When she graduated in June, Winsor refused to recommend her for Radcliffe; the advice of the school was that she take a year out before college to "do something responsible." Marquand thought this ought to be a secretarial course at the Katharine Gibbs School, but Adelaide, taking the suggestion more absolutely, sent Ferry to Germany where, after the collapse of other plans, she spent the winter working in a rest home as a maid.

For Ferry's brothers the years between Marquand's heart attack in 1953 and the actual divorce were also profoundly disturbing. In the great fraud of a home at One Reservoir Street, the boys' efforts to establish new patterns of play and school and household life were mocked by the preposterous space, the pomp of the furnishings in the huge rooms, which were now and then filled by Adelaide with large parties at which their father seemed imminently expected but never arrived. While Ferry had understood the basis for Marquand's rejection of their mother, the boys were only numbly aware that they had been abandoned, and being younger than she, were less capable of taking any initiative in establishing a new kind of relationship with him on their own. Marquand tried to establish a male comradeship with them during the holidays they spent at Kent's Island, but they were not quite ready, at thirteen and fifteen, to share his solitary country pleasures; they missed the friends they had finally made in Cambridge. And in September 1956, after the summer he spent with them, he admitted to Helen Howe that they had been able to "wear him down to a nub."

Timmy, less than two years younger than his sister, accepted the situation with least apparent difficulty. Unspectacularly, he got through the Shady Hill School and qualified for Exeter as his parents had planned for him, a boy whose distresses only announced themselves in the later problems of adult adjustment. But Lonny, outwardly more emotional and responsive, was in immediate trouble. At the Shady Hill School, where a considerable degree of self-direction was expected of the student, he felt helpless. At home he showed some of his sister's rebelliousness and a propensity to unexpected changes of mind and sullen resistances. Less aware in a conscious way of why he acted as he did, he seemed to want to reject his rejecting father. Expected to meet Marquand for dinner at Lucy Ames's, he would simply call up at the last moment to say he was not coming. He joined Ferry in refusing to spend the February vacation of 1957 at Pinehurst, declaring that he would be completely bored there, much as he was getting to like golf. He simply would not write, until his father threatened, as he had Ferry: "If I do not hear from Lonny within ten days, I think that in view of the difficulties which always arise when I try to see the children, I refuse to take any further initiative." And again, the threat was effective, and Lonny did pay the expected visit to his father after all. It was during this visit that Marquand discovered what he had overlooked till then: his youngest child was a very scantily educated fourteen-year-old whose knowledge of the subjects he was supposed to have studied—algebra, English literature and expression, history—was meager. Marquand attributed the situation to Shady Hill's "progressive" methods and called for a change of schools. After Lonny returned to Cambridge, "very academically discouraged," as Adelaide observed, he was got, with some effort, into Deerfield Academy. But his school troubles were not about to end. It was soon clear that he was totally lacking in self-confidence; Marquand himself had noted that the boy would become upset when challenged to learn anything, even a card game, though his intelligence was not inadequate. Like Ferry, he was now under a psychiatrist's observation. The doctor urged that he be allowed to have a carefree summer, that he be released from the parental tug-of-war that paralyzed him. But what Lonny himself wanted was more than he could decide. One moment he was going to Aspen with his mother and then he told his father that he would rather stay at Kent's Island. Finally, he chose Aspen: Adelaide, he wept, had threatened to sell the Colorado property if the children did not make regular use of it.

In August 1957, Potter began to make arrangements for divorce proceedings in Reno, and Marquand went off for a brief holiday in London and Paris. "I'm no longer going to harbor any hopes that I can behave in any sense like a father to these children, and I do not feel that the blame for this situation rests on me," he wrote Potter from this distance. At the same moment he wrote Marjorie Davis, now secretary to the cartoonist Al Capp, "There is nothing in the world that would be pleasanter than having you here right now." Potter just thereafter reported that the former Marquand governess had been seen in the neighborhood of Kent's Island on what he suspected was a mission of espionage, and Marquand responded that he had told Adelaide over a year before that "if she cared to divorce me for cause, I should be glad to supply it promptly." When he came back in October, he saw Marjorie in New York. He also saw Carol Brandt, who had just become a widow, Carl having at last expired of emphysema and chronic alcoholism.

He saw little of the children and continued to profess his surrender of interest in relationship with them. But in December, when Ferry was preparing to leave for her winter in Germany, she came down to New York to see *My Fair Lady* with him, and afterwards he took her to supper with Carol Brandt and Denny. The occasion impressed itself: "Mrs. Brandt seemed a Charles Addams lady, sinister, wearing black. In her manner to my father I noticed a kind of syrupy pampering and towards me an effort to ingratiate herself which I disliked." Everything about Mrs. Brandt and her apartment, even the duck that was served, seemed pretentious, insincere, to the girl. It was snowing heavily outside and when the time came for Ferry to leave to catch her train back to Boston, Mrs. Brandt suddenly clapped her hands like a duchess in her court and declared, "I think the best thing would be for Denny to take Ferry out for a nightcap and put her on the train." Ferry stood up then and shouted at her father, who had already nodded his assent, "I won't go, I won't go! *You* take me to the train, Goddammit!" "The idea," she said later, "of my father just sitting there while I was sent off for a 'nightcap,' of all things, with this strange woman's creep of a son!" And Marquand got up and took her to the train. Still, she did not forgive him, and a few weeks later, when he came up to Boston, she simply missed an appointment for lunch he had made with her. The next day he wrote her, uncomprehendingly: "I am sorrier than I like to think that you could not have lunch with me yesterday as I had hoped. But I am sorrier still that you did not feel able—as far as I can gather—either to write or telephone me saying that you could not—and at least to say good-bye before you leave for Germany. This means, I fear, that you did not have a good time with me in New York. This is a great disappointment to me, but such things cannot be helped—and I must remember that I have hardly laid eyes on you for more than two years and that people change rapidly, especially when they are growing up. As I am leaving for Pinehurst today there is no chance of seeing you until next summer. I can only hope that you will write me if you think that there is anything at all I can do to be of help to you—but this will, of course, be the last letter you get from me unless I hear from you because one has to stop somewhere sometime."

Thereafter Marquand pretty much gave up the contest for the children's company and began to blame them as much as Adelaide for not taking the initiative in choosing to come to him. Christmas at One Reservoir Street at the end of 1957 found them with their mother in attitudes it would have given him malicious pleasure to witness. As Adelaide herself said, "All the individuals in the family were at their most individual and my efforts to produce a sense of Christmas spirit with family feeling, religious fervor, sentiment, and all those things which I have been told the Sedgwicks and Hookers enjoyed, blew up in the face of the Marquand heritage." Ferry refused to decorate their tree but went instead to her best friend's house to festoon her best friend's tree. Timmy went so far as to buy a few presents for the family but he dumped them down with the remark that anyone who wanted wrapped presents could wrap them. He went out with his girl on Christmas Eve, and the next morning announced that since he had had a late breakfast he preferred to go to a movie by himself rather than sit through Christmas dinner, and, anyhow, he had never liked turkey. Ferry was preoccupied with her packing and farewells to her friends because she was leaving the next day for Germany, while the two boys and two friends of theirs were packing for Aspen. Ferry took a moment to call Pinehurst to say goodbye, after all—but the call was refused. (Marquand later claimed that he had been asleep after an injection of Demerol given for a recurrence of his stomach trouble and had ordered that he not be disturbed. When he was told about the call he had had the impression, anyhow, that it was Adelaide who had broken her promise not to bother him.) Such was the Marquand Christmas.

Lonny, that spring, while his father was preparing to go to Nevada, discovered a way to relieve himself altogether of the necessity of making continual choices. He asked his father to assume some sort of guardianship over him that would give the one parent complete authority to decide about his school problems, vacations and anything else that came under the head of parental decision making. The idea may not have been altogether his own; in any case, the thing was legally possible, as he was assured, and Brooks Potter had the petition by which he would nominate his father as his guardian ready for the boy's signature in a few days. Lonny himself felt that this act would make everything easier, "clear my mind of all emotional disturbances," help him to concentrate more effectively on his schoolwork, and "calm mother down and stop her from worrying about so many things." Instead, Adelaide was outraged, and she called Lonny at Deerfield to tell him that his father "didn't really want" him, or so he translated her statements. The document needed Adelaide's signature, and there was little likelihood of getting it. Her comment on Lonny's gesture came in a letter she wrote directly to Marquand: "This embattled child horrified the people in the community closest to him by the unhappy legal gesture born of his natural love and need for you, and suckled, I am afraid, by familiarity with soap operas." Nevertheless, Potter was glad to have the paper on hand "to be filed in court at such time as some serious situation arises which cannot be handled merely by threatening to file a petition"—which may have been the purpose all along for arousing or encouraging the boy's hopes of a way out of his situation.

Ferry's German experience proved a more violent translation into another universe than could have been imagined; it had the single virtue of taking her mind off her relations with her father that winter. Adelaide had sent her to visit a remarkable acquaintance from her own German sojourns, one who, as it happened, was a Sedgwick relative. This woman, very wealthy and a patron of the arts, numbered Albert Schweitzer and Chancellor Adenauer among her friends and kept a musician or two always in residence. At the end of about two months in this household Ferry was accused, as her mother related, "of sneaking away the grade B pianist with a gold tooth in the middle of his face" who was the current resident, and she was practically put out of the house by her hostess. Adelaide flew over and snatched her eighteen-year-old from between the fifty-five-year-old lady and the pianist, aged thirty-eight, and made other arrangements. For the rest of the winter, Ferry earned her living in Hamburg as a cleaning woman and kitchen maid in a Red Cross rest home for East Zone refugees and received in return courses in typing, first aid, and infant care, and five dollars monthly as pocket money.

In February she wrote to her father, her first letter to him in two years. It was a serious letter, in which she offered observations of the German scene and a description of her hostess—who had not yet decided to accuse her guest of being a wicked young siren. Marquand's reply, cordial in its obvious intent, was threaded with misogynist bitterness. He described his own amusements at Pinehurst and remarked that Ferry did not seem likely to become fascinated with the game of bridge: "I fear you are going to grow up to be one of those women who feel that bridge is a 'waste of time' and who demand nothing but bright conversation after dinner. Women in this class never seem to realize that few people can carry on bright conversation all the time and that most people who try it are crashing bores, and that a bridge game is much better. Having been married to two women who have believed that bridge is a waste of time and who have believed that conversation until after midnight and then carried on in the bedroom after the guests have left until the small hours of the morning, is better than bridge, I am something of an authority on the subject." He commented on Ferry's hostess as follows: "You make her sound to me like a matriarchal monster. I thought that German hausfraus gave their attention only to children, church and cooking and that America developed the matriarchs. How wrong I appear to be. Look at her carefully and try yourself not to be a tyrant in your later years. It seldom pays in the end."

He had come to identify Ferry as her mother's ally. When the girl returned to Cambridge in September to get ready for Radcliffe, to which she had finally been admitted, she was in time to witness her mother's last attempts to halt Marquand's deliberate progress towards divorce. Adelaide had been behaving with ludicrous and pitiable unreason; she had made, during the preceding week, long emotional and confessional calls to Carol Brandt and to Marquand's cousin Lucy Ames, begging for help from these unlikely quarters, and she had beseeched Marquand, through his lawyer, for the personal interview he dreaded above everything. Finally, Ferry herself called him and with savage calm told him that she did not ever wish to see or communicate with him again. Adelaide then wrote still another abject note beginning, "Please call this whole ghastly thing off," and pleading for their reunion for the sake of the children—which she made Timmy bring his father by hand.

Now Marquand wrote her what he called his "final letter": "I have gone on record previously, and I now repeat, that I will do anything possible for the children that might assist them in developing a sense of security, or in making adult adjustments. I am keenly aware that their lives are beginning, whereas my own is drawing to a close, and that the spare time that remains to me could not be better spent than in furthering such aims. Unfortunately, I feel more strongly than ever that an attempt on your part and mine to renew any sort of life together in order to give the children this security is impossible and would be doomed to such a failure as to make their attitudes worse instead of better." He charged "slanderous tongues"—which he did not identify—with having helped to do their past relationship to death and making a future one impossible. Perhaps it was only Adelaide herself whom he had in mind, though he did not say so, as the source of irresponsible "defamation of character" from which he had suffered. "I am more than ever before aware," he said, "that the result is devastating. The defection of my daughter Ferry is the only illustration I need to convince me of this painful truth." He concluded to Adelaide: "I regret that I am not equipped, in the light of all that has transpired, with the patience, the nervous or the physical strength, and above all the lack of pride, all of which would be essential requisites, were I to resume the life I left. What I have written to you is not, I hope you will understand, a basis for arguments or compromise. It is a picture of human failures which point, as far as I am concerned, to only one conclusion. This conclusion is, as I have repeated on numerous occasions, that it will be better for the peace of mind of the children, and I believe for yours and mine also, to have this wretched state of affairs ended in as rapid and dignified a manner as possible."

A few days after posting this, he flew to Reno.

23

The End of a Man

On October 2, 1958, a Mr. J. Philip Maynard registered at the Riverside Hotel in Reno. Despite the alias, he was not hard to identify—the flushed guardsman's face with its clipped military mustache and white hair had offered its slightly menacing surface to view on the jackets of his recent books and on the book pages of newspapers and magazines. Some, certainly, of the other guests at the hotel, like himself dwellers in a peculiar purgatory while they waited for their divorce decrees in the Nevada courts, were his readers. But even if they had not heard of him he was conspicuously "unbelievable," Ruth Whitman, in Reno for the common purpose, thought. He had hardly been at the hotel a day before large bundles marked "proofs" and addressed to J. P. Marquand began to arrive from the offices of the Book-of-the-Month Club, and the mailman was heard to speculate that this Mr. Maynard must be trying to masquerade under the queer, foreign-sounding name of Marquand, obviously "made up."

Mrs. Whitman was in on the secret. Another of Brooks Potter's clients, the wife of a Harvard classics professor, she had followed her lawyer's suggestion that she introduce herself. She was familiar with the faraway world of New England and she was herself a writer; Potter had calculated correctly that she would prove a companion in exile. Moreover, she could type. Marquand was working on a new book and he hired her to take dictation from him every morning at five dollars an hour. She would discover that she was needed in other ways besides. As usual, someone was required to assume the burden of mediating between him and the practical world; he hated even to dial a telephone. She became his chauffeur, driving him out into the country surrounding Reno in the afternoons. But, best of all, she was a good listener, a sympathetic and appreciative audience for his comments on the scene around him and on life in general, a confidante to whom nothing needed to be confided because it was understood that she already understood. So he might suddenly remark to her, "American women, particularly American upper-class women, are essentially unmarriageable. They are neither good wives nor good mothers. They are arrogant, stubborn and willful. They are extravagant." He might add ruefully, "Perhaps I wasn't meant for marriage or babies. I always found domestic life a terrible burden. It's always a wrench for an artist going from one world to another, from diapers to typewriters." In looking back at his latest novel, *Women and Thomas Harrow*, he felt not that it had expressed his extremity of gloom but that it had not gone far enough. If he could write it again, he would say it "even more clearly and bitterly." He would have to say that he felt "glad to be through with sex—like Sophocles—or was it Socrates." But he was through with the effort to say anything; he was telling others as well as Mrs. Whitman that *Women and Thomas Harrow* was his last novel. The new book he was working on was not a work of fiction. It was a rewrite of his early biography of Timothy Dexter, and this was going to be his last book of *any* kind.

As he observed to Marjorie Davis, in Reno he was "on another planet." He told his daughter-in-law Sue that the city was "the God damnedest place I have ever been in, except Las Vegas. If the latter is Sodom, this is Gomorrah. I cannot understand why God is so patient in this case, and he certainly does not seem to damn it up to date." To young Lonny he caustically remarked: "I should say to give you some idea of it that it is ten times worse than Aspen and you know how I have always loved that place. The only thing in its favor is that there are no Paepkes and no culture." The capital of Anything Goes was a revelation to this world traveler. He was diverted as much as repelled. As he observed the seething spectacle, he felt his acidulous humor come awake and he thought of changing his mind about writing no further fiction.

The corridors of his hotel reeked of the Chanel No. 5 of friendly call girls. If he wanted to enter either of the dining rooms he first had to pass through the hotel's gambling establishment with its battery of slot machines, two roulette tables and bars. The games were kept running day and night, including Sunday, and so were the bars, and when he went down at ten in the morning to see the World Series on television, he was able to lose five dollars playing faro with a lovely blonde and to get a whiskey sour almost at the same instant. Everyone seemed possessed by the gambling fever, chained to the mechanism of the roulette wheel. The very attendants at the tables had, he believed, no other life. He claimed to have heard that they often married each other and begat children but worked such hours that neither Mom nor Dad saw the kids for weeks. In the supermarkets, he observed, housewives asked for their change in nickels so that they could play the slot machines conveniently located in the store. Everyone drank all the time and not merely at the appointed ritual moments he was used to—

the luncheon highball, the cocktail hour, the after-dinner cordial, the night-cap. He had never seen alcohol consumed so unremittingly. He got to humming the old World War I army song:

> *I'm going to a Happy Land where everything is bright*
> *Where the hangouts grow on bushes and we stay out every night*
> *Where there are no more parades—and you don't have to wash*
> *your socks*
> *And little drops of Haig and Haig come trickling down the rocks.*

He was to remain six weeks—during which he tried to have as good a time as he might. In writing to Lonny, who had learned to like the scenery and recreations around Aspen, he kept up his pose of disdain: "I have never been a great lover of the West, because probably I was never taken out here in my infancy as you were. The altitude gives me the heaves, especially since my heart attack. I don't like the open spaces and the sage brush. Even the Indians bore me and so do the ghost towns, but here I am in the middle of them, doing the best I can." And he bought western boots, though he had so much trouble getting them on and off that one of Mrs. Whitman's first responsibilities was finding him a boot stretcher and helping him to use it. He wore plaid flannel shirts and frontier pants that bore a label reading "Made in the West for the West and Worn Proudly by Westerners." He also ordered a fringed and beaded buckskin shirt from an old Indian woman whom he met at the Piute Reservation north of Reno on one of his drives with Mrs. Whitman (this was not finished until the following spring, when it came to him in the mail at Kent's Island and was hung, never to be worn, incongruously among his Harris tweeds). The scenery of the area—the snowy Sierra Nevada, the sagebrush-covered foothills, the ranches and old mines, the dazzlingly clear air—seemed to him full of beauty he had not expected; from the balcony of his room at the Riverside he could see a big bare mountain that changed color every few moments. He wrote Marjorie Davis, who liked to do watercolors, that she ought to visit him and bring her paints. Also, at the crap tables at the Nugget he discovered, with some zest, that betting skills learned in his army days still worked.

After about two weeks, he moved out to a ranch near Carson City. Mrs. Whitman came every morning and worked with him on Timothy Dexter. Washoe Pines was a rustic establishment on the shores of Lake Washoe that was run for such divorce candidates as himself by a several-times-married-and-divorced lady named Elizabeth Cathles. When Mrs. Whitman had a car accident and had to suspend her visits, Mrs. Cathles took over the duties of amanuensis at the typewriter in the mornings and drove him where he wanted to be driven, even accompanying him to dinner away from the ranch occasionally—with such local celebrities as Perle Mesta or Lucius Beebe. Like others before her, Mrs. Cathles accepted the role of female prop that

Marquand expected of secretaries. He would lie abed mornings in his little guest cabin and she would carry his breakfast to him in her station wagon before they got to work. In the afternoon he would appear at the house where she lived with her two daughters and take his seat in an old wicker chair to enjoy his Cutty Sark highball and play chess with the girls. He seemed to take pleasure in acquaintances among the oddly assorted members of his "class of 1958" who were in residence at Washoe Pines, celebrating, as their decrees came through, each one's "graduation day" with fraternal good spirit. But, as Mrs. Whitman would remember, he talked eagerly to everyone he met during these weeks—to barkeeps, shills, storekeepers, and especially to the slightly counterfeit cowpunchers who worked or hung around the Washoe and other ranches. One lanky horseman, a former rodeo competitor named Spike, attached himself to Marquand and they went riding together. Marquand complained that the western saddle had never been designed for his anatomy, but he liked to listen to his new friend's denunciations of the decadent Reno scene and to his somewhat learned-from-the-movies nostalgia for the Old West, which was a sort of parody of his own nostalgia for an earlier America.

The divorce proceedings, meanwhile, were stalled by Adelaide's last-ditch refusal to "make an appearance" in the court or to give the power of attorney for doing so to her Reno lawyer. Marquand was furious that she might subject him to the awkwardness of an uncontested divorce with its inevitable consequence of gossip and further delay. To his lawyer he said: "She must be made to understand that she should not give me the wear and tear of an uncontested divorce at my time of life and compel me to take up permanent residence in Nevada or what have you. It will only make her ridiculous and what fragments of any relationship I may have left with the children nil. If necessary I shall stay out here all the rest of my life if this enables me to sever relations with her." He threatened to fill the gossip columns with his complaint that she had "succeeded in alienating my children from me by malicious defamation of character" if she did not soon sign the necessary power of attorney. To Carol Brandt he expostulated: "This business of sitting around here and waiting for a neurotic and hysterical woman to pull the strings if she will is humiliation. It makes me against all marriage at the moment. To think that any bitch can put me in this box is infuriating. It makes me lose my faith in the United States. In Manhood and the World!"

Then she suddenly demanded as a condition for signing that he grant her a last interview. At her hotel at Lake Tahoe, where Marquand met her, as agreed, three hours of discussion ended with his flight through the lobby of the hotel and out to the car where her attorney was waiting. Adelaide, in tears, ran at his heels. Standing at the car she finally said she would sign the paper—where was it? But Mr. Thatcher didn't have it with him. The next day a long letter from her was delivered by hand to the ranch. In it she said that she would sign the document if her husband would join her at the Mark in San Francisco for a couple of days. But Marquand wanted no further "confrontation scenes." "I am convinced these gave me my heart attack and I'd rather have another in a more agreeable manner," he told Potter.

Finally, Adelaide sent Marquand the signed paper on November 6, accompanied by a six-page (single-spaced, typewritten) letter which appealed to him to tear it up, and, once more, to begin again. She enclosed another item—a picture of the Easter Island monolith "which was what we talked about over fresh limeade on 73 Street the first time you ever called on me," and pathetically declared, "I still want us to go to Easter Island together." She argued and she begged and she reviewed the record. She listed the friends whom she felt sure would rejoice in their reunion—the McCutcheons (the owners of Salt Cay), the Gene Tunneys, the McGeorge Bundys and the Harvey Bundys, the Archibald MacLeishes, the Perry Millers, the Benjamin Fairbanks, the Nathan Puseys, the Randall Thompsons, the Dana Atchleys, the Harvey Coxes, the Harry Schermans, the Cedric Gibbonses, the King Vidors, the Francis Welches, Helen Howe and her brothers, Frances McFadden, Rosemary Benét, J. Donald Adams, Murray Forbes, Helen McIntyre, Serena Merck, Conney Fiske, Lucy Ames, and others. It was a vain, overconfident list of superrespectable witnesses to their life together—not all of the listees would have been willing to be named as supporters of the Marquand marriage—and Marquand must have read Adelaide's letter with revulsion. When his birthday arrived on the eleventh he remarked to Tina that it was, to him, the "gloomiest day of the year." On that day he told Johnny that Adelaide had been bombarding him "with long letters about the Brandts and poor Davis, etc. You would think if she wanted me to come back, which she really seems to want, she would say she would promise to be a good girl, to be quieter, less aggressive and not determined to impose her will on her whole family and not to win all the battles and all the wars. She seems utterly oblivious to this side of the situation, which, with her inability ever to finish anything or stay in one place, has always seemed to me the crux of the matter." On the fourteenth the divorce decree was granted in Carson City. Marquand had charged "extreme mental cruelty."

As the divorced so frequently discover, the act of severance brought no instant change. Everyone thought he would remarry. "Top tchit-tchat in literary circles," Walter Winchell immediately informed his readers, was that the famous novelist would marry "the widow of the prexy at the Brandt & Brandt Agency." But this possibility had already been put aside some months earlier. Carol had been nearly ready for it—she had for some time been visiting Kent's Island alone, causing local tongues to wag; she had supervised the redecoration of the house, giving things a Park Avenue touch that was as characteristic of her presence as her Shalimar. And yet the idea of marriage seemed, in the end, impossible to both of them. During the next year they must have reviewed the matter many times. She would later claim that he asked her to marry him and that she refused because she could not see herself in the context of his Newbury life. He told a friend that she had asked him to marry her—and that he had countered, "I will if you will give up Brandt and Brandt, but damned if I'll marry two Brandts"—by which he meant the agency, and also, maybe, that double-barreled authoritative self that, woman and agent, made her so potent in her attraction and so dangerous to the male ego. Their affair was to drift on quietly for a little while and quietly close in the spring of 1960, when she decided to marry a new admirer. Marquand then observed to Tina, "Mrs. Brandt, known to you since childhood as home-breaker, evil genius and bad influence, is marrying a very rich and highly intelligent New York lawyer, so we can all be perfectly delighted." There was, still, a general expectation that he would marry somebody—and his circle contained a number of possibilities besides Carol. Other widows of old friends were fond of him—Serena Merck, Helen McIntyre and Conney Fiske came to everyone's mind. Indeed, Conney would later declare that he had proposed to her—and that she had declined. He reportedly claimed, as in the case of Carol, that the woman had asked *him*, but he had not been able to see himself joining her Weston or Southern Pines horsy set. Quite deliberately he had, in fact, placed a certain distance between himself and this latter world of Conney's when he established himself in the nearby but separate golfing community of Pinehurst.

Christmas 1958 was much like the preceding Christmas. Adelaide had a "hideously eventful" holiday in Aspen entertaining ten teenagers—her children's friends, whom only one of her own, Lonny, consented in the end to join. Ferry, after inviting two guests to the party, decided that she would flunk out of Radcliffe if she did not spend the three weeks of vacation in Widener Library, and Timmy remained in Cambridge for all of his vacation to practice his trumpet and read. Marquand had always loathed family Christmases, but this solitary Pinehurst Christmas he called "one of the worst ones yet, a curious but excruciating combination of peace and utter loneliness, interspersed with perhaps an excessive ingestion of golf, games of bridge and duck shooting." He told Tina, "I cannot remember when I have felt so confused or disturbed"—and he even forgot to send greetings or presents to the Welches, the one branch of his family that gave him no woe. He was more and more out of touch with Johnny and Sue, who struck him as taking a whimsical direction that he could not understand. Johnny still failed to finish his second novel and they did not seem to desire stability or children, but amused themselves by travel and adopting unusual pets—a parrot or a bush baby. Marquand commented: "Of course they can afford these eccentricities financially but I wonder whether anyone can afford them spiritually for an indefinite period. This does not mean that they are not both perfectly delightful, but then, so was Peter Pan, and so too was Lord Byron, but his Lordship in his rather brief life did turn out quite a lot of work." He had vested in Johnny as well as in Tina his hope that some of his own feeling for tradition might be expressed in the next generation. Immediately following his divorce he had arranged to deed the Curzon's Mill real estate to Johnny and his wife, who were to divide off the old Mill building by the Artichoke as a summer home for Tina and her family. But to Brooks Potter he confessed his feeling that Johnny's desire to assume responsibility for the Mill was "tepid to say the least."

The divorce did not make for any improvement in his difficult relation with his younger children, who continued to occupy an area of maximum stress crossed by lines of tension still operating between their parents. Lonny had begun the new year of 1959 by at first refusing to go back to Deerfield Academy after his vacation. His state of mind was now almost constantly precarious, the walls of his ego caving in at every new buffet. But Marquand was not exceptionally callous, as parents go, in resisting the suggestion that his son was as much handicapped in some invisible way as he had been visibly handicapped by the broken leg he had acquired on the ski slope at Aspen. When the truant called Pinehurst from Cambridge, Marquand told him to get back immediately to the school. It had not been easy to get Headmaster Boyden to take him in, with his spotty record, in the first place, and he had been treated very kindly by all the teachers. What was it all about? "In fact it is my opinion that too much fuss and attention has been given this matter. I cannot have much sympathy about your peace of mind. It is not as though you were being starved, beaten or maltreated at Deerfield. If in June you don't want to go to Deerfield again, I shall appreciate your point of view." Marquand's inability to identify mental illness in its incipient stages was natural enough and no doubt a form of self-protection. It was also part of his contest with Adelaide to find fault with her for sending the children to psychiatrists at every behavioral blowup, and he threatened not to take any responsibility for their psychiatric bills, even in the case of Lonny, whom he had stood ready to adopt. When Lonny did return to school but made no answer to his father's invitation that he spend his next vacation at Pinehurst, Marquand responded with his usual renunciatory "As things are going, I am increasingly reluctant to assume any of his expenses after the end of his school year." And once again, he declared to Potter, "The behavior of my younger children has upset me greatly all winter, and for my own health and peace of mind, unless there is an improvement in the relationship I propose to withdraw all interest from them." Marquand complained that he had leased a more expensive house than he personally needed at Pinehurst because he had expected that the children, and Lonny in particular, would be visiting him there. It was Adelaide, he said to his friends, who had, of course, "suborned" the boy as she had "suborned" his older brother and sister. He had heard that plans were being made for Lonny to visit, instead, with Johnny and Sue, and he could only resent the preference, though it was natural enough for a sixteen-year-old to prefer a chance of holiday in New York at his stepbrother's apartment—where there were now *two* bush babies—to a sojourn among the aging golfers at Pinehurst. Marquand offered to return Lonny's guardianship petition: "I cannot assume financial responsibility if I am allowed no other"—a threat which, if Lonny heard of it, must have deepened his insecurity. By the end of April he had left school again and was under psychiatric care. But Marquand would say to Potter: "I am not as moved as I might be by Lonny's fits of depression, which I believe are an infantile means of calling attention to himself. The trouble with the boy really is that he is lacking in character and guts—an attribute shared by all those children except possibly Ferry."

From Ferry there had been no sign of a desire for communication since her telephone call in September 1958, when she declared that she never wished to see or hear from her father again. When he came back to Kent's Island in the middle of April, he learned from the caretaker that she and Timmy had paid a visit there in his absence during the spring vacation, and he wrote her, "I must ask you not to make another visit to Kent's Island until such time—if ever—your feelings toward me undergo great change." He was told that Ferry was playing Lady Blanche, the leading role in a college production of *Princess Ida* at Agassiz Theater—an unusual distinction for a freshman. Potter, who had more and more come to act as a representative of Marquand's own aggression, a sort of deputized ego, advised, "In view of Ferry's conduct towards you, I don't see any reason why you should go and see it." Still, on the day of his departure for an extended trip abroad at the beginning of June she called him, as Marquand triumphantly reported to the lawyer, "and said that she was sorry for what she had done and would be a good girl in the future." He therefore instructed that a codicil be added to his recently revised will so that she might, after all, share equally with her brothers in his estate.

At the end of May 1959, he flew to London. He promised himself a month in Italy and then a visit to Africa for another month, then, on the swing home, a few days in Athens. He would not be back until the tenth of August. He was accompanied by Marjorie Davis. She had returned as his secretary the previous January and would continue to assist him during the trip; he would be working, for another few weeks at any rate, on the last chapters of *Timothy Dexter Revisited.* But her role as indispensable companion was probably quite clear to both of them now, if not to others. Carol Brandt, devoted as ever in her own way, remained behind to manage, among the many matters under her management, various Marquand affairs, professional and personal, including ordering towels and sheets from Macy's for his new house in Pinehurst. Still benevolently smoothing his arrangements as—to Adelaide's annoyance—she had done for so long, she urged him to pay a visit to her friend and client Marcia Davenport while he was staying in Rome, and this time it was his turn to be annoyed. She had not seemed to realize—"bitcherisque" he called it—that he would not leave Marjorie behind (of course she had to drive the car!) and that the young woman, who was clearly not merely a chauffeur, would have to be accommodated by his hostess.

After a few days in Rome, Marquand and Miss Davis took the train to Stresa, where they had rooms in the Regina Palace Hotel overlooking Lago Maggiore. They worked in the morning and took walks in the afternoon. Marquand told Carol, "This is beautiful here, but if I did not have the writing to do, I should be bored stiff." After two weeks he and Marjorie took a trip by car to Lake Como, St. Moritz, Verona and Venice. "I saw your friend Willie Maugham in Venice. Krist!" Marquand wrote Carol, who was planning to come over herself for a short stay with Mrs. Davenport. Perhaps they would meet. "I miss you and I have to clack my own bangles," he had written her earlier, thinking of those noisy bracelets of hers that he had claimed to detest. Unquestionably, Miss Davis had a quieter taste in self-adornment. On the Fourth of July they left for the real heart of the trip—the journey into Africa that Marquand had planned with the help of a Pinehurst friend, George Shearwood.

Shearwood, an Englishman who had settled in Pinehurst after his marriage to an American and who ran a small travel agency there, had been a colonial administrator in the British army in the remote Karamojo region in northeast Uganda forty years before. One evening during the previous winter after a bridge session at The Wolves, Marquand had talked about his extensive travel in Asia, where he had gone far off the well-worn highways to places still unaltered by the "civilized" West. "I could take you in Africa where you could see some of that still, I think," Shearwood offered. Karamojo was not on the tourist route; in fact, one could not get into this "closed district" without permission from the local government, but Shearwood had kept up his connections. So plans were laid for a trip into the African interior, in the company of Shearwood and another Pinehurst friend, Mrs. Gertrude Page. Of course, Marquand might get professional mileage out of the trip—*Sports Illustrated*, the Brandt office quickly discovered, was willing to commission him to do six articles at $2,000 apiece plus expenses. But Marquand found that the trip was not the stuff for a big-game travelogue of the kind *Sports Illustrated* expected, and in the end he did only a single reflective piece for the *Atlantic*, which was inspired by his impressions of Karamojo.

He and Marjorie had met the other two in the Rome airport and flown directly to Nairobi. They had been able to drive themselves to Nyeri to spend the night at the famous Treetops, and from there to Nanyuki on the far side of Kenya. They had gone down into the Great Rift Valley. In the beautiful, fertile Kenya section of the Rift, they enjoyed the landscape and marveled at the cool dry air of the Kenya highlands. But when they reached Kitale, they were finally at the threshold of what Marquand had really come for, the adventure into the "back of beyond," as Shearwood called it. The Karamojo region, a huge area stretching from the shore of Lake Rudolf to the Abyssinian border, had a strange, unfamiliar beauty. The mountains

Marquand saw from a distance as they drove along were heavily wooded. They had, he would relate, "a forbidding blueish-green color" that contrasted almost shockingly with the reddish dust of the plain across which they were traveling. "When you raise your eyes to these hills in Karamojo, they give you the wordless message that you are a long way from anywhere and could be still further off if you trekked through their dark valleys and over the lower ridges," Marquand reflected.

Moroto, as Shearwood had first known it, had been a crude headquarters of a few huts; he told his friends that his own hut had had only holes in the walls for windows and doors. Now there was a permanent settlement of 120 persons, cement buildings and electric lights. Typewriters rattled busily in the commissioner's office, the bugle blew for parade, sundowners were served at the Moroto Club, and Hindu shopkeepers had arrived to establish a short commercial street of *dakans*, one-room shops that sold all the civilized essentials, including cotton cloth from Manchester, kitchen cutlery, tobacco and Coca-Cola. The visiting party from America was put up in the rest house where they were attended by barefoot servants in white robes, sashes and tarbooshes. At breakfast the next morning Marquand noticed a British major who had taken his golf clubs with him into the two-table dining room. Moroto had, it seemed, a nine-hole golf course—not bad considering, the major remarked; with time it could be expected to improve. After this he was silent a moment, reflecting, Marquand guessed, that there might not be much time for improving the golf course, "now that all the clocks in Africa were striking twelve." Later Marquand got a look at the golf course. The fairways, grazed by cattle, stretched across gullies, and the greens were packed sand.

Something about the white man's golf course, a "remoteness from spiritual and physical sources of supply," was matched by a track meet the visitors witnessed. It might have been a scene from Trollope, Marquand thought, a party for the tenantry with games on the village green graced by the presence of people from the Great House and the curate. Here the crowd was composed mostly of East Africans who had come to Moroto to work as mechanics or laborers or servants. The wives of some of the Europeans poured tea at a table. A group of Indian ladies in saris added an exotic note. Standing apart were some of the natives of the region, the Karamojo, the women bare to the waist in skirts of cowhide strips, the men naked except for necklaces of beaded wire. Marquand noticed one of them, obviously a headman, standing by a Ford automobile. His hair, stiffened by mud and braided elaborately, was crowned by white ostrich plumes. He wore a white shell ornament in his lower lip and held a spear and was tattooed on arms and chest. He seemed to be watching the track meet with patient condescension. Marquand, remembering that the Karamojo were reputed to have the swiftness of gazelles as they ran in pursuit of game, decided that the runners they were watching looked awkward and ridiculous.

The next day he had an opportunity to see the Karamojo at a convocation of their own. The tribesmen were planning a *nygona*, or dance to bring on rain. Marquand's party arrived at a Karamojo village of thatched huts to which over a thousand Karamojo had come, driving their cattle into a large circle. The guide introduced Marquand and his companions to two chiefs who were dressed in shirts and trousers and ties. One of them wore a tie with a nude girl sitting in a cocktail glass painted on it. White ostrich plumes were attached to their European felt fedoras. The chief of all the Karamojo was wearing an old pith helmet, a tweed coat, and tweed shorts. Despite these evidences of Westernization, the dance, as far as Marquand could tell, was as "authentic" as any researcher into aboriginal Africa could have desired. Plumed spearmen, bells jingling at their ankles, charged out of the thorn thicket at the blowing of a bass horn, their solemn faces painted with wood ash and ocher. Another party sprang forward from the opposite side to engage them in what looked like mock combat, writhing in magnificently simulated fury, then veering back into the shadows. At an altar, after a while, a bull was sacrificed. All around the little party of white persons the spectators had begun to leap and sing until, as Marquand said, "they looked like a pan of black bean soup coming to a boil." It was, he realized, time to go. "We did not belong there." They flew from Entebbe to Athens, where Marquand took the party to Delphi and put on a remarkable performance as cicerone, dramatizing the ancient scene when the oracle spoke to the Greeks. But soon they were in New York, and Marquand was back in his own constricted world.

Autumn went by without special incident at Kent's Island. When his "graduation date" came around again on November 14, Marquand realized with a shock that a year had passed since his divorce. At the end of the month he went down to Pinehurst, leaving the caretaker, Mr. Berry, strict instructions to keep not only Mrs. Marquand but her children off the premises in his absence: "The house is supposed to be closed, and they are irresponsible." His relation to them had not improved. As Christmas approached he felt his usual revulsion for the seasonal mood. He wrote Tina that he had awakened in the middle of the night, in spite of his sleeping pill, and "reached the decision to have no wreath on the front door." What he told no one was that his relation with Marjorie Davis had come to some sort of crisis. On the fifteenth of December she left for California to visit her sister, promising to be back in the spring. Marquand told Brooks Potter, "She hates Pinehurst because she says there is nothing for her to do; no boy friends, no social life, no one below the age of 70," but this was hardly an honest description of her real feelings. She had always found Marquand's company all-sufficient; more likely she was dissatisfied with the ambiguous, unacknowledged place she occupied in his life. He instructed Potter to send her two weeks' salary and traveling expenses to the Coast, but he remarked,

"I would not be surprised if she gets lost in the smog that hangs over Los Angeles and doesn't return." His Christmas solitude was mitigated by the arrival of Carol Brandt, who, her forthcoming marriage to the lawyer Edmund Pavenstedt nearly settled, came down to visit Marquand with her daughter and her poodle, and then returned with him for a week in New York.

At One Reservoir Street Adelaide prepared to spend Christmas in her own peculiar way. She rented Salt Cay for the children's school recess. She took Lonny and Ferry with her in an ill-fated effort to recapture something of their past happiness on the island. But Timmy remained in Cambridge. He must have felt a tremor of kinship with his father's ideas about the Season to Be Jolly, for he refused to stir at all in search of it. When Adelaide asked him "where he was going to see a little holly," he declared that the Christmas dinner at his Harvard dormitory—along with the hapless orphans or foreigners who could not get Home for the Holidays—would do. As it turned out, inclement weather kept Adelaide and her other two children marooned on the island for five and a half days, and on Christmas Eve the captain of the McCutcheon's boat got drunk in Nassau, cracked the rudder against a stone pier, and was unable to get it repaired till the weekend was over.

Lonny had been refused readmittance to Deerfield for the fall and was entered in the Belmont Hill School, but in January he was expelled once more. He had committed various infractions—climbing out his window and taking off in the middle of the night for Boston, for example—nothing really extraordinary as schoolboy escapades go. The trouble was that Lonny's state was not exactly that of youthful high jinks. His doctor now used the word "manic" in its exact clinical sense when his patient was hardly able to sleep or eat and was potentially dangerous to himself and others, and put him in McLean Hospital for a week. As soon as Lonny was discharged, Adelaide took steps to get him into a tutoring school in Cambridge in the hope that his purely educational problems could be handled. His emotional difficulties would prove too much for any school. For the moment he seemed recovered and wanted to come down to Pinehurst for a visit. When he did come, in April, the visit was apparently a disaster. Marquand wrote Potter, delegated as always to carry out his more punitive impulses: "I do not care, both for reasons of my own health and of impact on the community, to have him visit me again when he is in an elated state. I am not sure, in fact, that I wish to have him visit me again under any circumstances." He had become convinced that Lonny had been pilfering money and objects at Kent's Island and at Pinehurst during the visits of the past year. "I do not believe that theft has anything to do with his emotional instability," he declared, and ordered Lonny's allowance suspended until he made up the "stolen" sums.

Somewhat contradictorily he also expressed the opinion that Lonny ought to be immediately committed to an institution. But he wrote: "I personally see no reason why the money should be paid for an expensive sojourn at McLean's, which is a dismal enough place anyway, when he may be housed free or for a nominal sum at either Danvers or Medfield [state hospitals for the insane]. I have had occasion to visit both these institutions. Although the inmates are not all members of the Porcellian Club, they are not much worse than the McLean crowd, and from my observation and also from what I hear from alienists, they are on the whole given superior care to what they may receive at a private institution. Also, the place is rugged enough to make the patient want to get out. I am sorry to take this dim view about Lonny, but as of now I am fed to the teeth with him, and I am afraid in the end he is not much more than a spoiled brat developing vicious habits." Potter concurred in Marquand's view, writing back, "I am still of the opinion that Lonny is really not a 'sick' boy, and that a lot of his trouble stems from an effort to attract attention." Potter was even of the opinion that another school should be tried. He recommended one he had heard of that took on boys who needed training in better study habits. Marquand had to remind his lawyer, who had never seen Lonny "in one of his higher states of elation": "He is like someone with six drinks who can't stop talking, playing the guitar or writing. He gives all the indications of the classic symptoms of manic depression." The only place for him in these states, the father was positive, was "behind walls." Lonny was almost immediately placed in the Massachusetts Mental Health Center, a much less prestigious—and less expensive—place than McLean.

In this spring of 1960, the last of his life, Marquand's relations with Timmy and Ferry had no such dramatic and disastrous ending as those with Lonny, though in January he had said, "I feel the general write-off is inevitable." The two older children continued to disappoint him by resistance more unconscious and evasive, by failure to write or visit, rather than by overt repudiation. Timmy, whose long-term asthma had been recognized as psychosomatic in origin, now came down with a case of eczema bad enough to require hospitalization, but expressed his defiance of his parents—or of life in general—in no more explicit fashion. Once in the hospital he did, in fact, make his father long-distance calls such as he had previously been incapable of, chatting cheerfully from his hospital bed about literature (in which he was majoring at Harvard). Indeed, there was some final surrender of enmity on the part of both Timmy and Ferry. Ferry still seldom called, but she was beginning to turn to her father a little as her life in Cambridge became more and more insupportable. Reservoir Street was altogether too close to the Radcliffe campus. Adelaide had developed the habit of intruding herself continually in her daughter's dormitory, insisting, to Ferry's embarrassment, on making friends with her friends. Since the divorce she had become more eccentric than ever in appearance and behavior. In the evenings she now drank heavily and Ferry spent horrifying hours with her while she wept aloud and sometimes threw herself on the floor in sodden despair. Marquand listened to descriptions of such scenes with grim amusement and agreed that it was worth leaving Radcliffe to escape; he encouraged his daughter to apply to Bryn Mawr and Barnard and, finally, to Stanford, furthest away of all, where he was able to make her acceptance certain by writing to an old friend who was now a Stanford dean.

Like Johnny, she had begun to show, despite her rebellion, the impulse to imitation that is the child's sincerest tribute to the parent. Only a sophomore, she surprised everyone by winning the Radcliffe annual Phi Beta Kappa Award for the best creative work done by an undergraduate. This was a story that came out of her memories of the Bahamas—the happiest Marquand time—about an island whose inbred inhabitants all looked alike and had a common last name. She had remembered her father's own delight in the group of small islands off Eleuthera called Spanish Wells, which he had discovered to be populated almost entirely by the Pindar family. He had seen it as a literary subject himself and had written a description of the place that had been read to the Tuesday Night Club. Ferry, of course, deprecated the suggestion that she intended to take up the literary life. When newspaper reporters asked her what she would do with the prize money, she declared with determined frivolity that she was going to spend it on an orange sheath dress.

That April Ferry paid her first visit in a long time to Pinehurst. Marquand reported with a dryness: "Ferry is here now, in one of her more benign and affectionate moods. She has already chiseled a cocktail gown and a bathing suit." But their old feud was at an end. Her last letter to her father was full of long-suppressed admiration and the affection he aroused when he had appealed to her half-grown femininity. She was again at Aspen—at whose *longueurs* she griped, knowing how well he would understand—when she wrote: "If, as you say, this is the first letter I have written you in six years, it ought to have weight and significance. I am afraid it has neither. It is merely an attempt to communicate with a Grand Old Gentleman of American Letters who, in my humble and probably biased opinion, is more worthy of the title than Frost or Sandburg." Obscurely, she sensed that he needed assurance that his labors as a writer had been worthwhile.

His death could not have been more sudden, yet long before it he seemed to have felt that groundswell which sometimes seems to cause men to begin the final giving-over. In September 1959, he signed a new version of his will, which divided his personal estate—worth about $1.1 million—among his five children. The bulk went to Tina and Johnny (three fourths of the "residue" to Tina) because, he said, Ferry, Timmy and Lonny were "otherwise adequately provided for." To Marjorie Davis he assigned a legacy of $10,000, and the same amount to Newland Berry for his faithful management of Kent's Island. He knew now that he would never achieve the return to Curzon's Mill—and so he had already given it to Johnny and Tina. He wondered what would happen to Kent's Island when he died; he willed it to his three younger children but foresaw a time when they might not want it and imagined it enduring as a place of quiet marshes and undisturbed wildlife, perhaps under the protection of a preservation agency. The family heirlooms, which had meant so much to him as symbols of his Marquand–Curzon continuity, now weighed on his mind. He decided to give the most valuable of them all, the silver Tyng tray made by Paul Revere, valued at $18,000, to Harvard. He arranged to have a replica made for himself.

Timothy Dexter Revisited had been a consciously final work, a sort of personal testament that concealed autobiography under the disguise of the biography of someone else. Dexter and his times were to be invoked to afford a contrast with the contemporary age, and with his willed connection with an early American past. He was peculiarly fit to look backwards and forwards. He told the illustrator, Philip Kappel: "This one is not written, I hope, in the rather kittenish, overanxious way the first was. It is meant to be a comparison between the culture of Federalist Newburyport at the time of Lord Timothy Dexter and the town of the present. There are also quite a lot of my own adolescent reminiscences." Underneath the book's witty, objective comments about historical differences lay the peculiar poignancy of his own nostalgia, deeper now than ever. He remembered his great-aunt Mary Curzon and his own childhood at the Mill as well as the curmudgeon Dexter of a still earlier time. He inserted the strange dreamy recollection of the occasion when he drove his mother home to the Mill from the trolley line in a snowstorm, and gave as the excuse that all of its remembered details (the horse and sleigh, even the buffalo robe he had thrown over the horse) as well as the rural electric car line, had absolutely vanished from the modern world. But there was a more personal significance in that plunge into the deepest heart of memory, the very core of his first assumption of manhood. He was reaching back towards the image of self he had cherished all his life, despite all self-betrayals.

One intelligent reader who understood the book's true significance was an Ipswich friend, Katherine Thompson, who imagined a lecture being given by a professor of American studies at a Japanese university: "The unknown Marquand of 1925 began his career by writing about this forgotten eccentric; 35 years later, when Dexter's name had faded still more, and his own name was famous throughout the world, Marquand paused to re-examine and re-appraise the character which had first caught his interest. The young Marquand saw Dexter as a phenomenon, but the mature Marquand had learned that matrix maketh man; and so *he* saw Dexter as formed by the matrix of Federalist Newburyport and himself as similarly shaped. After his Japanese period, almost all of Marquand's most important novels were concerned with the theme of a man returning by accident or choice to the home of his childhood, and there achieving some self-knowledge. Nearly all the heroes of these novels suggest Marquand himself; the hometowns were, in ever thinner disguise, Newburyport. The crucial significance of *Timothy Dexter*

Revisited is that here, for the first time, Marquand, *in propria persona*, is returning to the actual Newburyport. Insofar as Marquand was able to carry out this plan, to identify the world of his ancestors and of his childhood with the world of Timothy Dexter, and his own ambivalent feelings toward the town and its toward him with those Dexter must have experienced, the subterfuge worked. The first part of the book, which used Marquand's recollections of his own childhood, and the recollections of his Newburyport elders whose memory and ways reached still further back into the past, brilliantly sustained the thesis. But toward the end of the book, Marquand appeared to lose interest in his puppet. Timothy Dexter, grown senile, lecherous and dull, had ceased to be an agreeable, or more importantly, an accurate symbol for his era, his town or his biographer." Without intending it, Mrs. Thompson suggested a further thought, the reverse of her own conclusion: the late, unregenerate Dexter was *still* Marquand self-viewed.

Marquand had thought of returning to Dexter for years. As early as 1938, Bernice Baumgarten had reported to Carl Brandt with some incredulity that the old Dexter book was "closest to John's heart" of anything he had done up till then. "I see no harm in a new edition if it doesn't take John too long and if he'd really like to see it done," she grudgingly conceded. The idea was laid aside, but it kept coming up. In 1947 John Farrar, the publisher, asked if Marquand might be interested in doing a book on Boston, perhaps an exercise in historic and personal recall such as *Timothy Dexter Revisited* would prove to be, and Marquand had regretfully declined, saying, "The time may come sooner than I think when I shall have to give up writing fiction, and then I should like to try a job like that very much." And now the time *had* come and the viewpoint of the Brandt office was still negative, although Arthur Thornhill encouraged the idea. Even after the book had been written, Carol remained convinced that it had been a waste of Marquand's time. Alex Williams, the Little, Brown editor who worked over the book with Marquand, felt immediately that Carol had reacted characteristically, despite her long attachment to Marquand: "There is nothing in it for her; she can't sell it to a magazine. There's no bread and butter in this for her." Marquand merely threatened to dedicate it to her.

Although Little, Brown did not expect to make a great deal of money out of the new Dexter, it was carefully "packaged" for the Christmas gift trade. After some difficulty, Philip Kappel, who had illustrated the 1925 volume, was located and engaged to do a new set of drawings. His pen-and-ink sketches captured the mood of a walk Marquand and Alex Williams and Kappel took together through the town, looking for significant pictures on one very hot midsummer day. As they strolled from one spot to another they became more and more discouraged. Dexter's mansion was a mess; the old streets had a seedy, not a romantic look. Along the rotted docks there was not a stir of life, except for two small boys who had stripped off their clothes and were about to dive into the Merrimack. Marquand said, "God,

I've had enough of this. Let's get a bottle of rum and Alex will make us some daiquiris and we'll have lunch." But Kappel had found one of his best subjects in the glimpse of the naked young swimmers.

Williams had taken over as Marquand's special editor when Cammann Newberry left Little, Brown in 1957, after having helped *Women and Thomas Harrow* into print. In the isolation into which Marquand had now drifted with the death of old friends, the divorce, the alienation of his children, he let himself be looked after by new caretakers. Carol had gone to Pavenstedt without causing him a pang. He leaned now on the slightly sycophantic, essentially detached solicitude of Williams and of Newberry. Williams, Newberry and Newberry's wife, Reddy, became a trio of companions who mitigated his loneliness. In February 1959, the three of them came to Pinehurst "to interrupt my vicious solitude," as Marquand observed, and the year following he visited with Williams the Newberry's winter place in Boca Grande, Florida. During the intervening summer they had seen each other frequently at Kent's Island and at the Newberrys' home in nearby Beverly Farms. Newberry and Williams were both cultivated and urbane companions with Somerset and Myopia Club habits. The Newberrys were golf enthusiasts, and the bachelor Williams was almost a professional clubman—he would write *A Social History of the Greater Boston Clubs*, which described the elite club world of which Marquand had long been a part. Neither asking nor receiving more intimacy, Marquand was glad to relax in comfortable sociabilities with such company.

They had begun to talk about taking some sort of holiday together. During Marquand's visit to Greece in 1959 he had heard from Shan Sedgwick about the possibility of chartering a yacht for a cruise among the Greek islands, and the following February Sedgwick wrote him about the forty-eight-foot *Stormie Seas*, which was available at $1,365 for three weeks. By the end of the month the Newberrys, Williams and Marquand had agreed to engage the yacht for the period September 15 to October 6, avoiding the unpleasant Meltimi winds. Captain Sam Barclay promised to take them via Poros, Hydra and Spetsai to Nauplia. They would go by car from Nauplia to see Mycenae and Epidaurus and then go down the coast of the Peloponnesus to see the island of Cythera. He knew of an anchorage at the western end of Crete where there was a Venetian fortress that had been "uninhabited for 150 years and was just as the Venetians left it." They would land at Iraklion (Candia) for Knossos and the other Minoan cities, then come back by way of Santorini, Nios, Naxos, Delos, Mykonos and Kythnos to Piraeus. The magical ancient names sprinkled the letter the captain wrote to Marquand.

The *Stormie Seas* was fitted out to accommodate four or even five passengers. There was to be another in their party, Marjorie Davis, though neither Williams or Newberry was aware of this until May, when they got together at Kent's Island. Marjorie had returned to Pinehurst from California in February. On what terms she had come back is not altogether clear but she remembered later that it was at this time that Marquand formally asked her to marry him. "I didn't think it was appropriate," she said. Nevertheless, she told him she would stay on. Her secretary's salary was resumed and her regular duties as Marquand's assistant began again. An apartment for her use with an adjoining office for their work together was built in the garage of the Pinehurst house. But they had, she would later say, talked about the possibility of marriage sometime in the future, and he had half-seriously introduced the idea to Johnny already: "Which shall it be, the agent or the secretary?" he had said some time before Carol's decision to marry Pavenstedt. The trip to Greece was not to be a honeymoon—they had no plans to be married before they took off on the *Stormie Seas*—but it was, possibly, a prenuptial flight.

For at the very last one pushes premonition aside and anticipates that one has more lives to live. He might marry again. He would, after all, begin another novel. When the Newberrys and Williams came down to Pinehurst in February 1959, he showed them the opening chapters of a new work of fiction. He wrote ninety pages of a first draft in which something of the old pattern of autobiographical compulsion was once more visible. He reached back to that extraordinary moment when a special signal had flashed among the stars for him, and the *Post* had taken his first story. His novel opens with the narrator-hero finding in his mailbox the note of summons to the "McCloud Building"—recognizably the headquarters of the Curtis Publishing Company, to which he had come, at Lorimer's beckoning, long ago. The mystery of such moments still stirred his wonder. The narrator acknowledges the banality of the scene: "It has been worked to death ever since there has been narrative prose and verse—by messengers, by heralds, by gods and goddesses, in the more stately forms of drama, and by kind fairies in nursery books, worn threadbare in the slick magazines, the slick movies, the slick TV, and the slick contemporary stage, and I use the word slick without attempting denigration. Art has a dangerous, slick, brittle brilliance when it is not obscure and clumsy. But the scene is equally hackneyed in our more serious breast-beating sectors. It, unfortunately, has become aggressively American."

This hero, we discern, is someone who like himself is going to make it by grace of luck and talent from modest beginnings. When we encounter him he is living in a scruffy New York apartment with his socially superior young wife. Then, in the old Marquand way, we are thrown back to an earlier scene of their first encounter when he was a newspaper reporter, and to his first sight of her parents. Almost wearily the trained humor splutters along with wry asides of social observation. Could he have confronted still another time the puzzle of his own history to see it more freshly? He may have been thinking of his own beginnings in May when he addressed the honors students of Newburyport High School at their graduation banquet. A few weeks later he entertained at Kent's Island the eighteen survivors of his own class at their fiftieth reunion. On the twenty-eighth of June he attended a meeting of the trustees of the Wheelwright Fund that had enabled him, in 1910, to go to Harvard.

His interest in the fate of the nation expressed itself in a personal way at the Harvard commencement. There, seignorial in his Overseer's hat, he had fallen into step beside John F. Kennedy in the academic procession and chatted affably while some of his arch-Republican fellow Overseers stalked aloofly past. He planned to vote for the senator in the coming presidential election. Up to the time of Kennedy's nomination, Marquand, who had supported Eisenhower in 1952, had favored Adlai Stevenson. He had offered to assist Stevenson in writing speeches for the fall campaign ("though he really needs no such assistance," he deferentially said). Stevenson and he had exchanged some ideas on the current "excessive fear of communism that borders on the paranoid," as Marquand expressed it. After the encounter with Kennedy in Cambridge he had observed to Stevenson, "He looked as young to me as an Horatio Alger hero, but at least he wasn't riding a golfmobile." Stevenson invited Marquand to come to Chicago for further conversation, and, indeed, a meeting had been planned for late in July.

Marching for the last of his term as Overseer, he was in visible good spirits. Johnny had gone up to Cambridge too. After the ceremonies were over that afternoon, father and son met on the bricks outside Quincy House, where Marquand had come to see his classmates. "With his heavy cutaway and black top hat, he was strutting in the hot sun, as vigorous as I ever saw him, and against a backdrop of the Lampoon building, where he had begun to be a writer forty-five years before. He was in the highest of spirits and at his most entertaining—secretly but obviously rejoicing in being a Harvard man," Johnny recalled to President Pusey. It turned out to be the last time he would see his father alive. One of Marquand's final gestures had declared his reconciliation with Harvard after the old resentments that had culminated in the gift of his manuscripts to Yale. He had decided that his bulky accumulations of professional correspondence should go to Houghton Library. Only some weeks before graduation Alex Williams had gone down to Kent's Island to pick up the boxes of letters, as well as a copy of Thoreau's *Walden* inscribed by the author to Margaret Fuller, and had taken them to Cambridge.

On the weekend of July 4, Williams came to see Marquand with a few dozen of *Timothy Dexter Revisited* for some of the Book-of-the-Month Club people who wanted autographed copies, and to talk about the planned excursion to Greece. Marquand autographed a copy for Williams on the spot and during the next week began, but did not finish, the job of signing the other copies. On the fourteenth he attended the judges' meeting of the Book-of-the-Month Club and shared a taxi with John Mason Brown on the ride uptown to the Knickerbocker Club. As always after one of the meetings he abounded in quick humorous talk, an overflow of the occasion which called out his talents as a sort of good-natured cerberus, snapping at the heels of books that tried to pass into the land of fame and dollars. The next day he lunched at the "long table" at the Century and was full of stories as usual. The other members clustered around to hear them as they had been doing for years, confident in their expectation of entertainment.

He was back at Kent's Island early enough in the afternoon to have a cookout dinner with Lonny, who was visiting him, and with Tina and her family from Curzon's Mill. He did not feel tired and planned to go out to Martha's Vineyard to see Johnny and Sue at their summer place the next morning. Floyd and Julia Ray, the black couple who had been working for him for two years, remembered him presiding paternally over the charcoal roasting while his three grandchildren and the three Ray children scampered over the lawn. It was Floyd Ray who found him dead when he brought Marquand's breakfast tray to him as usual at 8:30 A.M. and, setting it down, noticed as he went to open the curtains the unnatural stillness of the man on the bed. Ray telephoned Dr. Rogers, then Johnny, and then Marjorie Davis, who was with her family in Scituate.

Marquand's other children were in the West—Timmy with his mother in Aspen and Ferry visiting a friend in California. Ferry would remember the telephone summons from her mother and the meeting of the three of them in the airport at Phoenix, but most of all the ride east in the plane. Adelaide sat alone in the double seat across the aisle from her son and daughter with a great stack of newspapers beside her from which, as they watched, she was carefully clipping with a pair of shears one after another of the obituaries of her late ex-husband that had appeared that morning.

Notes and References

ABBREVIATIONS USED IN THE NOTES

ACS	Alexander C. Sedgwick
AHM	Adelaide Hooker Marquand
AL	Amy Loveman
AM	Alfred McIntyre
AM	*Atlantic Monthly*
AW	Alexander Williams
BB	Bernice Baumgarten
BFD	*B. F.'s Daughter*
BFH	Blanche Ferry Hooker
BFM	Blanche Ferry Marquand
BH	Boston *Herald*
BOMC	Book-of-the-Month Club
BP	Brooks Potter
BUMC	Boston University Marquand Collection
Carl B	Carl Brandt
Carol B	Carol Brandt
CMW	Christina Marquand Welch
CN	Cammann Newberry
CSM	Christina Sedgwick Marquand
CSM	*Christian Science Monitor*
EHH	Elon Huntington Hooker
EHM	Elon Huntington Marquand
EM	Elizabeth Marquand
EN	Eliot Noyes
FOK	*Four of a Kind*
GHL	George Horace Lorimer
GM	George Merck
GN	George Naylor
HE	*Haven's End*
HH	Helen Howe
HM	*Harper's Magazine*
HMP	*H. M. Pulham, Esquire*
HS	Harry Scherman
HUL	Harvard University Library
JPM	John P. Marquand
JPMj	John P. Marquand, Jr.
KR	Kenneth Roberts
LB	Little, Brown and Company
LBF	Little, Brown Files
LC	Library of Congress
LRS	Lydia Rogers Sedgwick
LGA	*The Late George Apley*
LHJ	*Ladies' Home Journal*
MD	Marjorie Davis
MFM	Margaret Fuller Marquand
MG	*Melville Goodwin, U.S.A.*
MMO	Margaret Marquand Oakman
MP	Maxwell Perkins
MW	Meredith Wood
N	*Nation*
NN	Newburyport *News*
NR	*New Republic*
NY	*New Yorker*
NYHT	New York *Herald Tribune*
NYT	New York *Times*
NYTBR	*New York Times Book Review*
NYWT	New York *World Telegram*
PM	Philip Marquand
PNR	*Point of No Return*
RB	Roger Burlingame
RBH	Robert Beverly Hale
RIH	*Repent in Haste*
RS	Roger Scaife
SCM	Susan Coward Marquand
SEP	*Saturday Evening Post*
SLT	*So Little Time*
SM	*Scribner's Magazine*

SR	*Saturday Review*
SRL	*Saturday Review of Literature*
SS	Alexander C. Sedgwick, Jr.
SWW	*Sincerely, Willis Wayde*
TBC	*The Black Cargo*
TC	Thomas Costain
TDR	*Timothy Dexter Revisited*
TFM	Timothy Fuller Marquand
TNC	Tuesday Night Club
TSH	Thomas Shaw Hale
TY	*Thirty Years*
UG	*The Unspeakable Gentleman*
WES	William Ellery Sedgwick
WH	*Warning Hill*
WP	*Wickford Point*
WTH	*Women and Thomas Harrow*
YUL	Yale University Library

PROFILES OF JPM

Butterfield	Roger Butterfield, "John P. Marquand: Novelist of Manners Would Make a Wonderful Character in One of His Own Books," *Life*, 7/31/44, pp. 65–73.
Hamburger	Philip Hamburger, *J. P. Marquand, Esquire: A Portrait in the Form of a Novel* (Boston: Houghton Mifflin, 1952).
Time Profile	"Spruce Street Boy," *Time*, 3/7/49, pp. 104–113.

MARQUAND'S LETTERS

The largest mass of Marquand letters is in the Boston University Marquand Collection and the Harvard University Library, the former containing family and personal correspondence, the latter his professional correspondence. Other letters are in the Yale University Library, the Library of Congress, the Scribner Archives at Princeton University and the Historical Society of Pennsylvania. Still others are in private collections.

1. CURZON'S MILL

A thirty-one-page typescript memoir describing Curzon's Mill and JPM's ancestry and childhood, meant to accompany a box of family papers left to the Harvard Library and written by JPM in the year before his death, was an important source of descriptive details for this chapter and is directly quoted from. In addition, important sources were his published essay "A Hearsay History of Curzon's Mill" (*AM* 11/57) and the typescript of a paper upon which it was based that was written twenty years earlier for delivery to the Newburyport Historical Society (YUL). *TDR* also provided autobiographical reminiscences of JPM's earliest years. The Marquand-Curzon Family Papers, now in the Houghton Library at Harvard, supplied not only letters utilized in my description of JPM's Curzon ancestors but also Samuel Curzon's manuscript journals, "My Early Days" and "My First Voyage," and notes on family history by other family members. JPM's own description of Federalist Newburyport is provided in his essay "Federalist Newburyport; or Can Historical Fiction Remove a Fly from Amber?" in *TY*, pp. 28–40. His history of the Newburyport eccentric was supplemented by that of Samuel L. Knapp, *Life of Lord Timothy Dexter; with Sketches of Eccentric Characters that Composed his Associates: Including his Own Writings, Dexter's Pickles for the Knowing Ones, etc., etc.* (Boston: J. E. Tilton, 1958). Other printed sources included *The History of Newbury, 1764–1909* by John J. Currier (Salem: Essex Institute, 1906–1909); *The Curzon Family of New York and Baltimore and Their English Descent* by J. Hall Pleasants (Baltimore, 1919); and the same author's *The Curzon Family* (Roland Park, Md., 1919); a letter from Pleasants to JPM (9/8/50) added details. For general and particular impressions of JPM's Newburyport background I am, as well, indebted to the opportunities for direct observation provided by visits to Curzon's Mill made possible by JPM's eldest son and daughter, JPMj and CMW, who showed me the old house and the memorabilia and furnishings, including portraits, still contained in it. JPM's novel, *WP*, also provided a suggestive and only slightly disguised description of Curzon's Mill.

PAGE

3 "Sometimes when I": "Hearsay History," p. 91.

6 "I think they were": JPM/Carl B, 1/23/40, a letter in which JPM proposed to write an essay about Knight for the *Reader's Digest*, although, he said, "I may have difficulty in explaining why he is so unforgettable"; the essay was not written.

6 "I have been impressed": "A Hearsay History," p. 88.

8 The secret marriage: JPM/Keyes D. Metcalf, 11/7/49.

10 "seen all together": *TDR*, p. 41.

10 "I have been to all": *TDR*, pp. 39-40.

11 "Still, still": Samuel Curzon/Margaret Searle Curzon, 1/23/1834.

11 "In all forms": Margaret Searle Curzon/Frances Searle, 3/14/1821.

11 "such energy": Margaret Searle Curzon/Catherine Norton, 4/18/1838.

11 "I have been": Margaret Searle Curzon/Mary Russell Curzon, n.d.

12 "floating lazily": J. G. Whittier/Celia Thaxter, 8/8/1867, quoted in Samuel T. Pickard, *Life and Letters of John Greenleaf Whittier* (Boston: Houghton Mifflin, 1894), II: 526.

12 "sprites of the river": "To ———: Lines Written After a Summer's Day Excursion," *Collected Works of J. G. Whittier* (Boston, 1948), p. 188.

12 ". . . maidens in the far off": quoted in "A Hearsay History," p. 88.

14 The red waistcoat: *TDR*, p. 88; JPM/Hon. Hilary A. Marquand, 8/12/54.

15 "There are two versions": *TDR*, p. 90.

15 "The speech": *TDR*, pp. 90-91.

16 JPM and Newburyport: in 1943 JPM considered doing a history of the Merrimack and its region for a Rivers of America series (JPM/Hervey Allen, 11/16/43).

17 Joseph Marquand's resignation from his congregation was related by JPM at the annual "Ancestor's Day" service of the Newburyport Unitarian Church in 1938 (*NN*, 6/27/38).

22 "to set foot": JPM/Warren Lynch, 10/28/58.

2. *FATHERS*

Among other sources supplying biographical facts about PM were the twenty-fifth *Annual Report* of the Harvard Class of 1889 and materials in the Harvard and MIT alumni archives. JPM's own recollections of his father and grandfather as well as other early memories were set down in the unpublished Curzon's Mill memoir, again an important source. Genealogical information concerning the Fullers was made available to me by the New England Genealogical Society of Boston; genealogy and other information about the Reeves family was supplied by Mrs. Helen Emery, research director of the Wayland Historical Society and Mrs. Eleanor C. Benjamin of the Wayland Free Library, Wayland, Mass., who also excerpted from the *Annals of Sudbury, Wayland and Maynard* a biographical summary of Richard F. Fuller and from the *Old Houses Under New Roofs* by Joseph Stowe Seabury a description of the Reeves Tavern. William Henry Moss, reference librarian of the Concord Public Library, located for me the Marquands' Concord address in local directories. In addition to description in the unpublished Curzon's Mill memoir of JPM's early years in Rye, his recollections of early school experience in both Rye and New York appear in his talk to the Lawrenceville School delivered in 1938, "Dear Old Golden Rule Days," the typescript of which is in YUL. JPM's Rye diary of 1906, now in BUMC, was shown me by his daughter, BFM. A number of details about his Concord and Rye years were supplied by JPM in interviews for the *NY* and *Life* profiles by Philip Hamburger and Roger Butterfield respectively. Descriptions of Heathcote Hall, now the Halcyon Rest Nursing Home, were given me by Richard E. Gavitt of the Rye Historical Society and Mrs. Hugh D. McKay, and other help regarding JPM in Rye, by Edith Zoe Wright, Rev. Wendell Phillips, Edmund J. Winsloe, William J. O'Shea, Robert J. Lane, Frank Parker, Mary D. Lyons, Karen Uhl and Horace Hotchkiss. Reference to the locale of the Marquand house and Heathcote Hall was found in *Fifty Years of Rye, 1905-1954* by Marcia Dolphin (Chronicle Press, 1955) and *A History of the Rye Presbyterian Church* by Ellen Cotton McKay (Rye Presbyterian Church, 1957). The history of PM's job hunting in California and subsequent employment in Panama was extracted from letters to JPM in BUMC. Information about the Marquand family in Wilmington was obtained from Mrs. Anna Cox, granddaughter of William Sellers, and Mrs. Adeline Strange, in personal interviews.

PAGE

23 "Tell old Phil": JPM Senior/MFM, 1/22/1900.

23 Letters from Russell Marquand are in BUMC.

24 PM's cups for the Featherweight Sparring Prize (as well as for the Freshman Mile) from Harvard and the Boston Athletic Association, and MIT Athletic Association Sparring Prizes are in the possession of JPMj.

24 JPM as his grandfather's namesake: although her sister-in-law, Laura Marquand Walker, had named her son John Marquand, JPM's mother would say that this did not count, "and besides, she always said, my grandfather hated it when he began to be called Marq, a disrespectful use of the family name" (Curzon's Mill memoir).

27 "took credit to herself": Julian Hawthorne, *Nathaniel Hawthorne and His Wife* (Boston: Houghton Mifflin, 1884), I: 261.

27 "I have often heard": JPM/Louise Hall Tharp, 5/13/53. Despite JPM's criticism of Margaret Fuller, he considered doing a biography of her (JPM/AM, 1/17/38) and even suggested that her life—he called it "a dramatic and particularly American career"—would make a good movie (JPM/King Vidor, 2/1/42).

28 "In my opinion": JPM/Townsend Scudder III, 6/10/40. A copy of *Recollections of Richard F. Fuller* (Boston, 1936) is in HUL.

30 "As time goes on": JPM/Robert L. Duane, 6/21/52; Robert L. Duane/JPM, 6/2/52.

34 "He was afraid": *PNR*, p. 360.

34 "Most of his life": *PNR*, p. 375.

34 "Is there ever": *WH*, p. 86.

35 JPM at the fire: Mary C. Westervelt/JPM, 10/4/54; JPM/Mary C. Westervelt, 10/22/54.

36 "just as I": JPM's 1906 diary.

37 JPM also described his Rye football opponents as "horrid little muckers who came from a school in Harrison, New York, and who did not understand the rules of sportsmanship and gentility" (JPM/JPMj, 10/6/36).

39 "I blew it in": Hamburger, p. 37.

39 "had no sympathy": *WH*, p. 63.

40 "Everyone knew": *PNR*, p. 169.

40 "You want to": *PNR*, p. 220.

3. NEWBURYPORT

JPM's Newburyport school days are recalled by a contemporary, Josephine Little Driver, in "The Young John Marquand," *AM*, 8/65, pp. 69-72; Mrs. Driver supplemented this account in a personal interview. Other interviews of importance were those with Mrs. Eleanor Little Baker, Marquand's only surviving high school teacher; with two of his classmates, Mrs. James Longstreet, the former Lillian Simpson, and Miss Amelia W. Little, whose copy of the Newburyport High School *Record* contained the class prophecy of Gladys Whitson and Lillian Simpson's class ode; and with Mrs. Morton Prince. Lispenard Phister and William L. Plante, Jr., editor of the Newburyport *Daily News*, furnished me with useful insights into the Newburyport of JPM's boyhood. *Yankee City*, the sociological study by W. Lloyd Warner (New Haven: Yale University Press, 1963), provided analysis of the demographic shifts in Newburyport. JPM's own recollections of this period were gathered from *TDR* as well as from comments in his "Good Old Golden Rule Days" talk to the Newburyport High School graduating class of 1944 (*NN*, 6/20/44) and to the high school's Honor Banquet in 1960 (*NN*, 5/18/60). Elliot Knight and John P. Pramberg gave me information concerning the Wheelwright Fund, and Donald J. Zabriskie, principal of the Newburyport High School, supplied JPM's high school record. His grades on the Harvard entrance examinations were obtained from the Harvard University registrar.

PAGE

43 JPM's reception for his high school class reunion (6/21/60): Eighteen guests, along with Eleanor Little Baker, "our beloved English teacher," are listed on the printed program provided by the host. JPM entertained with a recitation of "Casey at the Bat," and spoke of his travels, which he deprecated in comparison with the advantages of those who had not strayed from Newburyport. He was elected president of the class (letter by Sarah Ilsley Jaques, class secretary [*NN*, 7/19/60]); the *Heathcote* masthead for 2/09 shows John P. Marquand, '11, as assistant editor, but the "graduation number" of the Newburyport High School *Record* (6/10) does not include him among its editors or contributors.

46 "built in the days": *SLT*, p. 170.

48 "It isn't as though": *WTH*, p. 27.

48 "It's an old town": *TDR*, p. 119.

50 "The barn in back": *TDR*, pp. 245–248.

52 "The old buildings": *TDR*, pp. 122–124.

52 "Bossy" Gillis: When Gillis was elected mayor JPM wrote an article of humorous appreciation in which he cited the chamber-pot incident and remarked, "It almost seems as though another Timothy Dexter had arrived in Newburyport" (Boston *Evening Transcript*, 12/10/27).

54 The graduation: *SLT*, pp. 164–168.

4. HARVARD

The Harvard of JPM's time is completely documented in the university archives and Alumni Records Office, where I was able to obtain the particulars about entrance requirements, curriculum, faculty and other matters, and also to examine the files of the *Harvard Lampoon*. JPM's undergraduate record was made available to me by the registrar. Among many descriptions in print of undergraduate life at Harvard before the First World War, the most useful was the collection of reminiscences titled *College in a Yard*, edited by Brooks Atkinson (Cambridge, Mass.: Harvard University Press, 1957), which includes, along with other contributions, JPM's essay "New Bottle: Old Wine." Reminiscences of JPM at Harvard were supplied by contemporaries—Samuel T. Williamson (*NYTBR*, 10/12/52), Roger Burlingame (*Vogue*, 2/15/44), Edward Streeter (personal interview). For the accounts of the careers of JPM's classmates and other college friends the published class reports were useful, particularly the *25th Anniversary Report of 1915* (Cambridge, Mass., 1940). Robert Benchley's experiences at Harvard are related in *Robert Benchley: A Biography* by Nathaniel Benchley (New York: McGraw-Hill, 1955) and those of E. E. Cummings in *The Magic-Maker: E. E. Cummings* by Charles Norman (New York: Duell, Sloan & Pearce, 1958); those of John Dos Passos in *The Best Times: An Informal Memoir* (New York: New American Library, 1966); those of Roger Burlingame in his autobiographical *I Have Known Many Worlds* (New York: Doubleday, 1959); those of James B. Conant in *My Several Lives* (New York: Harper & Row, 1970). JPM's own recollections appear in, among other sources, his own class reports; the commencement speech he delivered when he received the honorary LL.D. on June 11, 1953, and his address to the Associated Harvard Clubs in Philadelphia in 1948 (both reprinted in *TY*, pp. 72-76, 41-46, the latter titled "The Social Function of the Harvard Man in the Free World of Tomorrow"); his speech to the thirty-fifth annual dinner of the class of 1915, 6/20/53, and the 1938 "Dear Old Golden Rule Days" (both typescripts in YUL). His freshman themes and other college papers, which were retained by him until his death, and his college letters to and from his parents are in BUMC. Imaginative recounting of his college scene and experience was available, also, in his short stories and novels, particularly *LGA*, *WP*, *HMP*, and *SLT*.

PAGE

58 "At five-thirty": RB, *I Have Known Many Worlds*, pp. 59-60.

58–59 JPM's commencement speech: *TY*, pp. 72–75.

60 "You and I": *WP*, p. 190.

60 The white tie: "I never tie a white tie without thinking of you and the time at 5 Linden Street when you came in to get me to do the job of necktie tying for you" (James B. Conant/JPM, 11/13/39).
60 "I do not think": *College in a Yard*, p. 176.
61 "showers on the third floor": *College in a Yard*, p. 73.
61 JPM's living arrangements: "It used to be called Mooney's Pleasure Palace in those days, an ironical term, because its facilities for pleasure were as limited as its central heating and its plumbing," JPM wrote when his name was used in an advertisement in the *Harvard Crimson* of the still-existing boardinghouse in 1952 (JPM/Carl B, 10/6/52; he also described it to Butterfield and Hamburger and in the *Time* profile; JPM's lease of a room at 5-7 Linden Street from Mary E. Mooney for the period 9/20/12 to 6/20/13 is in BUMC.
61 Wheelwright Scholarship: Lawrence B. Cushing/JPM, 9/14/11.
62 "It was a noisy place": S. T. Williamson.
62 "he was part": *SLT*, p. 175.
62 Edward William Mahan, class of 1916, was the unnamed fellow student in Hamburger's printed version of the wartime reencounter, but JPM had written before publication, "I'd rather you didn't use his name. Actually he did nod to me frequently in college and even called me by my first name. We took Geology I together and I feel I was of some help to him on occasion. As a matter of fact, I have always liked Eddie. He is one of my favorite football heroes, and so I hope you will say he nodded to me, though the rest of the story is essentially correct" (typescript, "Notes on New Yorker Profile," HUL).
62 "those early snubs": *Time* profile, p. 106.
63 "Those who": *SLT*, p. 176.
63 "When I finally": "Good Old Golden Rule Days."
64 "The Cinderella Motif," *SEP*, 3/5/27, pp. 5-7.
64 "the best story": TC/JPM, 1/14/27.
64 "The Harvard Square Student," *SEP*, 12/10/27, pp. 8-9.
65 "strange, earnest": *Vogue*, 2/15/44, p. 110.
65 "Harry was generally": *WP*, p. 204.
66 "He would make": *Vogue*, p. 110.
66 JPM's version of his *Lampoon* initiation was offered at the 1953 class dinner and is also recorded in Hamburger, but Otis's differing account was presented in a letter to the *Lampoon* (9/24/66), which was printed in *The Harvard Lampoon Centennial Celebration, 1876-1973* (Boston: Atlantic-Little, Brown, 1973, p. 153) and elaborated to me in a letter (12/31/71).
67 JPM's *Lampoon* contributions: "Lampy's Key to the Boston Elevated's Transfer Rules," 6/17/12, p. 370; "The Horror of the Infinite," 11/9/12, p. 138; "Fuzzy Wuzzy" (with RB), 11/21/12, p. 186; "How They Run the Paper, or Our Contemporary's Daily Notice," 12/14/12, p. 232; "The Rules of the Game, or A Dead Loss," 12/14/12, p. 239; "College Animals No. 5 (the Mouse)," 12/20/12, p. 279; "Gentle Jerry, or the Bung-seller's Christmas-Eve," 12/20/12, p. 280; "How Willie's Argument Came Back," 12/20/12, p. 284; "Breaking the Noonday Fast at Memorial," 1/22/13, p. 322; "Lampy's Subway Guide," 1/22/13, p. 322; "The Millennium or a Perfect Solution of the Eating Question," 3/8/13, p. 326; "Our Reading Notices," 3/8/13, p. 402; "Harvard University in Case of Fire in the Yard," 3/8/13, p. 404; "The Millennium No. 2, or the Automatic Dean," 3/14/13, p. 22; "On Board USS Lilypad," 3/14/13, n.p.; "What Our Catalogue Might Have Been, or a Prospectus for Some Universities," 3/27/13, p. 98; editorial (with George Merck), 4/3/13; "Radcliffe Wins Again, or the Prize Play at the Bijou Dream," 4/3/13, p. 134; editorial (with GM), 4/11/13, pp. 168-169; "Fun with the Microscope" (with GM), 4/11/13, p. 170.
68 "We were one": Dos Passos, *The Best Times*, p. 24.
68 Cummings's commencement talk was published in the *Harvard Advocate*, 6/15.
69 "an almost unspeakable": RB, *I Have Known Many Worlds*, pp. 55-56.
69 "He had an old-fashioned": *College in a Yard*, p. 65.
69 "It meant more to me": JPM/Ralph Mannis, n.d.

70 "You may not know": JPM/Homer T. Woodbridge, 12/22/49.
70 The "perfect squelch" anecdote was confirmed by Woodbridge (Ashley Halsey, Jr./JPM, 3/25/57) and by JPM (JPM/Ashley Halsey, 4/1/57).
71 "Now John": PM/JPM, n.d.
72 "If I got": PM/JPM, 12/3/11 and 12/20/11.
72 "I have never done": MFM/JPM, Nov. 1911.
72 "I know that": MFM/JPM, 12/8/11.
73 "Don't you think": MFM/JPM, 12/8/11.
73 "Your mother": PM/JPM, n.d.
73 The parental reproaches: MFM/JPM, 2/27/12; PM/JPM, 2/11/12; MFM/JPM, 4/2/12; PM/JPM, 3/13/12; PM/JPM, 3/24/12; PM/JPM, 4/2/12.
74 "Wickford Point": JPM/John P. Reinhard, 12/24/42.
74 "I do agree": JPM/JPMj, 10/11/45.
74 "You must not really": JPM/Conant, 12/18/53.
75 "Seeing that Yale": JPM/James T. Babb, 7/3/51.

5. *THE TRANSCRIPT*

General description of the Boston *Evening Transcript* in the pre-World War I period is contained in *The Boston Transcript: A History of Its First Hundred Years* (Boston: Houghton Mifflin, 1930) by Joseph Edgar Chamberlin and in the memoirs of Charles W. Morton, *It Has Its Charms* (Philadelphia: Lippincott, 1967). Personal recollections were given me by former Transcripter Karl Schriftgiesser. Clippings of JPM's *Transcript* stories are in the BUMC. Constance M. Fiske's "Battery A at the Border" (*Yankee*, 6/68, pp. 85, 162-167), gave an account of the service to which JPM was called up in 1917. *SLT* provided JPM's fictional version of his *Transcript* period.

PAGE

76 "I was obliged": JPM/Sgt. W. J. Briggs, 4/16/45.
76 "had known": *PNR*, p. 325.
76 "I still always": JPM/Sgt. W. J. Briggs, 4/16/45.
76-77 The *Transcript* staff: Karl Schriftgiesser observes: "Henry Cabot Lodge was recalled as one of the few Cold Roast Bostonians ever to be on the *Transcript*'s far from patrician staff. The *Transcript* was the bible of the Brahmins and reported their doings with reverence and even awe—but except for the proprietor, George Snell Mandell, hardly any of its staff were Brahmins—or even Harvard men" (letter to me, 5/17/71).
77 "Indeed it was": JPM/Sgt. W. J. Briggs, 4/16/45.
77 Description of Kline: JPM/H. Addington Bruce, 2/9/39, and Butterfield, p. 69.
77 JPM's collaboration with Macdonald was recounted by Robert van Gelder ("Marquand Unburdens Himself," *NYTBR*, 4/7/40) and also recalled by Karl Schriftgiesser. No trace of the MS survives among JPM's papers.
78 "The career": JPM/Ralph Block, 4/5/55.
78-79 *Transcript* recollections: JPM/H. Addington Bruce, 2/9/39.
79 The Jenks anecdote: *SLT*, p. 17.
79-80 Description of H. T. Parker and of JPM as school and college editor: Hamburger, p. 55.
81 A copy of *Prince and Boatswain* (Greenfield, Mass.: E. A. Hall, 1915) is in HUL; JPM described Clark to Dorothy Canfield Fisher (6/5/53).
81 "When I tell you": C. E. Clark/J. M. Morgan, 5/5/15 (letter printed in *Prince and Boatswain*).
81 "written at the insistence": JPM/Lowell Brentano, 7/9/43; the MS of the novel is in HUL.
82 "I don't know": Butterfield, p. 69.
82 "I can even": JPM/H. Addington Bruce, 2/9/39.
82 "Jeffrey could hear": *SLT*, p. 196.

84 The special article: "Tenting Tonight with the Boys of Battery A," Boston *Evening Transcript*, 7/8/16.
84 "For in those serried ranks": "When the Rio Grande's a Joke," Boston *Evening Transcript*, 9/9/17.
85 The back-pay incident: JPM/Charles A. Colton, 3/12/52.
85 "I can still": JPM/H. Addington Bruce, 2/9/39.
86 JPM's enlistment: JPM/Charles A. Colton, 3/12/52.
86 "In the afternoon": *SLT*, pp. 202-204.

6. WAR

General histories of the American army in the First World War enabled me to follow JPM's career from Plattsburg to the First Army Headquarters at Fort Greene and overseas to the Western Front, fitting his accounts to the locations and action of the military units to which he was attached. These sources included the publications of the American Battle Monuments Commission (Washington, D.C.: U.S. Government Printing Office): *American Armies and Battlefields in Europe: Guide and Reference Book* (1938); *4th Division: Summary of Operations in the World War* (1944); *77th Division: Summary of Operations in the World War* (1944), which provided detailed chronology and maps. Also useful were Maj. Frederick Palmer's *America in France* (New York: Dodd, Mead, 1918); Frederic L. Paxson's *America at War: 1917-1918* (New York: Cooper Square Publishers, 1966); Robert Alexander's *Memories of the World War, 1917-1918* (New York: Macmillan, 1931). JPM recalled Fort Devens in his address to the Lawrenceville School (3/16/43), which was published as "Time Is Like a Fashionable Host" in *Return to Freedom: The Affairs of Our Time and Their Impact Upon Youth*, edited by Thomas H. Johnson (New York: Putnam, 1944). He set down an account of his service in the Fourth Field Artillery Brigade Headquarters in France, including his short career as an intelligence officer, in a paper, "Military Intelligence," written for TNC in 1947 but never delivered (the typescript is in YUL). I have also drawn occasionally upon his own war description in *WP*, *HMP*, and *SLT* for aid in re-creating scenes that were recalled from life.

PAGE
88 "They tried to give": *SLT*, p. 231.
88 The Scott Mattaye stories: In 1931 the *SEP* printed six of them: "Solid South," "Jine the Cavalry," "Jack Still," "Far Away," "High Tide," "Dispatch Box No. 3."
90 The Second Field Artillery: JPM/EM, 6/24/18.
90 "First we were": *WP*, p. 242.
90 The photograph of JPM in uniform is in BUMC.
90 Camp Devens recalled: *Return to Freedom*, p. 124.
90 "I could smell": JPM/JPMj, 3/5/43.
91 "I am very glad": JPM/JPMj, 3/20/43.
92 Embarkation: postcard JPM/MFM and PM, 5/10/18.
92 Transport details: JPM/EM, n.d.
93 Gen. Babbitt: JPM/EM, n.d.
93 Bordeaux: JPM/PM, 7/4/18.
93 The police dog: JPM/PM, 7/4/18.
94 "It rather puts me": JPM/PM, 7/22/18.
94 The French instructor: Hamburger, pp. 58-59.
94 JPM into action: JPM/MFM, 6/22/18.
94 "'What big men'": JPM/PM, 7/4/18.
94 "The rest of us": JPM's "Military Intelligence."
95 "I am now": JPM/PM, 8/6/18.
95 "It seems funny": JPM/"cousin Elizabeth," 8/9/18.
95 "The country around": JPM/PM, 8/26/18.
95 "They were near": *SLT*, pp. 233-234.
96-110 JPM as intelligence officer: JPM's "Military Intelligence."

98 "I am now serving": JPM/PM, n.d.
98 "most of them": *HMP*, p. 122.
98 JPM as information officer: JPM/MFM, 9/6/18, 9/19/18.
99 In the Meuse-Argonne sector: JPM/MFM, 10/15/18.
99 "For the past month": JPM/PM, 11/11/18.
99 "Shells of various": "Looking Towards the New Grand Army of the Republic," New York *Tribune*, 3/16/19.
99 "I've been machine-gunned": JPM/PM, 11/2/18.
100 "If you only knew": JPM/MFM, 10/15/18.
100 Plummer's brief biography appears in the *25th Anniversary Report of the Class of 1914* (Cambridge, Mass., 1939).
100 "Somehow news": JPM/JPMj, 10/11/45.
100 "When I struck": JPM/PM, 11/2/18.
101 JPM's war experiences in retrospect: Butterfield, p. 69; *Time* profile, p. 106.
101 "he had no big memories": Hamburger, p. 59.
101 "He learned that": "Looking Towards the New Grand Army of the Republic," New York *Tribune*, 3/16/19.

7. *AFTER THE WAR WAS OVER*

There are many studies of the collegiate literary generation whose disillusion and intellectual rebellion, break with traditional behavior and voluntary exile were shared by a few famous and many obscure young men who had experienced the European war. What has not been sufficiently documented is the story of their more conforming companions among the same class who stayed at home after the war was over and chose to flourish as wits rather than struggle as rebels. They put their abilities to work, frequently at the newly booming trades of advertising and journalism, or in the writing of "stuff that will sell" in the market for magazine fiction, which promised golden rewards in the twenties. JPM's rise in this period is a part of this other generational history. In an interview, Edward Streeter gave me perspective on the general experience. The career-stories of Burlingame and Benchley were extracted from sources already cited. Accounts written by these men, as well as autobiographical statements by Paul Hollister, Richard Connell, Frederick Lewis Allen and others, were available to me in their Harvard class reports and other materials in the Harvard archives. The postgraduate histories of Dos Passos and Cummings are continued from sources listed for Chapter 6. For New York newspaper history, especially that of the *Tribune*, I referred to *Park Row* by Allen Churchill (New York: Rinehart, 1958). Clippings of JPM's own *Tribune* stories are in the BUMC. The Algonquin circle has been recently described in Scott Meredith's *George S. Kaufman and His Friends* (New York: Doubleday, 1974) and James R. Gaines's *Wit's End: Days and Nights of the Algonquin Round Table* (New York: Harcourt, Brace, Jovanovich, 1977). The Hale household in 1919 was recalled for me by Robert Beverly Hale, Thomas Shaw Hale and Albert Hubbell in interviews. The genesis of *UG* and the well-known story of its lost manuscript as well as other details of JPM's life up to 1922 are contained in an autobiographical summary written for publicity purposes at RB's request; the typescript is in the Scribner Archives at Princeton University together with letters from JPM and those written to him by RB and MP. John W. Tebbel, in *George Horace Lorimer and the Saturday Evening Post* (New York: Doubleday, 1948), usefully summarized the history of the magazine and provided details concerning JPM. JPM commented at length on the charge of "literary split personality" in his speech before the Columbia University Club (3/17/41); the typescript is in YUL.

PAGE

102 The homecoming: *MG*, p. 296.
102 "I was full of beans": *Time* profile, p. 106.
103 JPM's start as a writer: "I don't know when I started to write, but I began in earnest when it seemed to be the best means I could think of to be in business by myself" (JPM/Charles Lee of the Boston *Herald*, 4/3/39).
103 "Well, I'm out": JPM/EM, 1/2/19.

104 "Now I am back": *Harvard College, Class of 1913, Third Report*, June 1920, p. 57.
106 Lewis and Fitzgerald: When Lewis read and praised *HMP* in 1941, as well as the earlier *LGA* and *WP*, JPM wrote, "I don't know anything which has given me more pleasure than your note. This is particularly so since nearly everything I know about writing I have learned from you" (4/17/41). Of Fitzgerald's novel he would write: "*This Side of Paradise* was written by a great writer, the most naturally gifted and the most sensitive of any of his generation" (*SRL*, 8/6/49, p. 30), and added to Gregory Mason that Fitzgerald had "much more sympathy, insight and maturity than Hemingway will ever possess" (8/24/49).
107 "With the exception": JPM/Beatrice Kaufman, 8/9/44.
108 The Whistler painting, an uncompleted portrait painted over another one of someone else, is in the Hunterian Art Gallery of the University of Glasgow.
109 "Dudley Hale is today": JPM/Samuel Otis, n.d.
109 "Why should anyone": *WP*, p. 275.
109 "with that intangible": "Golden Lads," *SEP*, 2/14/31, p. 8.
109 Life at Aunt Greta's: JPM/EM, 1/2/19.
110 "Strange, that all": "The Subway as a Seat of Philosophy," N.Y. *Tribune* (undated clipping, BUMC).
110 Kline's firing: W. A. Swanberg, *Dreiser* (New York: Scribner's, 1965), p. 236.
111 JPM-Wortman collaboration: "I have often thought that this experience may have started your mind working on Mopey Dick and the Duke" (JPM/Denys Wortman, 5/12/53).
111 "a gentle idealist": JPM/Wade Fairchild, 8/5/51.
111 JPM's feature stories in the *Tribune*: "Blakelock Thinks He's World's Richest Man"; "William Waldorf Astor Lives in Retirement in England"; "Looking Towards the New Grand Army of the Republic"; "Was, Is, and Always Will Be—Greatest on Earth" (undated clippings, BUMC).
111 Mrs. Ogden Reid: "My services could not have been conspicuous, because Mrs. Ogden Reid told me last year that she couldn' remember my being around the place at all" (*25th Anniversary Report*).
112 "When I saw men": quoted in C. M. Fiske, *SRL*, 12/10/38, p. 11.
112 "a sequence of qualifications": *25th Anniversary Report*.
112 "The man for whom": *HMP*, pp. 126-127.
112 Hollister's recollections were communicated to JPMj, 8/1/60.
112-113 JPM at J. Walter Thompson: Butterfield, 69-70; *Time* profile, p. 106.
113 Dudley Hale: JPM/Samuel Otis, n.d.
114 "Eight Million Bubbles": *SEP*, 1/28/22.
114 "Son of a Sloganeer": in *Apes and Angels* (New York: Minton, Balch, 1924); praised by JPM in *25th Anniversary Report*.
114 "I promise you": RB, *Vogue*, 2/15/44.
114 "You Too Can Dream": *You Too* (New York: Scribner's, 1924), p. 7.
115 *HMP*, pp. 130-149 passim.
116 Thompson agency and customer survey: letter to me from Margaret King Eddy, 2/19/72.
117 The anecdote about "The Right That Failed" was related to me by Robert Hale.
117 "The Right That Failed," *SEP*, 7/23/21.
117 "knew practically nothing": in the typescript version of the Introduction to *TY* (YUL), the wording is "knew absolutely nothing."
117 "The houses were": *The Unspeakable Gentleman* (New York: Scribner's, 1922), p. 15.
118 JPM's savings: JPM/Sgt. W. J. Briggs, 4/16/45.
118 Writing at the Mill: Butterfield, p. 70; Frank Woolman/JPM, 10/31/54: "It seems only the day before yesterday when I discovered you with pencil and paper in the mill loft! No one else seemed in sympathy with your efforts. I asked, 'Where's John?' 'Oh, he's in the mill loft—thinks he can write!'"
118 "to prove everybody": quoted in Tebbel, p. 229.
119 "It so happens": JPM/RB, 2/19/21.
119 "I have never": *Time* profile, p. 108.
119 Date of loss of MS: Fiske, *SRL*, 12/10/38, p. 11.

120 JPM's third story: Tebbel, p. 98.
120 "tried to sew me up": JPM/Sgt. Briggs, 4/16/45.
121 "For many years": JPM/Sgt. Briggs, 4/16/45.
122 "The Saturday Evening Post": Stolberg, quoted in Tebbel, pp. 41-42.
123 "It would be": JPM/Carl B, 4/3/39.
123 "I share": JPM/Mrs. Marjorie Stoneman Douglas, 4/10/39.
123-124 "That enthusiasm": *WP*, pp. 229-232.
124 "I have prostituted": JPM/RB, 3/22/21.
124 The Scribner offer: RB/JPM, 3/31/21.
124 "We think it": RB/Carl B, 4/1/21.
124 "Critics say": RB/Carl B, 4/1/21.
124 "This sort of romance": RB/JPM, 4/2/21.
125 Printers' strike: Carl B/MP, 7/13/21.
125 "You are going": RB/JPM, 4/7/21.
125 "I was Lord Byron": *Time* profile, p. 108.

8. THE CINDERELLA MOTIF

Descriptions of the young Christina Sedgwick and her family were provided by a number of persons I interviewed—particularly SS, Mrs. Ellery Sedgwick, Ewen MacVeagh, Mrs. Morton Prince, Mrs. Lydia Bond Powel, Mrs. Warwick Potter. SS also lent me a manuscript of personal reminiscences describing his parents, his sister's upbringing, and the events leading to her engagement. For her later appearance as JPM's wife and for the anecdotes he told about her, numerous witnesses besides these have confirmed the details utilized here and in subsequent chapters. During a visit to Stockbridge I was shown the Sedgwick Mansion, burial plot and other family scenes by the late Gabriella Sedgwick and I interviewed Sedgwick family friends, notably Mrs. Margaret French Cresson and Miss Alice Riggs. Sedgwick family history and its part in the history of Stockbridge were found in *Stockbridge 1739-1939: A Chronicle* by Sarah Cabot Sedgwick and Christina Sedgwick (Great Barrington, Mass.: privately printed, 1939); in *Berkshire County* by Richard D. Birdsall (New Haven: Yale University Press, 1939); and in "The Sedgwicks of Berkshire" by H. D. Sedgwick in *Collection of the Berkshire Historical and Scientific Society* (Pittsfield, Mass., 1900), pp. 89-106. Insights were also gathered from talks with Prof. David Hall of Boston University, who let me see his Harvard undergraduate thesis on Catherine Sedgwick. Mrs. Harold Pierce, Jr., of the Stockbridge Public Library was helpful in locating clippings from local newspapers about the Sedgwick family. She also unearthed a typescript copy of a speech by ACS, "The History and Traditions of Stockbridge," and supplied me with a copy of *A Sedgwick Genealogy: Descendants of Deacon Benjamin Sedgwick*, compiled by Hubert M. Sedgwick (New Haven, 1961). Information about Nathalie Sedgwick Colby was drawn from her *Remembering* (Boston: Little, Brown, 1938) and from interviews with SS and Mrs. Ellery Sedgwick. Sedgwick family letters in the BUMC supplied details of Christina's early years. Many of these are undated.

PAGE

127 "rudely had the rug": Hamburger, p. 40.
129 Sedgwick graves: Prof. Hellmut Wohl of Boston University counted them for me in 1977.
129 Description of ACS: JPM/JPMj, 5/20/58.
130 "a feudal state": LRS/CSM, 7/4/29. JPM was thinking of the Davenports when he wrote Dorothy Canfield Fisher of "upstate New York families who still have a brand of arrogance which is different from the more democratic attitudes of our Saltonstalls, Cabots and Lowells" (6/5/53).
130 LRS's effect on her sons: she was not unaware of it. She would write CSM, "I guess John is right about the greater importance of a father's influence than a mother's and I begin to feel that it was my domination—your father notwithstanding—that ruined the boys' upbringing in the sense of making them unprepared to meet life" (n.d.).
130 "He was in love": JPM/JPMj, 5/20/58.

130–131 Christina in France: interview, Mrs. Warwick Potter; CSM/LRS, 8/1/14.
131 "How I hate": CSM/LRS, n.d.
131 "I'm not very": CSM/LRS, n.d.
131 "Do not": WES/CSM, n.d.
133 "Aunt Nathalie": CSM/LRS, 10/12/18.
134 Meetings at the Harvard Club: E. C. MacVeagh/JPMj, 9/29/60.
134 "We had an awful": CSM/LRS, 8/17/20.
134 "The Tyngs were here": CSM/LRS, 8/23/20.
134 "John Marquand is": CSM/LRS, 8/26/20.
135 "His latest story": CSM/LRS, n.d.
135 "He said everything": CSM/LRS, 9/n.d./20.
135 "He is a fearfully": CSM/LRS, 11/18/20.
135 "I dropped": CSM/LRS, 8/19/21.
135 The engagement: *Remembering*, p. 228. More precisely, the consent of ACS was accompanied by some expectable tearful outbursts—he wrote his son about this impending loss of "the ornament and shining light of his soul." Ellery commented: "Poor papa! His feeling is very natural and you must be patient." As for himself, this brother had "very nearly died" at the news of her engagement (W. E. Sedgwick/CSM, 1/23/22).
136 Fitzgerald: "He told me once in Paris in 1926 that his eyes were going bad on him because he got drunk every night and then read excessively in bed while his eyes were out of focus" (JPM/Andrew Turnbull, 6/5/57).
137 The near meeting with Lewis: JPM's "I Knew Sinclair Lewis Once" (typescript, YUL).
137 The D. H. Lawrence story: Hamburger, p. 31.
137 "The Ship": RB/JPM, 1/10/22; the story was published in *SM*, 1/3/23.
137 "Once, a long time ago": Era Licari sent this account to Joseph Verner Reed in 1953 (JPM/Joseph Verner Reed, 10/23/53).
138 "It's an awfully": JPM/RB, 3/15/22.
138 "How Willie Came Across," *SEP*, 7/8/22.
139 Publication date of *UG*: RB/Carl B, 2/2/22.
139 JPM's return: JPM/RB, 3/16/22.
139 "I think": RB/H. Brown, 4/12/22.
139 "Marquand is": RB/J. Williams, 4/12/22.
139 "a troubadour": J. H. Rosegen in Philadelphia *Ledger* (clipping, BUMC).
139 "It seems a shame": RB/JPM, 5/4/22.
139 "I am gagging": JPM/RB, 5/2/22.
139 "What I'm suggesting"; JPM/MP, 5/5/22.
139 "The place": JPM/RB, 5/2/22. The Marquand house at Edge Moor is visible in photos in BUMC.
140 JPM at York Harbor: Weeks, Boston *Globe*, 7/24/60 and *AM*, 10/n.d./60; interview with Dr. Elizabeth Councilman.
140 "tweedy and affable" (JPM/Blake Nevius, 2/25/59).
140 "Naturally I am": JPM/CSM, 8/11/22.
141 The wedding: *NYT*, 9/10/22.

9. PULLED BY STRINGS

My analysis of JPM's first marriage in this and the following chapters was evolved from the study of materials of several sorts. Basic documents were letters of CSM and JPM and a manuscript notebook written by the former during her divorce (BUMC). Certain assumptions grew out of the recollections communicated to me by friends and relatives. A few days before the wedding, according to SS, she sent a letter to her fiancé breaking their engagement (it is said that Mrs. Sedgwick persuaded the Stockbridge postmistress to open the bag of outgoing mail to retrieve it). When the divorce was in progress CSM confessed in the notebook mentioned, "I suppose I never really loved his nature" and compared her failure to her mother's:

"I am surely punished for my sins—even as poor mamma was punished for hers." JPM's continued correspondence with RB and MP was located in the Princeton Scribner Archives; that with *SEP* editors GHL and TC in the Historical Society of Pennsylvania, Philadelphia.

PAGE

143 "I know I am": CSM/LRS, 9/9/22.
143 "I am very happy": CSM/LRS, 9/10/22.
143 CSM's letters: all of those written on the honeymoon (except the first) and all those written during the first months of the marriage are undated.
145 "I am sorry": JPM/GHL, 11/21/22.
145 "The Sunbeam," *SEP*, 1/20/23.
145 "I don't think": CSM/LRS, n.d.
146 "As long as": CSM/LRS, 11/1/22.
146 "One thing is": CSM/LRS, 12/18/22. Her mother had already declared her sorrow at "losing" her daughter and CSM had pathetically written, "My darling Mamma, you must not feel 'it is better to have loved and lost' because you could never lose me really, separated though we may be by time and circumstances. I love you always more than most children love their mothers—and if I seem cross at times it's because I hate to feel in any way separated from you and of course one always has to be somewhat after one is married" (12/11/22).
146 "Only a Few of Us Left," first published *SEP*, 1/14/22.
147 "Different from Other Girls," first published *LHJ*, 7/22.
147 "The Land of Bunk," *SEP*, 9/16/22.
147 "I will be through": JPM/RB, 12/16/22.
147 "badly mutilated"; JPM/RB, 1/4/23.
147 "As I read over": JPM/RD, 1/4/23.
147 "The 'reaction'": RB/JPM, 1/4/23.
148 Review of *Four of a Kind*: Boston *Evening Transcript*, 6/27/23.
148 "I am convinced": JPM/J. M. Brown, 2/14/55.
148 "In a short time": JPM/Sgt. W. J. Briggs, 4/16/45.
148 JPM's fees: his price was raised to $2,250 in 1925 (TC/JPM, 10/21/25), to $3,000 in 1929 (GHL/JPM, 7/1/29).
149 The Hearst bribe and the gold mine: "John has just got back from New York where he had a very exciting time with Hearst's agents who tried to bribe him with dazzling sums into their employ. It seems all the good Saturday Evening Post writers have gone over to Hearst. It is all quite bewildering and exciting and thank goodness John has a level head. He has bought, however, a claim on a gold mine in Alaska" (CSM/LRS, n.d.).
149 "The Big Guys," *SEP*, 2/21/25.
149 "The Old Man," *SEP*, 6/6/25.
149 "The Educated Money," *SEP*, 2/14/25; the horse-betting townsman was Josiah Hale, not a relative.
149 "The Last of the Hoopwells," *SEP*, 12/5/25.
149 "Fun and Neighbors," *SEP*, 2/20/26.
150 "The rolls-royce": LRS/CSM, 5/27/24, 6/6/24.
150 Nursemaid quarrel: LRS/CSM, 1/11/24, 3/24/24, 8/4/24.
151 "I think it is": RB/JPM, 1/24/23.
151 "I am hoping": TC/JPM, 10/30/24.
151 "My wife, poor girl": JPM/Beatrice Kaufman, 8/9/44.
151 "I was not doing": JPM/B. Kaufman, 8/9/44.
152 Movies: RB/Mr. Ritchie, 2/28/24.
152 *FOK* earnings: after six months the royalties had not met the advance of $250 (Scribner's statement to Brandt and Kirkpatrick, 10/23/23).
152 "You must not be": RB/JPM, 12/21/23.
152 "It happens that": TC/JPM, 5/22/23.
152 Perkins's critique: MP/JPM, 11/23/23.
153 "As I glanced": JPM/MP, 12/8/28.
153 "Without being": JPM/Henry Allen Moe, 6/25/47.

154 "Glad to hear": TC/JMP, 12/6/23.
154 Publication of *TBC*: RB/JPM, 7/1/24; TC/RB, 7/11/24; RBJ/JPM, 7/21/24; RB/TC, 7/14/24; Adelaide Neal/RB, 7/18/24; RB/TC, 7/18/24; A. Neal/RB, 7/21/24; RB/JPM, 7/21/24.
154 "Mr. Lorimer": Erdman N. Brandt/JPM, 3/15/24.
154 "A Friend of the Family," *SEP*, 12/13/24; TC/JPM, 10/30/24; Carl B/JPM, 10/29/24.
154 "Pozzi of Perugia," *SEP*, 11/8/24, 11/15/24, 11/22/24.
155 "low in mind": JPM/RB, 5/14/24.
155 "I thought the story": RB/JPM, 9/18/24.
155 "On the strength": GHL/JPM, 10/21/25; JPM/GHL, n.d.
155 Douglas review: *N*, 6/10/25.
155 Sales of *TBC*: RB/JPM, 9/9/25; JPM/RB, 9/11/25.
155 "'The Black Cargo'": MP/JPM, 12/14/25.
155 "dug in": JPM/MP, 12/n.d.
155 "The fact is": MP/JPM, 1/20/26.
156 "Now that Balch": JPM/RB, 5/28/25.
156 "taking it": RB/JPM, 12/21/23.
157 "We know that": RB/JPM, 6/1/25.
157 "You are in": MP/JPM, 12/14/25; JPM/MP, 12/n.d./25.
157 Silas Talbot book: MP/JPM, 10/14/26.
157 "Much as I": JPM/MP, 11/2/26.
157 "I always felt": TC/JPM, 12/13/26.
157 "The best story": TC/JPM, 1/14/27.
157 Ethan Allen book: MP/JPM, 2/3/27.
158 "My plans are": JPM/MP, 2/n.d./27.
158 "if that were one": MP/JPM, 5/13/27.
158 JPM novel for 1928: MP/JPM, 8/31/27.
158 "Though I have": JPM/MP, 9/n.d./27.
158 "by long odds": TC/JPM, 10/25/28.
158 "Alfred would go": Carl B/JPM, 11/21/28.
158 "He was deeply": BB/JPM, 12/21/28.
159 "I thought it" and "I still regret": JPM/Carl Jonas, 4/21/55.
159 "Not the longest": *10th Anniversary Report*, 1925.
159 Macdonald story: Boston *Evening Transcript*, 6/19/26.
160 Aunt Molly: CSM/LRS, 10/n.d./25.
160 "I was in love": *Cosmopolitan* interview by Robert van Gelder, 3/47, p. 150.
160 "I have been loyal": JPM/GHL, 10/24/25.
161 "half Barnum": N.Y. *World*, 10/5/25.

10. DEPRESSION DAYS

Many Marquand and Sedgwick letters used in this chapter (and the letter to Carol B quoted on pp. 173–174) are undated—though a chronology can be established—and are used without further citation below. I owe my description of the Riggs Foundation system of therapy and of Austen Riggs to *The Riggs Story: The Development of the Austen Riggs Center for the Study and Treatment of Neuroses* by Lawrence S. Kubie (New York: Paul B. Hoeber, 1960) and to conversation with Alice Riggs, who recalled both her father and CSM. The officers of the Tavern Club gave me permission to visit it and examine records, and Alexander Cabot, the manager, assisted me. Shan Sedgwick related to me the story of his 1929 marriage.

PAGE

162 Plans for the trip to France: RB, *I Have Known Many Worlds.*
163 "It would be an education": ACS/CSM, 1/10/26.
163 "John and I": CSM/LRS, 7/6/26.
164 "The country is": CSM/LRS, 7/17/26.
165 "realizing": CSM/JPM, 8/6/26.

165 "I am glad": JPM/CSM, 8/8/26.
165 Saint-Malo excursions: LCS/CSM, 8/1/26, 8/10/26, 8/13/26.
165 Channel Is. trip: ACS/CSM, 8/12/26, 8/22/26, 8/26/26.
166 "I have shown": ACS/CSM, 9/1/26.
166 The picture of CSM is in BUMC.
167 "I can't begin": JPM/CSM, 9/4/26.
168 Accommodations on the *Orca*: JPM/CSM, 9/4/26.
168 "I feel they": CSM/LRS, 10/10/26.
169 "He thinks": CSM/LRS, 11/17/26.
169 "Riggs gathered": ACS/CSM, 2/25/27.
169 "Personally": SS/ACS, 10/11/26.
170 "I am sorry": JPM/CSM, 10/15/26.
171 The winter in Cambridge: CSM/LRS, 1/10/27.
171 "a small spot": CSM/LRS, 12/14/26.
172 "The college set": CSM/LRS, 6/15/27.
173 Price of W. Cedar St. house: deed, E. A. Codman to JPM, 4/25/27. When JPM remarked to the real estate agent that the price seemed high he was told, "You can't go wrong on Beacon Hill." Nevertheless, the house was sold in 1938 for only $11,000 (Hamburger, p. 72).
174 "It makes me feel": CSM/LRS, 8/19/27.
174 Uncle Ellery: in her undated letter to her mother she drew an outline of a hill labeled "Olympus," on which "Uncle Ellery" was placed at the top and on upper slopes Beacon Hill friends like Harford Powel and M. A. DeWolfe Howe.
175 JPM's apology: JPM/Stewart Forbes, 11/2/43.
175 "Now that I": JPM/CSM, 2/24/31. He became a trustee of the Athenaeum in 1936, and said later: "When I lived in Boston I was a trustee of the Boston Athenaeum, in case that interests you. It interested my mother-in-law. It made her very happy and very proud" ("Notes on the New Yorker Profile").
175-176 On PM: CSM/LRS, 4/2/28.
176 PM and MFM's legacy: Hamburger, pp. 42-43.
176 "a tragic": SS/CSM, 1/16/29.
177 Johnny's remark was quoted in LRS/CSM, 1/23/29.
177 "until they either": LRS/CSM, 1/11/29.
177 "I did not object": LRS/CSM, 1/16/29.
177 "*Don't* urge": LRS/CSM, 7/2/30.
177 "Several people": LRS/CSM, 10/21/31.
177 "I hope that": LRS/CSM, 4/1/32.
178 "Good Morning, Major" was first published in *SEP*, 12/11/26.
178 "Oh, Major, Major" was first published in *SEP*, 4/27/29.
178 "The Powaw's Head," *SEP*, 7/20/29. Nine other stories were published in *SEP* in 1929 and 1930 and also collected, with introductory and concluding chapters, in *HE*.
178-179 *Post* reception of "Captain Whetstone": GHL/JPM, 7/1/29; see also TC/JPM, 7/1/29.
179 Publication of *HE*: Carl B/JPM, 2/26/30.
181 "Golden Lads": *SEP*, 2/14/31.
181 "heavy atmosphere": JPM's introduction to *TY*, pp. 47-48.
182 "My position": JPM/John Gallishaw, 5/n.d./30. Gallishaw's two books were published by Putnam's in 1929.
182 "pretty terrible": JPM/R. V. Gery, 2/23/29.
182 "your 'trouble-shooter'": John Gallishaw/JPM, 5/3/29.

11. HEARTBREAK HOUSE

This chapter owes much for its description of Mark A. DeWolfe Howe and his family to the late HH's *The Gentle Americans, 1864-1960: Biography of a Breed* (New York: Harper & Row, 1965) and to two extended interviews in which she elaborated the picture given in the book of the Howes and the Marquands in Cotuit as well as providing background and information concerning her relationship to JPM; these interviews were of fundamental assistance in the writing of the next two chapters also. HH let me see the letters she had received from JPM and prepared for me a typescript statement, "The 'Story Line,' or Chronology of My Involvement with JPM." The picture of the Marquands in Hawaii in 1931 derives not only from letters but from *NYT* news stories about the Massie case, and other newspaper reports (JPM recommended for their veracity the NANA series of articles by Russell Owen which appeared in the Boston *Globe* [JPM/PM 3/26/32]). His impressions of Hawaii also appear in "Honolulu 1945," a TNC talk (typescript, YUL) and "The Road Turns Back: The Author in Search of Earthly Paradise," *Forum*, 9/36, pp. 138–139. Again, many letters by the Marquands during this period are undated, and will not be given specific citation.

PAGE

183 On Tina's return from the hospital Christina wrote: "John is on the rampage tonight. It seems to have come over him in a great wave that he is being dominated by Doctor Sisson. This is because the doctor advised the Cape for the summer" (CSM/LRS, 1/29/29). Two months later: "Dr. Thorndike prescribes the Cape for Tina" (CSM/LRS, 4/3/29). JPM, who may have wanted to go to Curzon's Mill, capitulated. In two weeks the Howe house was rented.

185 "the heartbreak quality": CSM/LRS, 12/7/29.

186 JPM's appeal for women: "There never was a man in the world more dependent on a 'sympathizer'—preferably an attractive female sympathizer" (HH, "The 'Story Line'").

187 "Dear Chrissy": JPM/CSM, 5/4/31.

187 "I feel badly": JPM/CSM, 5/4/31.

188 Notes to HH: CSM/HH, 10/3/31; JPM/HH, 10/3/31.

188 "must try to collect": CSM/LRS, 10/3/31.

188 The house at Kahala: CSM/LRS, 10/20/31, 10/30/31; CSM/HH, 11/1/31.

188 "A horrid feeling": CSM/LRS, 10/30/31.

189 The Withingtons: CSM/LRS, 10/18/31, 10/24/31.

189 "Any visitor": "Honolulu, 1945."

189 "We *cannot* admire": CSM/HH, 11/10/31, 11/12/31.

189 "When they say": "Honolulu, 1945."

189 JPM's writing arrangements: CSM/LRS, 10/30/31.

190 "Solid South" was published in *SEP*, 3/12/32; five more Civil War stories appeared in *SEP* in 1932.

190 "John has just sold": CSM/LRS, 12/18/31.

190 "all of them": JPM/HH, 3/n.d./32.

190 "I got word": JPM/HH, 5/23/32.

191 "If 'Posty'": JPM/HH, 12/1/31.

191 "Thank you": JPM/LRS, 3/26/32.

192 "I am so glad"; CSM/LRS, 3/28/32.

192 "I never get tired": JPM/HH, 12/1/31.

192–193 "On the upper crust": "Honolulu, 1945."

194 "None of us": JPM/LRS, 2/18/32.

194 "very distinguished-looking": CSM/LRS, 1/9/32. "She asked us to supper and we didn't go," CSM reported of Mrs. Fortescue.

194 "Frankly": JPM/HH, 3/25/32.

194 The NANA articles: CSM/LRS, 1/14/32.

195 "Really I wish": JPM/HH, 3/25/32.

195 "a seaport town": "The Road Turns Back."

196 "It's been such a joy": CSM/LRS, 5/6/32.

196 "John has": CSM/HH, 12/10/31.

196 "Stay for": JPM/HH, 3/25/32.

197 "I hope you've seen": CSM/HH, 5/24/32.

197 "It has come over": JPM/HH, 5/23/32.

197 "You have been": CSM/JPM, 6/n.d./32.

198 "He had admitted": "The 'Story Line.'"

198 Irmarita Kellers married the neurological surgeon Tracy Jackson Putnam in 1924.

She had studied medicine at the Rockefeller Hospital in New York before studying in Vienna with Freud (information supplied by her brother Charles F. Kellers). JPM wrote HH (11/17/33): "As you know I am in the midst of a series of pourparleys or whatever you may choose to call them with Irma Putnam, Mr. Freud's Girl Wonder." The same letter detailed Dr. Putnam's advice and JPM's concurrence. HH later said: "Dr. Putnam was confronted with the challenge of trying to con him into believing he was leaving his wife *only* because he was unhappily married, *not* because he had fallen in love with anyone else. The simple fact is that although I was not the *cause* of the breakup I was the occasion. John was determined, however, that Christina be told that there was nobody else in the picture, and Dr. Putnam aided and abetted" ("The 'Story Line'").

198–199 *HE*, published on 8/11/33, sold a total of 3,304 copies in the hardback edition, only a little more than the hardback sales, in 1935, of JPM's entertainment fiction *No Hero*.

199 "If you miss me": JPM/HH, 12/29/33.

200 The snapshots are in BUMC.

200 "I am trying": JPM/HH, 10/31/33.

200 "I said I might": JPM/HH, 11/17/33.

201 "I seem to love": JPM/HH, 11/17/33.

202 "A pretty scaly job": JPM/I. Putnam, 2/6/34.

202 "History, she says": JPM/HH, 2/9/34.

202 "They have been": JPM/HH, 1/22/34.

202 "The attitude": JPM/I. Putnam, 2/6/34.

12. JOURNEY TO THE EAST

JPM's experiences and observations in China in 1934 were recorded in a manuscript notebook (now in the BUMC), from which this chapter draws many details. In addition, JPM's letters to HH provided further description, for which specific citation is given. George Kates gave me, in two interviews, his own impressions of JPM in China and a detailed account in particular of the Priest expedition into Shansi. JPM's TNC talk, "Where Are You, Prince" (*TY*, pp. 395–408), provided JPM's report of the trip to Mongolia with Bosshard.

PAGE

204 JPM's summons: Tebbel, p. 87.

204 "I have finally": JPM/HH, 2/11/34.

205 "There comes": JPM/HH, 2/11/34.

205 Louisburg Square: JPM/HH, 3/4/34.

206–208 JPM's impressions of Japan: JPM/HH, 3/28/34.

209 "a cross between": JPM/HH, 4/2/34.

213 "I just got here": JPM/HH, n.d.

215 F. A. Larson: JPM/JPMj, 5/10/39.

216 A. Priest: JPM/HH, 5/17/34.

217 The dedication of *Thank You, Mr. Moto* read: "To R.S.M., that indefatigable traveller and sinologist."

218 "I remember": interview with Harvey Breit, *NYTBR*, 4/24/49.

218 The publication dates of the novels with an Oriental setting are as follows (the year in parentheses indicates the publication date in hard cover by Little, Brown): *Ming Yellow: SEP*, 12/8/34–1/12/35 (1935). *Mr. Moto Takes a Hand: SEP*, 3/30/35–5/4/35 (*No Hero*, 1935). *Thank You, Mr. Moto: SEP*, 2/8/36–3/7/36 (1936). *Think Fast, Mr. Moto: SEP*, 9/12/36–10/17/36 (1937). *Mr. Moto Is So Sorry: SEP*, 7/2/38–8/13/38 (1938). *Mercator Island: Collier's*, 9/6/41–10/25/41 (*Last Laugh, Mr. Moto*, 1942).

220 Publication of *Mercator Island*: Erdman Brandt/BB, 2/21/41; BB/Carl B, 3/26/41.

220 JPM's opinion of *Mercator Island*: "Between you and me it is a completely perfunctory piece of work. While I might devote a day to making a few minor changes your suggestion that I build up Mr. Moto by a few adroit additions would take more time than the project is worth" (JPM/AM, 5/5/41, 9/10/41).

13. ENDINGS AND BEGINNINGS AND A PERSIAN INTERLUDE

HH's recollections and opinions continued to be useful in the writing of this chapter. Because of the wealth of correspondence and other materials in the LBF it was possible to trace the early stages of JPM's professional career with a completeness rarely at the biographer's disposal; these materials will continue to play a part in all subsequent chapters. Mrs. Ray Slater Blakeman (formerly Ray Murphy) permitted me to use her typescript copy of JPM's journal dictated to her in 1935 when he accompanied the Schmidt expedition in Persia. This helped to form the basis of my description, along with the account sent to me by EN, who also lent me letters he had written his own family while he was JPM's companion on the same expedition. JPM's recollections of Cambodia were offered the TNC in 1945 (typescript, YUL). Mrs. Helen Hooker Roeloffs described for me the first meeting of JPM and her sister Adelaide.

PAGE

222 "must be utterly alone": JPM/HH, 5/15/34.
222 JPM and the Brandts in the fall of 1934: JPM/HH, 10/6/34.
222 "It did not seem": CSM/JPM, 8/26/34.
223 "proof enough": JPM/CSM, 9/17/34.
223 Separation agreement: dated 10/24/34, between JPM, Robert Cutler, Trustee, CSM and James Garfield, Trustee, amended by supplemental agreement, 2/23/35 (BUMC).
223 "I'm having": JPM/HH, 10/6/34.
223 E. Sedgwick's opinion: CSM/E. Sedgwick, n.d.
223 "Now that we": JPM/CSM, 11/n.d./34.
224 "If you have": JPM/CSM, 1/31/35.
224 "It is not": F. B. Riggs/JPM, 10/5/34.
224 Johnny's letters: JPMj/CSM, 1/17/34; JPMj/JPM, 2/23/34; JPMj/JPM, 7/n.d./34.
224 "I went down": written by CSM on the envelope of JPM's letter of 1/31/35.
225 "Our last interview": JPM/CSM, n.d.
225 JPM's reply to CSM's appeal: JPM/CSM, 3/24/35.
225 "I suppose": diary entry, 9/20/35.
225 "to eat his cake": HH interview.
226 "a good deal": JPM/HH, 11/13/34.
226 "We doubt if": HM/BB, 9/10/34.
226 "did not see why": AM/BB, 9/25/34.
226 "It is kind": JPM/Roger Scaife, 10/8/34.
227 "It is, as Carl says": AM/BB, 12/18/34.
227 "In spite of": JPM/Sgt. W. J. Briggs, 4/16/45.
227 "That's a good book": *Time* profile, p. 109.
227 The form of *LGA*: HH interview.
227 "'John Apley, Trustee'": JPM/HH, 11/13/34.
228 BB's opinion: BB/AM, 1/11/35.
228 "The last two months": JPM/AM, 1/11/35.
228 "I started": Upton Sinclair/Editor, LB, 12/31/36.
228 McIntyre's opinion: AM/BB, 1/22/35.
228–229 The typesetting of *LGA*: AM/JPM, 1/22/35.
229 The Mr. Moto series: "'No Hero' is the first book in which Mr. Moto appeared. I had not thought of him as a series character when I wrote the book as a serial for the Saturday Evening Post. I imagine it was due to some suggestion from the Post editors or my agent that caused me to write a series of serial stories using Mr. Moto" (JPM/Ellery Queen, 3/11/50).
229 "when I showed": JPM/JPMj, 2/19/46.
229 "privately, Carl thinks": BB/AM, 11/10/35 (see also AM/BB, 4/9/35; BB/AM, 4/10/35; AM/BB, 4/12/35).
229 "Mr. Scaife feels": AM/BB, 8/15/35.
230 "Personally I": JPM/HH, 6/13/35.
230 "If you picture": JPM/HH, 6/13/35.
231 "is about as tough": JPM/HH, n.d.
232 "was mopped up": JPM/HH, 6/13/35.

232 "Marquand is": EN/"Mom," n.d.
232 The skis: EN to me, 7/24/74.
232 "good company": EN/"Dad," 5/28/35.
233 Noyes on Persepolis: EN/"Family," 6/9/35.
233 JPM's mold: related by Ray S. Blakeman to JPMj, 6/19/69.
233 The watercolor: EN/"Family," 6/9/35.
233 "This means": JPM/HH, 6/13/35.
238 "like an English officer": Butterfield, p. 70.

14. ADELAIDE, *APLEY*, KENT'S ISLAND

Genealogical and other information about the Hooker family, particularly EHH, and information about the Hooker Electrochemical Co. were supplied me by R. Walcott Hooker. The fullest early account of Thomas Hooker's life is in Cotton Mather's *Magnalia Christi Americana* (Hartford, 1855), vol. I, bk. 3, and is interpreted by Norman Pettit in "Lydia's Conversion: An Issue in Hooker's Departure," *Cambridge Historical Society Proceedings* (1964-66) 40:59-83. The privately published memorial tribute *Elon Huntington Hooker: Engineer, Industrialist, Patriot, Public Servant, Author, Humanitarian* (n.p., n.d.) supplied biographical data, and *Salt & Water, Power & People: A Short History of the Hooker Electrochemical Company* by Robert E. Thomas (Niagara Falls, N.Y., 1955) gave further details of his career as an industrialist as well as of the development of the company he founded. Impressions of EHH's family life and of AHM's childhood were given me by Blanchette Hooker (Mrs. John D.) Rockefeller and by Helen Hooker (Mrs. Richard) Roeloffs and by early friends such as Frances McFadden and Randall Thompson, all of whom granted me extensive interviews. Other friends contributed recollections of AHM at Vassar and in later life: Claire (Mrs. Robert) Emerson; Lucy (Mrs. Franklin) Beardsley; Lauralee (Mrs. F. Day) Tuttle; Judith M. (Mrs. John C.) Borden; Grace L. (Mrs. Arthur) Case; Elizabeth Coonley (Mrs. Waldron) Faulkner; Winifred C. Bowman, and Delia W. Kuhn. AHH's trip with her sister Helen to Russia was recounted to me by Mrs. Roeloffs; AHM's own description of the adventure was published in three articles in *Good Housekeeping*: "A High Time in Red Russia" (7/30); "How Red Is Red Russia?" (8/30); "Prisoners of the Cheka" (9/30). Early letters of AHM to her parents were shown me by BFM, and Randall Thompson recalled her during her post-college years. Mrs. Constance M. Fiske was able to give me in an interview an idea of the role that she and her husband Gardiner played in JPM's life between marriages and after his marriage to AHM. Kent's Island in its early and later stages of development was described to me by many persons. Early published descriptions were offered by RB and Frances C. Alexander (*Vogue*, 2/44), Alice Dixon Bond (Boston *Herald*, 7/15/42), Robert van Gelder (*Cosmopolitan*, 3/47). It is also described by Hamburger (pp. 91 ff.) and Lewis Nichols (*NYTBR*, 8/5/58). I visited Kent's Island on a number of occasions ten years after JPM's death when its final appearance and interior arrangement were still more or less as JPM had left it (my visits were made possible by JPM's children, particularly by JPMj, TFM, and EHM).

PAGE

239 "The old devil!": AHM/BHF, 3/9/36.
242 AHM's Vassar connections: while AHM was a student her aunt, Queene Ferry Coonley '96, was an alumnae trustee and her mother, BFH '94, a director of the Alumnae Association.
245 "serious purpose": EHH/AHM, n.d.
246 The invitation to Chelmsford: JPM/AHM, 11/8/35.
247 "John M. is": AHM/BFH, 3/28/36.
247 "Don't worry": AHM/BFH, n.d.
248 "we are still married": JPM's MS notebook (in BUMC).
249 "was most impressed": AHM/BFH, 3/28/36.
249 "We still have": AM/BB, 7/13/36.
249 "carrying forward": Carl B/JPM, 11/29/35.
249 "I have just": AHM/BFH, 3/28/36.

249–250 Publication of *LGA* under a pseudonym: AM/BB, 9/5/35; AM/JPM, 3/13/36; Carl B/AM, 3/24/36. Yet JPM, as he told Robert van Gelder in 1947, continued to believe that AM had suggested the publication of the novel under a pseudonym because of doubts of its success (*Cosmopolitan*, 3/47, p. 150). At this time AM reminded him privately that the suggestion had been put forward when only a portion of the manuscript was seen, and that he later made the modified suggestion that only the first printing omit the author's name "as a piece of stunt publishing to arouse speculation" (AM/JPM, 3/18/47). JPM remained unconvinced and nine years later wrote again: "When I began *The Late George Apley*, I was told frankly that this sort of thing would ruin my market and that I would face serious financial loss. I can even recall that an officer of Little, Brown & Company, who were then and still are my publishers, suggested that the novel should appear under a pseudonym because it was so markedly different from any of my previous work" ("Apley, Wickford Point and Pulham," *AM*, 9/56, p. 71).

250 *SEP* opinion *LGA*: Tebbel, p. 100. JPM wrote to Adelaide Neall (1/14/37), "I will always remember that you and Mr. Lorimer were among the few that thought 'Apley' had any real possibilities."

250 AM on excerpting of *LGA*: AM/BB, 1/5/37; AM/BB, 5/6/38; AM/George Stevens, 5/6/38.

251 "Every incident": "Boston Satirist Wonders Why: What Makes People Think I Am Making Fun of My Own Sort, Asks John Marquand," by Louis M. Lyons, Boston *Sunday Globe*, 1/10/37.

251 Peter M. O'Reilly sued the Curtis Publishing Co. and LB for libel in 1/38.

251 "Anyone reading": JPM/RS, 9/18/41.

252 "For better or worse": *LGA*, p. 217.

252 "Everything I have done": *LGA*, p. 344.

252 "The world": *LGA*, p. 346.

252 "not a Bostonian": Boston *Evening Transcript*, 1/9/37.

252 Interview by A. Lawrence Mackenzie, Boston *Sunday Post*, 1/10/37.

252 Interview by Louis M. Lyons, Boston *Sunday Globe*, 1/10/37.

253 "Mr. Marquand": Boston *Herald*, 1/9/37.

253 "I realize": Arthur Pier/JPM, 1/24/37.

253 "I think it is": Bliss Perry/RS, 12/17/36.

253 "There were plenty": Robert Grant/RS, 12/20/36.

254 "sympathetic and ironic": *NYTBR*, 1/3/37.

254 "an essay in": *SRL*, 1/2/37.

254 "Before he gets": "Books," *NYHT*, 1/3/37.

254 "a double edge": *NYHT*, 1/3/37.

254 "In comparing": George Santayana/Elizabeth Bolton, 12/14/36.

254 "It looks": AM/BB, 1/5/37.

255 Sales of *LGA*: AM/BB, 1/8/37; AM/JPM, 1/2/37; AM/JPM, 11/26/37.

255 "Now that John": AM/BB, 5/6/38.

255 *Three-Three-Eight*: BB/AM, 2/8/37.

255 "No doubt if John": AM/BB, 3/3/37.

256 Book publication of *Mr. Moto Is So Sorry*: AM/BB, 2/21/38.

256 Book publication of March stories: BB/AM, 4/6/37. BB claimed that JPM told her that he would like to see the March stories in book form but AM reported back that JPM had merely given his consent for their publication in England (AM/BB, 6/8/37). JPM said that her recommendation had been "based entirely on her own authority" (JPM/AM, 6/7/37).

256 "there is just": AM/BB, 5/3/37.

256 The "very serious" thing: AM/BB, 10/4/37.

256 The *Collier's* advance: JPM/Carl B, 11/16/37; Carl B/JPM, 11/16/37; JPM/E. Sohier Welch, 11/16/37.

256 "Taxation may be": Boston *Herald*, 7/15/42.

257 "Pull, Pull Together": *SEP*, 7/24/37. The reading of this story by the headmaster of the Lawrenceville School resulted in the invitation to address the school in 1938.

JPM's address, "Dear Old Golden Rule Days," described the response of the *Post* editors to the story.

257 JPMj's school: Indian Mountain report, 10/25/35; JPM/CSM, 4/24/36, 5/1/36, 5/5/36.
257 "For the first time": JPM/AHM, 8/3/36.
258 "This article": Carl B/George Stevens, 11/23/38.
259 "Although he": *SRL*, 12/10/38, p. 11.
259 "You know the way": JPM/Carl B, 4/3/39.
259 "We are aware": Wesley Stout/JPM, 4/12/39. And JPM went further: "I really feel that the backlog of any literature we have in America lies in the magazines. Granted a lot of the work there may be second rate, it is technically very competent and it furnishes a real impetus for literature" (JPM/Mrs. M. S. Davis, 4/10/39).
260 Sinclair Lewis anecdote: related by Mark Schorer in *Sinclair Lewis: An American Life* (New York: McGraw-Hill, 1961), p. 572.
260 Kent's Island purchase and history: *NN*, "John Marquand, Famous Novelist, Buys Kent's Island," 10/30/35.
261 "I should like to have you": JPM/JPMj, 4/13/39.
261 "I should like him": JPM/CSM, 5/25/39.
261 Appraisal of Kent's I. property: report by Hunneman & Co., Inc., in BUMC.
262-263 The wedding and Fosdick story: Frances McFadden and other friends of AHM's.
263 "returned to the old town": JPM/AHM, 7/3/36.
263 The Pulitzer awards for 1937 were announced on 5/2/38.
263 Ancestors' Day address: *NN*, 6/27/38.

15. THE SQUIRE OF NEWBURYPORT

JPM's participation in the meetings of the TNC was recorded and summarized in *The Records of the Tuesday Night Club of Newburyport* (privately printed; nos. 1934-40, 1940-45, 1946-51), which were lent to me by CMW. The club was described by Mignon and Robert McLaughlin (*Vogue*, 7/15/47), and one particular meeting by Hamburger, pp. 106-114. Conversation with Lispenard Pfister and Joseph Murphy of the Newburyport Firemen's Association gave me a picture of the traditions of the Neptunes and the institution of the annual muster, and of JPM's role as a member; JPM's own description of a muster was available in "When We Ran with the Old Machine" (typescript essay, YUL) and in the fictional evocation in *PNR*. The Hale family circle was described for me by Robert B. Hale and Thomas Shaw Hale. The former helped to confirm the identifications, generally assumed by acquaintances, of the characters in *WP*. These identifications were often denied by JPM, even as late as 1956: "I was greatly surprised, and still am, that some of my near relatives identified themselves with people in this book and should have thought that Wickford Point, which is at least eighty percent a figment of imagination, bore any resemblance to Newburyport, Massachusetts" ("Apley, Wickford Point and Pulham," p. 73). This insistence had doubtless been strengthened in the interval by the fact that in the 1948 lawsuit to be described on pp. 377-380, JPM's Hale cousins had charged him with exploitation of their private lives. Then, *Life* published a picture story, "Trouble at Wickford Point: Cousins Who Claim to Be John Marquand 'Characters' Squabble with Author Over the Ancestral Estate" (11/9/48, pp. 42-43). Henry Lee Shattuck's version of his dispute with JPM over his vote against *HMP* in the Boston City Council is given in "Some Experiences of My Political Life," *Proc. Mass. Historical Society*, LXXIII Jan.-Dec. 1961 (Boston, 1963), 81-91. JPM's experiences in Hollywood during the filming of *HMP* were related in a TNC talk (12/9/41; typescript, YUL) which is the basis of the description here.

PAGE

265 "Perhaps Newburyport": JPM/PM, 1/30/39.
266 "They want to be": JPM/Gardiner Fiske, 2/3/39.
266 The tape cutting: "Novelist Wields Big Shears at A & P Ceremony," *NN*, 6/2/49. A month later (7/10/49) he is reported delivering an address in the Unitarian Church in connection with the dedication of a new steeple.

266 "There was the gallstone": *PNR*, p. 272.
268 "The way to learn": *PNR*, p. 166.
269 "I personally feel" and "inclined to do": JPM/Dr. Frank Snow, 1/2/41.
269 "Lapses of memory": JPM/H. Patterson Hale, 3/28/47.
269 JPM's house-moving idea: he mentioned it to Robert van Gelder (*NYT*, 4/7/40).
270 "[Aunt Bessie] left me": JPM/PM, 9/7/41.
270 Identification of characters in *WP*: see the paragraph on sources above. About two dozen letters exist in JPM's file of correspondence from readers (HUL) who claimed to identify the *WP* characters. There even turned out to be a Clothilde Brill, and in October 1939, JPM was heckled during the Boston Book Fair by a young man named Richard Brill (JPM/J. B. Conant, 10/30/39). To all these and even to friends like George Merck and his old professor Woodbridge (JPM/GM, 3/18/39 and JPM/Homer Woodbridge, 10/21/52) he maintained that his fiction had no basis in actuality.
271 "Bella the Bitch": "Trouble at Wickford Point," p. 43.
272 "When one was": *WP*, p. 232.
272 "They'll be": *WP*, p. 190.
272 "This cheers me": JPM/GM, n.d.
273 "In spite of": *WP*, pp. 24-25.
273 "He is not inclined": "Record of conversation with JPM" (AM), 5/26/38.
273 The advance for *WP*: AM/BB, 10/10/38.
273-274 Payment of *WP* royalties: AM/BB, 2/6/39.
274 "The *Post*'s seven": *Time*, 3/20/39.
274 "the book and the serial": AM/BB, 2/15/39; the circulars and posters are in LBF.
274 "Isn't this liberal": AM/BB, 8/16/39. JPM was so disturbed by the suggestion that *WP* had been mishandled by the publisher that he spoke of going back to Scribner's (memo, CB/BB, 5/18/39).
275 "What about this": Carl B/JPM, 7/25/39.
275 "I think": JPM/Carl B, 7/27/39.
275 "they want a story": Carl B/JPM, 8/14/39.
276 The writing of *HMP*: JPM/Carl B, 8/31/39; JPM/Carl B, 10/10/39.
276 "After struggling": JPM/Mrs. I. A. R. Wylie, 12/11/40.
276 Brandt's advice: Carl B/JPM, 11/7/39.
276 "It has been difficult" and "My feeling is": Carl B/JPM, 5/6/40.
276 The telegram: Carl B/JPM, 11/25/40.
276 "I hope Carl": JPM/Mrs. I. A. R. Wylie, 12/11/40.
276 "It seems to me": JPM/Carl B, 11/29/40.
277 "As to your feelings": Carl B/JPM, 12/3/40.
278 "The one silver": JPM/GM, 9/22/39.
278 "some real heart": J. Garland/JPM, 9/26/39.
278 "I hope": JPM/J. Garland, 10/9/39.
278 "A favorable reply": quoted in John Rock/JPM, 1/3/40.
278-279 JPM's script: JPM/E. Munro, 2/10/40; JPM/Charles Codman, 2/26/40, 2/29/40; JPM/John Rock, 3/11/40. Minutes of the "Harvard 1915 Monday Night Show Committee" and the script, which lists JPM for the part of Peavey, are in the archives of HUL.
279 "It may be": JPM/GM, 5/18/40.
279-280 "I just went": JPM/B. Atkinson, 3/13/41.
280 The early draft of *Pulham* is in YUL.
281 "The office of": JPM/Stanley Resor, 12/11/40.
281 "As you will see": JPM/Edward Thayer, 12/11/40.
281 "I hope Bo-jo": JPM/Frederick Bradlee, Jr., 12/11/40.
281 "the late summer": "Apley, Wickford Point and Pulham," p. 74.
282 "I thought": JPM/J. B. Conant, 12/11/40.
282 "Of course my experience": Boston *Herald*, 3/14/41.
282 "disrespectful to": Boston *Herald*, 3/23/41.
282 Sales of *HMP* doubled: *NYT*, 4/14/41.
282-283 Shattuck's vote: Shattuck, "Some Experiences," p. 89.
283 "I gather that": JPM/H. L. Shattuck, 4/21/41.

283 Shattuck's reply: H. L. Shattuck/JPM, 4/23/41. Shattuck read *HMP* two months later and wrote RS that he found nothing in it to justify Sullivan's order, but he had not liked the book. It was an example, he thought, of the "vogue for depicting frowsy back-yards" (6/25/41).
283 The *Pulham* MS: W. Lewis confirmed to me the story of its acquisition for Yale.
283 The *Pulham* movie script: Boston *Herald*, 12/3/41.
283 "It seems since": "Apley, Wickford Point and Pulham," p. 73.
284 "Marquand's Boston": *Life*, 3/24/41.
284 "My Boston": *Life*, 3/24/41; Boston *Herald*, 3/22/41; JPM/Paul Peters, 4/24/41.
284 "written off": teletype, Harry Sions/Carl B, 1/n.d./53.
284 *HM* poll: "The Critics' Poll," *HM*, 5/41.
285 *Transcript* review: 2/21/41.
285 Bisbee review: *SRL*, 7/5/51.
285 "The nation could not": Van Wyck Brooks, *New England: Indian Summer* (New York: Dutton, 1941), pp. 541–542.
285 Fadiman review: *NY*, 2/22/41.
285 Cowley review: *NR*, 3/3/41.
285 *Time* review: 3/3/41.
285 Marshall review: *N*, 3/8/41.
286 "There does seem": JPM/JPMj, 3/5/41.
286 S. Lewis's opinion: Lewis/JPM, 3/20/41.
286 JPM's suggestions: JPM/King Vidor, 3/21/41.
286 Vidor's invitation: telegram to JPM, 4/12/41.
286 Interview with Parsons: "JPM Goes to Hollywood," INS syndicated column by Louella O. Parsons, 5/31/41.
287 "We were all": Helen Eager, Boston *Herald*, 12/13/41.
287 The casting: JPM/Hedy Lamarr, 11/29/41.
287 The dinner: JPM/AHM, 5/17/41.

16. SO LITTLE TIME

I am indebted for historical background of the pre-Pearl Harbor period to William L. Langer and S. Everett Gleason, *The Undeclared War, 1940–1941* (New York: Harper, 1953) and the same authors' *The Challenge to Isolation, 1937–1940* (New York: Harper, 1952); Manfred Jonas, *Isolationism in America, 1935–1941* (Ithaca: Cornell University Press, 1966); Walter Johnson, *The Battle Against Isolation* (Chicago: University of Chicago Press, 1944); Wayne S. Cole, *America First: The Battle Against Intervention, 1940–1941* (Madison, Wis.: University of Wisconsin Press, 1953) and the same author's *Charles A. Lindbergh and the Battle Against American Intervention in World War II* (New York: Harcourt Brace Jovanovich, 1974). AHM's own files of papers and clippings now stored in Curzon's Mill and shown me by courtesy of her children, provided many details of America First activities. A long interview with Mr. and Mrs. Charles A. Lindbergh also amplified this account and illuminated AHM's role (Lindbergh's *Wartime Diaries* [New York: Harcourt Brace Jovanovich, 1970] contains several important entries reflecting AHM's participation). My view of the relationship between JPM and JPMj depends heavily for many details in this and the following chapters on conversations with JPMj. The latter provided description and a log of his trip to Ecuador with his father. CMW described for me her own relation with JPM and narrated her flight from Westover in a letter (1/21/71).

PAGE

291 "Most of": *SLT*, p. 31.
291 "It seems to me": JPM/Lester Walker, 7/26/39.
291 The article: Heinrich Hauser's "The Romans Did It," *Commentator*, 7/39.
292 "We have been told": JPM/Quincy Howe, 7/11/42.
292 "keeping America": JPM/GM, 9/22/39.
293 JPM and the Committee to Defend: JPM received a letter from H. S. Canby and Christopher La Farge of the committee, asking him to join "a group of prominent

writers" in signing a protest against the congressional filibustering that was holding up the vote on the Lend-Lease Bill (3/4/40).

293 JPM and the AFS: Gerald Willis/JPM, 10/19/39, 10/24/39; JPM/G. Willis, 1/12/40; G. Willis/JPM, 1/13/40.

293 "I believe": JPM/Mary C. Dupee, 4/11/40.

293 "swing over to": JPM/Col. Theodore Roosevelt, 6/12/40.

293 AHM and America First: stationery of the New York Chapter of America First carried the name of AHM as a member of the Executive Committee, to which she was named at the end of November. On 5/19/41, she signed a letter, as chairman of the Platform Committee, that was sent out to solicit sponsorship for the Madison Square Garden meeting on the 23rd, at which Lindbergh and Sen. Burton K. Wheeler were to speak. "This will be one of the most thrilling and decisive events in contemporary history," she wrote. Upon repeal of the Neutrality Act she signed the statement, along with Chairman John T. Flynn, which called the close congressional vote a triumph for the antiwar faction and demanded that the President keep his pledge of nonintervention.

294 "Although I feel": JPM/Verne Marshall, 1/3/41.

294 "I find myself": JPM/Robert Littell, 12/24/40.

295 "Right now": JPM/H. S. Canby, 2/4/41. In June he declared that he still felt unable either to "'pipe for peace' or 'beat the drums for battle'" (JPM/Mrs. Cropsey, 6/2/41).

295 "Don't bother": JPM/W. Edmonds, 3/14/41.

295 JPM and the interventionists: JPM/H. S. Canby, 3/21/41.

296 The America First meeting: *NYT* news report, 4/23/41.

296 The cocktail party: *War Diaries*, p. 476.

296 AHM's war hysteria: AHM/JPM, 5/14/41.

296 "I'm sorry": JPM/AHM, 5/17/41.

297 "I think America First": JPM/AHM, 7/n.d./41.

297 "It might change": JPM/AHM, 7/19/41.

297 The America First dinner: Freda Utley, *The Odyssey of a Liberal* (Washington, D.C.: Washington National Press, 1970), p. 267.

297 "New York this winter": JPM/G. Williams, 11/26/41.

297 "Mrs. Marquand": interview with Ira Wolfert, Boston *Herald*, 11/12/41.

298 "I hate the guts": JPM/Ralph Thompson, 1/18/56.

299 "Even I": JPM/JPMj, 11/23/40.

299 JPMj and *WP*: JPM/JPMj, 2/6/38; JPM/JPMj, 1/30/39.

299 JPM appeared on "Information Please" 5/16/39.

299 Admiral Byrd and *Lord Timothy Dexter*: JPMj/JPM, 5/10/39.

299 JPMj and the Episcopal Church: JPMj/JPM, 3/7/39.

299 Johnny and money: Marquand would remind his son, who had gone through his school account: "When I started as a reporter on the Transcript I was paid fifteen dollars a week, and I had to live on that salary for a year. In order to give you fifty dollars in those days, I should have had to have worked a little more than three weeks. I am making plenty of money now, but it's only because I have worked for years—and any day I may not make any more. Think of this the next time you want something, and go easy. I should much rather have you learn to do without things than want to have too much, although I know this point of view is hard for you in the school you are attending" (JPM/JPMj, 1/31/37).

299–300 Johnny's charge accounts: JPM/W. P. Donnelly, 2/7/41; JPM/JPMj, 11/5/41.

300 "habits": JPM/CSM, 12/11/39.

300 Nonquitt: JPM/CSM, 3/9/39, 5/25/39.

300 Weekend liberty for schoolboys: JPM/Francis Parkman, 4/3/40.

300 "on the verge": JPM/JPMj, 1/3/41.

300 JPMj's school difficulties: R. E. Sawyer, Jr./JPM, 5/26/41.

300 The Exeter alternative: JPM/Lewis Perry, 4/24/41; L. Perry/JPM, 4/18/41.

300 "written promise": JPM/JPMj, 12/4/41.

300 "I am very sorry": JPM/CSM, 9/29/41.

301 "He may think": R. E. Sawyer, Jr./JPM, 2/10/42.

301 JPM's blame: JPM/R. E. Sawyer, Jr., 2/24/42.

301 Venezuela trip: JPM/J. W. Chapman, 4/15/41.
301 Organization of Ecuador Trip: Sewell Tyng/Carl B, 5/21/41.
301 "All day long": JPM/AHM, n.d.
302 "The souvenir dealer": script of television speech, 1/11/42 (YUL).
302 The Ecuador trip: JPM/AHM, 7/19/41.
303 "good will tour": AHM/JPM, 6/21/41.
303 "You mustn't get": JPM/JPMj, 12/11/41.
303 The teapot story: Butterfield, p. 73.
303 "As far as I": JPM/JPMj, 12/11/41.
303 "People with Mongoloid eyes": *SLT*, p. 388.
304 "Before long": JPM/JPMj, 12/11/41.
304 JPMj's interview: Boston *Globe*, 6/26/42.
304 "I am naturally": JPM/CSM, 10/23/42.
304 "I imagine": JPM/JPMj, 1/26/43. At the Lawrenceville Forum, JPM gave the John Humbert Kendrick Williams Memorial Lecture on 3/16/43.
305 "Do write him": AHM/JPMj, 3/13/43.
305 "Fort Sill": JPM/JPMj, 3/5/43.
305 The barracks-mates: JPMj/JPM, 3/4/43.
305 "as they get older": JPM/JPMj, 3/20/43.
306 "As part of": JPM/JPMj, 3/20/43.
306 The apartment offer: Carol B/JPMj, 7/15/43.
306 "I have a shrewd": JPM/AHM, 2/3/42.
307 "There are some": JPM/AHM, 2/13/42.
307 "I only hope": JPM/Walter Paepcke, 5/8/42.
307 "I have been": JPM/T. W. Lamont, 8/20/42.
308 Plans for trip: JPM/JPMj, 3/5/43; Carol B/JPMj, 2/26/43.
308 "I have been planning": JPM/JPMj, 3/27/43.
308 The new baby: JPMj/AHM, 3/29/43.
308 "I was away": JPM/JPMj, 4/19/43.
309 Tina's IQ: JPM/CSM, 6/27/39, 4/28/42.
309 "The war news": CMW/JPM, n.d.
309 "There are several": JPM/CMW, 12/9/42.
310 "I have been impressed": JPM/CMW, 3/20/43.
310 "Everybody assures": JPM/J. S. Bolles, 6/14/43.
311 "I think the army": JPM/CSM, 7/20/43.
311 "I would not feel": JPM/CSM, 10/28/43.
311 "the only remaining": JPMj/JPM, 2/15/44.
312 JPMj's engagement: JPM/JPMj, 4/24/45.
312 "It is completely": JPM/JPMj, n.d.
312 "Catholic families": AHM/JPMj, n.d.
312 "I know a B-17 pilot": JPM/JPMj, 3/30/45.

17. WAR AGAIN

Among general histories of World War II, Louis L. Snyder's *The War: A Concise History, 1939–1945* (New York: Messner, 1960) provided a convenient source of information as background for this chapter. The history of the biological warfare program was set forth in Theodore Rosebury, *Peace or Pestilence: Biological Warfare and How to Avoid It* (New York: Whittlesey, 1949), and in Seymour Hersh, *Chemical and Biological Warfare: America's Hidden Arsenal* (Indianapolis, Bobbs-Merrill [1968]). BUMC contains correspondence and documents referring to JPM's war service record after his appointment as director of intelligence and information, Federal Security Agency (GM/Carl B, 11/25/42). It also has his travel orders and reports by Merck, such as "Biological Warfare: Report to the Secretary of War" (1/3/46) and *Peace-Time Implications of Biological Warfare* (Pittsburgh: Westinghouse Forum, 5/16/46), which JPM probably helped to compose. Charles R. Codman's posthumous *Drive* (Boston: Atlantic-Little, Brown, 1957) gives a view of General Patton in Sicily when JPM visited him. JPM's introduction (in the fuller version [typescript, YUL]) was an important source of my description. JPM remarked to Edward Weeks that the published introduction omitted "one of Charley's main reasons for coming to Algiers, namely to buy liquor for General Patton to present to the officers of the Seventh Army" and "the paragraph about general officers laughing according to rank at other officers' jokes" (12/27/56, 3/17/57). JPM prepared but never delivered a TNC talk, "The General," which gives his vision of Patton (typescript, YUL). When this was considered for inclusion in *TY*, JPM wrote Stanley Salmen of Little, Brown: "I do not want to print it under any circumstances. It is too personal and too careless and makes my friend Charles Codman say a lot of things he would not want to say in print" (12/31/53). Other TNC talks drawn upon for this chapter were "On Biological Warfare," "Military Intelligence," and "Honolulu 1945" (typescripts, YUL) and "Ascension Island," reprinted in *TY*. For *HM*, JPM wrote the usefully descriptive "Lunch at Honolulu" (8/45), "Iwo Jima Before H-Hour" (5/45) and "Why the Navy Needs Aspirin" (8/47). JPM's correspondence with the editors of *HM*, now in LC, was made available to me by courtesy of the magazine. JPM's visit to Truk was recalled by him in "Return Trip to the Stone Age" (*AM*, 4/49).

PAGE

314 JPM's list of ideas for articles is in BUMC, together with letters suggesting devices for promoting the sale of war bonds (to Julian Street, of the Defense Savings staff).
317 The killing dose: *Science News Letter*, 5/25/46.
317 JPM's discovery of invasion plans: JPM/PM, 12/15/42.
317 "Mr. Bundy has": JPM/JPMj, 3/13/43.
318 "There was, for example": JPM/JPMj, 3/13/43.
318 "now smells": JPM/JPMj, 4/10/43.
318 The train to Washington: JPM/CMW, 3/20/43.
318 "Meat is almost": JPM/JPMj, 4/10/43.
318 "I asked them": JPM/JPMj, 7/n.d./43.
319 "machine shops": JPM/Joseph Collins, 10/20/43.
326 Allen's proposal: F. L. Allen/JPM, 8/18/43.
326 JPM's turndown: JPM/F. L. Allen, 12/18/43; JPM/Carl B, 10/23/43.
326 "It is a difficult": JPM/Carl B, 11/9/43.
326 JPM's hospitalization: JPM/JPMj, 4/5/43.
326 "After this tour": JPM/HH, 12/20/43.
327 JPM's advice: JPM/GM, 9/7/45.
327 The Merck report: War Dept. Press Release, "Biological Warfare, Report to the Secretary of War by G. W. Merck" (1/3/46).
327 Arrangements for JPM's trip: JPM received Navy credentials as *HM* representative on 12/15/44; Karig's drawing was sent JPM by F. L. Allen (7/30/44); correspondence between Navy officials and *HM* and between JPM and *HM* over his Pacific assignment began in 8/43 and continued for over a year before JPM departed. The financial arrangements are given in F. L. Allen/JPM, 7/9/44.
328 JPM's departure: JPM/JPMj, 3/30/45.
328 Play version of *Apley*: JPM/JPMj, 9/28/44.
328 "Traveling with him": JPM/AHM, 1/21/45.
328 "Those were the days": JPM review of *Don't Go Near the Water* by William Brinkley (New York: Random House, 1956) for the BOMC *News* (typescript, YUL).
328–329 JPM's description of Honolulu: JPM/AHM, 1/21/45, 1/31/45, 2/10/45.
329 JPM's *Tabberer* report: BUMC has the Navy memo (Winston Norman/JPM, 1/28/45) with attached six-page transcript, "Excerpts, *Tabberer* Press conference."
329 "I know a bit": JPM/AHM, 1/31/45.
330 "The coral reef": JPM/JPMj, 3/30/45.
331 Housing the VIP's: Brinkley's *Don't Go Near the Water*.
331 On the *Nevada*: JPM/Mrs. Howard Yeager, 3/27/45.
332 "It seemed to me": JPM/Mrs. Howard Yeager, 3/27/45.
333 Morison's assessment: S. E. Morison, *History of United States Naval Operations in World War II*, vol. XIV, *Victory in the Pacific* (1960), pp. 29–33.
333 "The boys were": JPM/JPMj, 3/30/45.
333 "The fighting": JPM/F. L. Allen, 3/24/45.

334 "I am rather": JPM/JPMj, 7/19/45.
335 "an invitation": JPM/JPMj, 4/1/47.
335 "The Peking Man": JPM/Col. Parker Tenney, 12/11/47.
335 The mayor of Peking's dinner: "The Social Future of the Harvard Man in the Free World of Tomorrow," *TY*.

18. WRITING THE WAR

PAGE
338 "When I boarded": *MG*, p. 111.
339 "I have never": "Return Trip to the Stone Age," *AM*, 4/49.
339 "Lord knows": JPM/JPMj, 3/27/43.
340 "However, I am": JPM/Col. R. A. D. Ford, 7/17/45.
340 JPM's nervous indigestion: JPM/T. W. Lamont, 8/20/42.
341 The first draft of *SLT*: JPM/AM, 12/15/42.
342 "I don't see": AM/JPM, 3/15/43.
342 Brandt's views on cutting: LB office memo, telephone conversation AM/JPM, 3/16/43.
342 JPM's decision: LB office memo, AM/Ray Everitt, 8/12/43.
342 "John, you know": JPM/Dr. Joseph Collins, 10/26/43.
342 "Most of them": JPM/Edward Sheldon, 10/29/43.
342 "the most remarkable": Marcia Davenport/JPM, 8/9/43.
343 Proposed titles: Carl B/JPM, 12/15/42; JPM/AM, 3/16/43; AM/JPM, 3/17/43, 4/15/43, 5/3/43; JPM/Ray Everitt, 4/29/43.
343 "I am afraid": Edward Sheldon/JPM, 5/n.d./43.
343 The ending: AM also recommended a change in it (4/1/43) but JPM refused (JPM/Carl B, 5/29/43). The argument continued: BB/RS, 6/18/43. JPM concluded to Sheldon: "Although this ending has been considerably criticized in high places I still cannot avoid the personal conviction that it is the proper artistic ending for that particular book" (10/29/43).
343 "A girl": *SLT*, p. 591.
344 "It was very hard": *NY*, 10/23/43, p. 20.
344–345 The reviews of *SLT*: Gannett, *NYT*, 8/20/43; Hansen, *NYWT*, 11/1/43; Powell, *Mademoiselle*, 10/43; Chamberlain, *HM*, 9/43; Beach, *NYTBR*, 8/22/43; Feld, *NYHT*, 8/22/43; Mayberry, *NR*, 8/23/43; Redman, *SRL*, 8/21/43; Rahv, *American Mercury*, 11/43; Omaha *World-Herald*, 8/22/43; Todd, Houston *Press*, 8/27/43.
345 First printing: *Esquire*, 12/43.
346 "This, as you": JPM/JPMj, n.d.
347 JPM's earnings of $90,000: AM/Carl B, 11/23/43.
347 Selznick's purchase: *NYT*, 9/11/43.
347 Movie rights: MGM archives.
347 D. Trilling piece: *HM*, 5/44.
348 H. Hansen's column: *NYWT*, 11/1/43.
348 "The truth is": JPM/AM, 11/9/43.
349 "The best escape": JPM/HH, 12/20/43.
349 "the most amazing": JPM/AM, 9/20/41.
349 "It seems to me": JPM/AM, 11/9/43.
349 "And after that": JPM/Carl B, 11/9/43.
349 "Personally": JPM/Norman Cousins, 8/22/45.
350 JPM's own account of Mayes's role in the genesis of "The End Game": *TY*, p. 144.
351 "It doesn't matter": *TY*, p. 145.
351 "if you are born": *TY*, pp. 187–188.
351 "the ridiculously": JPM/P. H. Bonner, 11/1/54.
352 "Just remember": *RIH*, p. 150.
352 "I mean": *RIH*, pp. 39, 41, 42.

352 "It is honestly": JPM/Carl B, 7/30/45. *Liberty* had wanted to print a condensed version of *RIH* but JPM said no.
352–353 *RIH* and the critics: even the *HM* editor F. L. Allen felt that *RIH* had a "sort of old-timey, romantic novel-of-marriage flavor."
353 "With the war": Philadelphia *Record*, 11/15/45.
353 "Actually the evidence": *NYWT*, 11/9/45.
353 "Everything Marquand": North column, 11/18/45.
353 Spectorsky review: *Junior Bazaar*, 1/46.
353 Purdy review: *SRL*, 11/10/45.
353 Screen rights to *RIH*: JPM/Carl B, 9/7/45.
353 "I can only": JPM/R. Gros, 12/17/45.
354 "The story creates": *NY*, 11/10/45.
354 "Bunny Wilson": JPM/Carl B, 11/10/45.
355 J. Lardner review: *NY*, 11/9/46.
355 McBride review: *NYTBR*, 11/3/46.
355 Weeks review: AM, 12/46.
355 Prescott review: *Yale Review*, Winter/47.
356 "No one ever": told to Marjorie Adams, *BH*, 12/2/41.
357 "I must have felt": *Wings*, 11/46.
357 First draft of *BFD*: AM/JPM, 8/21/45.
357–358 Beecroft on *BFD*: AM/JPM, 6/18/46.
358 *BFD* printings: LB memo, Sutliffe/AM, 1/14/47.
358 Movie version of *BFD*: Al Weitschat, Detroit *News*, 5/28/48; B. Crowther, *NYT*, 3/25/48; H. Barnes, *NYHT*, 3/25/48.
358 "The other day": JPM/Mrs. Robert McLaughlin, 3/17/47.
359 Movie script of *SLT*: JPM/Carl B, 3/29/48.
360 "Up to date": JPM/H. A. Yeager, 7/6/47.
360 "he's got": *MG*, p. 408.
360 "Any general": *NYT Magazine*, 3/30/52.
361 Col. Greene's report is in LBF.
361 "the armed forces as": *Combat Forces Journal*, 10/51, p. 46.
362 "The widely advertised": Moscow, Soviet Home Service, 1/5/51, article by E. S. Romanova (reported, Dept. of State, U.S. International Information Admin.).
362 "I must accept": JPM/S. Salmen, n.d.
362–363 Reviews of *MG*: *Time*, 10/1/51; *SRL*, 9/29/51; Chicago *Tribune*, 9/30/51; Kansas City *Star*, 9/30/51; *Newsweek*, 10/6/51; Savannah *Journal*, 9/30/51; Minneapolis *Tribune*, 10/14/51; New York *Daily News*, 10/14/51.

19. THE SECOND POSTWAR

My account of JPM's struggle with his Hale relatives for possession of Curzon's Mill has been drawn from a mass of documents and letters in the BUMC, which also contains clippings from the wide press coverage given the case. I gained help in interpreting these from F. Murray Forbes, RBH, TSH and James Connolly, who offered their recollections and analyses in interviews. Salt Cay was described for me by JPMj, TFM, SCM, and Mrs. Gardiner Fiske, whose descriptive essay "Treasure Island with John Marquand" was very useful; other details were found in JPM's TNC talk "When We Sailed on the Sloop John B" (typescript in YUL).

PAGE

364 The meeting with Gordon and Kaufman: BFM showed me the diary begun by JPM in 1944, which records it (1/18/44).
364 "I think it would": Edward Sheldon/JPM, 5/n.d./43.
364 "I feel": JPM/JPMj, 9/28/44.

365 Barley Sheaf Farm: JPM/Katharine Scherman, 8/8/44.
365 "You may call": AHM/JPMj, 9/28/44.
365 "you must be" and "It is well": JPM/JPMj, 11/17/44.
365 "Though the customers": JPM/JPMj, 11/17/44.
365-366 *LGA* (play): closed in New York 11/17/45.
366 Carroll and his role: William Lindsay Gresham's interview with Carroll, *Theatre Arts Monthly*, 3/45; JPM/George Kaufman, 6/27/45.
366 J. M. Brown review: *SRL*, 12/9/44.
367 Crowther review: *NYT*, 3/21/47.
367 "It was most": JPM/Stewart Forbes, 11/2/43.
367 "forget his courage": JPM/Robert Sherwood, 12/29/52.
368 "intellectual dishonesty": JPM/HS, 2/6/50.
368 "When Sherwood": JPM/HS, 4/12/48.
368 "When you get": JPM/JPMj, 11/17/44.
368 "The *rentier* class": JPM/JPMj, 10/11/45.
368 "I think it is": JPM/JPMj, 11/17/44.
369 "now a very": JPM/JPMj, 7/19/45.
369 "I once had": JPM/JPMj, 7/19/45.
370 "go to pot": JPMj/JPM, 8/23/45.
370 "Your educational": JPM/JPMj, 10/11/45.
370 "It appears": JPM/JPMj, 7/19/45.
371 Rita's hair: JPM/JPMj, 2/22/47.
371 "a humdrum": JPM/Mrs. Robert Lovett, 6/7/51.
371 "Take her": Frances Alexander, in *Vogue*, 2/15/44.
371 "obliged to read": JPM/Mrs. Robert Lovett, 6/7/51.
372 "Aside from": *35th Anniversary Report of the Class of 1915* (1960).
372 "The Marquand farm": F. Alexander, in *Vogue*, 2/15/44.
373 "either to milk": JPM/KR, 3/13/44.
373 "I have been": JPM/Roger Butterfield, 4/22/44.
373-374 Kent's I. problems: JPM/Louis Denfield, 8/18/47; KR/JPM, 9/26/50, 10/6/50, 10/12/50; JPM/KR, 10/11/50, 10/25/50; JPM/JPMj, 4/5/44.
374 Problems with PM: JPM/MMO, 3/24/47, 3/10/47; JPM/F. Snow, 2/4/47; JPM/Ralph Webb, 7/21/47.
374 The vandalization: JPM/David Erickson, 1/29/47.
375 "I have a deep": JPM/MMO, 3/10/47.
375 JPM's other proposals: JPM/E. Sohier Welch, 8/25/47; JPM/RBH, 9/18/47, 9/20/47.
376 "You see": HDH/JPM, 11/19/47.
376 "brought on": RBH/J. M. Lowell, 11/22/47.
376 JPM's last proposal to Aunt Greta: J. M. Lowell/MMO, 1/26/48.
376 "Needless to say": JPM/F. M. Forbes, 1/26/48.
377 Percentages of ownership: JPM/Forbes, 2/13/48.
377 "Difficult as": JPM/F. M. Forbes, 2/4/48.
377 JPM's withdrawal of his offer: JPM/F. M. Forbes, 3/11/48.
377 "to face the problem": JPM/F. M. Forbes, 6/14/48.
377 The cousins' awareness of JPM's opinion: F. M. Forbes/TSH, 7/1/48.
377 PM as co-owner: F. M. Forbes/JPM, 2/2/48.
377 "He may very well": JPM/F. M. Forbes, 2/4/48.
379 "I don't think": JPM/CMW. 3/8/51.
379 "Did you filch it": JPM/AHM, 8/27/52.
380 The apartment: 115 East 67th St.
380 "it was due to": AHM/JPMj, 10/5/44.
381 "At noon": JPM/CMW, 3/23/45.
381 "It is too bad": JPM/JPMj, 3/30/45.
381 "a terrific-looking": AHM/JPMj, 4/18/45.
382 "I find": JPM/AM, 4/6/46.
382 Hobe Sound in 1955: JPM/H. S. Canby, 2/1/55.
382 "Adelaide loves": JPM/Parker Tenney, 8/24/49.

382 "Though Adelaide": JPM/King Vidor, 7/13/50.
383 "Sun, Sea and Sand," *Hearst's International Cosmopolitan*, 5/50; "King of the Sea," *McCall's*, 11/52. Both were reprinted in *TY*.
383 "I doubt": JPM/Paul Hollister, 5/19/50.
384 "I thought when": *TY*, p. 210.
384 "a nice guy": JPM/Cedric Gibbons, 4/9/48.
384 JPM's address: "The Social Future of the Harvard Man in the Free World of Tomorrow," *TY*, p. 46.
385 "I wish you": JPM/Parker Tenney, 2/4/50.
385 "Not for": JPM/HS, 1/12/50.
386 "The days pass": JPM/E. Hoxie, 2/2/50.

20. POINT OF NO RETURN

Edward Streeter described to me the appearance and workings of the Fifth Avenue Bank and his help to JPM in providing authentic banking details for *PNR*. Ruth Mehrtens Galvin recalled the writing of the 1949 *Time* cover story for me. Meredith Wood described the procedures of the BOMC and JPM's role as a judge. The influence of the Club was studied in 1951 by Prof. Riley Hughes of Georgetown University; I have drawn upon his summary article in the *Catholic Standard* (11/2/51).

PAGE

388 Hooker Electrochemical statistics: *Salt & Water, Power & People* (privately printed).
389 "to be expensive": *SWW*, p. 273.
390 "I would like": E. Streeter/JPM, 10/2/47.
390 Streeter's log is in BUMC.
390 Fifth Avenue Bank personnel and *PNR*: *NY*, 6/18/49.
390 Bank-vault scene: *SRL*, 5/28/49.
393 "swatting it out": *Time*, 3/7/49.
393–394 Narrative method for *SWW*: JPM/HH, 9/11/45.
394 Mizener's review: *NYTBR*, 2/27/55.
394 The *Time* and *Newsweek* cover stories appeared 3/7/49.
395 JPM's speech: Boston *Globe*, 6/8/49.
395 "are the distillation": JPM/Sidney Horler, 5/19/49.
396 "Much as I": JPM/———Club Comm. on Admissions, 6/17/53.
396 Gissen and Eisenhower: *Time*, 5/19/52.
396 "the orange chintz": Hamburger, p. 1.
396 "things might have": Hamburger, p. 9.
397–398 Reviews of *PNR*: San Francisco *Chronicle*, 3/6/49; *NYWT*, 3/8/49; Philadelphia *Inquirer*, 3/6/49; *AM*, 3/49; *NYT*, 3/6/49; *SRL*, 3/5/49; *NYHT Book Review*, 3/6/49; *NY*, 3/19/49; *NYTBR*, 3/6/49.
398 "makes the play": *SRL*, 1/28/52.
398 "You can't charge": *NYHT*, 12/9/51.
399 JPM's approval of the play: he also praised it to Hayward (7/30/51).
399 Rewrite of ending: *Theatre Arts Monthly*, 3/53.
399 "I really had": JPM/HH, 3/12/55.
400 "flatulently": JPM/H. S. Canby, 2/23/55.
400 "Only a craftsman": *NY*, 2/26/55.
400 *N* review: 1/4/55.
400 Barrett review: *SRL*, 2/26/55.
400 "You will find": JPM/JPMj, 12/23/55.
401 "recognized": JPM/CMW, 11/30/55.
401 "general pessimism": JPM/Mrs. Fred Wanger, 1/22/52.
401 "You would think": *CSM*, 2/17/55.
402 JPM as LB "creditor": F. M. Forbes/BP, 12/27/55; BP/JPM, 3/31/58.

403 JPM and Brandt: JPM/Carl B, 9/3/48.
403 "He had been": JPM/CMW, 10/16/57.
405 MacDuffie's efforts: he had protested its publication by Harper in a twelve-page letter to the chairman of the board (M. MacDuffie/Cass Canfield, 1/10/47) and met with the members of the BOMC board (JPM/HS, 1/14/47, 1/20/47). MacDuffie wrote again at length to the BOMC officers (M. MacDuffie/HS, 1/24/47) and John Fischer's reply (also twelve pages) to MacDuffie was studied by the Club (J. Fischer/Cass Canfield, 1/24/47), which decided that Fischer's alterations had met objections (H. S. Canby/M. MacDuffie, 1/28/47). JPM wrote a laudatory review for the *BOMC News* (4/47).
405 Gannett review: *NYHT*, 4/23/47.
405 "I don't think": JPM/HS, 1/13/48.
405 "political slant": JPM/Ralph Thompson, 12/18/53.
405 "I believe": JPM/HS, 3/25/48.
405 "This implies": JPM/HS, 12/13/51.
405 "no historian": *BOMC News*, 6/60 (typescript in HUL).
406 "a darn good": JPM/HS, 4/5/47.
406 "that we might": JPM/MW, 5/11/53.
406 "who stick": JPM/Mrs. H. S. Canby, 12/2/54.
406 JPM on BOMC choices: JPM/HS, 9/30/47; JPM/Charles Lee, 12/30/52.
406 "for some peculiar": JPM/AL, 8/2/48.
406 "John would moan": *SRL*, 8/3/60.
406 "*Prater Violet*": JPM/AL, 9/3/45.
406 "J. B. Priestley's": JPM/MW, 6/27/46.
406 "Robert Penn Warren": JPM/MW, 6/15/59.
406-407 "James Michener": JPM/HS, 2/12/48.
407 "one novel in": JPM/HS, 2/12/48.
407 "in spite of": JPM/HS, 11/15/50.
407 Jones's response: Jones/JPM, 2/4/51.
407 Cerf's letter: B. Cerf/HS, 7/12/48.
407 "I do not agree": JPM/HS, 7/18/48.

21. WOMEN AND JOHN P. MARQUAND

My description of AHM in the later years of her marriage and after her divorce is dependent upon help from friends and acquaintances, some already listed for Chapter 14. Particularly useful at this stage were interviews with Mr. and Mrs. Randall Thompson, Prof. and Mrs. Mason Hammond, Prof. Roy Lamson, Anne Morrow Lindbergh and Frances McFadden. JPM's three younger children all shared their early memories with me in extensive interviews that assisted this and the following two chapters to a major degree. JPMj and CMW continued to contribute their recollections of their father and of his second wife, and CMW lent me letters received from AHM. I also owe much to the frank accounts of their own experience with JPM given me in interviews by Carol B and MD. Both shared with me letters they had received from JPM, the former also showing me the letter from her husband to herself quoted on p. 424 (most of JPM's letters to Carol B are undated and will not be cited individually below). Prof. Hammond recalled for me the visit of the Marquands in Rome and Randall Thompson gave an account of his travels with them in Greece in 1952. Other friends provided glimpses of the Marquand family at Salt Cay—Constance Fiske and Anne Lindbergh—or traveling together on the West Coast—Robert Gros. I was able to put together a description of JPM's coronary attack and convalescence in 1953 as a result of conversations with his children, particularly BFM and TFM, with Drs. Dana Atchley and Howard Rogers and with F. Murray Forbes and MD. Descriptions of One Reservoir Street were offered by many visitors. Prof. Roy Lamson recalled, as did others, impressions of AHM in her last years, and he also permitted me to share his memory of his discovery of her drowned body.

PAGE

411 "in the end": *WTH*, p. 497.
413 "This winter": JPM/CMW, 5/16/53.
414 AHM's Collections of JPM's early work: AJM/BB, 9/4/43, 3/24/44. AHM's scrapbooks are now at Curzon's Mill; the sets of first editions she ordered (GN/BP, 2/2/57) have been retained by her children.
414 "Adelaide and I": JPM/JPMj, 3/27/43.
415 "She would love": JPM/Edward Sheldon, 5/4/43.
415 Title choice: AHM/JPMj, 6/10/43.
415 AHM and JPM's works: AM/AHM, 9/7/43; AHM/Carl B, 9/25/43.
415 The double portrait: Although Cox later declared that the portrait had not been rejected by Marquand but simply withdrawn by the artist, who was himself dissatisfied with it, Marquand's version of the story was remembered by others.
416 "I think you": JPM/JPMj, 7/25/46.
416 "despite flowing dresses": JPM/HH, 10/30/34.
417 "Perhaps this is": quoted in "Roughing It with the Late George Apley" by Ruth Whitman (MS lent me by Mrs. Whitman).
419 The copyrights: Carl B/AM, 5/14/46.
419 The itinerary: AM/BB, 5/15/46.
419 "After observing": JPM/GM, 10/11/46.
419 "had been *anything*": AHM/Mrs. H. W. Rogers, 4/15/47.
420 "a writer's apt": *Time*, 8/4/47.
421 "I do not suppose": 35th reunion dinner speech, 6/20/50 (typescript in YUL).
422 "a nervous": JPM/Col. Parker Tenny, 7/6/49.
422 "You may have": JPM/Carl Jonas, 4/15/49.
422 "a gruesome occupation": JPM/AHM, 4/30/49.
422 "a great extravagance": JPM/GM, 8/24/49.
424 "He only likes": AHM, undated memo (BUMC).
424 "There is a dreamy": JPM/Harry Emerson Fosdick, 4/11/50.
424 "I have seen": JPM/AHM, 9/12/50.
425 "I know what": JPM/AHM, 8/21/50.
425–426 K. Roberts anecdote: AHM/JPM, 10/29/51.
426 "the children are": JPM/AHM [10/51].
427 "I've had": Harford Powel/JPM, 3/24/51.
427 "vastly worse": JPM/JPMj, 11/14/55.
427 At Hadrian's villa: JPM/Mason Hammond, 5/20/59.
427 At Chartres: JPM/Robert Littell, 6/24/52.
428 "Although we were": JPM/BFM, 5/16/52.
428 "the place where": JPM/BFM, 5/16/52.
429 "author Marquand": "How They Win Friends and Influence Money: The Eve Perrick Column," *Daily Express*, 5/31/52.
429 "a little overpowering": JPM/Sir Gordon Covell, 6/7/52.
429 "The truth is": JPM/BFM, 8/27/52.
429 "I do wish": BFM/JPM, 8/29/52.
430 "to be engaged": JPM/P. Hamburger, 10/22/52.
430 "to take the children": JPM/CMW, 12/29/52.
430 "took place": AHM/JPM, n.d./58.
431 "Madam, madam"; recalled by THM.
431 "I realize": A. M. Lindbergh/JPM, 4/22/53.
431 JPM at the Harvard exercises: JPM/CMW, 5/16/53.
431 "I have decided": JPM/AHM, 6/30/53.
432 "death upon": JPM/HH, 11/19/53.
432 Prohibited vists: JPM/AHM, n.d.
432–433 Description of One Reservoir St.: AHM/Dana Atchley, 8/6/53; AHM/JPM, 8/12/54.
433 "On Saturday night": JPM/Carl B [8/53].
433 "which I know": JPM/AHM, 9/17/53.
434 Two separate establishments: JPM/AHM, 9/30/53, [12/53], 1/1/54, 1/18/54.
434 "I shall secretly": JPM/CMW, n.d./[54].

434 AHM's death: the friend was Prof. Roy Lamson of MIT; the date, 10/11/63.
434–435 JPM's health: JPM/D. C. Fisher, 10/6/53.
435 "You and I": JPM/D. C. Fisher, 12/9/53.
435 AHM's appeals: AHM/JPM, 12/14/53. Enclosed were "alternative plans for the next two months"—six pages of complaints and proposals.
435 "It seemed to me": AHM/JPM [12/53].
435 AHM's proposals: AHM/JPM, 12/14/53.
436 "According to my": JPM/CMW, 12/18/53.
436 Custody petition: John G. Jackson, Jr./BP, 12/24/53; BP/John G. Jackson, Jr., 12/29/53.
436 The telegram to Ferry was undated.
436 Grenada trip: JPM/Samuel Hopkins Adams, 12/24/53; JPM/AHM, 1/18/54.
436 "I ought to be": JPM/GM, 2/8/54.
436–437 Instructions to AHM: JPM/AHM, 2/15/54.
437 PM's funeral: AHM/JPM, 3/1/54.
437 "Well, the house": JPM/CMW, 10/29/54.
437 "The Boss": AHM/CMW, 5/25/54.
438 "Every year": JPM/CMW, 12/28/54.
438 "The damage is": JPM/CMW, 10/29/54.

22. *ALL MY CHILDREN*

This chapter is particularly indebted to the generous fashion in which all five of JPM's children—JPMj, CMW, BFM, TFM, and EHM—shared with me (in extensive interviews) their memories of their lives with their parents whether those memories were pleasant or painful. BP was also generous in opening to my examination his files of correspondence during a period when his function as lawyer made him a close participant in the affairs of the family. My impressions of Pinehurst were gained by a visit there in 1971, when I viewed JPM's home and interviewed George F. Shearwood and Floyd Ray. JPM's own comments on Pinehurst appear in a description written for the *Ford Times* (12/14/59). JPMj provided me with an itinerary and a written reminiscence of his trip with his father in 1955.

PAGE

439 "I really think": JPM/Paul Brooks, 5/31/50.
440 "Please give her": JPM/Harford Powel, 3/14/52.
440 "As the book stands": JPM/JPMj, 7/14/52.
440 "I wonder": JPM/AHM, 8/27/52.
441 "Johnny acts": JPM/AHM, 9/2/52.
441 "I am glad": JPM/JPMj, 1/6/53.
441 "It is no secret": *NYWT* (undated clipping, BUMC).
442 "They were all": *The Second Happiest Day* (New York: Harper, 1953), p. 28.
442 Mizener review: *SR*, 1/31/53.
442 "dense and uncharitable": JPMj/JPM, 3/2/53.
442 Gissen review: 2/2/53.
442 "One thing": JPMj/JPM, 3/2/53.
443 "I wonder": JPM/CMW, 5/16/53.
444 "Whether you": JPM/JPMj, n.d.
445 "a long talk": JPMj/JPM, 7/30/53.
445 "Johnny did not": JPM/CMW, 10/29/54.
445 "he is making": JPM/CMW, 4/8/55.
445 "I frankly think": JPM/CMW, 5/13/55.
445 Interview with Walter Hackett: Boston *Globe*, 3/24/55.
445 "I kept thinking": JPM/H. S. Canby, 2/23/55.
446 "a place devoid": JPM/H. S. Canby, 12/9/59.
446 The new mystery novel: JPM/JPMj, 11/14/55.
446 The dinner guests: JPM/CMW, 2/12/57.

446 The brick house: JPM/CMW, 4/19/57.
446–447 The leases and purchase agreement (4/59) are in BUMC.
447 "All the big brass": JPM/Robert Gros, 3/10/55.
447 "I told him": JPM/CMW, 4/25/55.
448 "a neater": JPM/Sir Gordon Covell, 11/15/55.
449 "I should have": JPM/JPMj, 11/14/55.
449 JPM's letters to M. Davis: 7/3/55, 7/15/55, 8/30/55.
450 "I do hope": JPM/SCM, 6/11/56.
450 "Your grandmother": JPM/JPMj, 11/16/55.
450 "I do not blame": JPM/JPMj, 12/29/55.
450 "does not stem": JPM/SCM, 4/19/56.
450 Curzon's Mill: JPM/JPMj, 3/16/56.
451 "The place has me": JPMj/JPM, 4/10/56.
451 "the tiresome band": JPM/JPMj, 6/25/56.
451 "Johnny works": JPM/CMW, 5/7/57.
451 "Johnny, I fear": JPM/CMW, 6/10/57.
451 "What happens is": JPMj/JPM, 6/14/57.
452 "The seven years": JPM/BP, 2/4/59.
452 "Of all": JPM/CMW, 11/n.d./58.
452 "You are going": J. G. Jackson/BP, 7/5/55.
452 "During my trip": JPM/AHM, 9/12/55.
453 "My dearest": AHM/JPM, n.d.
453 "I do not feel" and "Unfortunately": JPM/BP, 11/28/55.
454 The children's incomes: each received about $6,000 a year from trust accounts with a market value of $170,000 (Arthur Barton/BP, 4/8/58).
455 "the advisability": JPM/BP, 12/16/55.
455 "I have never": JPM/BFM, 12/14/55.
455 "It may not": JPM/JPMj, 11/14/55.
455 "for some reason": JPM/CMW, 1/19/56.
455 "She wanted them": JPM/BP, 3/28/56.
455 The calendar: BP/GN, 5/21/56.
456 "Here in America": JPM/BFM, 12/25/55.
456 "Oh, Daddy": BP/GN, 3/13/56.
457 "Let's face it": JPM/BFM, 10/22/55.
457 "refused to be": JPM/GM, 10/12/54.
457 "took a contemptuous": JPM/Valeria Knapp, 2/10/55.
457 "You will not": JPM/BFM, 9/4/56.
458 "wear him down": JPM/HH, 9/21/56.
458 Lonny and JPM: JPM/BP, 1/21/57; JPM/CMW, 1/21/57.
459 "If I do not hear": JPM/BP, 1/21/57.
459 Lonny's schooling: JPM/BP, 2/25/57.
459 "very academically": AHM/BP, 3/6/57.
459 Lonny's choice: JPM/BP, 6/18/57.
459 "I'm no longer": JPM/BP, 9/1/57.
459 "There is nothing": JPM/MD, 9/23/57.
459 "if she cared": JPM/BP, 10/1/57.
459 JPM sees MD: JPM/MD, 9/23/57.
460 "I am sorrier": JPM/BFM, 12/16/57.
460 Christmas, 1957: AHM/CMW, 1/20/58.
461 JPM and Ferry's call: JPM/BFM, 1/11/58.
461 "clear my mind": AHM/BP, 4/18/58.
461 "didn't really": BP/GN, 4/23/58.
461 "This embattled child": AHM/JPM, 5/16/58.
461 "of sneaking away": AHM/CMW, 5/28/58.
462 "I fear you": JPM/BFM, 2/14/53.
462 Ferry's call: JPM/BFM, 9/19/58, 4/16/59.
462 "I have gone": JPM/AHM, 9/24/58.

23. END OF A MAN

Ruth Whitman let me draw upon her unpublished essay recalling her Reno acquaintance with JPM, "Roughing It with the Late George Apley." Mrs. Betty Brewster (Elizabeth Cathles) wrote me a letter containing recollections of him during the same period. Constance Fiske and Carol B each gave me her own version of JPM's supposed proposals after his divorce. The latter also supplied letters used here, mostly undated. MD recounted the history of her own relation to JPM in its final stages, providing me with an itinerary of the trip to Africa in 1959. For this trip George Shearwood supplied a complete account in the interview I had with him, and this was supplemented by the memories of Gertrude Page, also in an interview. JPM's own travel report was set down in "Afternoon at Moroto" (*AM*, 1/60). Cammann Newberry and Alexander Williams contributed, in interviews, a picture of JPM's relation to his editors in his last years. CMW lent me a copy of the typescript of JPM's uncompleted draft of a final novel. Floyd Ray described JPM's last afternoon and also how he found him dead the next morning. As before, the five Marquand children and the late SCM, JPM's daughter-in-law, gave me major assistance in the writing of this chapter by recounting to me their memories of JPM.

PAGE

464 The employment of R. Whitman: JPM/BP, 10/14/58.
465 "on another": JPM/MD, 10/8/58.
465 "the God damnedest": JPM/SCM, 10/6/58.
465 "I should say": JPM/EHM, 10/14/58.
465 Gambling at the Riverside Hotel: JPM/MD, 10/7/58.
466 "I have never": JPM/EHM, 10/21/58.
467 "She must be": JPM/BP, 10/25/58; 10/31/58.
467 "succeeded in alienating": JPM/BP, 10/14/58.
468 "I am convinced": JPM/BP, 10/25/58.
468 "which was what": AHM/JPM, 11/7/58.
468 "gloomiest day": JPM/CMW, 11/11/58.
468 "with long letters": JPM/JPMj, 11/11/58.
468 "Top tchit-tchat": Walter Winchell, "On Broadway" (syndicated column), 11/25/58.
469 "Mrs. Brandt": JPM/CMW, 4/27/60.
469 Christmas, 1958: AHM/CMW, 1/16/59.
469 "one of the worst": JPM/CMW, 1/13/59.
469 "Of course they": JPM/CMW, 1/13/59.
470 "tepid to say the least": JPM/BP, 2/4/59.
470 Lonny's difficulties: JPM/EHM, 1/22/59.
470 "The behavior": JPM/BP, 2/19/59.
471 "I cannot assume": JPM/BP, 1/20/59.
471 "I am not": JPM/BP, 6/15/59.
471 "I must ask": 4/16/59.
471 "In view of": BP/JPM, 5/6/59.
471 "and said that": JPM/BP, 6/7/59.
471 Carol B as manager: JPM/Carol B, 6/16/59.
472 *Sports Illustrated* articles: Richard Johnston/Carol B, 6/25/59.
473 "a forbidding": "Afternoon in Moroto," p. 31.
474 "The house is": JPM/N. L. Berry, 11/27/59.
474 "reached the decision": JPM/CMW, 12/9/59.
475 "I would not": JPM/BP, 12/21/59.
475 Christmas on Salt Cay: AHM/CMW, 1/28/60.
475 "I do not care": JPM/BP, 4/12/60.
475 "I personally": JPM/BP, 4/12/60.
476 "I am still": BP/JPM, 4/22/60.
476 "in one of his": JPM/BP, 4/25/60.
476 "I feel": JPM/BP, 1/11/60.
476–477 AHM's behavior: JPM/BP, 4/17/60.

477 Ferry's prize: "Another Marquand Wins a Literary Prize," Boston *Traveler*, 3/28/60.
477 "Ferry is here": JPM/BP, 4/5/60.
477 "If, as you say": BFM/JPM, 7/7/60.
477 The new will: signed, 9/1/59, proved, 9/6/60 (Essex County Probate Office).
477-478 Future of Kent's I.: JPM/J. Coolidge, 12/21/59.
478 The Tyng tray: J. Coolidge/JPM, 1/8/60.
478 "This one": JPM/Philip Kappel, 5/5/59.
478 "The unknown": K. Thompson/JPM, 12/19/59.
479 "I see no": BB/Carl B, 12/14/38.
479 "The time may": JPM/BB, 2/28/47.
479 "There is nothing": AW/JPM, 3/4/59.
480 "to interrupt": JPM/AW, 1/17/59.
480 The Greek cruise: SS/JPM, 2/14/60, 2/16/60, 2/18/60; JPM/Mrs. CN, 2/19/60; SS/JPM, 2/21/60; JPM/AW, 2/27/60; JPM/SS, 2/27/60; Sam Barclay/JPM, 2/27/60, 3/7/60; JPM/Sam Barclay, 3/1/60; JPM/AW, 3/1/60; AW/JPM, 3/3/60; JPM/AW, 3/17/60; AW/JPM, 3/7/60, 3/22/60.
481 The new work of fiction: JPM/AW, 1/17/59.
481 JPM's address: *NN*, 5/18/60.
481-482 The fiftieth reunion: printed invitation, "50th Anniversary, Newburyport High School Class of 1910, Kent's Island," 6/21/60.
482 JPM's support of JFK: as he told a *NY* reporter five days before he died (*NY*, 8/6/60).
482 JPM's support of Eisenhower: in 1952 he had made a statement to *Life* that Eisenhower was "far better for the Presidency than Adlai Stevenson" (JPM/John K. Jessup, 10/23/52).
482 JPM and Stevenson: JPM/Ernest Ives, 5/24/60; Adlai Stevenson/JPM, 6/9/60; JPM/Adlai Stevenson, 6/18/60; Adlai Stevenson/JPM, 6/28/60.
482 "With his heavy": JPMj/Nathan Pusey, 8/9/60.
482-483 JPM at the judges' meeting: *SRL*, 8/3/60.

Marquand's Works

Below are listed, chronologically, those of Marquand's works discussed in the text.

1915 *Prince and Boatswain: Sea Tales from the Recollections of Rear Admiral Charles E. Clark as Related to James Moran and John Philip* [sic] *Marquand*
1921 "The Right That Failed"
1922 *The Unspeakable Gentleman*
"Only a Few of Us Left"
"Eight Million Bubbles"
"Different from Other Girls"
"How Willie Came Across"
"The Land of Bunk"
"Captain of His Soul"
1923 *Four of a Kind*
"The Ship"
"The Sunbeam"
1924 "Pozzi of Perugia"
"A Friend of the Family"
1925 *The Black Cargo*
Lord Timothy Dexter of Newburyport, Mass.
"The Educated Money"
"The Big Guys"
"The Old Man"
"The Last of the Hoopwells"
1926 "The Artistic Touch"
"Fun and Neighbors"
"The Spitting Cat"
"Good Morning, Major"
1927 "The Cinderella Motif"
"Once and Always"
"The Harvard Square Student"
1929 "Oh, Major, Major"
"The Powaw's Head"
"Captain Whetstone"
1930 *Warning Hill*
1932 "Ask Him"
"The Music"
"Golden Lads"
"Deep Water"
"Solid South"
"High Tide"
1933 *Haven's End*
1935 *Ming Yellow*
No Hero (serial title: *Mr. Moto Takes a Hand*)
1936 *Thank You, Mr. Moto*
"The Road Turns Back" (essay)
1937 *Eight-Three-Eight*
The Late George Apley
Think Fast, Mr. Moto
"Pull, Pull Together"
"Everything Is Fine"
1938 *Mr. Moto Is So Sorry*
"Castle Sinister"
1939 *Wickford Point*
1941 *H. M. Pulham, Esquire* (serial title: *Gone Tomorrow*)
"My Boston: A Note on the City by Its Best Critic" (essay)
1942 *Last Laugh, Mr. Moto* (serial title: *Mercator Island*)
1943 *So Little Time*
"The End Game"
1945 *Repent in Haste*
"Lunch at Honolulu"
1946 *B. F.'s Daughter*
"Why I Wrote *B. F.'s Daughter*" (essay)
1947 "Why the Navy Needs Aspirin" (essay)
1948 "King of the Sea"
1949 *Point of No Return* (serial title: *Banking Is an Art*)

1951 *Melville Goodwin, U.S.A.*
1954 *Thirty Years*
1955 *Sincerely, Willis Wayde*
1957 *Stopover Tokyo* (serial title: *Rendezvous in Tokyo*)
Life at Happy Knoll
1958 *Women and Thomas Harrow*
"An Inquiry into the Military Mind" (essay)
"Sun, Sea and Sand"
1960 *Timothy Dexter Revisited*

Index